# Modeling, Analysis and Design of Control Systems in MATLAB and Simulink

# MODELING, ANALYSIS AND DESIGN OF CONTROL SYSTEMS IN MATLAB AND SIMULINK

## Dingyü Xue

Northeastern University, China

## YangQuan Chen

University of California, Merced, USA

**World Scientific**

NEW JERSEY · LONDON · SINGAPORE · BEIJING · SHANGHAI · HONG KONG · TAIPEI · CHENNAI

*Published by*

World Scientific Publishing Co. Pte. Ltd.

5 Toh Tuck Link, Singapore 596224

*USA office:* 27 Warren Street, Suite 401-402, Hackensack, NJ 07601

*UK office:* 57 Shelton Street, Covent Garden, London WC2H 9HE

**Library of Congress Cataloging-in-Publication Data**
Xue, Dingyu.
    Modeling, analysis and design of control systems in MATLAB and Simulink / Dingyu Xue, Northeastern University, P.R. China, YangQuan Chen, University of California, Merced, USA.
      pages cm
    Includes bibliographical references and index.
    ISBN 978-9814618458 (hardbound : alk. paper) -- ISBN 9814618454 (hardbound : alk. paper)
    ISBN 978-9814618472 (e-book) -- ISBN 9814618470 (e-book)
    ISBN 978-9814618489 (mobile) -- ISBN 9814618489 (mobile)
    1. Automatic control--Computer simulation. 2. Control theory--Data processing. 3. MATLAB.
4. Simulink. I. Chen, YangQuan, 1966–   II. Title.
    TJ213.X84 2014
    629.80285'53--dc23

                                                        2014018317

**British Library Cataloguing-in-Publication Data**
A catalogue record for this book is available from the British Library.

Printed in Singapore

# Foreword

Most people are familiar with the "mad scientist," usually a brilliant, sometimes comical figure found in books and movies. Years ago I developed the motif of the "MAD control engineer" as a way to inspire a bit of passion and even brilliance in the students taking my feedback control classes. As such, I am pleased to see the new edition of this book, *Modeling, Analysis and Design of Control Systems in MATLAB and Simulink*, by Professors Xue and Chen, which follows the same motif.

"MAD" is an acronym that stands for <u>M</u>odeling, <u>A</u>nalysis, and <u>D</u>esign. My particular perspective is that these are the three essential activities required to design a control system. Specifically, given a physical system that we want to control, along with a desired behavior or performance for the controlled system, we determine a control law that will cause the closed-loop system to exhibit the desired behavior by:

(1) **<u>M</u>odeling** (mathematically) the system, based on measurement of essential system characteristics.
(2) **<u>A</u>nalysis** of the model to determine the properties of the system.
(3) **<u>D</u>esign** of the controller which, when coupled with the model of the system, produces the desired closed-loop behavior. This will involve development of

   (a) Control law algorithms.
   (b) Measurement and testing techniques for the specific physical system.
   (c) Signal processing and signal conditioning algorithms necessary for interfacing the sensor and controller to the physical system and to each other.
   (d) Simulation studies of the individual components of the control system as well as simulation of the closed-loop system in which all the components are interconnected. Simulation studies are an essential part of the design and development process and are highly dependent on the models obtained from the measurement process.

Wrapped around these three activities are two other key parts of the controller development process:

(1) **Development of performance specifications** that define the objective of

the control design.

(2) **Implementation of the controller** through software and hardware realizations of the control law, including complete specification of the sensor, signal processing, and control elements, and final assembly, testing and validation, delivery, and operation of the control system.

The five activities described above are summarized in Fig. 0-1, which shows an overall conceptual flowchart of the control system design process. As shown in the figure, starting with the original system we wish to control (defined as including the plant, sensors, and actuators), we proceed with two tasks in parallel: defining the required performance specifications and developing a model of the process. The modeling activity will often include some form of measurement to determine key system properties. Note that mathematical modeling is a particularly important part of the process of control system development. By having a framework for describing the system in a precise way, it is possible to develop rigorous techniques for analyzing and designing systems. Once a math model is available and we have decided the goal of the design, it is possible to proceed with the analysis of the model and design of the control law. Finally, once the control law is finalized the implemented controller is combined with the physical system to collectively act as a new system - one that meets the desired performance.

Central to the process shown in Fig. 0-1 is the iteration of simulation, modeling, and design. Indeed, in today's world simulation cannot be separated from analysis and design. Further, the process of arrive at a math model of the controller is itself a feedback process. Once a controller model is defined it is necessary to evaluate its effectiveness in combination with the math model of the process (via simulation of the complete control system) before proceeding to implementation. We also note that today the process of going from a completed math model of the controller to its implementation is typically highly coupled to the same software environment used for simulation, using a hardware-in-the-loop approach to rapid prototyping. One such environment is the MATLAB/Simulink package.

This discussion then brings me back to the present book by Professors Xue and Chen. My pleasure in the new edition comes from seeing how first they have developed an exposition that embodies the perspective of the MAD Control Engineering and second they have integrated the real-world practices of simulation as part of analysis and design process together with controller implementation using rapid prototyping tools, using MATLAB/Simulink. I believe students who study and follow this text will be well-equipped to "hit the ground running!"

*Kevin L. Moore, Colorado School of Mines, Golden, Colorado, United States*

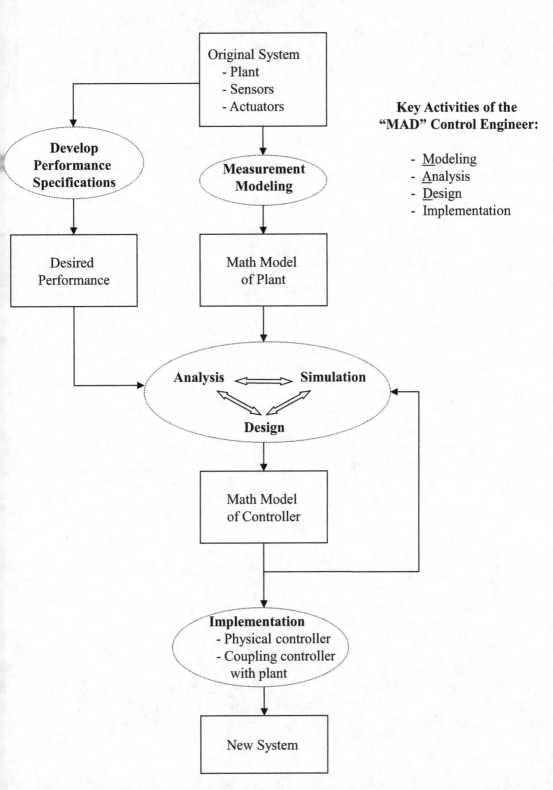

Fig. 0-1  Flowchart of the control system design process.

# Preface

Although the benefits from the wise use of control engineering such as improved product/life quality, minimized waste materials, reduced pollution, increased safety, reduced energy consumption etc. are widely recognized, as per Professor Karl J. Åström, "Control is a hidden technology." To promote the appreciation of control subject, an interesting book "*Feedback and Control for Everyone*"(2010, Pedro Albertos and Iven Mareels, Springer) serves the purpose. Conventional control systems are mostly signal-based control systems which are the foundation to our modern life. While moving from signal-based control to information-based control systems, the basic ideas of control systems are ubiquitous even in this increasingly information-rich world.

This textbook is about signal-based control systems following the so-called "MAD (modeling, analysis and design) notion" suggested by Professor Kevin L. Moore of Colorado School of Mines in 1990s. To have a good control system, one needs to be asked on "What do you have?" and "What do you want?" Many iterations may be needed to design a controller with knowledge about plant model ("What do you have?") and performance and constraints ("What do you want?"). Clearly, a computer-aided design (CAD) platform must be used. MATLAB and Simulink are considered as the dominant software platform for control system modeling, analysis and design, with numerous off-the-shelf toolboxes and blocksets dedicated to control systems and related topics. The major objective of this book is to provide first-hand information on how MATLAB/Simulink can be used in control system modeling, analysis, design as well as hardware-in-the-loop rapid prototyping. The main structure of the book is outlined as follows:

Foundation: Chapters 1, 2 and 3;

Modeling: Chapters 4, 6, 11

Analysis: Chapters 5, 6, 11

Design: Chapters 7, 8, 9, 10, 11

Rapid Prototyping: Chapter 12

The inclusion of Chapter 12 is on purpose since in industry, MATLAB/Simulink is widely used for control system MAD and even deployment via the hardware-in-the-loop real time simulation and targeting onto various microprocessors. Another distinguishing feature is the inclusion of a dedicated PID control design chapter (Chapter 8) with various tuning methods introduced with the dedicated handy tools (e.g., OCD, PID_Tune and OptimPID) developed for this book. Chapters 10 and 11 are both interesting and useful with emerging topics for potential further research and development. Chapter 10 presented concise introduction to some major adaptive and intelligent control system design methods with illustrative design examples. Chapter 11 serves as a survival guide to the analysis and design of fractional-order systems governed by fractional-order differential equations with differentiation or integration of non-integer orders. Extensive illustrative examples are presented in cartoon style so the readers can reproduce the results and gain hands-on working experience on fractional-order control systems analysis and design. This is a nice feature of this book consistently seen in each section with smooth mixture of MATLAB scripts and figures. These scripts are carefully designed so the readers can mimic and even reuse the codes in their own future work.

This book can be used as a reference text in the introductory control course for undergraduates in all engineering schools. The coverage of topics is broad, yet balanced, and should provide a solid foundation for the subsequent control engineering practice in both industry and research institutes. For graduates and researchers not majoring in control, this textbook is useful for knowledge enhancement. The authors also believe that this book will be a good desktop reference for control engineers and many codes and tools in this book may be directly applicable in real world problem solving.

The first version of this textbook, entitled *"Computer-aided design of control systems — MATLAB and its Applications"*, was published by the first author in Chinese by Tsinghua University Press, Beijing, China in 1996. It was the earliest textbook on CADCS (computer aided design of control systems) in MATLAB in China and together with its several later editions, it has been among the most popular textbooks on control systems in China with more than 60,000 copies sold. This new English edition has leveraged all welcoming aspects of the past Chinese editions in terms of the presentation style that has been optimized for self-learning as well as classroom teaching. Most importantly, we followed the MADCS (modeling, analysis and design of control systems) notion and organized the contents in the MADCS way as outlined above. The enhancement in contents includes the intelligent control, fractional-order control as well as rapid prototyping of real-time control systems etc.

This textbook has a book companion website (`http://mechatronics.ucmerced.edu/MADbook`) which contains downloadable resources such as teaching slide set with over 1,000 PPTs, solution manual (for instructors only), all codes/scripts for reproducing the figure/results in this textbook, as well as several useful MATLAB tools developed exclusively for this textbook.

We would like to thank Professor Kevin L. Moore for preparing a foreword for this book sharing his further insights in MAD.

During the evolution of this book, many researchers, professors, and students have provided useful feedback, comments, and inputs. In particular, we thank the following professors: Xinhe Xu, Xingquan Ren, Derek P. Atherton, Yuanwei Jing, Feng Pan, Dali Chen, Igor Podlubny, Blas M. Vinagre. The writing of the materials on fractional-order systems is partly supported by the National Natural Science Foundation of China under grant number 61174145. The "Book Program" from MathWorks Inc., is acknowledged for the latest MATLAB software access.

Moreover, we are grateful to Chandra Nugraha of World Scientific Publishing Co. who helped on detailed copyediting of this textbook.

Last, but not least, Dingyü Xue would like to thank his wife Jun Yang and his daughter Yang Xue; YangQuan Chen would like to thank his wife Huifang Dou and his sons Duyun, David, and Daniel, for their patience, understanding and complete support throughout this work.

*Dingyü Xue, Northeastern University, Shenyang, China*
*YangQuan Chen, University of California, Merced, United States*

# Contents

# Chapter 1

# Introduction to Simulation and Computer-aided Design of Control Systems

Automation science originated in the beginning of the 20th century. The theoretical foundation of automation science and technology is established on physical sciences, mathematics, system sciences and social sciences[1]. In the opening speech of the 40th IEEE Conference of Decision and Control held in 2000, Professor John Doyle quoted the words of a well-known scientist in control, Professor Larry Yu-Chi Ho of Harvard University, "Control will be the physics of the 21st century"[2].

The progresses of automation science are inseparable from the development of automatic control theory. At the very beginning of control system applications, trial-and-error methods were used in control systems design, which is usually done with slide-rules and calculators. With the rapid development of control theory, especially with the rapid development of hardware and software in computers, computer-aided design of control systems (CACSD) emerged as an important research area in automation science. In this chapter, the development of the area of CACSD is briefly introduced, and the development of the subjects of computer software and languages, which are closely related to the area, will also be given. In particular, the development of MATLAB language will be presented. The framework of the book will be summarized briefly in the chapter so that the readers can better study the materials in the book.

## 1.1 A Brief Historic Review of the Development of Computer-aided Design of Control Systems

In the past, control systems design problems were often solved simply with pens and papers. For instance, the tuning of PID controllers can easily be worked out using the empirical formula proposed by Ziegler and Nichols in 1942[3]. With the rapid development of control theory, and the ever-growing demanding to the advanced controllers, the design of controllers are more and more complicated, the mere use of pens, papers and calculators are no longer possible. Meanwhile, with the rapid development of computers and software, the emergence of the CACSD techniques is inevitable.

The development of CACSD techniques now achieved an extremely high level, and continuously received the attentions from the scholars and researchers in control community worldwide. Dating back to the years of 1982, and 1984, special issues on CACSD were first published by *Control Systems Magazine* of IEEE Control Systems Society and *Proceedings of IEEE*[4, 5]. Two collective books reporting the recent progresses in CACSD were published by Jamshidi and Herget in 1985 and 1992[6, 7]. In the important conferences in control engineering, such as IFAC World Congress, American Control Conference (ACC) and IEEE Conference on Decision and Control (CDC), special sessions were arranged. The CACSD techniques are sometimes referred to as computer-aided control systems engineering (CACSE)[6, 7].

In the last thirty years, with the rapid development of computer technology, many splendid application software emerged, and a great variety of CACSD software also appeared. Some of the CACSD software and packages were written in Fortran, while many were interactive languages. Also special simulation languages were released. Many of the software were mostly used in control community. Since the depute of MATLAB, as a language, it was welcome by the scholars and students in control community worldwide, and it has become the *de facto* most influential and top choice among the control researchers and educators.

In the earlier textbooks in CACSD, the general-purpose computer languages such as BASIC[6, 8], Fortran[9] and C were used as the supporting languages. With the development and progresses of computer tools, especially the leading-edge MATLAB in control and scientific computation, recent textbooks used MATLAB as the major tool in addressing the CACSD algorithms and implementations[10–17]. The trend is also extended to classical control textbooks, such as in [18–20]. Equipped with the powerful computer tool, control researchers can concentrate on the efforts of control theory and approaches, instead of spending their valuable time on repetitive low-level mechanic work. In this way, the researchers should have better understanding on the overall CACSD techniques. The understanding deviation of "can't see the wood for the trees" can be avoided, and effectiveness and reliability of controller design can be expected.

It was pointed out by the greatest ancient Chinese philosopher, Confucius, that "*The mechanic, who wishes to do his work well, must first sharpen his tools*". The major objective of this book is to systematically introduce the recent progresses in the area of control systems analysis and design, with the most advanced tools, to solve directly the problems in control systems design with minimum efforts.

## 1.2    Introduction to the CACSD Languages and Environments

In 1973, a monograph on CACSD was published by Professors James L Melsa and Stephen K Jones[9], and in the book, many of the Fortran subroutines related to control problems were provided, including root locus, frequency responses of linear systems, as well as those used in Luenberger observers and Kalman filters.

Professor Karl J Åström in Lund Institute of Technology in Sweden proposed a set of interactive software package INTRAC[21] for solving CACSD problems, including IDPAC, MODPAC, SYNPAC, POLPAC, as well as a simulation language SIMNON[22], where SIMNON allows the user to model and simulate systems in a Fortran-like programming style. Professor Katsuhisa Furuta of Japan developed the DPACS-F[23] and it is useful in handling multivariable systems. The leading simulation languages such as ACSL, CSMP, TSIM (Cambridge Control Ltd.) and ESL provide some model blocks, and the users can express the system model by writing simulation programs. There are also dedicated packages for control systems, including CLADP (Cambridge linear analysis and design programs)[24, 25] developed in Cambridge University, and ORACLS (optimal regulator algorithms for the control of linear systems) developed by Dr Ernest S Armstrong of NASA Langley Research Center[26].

In the late 1970's, American mathematician Cleve B Moler proposed the interactive MATLAB, and it received great attention from the researchers in control community. Many toolboxes were developed with MATLAB devoted to a varieties of control problems, and these facilities are very convenient in the analysis and design of control systems; also, powerful functions were provided to test new controller design algorithms with ease. The emerge of Simulink, an interactive graphical modeling and simulation environment, promoted the application of MATLAB. Now MATLAB is the top choice and most popular and welcomed computer language among the researchers in control community worldwide.

Along with the rapid development of MATLAB, many other software and languages dedicated to control also appeared. Among them, some of the representative ones are, CTRL-C[27] developed by Jack Little in Systems Control Technology Inc., EASY 5 and EASY5x by Boeing Corporation, MATRIX$_X$ and Xmath by Integrated Systems[28], CC by Systems Technology Incorporated[29], VisSim/O-Matrix by Visual Simulation Corporation, CemTool by Professor Kwon of Seoul National University. Also, the free software Octave[30] and Scilab[31] are still active. Although some of the above mentioned software and languages are developed independently and in parallel with MATLAB, the impact of MATLAB can easily be witnessed from them. Thus, it is a good way to introduce CACSD techniques with the support of the most popular computer tool, and MATLAB is the top choice.

There are some stages in the development of CACSD techniques, such as software packages, interactive languages, and the modern object-oriented environment[32].

In earlier days, the work of CACSD concentrated on the design of software packages. The work of Melsa and Jones mentioned earlier is a good example. Several supporting packages in numerical analysis also appeared, such as eigen-system computation package EISPACK[33, 34], linear algebra package LINPACK[35], NAG package[36] by Numerical Algorithm Group in Oxford, and the "Numerical Recipe" software package[37]. In the area of control, the SLICE (subroutine library in control engineering)[38] developed by Kingston Polytechnic, and the packages DPACS-F, ORACLS mentioned earlier are also good examples. Most of these software package were developed in Fortran, and good user interface was provided, however, the use of the packagers are far more complicated and inconvenient compared with MATLAB.

If one wants to find all the eigenvalues of an $N \times N$ real matrix $A$, and the arrays $W_R$ and $W_I$ for real and imaginary parts of the eigenvalues, the suggested sequence of subroutine call of EISPACK package is[33]:

```
CALL BALANC(NM,N,A,IS1,IS2,FV1)
CALL ELMHES(NM,N,IS1,IS2,A,IV1)
CALL ELTRAN(NM,N,IS1,IS2,A,IV1,Z)
CALL HQR2(NM,N,IS1,IS2,A,WR,WI,Z,IERR)
IF (IERR.EQ.0) GOTO 99999
CALL BALBAK(NM,N,IS1,IS2,FV1,N,Z)
```

Besides, to find the eigenvalues and eigenvectors of a matrix, some other statements are needed. For instance, one has to write further statements to load the matrix into the program, and when the eigenvalues are found, other statements are needed to feedback the results back to the user. The source code should be compiled and linked to form an executable program. From the above subroutine calls it can be found that the procedures are rather tedious to use packages for solving certain problems. The major problems of using software packages, therefore are:

(1) **Inconvenience in use**. For the users who are not proficient in the packages, it is difficult to write programs and the programs are error prone. A slight carelessness may result in incorrect or misleading results.

(2) **The calling sequence is tedious**. A main program should be written and compiling and linking processes are expected. A great amount of time is needed in debugging the program to ensure the correctness of the results, which may not immediately available.

(3) **Too many executable files**. Each specific problem needs one executable file, and it may require maintenance of a certain amount of executables, which may be not economic; besides, the executables may cause problems to maintain.

(4) **Inconvenience in data transfer**. Each executable is an independent and isolated file, and it might be very difficult to share data by several executables.

(5) **Array size allocation problems**. Matrix is the essential data type in CACSD problems. If the size of the matrices are allocated too low, it cannot be used for some high-order systems. For instance, the matrix dimensions were allocated to $10 \times 10$ in the packages of Reference [9]. In successful softwares, dynamic allocation approaches are adopted.

Besides, most of the earlier packages were developed in Fortran, and in the earlier version of Fortran, graphics are not well supported, other packages such as GINO-F[39] should be used. Fundamental plotting facilities are provided in these packages and low-level programming are needed to draw satisfactory plots.

The CLADP program developed by Jan Maciejowski and Alistair MacFarlane of Cambridge University is also very influential and it includes many analysis and design methods for multivariable systems, where frequency domain Nyquist methods, characteristic loci methods and time domain methods like linear quadratic Gaussian (LQG) and Kalman filter are implemented. The DPACS-F package developed by Professor Katsuhisa Furuta of Tokyo Institute of Technology analyzes multivariable systems, and the design methods such as pole placement and LQG are implemented, and the subroutines of identification of multivariable systems are also supported. The ORACLS package developed by Ernest S Armstrong of NASA are equipped with the facilities of LQG design of multivariable systems. Those packages were also developed in Fortran.

In late 1970's and earlier 1980's, a great amount of practical interactive software were released, and MATLAB is a good representative. Besides, INTRAC and CTRL-C mentioned earlier are also good examples.

Since there exists a great variety of such CACSD software, and each has its own characteristics, there were several attempts to integrate some of these software together. For instance, Professor Spang III tried to integrate SIMNON, CLADP, IDPAC and his own SSDP (state space design program) together in 1984 to form a new powerful software[40]. The interchange of data among the components was made though data files. The other example was the SERC ECSTASY (environment for control system theory and synthesis) project by Professors Howard H Rosenbrock and Neil Munro in 1986[41], where MATLAB, ACSL, TSIM, and the brand new Mathematica[42] were under the same framework. Scientific documentation systems such as LATEX[43] and FrameMaker were also integrated. The data transfer among the components were made through databases. In ECSTASY, some advanced new CACSD commands were defined, which were better than the then MATLAB. The ECSTASY project was a good attempt, however, it can only run on SUN workstations, and the compatibilities with personal computers was not considered.

In the authors' opinion, these software by mere integration are not successful, since the expected targets were not achieved. In fact, the facilities of each individual software has significant improvement. For instance, the simulation facilities of MATLAB evolved a lot, and the interface to Simulink is far much better than that of ACSL. There are better interfaces to Mathematica, and MATLAB itself was equipped with powerful Symbolic Math Toolbox.

Meanwhile, the influential works on CACSD in China include the key national natural science foundation project, CADCSC (CADCS in China), chaired by Professor Jingqing Han[44], and the books and codes by Professors Zengqi Sun and Zengren Yuan of Tsinghua University[8] and Professors Chongguang Wu and Chenglin Shen of Beijing Institute Chemical Engineering[45].

## 1.3 Development of Simulation Software

From the limitations of the software packages summarized earlier, it can be seen that it might be very difficult to call them in simulation directly, since one has to master the interfaces of all the blocks. Besides, the results from some of the software packages may not be very reliable, since the qualities of packages are different.

Simulation techniques received attentions from the scholars and experts around the world, and the Simulation Councils Inc. was established, and in 1967, the standard of simulation languages was publicized. CSMP (computer simulation modelling program) was the earliest simulation language released obeying that standard. Professor Jihu Ma of Shenyang Institute of Automation, Academia Sinica of China extended it to CSMP-C, in 1988.

In earlier 1980's, Mitchell and Gauthier Associates Ltd in USA released the ACSL (advanced continuous simulation language)[46]. Since its powerful and high standard simulation capabilities and some of system analysis facilities, it soon became dominant in the simulation communities.

During a similar period as ACSL, Professor Karl J Åström of Lund Institute of Technology in Sweden developed the SIMNON language, and the ESL language[47] developed by Salford University in England. The interface and programming of these languages are similar, since they all obey the same standard.

Computer algebra system is another attractive topic in the related field. Analytical computation is sometimes not possible even for the most experienced C programmers. The muMATH system[48] and REDUCE[49] are good examples of this kind of computer algebra systems. The new comers Maple and Mathematica soon dominanted the market and becoming the leading computer algebra systems.

There is interaction between MATLAB and earlier versions of Mathematica, via the interface called MathLink. To solve computer algebra problems, MATLAB released its own Symbolic Math Toolbox, where Maple was used as its symbolic computation engine, so that the benefit of the two languages is combined perfectly. Now the symbolic engine adopted in MATLAB is MuPAD.

Some softwares and languages are extremely expensive, thus many researchers tend to use freely available softwares instead. For instance, the programming styles of Octave[30] and Scilab are very similar to MATLAB. The Scicos environment under Scilab can also be used to draw block diagrams and perform simulation. All their source codes are available and transparent; however, the global standard of them is not as good as the current versions of MATLAB.

System simulation has its own characteristics. If we select a leading-edge simulation tool to deal with control systems, the readers can then use it to further investigate the behaviors of the systems. It is demonstrated already that MATLAB/Simulink is such a simulation tool. In this book, we shall extensively introduce MATLAB and Simulink,

## 1.4   MATLAB/Simulink and Their CACSD Toolboxes

The creator of MATLAB, Professor Cleve Moler, is a famous mathematician, and his research work in numerical linear algebra are very influential[33–35, 50–52].

He served professorship in Universities of Michigan, Stanford and New Mexico. In the late 1970's, while he was the chinaman of the Department of Computer Science at University of New Mexico, and was teaching linear algebra, he began to realize that the original programming with EISPACK was very tedious. He conceived and implemented MATLAB, meaning matrix laboratory[53]. MATLAB was established upon the two software packages EISPACK[34] and LINPACK[35], and it is an interactive system integrating facilities such as command parser, scientific computation. The original version of MATLAB was written in Fortran.

The so-called interactive language means that if you give a command, the results can be obtained immediately. There is no need to compile, link to generate executables, like the C and Fortran languages. This has undoubtedly brought much convenience to the users. Matrix computation was made much easier in MATLAB at that time, thus it received welcome attentions from engineers once it appeared.

The earlier version of MATLAB could only be used to perform matrix computation, and the plotting facilities were very primitive, where asterisks were used to label points on curves. The total number of built-in functions was only about 40 to 50. Even so, it attracted many users since it first appeared.

Cleve Moler and Jack Little co-founded a company named "The MathWorks" in 1984, to develop and promote MATLAB, and Cleve Moler became the chief scientist. MATLAB was completely rewritten in C, and other useful facilities were introduced and it became more and more powerful. The earlier version running on personal computers was named PC-MATLAB, and the one on workstations was named Pro MATLAB. In 1990, MATLAB 3.5i was released and it was the first version executable on Microsoft Windows. Two windows could be opened, one for command line, and the other one for graphics display. Later the block diagram-based modeling and simulation interface SimuLAB was released, and it was renamed to Simulink one year later. In 1992, the epoch-making MATLAB 4.0 was released, which fully support Microsoft Windows programming. In 1996, MATLAB 5.0 was released and more data types such as cells, objects are supported. In 2000, MAT-LAB 6.0 was released and in the computation kernel, LAPACK and FFTW were adopted, instead of the traditional LINPACK and EISPACK packages. MATLAB 7.0 was released in 2004, and multiple domain physical modeling technique was supported, and the brand new Simulink modeling facilities are useful for control engineers. In 2012, MATLAB 8.0 was released and the interface is shown in Fig. 1-1. The new facilities in Simulink modeling interface were more powerful.

MathWorks releases two versions each year, and labeled a and b respectively. The most recent version is MATLAB R2014a. Since the symbolic engine is changed from Maple to MuPAD, and from the authors' point of view, the capabilities of symbolic computation are reduced. For users involved in extensive symbolic computations, MATLAB R2008a or earlier versions are recommended. Two versions are suggested if possible — R2008a and the latest version. MATLAB R2014a is used in the book, however, most of the materials are applicable to earlier versions

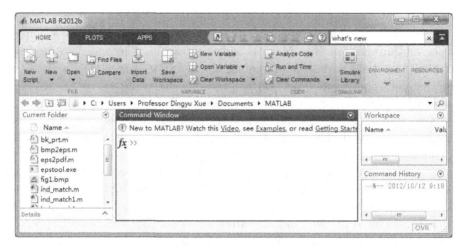

Fig. 1-1    MATLAB 8.0 interface.

of MATLAB.

MATLAB is now the leading and most popular tool in the area of scientific and engineering computation. MATLAB is not merely a matrix laboratory; it is a promising advanced programming language with great application prospect. It is referred to as the fourth generation computer language, and is playing an important role in education and scientific research. MATLAB is becoming more and more powerful. Its long time competitor, Matrix-X, was acquired by MathWorks. It can be expected that MATLAB will keep its unique position in scientific computation and system simulation.

Apart from its classical interactive programming style, MATLAB is an object-orient computer language with its reliable matrix computation, scientific visualization, data processing, and and image processing capabilities. Many famous scholars in control have developed relevant toolboxes of their own research area in MATLAB. For instance, there are Control System Toolbox, System Identification Toolbox, Robust Control Toolbox, Multivariable Frequency Design Toolbox, $\mu$-Analysis and Synthesis Toolbox, Neural Network Toolbox, Optimization Toolbox, Signal Processing Toolbox. The developers of the toolboxes are famous scholars in control community, including Professors Alan Laub, Michael Sofanov, Leonard Ljung, and Jan Maciejowski. This of course earned the reputation and credibility of MATLAB, and MATLAB gradually becomes the most popular and effective computer tool in control community.

More information about MATLAB can be found from its official web-site
http://www.mathworks.com

## 1.5    Overview of CACSD Approaches

At the beginning of the development of control theory and applications, the controller design problems studied are much simpler. For instance, practical

PID controllers can be tuned with Ziegler–Nichols empirical formula[3]. This phenomenon lasted for a few decades.

With the development of computer technology, especially with the popularization of the flexible and powerful tool like MATLAB, great achievement is witnessed in the CACSD area. Researchers and engineers are no longer happy to accept the controllers designed with pens and papers. There are more and more demanding in the quality and robustness of the controllers. For instance, engineers are expecting optimum behaviour of the controllers, and this kind of effect cannot be obtained with pens and papers any more. Thus, a new area — computer-aided design techniques are developed.

Earlier work of CACSD focused on the computer-aided analysis of control systems. Powerful facilities were implemented to enable researchers to draw frequency response curves, and design controllers based on the curves, with usually trial-and-error methods, and then the time domain responses are observed. These kinds of approach worked well for simple single variable systems. The British School represented by Professors Rosenbrock and MacFarlane concentrated on the design of frequency domain methods for multivariable systems. Professor Issac Horowitz created a new way in frequency domain design methods, where he introduced the quantitative feedback theory (QFT)[54]. Many scholars develop software packages in their own research area, for instance, the CLADP mentioned earlier. With the development of MATLAB, MATLAB toolboxes are also developed, for instance, the Multivariable Frequency Design (MFD) Toolbox, developed by Professor Jan Maciejowski of Cambridge University[55]. The QFT Toolbox was developed by Craig Borghesani and Yossi Chait of University of Masseusutes[56].

Apart from the classical multivariable frequency domain approaches, some scholars use optimization techniques to design optimal controllers; for instance, the parameter optimization method by Dr. John Edmunds, and the method of inequalities by Dr. Zakian[57]. These methods are all very effective practical approaches.

At the same time, American scholars are interested in state space representation and design methods, these methods are time domain methods. Linear quadratic criterion was first used, and linear quadratic optimal regulators were designed. The weighting matrices can be selected by the users such that optimum performance can be achieved. State feedback and state observers can be designed and implemented. Due to the limitations in linear quadratic Gaussian control, loop transfer recovery (LTR) and other new control techniques are proposed.

There are also a lot of design approaches proposed, aiming at rising the robustness of the closed-loop systems. The minimum sensitivity control strategy proposed by Professor George Zames attracted the attention of researchers, and various optimal $\mathcal{H}_\infty$ norm controllers were also published. The so-called $\mathcal{H}_\infty$ means physically realizable systems, where $\mathcal{H}$ for Hardy space. A key problem in $\mathcal{H}_\infty$ is that with Youla parameterization, a class of controllers can be generalized. There are various ways in solving $\mathcal{H}_\infty$ problems, all the stabilizing controllers can be formulated with Youla parameterization approach. State space methods are now usually used, since closed-form design scheme can be proposed. Because the orders of the controllers thus designed are usually too high, controller reduction approaches are always adopted. Linear matrix inequalities (LMI) and $\mu$-synthesis approaches are the other forms for solving robust controller design problems. These methods cannot be used without the use of computers and relevant software tools.

The work of Professor Karl Åström in Sweden are closer to practical control engineering applications, rather than applied mathematics. Innovative work can usually be witnessed from his publications. His work on automatic tuning of PID controllers[58] is now widely used in process industry. His pioneer work on self-tuning controllers opened a new era in the area of adaptive control. Intelligent control systems are important in theory and applications. Predictive control, learning control, fuzzy logic control and neural network-based control are good examples actual intelligent control systems.

Fractional-order control is another promising new research area[59] and many new achievement are being made.

Many textbooks and monographs are published on MATLAB and CACSD applications[10–12]. Most of the existing books are only introductory ones of MATLAB. Extensive and systematic applications in control with MATLAB were not fully provided. This is the main target of this book.

## 1.6  Fundamental Structures and Contents of This Book

The tasks involved in the simulation and design of control systems are always composed of three procedures, the so-called MAD processes — the modeling, analysis, design processes. The model of the system should be established first, and if it is found that the model is not correct in the analysis process, the model should be modified. When an exact model is established and complete analysis to the system is made, controllers can then be designed for the target system. Closed-loop behaviours of the system under the new controllers should then be analyzed again. If the behaviour of the closed-loop system is not satisfactory, the control design process should be performed again to redesign the controllers.

According to the processes involved in the simulation and design of control systems, the following materials are organized in the book, as follows:

In Chapter 1, the popular CACSD softwares such as ACSL, MATLAB and Mathematica are summarized, and the CACSD strategies are also briefly introduced. Also, in the chapter, the question "Why MATLAB in the book" will be answered.

In Chapter 2, essential knowledge of MATLAB programming is presented, including data types, statements, control structure, function programming and graphics. Object-oriented programming techniques for graphical user interfaces are also demonstrated in examples.

Chapter 3 presents the scientific computation problem solutions with MATLAB, and those problems mainly presented are closely related to control systems. The computation problems are linear algebra, nonlinear equations, differential equations, optimization and Laplace/$z$ transforms.

Chapter 4 presents the model representation of various linear systems, including continuous/discrete, single variable/multivariable, transfer function, state space and zero–pole–gain models. The topics of block diagram modeling and simplification, as well as conversions among different model representations will also be covered. Further, model reduction and system identification will be addressed in the chapter.

Chapter 5 covers the basic analysis problems for linear control systems. The properties such as stability, controllability and observability are presented first, and then, root locus, time/frequency domain system analysis approaches are presented. Multivariable frequency domain responses are also presented in the chapter. These approaches are useful in system design topics.

In Chapter 6, nonlinear system modeling and analysis approaches with Simulink are presented. A brief introduction to Simulink block library is given, then examples on various control system modeling are given. Subsystem, model masking and S-function programming are also talked about in the chapter. Theoretically, equipped with the methodology presented in the chapter, systems of any complexity can be modeled and simulated.

Chapter 7 presents various classical controller design methods, including series lead–lag compensator design, linear quadratic optimal controller design and pole placement, observers and observer-based control, optimal controller design, frequency domain design and decoupling control of multivariable systems.

Chapter 8 presents PID controller design methods, including PID controller structures, regular PID controller tuning algorithms and in particular, with the use of OptimPID graphical user interface, optimal PID controllers can be obtained. Also, some of the PID design interfaces provided in MATLAB are illustrated.

In Chapter 9, some of the typical robust controller design approaches are given, including LQG/LTR-based robust controller design, $\mathcal{H}_\infty$ optimal controller design. Also, design method and tool of quantitative feedback theory will be introduced. Linear matrix inequality and quantitative feedback theory-based robust control system design approaches are also presented.

Chapter 10 presents an introduction to the modeling, design and simulation of adaptive control and intelligent control design problems. Model reference adaptive control, self-tuning control and generalized predictive control will be shown first. Then the design and simulation of fuzzy logic control, various neural network control systems will be introduced. Finally genetic algorithm, particle swarm optimization algorithm and their applications in optimal controller design will be illustrated. Also, in the chapter, model predictive control and iterative learning control systems are introduced and illustrated.

In Chapter 11, fractional-order control systems are presented. This covers the topics of the definitions and solutions of fractional-order calculus problems, block diagram approximation of fractional-order systems. Fractional-order transfer function is used as an example to demonstrate object-oriented modeling and class object programming. Simulation analysis of complicated fractional-order systems are illustrated. Also, the optimal design of fractional-order PID controllers will be illustrated.

Chapter 12 bridges the gap between software analysis and hardware control. Hardware-in-the-loop framework is presented, based on the dSPACE, Quanser and low-cost Arduino software/hardware systems. This chapter can be a starting point of real-time applications of control theory.

Several benchmark problems of control systems are given in Appendix and the readers can use these plant models as the starting point to test a variety of their own controllers and get fair comparisons.

## 1.7   Problems

(1) The whole set of manuals of MATLAB and its toolboxes are provided in MathWorks web-site at `http://www.mathworks.cn`. If necessary, you can download the relevant manuals for further reading. It is not possible to cover all the topics with a single book, this book can only be used as introductive materials of MATLAB applications in control problems.

(2) MATLAB language is the top selected language in control systems research, and it is the major tool to implement the materials in the book. Install MATLAB on your machine, and execute `demo` command to run demonstrations. You can appreciate the facilities of MATLAB.

(3) Learn to use the on-line help facilities of MATLAB language, and learn MATLAB with these facilities. The MATLAB command `help` or Help menu can be used to find on-line information, and `doc` command can also be used.

(4) When the user wants to write his own program, makes sure that there is no file with the same name on MATLAB search path, otherwise there may exist conflicts in the future. To check whether there is any file with the same name, use `which` command to confirm it.

(5) In MATLAB, the multiplication of two matrices can be obtained directly with $C = A * B$. Try to write a general function in C for the multiplication of two matrices, and experience the problems and bugs you may encounter in low-level programming.

(6) Matrix computation is the classical characteristics of MATLAB, the inverse matrix of matrix $A$ can be evaluated with $B = \text{inv}(A)$ command. You can experience the high-level facilities and efficiency of MATLAB in matrix inversion. Assume that one can declare an $n \times n$ random matrix $A$, with $n = 550$ and $n = 1550$, respectively, validate the results and elapsed time with the following statements

```
>> tic,  A = rand(550);  B = inv(A); toc
>> norm(A*B-eye(size(A)), norm(B*A-eye(size(A)))
```

Please note that it is known from linear algebra that $AB = BA = I$, where $I$ is an identity matrix. Thus, $\|AB - I\|$ can be used to validate the results, $\|A\|$ evaluates the norm of matrix $A$.

(7) In the solution of mathematical problems, different algorithms may have different precision and speed. For instance, to find the determinant of an $n \times n$ matrix, algebraic complement method can be used, and the original problem can be converted to find $n$ determinants of $(n-1) \times (n-1)$ matrices, and the determinant of $(n-2) \times (n-2)$ matrices can in turn be converted to the determinants of $(n-3) \times (n-3)$ matrices, and so on. Thus, the conclusion below can be proposed. "The analytical solution of the determinant of any square matrix can be found". Unfortunately, this conclusion is wrong, since it neglected the computability problem. When $n = 25$, the working load is about 65 years on the today's fastest mainframe computers in the world.

From numerical linear algebra, it is known that the determinant can be evaluated by LU decomposition method, with much less computation effort. Try to find the analytical solution of the determinant of a $25 \times 25$ matrix, and measure the time elapsed. You can reference the following commands:

```
>> tic, A=sym(hilb(25)); det(A); toc
```

(8) Try to solve analytically and numerically the expanded form of the equation

$$(x + 1)^{20} = x^{20} + C_{20}^1 x^{19} + \cdots + C_{20}^{19} x + C_{20}^{20} = 0,$$

where $C_n^m = n! / \left[ n! \cdot (n - m)! \right]$ are binomial coefficients. Of course the coefficients can be generated with loops. With Mathematica, Maple or MATLAB and its Symbolic Math Toolbox, and try to explain what is happening. The sample code is

```
>> p=1; for i=1:20, p=conv(p,[1 i]); end, p, roots(p)
   syms x; p=sym(1); for i=1:20, p=p*(x+i); end, p, solve(p)
```

(9) Simulink environment in MATLAB can be used in modeling of complicated block diagrams. Try to use Simulink to establish a simulation model for the nonlinear feedback control system shown in Fig. 1-2. Evaluate the unit step response of the system with the dead zone parameter of $\delta = 0.3$. See what kind of impact on the system response for different values of $\delta$'s and understand the simplicity of block diagram modeling and simulation approaches.

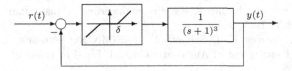

Fig. 1-2   Block diagram of a nonlinear feedback control system.

## Bibliography and References

[1] Dai X Z. Contents, status and architecture of the descipline of automation science and technology. Beijing: Higher Education Press, 2003. (In Chinese)

[2] Doyle J C. A new physics? 40th IEEE Conference on Decision and Control, Plenary Speech. Orlando: IEEE Publisher, 2000

[3] Ziegler J G, Nichols N B. Optimum settings for automatic controllers. Transaction of ASME, 1944, 64:759–768

[4] Herget C J, Laub A J (eds.). Special issue on computer-aided control system design. IEEE Control Systems Magazine, 1982, 2(4):2–37

[5] Herget C J, Laub A J (eds.). Special issue on computer-aided control system design. Proceedings of IEEE, 1984, 72:1714–1805

[6] Jamshidi M, Herget C J. (eds.). Computer-aided control systems engineering. Amsterdam: Elsevier Science Publishers B V, 1985

[7] Jamshidi M, Herget C J. (eds.). Recent advances in computer-aided control systems engineering. Amsterdam: Elsevier Science Publishers B V, 1992

[8] Sun Z Q, Yuan Z R. Computer-aided design of control systems. Beijing: Tsinghua University Press, 1988. (In Chinese)

[9] Melsa J L, Jones S K. Computer programs for computational assistance in the study of linear control theory. New York: McGraw-Hill, 1973

[10] Shahian B, Hassul M. Computer-aided control system design using MATLAB. Englewood Cliffs: Prentice-Hall, 1993

[11] Leonard N E, Levine W S. Using MATLAB to analyze and design control systems. Redwood City: Benjamin Cummings, 1993

[12] Ogata K. Solving control engineering problems with MATLAB. Englewood Cliffs: Prentice Hall, 1994

[13] Mościński J, Ogonowski Z. Advanced control with MATLAB and Simulink. London: Ellis Horwood, 1995

[14] Xue D Y. Computer-aided design of control systems — MATLAB language and applications. Beijing: Tsinghua University Press, 1996. (In Chinese)

[15] Zhang X H. Computer simulation and CAD of control systems. Beijing: China Machine Press, 1999. (In Chinese)

[16] Xue D Y. Design and analysis of feedback control systems with MATLAB. Beijing: Tsinghua University Press, 2000. (In Chinese)

[17] Xue D Y. Simulation and computer-aided design of control systems. Beijing: China Machine Press, 2005. (In Chinese)

[18] Kuo B C. Automatic control systems. Wiley, 8th edition, 2003

[19] D'Azzo J J, Houpis C H. Linear control system analysis and design: conventional and modern. New York: McGraw-Hill, 4th edition, 1995

[20] Ogata K. Modern control engineering. Englewood Cliffs: Prentice Hall, 4th edition, 2001

[21] Åström K J. Computer aided tools for control system design, In: Jamshidi M, Herget C J. Computer-aided control systems engineering. Amsterdam: Elsevier Science Publishers B V, 1985, 3–40

[22] Elmqvist H, Åström K J, Schönthal T. SIMNON — user's guide for MS-DOS computers. Department of Automatic Control, Lund Institute of Technology, Lund, Sweden, 1986

[23] Furuta K. Computer-aided design program for linear control systems. Proceedings of IFAC Symposium on CACSD, 1979, 267–272. Zurich, Switzerland

[24] Edmunds J M. Cambridge linear analysis and design programs. Proceedings IFAC Symposium on CACSD, 1979, 253–258. Zurich, Switzerland

[25] Maciejowski J M, MacFarlane A G J. CLADP: the Cambridge linear analysis and design programs, In: Jamshidi M, Herget C J. Computer-aided control systems engineering. Amsterdam: Elsevier Science Publishers B V, 1985, 125–138

[26] Armstrong E S. ORACLS — a design system for linear multivariable control. New York: Marcel Dekker Inc., 1980

[27] Little J N, Emami-Naeini A, Bangert S N. CTRL-C and matrix environments for the computer-aided design of control systems, In: Jamshidi M, Herget C J. Computer-aided control systems engineering. Amsterdam: Elsevier Science Publishers B V, 1985, 191–205

[28] Shah S C, Floyd M A, Lehman L L. MATRIX$_X$: Control and modeling building CAE capability, In: Jamshidi M, Herget C J. Computer-aided control systems engineering. Amsterdam: Elsevier Science Publishers B V, 1985, 181–207

[29] Thompson P M. Program CC: Technical information. Proceedings of the 2nd IEEE Control Systems Society Symposium on Computer-aided Control System Design (CACSD), Santa Barbara, California, 1985

[30] Octave webpage. http://www.octave.org

[31] SciLAB webpage. http://scilabsoft.inria.fr

[32] Jobling C P, Grant P W, Barker H A, Townsend P. Object-oriented programming in control system design: a survey. Automatica, 1994, 30:1221–1261

[33] Smith B T, Boyle J M, Dongarra J J. Matrix eigensystem routines — EISPACK guide, *Lecture Notes in Computer Sciences*, volume 6. New York: Springer-Verlag, 2nd edition, 1976

[34] Garbow B S, Boyle J M, Dongarra J J, Moler C B. Matrix eigensystem routines — EISPACK guide extension, *Lecture Notes in Computer Sciences*, volume 51. New York: Springer-Verlag, 1977

[35] Dongarra J J, Bunch J R, Moler C B, Stewart G W. LINPACK user's guide. Philadelphia: Society of Industrial and Applied Mathematics (SIAM), 1979

[36] Numerical Algorithm Group. NAG FORTRAN library manual, 1982

[37] Press W H, Flannery B P, Teukolsky S A, Vitterling W T. Numerical recipes, the art of scientific computing. Cambridge: Cambridge University Press, 1986

[38] Atherton D P. Control systems computed. Physics in Technology, 1985, 16:139–140

[39] CAD Center. GINO-F Users' manual, 1976

[40] Spang III H A. The federated computer-aided design system, In: Jamshidi M, Herget C J. Computer-aided control systems engineering. Amsterdam: Elsevier Science Publishers B V, 1985, 209–228

[41] Munro N. ECSTASY — a control system CAD environment. Proceedings IEE Conference on Control 88, 1988, 76–80. Oxford

[42] Wolfram S. Mathematica: a system for doing mathematics by computer. Redwood City, California: Addison-Wesley Publishing Company, 1988

[43] Lamport L. LaTeX: a document preparation system — user's guide and reference manual. Reading MA: Addision-Wesley Publishing Company, 2nd edition, 1994

[44] Wang Z B, Han J Q. CADCSC software system — computer-aided design of control systems. Beijing: Science Press, 1997. (In Chinese)

[45] Wu C G, Shen C L. Computer-aided design of control systems. Beijing: Mechanical Industry Press, 1988. (In Chinese)

[46] Mitchell E E L, Gauthier J S. Advanced continuous simulation language (ACSL) — user's manual. Mitchell & Gauthier Associates, 1987

[47] Hay J L, Pearce J G, Turnbull L, Crosble R E. ESL software user manual. Salford:

ISIM Simulation, 1988

[48] Wooff C, Hodgkinson D.  muMATH: A microcomputer algebra system.  London: Academic Press, 1987

[49] Rayna G.  REDUCE software for algebraic computation.  New York: Springer-Verlag, 1987

[50] Forsythe G E, Malcolm M A, Moler C B.  Computer methods for mathematical computations.  Englewood Cliffs: Prentice-Hall, 1977

[51] Forsythe G E, Moler C B.  Computer solution of linear algebraic systems.  Englewood Cliffs: Prentice-Hall, 1967

[52] Molor C B.  Numerical computing with MATLAB.  MathWorks Inc, 2004

[53] Moler C B.  MATLAB — An interactive matrix laboratory.  Technical Report 369, Department of Mathematics and Statistics, University of New Mexico, 1980

[54] Horowitz I.  Quantitative feedback theory (QFT).  Proceedings IEE, Part D, 1982, 129:215–226

[55] Boyel J M, Ford M P, Maciejowski J M.  A multivariable toolbox for use with MATLAB.  IEEE Control Systems Magazine, 1989, 9:59–65

[56] Borghesani C, Chait Y, Yaniv O.  The QFT frequency domain control design toolbox for use with MATLAB.  Terasoft Inc, 2003

[57] Zakian V, Al-Naib U.  Design of dynamical and control systems by the method of inequalities.  Proceedings of IEE, Part D, 1973, 120:1421–1427

[58] Åström K J, Hägglund T.  Automatic tuning of simple regulators with specification on phase and amplitude margins.  Automatica, 1984, 20:645–651

[59] Monje C A, Chen Y Q, Vinagre B M, Xue D Y, Feliu V.  Fractional-order systems and controls — fundamentals and applications.  London: Springer, 2010

# Chapter 2

# Fundamentals of MATLAB Programming

MATLAB language is the top choice in modern control engineering, it is also the top choice of many other engineering disciplines. MATLAB language will be extensively used in the book, and we shall systematically introduce its applications in modeling, analysis, simulation and design of control systems. A good working knowledge of MATLAB language will enable one not only understand in depth the concepts and algorithms in research but also increase the ability to do creative research work and apply MATLAB to actively tackle the problems in other related courses.

Compared with other programming languages, MATLAB has mainly the following advantages:

(1) **Clarity and high efficiency**. MATLAB language is a highly integrated language. A few MATLAB sentences may do the work of hundreds of lines of source code of other languages. Thus, the MATLAB program is more reliable and easy to maintain.

(2) **Scientific computation**. The basic element in MATLAB is a complex matrix of double-precision. Matrix manipulations can be carried out directly. Numerical computation functions provided in MATLAB, such as the ones for solving optimization problems or other mathematical problems, can be used directly. Also, symbolic computation facilities are provided in MATLAB's Symbolic Math Toolbox to support formula derivation.

(3) **Graphics facilities**. MATLAB language can be used to visualize the experimental data in an easy manner. Moreover, the graphical user interface is also supported in MATLAB, and the programming is quite similar to Visual Basic.

(4) **Comprehensive toolboxes and blocksets**. Although MATLAB was invented by a mathematician, it was indeed promoted to the current status by control people, since many of the toolboxes are written by well-known scholars in control community. In other related engineering fields, more and more toolboxes are being developed.

(5) **Powerful simulation facilities**. The powerful block diagram-based modeling technique provided in Simulink can be used to analyze systems with almost any complexity. In particular, under Simulink, the control blocks, electronic blocks

and mechanical blocks can be modeled together under the same framework, which is currently not possible in other computer mathematics languages.

The arrangement of the materials in this chapter is: In Section 2.1, fundamental knowledge in MATLAB programming is given, including data structure, basic syntaxes, colon expression and sub matrix extraction. Section 2.2 describes various basic operations in MATLAB, such as algebraic operation, logic operation, comparisons and so on. In Section 2.3, basic program structures such as loops, switches, conditional structures and trial statements are presented. Section 2.4 presents the main stream program structure — M-function programming, with useful hints on high-level programming. In Sections 2.5 and 2.6, two-dimensional and three-dimensional plotting facilities are presented. In Section 2.7, brief introduction to graphical user interface design and programming are given.

## 2.1 Basics in MATLAB Programming

### 2.1.1 *Variables and Constants in MATLAB*

By convention, variable names in MATLAB should be led by an alphabet letter, followed by letters, numbers, underscores. For instance, MYvar12, MY_Var12 and MyVar12_ are valid variable names, while 12MyVar and _MyVar12 are not. Variable names in MATLAB are case-sensitive, that is to say, Abc and ABc are two different variable names.

Many names are reserved in MATLAB, and used as constants. These names can of course be redefined to other values, it is suggested not to redefine them, unless necessary, to avoid unnecessary confusion.

(1) eps. Machine precision. On personal computers, the value is $2.2204 \times 10^{-16}$. If the absolute value of a variable is smaller than it, the quantity can be regarded as zero.

(2) i and j. If the two names were unchanged, they represent pure imaginary unit j, which is $\sqrt{-1}$. However, in many actual programming, if loops are expected, these two names are usually used as loop variables, one has to be very careful with that. If one wants to restores their original value, the command $i = \mathtt{sqrt(-1)}$ should be given.

(3) Inf. It represents infinity $+\infty$ in MATLAB, and it can also be noted as inf. Similarly $-\infty$ can be specified by $-$Inf. In MATLAB execution, a zero in denominator may generate Inf, and it does not terminate the execution of the program. Only "Divide by zero" warning is given. This agrees with the IEEE standard. For mathematical computation, this definition has its advantages over C language.

(4) NaN. Not a number, which is often obtained by the operations 0/0, Inf/Inf and others. It should also be noted that NaN times Inf will return NaN.

(5) pi. Double-precision representation of the circumference ratio $\pi$.

## 2.1.2 Data Structures

### 1. Numeric data type

Numerical computation is the most widely used computation form in MATLAB. To ensure high-precision computations, double-precision floating-point data type is used, which is 8 bytes (64 bits). According to the IEEE standard, it is composed of 11 exponential bits, 52 number bits and a sign bit, representing the data range of $\pm 1.7 \times 10^{308}$. The MATLAB function for defining this data type is double(). In other special applications, i.e., in image processing, unsigned 8 bit integer can be used, whose function is uint8(), representing the value in $(0, 255)$. Thus, significant memory space is saved. Also, the data types such as int8(), int16(), int32(), uint16() and uint32() can be used.

### 2. Symbolic data type

Symbolic variables can be declared in MATLAB, in contrast to numeric ones. Symbolic variables are used in deriving formula or finding the analytical solutions. Before used, it should be declared with syms command, with the syntax syms *vars props* , where *vars* can be composed of several variable names, separated by spaces (please note, not commas). For certain variables, *props* can be used to declare the properties of these variables, with possible options real, positive, and so on. The command syms *a b* can declare *a, b* as symbolic variables, and syms *a* real declares a real variable *a*.

The specific data of a symbolic variable can be converted with variable precision algorithm function vpa(), with the syntax vpa($A$) , or vpa($A, n$) , where $A$ is the name of the variable, and $n$ is the number of digit one wants to display. The default value of $n$ is 32.

**Example 2.1.** The first 300 digits of the base e in natural logarithmic number can be displayed directly with the following statement

```
>> vpa(exp(sym(1)),300) % one should convert 1 to symbolic variable first
```

The displayed result is 2.71828182845904523536028747135266249775724709369995957496696762772407663035354759457138217852516642742746639193200305992181741359662904357290033429526059563073813232862794349076323382988075319525101901157383418793070215408914993488416750924476146066808226480016847741185374234544243710753907774499207. If 300 is not specified, the default display is the first 32 digits.

### 3. Other data types

Apart from those used in computation, the following data types are also supported by MATLAB:

(1) **Strings**. Strings can be specified in MATLAB using single quotation marks, and it can be used to store text information. Please note the difference between MATLAB and C, in the latter, double quotation marks are used.

(2) **Multiple dimensional arrays**. Three dimensional arrays are direct extension to matrices. In control system analysis, frequency domain responses of

multivariable systems, three-dimensional arrays are used. In practical programming, arrays with even higher dimensions can also be used.

(3) **Cells.** Cells are direct extension to matrices, whose elements are no longer numbers. The elements in cells can be of any data type. The command $A\{i,j\}$ extracts the contents of the $i$th row, $j$th column in cell array $A$.

(4) **Classes and objects.** MATLAB allows the use of classes in programming. For instance, the transfer function class in control can be used to represent a transfer function of a system in one single variable. An example of the creation and overload function programming of an object is given in Chapter 11.

### 2.1.3    *Basic Statement Structures of MATLAB*

Two types of MATLAB statements can be used:

**1. Direct assignment**
The basic structure of this type of statement is

variable $=$ *expression*

and *expression* can be evaluated and assigned to the variable defined in the left-hand-side, and established in MATLAB workspace. If there is a semicolon used at the end of the statement, the result is not displayed. Thus, the semicolon can be used to suppress the display of intermediate results. If the left-hand-side variable is not given, the expression will be assigned to the reserved variable **ans**. Thus, the reserved variable **ans** always stores the result of the latest statements without a left-hand-side variable.

**Example 2.2.** Matrix input is very simple and straightforward in MATLAB. Consider the following matrix

$$A = \begin{bmatrix} 1 & 2 & 3 \\ 4 & 5 & 6 \\ 7 & 8 & 0 \end{bmatrix}.$$

The matrix $A$ can easily be entered into MATLAB workspace, with the statement

```
>> A=[1,2,3; 4 5,6; 7,8 0]
```

where >> is the prompt given by MATLAB automatically. Under the prompt, various MATLAB commands can be specified. For matrices, square brackets should be used to describe matrices, with the elements in the same row separated by commas or spaces, and the rows are separated by semicolons. The double-precision matrix variable $A$ can then be established in MATLAB workspace. The matrix $A$ can be displayed in MATLAB command window

A semicolon at the end of the statement suppresses the display of such a matrix. The size of a matrix can be expanded or reduced dynamically, with the following statements.

```
>> A=[1,2,3; 4 5,6; 7,8 0];      % assignment is made, however no display
   A=[[A; [1 2 3]], [1;2;3;4]];  % dynamically update the size of matrix
```

**Example 2.3.** Complex matrices can equally entered into MATLAB simply and straightforwardly. Now consider the following complex matrix

$$B = \begin{bmatrix} 1+9j & 2+8j & 3+7j \\ 4+6j & 5+5j & 6+4j \\ 7+3j & 8+2j & 0+j \end{bmatrix}.$$

The two notations i or j can be used to denote complex numbers. The following commands can be used

```
>> B=[1+9i,2+8i,3+7j; 4+6j 5+5i,6+4i; 7+3i,8+2j 1i]
```

**2. Function call statement**

The basic function call statement statement is

$[returned\_arguments] = function\_name (input\_arguments)$

where the regulation for function names are the same as in variable names. Generally the function names are the file names in the MATLAB path. For instance, the function name my_fun corresponds to the file my_fun.m. Of course, some of the functions are built-in functions in MATLAB kernel, such as the inv() function.

More than one input arguments and returned arguments are allowed, in which case, commas should be used to separate the arguments. For instance, the function call $[U \ S \ V] = \text{svd}(X)$ performs singular value decomposition to a given matrix $X$, and the three arguments $U, S, V$ will be returned. If a certain returned variable is not necessary, $\sim$ can be used at the desired place. For instance, the function call can be $[\sim \ S \ V] = \text{svd}(X)$.

### 2.1.4 *Colon Expressions*

Colon expression is a useful expression in MATLAB. It is especially useful in vector creation and sub-matrix extraction. The full form of colon expression is $v = s_1 : s_2 : s_3$, and a row vector $v$ can be created. In the expression, $s_1$ and $s_3$ are respectively the starting and terminate values, and $s_2$ is the increment. The vector is created from point $s_1$, with increment $s_2$ to generate a series of points, until $s_3$. If $s_2$ is missing, the default increment of 1 is used.

**Example 2.4.** With increment 0.3, the vector in the interval $t \in [0, \pi]$ is created

```
>> v1=0: 0.3: pi   % the maximum value is 3 rather than π
```

and the generated vector is $v_1 = [0, 0.3, 0.6, 0.9, 1.2, 1.5, 1.8, 2.1, 2.4, 2.7, 3]$. Please note that the last element in the vector is 3, rather than $\pi$.

Different increments and other information can be specified

```
>> v2=0: -0.1: pi   % negative increment leads to empty vector
   v3=0:pi           % with increment of 1
   v4=pi:-1:0        % vector generated in reverse order
```

The above statements will assign a $1 \times 0$ empty matrix to $v_2$, and with $v_3 = [0, 1, 2, 3]$ and $v_4 = [3.1416, 2.1416, 1.1416, 0.1416]$.

### 2.1.5  *Sub-matrix Extraction*

Sub-matrix extraction is often handled in MATLAB programming. Sub-matrix extraction can be made using the syntax $B = A(v_1, v_2)$ , where $v_1$ and $v_2$ vectors specify the rows and columns to extract from matrix $A$. The extracted matrix can be returned in matrix $B$. If $v_1$ is :, all the rows are extracted. Similar specification to vector $v_2$. The keyword **end** represents the last row (or column, depending on its position).

**Example 2.5.** With the following statements, different sub-matrices can be extracted from the given matrix $A$, such that

```
>> A=[1,2,3; 4,5,6; 7,8,0];
   B1=A(1:2:end, :)       % extract all the odd rows of matrix A
   B2=A([3,2,1],[1 1 1])  % copy the reversed first column to all columns
   B3=A(:,end:-1:1)       % flip left-right the given matrix A
```

and the sub-matrices extracted with the above statements are

$$B_1 = \begin{bmatrix} 1 & 2 & 3 \\ 7 & 8 & 0 \end{bmatrix}, \ B_2 = \begin{bmatrix} 7 & 7 & 7 \\ 4 & 4 & 4 \\ 1 & 1 & 1 \end{bmatrix}, \ B_3 = \begin{bmatrix} 3 & 2 & 1 \\ 6 & 5 & 4 \\ 0 & 8 & 7 \end{bmatrix}.$$

## 2.2   Basic Mathematical Operations

### 2.2.1   *Algebraic Calculations of Matrices*

Suppose matrix $A$ has $n$ rows and $m$ columns, it is then referred to as an $n \times m$ matrix. If $n = m$, then matrix $A$ is also referred to as a square matrix. The following algebraic operations can be defined:

**1. Matrix transpose**

Transpose of matrices are usually denoted mathematically $B = A^{\mathrm{T}}$, whose elements are $b_{ji} = a_{ij}$, $i = 1, 2, \cdots, n$, $j = 1, 2, \cdots, m$. Thus, $B$ is an $m \times n$ matrix. Ff matrix $A$ contains complex elements, the transpose $B$ may alternatively be defined as $b_{ji} = a_{ij}^*$, $i = 1, 2, \cdots, n$, $j = 1, 2, \cdots, m$, i.e., take transpose first, then take complex conjugate to each element. This kind of transpose is also known as Hermitian transpose, denoted as $B = A^*$. In MATLAB, $A$' can be used to get the Hermitian transpose, while $A.$' can be used to find direct transpose. For a real matrix $A$, $A$' is the same as $A.$'.

**2. Summation and subtraction of matrices**

Assume that there are two matrices $A$ and $B$ in MATLAB workspace, the statements $C = A + B$ and $C = A - B$ can be used respectively to evaluate the addition and subtraction of these two matrices. If the matrices $A$ and $B$ are with the same size, the relevant results can be obtained. If one of the matrices is a scalar, it can be added to or subtracted from the other matrix. If the sizes of the two matrices are different, error messages can be displayed.

### 3. Matrix multiplication

Assume that matrix $A$ of size $n \times m$ and matrix $B$ of size $m \times r$ are two variables in MATLAB workspace, and the columns of $A$ equal the rows of $B$, the two matrices are referred to as compatible. The product can be obtained from

$$c_{ij} = \sum_{k=1}^{m} a_{ik} b_{kj}, \text{ where } i = 1, 2, \cdots, n, \ j = 1, 2, \cdots, r. \tag{2.1}$$

If one of the matrices is a scalar, the product can also be obtained. In MATLAB, the multiplication of the two matrices can be obtained with $C = A * B$. If the two matrices are not compatible, an error message will be given.

### 4. Matrix left division

The left division of the matrices $A \backslash B$ can be used to solve the linear equations $AX = B$. If matrix $A$ is non-singular, then $X = A^{-1}B$. If $A$ is not a square matrix, $A \backslash B$ can also be used to find the least squares solution to the equations $AX = B$.

### 5. Matrix right division

The statement $B / A$ can be used to solve the linear equations $XA = B$. More precisely, $B / A = (A' \backslash B')'$.

### 6. Matrix flip and rotation

The left-right flip and up-down flip of a given matrix $A$ can be obtained with $B = \texttt{fliplr}(A)$ and $C = \texttt{flipud}(A)$ respectively, such that $b_{ij} = a_{i,n+1-j}$ and $c_{ij} = a_{m+1-i,j}$. The command $D = \texttt{rot90}(A)$ rotates matrix $A$ counterclockwise by $90°$, such that $d_{ij} = a_{j,n+1-i}$.

### 7. Matrix power

$A^x$ computes the matrix $A$ to the power $x$ when matrix $A$ is square. In MATLAB, the power can be evaluated with $F = A\char`^x$, where $x$ can be any scalar.

### 8. Dot operation

A class of special operation is defined in MATLAB. The statement $C = A.*B$ can be used to obtain element-by-element product of matrices $A$ and $B$, such that $c_{ij} = a_{ij} b_{ij}$. The dot product is also referred to as the Hadamard product.

Dot operation plays an important role in scientific computation. For instance, if a vector $x$ is given, then the vector $[x_i^5]$ cannot be obtained with $x\char`^5$. Instead, the command $x.\char`^5$ should be used. In fact, some of the functions such as $\texttt{sin}()$ can also be used in element-by-element operation.

Dot operation can be used to deal with other problems, for instance, the statement $A.\char`^A$ can be used, with the $(i,j)$th element then defined as $a_{ij}^{a_{ij}}$. Thus the matrix can be obtained

$$\begin{bmatrix} 1^1 & 2^2 & 3^3 \\ 4^4 & 5^5 & 6^6 \\ 7^7 & 8^8 & 0^0 \end{bmatrix} = \begin{bmatrix} 1 & 4 & 27 \\ 256 & 3125 & 46656 \\ 823543 & 16777216 & 1 \end{bmatrix}.$$

### 2.2.2   Logic Operations of Matrices

Logical data was not implemented in earlier versions of MATLAB. The non-zero value is regarded as logic 1, while a zero value is defined as logic 0. In new versions of MATLAB, logical variables are defined and the above rules also apply.

Assume that the matrices $A$ and $B$ are both $n \times m$ matrices, the following logical operations are defined:

(1) **"And" operation.** In MATLAB, the operator & is used to define element-by-element "and" operation. The statement $A \& B$ can then be defined.

(2) **"Or" operation.** In MATLAB, the operator | is used to define element-by-element "or" operation. The statement $A \,|\, B$ can then be defined.

(3) **"Not" operation.** In MATLAB, the operator $\sim$ can be used to define the "not" operation such that $B = \sim A$ .

(4) **Exclusive or.** The exclusive or operation of two matrices $A$ and $B$ can be evaluated from $\texttt{xor}(A,B)$ .

### 2.2.3   Relationship Operations of Matrices

Various relationship operators are provided in MATLAB. For example, $C = A > B$ will perform element-by-element comparison, with the element $c_{ij} = 1$ for $a_{ij} > b_{ij}$, and $c_{ij} = 0$ otherwise. The equality relationship can be tested with $==$ operator, while the other operators $>=$, $\sim=$ can also be used.

The special functions such as find() and all() can also be used to perform relationship operations. For instance, the index of the elements in $C$ equal to 1 can be obtained from $\texttt{find}(C == 1)$ . The following commands can be used:

```
>> A=[1,2,3; 4 5,6; 7,8 0]; % enter a matrix
   i=find(A>=5)' % find all the indices in  A whose value is larger than 5
```

and the indices can be found as $i = 3, 5, 6, 8$. It can be seen that the function arranges first the original matrix $A$ in a single column, on a columnwise basis. The indices can then be returned.

The functions all() and any() can also be used to check the values in the given matrices. For instance

```
>> a1=all(A>=5) % check each column whether all larger than 5
   a2=any(A>=5) % check each column whether any larger than 5
```

and it can be found that $a_1 = [0, 0, 0]$, $a_2 = [1, 1, 1]$.

### 2.2.4   Simplifications and Presentations of Analytical Results

The Symbolic Math Toolbox can be used to derive mathematical formulas. The results however are often not presented in their simplest form. The results should then be simplified. The easiest way of simplification is by the use of simple() function, where different simplification methods are tested automatically until the simplest result can be obtained, with the syntaxes

$s_1$=simple($s$),   % try various simplification methods and find the simplest
[$s_1$,how]=simple($s$),    % return the simplest form and the method used

where $s$ is the original expression, and $s_1$ is the simplified result. The string argument how will return the method of simplification. Apart from the easy-to-use simple() function, the function collect() can be used to collect the coefficients, and function expand() can be used to expand a polynomial. The function factor() can be used to perform factorization of a polynomial. The function numden() can be used to extract the numerator and denominator from a given expression. further information of these functions can be obtained with help command.

**Example 2.6.** Consider a polynomial $P(s)$ is given by

$$P(s) = (s+3)^2(s^2 + 3s + 2)(s^3 + 12s^2 + 48s + 64).$$

A symbolic variable $s$ should be declared first, then the full polynomial can be expressed easily and the polynomial can then be established in MATLAB workspace. With the polynomial, one can first simplify it with the simple() function

```
>> syms s; P=(s+3)^2*(s^2+3*s+2)*(s^3+12*s^2+48*s+64)
   [P1,m]=simple(P) % a series of simplications made, find the simplest
```

and one finds that $P_1 = (s+3)^2(s+2)(s+1)(s+4)^3$, with the method $m$=factor, which means that factorization method is used to reach the conclusion. Also, the expand() function can be tested

```
>> P1=expand(P)       % expand the polynomial
```

and the expanded polynomial is

$$P_1(s) = s^7 + 21s^6 + 185s^5 + 883s^4 + 2454s^3 + 3944s^2 + 3360s + 1152.$$

The function subs() provided in the Symbolic Math Toolbox can be used to perform variable substitution, and the syntaxes are

$f_1 = $ subs($f, x_1, x_1^*$)                              % substitute one variable
$f_1 = $ subs($f, \{x_1, x_2, \cdots, x_n\}, \{x_1^*, x_2^*, \cdots, x_n^*\}$)   % substitute several

where $f$ is the original expression. With the statement, the variable $x_1$ in the original function can be substituted with a new variable or expression $x_1^*$. The result is given in the variable $f_1$. The latter syntax can be used to substitute many variables simultaneously.

**Example 2.7.** Consider the polynomial $P(s)$ in Example 2.6, use subs() to change the variable $s$ into $z$ using bilinear transform $s = (z+1)/(z-1)$. The following commands can be used

```
>> syms z s; P=(s+3)^2*(s^2+3*s+2)*(s^3+12*s^2+48*s+64);
   P2=simple(subs(P,s,(z+1)/(z-1)))
```

and the substitution result is

$$P_2(s) = \frac{8(2z-1)^2 z(3z-1)(5z-3)^3}{(z-1)^7}.$$

### 2.2.5  Basic Number Theory Computations

Basic data transformation and number theory functions are provided in MAT-LAB, as shown in Table 2-1. The following examples are used to illustrate the functions. Through the example, the readers can observe the results.

Table 2-1   Functions for data transformations.

| function | syntax | function description |
|---|---|---|
| floor() | $n = \text{floor}(x)$ | round towards $-\infty$ for each value in variable $x$, mathematically denoted as $n = \lfloor x \rfloor$ |
| ceil() | $n = \text{ceil}(x)$ | round towards $+\infty$ for $x$ |
| round() | $n = \text{round}(x)$ | round to nearest integer for $x$ |
| fix() | $n = \text{fix}(x)$ | round towards zero for variable $x$ |
| rat() | $[n,d] = \text{rat}(x)$ | find rational approximation for variable $x$, and the numerator and denominator are returned respectively in $n$ and $d$ |
| rem() | $B = \text{rem}(A,C)$ | find the reminder after division to variable $A$ |
| gcd() | $k = \text{gcd}(n,m)$ | compute the greatest common divisor for $n$ and $m$ |
| lcm() | $k = \text{lcm}(n,m)$ | compute the least common multiplier for $n$ and $m$ |
| factor() | $\text{factor}(n)$ | prime factorization |
| isprime() | $v_1 = \text{isprime}(v)$ | check whether each component in $v$ is prime or not. Set the corresponding value in $v_1$ to 1 for prime numbers, otherwise set to 0 |

**Example 2.8.** For a given data set $-0.2765, 0.5772, 1.4597, 2.1091, 1.191, -1.6187$, observe the integers obtained using different rounding functions. The following statements can be used to round the original vector such that

```
>> A=[-0.2765,0.5772,1.4597,2.1091,1.191,-1.6187];
   v1=floor(A), v2=ceil(A) % round towards -∞ and +∞ respectively
   v3=round(A), v4=fix(A)   % round towards 0 and nearest integers
```

and the integer vectors obtained are $v_1 = [-1,0,1,2,1,-2]$, $v_2 = [0,1,2,3,2,-1]$, $v_3 = [0,1,1,2,1,-2]$, $v_4 = [0,0,1,2,1,-1]$.

**Example 2.9.** Assume that a $3 \times 3$ Hilbert matrix can be generated with $A = \text{hilb}(3)$, the following statements can be used to get the rational fitting, and the results are

$$n = \begin{bmatrix} 1 & 1 & 1 \\ 1 & 1 & 1 \\ 1 & 1 & 1 \end{bmatrix}, \quad d = \begin{bmatrix} 1 & 2 & 3 \\ 2 & 3 & 4 \\ 3 & 4 & 5 \end{bmatrix}.$$

```
>> A=hilb(3); [n,d]=rat(A)
```

If $B = \text{sym}(A)$ function is used, the matrix will be converted to symbolic form, and $B$ will be given in rational form.

**Example 2.10.** Consider two polynomials $P(s) = s^6 + 10s^5 + 42s^4 + 96s^3 + 125s^2 + 86s + 24$ and $Q(s) = s^5 + 5s^4 + 12s^3 + 28s^2 + 35s + 15$, which can be entered after declaring $s$ a symbolic variable. The functions $\text{lcm}()$ and $\text{gcd}()$ can be used to find the least common multiplier and greatest common divisor of them. The factorized form of their least common multiplier can be obtained with function $\text{factor}()$, while the expanded form can be found with function $\text{expand}()$.

```
>> syms s; P=s^6+10*s^5+42*s^4+96*s^3+125*s^2+86*s+24;
   Q=s^5+5*s^4+12*s^3+28*s^2+35*s+15;
   F1=factor(lcm(P,Q)), F2=expand(F1)
```

The factorized and expanded forms of the lease common multiplier are

$$F_1 = (s + 2)(s^2 + 3s + 4)(s + 1)^2(s^2 + 5)(s + 3),$$

$$F_2 = s^8 + 10s^7 + 47s^6 + 146s^5 + 335s^4 + 566s^3 + 649s^2 + 430s + 120.$$

Similarly the factorized greatest common divisor is $(s+3)(s+1)^2$, with the command `factor(gcd(P,Q))`.

## 2.3   Flow Control Structures in MATLAB Programming

As a programming language, the loop control structures, conditional control structures, switch structures and trial structures are provided in MATLAB. These structures are illustrated in this section.

### 2.3.1   *Loop Control Structures*

Loop structures can be started with `for` and `while` commands, and terminated by `end`. The statements between them are referred to the loop body.

**1. For loop.**   `for `$i = v$`, loop body, end`

In `for` loop structure, $v$ is a vector, the loop variable $i$ selects one element from vector $v$ each time, and execute the loop body once. Then $i$ takes another element from vector $v$, and executes the loop body once more. The loop structure will not terminate until all the elements in vector $v$ are selected. Compared with C, the MATLAB loop structure is more flexible, since any combination of $v$ can be pre-assigned.

**2. While loop.**   `while (`*condition*`), loop body, end`

The *condition* in `while` loop is a logic expression. If it is true, the loop body will be executed once. Then the *condition* execution is evaluated again. The loop will not terminate until the *condition* is true.

The `while` and `for` loops are different, and we shall demonstrate them through simple examples below, and the application situations will be pointed out.

**Example 2.11.** Find $\sum\limits_{i=1}^{100} i$ through loop structures. Similar to C language, `for` and `while` loops can be used to compute the sum below, and both methods yield the same results, $s = 5050$.

```
>> s=0; for i=1:100, s=s+i; end, s
   s=0; i=1; while (i<=100), s=s+i; i=i+1; end, s
```

The `for` structure is simpler for this example. In fact, with a simpler command `sum(1:100)`, the sum can also be evaluated. We used this example here merely show the loop structure.

Loops can be nested in application, or alternative nested use of `for` and `while` are possible. The command **break** can be used to terminate the last level of loop.

In MATLAB, the execution of loop structure is relatively slow, thus in actual programming, to improve the program efficiency, vectorized operation can be used to avoid loops.

**Example 2.12.** Loops and vectorized programming can both be used in calculate

$$S = \sum_{i=1}^{100000} \left( \frac{1}{2^i} + \frac{1}{3^i} \right).$$

The command pairs `tic` and `toc` can be used to measure the time elapsed. With loops, the time is 0.095 s, and 0.061 s without loops. For this example, about 2/3 time is used in vectorized programming.

```
>> tic, s=0; for i=1:100000, s=s+1/2^i+1/3^i; end; toc
   tic, i=1:100000; s=sum(1./2.^i+1./3.^i); toc
```

**Example 2.13.** Now consider a variation of the problem of Example 2.11. How can we find the minimum of $m$ such that $\sum_{i=1}^{m} i > 10000$ is satisfied? Since $m$ is not known, `for` loop cannot be used alone to solve the problem. The `while` loop should be used instead. With `while` loop, the following results can be obtained, $s = 10011$, and $m = 141$.

```
>> s=0; m=0;
   while (s<=10000), m=m+1; s=s+m; end, s, m
```

### 2.3.2 Conditional Structure

Conditional structure is supported and used in all programming languages. In MATLAB, the basic structure is `if` $\cdots$ `end`, and it is usually associated with `else` and `elseif` to establish extended conditional structures.

```
if (condition 1)        % if condition 1 is satisfied, execute statements 1
    statements 1        % lower level if can be nested here as well
elseif (condition 2)    % if condition 2 is satisfied, execute statements 2
    statements 2

        :               % other condition's
else                    % if none of the conditions are satisfied
    statements n + 1    % execute statements n + 1
end
```

**Example 2.14.** The problem in Example 2.13 can be solved with the combination of `for` loop and `if` statements as follows. It can be seen that although the result is the same, the program structure is rather complicated, compared with the `while` loop.

```
>> s=0; for i=1:10000, s=s+i; if s>10000, break; end, end
```

### 2.3.3  *Switch Structure*

The syntax of switch structure is

```
switch expression
    case expression 1
        statements 1
    case {expression 2, expression 3, ···, expression m}
        statements 2
            ⋮
    otherwise
        statements n
end
```

where the crucial part in switch structure is the evaluation of *expression*. If it matches a value in a case statement, the statements after the case statement should be executed. Once completed, the switch structure is terminated.

There exist differences between the switch statements in MATLAB and in C languages. The following tips should be noted in programming with MATLAB:

(1) When the value of the switch expression equals *expression* 1, the *statements* 1 should be executed. After execution, the structure is completed. There is no need to introduce a `break` statement before the next `case`.

(2) If one is checking whether one of several expressions is satisfied, the expressions must be given in cell format.

(3) If none of the expressions are satisfied, the paragraph in `otherwise` should be executed. It is similar to the `default` statement in C language.

(4) The execution results are independent of the orders of the `case` statement. When there exist two or more `case` statements having the same expressions, those listed behind may never be executed.

### 2.3.4  *Trial Structure*

Trial structure in MATLAB is

```
try,  statement group 1,  catch,  statement group 2,  end
```

Normally, only the *statement group* 1 is executed. However, if an error occurs during execution of any of the statements, the error is captured into `lasterror`, and the *statement group* 2 is executed. The new structure is not available in languages such as C. The trial structure is useful in practical programming.

Suppose for a certain problem, two algorithms are available. One is fast but may lead to errors sometimes, while the other is reliable but is extremely slow. The fast one is tried, and if the results are obtained successfully, the program is completed. If the fast algorithm fails, the second algorithm is executed.

## 2.4   Function Writing and Debugging

Two kinds of programming styles are supported in MATLAB. One is standard ASCII code, which can be sequentially executed, similar to DOS batch files. This kind of code is also known as M-script. The execution is rather simple. The user can simply type the file name under MATLAB prompt >>, and the sentences in the M-script file can be executed sequentially. M-script files can only be used in small-scale computations.

**Example 2.15.** Consider again the Example 2.13. The code can be saved into an M-script file. However, if the target is changed from 10000 to 20000 or 30000, one has to modify the source M-script file. This is sometimes complicated. If a mechanism can be established such that the target can be assigned to the problem, rather than modify the low-level source code, the programming style will be more reasonable. M-function is the programming style satisfy the above requirement.

M-function is the major structure in MATLAB programming. In practical programming, M-script programming is not recommended. In this section, MATLAB functions and some tricks in programming are given.

### 2.4.1   *Basic Structure of MATLAB Functions*

MATLAB functions are led by the statement of `function`, with

```
function [return argument list] =funname(input argument list)
    comments led by % sign
    input and output variables check
    main body of the function
```

Moreover, the actual number of input and returned arguments can be measured by `nargin` and `nargout`. If the numbers of input and returned variable are more than 1, the variables names should be separated by commas. The code lead by percentage mark (%) will be regarded as comments, and the message can be displayed with `help` or `doc` commands. Besides, the formal judgement of the numbers and types of the arguments are usually necessary.

From system viewpoint, a function can be regarded as an information processing unit. The input arguments are fed into the system and get processed, the output of the system can be returned to the calling procedure as returned variables, In M-functions, the variables beside the input and returned arguments are local ones, they will disappear when the function is completed. The following examples are given to show function programming.

**Example 2.16.** Consider the M-function implementation of Example 2.15. The input variable $k$ is the input while $m$ and $s$ are the outputs. Thus, M-function implementation is

```
function [m,s]=findsum(k)
```

```
s=0; m=0; while (s<=k), m=m+1; s=s+m; end
```

Having written the above function, we can save it into findsum.m file. Then the function can be called directly. For instance, if the target sum is $k = 123456$ and find the minimum value of $m$, the following statements can be issued and get the results $m_1 = 497$, $s_1 = 123753$.

```
>> [m1,s1]=findsum(123456)
```

It can be seen that the calling format is quite flexible, and we may find the needed results without modifying the original program. Thus, this kind of method is recommended in programming.

**Example 2.17.** Assume that we want to generate an $n \times m$ Hilbert matrix, whose $(i,j)$th element is $h_{i,j} = 1/(i+j-1)$, and $n$ and $m$ are any given numbers. There are also additional requests

(1) If only one argument is specified, generate a square matrix.

(2) Give reasonable help information.

In fact, in actual programming, it is a good habit that detailed comments are written, along with the program itself. This is useful both to the programmer and those who uses or maintains the program.

According to the request given above, a MATLAB function myhilb() can be written and saved into the file myhilb.m, and the file should be placed in MATLAB search path.

```
function A=myhilb(n,m)
%MYHILB  The function is used to illustrate MATLAB functions.
%   A=MYHILB(N, M) generates an NxM Hilbert matrix A;
%   A=MYHILB(N) generates an NxN square Hilbert matrix A;
%   See also: HILB.

% Designed by Professor Dingyu XUE, Northeastern University, PRC
%      5 April, 1995, Last modified by DYX at 30 July, 2001
if nargout>1, error('Too many output arguments.'); end
if nargin==1, m=n; end
for i=1:n, for j=1:m, A(i,j)=1/(i+j-1); end, end
```

The comments are led by % sign. The on-line help command **help myhilb** will display the help information. It should be noted that only the first few lines of comment information are displayed when **help** command is used, while the author information is not displayed, because there is a blank line before the author information.

To implement the requirement in (1), one should check whether the number of input argument is 1, i.e., whether **nargin** is 1. If so, the column number $m$ is set to $n$, the row number, thus a square matrix can be generated. If the numbers of input or returned arguments are not correct, the error messages can be given. The double **for** loops will generate the required Hilbert matrix.

Having written the above file, the following statements can be used to generate different Hilbert matrices, in different calling syntaxes.

$$A = \begin{bmatrix} 1 & 0.5 & 0.3333 & 0.25 \\ 0.5 & 0.3333 & 0.25 & 0.2 \\ 0.3333 & 0.25 & 0.2 & 0.1667 \end{bmatrix}, \quad B = \begin{bmatrix} 1 & 0.5 & 0.3333 & 0.25 \\ 0.5 & 0.3333 & 0.25 & 0.2 \\ 0.3333 & 0.25 & 0.2 & 0.1667 \\ 0.25 & 0.2 & 0.1667 & 0.1429 \end{bmatrix}.$$

```
>> A=myhilb(3,4), B=myhilb(4)
```

**Example 2.18.** MATLAB functions can be called recursively, i.e., a function may call itself. Please write a recursive function to evaluate the factorial $n!$.

It is know that for factorials, we have $n! = n(n-1)!$, thus the factorial of $n$ can be obtained with the factorial of $n-1$, which in turn, factorial of $n-2$, and so on. With the exits at $1! = 0! = 1$, the recursive function can be written as

```
function k=my_fact(n)
if abs(n-floor(n))>eps | n<0 % test whether n is a nonnegative integer
    error('n should be a nonnegative integer');
end
if n>1, k=n*my_fact(n-1); % if n > 1, recursive call is performed
elseif any([0 1]==n), k=1; % 0! = 1! = 1 as the exits of the function
end
```

It can be seen that in the function, the judgement whether $n$ is a nonnegative integer is made. If the judgement is not passed, an error message will be declared. If it is, the recursive function calls will be used such that when $n = 1$ or 0, the result is 1, which can be used as an exit to the function. For instance, 11! can be evaluated with `my_fact(11)`, and the result obtained is 39916800.

In fact, the factorial for any nonnegative integer can be evaluated directly with function `factorial(n)`, and the kernel of such a function is `prod(1:n)`.

**Example 2.19.** It is certain that the recursive algorithm is an effective method for a class of problems. However, this method should not be misused. A counter-example is shown in this example. Consider the Fibonacci array, where $a_1 = a_2 = 1$, and the $k$th term can be evaluated from $a_k = a_{k-1} + a_{k-2}$ for $k = 3, 4, \cdots$. A MATLAB function can be written for the problem

```
function a=my_fibo(k)
if k==1 | k==2, a=1; else, a=my_fibo(k-1)+my_fibo(k-2); end
```

and for $k = 1, 2$, the exit can be made such that it returns 1. If the 29th term is expected, the following statements can be used and the time required is 7.6 s.

```
>> tic, my_fibo(29), toc % find the 29th term, and measure the time elapsed
```

If one is expecting the term $k = 35$, several hours of time might be required. If the loop structure is used, within 0.02 s, the whole array can be obtained for $k = 100$.

```
>> tic, a=[1,1];
    for k=3:100, a(k)=a(k-1)+a(k-2); end, toc
```

It can be seen that the ordinary loop structure only requires a very short execution time. Thus the recursive function call should not be misused.

### 2.4.2  Functions with Variable Numbers of Inputs and Outputs

In the following presentation, the variable number of input and returned arguments is introduced, based on the cell data type. It should be mentioned that most of the MATLAB functions are implemented in this format.

**Example 2.20.** The `conv()` function provided in MATLAB can be used to get the product of two polynomials. For more than two polynomials, nested use of the function should be made. Our target now is to write an extended function `convs()` such that any number of polynomials can be multiplied together to get the final product. Cells `varargin` can be used to accept all the input arguments of any number, such that the following function can be written.

```
function a=convs(varargin)
a=1; for i=1:length(varargin), a=conv(a,varargin{i}); end
```

In the function, all the input arguments are fed into the function through cell variable `varargin`, and the $i$th argument can be extracted with `varargin{i}`. Thus, the above function can be used to handle the product of any number of polynomials. Below is a few examples to use such a function.

```
>> P=[1 2 4 0 5]; Q=[1 2]; F=[1 2 3]; D=convs(P,Q,F)
   E=conv(conv(P,Q),F)   % if necessary, conv() function can be nested
   G=convs(P,Q,F,[1,1],[1,3],[1,1])
```

The results are $D = [1, 6, 19, 36, 45, 44, 35, 30]$, $E = [1, 6, 19, 36, 45, 44, 35, 30]$, and $G = [1, 11, 56, 176, 376, 578, 678, 648, 527, 315, 90]$.

### 2.4.3  Anonymous and Inline Functions

Anonymous function is supported since MATLAB 7.0, and its syntax is `f = @(var_list) func` . For instance, $f = @(x,y)\sin(x.\char`^2+y.\char`^2)$ can be used to express the function $f(x, y) = \sin(x^2 + y^2)$. MATLAB workspace variables can be used directly in anonymous functions. For instance, if there are variables $a$ and $b$ in MATLAB workspace, the formula $f(x, y) = ax^2 + by^2$ can be expressed with anonymous function $f = @(x,y)a*x.\char`^2+b*y.\char`^2$ directly. Please note that if $a$ or $b$ is changed after the definition of the anonymous function, the old values of $a$, $b$ will still be used. If one wants to use new values of $a$ or $b$, the anonymous function should be declared again.

In earlier versions of MATLAB, `inline()` function is also supported, with the syntax `fun = inline(func, var_vars)` , where the definitions of the two arguments are almost the same as in the anonymous functions. For instance, $f(x, y) = \sin(x^2 + y^2)$ function can be expressed as $f = $ `inline('sin(x.^2+y.^2)','x','y')`.

Compared with anonymous functions, `inline()` function is not as good and the use of it is more complicated, and the efficiency is lower. Unless very early versions of MATLAB is used, `inline()` function is not recommended.

### 2.4.4 Pseudo Codes

There are two major applications of MATLAB pseudo code techniques, one of which is to speed up the program execution, since the *.m file can be converted to executable code. Another application of pseudo code techniques is that the ASCII code in the source MATLAB function can be transformed into binary code. This prevents other people from reading the source code.

Command `pcode` provided in MATLAB can be used to transform the .m functions into pseudo code files, with a suffix of p. To convert file `mytest.m` into pseudo code, the command `pcode mytest` should be issued. To generate p files in the same folder as the original .m files, the command `pcode mytest -inplace` should be used. To convert all the *.m files in a folder to *.p files, use the `cd` command in that folder, and issue the command `pcode *.m` . If there is a grammar error in the files, the conversion process will be aborted and error messages will be given. Users can find potential errors in the code in this way. If both *.m and *.p files with the same name exist, the *.p files have the priority in execution.

It is extremely important to note that the source *.m files should be saved in a safe place, so that they cannot be deleted by mistake, since the *.p file cannot be converted back.

## 2.5 Two-dimensional Graphics

Computer graphics and visualization are the most significant advantages of MATLAB. A series of straightforward and simple functions are provided in MATLAB for two-dimensional and three-dimensional graphics. Experimental and simulation results can be easily interpreted in graphical form. In this section, the two-dimensional graphics functions will be illustrated.

### 2.5.1 Basic Statements of Two-dimensional Plotting

Assume that a sequence of experimental data is acquired. For instance, at time instances $t = t_1, t_2, \cdots, t_n$, the function values are $y = y_1, y_2, \cdots, y_n$. The data can be entered to MATLAB workspace such that $t = [t_1, t_2, \cdots, t_n]$ and $y = [y_1, y_2, \cdots, y_n]$. The command `plot(t,y)` can be used to draw the curve for the data. The "curve" is, in fact, represented by poly-lines, joining the sample points. If the sample points are densely distributed, the poly-lines may look like curves.

In practical situations, the `plot()` function can further be extended

(1) $t$ is a vector, while $y$ is a matrix, such that

$$y = \begin{bmatrix} y_{11} & y_{12} & \cdots & y_{1n} \\ y_{21} & y_{22} & \cdots & y_{2n} \\ \vdots & \vdots & \ddots & \vdots \\ y_{m1} & y_{m2} & \cdots & y_{mn} \end{bmatrix},$$

then, the `plot()` function will draw $m$ curves, each curve corresponds to a row in matrix $y$. Please note that the row number should equal to the length of vector $t$.

(2) $t$ and $y$ are both matrices, and the sizes of the two matrices are the same. The plots between each row of $t$ and $y$ can be drawn.

(3) Assume that there are many pairs of such vectors or matrices, $(t_1, y_1)$, $(t_2, y_2)$, $\cdots$, $(t_m, y_m)$, the following statement can be used directly to draw the corresponding curves.

```
plot(t₁,y₁,option₁,t₂,y₂,option₂,···,tₘ,yₘ,optionₘ)
```

where *option$_i$* can be assigned according to the combinations in Table 2-2. For instance, to draw red dash dot lines for a curve, and indicate the data points by pentagrams, the option string `'r-.pentagram'` can be used, meaning red dash dot lines, with sample points marked by pentagrams.

Table 2-2　Options in MATLAB graphics.

| line styles | | color specification | | | | mark specification | | | |
|---|---|---|---|---|---|---|---|---|---|
| options | for | options | for | options | for | options | for | options | for |
| '-' | solid line | 'b' | blue | 'c' | cyan | '*' | * | 'pentagram' | ☆ |
| '--' | dash line | 'g' | green | 'k' | black | '.' | . | 'o' | ○ |
| ':' | dotted line | 'm' | magenta | 'r' | red | 'x' | × | 'square' | □ |
| '-.' | dash dot | 'w' | white | 'y' | yellow | 'v' | ▽ | 'diamond' | ◇ |
| 'none' | no line | | | | | '^' | △ | 'hexagram' | ✿ |
| | | | | | | '>' | ▷ | '<' | ◁ |

Once the graph is drawn, the `grid on` command can be issued to draw grid lines, and `grid off` command to delete the grids. Besides, `hold on` command can be used to reserve the current axis, so that `plot()` command used later can be drawn on top of the original plots. The command `hold off` can be used to cancel the "hold on" status. The `title()` function adds title to the plot, and `xlabel()` and `ylabel()` function add information to $x$ and $y$ axes. Low-level command `line()` can be used to draw new lines on top of the current axis.

**Example 2.21.** To draw curve for the explicit function $y = \sin(\tan x) - \tan(\sin x)$ over the interval $x \in [-\pi, \pi]$, the following commands can be used directly.

```
>> x=[-pi : 0.05: pi];        % select an increment of 0.05, form horizontal axis
   y=sin(tan(x))-tan(sin(x)); % find the function value
   plot(x,y)                  % draw curve
```

The plot obtained is shown in Fig. 2-1(a). It can be seen that the curve around $t = \pm\pi/2$ looks odd. Smaller increments can be tried, to get the curve shown in Fig. 2-1(b). Normally when the curves are drawn, make sure validations are made. The simplest way is to try different increment and see whether the same results can be obtained.

**Example 2.22.** Consider the saturation function

$$y = \begin{cases} 1.1\,\text{sign}(x), & |x| > 1.1, \\ x, & |x| \leqslant 1.1. \end{cases}$$

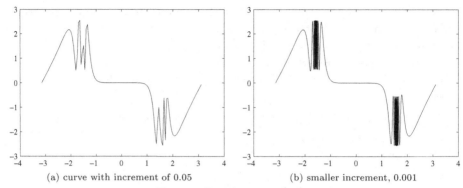

(a) curve with increment of 0.05          (b) smaller increment, 0.001

Fig. 2-1     Two-dimensional plots.

Of course, **if** statement can be used to get the values of $y$ for each point in $x$. In fact, a better and practical way is to use relational operations. Construct an $x$ vector first, and the relationship with command **$x$>1.1** generates a vector whose length is the same with vector $x$. For the points satisfy $x_i > 1.1$, the vector values are one, otherwise the values are zero. Based on such an idea, the following code can be used to draw the curve shown in Fig. 2-2.

```
>> x=[-2:0.02:2]; % generate an independent variable vector
   y=1.1*(abs(x)>1.1) + x.*(abs(x)<=1.1); plot(x,y)
```

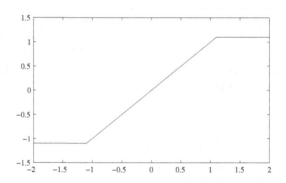

Fig. 2-2     Plot of the piecewise function.

Please note that the relational operation should be repeated points or intervals. For instance, if the first condition is changed to **1.1\*($x$>=1.1)**, the two conditions overlap at $x_i = 1.1$, the value $y_i$ will be double computed, which leads to a wrong $y$ vector.

Besides, since **plot()** function joins given sample points, if the turning points are specified, exactly the same plot as shown in Fig. 2-2 can be obtained with

```
>> plot([-2,-1.1,1.1,2],[-1.1,-1.1,1.1,1.1])
```

In MATLAB graphics, each curve is an object, so are the axes and windows. The properties of objects can be accessed with **get()** and **set()** functions, with

```
set(handle,'pname₁',pvalue₁,'pname₂',pvalue₂,···)
v = get(handle,'pname')
```

These two functions are useful in graphical user interface design, and will be demonstrated further later.

### 2.5.2  *Other Graphics Functions with Applications*

Apart from the standard two-dimensional plotting functions, special two-dimensional functions are also supported in MATLAB. The commonly used functions and syntaxes are given in Table 2-3, where the arguments $x$ and $y$ store the data for the $x$ and $y$ axes, respectively. The argument c is the color option, while $u$ and $l$ are the upper and lower bounds in the error plots. The following examples can be used to demonstrate the plotting functions.

Table 2-3   Special two-dimensional plotting functions provided in MATLAB.

| function names | plotting facilities | commonly used syntaxes |
| --- | --- | --- |
| bar() | bar plot | bar($x,y$) |
| comet() | comet plots to show trajectories | comet($x,y$) |
| compass() | arrow plots from origin | compass($x,y$) |
| errorbar() | curves with error bars | errorbar($x,y,l,u$) |
| feather() | velocity vector plots | feather($x,y$) |
| fill() | filled polygons | fill($x,y$,c) |
| hist() | histogram | hist($y,n$) |
| loglog() | both axes are in logarithmic scales | loglog($x,y$) |
| polar() | polar plots | polar($x,y$) |
| quiver() | quiver or velocity plots | quiver($x,y$) |
| stairs() | stairstep graphs | stairs($x,y$) |
| stem() | discrete sequence stem plots | stem($x,y$) |
| semilogx() | one of the axis in logarithmic scale | semilogx($x,y$),  semilogy($x,y$) |

**Example 2.23.** Consider the Polar function

$$\rho = \frac{\sin(8\theta/3)}{2 - \cos^2(3\theta/2)}, \ \theta \in (0, 4\pi).$$

Polar plot can be drawn with the polar() function call, as shown in in Fig. 2-3(a).

```
>> t=0:0.01:4*pi; r=sin(8*t/3)./(2-cos(3*t/2).^2);
   polar(t,r); axis('square') % draw polar plot and assign the shape of axis
```

In fact, the curve obtained seems to be incomplete. A larger range of $\theta$ can be tried. For instance, select $\theta \in (0, 6\pi)$, the new complete polar plot can be obtained as shown in Fig. 2-3(b). Further increase of the range will not change the shape of the plot, since the original polar function is a periodic one.

```
>> t=0:0.01:6*pi; r=sin(8*t/3)./(2-cos(3*t/2).^2); polar(t,r)
```

Graphics window can be divided into several small regions, and the user may specify a certain region to draw plots. Region division can be made by calling the

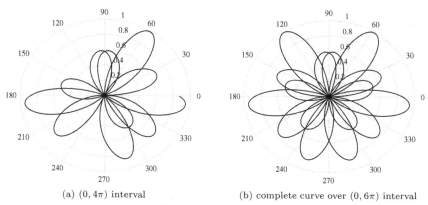

(a) $(0, 4\pi)$ interval          (b) complete curve over $(0, 6\pi)$ interval

Fig. 2-3   Polar plots.

function `subplot(m,n,k)` or `subplot(mnk)` , where the graphics window can be divided into $m \times n$ regions, and $k$ is the division to draw plots. Irregular division of windows can be made by the menu item Insert → Axes, and arbitrary subplot can be added to a graphics window.

**Example 2.24.** We still use sinusoidal curve to demonstrate the use of `subplot()` function. Suppose we want to divide the graphics window into $2 \times 2$ regions and in each region we draw different plots. The following statements can be used, and the results are shown in Fig. 2-4.

```
>> t=0:.2:2*pi; y=sin(t);        % generate data for plots
   subplot(2,2,1), stairs(t,y)    % draw stairs plot at (1,1) region
   subplot(2,2,2), stem(t,y)      % draw stem plot at (1,2) region
   subplot(2,2,3), bar(t,y)       % bar plot
   subplot(2,2,4), semilogx(t,y)  % logarithmic scale in horizontal axis
```

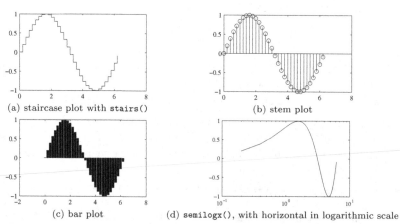

(a) staircase plot with `stairs()`          (b) stem plot

(c) bar plot          (d) `semilogx()`, with horizontal in logarithmic scale

Fig. 2-4   Different plots in divided regions.

### 2.5.3 *Implicit Function Visualizations*

Implicit function is the function described by $f(x, y) = 0$. Normally the `plot()` function described earlier cannot be used in drawing the curves of implicit functions, since the explicit relationship of $x$ and $y$ cannot easily be obtained. In this case, implicit function drawing facilities are needed. The syntax of the function is `ezplot(Fun,[`$x_m$`,`$x_M$`])`, where `Fun` can be given by a string or a symbolic expression describing the implicit function. The arguments $x_m$ and $x_M$ are the range of independent variable $x$, with default interval $(-2\pi, 2\pi)$. The example follows will be used to show the function call.

**Example 2.25.** Consider an implicit function

$$f(x, y) = xy \sin(x^2 + y^2) + (x + y)^2 e^{-(x+y)} = 0.$$

It can be seen that it is not possible to find the explicit expression between $x$ and $y$. The following MATLAB statements can be used directly to draw the implicit function, shown in Fig. 2-5.

```
>> ezplot('x*y*sin(x^2+y^2)+(x+y)^2*exp(-(x+y))')
```

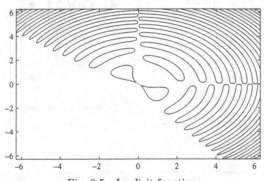

Fig. 2-5   Implicit function.

### 2.5.4 *Graph Editing and Decorations*

Various tools are provided in the toolbar of the MATLAB graphics window, allowing the users to add decorations to the plots. For instance, the user can add text, arrows and lines to the graph. A subset of the well-established LATEX commands[1] can be used to represent formatted text or mathematical formulae on the plots. For instance, the commands \bf, \it and \rm can be used to specify bold, italic and normal font. For example, `The {\bf word is bold}` will give display of "The **word is bold**" in the graphics window. Superscripts and subscripts can be assigned. For instance, `y=x^{abc}` will give a display of $y = x^{abc}$, while `y=x^abc` will produce $y = x^a bc$. Similarly, underscores can be used to describe subscripts.

Unfortunately, the quality of the mathematical formulae thus generated is not very high. In order to embed such a graph into a LaTeX documentation system, the package overpic should be used to superimpose the text on the graphs.

MATLAB graphics window provides various tools to decorate the graphs. The View → Figure Palette menu can be used to display figure decorating toolbar, as shown in Fig. 2-6, where lines, arrows and text can be superimposed on the graph. Two- and three-dimensional axes can also be inserted. The Property Editor menu allows the user to modify the properties such as color, line style and fonts of the selected objects. The View → Plot Browser menu (or button ▣) allows the user to edit graphical elements, or add new data to superimpose new plots.

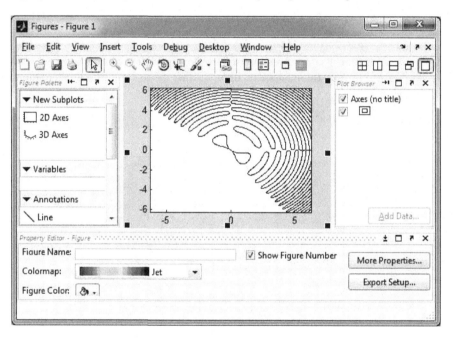

Fig. 2-6    Graph editing interface of MATLAB R2012b.

In the new versions of MATLAB, such as MATLAB 2012b, a plot editing toolbar can be displayed, with View → Plot Editing Toolbar menu, as shown in Fig. 2-7. The existing plots in the graphics window can be edited with the tools.

Fig. 2-7    Plot editing toolbar in MATLAB graphics window.

In the toolbar of the graphics window, the coordinates of points on plots can be selected and displayed, with button 🔄. The 🔄 button can be used to rotate the plots, and to display two-dimensional plots in three-dimensional coordinates, as shown in Fig. 2-8.

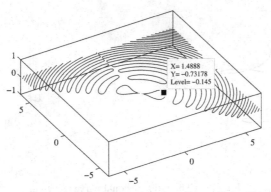

Fig. 2-8　Three-dimensional representation of two-dimensional plots.

## 2.6　Three-dimensional Visualization

### 2.6.1　*Three-dimensional Curves*

Similar to two-dimensional plots, a function `plot3()` can be used to drawn three-dimensional plots, with the syntax $\boxed{\texttt{plot3}(x,y,z,options)}$ , where $x$, $y$ and $z$ are vectors of the same length, storing the coordinates, and the options available are exactly the same, as shown in Table 2-2.

Similarly, there are other extended three-dimensional visualization functions, such as `stem3()`, `fill3()` and `bar3()`.

**Example 2.26.** Consider the parametric equation of a particle in three-dimensional space whose position can be described by

$$x(t) = t^3 \sin(3t)e^{-t}, y(t) = t^3 \cos(3t)e^{-t}, z = t^2.$$

The trajectory of the particle can be drawn with the following statements, as shown in Fig. 2-9(a). It can be seen that the statements are quite straightforward.

```
>> t=0:.1:2*pi;        % construct vector t, pay attention to dot operation
   x=t.^3.*sin(3*t).*exp(-t); y=t.^3.*cos(3*t).*exp(-t); z=t.^2;
   plot3(x,y,z), grid
```

Function `stem3()` can also be used, and the new three-dimensional plot is obtained as shown in Fig. 2-9(b).

```
>> stem3(x,y,z); hold on; plot3(x,y,z), grid
```

### 2.6.2　*Three-dimensional Surfaces*

If a two-variable function $z = f(x,y)$ is given, three-dimensional surfaces and mesh grid plots can be drawn with the functions `surf()` and `mesh()`. Mesh grid $x$-$y$ plane should be generated first, then the function $z$ can be evaluated with dot operations. Three-dimensional plot can the be drawn with of $\boxed{\texttt{mesh}(x,y,z,c)}$ , where $x$ and $y$ are matrices of the mesh grid coordinates on the $x$-$y$ plane. The

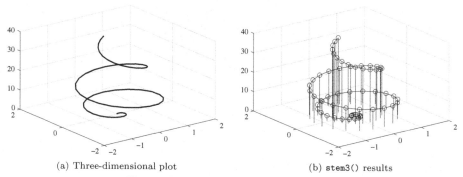

(a) Three-dimensional plot                    (b) `stem3()` results

Fig. 2-9   Three-dimensional curve drawing.

variable $z$ is the height matrix. The argument $c$ is the color matrix, indicating the range of colors. If the $c$ argument is omitted, MATLAB will assign it to $c = z$, that is the setting of the color is proportional to the value of $z$. The syntax of `surf()` is the same as `mesh()`. MATLAB implementation of 3D plots is

```
[x,y] = meshgrid(v₁,v₂)        % generate mesh grid on x-y plane
z = ···,  e.g., z = x.*y        % calculate matrix z, dot operations
surf(x,y,z) or mesh(x,y,z)     % draw surface of mesh grid plots
```

where vectors $v_1$ and $v_2$ specify the grid scales of $x$ and $y$ axes. Three-dimensional contours can be drawn with `surfc()`, `contour()`, `contour3()` functions. Waterfall type of plot can also be drawn with function `waterfall()`. Examples will be given below to demonstrate three-dimensional graphics.

**Example 2.27.** Consider the two-variable function $z = f(x,y) = (x^2 - 2x)e^{-x^2-y^2-xy}$. Select a region in $x$-$y$ plane, in $x$-axis, from $-3$ to $3$ with increment of 0.1, and in $y$-axis, from $-2$ to $2$, with increment of 0.1. Then mesh grid can be generated, and the value of $z$ can be evaluated from $z = f(x,y)$. The function `mesh()` can be used to draw the 3D mesh plot, as shown in Fig. 2-10(a).

```
>> [x,y]=meshgrid(-3:0.1:3,-2:0.1:2);   % generate mesh grid
   z=(x.^2-2*x).*exp(-x.^2-y.^2-x.*y); mesh(x,y,z)
```

If `surf()` function is used to replace `mesh()` in above statements, the 3D surface plot can be obtained, as shown in Fig. 2-10(b).

```
>> surf(x,y,z)   % draw 3D surface plot
```

Command **shading** can be used to further decorate 3D surface plots with three options. The **flat** option redraw the 3D surface without grid lines, as shown in Fig. 2-11(a), **interp** option draws the smoothly interpolated surface shown in Fig. 2-11(b). The default **faceted** option draws the surface with grid, shown in Fig. 2-10(b).

Other 3D plots are supported in MATLAB. The `waterfall(x,y,z)` function draws the plot in waterfall-like form, shown in Fig. 2-12(a), while `contour3(x,y,z,30)` command shows 3D contour shown in Fig. 2-12(b), with 30 contours.

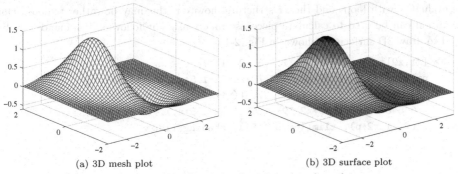

(a) 3D mesh plot    (b) 3D surface plot

Fig. 2-10    Three-dimensional mesh and surface plots.

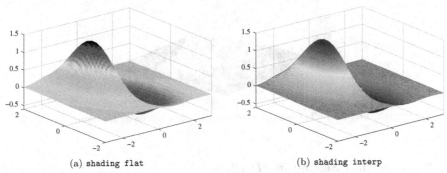

(a) `shading flat`    (b) `shading interp`

Fig. 2-11    Surface plots with `shading` decorations.

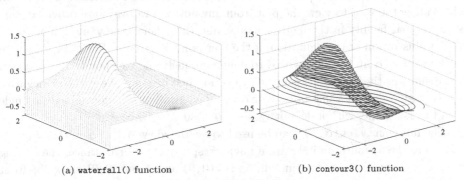

(a) `waterfall()` function    (b) `contour3()` function

Fig. 2-12    Other 3D plots.

**Example 2.28.** Assume that a joint probability density function can be expressed by a piecewise function [2]

$$p(x_1, x_2) = \begin{cases} 0.5457 \exp(-0.75x_2^2 - 3.75x_1^2 - 1.5x_1), & x_1 + x_2 > 1 \\ 0.7575 \exp(-x_2^2 - 6x_1^2), & -1 < x_1 + x_2 \leqslant 1 \\ 0.5457 \exp(-0.75x_2^2 - 3.75x_1^2 + 1.5x_1), & x_1 + x_2 \leqslant -1. \end{cases}$$

Mesh grid in the $x_1$–$x_2$ plane can be generated first. Of course, the value of $p$ can be evaluated with loops and the `if` structure; however, this may be rather tedious. Dot operation can be used to calculate piecewise functions. The following commands can be used to draw 3D surface, as shown in Fig. 2-13.

```
>> [x1,x2]=meshgrid(-1.5:.1:1.5,-2:.1:2);
   p=0.5457*exp(-0.75*x2.^2-3.75*x1.^2-1.5*x1).*(x1+x2>1)+...
     0.7575*exp(-x2.^2-6*x1.^2).*((x1+x2>-1)&(x1+x2<=1))+...
     0.5457*exp(-0.75*x2.^2-3.75*x1.^2+1.5*x1).*(x1+x2<=-1);
   surf(x1,x2,p), xlim([-1.5 1.5]); shading flat
```

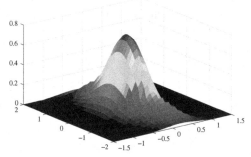

Fig. 2-13    Three-dimensional surface of a piecewise function.

### 2.6.3   *Viewpoint Setting in 3D Plots*

In the MATLAB 3D graphics facilities, viewpoint setting functions are provided, which allow the user to view the plot from any angle. Two ways are provided: one is the toolbar facility in the figure window, and the other is the `view()` function.

An illustration of the definition of the viewpoint is given in Fig. 2-14(a), where the two angles $\alpha$ and $\beta$ can be used to define uniquely the viewpoint. The azimuth $\alpha$ is defined as the angle between the projection line in $x$-$y$ plane with the negative $y$-axis, with a default value of $\alpha = -37.5°$. The elevation $\beta$ is defined as the angle with the $x$-$y$ plane, with a default value of $\beta = 30°$.

The function `view(`$\alpha,\beta$`)` can be used to set the viewpoint, where the angles $\alpha$ and $\beta$ are the azimuth and elevation angles respectively. For instance, the setting `view(0,90)` shows the planform, while `view(0,0)` and `view(90,0)` show the front view and the side elevation respectively.

For the plot shown in Example 2-13, if the azimuth angle is set to $\alpha = 80°$, while the elevation angle is set to $\beta = 10°$, the new plot is shown in Fig. 2-14(b).

```
>> view(80,10), xlim([-1.5 1.5])
```

**Example 2.29.** The following commands can be used to show the orthographic views of the plot in Fig. 2.27 in one window, as shown in Fig. 2-15.

```
>> [x,y] = meshgrid(-3:0.1:3,-2:0.1:2);
   z=(x.^2-2*x).*exp(-x.^2-y.^2-x.*y);
```

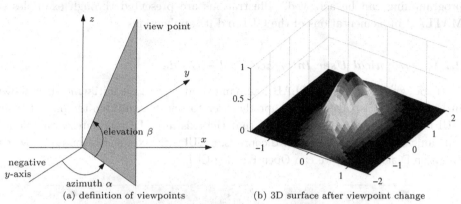

(a) definition of viewpoints        (b) 3D surface after viewpoint change

Fig. 2-14   Viewpoint settings of three-dimensional surfaces.

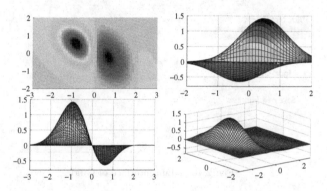

Fig. 2-15   Orthographic views of the two-variable function.

```
subplot(221), surf(x,y,z), view(0,90); axis([-3 3 -2 2 -0.8 1.5]);
subplot(222), surf(x,y,z), view(90,0); axis([-3 3 -2 2 -0.8 1.5]);
subplot(223), surf(x,y,z), view(0,0); axis([-3 3 -2 2 -0.8 1.5]);
subplot(224), surf(x,y,z), axis([-3 3 -2 2 -0.8 1.5]);
```

## 2.7   Graphical User Interface Design in MATLAB

For a successful software, of course, its contents and functions are the most important factors. The graphical user interface is also very important, since it determines the quality and level of the software. The graphical user interface in this case acts like the outward appearance of the product. Thus, by mastering the skills of graphical user interface techniques, it is possible to design high-quality software for general purposes.

The GUI design interface, named "Guide" (which stands for GUI development environment), is a very powerful tool for designing GUIs, in a visual manner. Equipped with MATLAB programming experiences and skills, high-standard GUI programming can be achieved. Illustrations are presented through examples of MATLAB implementations of the GUI and its applications.

### 2.7.1  *Graphical User Interface Tool – Guide*

Type **guide** in the MATLAB command window, and the initial interface shown in Fig. 2-16 is displayed to prompt the user to select a suitable template for the GUI to be designed. It can be seen that the existing GUI templates available are a default Blank GUI, a GUI with Uicontrols, a GUI with Axes and Menu and a Modal Question Dialog. Also, we can Open Existing GUI.

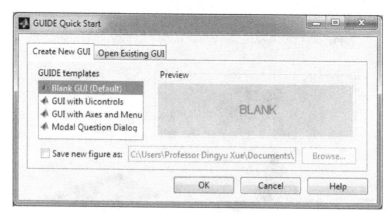

Fig. 2-16    Main interface of Guide.

Here we shall only discuss the blank GUI design method. Selecting the Blank GUI template from the list, and clicking the OK button, the GUI design interface shown in Fig. 2-17(a) is displayed. The prototype blank interface is also shown in the figure.

From the palette of icons on the left, it can be seen that different types of icons for designing GUI objects are provided. We can click the icon to select an object, and drag it to the blank prototype window.

The user can click an icon from the palette, and drag it to the blank interface then release the mouse button. The object can be copied into the interface window, and can be resized or moved easily with the mouse. In this way, the desired interface can then be drawn.

In the following, basic knowledge of handle graphics will be presented, and GUI design methods will be demonstrated through an example.

### 2.7.2  *Handle Graphics and Properties of Objects*

The major techniques used in object-oriented programming are to extract and assign properties to different objects. In order to manipulate the properties of the

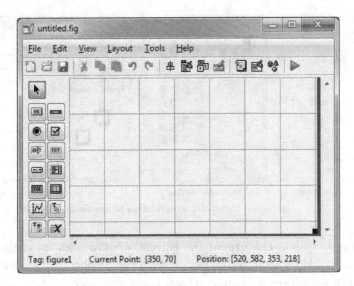

Fig. 2-17   Guide interface.

objects, the method of obtaining handles for the objects is very important. The handle graphics technique proposed by MathWorks Inc in the 1990s is very useful in this kind of programming. Details of handle graphics can be found in [3].

In MATLAB interface design, object-oriented methodology is extensively used. The window is an object, and the controls, such as buttons and edit boxes, on the window are also objects. In object-oriented programming, each object has its handle and properties.

Double click the prototype window, and a **Property Inspector** window shown in Fig. 2-18(a) will be displayed. The inspector shows the properties, and their values, of the selected object, in this case the window object, and the user can set or change the properties easily by using the mouse. For instance, if we want to change the color of the window, the box to the right of the **Color** property can be clicked, and a dialog box shown in Fig. 2-18(b) is opened. More colors can be selected when the button **More Colors** button is clicked. The standard color dialog box is shown in Fig. 2-18(c), from which more colors can be selected. The new color will take effect immediately in the prototype window.

It can be seen from the property browser that many properties are provided for the window object. It is not necessary to modify all of them. The commonly used window properties are:

- **MenuBar** property describes the form of the menu bar of the proposed window, and the available options are **figure** (for standard figure window menu — the default) and **none** (a window with no menu bar, for the time being). If necessary, the new menu system can be added, or appended to the existing ones, with the menu editor to be discussed later.

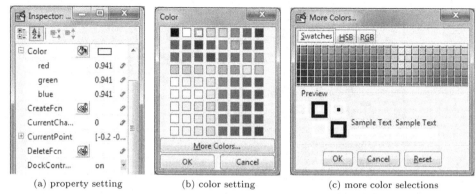

(a) property setting          (b) color setting          (c) more color selections

Fig. 2-18    Parameter modification of interfaces.

- **Name** property sets the title of the current window with its string property value. It should be used in conjunction with the **NumberTitle** property.

- **NumberTitle** property determines whether or not to prefix the window title with "Figure No *:". The property values are **on** (default) and **off**.

- **Units** property specifies the length unit used in the window property. The possible options are **pixels** (default), **inches**, **centimeters**, **normalized** (between 0, 1) and so on. The **Units** property can also be set with the property editor. When the property value box is clicked in the **Units** property, a listbox will appear, as shown in Fig. 2-19(a), and we can choose from it the desired property value.

- **Position** property determines the size and position of the current window. The property value is a $1 \times 4$ vector, with the first two elements specifying the coordinates of the lower left corner of the window, while the latter two values specify the width and height of the window, as shown in Fig. 2-19(b). The property should be used in conjunction with the **Unit** property. The best way to set the **Position** property is to directly move and resize the prototype window by using the mouse. The current position and size will be filled to the property value automatically.

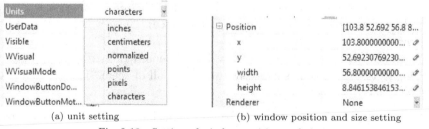

(a) unit setting                    (b) window position and size setting

Fig. 2-19    Setting of window position and size.

- **Resize** property determines whether the window is resizable or not. Two options are available, **off** and **on** (default).

- Toolbar property indicates whether or not to add visible toolbars to the window. The available options are none, figure (standard toolbar for the figure window) and auto (default). Toolbars can be designed visually by the Toolbar Editor.
- Visible property determines whether the window is visible or not, initially, with the options on (default) and off.

Object property extraction and setting in handle graphics can be implemented with two functions: set() and get(), with the syntaxes

```
v = get(h, property value)    % e.g., v = get(gcf, 'Color')
set(h, property name 1, property value 1, property name 2, property value 2, ···)
```

where h is the handle of the object. The command gcf can be used to get the handle of the current window object, while gco can be used to get the handle of the current object. Extraction of other handles will be shown later.

The following examples can be used to demonstrate the design process and skills of graphical user interfaces.

**Example 2.30.** Suppose we need to add two control items in a blank window: one a button and the other a text box. What we are expecting is that when the button is clicked, the "Hello World!" string will appear in the text box. The GUI design can be achieved with the following procedures:

(1) **Draw the prototype window**. Open a blank prototype window and draw the two control items onto the window, by directly selecting and dragging from the control item palette, and the layout of the prototype windows will be as shown in Fig. 2-20(a).

(2) **Control property modification**. Double click the text box control item, and the property editor windows will be displayed. We can set the String property to an empty one, which means nothing initially will be displayed, before the button is clicked. Also, the Tag property of the control item should be set so that the handle of it can be found easily by other objects. Here the Tag property can be set to txtHello, as shown in Fig. 2-20(b). Please note that a unique string should be assigned to each object, so that other objects can find its handle easily and without any conflict. By convention here, the string of the Tag property can be composed of two strings, the first one describing its type, the second one indicating its use. For instance, we have used txtHello here. Meanwhile we can set the tag of the button to btnOK.

(3) **Automatic generation of the framework of the program**. When the prototype window is designed, it can be saved into a .fig file, say, to file c2eggui1.fig. The framework of the MATLAB function, named c2eggui1.m can be generated, and the main part of it is show below.

```
function varargout = c2eggui1(varargin)
gui_Singleton = 1;
gui_State = struct('gui_Name',      mfilename, ...
                   'gui_Singleton',  gui_Singleton, ...
                   'gui_OpeningFcn', @c2eggui1_OpeningFcn, ...
                   'gui_OutputFcn',  @c2eggui1_OutputFcn, ...
                   'gui_LayoutFcn',  [] , ...
```

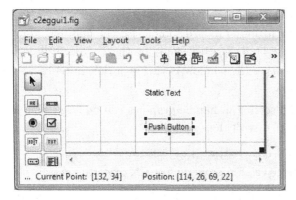 

(a) add control items                              (b) modify control properties

Fig. 2-20   Prototype windows design and modifications.

```
                    'gui_Callback',   []);
if nargin && ischar(varargin{1})
   gui_State.gui_Callback = str2func(varargin{1});
end
if nargout
   [varargout{1:nargout}]=gui_mainfcn(gui_State, varargin{:});
else
   gui_mainfcn(gui_State, varargin{:});
end
function c2eggui1_OpeningFcn(hObject, eventdata, handles, varargin)
handles.output = hObject; guidata(hObject, handles);
function varargout = c2eggui1_OutputFcn(hObject, eventdata, handles)
varargout{1} = handles.output;
% End of the main framework. No modification of the previous code is advised to
% be modified. The rest of the code are the frameworks of the callback functions
function btnOK_Callback(hObject, eventdata, handles)
```

(4) **Writing callback functions**. We can rewrite the requests given earlier: When the button is clicked, the string "Hello World!" is to be displayed in the text box. The request can be rephrased as follows, "when the button is clicked" means that we should write a callback function for the button. "Display the string in the text box" means that in the callback function, we should find the handle of the text box first, then we can assign the string to its String property. Since the tag of the text box is txtHello, the handle of it is handles.txtHello. The following callback function can be written for the button object

```
function varargout = btnOK_Callback(hObject, eventdata, handles)
set(handles.txtHello,'String','Hello World!');
```

Another important thing to note in MATLAB GUI design is that beside the typical callback functions, other types of callback functions are also supported. The so-called callback function actually means that when an event happens to an object, a function is invoked automatically by MATLAB's internal mechanisms.

Other commonly used callback functions are:

- CloseRequestFcn. The callback function when a window is closed.
- KeyPressFcn. The callback function when a key in keyboard is pressed.
- WindowButtonDownFcn. The callback function when a mouse button is clicked.
- WindowButtonMotionFcn. The callback function when the mouse is moved.
- WindowButtonUpFcn. The callback function when a mouse button is released.
- CreateFcn and DeleteFcn. They automatically call functions when an object is created or deleted.

Some of the callback functions are related to the window object, and some are for specific control items. If one masters the skills of callback function programming, the efficiency of MATLAB GUI programming can be improved.

Various properties are also provided for different types of control items. Some of the commonly used properties for the control items are listed below:

- Units and Position properties. The definitions are the same as the ones given in window properties. It should be noted that the lower left corner here refers to the corner of the window, not of the screen.
- String property. The property is used to assign a string in the control object. Normally it is used for labels or prompts.
- CallBack function. This is the most important property in GUI design. If an object is selected or an action is done to the object, for instance, a button is clicked, the callback function can be executed automatically.
- Enable property. This indicates whether the control item is enabled, with options on (default) and off. Visible property is also provided.
- CData property. A true color bitmap is to be drawn on the control item. It is a three-dimensional array.
- TooltipString property. This stores a string variable for displaying help information when the mouse is moved on top of the control object, when the mouse button is not clicked.
- UserData property. This can be used to store and exchange information with other controls.
- Interruptible property. This indicates whether interrupts are allowed in the execution of the callback functions, with available options on (default) and off.
- The properties related to the font, such as FontAngle, FontName and so on.

Functions gco and gcbo can be used to get the handles of the current object. All the property names and property values of the current object can be listed either with the command `set(gco)`, or by the View → Object Browser menu item in the Guide window. In the latter case the users can modify the properties interactively.

### 2.7.3 *Menu System Design*

With the facilities provided in Guide, not only dialog boxes, but also windows with menu systems can be designed. The menu editor can be launched by choosing the Tools → Menu Editor menu item, as shown in Fig. 2-21(a), and the menu editor interface is shown in Fig. 2-21(b). Menu tools also provide facilities such as Align Objects and Grid and Ruler.

(a) Tools menu                              (b) menu editor

Fig. 2-21    Menu tool and menu editor.

With the menu editor interface, the menu system shown in Fig. 2-22(a) can be easily designed. The execution results shown in Fig. 2-22(b) are produced. The program can be saved in the file c2eggui2.m.

(a) menu editor results                          (b) menu system

Fig. 2-22    Interface design and modifications.

### 2.7.4 *An Illustrative Example in GUI Design*

In this section, a control-related example is given to demonstrate the concept and methods in designing graphical user interfaces.

**Example 2.31.** Suppose we want to design a GUI to analyse linear control systems. The draft of the expected interface is shown in Fig. 2-23. The user can specify the numerator and denominator polynomials in the two edit boxes on the upper left corner. The button on the upper right corner can be used to load the model into the interface. Then from the listbox on the right, the user can select different analysis plots, such as Bode diagram, Nyquist plot, root locus and step response. The selected plots of the system are expected to be drawn in the axis on the lower left.

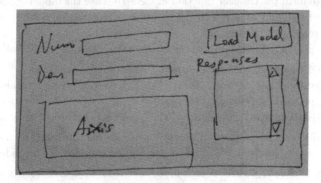

Fig. 2-23   Draft of the expected interface.

The prototype interface can be drawn directly with Guide as shown in Fig. 2-24. We have to assign the objects with meaningful tags, so that they can be accessed by other objects. For instance, we may assign the tags of the two edit boxes to edtNum and edtDen, the Load Model button to btnModel, listbox to lstResp, axis to axPlots.

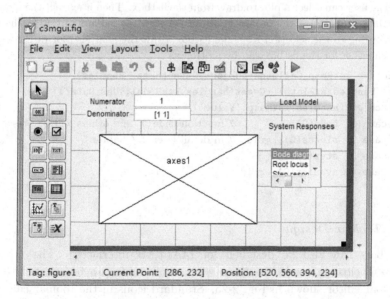

Fig. 2-24   Prototype of the expected interface.

Then the most important thing in interface design is to assign tasks (or propose "callbacks") to each of the relevant objects. The axis and two edit boxes are the objects to accept actions from other objects. There is no need for them to be assigned callbacks. The other two objects should be assigned tasks, specifically:

(1) The btnModel extracts the numerator and denominator polynomials from the two

edit boxes, edtNum and edtDen, then the transfer function model should be composed with the two arrays to form the transfer function model. To make the model accessible by other objects, the model should be saved to the an object. This can be done by assigning it to the UserData property of the button.

For this purpose, the callback function to the button can be written as

```
function btnModel_Callback(hObject, eventdata, handles)
n=eval(get(handles.edtNum,'String'));   % convert string to a numeric vector
d=eval(get(handles.edtDen,'String')); G=tf(n,d);   % construct TF object
set(handles.btnModel,'UserData',G);      % save TF object for later use
```

Since the edit box can be used to accept input information from the user, and wrong information is usually unavoidable. Error traps can be assigned to the code

```
function btnModel_Callback(hObject, eventdata, handles)
try
   n=eval(get(handles.edtNum,'String'));
   d=eval(get(handles.edtDen,'String')); G=tf(n,d);
   set(handles.btnModel,'UserData',G);
catch
   errordlg('Errors in the edit boxes, please check them','Error ...')
end
```

(2) The user can select a plot to draw from the listbox. Then it extract the model from the UserData property of the btnModel object. Assign the axPlots object to the current axis. According to the selection from the listbox, draw the analysis plot in the axis. The callback function for the listbox can be written as

```
function lstResp_Callback(hObject, eventdata, handles)
axes(handles.axPlots); G=get(handles.btnModel,'UserData');
switch get(handles.lstResp,'Value')
    case 1, bode(G);          % function bode() and others will be presented
    case 2, rlocus(G); grid   % in detail later in Chapter 5
    case 3, step(G);
    case 4, nyquist(G); grid
end
```

### 2.7.5   *Toolbar Design*

Toolbars can also be designed for MATLAB interfaces. The menu item Tools → Toolbar Editor in the main window of Guide can be selected to launch the toolbar editor shown in Fig. 2-25. Standard icons in the toolbar can be used directly, and new icons can also be designed.

In the toolbar editor, button **P** allows the user to design toolbar buttons, and button **T** allows the user to design tangle buttons. The new icons of the buttons can be described by the CData data type, or can use the existing icons provided.

**Example 2.32.** We can design a new user interface where a sinusoidal curve can be generated automatically on the interface. A toolbar system can be designed for this new

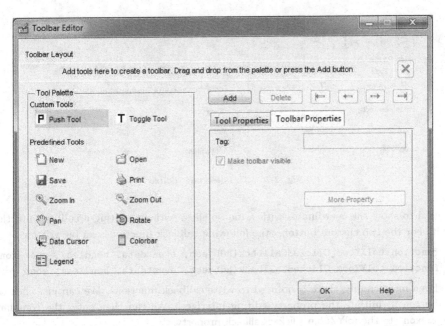

Fig. 2-25  Toolbar editor.

interface, with several standard buttons on it. Also, we can add more toolbar buttons to it, including the zooming buttons $\wp$ , $\wp$ for the $x$ and $y$ axes.

A blank prototype window can be designed first with Guide. An axis object can be added to it, with a tag of axPlot. The interface framework can be saved to the file c2eggui4.fig. Open the toolbar editor, and copy directly some of the standard icons to the editor. This can be done by first selecting the icons to be added, then clicking the Add button. A series of standard icons can be added to the Toolbar Layout in this way. If we want to add the custom icon $\wp$ button in the new toolbar, we can click the P button, and then click the Add button. Then the Tag property of the new custom button can be assigned to tolXZoom. Click the Edit button, and then select an existing bitmap file or CData data, and the picture can be assigned directly to the icon of the object. The designed toolbar is shown in Fig. 2-26. In the same way, the custom buttons $\wp$ , $\wp$ and $\wp$ can be added to the new toolbar, and their tags can be assigned to tolYZoom, tolZoom and tolZOff, respectively.

A file c2eggui4.m can be generated automatically by Guide, and the listings are exactly the same as the other framework files. If we want to automatically draw the sinusoidal curve when the interface is invoked, the OpeningFcn function in the main window should be written. In the function, the tag handles.axPlot can be activated, and the sinusoidal plot can be displayed automatically.

```
function varargout = c2eggui4_OpeningFcn(hObject, eventdata, handles)
varargout{1} = handles.output;      % this statement is already there
t=0:0.01:2*pi; y=sin(t); axes(handles.axPlot); plot(t,y)
```

When the program is written, the standard buttons in the new toolbar inherit the properties and callback functions of the original buttons. For instance, the button $\wp$ can

Fig. 2-26    The designed toolbar.

be used to show the coordinates with a mouse click, without writing a callback function for it. For the two custom buttons, the following callback functions can be written

```
function tolXZoom_ClickedCallback(hObject, eventdata, handles), zoom xon
function tolYZoom_ClickedCallback(hObject, eventdata, handles), zoom yon
```

Even more simply, there is no need to write callback functions. We can just click the ⊘ button to initiate the property editing interface. We can then enter the command 'zoom xon' to the tolYZoom_ClickedCallback property.

### 2.7.6    Embedding ActiveX Components in GUIs

ActiveX usually refers to reusable components, such as the Windows Media Player components, database components, developed by software providers, such as Microsoft. The ActiveX components can be adopted and embedded in the MATLAB GUI to make the interfaces more powerful, without the need for low-level programming. These ActiveX components can be embedded in MATLAB GUIs by clicking the ⧓X button, then a dialog box shown in Fig. 2-27 will be displayed, to allow the user to select a proper ActiveX component from the listbox. An example is given below to show how to use ActiveX in GUI design.

**Example 2.33.** A blank prototype GUI window can be opened with the guide command, and an ActiveX control can be drawn on the window. The Windows Media Player item can be selected from the ActiveX listbox, as shown in Fig. 2-28(a). Press the Create button, a Windows Media Player control will appear on the prototype window, and the Tag property can be set as activex3, as shown in Fig. 2-28 (b). A button can be drawn beside it, with the Tag set to btnFile, and the String property set to empty. We can also get the standard icon ☐, and save it to the file btnFile.bmp. With the $W = $ imread('btnFile.bmp') command, the image can be loaded into MATLAB workspace as variable $W$, and it can be set to the CData property, and the prototype window can be established as shown in 2-28 (b).

The callback function can also be established as (see file c2mmplay.m)

```
function btnLoad_Callback(hObject, eventdata, handles)
[f,p]=uigetfile('*.*','Select a media file');
if f~=0, set(handles.activex3,'URL',[p,f]); end
```

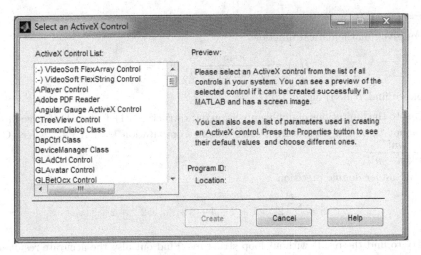

Fig. 2-27  Dialog box of ActiveX components.

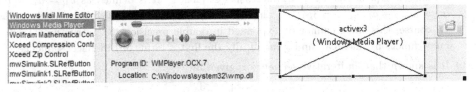

(a) Windows Media Player component          (b) prototype window

Fig. 2-28  Development of an interface with a Windows Media Player component.

It can be seen from the example that with only a few simple MATLAB statements, the interface can make use of the powerful Windows Media Player facilities. Thus, standard ActiveX components can provide great potential for MATLAB GUI programming.

## 2.8  Problems

(1) Enter the matrices $A$ and $B$ into MATLAB

$$A = \begin{bmatrix} 1 & 2 & 3 & 4 \\ 4 & 3 & 2 & 1 \\ 2 & 3 & 4 & 1 \\ 3 & 2 & 4 & 1 \end{bmatrix}, \quad B = \begin{bmatrix} 1+4j & 2+3j & 3+2j & 4+1j \\ 4+1j & 3+2j & 2+3j & 1+4j \\ 2+3j & 3+2j & 4+1j & 1+4j \\ 3+2j & 2+3j & 4+1j & 1+4j \end{bmatrix}.$$

What will happen in the $4 \times 4$ matrix, if a command $A(5,6) = 5$ is given?

(2) Find all the integers that have a reminder of 2 for modulo 13 operation, in the range of $0 \sim 1000$.

(3) For a given $A$, extract its all even rows and assign the results to matrix $B$. Test the code and see whether it is correct, with $A = \text{magic}(8)$.

(4) Express symbolically the polynomial $f(x) = x^5 + 3x^4 + 4x^3 + 2x^2 + 3x + 6$. Let

$x = (s - 1)/(s + 1)$, substitute $f(x)$ into a function of $s$.

(5) For given mathematical functions

$$f(x) = \frac{x \sin x}{(x + 5)\sqrt{x^2 + 2}}, \quad g(x) = \tan x,$$

please find $f(g(x))$ and $g(f(x))$.

(6) Due to the limitations of double precision data structure, the factorials of large integers cannot be found accurately. Use symbolic computation to find $C_{50}^{10}$, where $C_m^n = \frac{m!}{n!(m-n)!}$.

(7) Find under double precision

$$S = \sum_{i=0}^{63} 2^i = 1 + 2 + 4 + 8 + \cdots + 2^{62} + 2^{63}.$$

Try to find the result without loop structure. Find out also the accurate result using symbolic computation.

(8) Fibonacci sequence is a rapidly increasing sequence. It is defined as $a_1 = a_2 = 1$, $a_n = a_{n-1} + a_{n-2}$, $n = 3, 4, \cdots$, and its 120th term is 5358359254990966640871840. Of course, this value cannot be expressed in double precision data structure. Write an M-function which can find symbolically the first $n$ terms of Fibonacci sequence.

(9) It is known that an iterative sequence is given by

$$x_{n+1} = \frac{x_n}{2} + \frac{3}{2x_n},$$

with $x_1 = 1$; if $n$ is large enough, the sequence may converge to a certain value $X$. Select a suitable $n$ and find the steady-state value $X$, with the error tolerance of $10^{-14}$.

(10) Find all prime numbers smaller than 1000 with loop structure.

(11) Find $S = \prod_{n=1}^{\infty} \left(1 + \frac{2}{n^2}\right)$, with the error tolerance of $10^{-12}$.

(12) For $\arctan(x) = x - \frac{x^3}{3} + \frac{x^5}{5} - \frac{x^7}{7} + \cdots$, let $x = 1$, the approximate value of $\pi$ can be found

$$\pi \approx 4\left(1 - \frac{1}{3} + \frac{1}{5} - \frac{1}{7} + \frac{1}{9} - \frac{1}{11} + \cdots\right).$$

Use loop structure to find the approximate value of $\pi$, with the error tolerance of $10^{-6}$.

(13) Solve the algebraic equation $f(x) = x^2 \sin(0.1x + 2) - 3 = 0$ using the two algorithms:

(i) **Bisection method**. If in an interval $(a, b)$, $f(a)f(b) < 0$, there will be at least one solution. Take the middle point $x_1 = (b - a)/2$, and based on the relationship of $f(x_1)$ and $f(a)$, $f(b)$, determine in which half interval there exists solutions. Middle point in the new half interval can then be taken. Repeat the process until the size of the interval is smaller than the pre-specified error tolerance $\epsilon$. Find the solution with bisection method in interval $(-4, 0)$, with $\epsilon = 10^{-10}$.

(ii) **Newton–Raphson method**. Select an initial guess of $x_n$, the next approximation can be obtained with $x_{n+1} = x_n + f(x_n)/f'(x_n)$. If the two points are close enough, i.e., $|x_{n+1} - x_n| < \epsilon$, where $\epsilon$ is the error tolerance. Find the solution with $x_0 = -4$, and $\epsilon = 10^{-12}$.

(14) Write an M-function for the following piecewise function, where $D$, $h$ and $x$ are input arguments, and $y$ is the output.

$$y = f(x) = \begin{cases} h, & x > D \\ h/Dx, & |x| \leqslant D \\ -h, & x < -D. \end{cases}$$

(15) Write an M-function `mat_add()` such that any number of matrices can be added up with the function. The syntax of the function is $A = \texttt{mat\_add}(A_1, A_2, A_3, \cdots)$.

(16) Write an M-function which can generate an $m \times m$ Hankel matrix, whose syntax is $H = \texttt{myhankel}(v)$, with $v = [h_1, h_2, \cdots, h_m, h_{m+1}, \cdots, h_{2m-1}]$.

(17) It is known from matrix theory that a matrix $M$ expressed by $M = A + BCB^{\mathrm{T}}$. The inverse matrix $M$ can be obtained with the following formula

$$M^{-1} = \left(A + BCB^{\mathrm{T}}\right)^{-1} = A^{-1} - A^{-1}B\left(C^{-1} + B^{\mathrm{T}}A^{-1}B\right)^{-1}B^{\mathrm{T}}A^{-1}.$$

(18) The well-known Mittag–Leffler is defined as

$$f_\alpha(z) = \sum_{k=0}^{\infty} \frac{z^k}{\Gamma(\alpha k + 1)},$$

where $\Gamma(x)$ is $\Gamma$-function which can be evaluated with `gamma(x)`. Write an M-function with syntax $f = \texttt{mymittag}(\alpha, z, \epsilon)$, where $\epsilon$ is the error tolerance, with default value of $\epsilon = 10^{-6}$. Argument $z$ is a numeric vector. Draw the curves for Mittag–Leffler functions with $\alpha = 1$ and $\alpha = 0.5$.

(19) Write an M-function for an iterative model

$$\begin{cases} x_{k+1} = 1 + y_k - 1.4x_k^2 \\ y_{k+1} = 0.3x_k. \end{cases}$$

For the initial values $x_0 = 0$, $y_0 = 0$, take 30000 iterations to get two vectors $x$ and $y$, then get the plot with `plot(x,y,'.')`. The plot is known as Hénon attractor.

(20) A regular triangle can be drawn by MATLAB statements easily. Use the loop structure to design an M-function that in the same coordinates, a sequence of regular triangles can be drawn, each by rotating a small angle from the previous one.

(21) Select suitable step-sizes and draw the function curve for $\sin(1/t)$, where $t \in (-1,1)$.

(22) Assume that the power series expansion of a function is

$$f(x) = \lim_{N \to \infty} \sum_{n=1}^{N} (-1)^n \frac{x^{2n}}{(2n)!}.$$

If $N$ is large enough, power series $f(x)$ converges to a certain function $\hat{f}(x)$. Please write a MATLAB program that plots the function $\hat{f}(x)$ in the interval $x \in (0, \pi)$. Observe and verify what function $\hat{f}(x)$ is.

(23) For properly chosen interval of $\theta$, plot the following polar plots.

(i) $\rho = 1.0013\theta^2$, (ii) $\rho = \cos(7\theta/2)$, (iii) $\rho = \sin\theta/\theta$, (iv) $\rho = 1 - \cos^3 7\theta$.

(24) Use graphical method to find the approximate solution to the following simultaneous equations

(i) $\begin{cases} x^2 + y^2 = 3xy^2 \\ x^3 - x^2 = y^2 - y, \end{cases}$
(ii) $\begin{cases} e^{-(x+y)^2 + \pi/2} \sin(5x + 2y) = 0 \\ (x^2 - y^2 + xy)e^{-x^2 - y^2 - xy} = 0. \end{cases}$

(25) Draw the surface plot and contour plots for the following functions. Draw also with the functions `surfc()`, `surfl()`, and `waterfall()`, and observe the results.

(i) $xy$,    (ii) $\sin xy$,    (iii) $\sin(x^2 - y^2)$,    (iv) $-xye^{-2(x^2 + y^2)}$.

(26) In graphics command, there is a trick in hiding certain parts of the plot. If the function values are assigned to NaNs, the point on the curve or the surface will not be shown. Draw first the surface plot of the function $z = \sin xy$. Then cut off the region that satisfies $x^2 + y^2 \leqslant 0.5^2$.

(27) An Excel-like control object is available in MATLAB's GUI design tool. Build a matrix processor with such a control, to accept a matrix in a visible way. Also, add push buttons to find the matrix analysis results of $A^{-1}$, $e^A$ and $\sin A$.

## Bibliography and References

[1] Lamport L. LATEX: a document preparation system — user's guide and reference manual. Reading MA: Addision-Wesley Publishing Company, 2nd edition, 1994

[2] Atherton D P, Xue D Y. The analysis of feedback systems with piecewise linear nonlinearities when subjected to Gaussian inputs, In: Kozin F and Ono T. Control systems, topics on theory and application. Tokyo: Mita Press, 1991

[3] The MathWorks Inc. Creating graphical user interfaces

# Chapter 3

# MATLAB Solutions to Scientific Computation Problems

Research on control systems involves various mathematical problems. For instance, stability analyses involve the solution of eigenvalues of matrices, while controllability and observability analyses need the evaluation of matrix ranks. The evaluation of state transition matrix is, in fact, a matrix exponential problem. The above examples are closely related to linear algebra problems. Simulation of control systems is, in fact, numerical solutions of ordinary differential equations. Also, optimal controller problems involve optimization problems. If one can master the methods and skills of using MATLAB in scientific computation, the ability to solve problems in the analysis and design of control systems will greatly enhanced.

In this chapter, an introduction is provided in MATLAB applications in scientific computation. Here the keyword "computation" includes both numerical and symbolic computation. MATLAB originated from numerical linear algebra, and in its long-term development, dedicated toolboxes cover almost all mathematical branches. Since symbolic computation is also supported, MATLAB can also be used in formula derivations. Thus, normally with a single command, the solution to a mathematical problem can be solved.

The applications of MATLAB in scientific computations attract many scientists and engineers. Its capabilities in scientific computation is one of the distinguished features of MATLAB. In this chapter, mathematical problems related closely to control engineering will be addresses with MATLAB. This will establish a solid basis for the investigation of control problems. Section 3.1 presents the analytical and numerical solutions to linear algebra problems, including matrix analysis, matrix transformation and matrix functions. In Section 3.2, various algebraic equations are explored, including matrix equations and nonlinear equations. Section 3.3 introduces the numerical solutions to first-order explicit ordinary differential equations, and the methods converting an ordinary differential equations to the explicit ones. Analytical solutions to a certain class of differential equations will also be explored. In Section 3.4, optimization problem solutions will be given to unconstrained and constrained problems. Least squares curve fitting will also be presented. In Section 3.5, Laplace and $z$ transforms will be presented.

It seems that this chapter is on mathematics and involves a huge amount of mathematical formulas, however, the basic idea in this chapter is to try to avoid tedious low-level mathematics, and with the use of MATLAB, extremely difficult problems can be solved easily. Further information on MATLAB applications on scientific computation may refer to a more dedicated works in [1].

## 3.1   MATLAB Solutions to Linear Algebra Problems

Many linear algebra problems have analytical solutions, and for those analytical solutions that do not exist, numerical solutions can be obtained instead. In the section, linear algebra computations will be presented.

### 3.1.1   *Fundamental Analysis of Matrices*

Matrix analysis may sometimes reveal certain characteristics of the matrices. For instance, in control, eigenvalues reflect the stability, while rank of matrices reflect the controllability and observability of the systems. Here systematic introduction and MATLAB implementation will be presented.

**1. Determinant**

The built-in function `det(A)` in MATLAB can be used to find directly the determinant of matrix $A$. If $A$ is a numerical matrix in MATLAB, the function finds the determinant with numerical method. However, if $A$ is a symbolic variable, analytical solutions will be calculated. For matrices which are very close to singularity, the two results may have significant differences.

**Example 3.1.** The general term in Hilbert matrix is $h_{i,j} = 1/(i+j-1)$. With MATLAB command $H = \text{hilb}(n)$, the Hilbert matrix can be created. The function `sym()` can be used to convert a thus created matrix into symbolic variable. The determinant of a $15 \times 15$ Hilbert matrix can be obtained with

```
>> H=hilb(15); d1=det(H)          % find numerical solution
   H=sym(H); d2=det(H), vpa(d2) % convert to symbolic, find analytical solution
```

The numerical solution is $d_1 = -1.8701 \times 10^{-120}$, and it is not accurate. An analytical solution can be obtained

$$d_2 = \frac{1}{\begin{array}{l}9446949653634668571373109351236989087975627994978804269595338137635022705891424600259116300098090513203200000000000000000000\end{array}} \approx 10^{-124}.$$

**Example 3.2.** Consider a Vandermonde matrix

$$A = \begin{bmatrix} 1 & 1 & 1 \\ a & b & c \\ a^2 & b^2 & c^2 \end{bmatrix}$$

with variables. The variables can be declared as symbolic variables $a$, $b$, $c$ first, then the following command can find the analytical solution to the determinant $-(a-b)(a-c)(b-c)$.

```
>> syms a b c; v=[a b c]; A=[v.^0; v; v.^2]; % create a Vandermonde matrix
   det(A); simple(factor(ans))      % find the factorized form of the determinant
```

## 2. Trace

For a square matrix $A = \{a_{ij}\}$, the trace of the matrix $A$ is defined as the sum of the diagonal elements. From algebraic theory, it is known that the trace equals the sum of eigenvalues. The trace of matrix $A$ can be obtained with `trace(A)`. In MATLAB, the function `trace()` can be used in rectangular matrices.

## 3. Rank

The maximum number of linearly independent rows and columns is called the rank of the matrix, denoted as rank($A$). If the rank of its row or column, the matrix is called full-rank matrix. A built-in function `rank()` can be used to find the rank of a matrix, with `rank(A,ε)`, where $\varepsilon$ is the error tolerance and can be omitted.

## 4. Norms

Commonly used matrix norms are

$$||A||_1 = \max_{1 \leqslant j \leqslant n} \sum_{i=1}^{n} |a_{ij}|, \quad ||A||_2 = \sqrt{s_{\max}(A^T A)}, \quad ||A||_\infty = \max_{1 \leqslant i \leqslant n} \sum_{j=1}^{n} |a_{ij}|, \quad (3.1)$$

where $s(X)$ is an eigenvalue of $X$, and $s_{\max}(A^T A)$ is the maximum eigenvalue of matrix $A^T A$. In fact, $||A||_2$ is the maximum singular value of $A$. Function `norm()` can be used to find the norms of a matrix, with `norm(A)`, which evaluates the 2-norm, while `norm(A,1)` and `norm(A,inf)` evaluate the norms $||A||_1$ and $||A||_\infty$, respectively. In earlier versions of MATLAB, this function can only be used for numerical matrices.

## 5. Characteristic polynomials and eigenvalues

The determinant of matrix $sI - A$ can be expressed by a polynomial of $s$

$$C(s) = \det(sI - A) = s^n + c_1 s^{n-1} + \cdots + c_{n-1}s + c_n, \quad (3.2)$$

and such a polynomial is referred to as the characteristic polynomial of matrix $A$, and the coefficients $c_i$, $i = 1, 2, \cdots, n$ are referred to as the coefficients of characteristic polynomials.

MATLAB function `p=poly(A)` can be used to find the characteristic polynomial and the returned $p$ is a row vector, containing all the coefficients in the descending order of $s$. If $A$ is a vector, the same function can be used in creating a matrix whose eigenvalues are specified in $A$.

For a square matrix $A$, if there exists a nonzero vector $x$, and there is a scalar $\lambda$ such that $Ax = \lambda x$, $\lambda$ is referred as an eigenvalue of $A$, and $x$ is the corresponding eigenvector. The eigenvalues and eigenvectors can be found with function `[V,D] = eig(A)`, and $A$ is the given matrix, and $V$ and $D$ are eigenvector matrix and eigenvalues, respectively.

## 6. Polynomials and evaluation of polynomial matrices

Function $C$=`polyval(a,x)` evaluates the polynomial in a dot operation manner, $C = a_1 x.\hat{}\ n + \cdots + a_{n+1}$, where $a = [a_1, a_2, \cdots, a_n, a_{n+1}]$ is the coefficients of the polynomial in descending order of $s$.

If the polynomial matrix is expected, i.e.

$$B = a_1 A^n + a_2 A^{n-1} + \cdots + a_n A + a_{n+1} I, \tag{3.3}$$

where $I$ is an identity matrix, and $A$ is a square matrix, the polynomial matrix is obtained as $B$=`polyvalm(a,A)`.

## 7. Inverse and pseudo inverse

For an $n \times n$ nonsingular matrix $A$, if there exists a matrix $C$, satisfying

$$AC = CA = I, \tag{3.4}$$

then $C$ is referred to as the inverse matrix, denoted as $C = A^{-1}$. In MATLAB, inverse can be obtained as $C$=`inv(A)`.

If the "inverse" is of a rectangular or a singular matrix, generalized inverse or pseudo inverse matrix should be introduced. For a matrix $A$, matrix $M$ is referred to as pseudo inverse, or Moore–Penrose generalized inverse matrix, if the following three conditions are satisfied

(1) $AMA = A$

(2) $MAM = M$

(3) $AM$ and $MA$ are both symmetric matrices.

Moore–Penrose generalized inverse matrix is unique and is denoted by $M = A^+$. For a complex matrix, the third condition is extended as, both $MA$ and $AM$ are both Hermitian matrices. In MATLAB, pseudo inverse can be obtained with the function $M$=`pinv(A)`.

### 3.1.2  *Matrix Decomposition*

Similarity transform is useful in state space analysis. Here matrix transform and decomposition are presented. In particular, triangular and singular value decomposition are presented.

## 1. Similarity transform

For an $n \times n$ square $A$, if there exist a nonsingular matrix $T$ of the same size, the following transform to $A$ can be performed

$$\widehat{A} = T^{-1} A T, \tag{3.5}$$

this kind of transform is referred to as similarity transform. It can be shown that the eigenvalues of $\widehat{A}$ are the same as those of $A$.

## 2. Triangular decomposition

Triangular decomposition decomposes an arbitrary matrix $A$ into the product of a lower triangular matrix $L$ and an upper triangular matrix $U$, i.e., $A = LU$.

Triangular decomposition is also referred to LU decomposition. The two triangular matrices are

$$
L = \begin{bmatrix} 1 & & & \\ l_{21} & 1 & & \\ \vdots & \vdots & \ddots & \\ l_{n1} & l_{n2} & \cdots & 1 \end{bmatrix}, \quad U = \begin{bmatrix} u_{11} & u_{12} & \cdots & u_{1n} \\ & u_{22} & \cdots & u_{2n} \\ & & \ddots & \vdots \\ & & & u_{nn} \end{bmatrix}. \tag{3.6}
$$

MATLAB function $[L,U] = \text{lu}(A)$ can be used to perform LU decomposition. Since numerical method is used, pivots are considered. Thus, the matrix $L$ is usually not a lower triangular matrix, but a permutation of such a matrix.

**3. Cholesky decomposition**

If $A$ is a symmetric matrix, triangular decomposition can still be made, such that $A = D^T D$. This kind of decomposition is referred to as Cholesky decomposition. In MATLAB, $[D,p] = \text{chol}(A)$ function can be used in Cholesky decomposition, and $p - 1$ is the order of positive definite sub-matrix of $A$. If matrix $A$ is positive definite, $p = 0$.

**4. Orthogonal basis**

If a matrix $T$ satisfies $T^{-1} = T^*$, where $T^*$ is a Hermitian transpose of $T$, $T$ is referred to as an orthogonal matrix, and denoted as $Q = T$. It can be seen that orthogonal matrix $Q$ satisfies the following conditions:

$$
Q^* Q = I, \quad \text{and} \quad Q Q^* = I, \tag{3.7}
$$

where $I$ is an $n \times n$ identity matrix. The MATLAB function $Q = \text{orth}(A)$ can be used to find the orthogonal basis of $A$, and the columns of $Q$ is the rank of $A$.

**5. Singular value decomposition**

For an $n \times m$ matrix $A$, and rank$(A) = r$, the matrix $A$ can be decomposed as $A = L \Lambda M^T$, where $L$ and $M$ are both orthogonal matrices, and $\Lambda = \text{diag}(\sigma_1, \sigma_2, \cdots, \sigma_n)$ is a diagonal matrix, whose diagonal elements $\sigma_1, \sigma_2, \cdots, \sigma_n$ satisfy $\sigma_1 \geqslant \sigma_2 \geqslant \cdots \geqslant \sigma_n \geqslant 0$.

MATLAB function $[L, A_1, M] = \text{svd}(A)$ can be used to find singular value decomposition, such that $A = L A_1 M^T$.

**6. Condition number**

The condition number of $A$ is defined as the ratio of maximum and minimum singular values, denoted as cond$(A) = \sigma_{\max}/\sigma_{\min}$. In MATLAB, condition number can be evaluated with $\text{cond}(A)$. Condition number determines the numerical behavior of the matrix. If the condition number is extremely large, the matrix is referred to as bad-conditioned, or ill-conditioned matrix. Slight change in the ill-conditioned matrix may result in significant changes in the numerical properties of the matrix.

### 3.1.3  *Matrix Exponential* $e^A$ *and Exponential Function* $e^{At}$

Matrix exponential can be evaluated from MATLAB function `expm(A)`. Other matrix functions, such as $\cos A$, of matrix $A$ can be evaluated with `funm(A,'cos')`. It should be noted that `funm()` function may lead to significant errors if matrix $A$ has repeated eigenvalues. In this case, Taylor series expansion may be considered[2]. Complicated matrix function problems can be solved with the analytical method in [1].

**Example 3.3.** For matrix

$$A = \begin{bmatrix} -11 & -5 & 5 \\ 12 & 5 & -6 \\ 0 & 1 & 0 \end{bmatrix},$$

the exponential matrix $e^A$ and exponential function $e^{At}$ can be evaluated with

```
>> A=[-11,-5,5; 12,5,-6; 0,1,0]; F1=expm(A)    % numerical solution
   A=sym(A); F2=expm(A), syms t; expm(A*t)     % symbolic solutions
```

and the results are

$$F_1 = \begin{bmatrix} 0.24737701 & 0.30723864 & 0.42774107 \\ 0.14460292 & -0.00080692801 & -0.51328929 \\ 0.88197566 & 0.82052793 & 0.30643171 \end{bmatrix},$$

$$F_2 = \begin{bmatrix} 15e^{-3} - 20e^{-2} + 6e^{-1} & 5e^{-1} - 15e^{-2} + 10e^{-3} & 5e^{-2} - 5e^{-3} \\ 24e^{-2} - 18e^{-3} - 6e^{-1} & -12e^{-3} - 5e^{-1} + 18e^{-2} & -6e^{-2} + 6e^{-3} \\ 6e^{-1} - 12e^{-2} + 6e^{-3} & -9e^{-2} + 4e^{-3} + 5e^{-1} & -2e^{-3} + 3e^{-2} \end{bmatrix},$$

$$e^{At} = \begin{bmatrix} 15e^{-3t} - 20e^{-2t} + 6e^{-t} & 5e^{-t} - 15e^{-2t} + 10e^{-3t} & 5e^{-2t} - 5e^{-3t} \\ 24e^{-2t} - 18e^{-3t} - 6e^{-t} & -12e^{-3t} - 5e^{-t} + 18e^{-2t} & -6e^{-2t} + 6e^{-3t} \\ 6e^{-t} - 12e^{-2t} + 6e^{-3t} & -9e^{-2t} + 4e^{-3t} + 5e^{-t} & -2e^{-3t} + 3e^{-2t} \end{bmatrix}.$$

## 3.2  Solutions of Algebraic Equations

### 3.2.1  *Solutions of Linear Algebraic Equations*

In this part of presentation, linear equations, Lyapunov equations and Sylvester equations are presented.

**1. Linear matrix equation**

Left and right divisions discussed earlier can be used in solving linear matrix equations. For the linear equation $AX = B$, function $X = A\backslash B$ can be used. If the equation is $XA = B$, function $X = B/A$ can be used.

More precisely, in solving linear algebraic equation $AX = B$, the following three cases should be considered[1]:

(1) If matrix $A$ is a nonsingular square matrix, there is a unique solution, $X = \text{inv}(A)*B$.

(2) If $A$ is a singular or rectangular matrix, and the rank of the two matrices, $A$ and $C = [A, B]$ is the same, all equal to $m$, the equation has infinite number of solutions. With $\hat{x} = \text{null}(A)$ , the basic set of solutions, or null space, of the homogeneous equation $A\hat{x} = 0$. With $x_0 = \text{pinv}(A)*B$ , a particular solution can be found. Thus, for arbitrary constants $a_1, a_2, \cdots, a_{n-m}$, all the solutions to the original equation can be written as

$$x = a_1 * \hat{x}(:,1) + a_2 * \hat{x}(:,2) + \cdots + a_{n-m} * \hat{x}(:,n-m) + x_0$$

(3) If the ranks of $A$ and $C = [A, B]$ are different, the equation has no solution. Least squares solution can be obtained with $x = \text{pinv}(A)*B$ .

Besides, the function $\text{rref}(C)$ can be used to find the reduced row echelon form of the matrices and the analytical solution can be found.

**Example 3.4.** For the linear algebraic equation

$$\begin{bmatrix} 1 & 2 & 3 & 4 \\ 2 & 2 & 1 & 1 \\ 2 & 4 & 6 & 8 \\ 4 & 4 & 2 & 2 \end{bmatrix} X = \begin{bmatrix} 1 \\ 3 \\ 2 \\ 6 \end{bmatrix}.$$

The following statements can be used to find the ranks of $A$ and $C = [A, B]$, they all equal to 2.

```
>> A=[1 2 3 4; 2 2 1 1; 2 4 6 8; 4 4 2 2]; B=[1;3;2;6];
   C=[A B]; [rank(A), rank(C)]
```

Thus, it can be concluded that there is an infinite number of solutions. To solve the equation, the null space should be obtained first. A particular solution $x_0$ can also be found. Then the infinite number of solutions can be established

```
>> syms a1 a2; Z=null(sym(A)); x0=sym(pinv(A))*B;
   x=a1*Z(:,1)+a2*Z(:,2)+x0, A*x-B
```

From the results, the analytical solution can be written as

$$x = \alpha_1 \begin{bmatrix} 2 \\ -5/2 \\ 1 \\ 0 \end{bmatrix} + \alpha_2 \begin{bmatrix} 3 \\ -7/2 \\ 0 \\ 1 \end{bmatrix} + \begin{bmatrix} 125/131 \\ 96/131 \\ -10/131 \\ -39/131 \end{bmatrix} = \begin{bmatrix} 2a_1 + 3a_2 + 125/131 \\ -5a_1/2 - 7a_2/2 + 96/131 \\ a_1 - 10/131 \\ a_2 - 39/131 \end{bmatrix}.$$

If $D = \text{rref}(C)$ function is used, the reduced row echelon form is obtained as

$$D = \begin{bmatrix} 1 & 0 & -2 & -3 & 2 \\ 0 & 1 & 5/2 & 7/2 & -1/2 \\ 0 & 0 & 0 & 0 & 0 \\ 0 & 0 & 0 & 0 & 0 \end{bmatrix}.$$

The solutions to the linear equation can be written as $x_1 = 2x_3 + 3x_4 + 2$, $x_2 = -5x_3/2 - 7x_4/2 - 1/2$, for arbitrary choices of $x_3$ and $x_4$.

## 2. Lyapunov equation

The equation below is referred to as Lyapunov equation

$$AX + XA^{\mathrm{T}} = -C, \tag{3.8}$$

where $A$ and $C$ are given matrices, and $C$ is a symmetrical matrix. The `lyap()` function provided in the Control System Toolbox can be used to solve the Lyapunov equation, with $X = \text{lyap}(A, C)$. This function can also be used to deal with asymmetrical matrix $C$.

The standard form of Lyapunov equation for discrete system is

$$A X A^{\mathrm{T}} - X + Q = 0, \tag{3.9}$$

and the equation can be solved directly with $X = \text{dlyap}(A, Q)$.

### 3. Sylvester equation

Sylvester equation given below is, in fact, an extended version of Lyapunov equations. Sometimes Sylvester equation is also known as generalized Lyapunov equation. The Sylvester equation is given by

$$A X + X B = -C, \tag{3.10}$$

where $A, B, C$ are all given matrices. Again the function `lyap()` can be used in solving Sylvester equations with $X = \text{lyap}(A, B, C)$.

A MATLAB function for finding analytical solution of Sylvester equation is given in [1]. The original overload function name was lyap.m, placed under @sym folder. Since this format is no longer supported in new versions of MATLAB, a new name, `lyapsym()` is assigned.

```
function X=lyapsym(A,B,C)
if nargin==2, C=B; B=A'; end
[nr,nc]=size(C); A0=kron(A,eye(nc))+kron(eye(nr),B');
try
    C1=C'; x0=-inv(A0)*C1(:); X=reshape(x0,nc,nr)';
catch, error('singular matrix found.'), end
```

For different types of equations, the following syntaxes can be used

$X = \text{lyapsym}(\text{sym}(A), C)$         % Lyapunov equation
$X = \text{lyapsym}(\text{sym}(A), -\text{inv}(A'), Q*\text{inv}(A'))$ % discrete Lyapunov
$X = \text{lyapsym}(\text{sym}(A), B, C)$         % Sylvester equation

**Example 3.5.** For the following Sylvester equation

$$\begin{bmatrix} 8 & 1 & 6 \\ 3 & 5 & 7 \\ 4 & 9 & 2 \end{bmatrix} X + X \begin{bmatrix} 16 & 4 & 1 \\ 9 & 3 & 1 \\ 4 & 2 & 1 \end{bmatrix} = \begin{bmatrix} 1 & 2 & 3 \\ 4 & 5 & 6 \\ 7 & 8 & 0 \end{bmatrix}.$$

The numerical and analytical solutions can be found with

```
>> A=[8,1,6; 3,5,7; 4,9,2]; B=[16,4,1; 9,3,1; 4,2,1];
   C=-[1,2,3; 4,5,6; 7,8,0]; X1=lyap(A,B,C), norm(A*X1+X1*B+C)
   X2=lyapsym(A,B,C), norm(A*X2+X2*B+C)
```

The numerical and analytical solutions are respectively. The numerical solution has an error or $9.5337 \times 10^{-15}$.

$$X_1 = \begin{bmatrix} 0.0749 & 0.0899 & -0.4329 \\ 0.0081 & 0.4814 & -0.216 \\ 0.0196 & 0.1826 & 1.1579 \end{bmatrix},$$

$$X_2 = \begin{bmatrix} 1349214/18020305 & 648107/7208122 & -15602701/36040610 \\ 290907/36040610 & 3470291/7208122 & -3892997/18020305 \\ 70557/3604061 & 1316519/7208122 & 8346439/7208122 \end{bmatrix}.$$

## 4. Riccati equation

The following equation is referred to as Riccati equation

$$A^{\mathrm{T}}X + XA - XBX + C = 0, \tag{3.11}$$

where $A, B, C$ are given matrices, and $B$ is symmetrical nonnegative definite matrix, and $C$ is a symmetrical matrix. The function is a quadratic equation, and there is no analytical solutions exist. MATLAB function are() can be used to solve numerically Riccati equation, with $X = \mathrm{are}(A,B,C)$, and $X$ obtained is also a symmetrical matrix. Discrete Riccati equation can be solved with dare() function.

**Example 3.6.** Consider the Riccati equation

$$\begin{bmatrix} -2 & -1 & 0 \\ 1 & 0 & -1 \\ -3 & -2 & -2 \end{bmatrix} X + X \begin{bmatrix} -2 & 1 & -3 \\ -1 & 0 & -2 \\ 0 & -1 & -2 \end{bmatrix} - X \begin{bmatrix} 2 & 2 & -2 \\ -1 & 5 & -2 \\ -1 & 1 & 2 \end{bmatrix} X + \begin{bmatrix} 5 & -4 & 4 \\ 1 & 0 & 4 \\ 1 & -1 & 5 \end{bmatrix} = 0.$$

Compared with Eqn. (3.11), the standard form is

$$A = \begin{bmatrix} -2 & 1 & -3 \\ -1 & 0 & -2 \\ 0 & -1 & -2 \end{bmatrix}, \quad B = \begin{bmatrix} 2 & 2 & -2 \\ -1 & 5 & -2 \\ -1 & 1 & 2 \end{bmatrix}, \quad C = \begin{bmatrix} 5 & -4 & 4 \\ 1 & 0 & 4 \\ 1 & -1 & 5 \end{bmatrix}.$$

The numerical solution of the equation can be found

```
>> A=[-2,1,-3; -1,0,-2; 0,-1,-2]; B=[2,2,-2; -1 5 -2; -1 1 2];
   C=[5 -4 4; 1 0 4; 1 -1 5]; X=are(A,B,C); norm(A'*X+X*A-X*B*X+C)
```

the solution with an error of $1.4215 \times 10^{-14}$ can be obtained

$$X = \begin{bmatrix} 0.98739 & -0.79833 & 0.41887 \\ 0.57741 & -0.13079 & 0.57755 \\ -0.28405 & -0.073037 & 0.69241 \end{bmatrix}.$$

### 3.2.2 Solutions of Nonlinear Equations

#### 1. Analytical solutions of nonlinear equations

The function solve() provided in the Symbolic Math Toolbox can be used to find analytical solutions to some nonlinear equations. All the equations can be expressed in strings. The analytical or high-precision numerical solutions can be found. This function is especially useful in finding the analytical solutions of polynomial-type equations[1].

**Example 3.7.** Consider the following equation

$$\begin{cases} \dfrac{1}{2}x^2 + x + \dfrac{3}{2} + 2\dfrac{1}{y} + \dfrac{5}{2y^2} + 3\dfrac{1}{x^3} = 0 \\[2mm] \dfrac{y}{2} + \dfrac{3}{2x} + \dfrac{1}{x^4} + 5y^4 = 0. \end{cases}$$

It is not possible to find solutions of the original equations without powerful tools. The `solve()` function can be tried, with the following statements, and 26 solutions can be found, with norm of the error matrix $1.738 \times 10^{-33}$.

```
>> f1='x^2/2+x+3/2+2/y+5/(2*y^2)+3/x^3'; f2='y/2+3/(2*x)+1/x^4+5*y^4';
   syms x y; [x0,y0]=solve(f1,f2,'x,y'); size(x0),
   norm([subs(f1,{x,y},{x0,y0}),subs(f2,{x,y},{x0,y0})])
```

## 2. Graphical approach in nonlinear equations

As presented earlier, implicit function can be drawn directly with `ezplot()` function. If two simultaneous equations are provided, the solutions to the first equation can be drawn, then with `hold on` command, the second equation can also be drawn in the same axis. The intersections of the two set of plots are, in fact, the solutions to the simultaneous equations. Zoom facilities in MATLAB can be used to find details of a particular equation.

**Example 3.8.** Consider the simultaneous equations

$$\begin{cases} x^2 e^{-xy^2/2} + e^{-x/2}\sin(xy) = 0 \\[2mm] y^2\cos(y + x^2) + x^2 e^{x+y} = 0. \end{cases}$$

The following statements can be used to draw the curves of the two equations, as shown in Fig. 3-1(a). It can be seen that there are many intersections, which are solutions to simultaneous equations. If one wants to find a particular solution, for instance, point A, zooming facilities can be used, until the scales on both $x$ and $y$ axes read the same, as shown in Fig. 3-1(b). The solution at point A is $x = 2.7795$, and $y = -3.3911$. Substitute the solution back to the original equation, the errors are 0.0002 and $-0.0516$. It can be seen that the precision of the graphical method is not satisfactory.

```
>> ezplot('x^2*exp(-x*y^2/2)+exp(-x/2)*sin(x*y)=0')
   hold on; ezplot('y^2 *cos(y+x^2) +x^2*exp(x+y)=0')
```

## 3. Numerical solutions of nonlinear equations

The two approaches presented earlier have limitations. For instance, function `solve()` function is suitable only for those which can be converted to polynomial-type equations, and for other types of nonlinear equations, at most one solution can be found. The graphical approach can only be used in finding solutions to equations with one or two unknowns, with usually extremely low accuracy.

A solution function `fsolve()` for nonlinear equations is provided in MATLAB, and it can be used in finding numerically the solutions of nonlinear equations. The procedures are

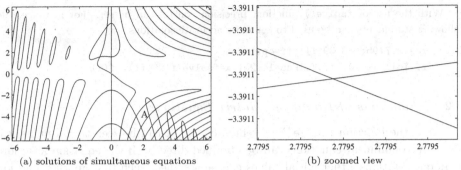

(a) solutions of simultaneous equations      (b) zoomed view

Fig. 3-1   Graphical illustration of simultaneous equations.

(1) **Convert equations to standard form** $Y = F(X) = 0$, where $X$ and $F$ are matrices of the same sizes.

(2) **Describe equations in MATLAB**. Anonymous function or M-function can be used in describing the equations.

(3) **Select an initial point and solve the equation**. Solve equations with

$$[x, f_1, \texttt{flag}] = \texttt{fsolve}(fun, x_0, \texttt{options})$$

where *fun* is the MATLAB description of the MATLAB function created in (2), $x_0$ is an initial point. The variable $x$ is the solution found, $f_1$ is the error matrix. The quantity `flag` indicates whether the solution is successful, with positive `flag` meaning successful. If the error tolerance is expected, the `options` template can be modified, with `optimset()` function.

**Example 3.9.** Consider again the simultaneous equations in Example 3.8. Since there are two independent variables, $x$ and $y$, rather than the standard independent vector $x$, new variables can be introduced such that $x_1 = x$ and $x_2 = y$, and the new equations can be expressed in the following standard form

$$y = f(x) = \begin{bmatrix} x_1^2 e^{-x_1 x_2^2/2} + e^{-x_1/2} \sin(x_1 x_2) \\ x_2^2 \cos(x_2 + x_1^2) + x_1^2 e^{x_1 + x_2} \end{bmatrix} = 0,$$

where $x = [x_1, x_2]^{\mathrm{T}}$. The anonymous function below can be used to describe the original nonlinear equations

```
>> f=@(x)[x(1)^2*exp(-x(1)*x(2)^2/2)+exp(-x(1)/2)*sin(x(1)*x(2));
          x(2)^2*cos(x(2)+x(1)^2)+x(1)^2*exp(x(1)+x(2))];
```

Select point A obtained earlier as the initial point, the more accurate solution can be found at $x = 2.7800$ and $y = -3.3902$. Substituting it back to the original equations, the error norm is $10^{-11}$, much higher than the graphical method.

```
>> x0=[2.7795; -3.3911]; x=fsolve(f,x0); y=x(2), x=x(1)
```

Change the initial point $x_0$, another real solutions may be obtained. For instance, the solution $x = 0$, $y = 1.5708$, with error of $10^{-7}$. Repeated use of the above code may yield more real solutions.

```
>> x0=rand(2,1); x=fsolve(f,x0), f(x)
```

With the use of `fsolve()` function, precision control can be set. For instance, the following statements can be used to get more accurate solutions.

```
>> x0=[2.7795; -3.3911]; ff=optimset;
   ff.TolX=1e-20; ff.TolFun=1e-20; x=fsolve(f,x0,ff), f(x)
```

### 3.2.3  Solutions of Nonlinear Matrix Equations

Using the function `fsolve()` presented earlier, it can be seen that a numerical solution to nonlinear equations can be obtained directly. If the equation has more than one solutions, other initial values can be assigned, such that another solution can be found. Repeated use of the methods may find other solutions.

Based on such an idea, a MATLAB function can be written such that all the solutions within the interested region can be found with a single call of the function. The listing of the function is

```
function more_sols(f,X0,A,tol,tlim)
if nargin<=4, tlim=60; end
if nargin<=3, tol=eps; end
if nargin<=2, A=1000; end
if length(A)==2, a=A(1); b=A(2); else, a=-0.5*A; b=0.5*A; end
ff=optimset; ff.Display='off'; ff1=ff; ff.TolX=tol; ff.TolFun=tol; X=X0;
try, err=evalin('base','err'); catch, err=0; end
[n,m,i]=size(X0); if i<=1; err=0; end, tic
while (1)
  x0=a+(b-a)*rand(n,m); [x,aa,key]=fsolve(f,x0,ff1);
  t=toc; if t>tlim, break; end
  if key>0, N=size(X,3); % compared with the solutions, is this new?
    for j=1:N, if norm(X(:,:,j)-x)<1e-5; key=0; break; end, end
    if key>0, [x1,aa,key]=fsolve(f,x,ff); % if this is new, save it
      if norm(x-x1)<1e-5 & key>0; err=max(norm(aa),err); X(:,:,i+1)=x1;
        assignin('base','X',X); assignin('base','err',err); i=i+1, tic
end, end, end, end
```

The syntax of the function is **more_sols**$(f,X_0,A,\epsilon,t_{\text{lim}})$ , where $f$ is the MATLAB description of the nonlinear matrix equations, it may be an anonymous function or an M-function. Default parameters in other arguments can normally be used. For inexperienced users, it is not necessary to specify them. $X_0$ is a three-dimensional array, storing the initial solution of solutions found. The argument $A$ is the range of random numbers. For the current version of the function, $(-A/2, A/2)$ specify the interested region. The argument $\epsilon$ is the error tolerance, with a default value of $10^{-20}$. The argument $t_{\text{lim}}$ is the allowed waiting time, with a default value of 60, meaning one minute. If no new solutions found, the function will normally terminate.

Since infinite loop `while(1)` is used, the function may be forced to terminate by pressing Ctrl+C keys. There is no returned arguments, instead, the solutions found are returned to MATLAB workspace with `assignin()` function. $X$ is a three-dimensional array, and $X(:,:,i)$ is the $i$th solution. The total number of solutions found can be measured with `size(X,3)`.

**Example 3.10.** Consider the Riccati equation in Example 3.6. With `are()` function, only one solution is found. Now let us try the `more_sols()` function. Anonymous function can be used to present the original equations, and the following statements can be used to find all the 8 solutions.

```
>> A=[-2,1,-3; -1,0,-2; 0,-1,-2]; B=[2,2,-2; -1 5 -2; -1 1 2];
   C=[5 -4 4; 1 0 4; 1 -1 5]; f=@(X)A'*X+X*A-X*B*X+C;
   X0=zeros(3,3,0); more_sols(f,X0) % size of the solution matrix described
```

It can be seen that the syntax is very simple and straightforward. With such a function call, all the 8 solutions can be listed, with maximum error of $2.1098 \times 10^{-13}$. The one obtained by `are()` is just one of them.

$$X_1 = \begin{bmatrix} 0.8878 & -0.9608 & -0.2446 \\ 0.1071 & -0.8984 & -2.5562 \\ -0.0185 & 0.3604 & 2.4619 \end{bmatrix}, \quad X_2 = \begin{bmatrix} -0.1538 & 0.1086 & 0.4622 \\ 2.0277 & -1.7436 & 1.3474 \\ 1.9003 & -1.7512 & 0.5057 \end{bmatrix},$$

$$X_3 = \begin{bmatrix} 1.2212 & -0.4165 & 1.9775 \\ 0.3577 & -0.4893 & -0.8863 \\ -0.7414 & -0.8197 & -2.3559 \end{bmatrix}, \quad X_4 = \begin{bmatrix} -2.1032 & 1.2977 & -1.9697 \\ -0.2466 & -0.3563 & -1.4899 \\ -2.1493 & 0.7189 & -4.5464 \end{bmatrix},$$

$$X_5 = \begin{bmatrix} 0.9873 & -0.7983 & 0.4188 \\ 0.5774 & -0.1307 & 0.5775 \\ -0.284 & -0.073 & 0.6924 \end{bmatrix}, \quad X_6 = \begin{bmatrix} 0.6664 & -1.3222 & -1.72 \\ 0.312 & -0.564 & -1.191 \\ -1.2272 & -1.6129 & -5.5939 \end{bmatrix},$$

$$X_7 = \begin{bmatrix} -0.7618 & 1.3312 & -0.84 \\ 1.3182 & -0.3173 & -0.1718 \\ 0.6371 & 0.7884 & -2.1996 \end{bmatrix}, \quad X_8 = \begin{bmatrix} 23.9469 & -20.6673 & 2.4528 \\ 30.146 & -25.983 & 3.6699 \\ 51.9666 & -44.9108 & 4.6409 \end{bmatrix}.$$

With the new `more_sols()` function, traditionally difficult matrix equations can be found. For instance, the variations of Riccati equation given below can also be solved easily with the new function.

$$AX + XD - XBX + C = 0, \tag{3.12}$$

$$AX + XD - XBX^{\mathrm{T}} + C = 0. \tag{3.13}$$

**Example 3.11.** Consider the matrix equation given in Eqn. (3.13), where

$$A = \begin{bmatrix} 2 & 1 & 9 \\ 9 & 7 & 9 \\ 6 & 5 & 3 \end{bmatrix}, \quad B = \begin{bmatrix} 0 & 3 & 6 \\ 8 & 2 & 0 \\ 8 & 2 & 8 \end{bmatrix}, \quad C = \begin{bmatrix} 7 & 0 & 3 \\ 5 & 6 & 4 \\ 1 & 4 & 4 \end{bmatrix}, \quad D = \begin{bmatrix} 3 & 9 & 5 \\ 1 & 2 & 9 \\ 3 & 3 & 0 \end{bmatrix}.$$

The following MATLAB commands can be used to solve the equation. After a while, all the 16 solutions can be found.

```
>> A=[2,1,9; 9,7,9; 6,5,3]; B=[0,3,6; 8,2,0; 8,2,8];
   C=[7,0,3; 5,6,4; 1,4,4]; D=[3,9,5; 1,2,9; 3,3,0];
   f=@(X)A*X+X*D-X*B*X.'+C; X0=zeros(3,3,0); more_sols(f,X0)
```

**Example 3.12.** The nonlinear equations in Example 3.8 can also be regarded as a special matrix equation. Suppose a solution $x = 0$ and $y = 0$ is known, the following MATLAB functions can be used in solving numerically the nonlinear equations.

```
>> f=@(x)[x(1)^2*exp(-x(1)*x(2)^2/2)+exp(-x(1)/2)*sin(x(1)*x(2));
          x(2)^2*cos(x(2)+x(1)^2)+x(1)^2*exp(x(1)+x(2))];
   more_sols(f,[0,0],10)   % alternatively initial point can be zeros(1,2,0)
```

After a while, the program may terminate automatically, or the user may terminate the program at any time by pressing Ctrl+C keys. With the following MATLAB statements, all the solutions found can be displayed graphically in Fig. 3-2. It can be seen that all the solutions in the interested area are found, with the norm of error $e = 9.333 \times 10^{-13}$, and the precision of this method is much higher than the graphical approach.

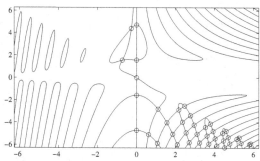

Fig. 3-2   Graphical display of the solutions of the simultaneous equations.

```
>> ezplot('x^2*exp(-x*y^2/2)+exp(-x/2)*sin(x*y)=0')
   hold on; ezplot('y^2*cos(y+x^2)+x^2*exp(x+y)=0')
   x=X(1,1,:); x=x(:); y=X(1,2,:); y=y(:); plot(x,y,'o')
   e=norm([x.^2.*exp(-x.*y.^2/2)+exp(-x/2).*sin(x.*y),...
           y.^2.*cos(y+x.^2)+x.^2.*exp(x+y)])
```

## 3.3   Solutions of Ordinary Differential Equations

Ordinary differential equations (ODEs) are the kernel of simulation of dynamical systems. With the use of powerful MATLAB, first-order explicit ODEs can be solved directly with a set of functions. Other types of differential equations can be solved, if the equations are converted to first-order explicit ODEs. For certain differential equations, analytical solutions can be found.

### 3.3.1   *Numerical Solutions to First-order Explicit ODEs*

Assume that the first-order explicit ODE is given by

$$\dot{x}_i = f_i(t, \boldsymbol{x}), \quad i = 1, 2, \cdots, n, \tag{3.14}$$

where $\boldsymbol{x}$ is the state vector of variables $x_i$, such that $\boldsymbol{x} = [x_1, x_2, \cdots, x_n]^{\mathrm{T}}$. The value of $n$ is called the order of the system. Functions $f_i(\cdot)$ can be any nonlinear function, and $t$ is independent variable, usually it denotes time. If the initial state vector $\boldsymbol{x}(0)$ is known, numerical solutions of the states can be obtained.

The procedures of the numerical solution methods are summarized below:

(1) **Convert the standard form.** Since only first-order explicit ODEs

$$\dot{\boldsymbol{x}} = \boldsymbol{f}(t, \boldsymbol{x}), \text{ with known } \boldsymbol{x}_0 \tag{3.15}$$

can be solved with existing solvers, ODEs of other form must be converted to this standard form first.

(2) **Describe the standard ODE in MATLAB.** Anonymous function of M-function should be written to express the ODE in standard form. If the ODE is simple, anonymous functions are suggested to use.

(3) **Solve the ODE.** There are various algorithms in solving ODEs. The commonly used ones are Euler algorithm, Runge–Kutta algorithm, Adams multi-step algorithm, and Gear algorithm. To solve stiff ODEs, dedicated algorithms should be used. If the systems contain algebraic constrains or delays, the equations can also be solved. If the equations are not given in the standard form of first-order explicit ODEs, conversion suggestions are given.

Several functions such as ode23(), ode45(), ode15s() are provided in MAT-LAB, and the syntaxes of them are nearly the same

$$[t, x] = \text{ode45}(Fun, tspan, x_0, \text{options}, pars)$$

where $t$ is the calculated time sequence. Normally variable-step algorithms are used, thus $t$ may not be evenly distributed. The returned variable $x$ is a matrix with $n$ columns, and $n$ is the order of the system. *Fun* is the MATLAB description of the original ODE, in either anonymous or M-functions. The argument *tspan* can be time information, usually it can be terminate time. The argument $x_0$ is the initial state vector. The argument options contains some controls to the ODE solver, and *pars* may pass some additional variables. Examples will be given next to show the solutions of ODEs.

(4) **Validate the solutions.** Variable-step algorithms are normally used in solving ODEs, and the crucial monitoring quantity is the relative tolerance RelTol. Its default value is $10^{-3}$, and a small value can be tried to see whether the same results. If they are not the same, even smaller RelTol value can be tried. Besides, the selection of different solvers is another way in validating the solutions. The controls of the RelTol options can be assigned with

```
options = odeset; options.RelTol = 1e-7;
```

**Example 3.13.** Consider the well-known Rössler ODE given by

$$\begin{cases} \dot{x}(t) = -y(t) - z(t) \\ \dot{y}(t) = x(t) + ay(t) \\ \dot{z}(t) = b + [x(t) - c]z(t). \end{cases}$$

If $a = b = 0.2$, and $c = 5.7$, with $x(0) = y(0) = z(0) = 0$. Since the equation set is nonlinear, there is no analytical solutions. Numerical solution is the only way for studying such equations.

Before starting the solution process, three state variables should be introduced, $x_1 = x, x_2 = y, x_3 = z$, and the equation can be manually rewritten as

$$\begin{cases} \dot{x}_1(t) = -x_2(t) - x_3(t) \\ \dot{x}_2(t) = x_1(t) + ax_2(t) \\ \dot{x}_3(t) = b + [x_1(t) - c]x_3(t), \end{cases}$$

and the matrix form is written as

$$\dot{\boldsymbol{x}}(t) = \begin{bmatrix} -x_2(t) - x_3(t) \\ x_1(t) + ax_2(t) \\ b + [x_1(t) - c]x_3(t) \end{bmatrix}.$$

The following statements can be used to describe the original ODE in anonymous function $f$

```
>> f=@(t,x)[-x(2)-x(3); x(1)+0.2*x(2); 0.2+(x(1)-5.7)*x(3)];
```

Alternatively, M-function can also be written and saved in rossler.m file.

```
function dx=rossler(t,x)  % although time is not explicitly given, it is still used
dx=[-x(2)-x(3);            % describe the first equation. Other equations
   x(1)+0.2*x(2); 0.2+(x(1)-5.7)*x(3)]; % are expressed in this line
```

The following statements can be used to solve numerically the ODE within $t \in [0, 100]$, and the time responses and phase space trajectory of the equations are shown respectively in Figs. 3-3(a) and (b).

```
>> x0=[0; 0; 0]; [t,y]=ode45(@rossler,[0,100],x0); % solve equation
       % or alternatively with [t,y]=ode45(f,[0,100],x0);
   plot(t,y)     % draw time responses of the state variables
   figure; plot3(y(:,1),y(:,2),y(:,3)), grid  % draw phase space trajectory
```

Function `comet3()` can be used to replace `plot3()` in the above code, and observe the animation display of the phase space trajectory.

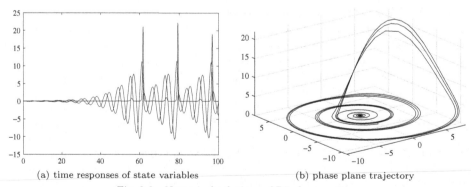

(a) time responses of state variables          (b) phase plane trajectory

Fig. 3-3    Numerical solutions of Rössler equation.

Now let us learn the use of additional variables in solving ODEs. In the example, $a$, $b$, $c$ can be regarded as additional variables. Thus, in describing the ODE's, additional variables should be listed as the input arguments.

```
function dx=rossler1(t,x,a,b,c) % define additional variables
   dx=[-x(2)-x(3); x(1)+a*x(2); b+(x(1)-c)*x(3)];
```

Thus, the following statements can be used to solve the original ODE, with additional variables in the solution function call.

```
>> a=0.2; b=0.2; c=5.7; % define three additional variables
   [t,y]=ode45(@rossler1,[0,100],x0,[],a,b,c); % solve the ODE again
```

There are a few benefits in this kind of programming. If one wants to change only the value of $\beta$, there is no need to rewrite the source code. Let $b = 2$, the following statements can be issued to solve the new ODE.

```
>> b=2; [t,y]=ode45(@rossler1,[0,100],x0,[],a,b,c);
```

In fact, the additional variables are useful in M-function modeling. For simple ODEs, a better way is to use anonymous function to describe the ODEs.

```
>> a=0.2; b=0.2; c=5.7;
   f=@(t,x)[-x(2)-x(3); x(1)+a*x(2); b+(x(1)-c)*x(3)];
   [t,y]=ode45(f,[0,100],x0); % use anonymous function to solve again the ODE
```

In many fields, some special ODEs are encountered, where some solutions change very rapidly, while others change slowly. This kind of ODEs is referred to as stiff equations, and they are usually difficult to solve numerically. Special dedicated functions such as ode15s() should be used instead. The syntax of the function is exactly the same as that of ode45().

### 3.3.2 Conversions of ODEs

The ODE solvers in MATLAB can only be used in solving first-order explicit ODEs. If the ODEs to be solved are not in standard form, conversions should be made first, before the ODEs can be solved. Here systematic ways are suggested in solving ODEs.

Let us first consider a single high-order differential equation

$$f(t, y, \dot{y}, \ddot{y}, \cdots, y^{(n)}) = 0, \tag{3.16}$$

The simplest and most straightforward way is to introduce the state variables

$$x_1 = y, x_2 = \dot{y}, \cdots, x_n = y^{(n-1)}. \tag{3.17}$$

It is obvious that we have $\dot{x}_1 = x_2, \dot{x}_2 = x_3, \cdots, \dot{x}_{n-1} = x_n$. Besides, from Eqn. (3.16), the explicit form of $y^{(n)}$ should be derived, with

$$y^{(n)} = \hat{f}(t, y, \dot{y}, \cdots, y^{(n-1)}). \tag{3.18}$$

However, if the explicit expression of $y^{(n)}(t)$ cannot be obtained, nonlinear equation solution function should be embedded in the description of the function $\hat{f}(t, y, \dot{y}, \cdots, y^{(n-1)})$. The first-order explicit ODE can be written as

$$\begin{cases} \dot{x}_i = x_{i+1}, \quad i = 1, 2, \cdots, n-1 \\ \dot{x}_n = \hat{f}(t, x_1, x_2, \cdots, x_n). \end{cases} \tag{3.19}$$

The converted equations can be solved directly then with MATLAB functions `ode45()` or `ode15s()`.

Consider again the conversion approach for several high-order differential equations. Assume that the high-order differential equations are given by

$$\begin{cases} f(t, x, \dot{x}, \cdots, x^{(m-1)}, x^{(m)}, y, \cdots, y^{(n-1)}, y^{(n)}) = 0 \\ g(t, x, \dot{x}, \cdots, x^{(m-1)}, x^{(m)}, y, \cdots, y^{(n-1)}, y^{(n)}) = 0. \end{cases} \tag{3.20}$$

The state variables can be selected such that $x_1 = x, x_2 = \dot{x}, \cdots, x_m = x^{(m-1)}$, $x_{m+1} = y, x_{m+2} = \dot{y}, \cdots, x_{m+n} = y^{(n-1)}$, and with Eqn. (3.20), the following equations can be established

$$\begin{cases} f(t, x_1, x_2, \cdots, x_m, \dot{x}_m, x_{m+1}, \cdots, x_{m+n}, \dot{x}_{m+n}) = 0 \\ g(t, x_1, x_2, \cdots, x_m, \dot{x}_m, x_{m+1}, \cdots, x_{m+n}, \dot{x}_{m+n}) = 0. \end{cases} \tag{3.21}$$

Solve the above equations can directly find $\dot{x}_m$ and $\dot{x}_{m+n}$, from which first-order explicit ODE can be found. Then MATLAB functions `ode45()` can be used in finding the solutions of the differential equations.

**Example 3.14.** Consider the well-known Van der Pol equation

$$\ddot{y}(t) + \left[ y^2(t) - 1 \right] \dot{y}(t) + y(t) = 0, \text{ with } y(0) = -0.2, \dot{y}(0) = -0.7.$$

This equation is not an explicit differential equation, thus the state variables can be selected such that $x_1 = y, x_2 = \dot{y}$. The original equation can then be converted to

$$\begin{cases} \dot{x}_1(t) = x_2(t) \\ \dot{x}_2(t) = -\left[ x_1^2(t) - 1 \right] x_2(t) - x_1(t), \end{cases}$$

and the matrix form is

$$\dot{x} = \begin{bmatrix} x_2(t) \\ -\left[ x_1^2(t) - 1 \right] x_2(t) - x_1(t) \end{bmatrix},$$

with initial state vector $x_0 = [-0.2, -0.7]^{\mathrm{T}}$. The following statements can be used to describe the new equations, and then MATLAB commands can be used in solving the equations. The time responses and phase plane trajectory can be drawn, as shown in Figs. 3-4(a) and (b).

```
>> f=@(t,x)[x(2); -(x(1)^2-1)*x(2)-x(1)];  % express the equations
   x0=[-0.2; -0.7]; tf=20; [t,x]=ode45(f,[0,tf],x0);  % solve numerically
   plot(t,x)                 % draw time responses of state variables
   figure; plot(x(:,1),x(:,2))   % phase plane trajectory
```

### 3.3.3  *Validations of Numerical Solutions*

The most important step in the solutions of ODEs is that the results must be validated before they can be used. In this section, an example is given to show the necessities in the validation process.

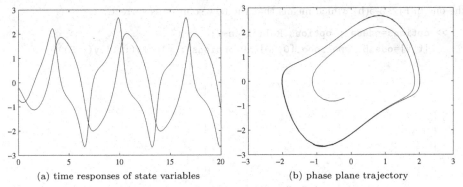

(a) time responses of state variables          (b) phase plane trajectory

Fig. 3-4   Numerical solutions of Van der Pol equation.

**Example 3.15.** For a given Apollo satellite model, the trajectory $(x, y)$ satisfies[3]

$$\ddot{x} = 2\dot{y} + x - \frac{\mu^*(x + \mu)}{r_1^3} - \frac{\mu(x - \mu^*)}{r_2^3}, \quad \ddot{y} = -2\dot{x} + y - \frac{\mu^* y}{r_1^3} - \frac{\mu y}{r_2^3},$$

where $\mu = 1/82.45$, $\mu^* = 1 - \mu$, $r_1 = \sqrt{(x + \mu)^2 + y^2}$, $r_2 = \sqrt{(x - \mu^*)^2 + y^2}$, with initial values $x(0) = 1.2$, $\dot{x}(0) = 0$, $y(0) = 0$, $\dot{y}(0) = -1.04935751$.

Selecting state variables $x_1 = x, x_2 = \dot{x}, x_3 = y, x_4 = \dot{y}$, the standard form of ODE can be obtained

$$\begin{cases} \dot{x}_1 = x_2 \\ \dot{x}_2 = 2x_4 + x_1 - \mu^*(x_1 + \mu)/r_1^3 - \mu(x_1 - \mu^*)/r_2^3 \\ \dot{x}_3 = x_4 \\ \dot{x}_4 = -2x_2 + x_3 - \mu^* x_3/r_1^3 - \mu x_3/r_2^3, \end{cases}$$

where $r_1 = \sqrt{(x_1 + \mu)^2 + x_3^2}$, $r_2 = \sqrt{(x_1 - \mu^*)^2 + x_3^2}$, and $\mu = 1/82.45, \mu^* = 1 - \mu$.

With the converted ODE model, the following MATLAB function can be written

```
function dx=apolloeq(t,x)
mu=1/82.45; mu1=1-mu; r1=sqrt((x(1)+mu)^2+x(3)^2);
r2=sqrt((x(1)-mu1)^2+x(3)^2); % with intermediate statements, anonymous
dx=[x(2);                      % functions are not suitable
   2*x(4)+x(1)-mu1*(x(1)+mu)/r1^3-mu*(x(1)-mu1)/r2^3;
   x(4);
  -2*x(2)+x(3)-mu1*x(3)/r1^3-mu*x(3)/r2^3];
```

With `ode45()` function call, the solution of the ODE can be obtained as shown in Fig. 3-5(a).

```
>> x0=[1.2; 0; 0; -1.04935751];
   [t,y]=ode45(@apolloeq,[0,20],x0); plot(y(:,1),y(:,3))
```

It is necessary to validate the results, with the following statements, and the new solution is shown in Fig. 3-5(b). It can be seen that the new result is completely different. This means that the solution obtained under the default `RelTol` setting is incorrect. Further reduce the value of `RelTol`, the solutions thus obtained are still the same as the one in Fig. 3-5(b), which means that the new solution is correct.

```
>> options=odeset; options.RelTol=1e-7;
   [t,y]=ode45(@apolloeq,[0,20],x0,options); plot(y(:,1),y(:,3))
```

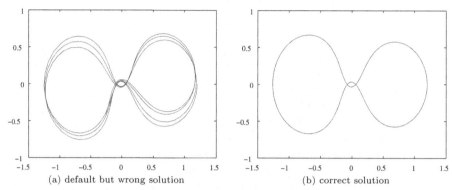

(a) default but wrong solution          (b) correct solution

Fig. 3-5   Trajectory of Apollo satellite.

Herein, it is important to note that do not rely too much on the computer results, even if they are obtained by the powerful MATLAB. The results must be validated if an actual problem is solved.

### 3.3.4   *Analytical Solutions to Linear ODEs*

It is known from the theory of differential equations that there exist analytical solutions to linear time-invariant differential equations. Also, some of the very special nonlinear differential equations may have analytical solutions. In MATLAB, dsolve() function is provided and it can be used in finding the analytical solutions to differential equations. To solve the equations, one has to declare symbolic variables with syms command, and then describe the original differential equations by strings. Then dsolve(*equation*) command can be used to solve the differential equations expressed by the string variable *equation*. Some examples are given to show the analytical solution approach.

**Example 3.16.** Consider the time-invariant linear differential equation

$$\frac{\mathrm{d}^4 y(t)}{\mathrm{d}t^4} + 11\frac{\mathrm{d}^3 y(t)}{\mathrm{d}t^3} + 41\frac{\mathrm{d}^2 y(t)}{\mathrm{d}t^2} + 61\frac{\mathrm{d}y(t)}{\mathrm{d}t} + 30y(t) = \mathrm{e}^{-6t}\cos 5t.$$

With MATLAB, the following statements can be issued to solve the equation, where the notation D$ny$ is used for $y^{(n)}(t)$

```
>> syms t y;   % declare symbolic variables
   Y=dsolve('D4y+11*D3y+41*D2y+61*Dy+30*y=exp(-6*t)*cos(5*t)'); % solve
   pretty(simple(Y))   % display with better readable form
```

In fact, the result can better be written mathematically as

$$y(t) = -\frac{79}{181220}e^{-6t}\cos 5t + \frac{109}{181220}e^{-6t}\sin 5t + C_1 e^{-t} + C_2 e^{-2t} + C_3 e^{-3t} + C_4 e^{-5t},$$

where $C_i$ are undetermined coefficients, which can be determined by initial or other known conditions. Function `dsolve()` can also be used to solve differential equations with initial or other conditions. For instance, if the initial conditions are $y(0) = 1, \dot{y}(0) = 1, \ddot{y}(0) = 0, y^{(3)}(0) = 0$, the following statements can be given to find the analytical solution of the differential equations.

```
>> Y=dsolve('D4y+11*D3y+41*D2y+61*Dy+30*y=cos(5*t)*exp(-6*t)',...
        'y(0)=1','Dy(0)=1','D2y(0)=0','D3y(0)=0');
```

and the solution can be mathematically written as

$$y(t) = -\frac{79}{181220}e^{-6t}\cos 5t + \frac{109}{181220}e^{-6t}\sin 5t + \frac{611}{80}e^{-t} - \frac{1562}{123}e^{-2t} + \frac{921}{136}e^{-3t} - \frac{443}{624}e^{-5t}.$$

**Example 3.17.** Very few nonlinear differential equations may have analytical solutions. Here is one example of them

$$y = \left( x\dot{y} + 2y \right)^2.$$

The differential equation can be solved analytically with

```
>> syms x; y=dsolve('y=(x*Dy+2*y)^2','x'); y=simple(y)
```

and the results are composed of four branches

$$y(x) = \frac{\left(x + 2e^{C_1}\right)^2}{4x^2}, \quad y(x) = \frac{\left(x - 2e^{C_2}\right)^2}{4x^2}, \quad y(x) = 0, \text{ and } y(x) = \frac{1}{4}.$$

Please note the `'x'` at the end of the statement. Since the original independent variable is $x$, rather than the default $t$, such a notation must be used, otherwise the results obtained are wrong.

## 3.4 MATLAB Solutions to Optimization Problems

Optimization problems play an important role in system simulation and computer-aided design of control systems. There are various optimization problems and solution algorithms. In MATLAB, systematic solutions to unconstrained and constrained optimization problems can be solved directly. Least squares curve fitting facilities are also supported.

### 3.4.1 *Unconstrained Optimization Problems*

The mathematical form of unconstrained optimization problem is given by

$$\min_{x} f(x), \tag{3.22}$$

where $x = [x_1, x_2, \cdots, x_n]^T$, and is called the optimization variables or decision variables. The physical meaning of the mathematical formula is that how should we select the values of the decision variables $x$, which minimizes the scalar objective function $f(x)$. This kind of optimization problem is often referred to as minimization problems, since the target is to minimize the objective function. In practice, there are often maximization problems, and the maximization problems can be converted to the standard minimization problems by simply multiplying the objective function with $-1$.

MATLAB function implements the simplex algorithm[4] and provides the functions `fminsearch()` and `fminunc()`, and the syntaxes of them are the same

$$[x, f_{\mathrm{opt}}, key, c] = \texttt{fminsearch}(Fun, x_0, \texttt{options})$$

where *Fun* is the MATLAB description of the objective function. It can be an M-function, and also it can be an anonymous function. The argument $x_0$ is an initial search point, and `options` are the options to further set the parameters of the algorithm. The returned variable $x$ is the optimal decision variable, $f_{\mathrm{opt}}$ is the minimized value of the objective function, and *key* indicates whether solution is successful, positive number means successful. Extra information is returned in variable c, which contains the number of function calls, the number of iterations and algorithms used. Further in Chapters 7 and 8, we shall explore the applications of optimization approaches in optimal controller design problems.

Besides, the decision variable $x$ may satisfy the lower and upper boundaries, such that $x_{\mathrm{m}} \leqslant x \leqslant x_{\mathrm{M}}$. This can be solved by constrained optimization methods discussed later, alternatively, the MATLAB function `fminsearchbnd()` by John D'Errico can be used to solve directly this kind of problems[5], with similar syntaxes.

### 3.4.2   *Constrained Optimization Problems*

The general form of constrained nonlinear programming is given by

$$\min \quad f(x), \tag{3.23}$$

$$x \text{ s.t.} \begin{cases} Ax \leqslant B \\ A_{\mathrm{eq}}x = B_{\mathrm{eq}} \\ x_{\mathrm{m}} \leqslant x \leqslant x_{\mathrm{M}} \\ C(x) \leqslant 0 \\ C_{\mathrm{eq}}(x) = 0 \end{cases}$$

where $x = [x_1, x_2, \cdots, x_n]^{\mathrm{T}}$. In the constraints, linear constraints $A_{\mathrm{eq}}x = B_{\mathrm{eq}}$ and $Ax \leqslant B$ are given separately such that the algorithm may deal with them individually. Nonlinear constraints include nonlinear inequalities $C(x) \leqslant 0$ and nonlinear equations $C_{\mathrm{eq}}(x) = 0$. Besides, there are lower and upper boundaries $x_{\mathrm{m}} \leqslant x \leqslant x_{\mathrm{M}}$ for the decision variables. Please note that all the inequalities are, in fact, $\leqslant$ inequalities. If there exist $\geqslant$ inequalities, both side should be multiplied by $-1$, such that they can be converted to $\leqslant$ ones.

The physical meaning of the mathematical formula is that under the constraints, how should we choose the decision variables, which minimize the objective function. Besides, all the solutions satisfying the constraints are referred to as feasible solutions.

Function `fmincon()` is provided in MATLAB Optimization Toolbox, and it can be used to solve constrained optimization problems. The syntax of the function is

$$[x, f_{\text{opt}}, \texttt{key}, \texttt{c}] = \texttt{fmincon}(Fun, x_0, A, B, A_{\text{eq}}, B_{\text{eq}}, x_{\text{m}}, x_{\text{M}}, CFun, options)$$

where *Fun* is still the MATLAB descriptions of the objective function, $x_0$ is the initial search point. If any of the constraints do not exist, empty matrices should be specified instead. *CFun* is the MATLAB function to describe the nonlinear equations and inequalities. In the function, two arguments are returned, such that it cannot be described by anonymous functions, M-function is the only way to use. The argument *options* is the control options.

The procedures in numerical optimization problems are

(1) **Mathematical model**. Write out the standard mathematical expression in Eqn. (3.23).

(2) **Express the problem in MATLAB**. Express the objective functions and constraints in MATLAB, with either MATLAB functions or anonymous functions.

(3) **Call optimization solver**.

(4) **Validate the results**. Numerical optimization solvers sometimes depend upon the selection of initial search points. Try different random initial points a couple of times and see whether the same results can be obtained.

**Example 3.18.** Consider the following nonlinear optimization problem

$$\min \quad e^{x_1}\left(4x_1^2 + 2x_2^2 + 4x_1x_2 + 2x_2 + 1\right).$$

$$x \text{ s.t.} \begin{cases} x_1 + x_2 \leqslant 0 \\ -x_1x_2 + x_1 + x_2 \geqslant 1.5 \\ x_1x_2 \geqslant -10 \\ -10 \leqslant x_1, x_2 \leqslant 10 \end{cases}$$

To solve the problem, the objective function and nonlinear constraints can be written

```
function y=c3exmobj(x)
y=exp(x(1))*(4*x(1)^2+2*x(2)^2+4*x(1)*x(2)+2*x(2)+1);
function [c,ce]=c3exmcon(x)
ce=[]; c=[x(1)+x(2); x(1)*x(2)-x(1)-x(2)+1.5; -10-x(1)*x(2)];
```

The objective function can alternatively be described with an anonymous function

```
f=@(x)exp(x(1))*(4*x(1)^2+2*x(2)^2+4*x(1)*x(2)+2*x(2)+1);
```

Note that the constraint function returns two arguments, inequality constraint `c` and equation constraint `ce`. Anonymous functions cannot be used to describe them. The second and third constraints can be converted to $\leqslant$ inequality by multiplying both side by $-1$. Also, from the constraints, it can be seen that the first one is, in fact, linear inequality, and it can alternatively be described by matrices $A$, $B$ as well. Us the optimization problem solver, the following results can be obtained, $x^{\text{T}} = [0.4195, 0.4195]$. Besides, the warning message "`fmincon` stopped because it exceeded the function evaluation limit, `options.MaxFunEvals = 200`" is also displayed.

```
>> A=[]; B=[]; Aeq=[]; Beq=[]; xm=[-10; -10]; xM=[10; 10]; x0=[5;5];
   ff=optimset; ff.TolX=1e-10; ff.TolFun=1e-20;
   x=fmincon(@c3exmobj,x0,A,B,Aeq,Beq,xm,xM,@c3exmcon,ff)
```

From the warning message, it can be seen that the solution process is not successful. The above results can be used as the initial search point and call the `fmincon()` function again. With the following loop structure, the optimal result $x^T = [1.1825, -1.7398]$ can finally be found. The loop execution is $i = 5$.

```
>> i=1; x=x0;
   while (1)
       [x,a,b]=fmincon(@c3exmobj,x,A,B,Aeq,Beq,xm,xM,@c3exmcon,ff);
       if b>0, break; end    % if successful, then terminate the loop
       i=i+1;                % otherwise continue searching
   end
```

Some special cases of constrained optimization problems are linear programming and quadratic programming problems, they can be solved with functions `linprog()` and `quadprog()`. Besides, mixed integer programming and binary programming problems can also be solved, with dedicated tools[1].

### 3.4.3   *Least Squares Curve Fitting*

Assume that there is a set of experimental data $x_i, y_i, i = 1, 2, \cdots, N$ and it is known that the data satisfies a certain prototype function $\hat{y}(x) = f(a, x)$, with $a$ the undetermined coefficients. The target of the least squares curve fitting method is to find the unknown coefficients, such that the total fitting error is minimized

$$J = \min_a \sum_{i=1}^N \left[ y_i - \hat{y}(x_i) \right]^2 = \min_a \sum_{i=1}^N \left[ y_i - f(a, x_i) \right]^2. \qquad (3.24)$$

In Optimization Toolbox of MATLAB, function `lsqcurvefit()` is provided to solve least squares curve fitting problems. The syntax of the function is

$$[a, J_m] = \texttt{lsqcurvefit}(Fun, a_0, x, y, a_m, a_M, \texttt{options})$$

where $a_0$ is the initial search point, $x$, $y$ are experimental data vectors for the sample points. *Fun* is the MATLAB description of the prototype function. It can either be an anonymous function or an M-function. The function can also assign minimum and maximum boundaries, $a_m$ and $a_M$, for the decision variable $a$. Search `options` can also be assigned. The least squares fitting coefficients are returned in vector $a$.

**Example 3.19.** Assume that a set of simulation data is generated from a given function. The set of data can be used to find the least squares curve fitting results. The following commands can be used to generate the samples, as shown in Fig. 3-6(a).

```
>> x=[0:0.01:0.1, 0.2:0.1:1,1.5:0.5:10]; % generate horizontal vector
   y=0.56*exp(-0.2*x).*sin(0.8*x+0.4).*cos(-0.65*x); % generate data
   plot(x,y,'o',x,y)                       % sample data
```

Assume also that the prototype function is given by

$$F(x) = a_1 e^{a_2 x} \sin(a_3 x + a_4) \cos(a_5 x),$$

where $a_i$ are the undetermined coefficients. Least squares curve fitting by MATLAB is needed. An anonymous function can be written for the prototype function, and with the `lsqcurvefit()` function. The fitting results obtained are $\boldsymbol{a} = [0.56, 0.2, 0.8, 0.4, 0.65]^{\mathrm{T}}$, which is the same as the known parameters. The fitting error is $4.4177 \times 10^{-7}$, and the fitting curve is exactly the same as the one shown in Fig. 3-6(a)

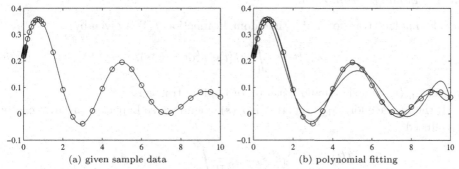

(a) given sample data        (b) polynomial fitting

Fig. 3-6    Curve fitting for the sample points.

```
>> F=@(a,x)a(1)*exp(-a(2)*x).*sin(a(3)*x+a(4)).*cos(-a(5)*x);
   f=optimset; f.RelX=1e-10; f.TolFun=1e-15; % high precision setting
   a=lsqcurvefit(F,[1;1;1;1;1],x,y,[0,0,0,0,0],[],f) % curve fitting
   a0=[0.56;0.2;0.8;0.4;0.65]; norm(a-a0)    % comparison with true data
   x0=0:0.01:10; y0=F(a0,x0);                % curve fitting plotting
   y1=F(a,x0); plot(x0,y0,x0,y1,x,y,'o')
```

Polynomial fitting function `a = polyfit(x,y,n)` is also provided, and it may find an $n$th order polynomial for the given sample points $x$ and $y$. The returned variable $\boldsymbol{a}$ is the coefficient vector of the polynomial, in descending order of $s$. Function `polyval()` can be used to evaluate polynomial functions. Fig. 3-6(b) displays the fitting results for 6th and 8th order polynomials.

```
>> p=polyfit(x,y,6), y2=polyval(p,x0); % 6th order polynomial fitting
   p=polyfit(x,y,8); y3=polyval(p,x0); % 8th order polynomial fitting
   plot(x0,y0,x,y,'o',x0,y2,x0,y3)       % comparisons of fitting results
```

The 6th order polynomial obtained is

$$P_6(x) = -0.0002x^6 + 0.0054x^5 - 0.0632x^4 + 0.3430x^3 - 0.8346x^2 + 0.6621x + 0.2017.$$

## 3.5   Laplace and $z$ Transforms and MATLAB Solutions

In earlier control systems research, ordinary differential equation was the major modeling tool. Since differential equations are more complicated than algebraic equations, an integral transform — Laplace transform can be adopted, which can map the systems described by ordinary differential equations into algebraic equations. Transfer function models were then introduced, and this created the theoretical background of classical control theory. In the analytical solutions to linear control systems, inverse Laplace transforms can be used. Similarly, for discrete systems, $z$ transforms can be used, and discrete transfer function model can be established.

### 3.5.1   *Laplace Transform*

The Laplace transform of a time domain function $f(t)$ is given by

$$\mathscr{L}\big[f(t)\big] = \int_0^\infty f(t)\mathrm{e}^{-st}\mathrm{d}t = F(s), \tag{3.25}$$

where $\mathscr{L}\big[f(t)\big]$ is a shorthand notation of Laplace transform.

If the Laplace form of a function is $F(s)$, then inverse Laplace transform can be introduced

$$f(t) = \mathscr{L}^{-1}\big[F(s)\big] = \frac{1}{2\pi\mathrm{j}} \int_{\sigma-\mathrm{j}\infty}^{\sigma+\mathrm{j}\infty} F(s)\mathrm{e}^{st}\mathrm{d}s, \tag{3.26}$$

where $\sigma$ is larger than the real part of the poles of function $F(s)$.

The functions `laplace()` and `ilaplace()` in the Symbolic Math Toolbox can be used to take Laplace and inverse Laplace transforms of functions. The procedure of the transforms is as follows:

(1) **Declare symbolic variables** with `syms` command.

(2) **Describe the original function.** Represent original function in MATLAB.

(3) **Integral transform evaluation.** Laplace and its inverse transform can be obtained with the functions `laplace()` and `ilaplace()` respectively. Also, `fourier()` and `ifourier()` functions can be used to evaluate Fourier transforms.

(4) **Simplify the results** with `simple()` function.

**Example 3.20.** Assume that a time domain function is given by

$$f(t) = 1 - (1 + at)\mathrm{e}^{-at},$$

the following commands can be used to find the Laplace transform directly.

```
>> syms a t              % declare symbolic variables
   f=1-(1+a*t)*exp(-a*t); % express the time domain function
   F=laplace(f)          % take Laplace transform
```

The transform obtained is

$$F = \frac{1}{s} - \frac{1}{s+a} - \frac{a}{(s+a)^2}.$$

The `ilaplace()` function can be used to take the inverse Laplace transform, and the original time domain function can be retained.

**Example 3.21.** For a given Laplace expression

$$G(s) = \frac{s+3}{s(s^4 + 2s^3 + 11s^2 + 18s + 18)},$$

the following MATLAB statements can be given to take the inverse Laplace transform

```
>> syms s, G=(s+3)/s/(s^4+2*s^3+11*s^2+18*s+18); y=ilaplace(G)
```

and the results is

$$y(t) = \frac{1}{255}\cos 3t - \frac{13}{255}\sin 3t - \frac{29}{170}e^{-t}\cos t - \frac{3}{170}e^{-t}\sin t + \frac{1}{6}.$$

**Example 3.22.** To find the inverse Laplace transform of

$$\mathscr{L}^{-1}\left[\frac{3a^2}{s^3 + a^3}\right], \quad a > 0,$$

symbolic variables must be declared first. In particular, declare a positive $a$. Then the inverse Laplace transform can be found with the following statements

```
>> syms s t; syms a positive; F=3*a^2/(s^3+a^3);
   f=simple(ilaplace(F))   % perform inverse Laplace transform and simplify
```

The result is

$$\mathscr{L}^{-1}\left[\frac{3a^2}{s^3 + a^3}\right] = e^{-at} + e^{at/2}\left(-\cos\frac{\sqrt{3}}{2}at + \sqrt{3}\sin\frac{\sqrt{3}}{2}at\right).$$

**Example 3.23.** For the Laplace transform

$$F(s) = \frac{e^{-\sqrt{s}}}{\sqrt{s}(\sqrt{s} - 1)},$$

the inverse Laplace transform can be obtained with the following statements

```
>> syms s; z=sqrt(s); f=ilaplace(exp(-z)/z/(z-1))
```

The result obtained below is, in fact, an example of fractional-order systems. Please note that the results can only be obtained with old version of MATLAB, where Maple was used as its symbolic computation engine.

$$f(t) = e^{t-1}\text{erfc}\left(-\frac{2t-1}{2\sqrt{t}}\right).$$

### 3.5.2  z Transform

The $z$ transform of a discrete sequence signal $f(k)$ is defined by

$$\mathscr{Z}\big[f(k)\big] = \sum_{i=0}^{\infty} f(k)z^{-k} = F(z). \tag{3.27}$$

For a given $z$ transform $F(z)$, its inverse $z$ transform is defined as

$$f(k) = \mathscr{Z}^{-1}\big[f(k)\big] = \frac{1}{2\pi\mathrm{j}}\oint F(z)z^{k-1}\mathrm{d}z. \tag{3.28}$$

MATLAB functions `ztrans()` and `iztrans()` can be used to solve directly the $z$ and its inverse transforms, with the syntaxes similar to `laplace()`. Please reference the procedures for Laplace transforms.

**Example 3.24.** In ordinary textbooks, the inverse $z$ transform of

$$F(z) = \frac{q}{(z^{-1} - p)^m}, \quad p \neq 0$$

is normally not presented, however, this is useful in finding the analytical solutions of discrete systems. For different values of $m$, the inverse $z$ transform is taken, and general formula may be summarized. The inverse $z$ transform to the function for $m = 1, 2, \cdots, 5$ can be obtained with the following statements.

```
>> syms p q z;
   for i=1:5, disp(simple(iztrans(q/(1/z-p)^i))), end
```

and the results obtained are

$$F_1 = -\frac{q}{p^{1+n}}, \quad F_2 = \frac{q(1+n)}{p^{2+n}}, \quad F_3 = -\frac{q(1+n)(2+n)}{2p^{3+n}},$$

$$F_4 = \frac{q(3+n)(2+n)(1+n)}{6p^{4+n}}, \quad F_5 = -\frac{q(4+n)(3+n)(2+n)(1+n)}{24p^{5+n}}.$$

Summarizing the results above, the general formula for $m$ can be written as

$$\mathscr{Z}^{-1}\left\{\frac{q}{(z^{-1} - p)^m}\right\} = \frac{(-1)^m q}{(m-1)! \, p^{n+m}}(n+1)(n+2)\cdots(n+m-1).$$

**Example 3.25.** Assume that the inverse $z$ transform of a function is

$$H(z) = \frac{z(5z - 2)}{(z-1)(z-1/2)^3(z-1/3)},$$

the following statements can be used to take the inverse $z$ transform

```
>> syms z; H=z*(5*z-2)/((z-1)*(z-1/2)^3*(z-1/3)); h=iztrans(H)
```

and the result is

$$h(n) = \mathscr{Z}^{-1}\big[H(z)\big] = 36 + (72 - 60n - 12n^2)(1/2)^n - 108(1/3)^n.$$

## 3.6  Problems

(1) Analyze the parameters such as determinants, traces, ranks, characteristic polynomials, and norms to the following matrices. Also, find the analytical solution to the problems.

$$A = \begin{bmatrix} 7.5 & 3.5 & 0 & 0 \\ 8 & 33 & 4.1 & 0 \\ 0 & 9 & 103 & -1.5 \\ 0 & 0 & 3.7 & 19.3 \end{bmatrix}, \quad B = \begin{bmatrix} 5 & 7 & 6 & 5 \\ 7 & 10 & 8 & 7 \\ 6 & 8 & 10 & 9 \\ 5 & 7 & 9 & 10 \end{bmatrix}.$$

(2) Find the ranks and Moore–Penrose generalized inverse matrices to the following matrices, and check whether the conditions of Moore–Penrose generalized inverse matrices are satisfied.

$$
A = \begin{bmatrix} 2 & 2 & 3 & 1 \\ 2 & 2 & 3 & 1 \\ 4 & 4 & 6 & 2 \\ 1 & 1 & 1 & 1 \\ -1 & -1 & -1 & 3 \end{bmatrix}, \quad
B = \begin{bmatrix} 4 & 1 & 2 & 0 \\ 1 & 1 & 5 & 15 \\ 3 & 1 & 3 & 5 \end{bmatrix}.
$$

(3) Solve the following linear algebraic equation, and validate the results

$$
X \begin{bmatrix} 7 & 6 & 9 & 7 \\ 7 & 1 & 3 & 2 \\ 2 & 1 & 5 & 5 \\ 6 & 4 & 2 & 6 \end{bmatrix} = \begin{bmatrix} 2 & 1 & 0 & 1 \\ 0 & 3 & 1 & 2 \end{bmatrix}.
$$

(4) For the special matrix $A$, find the inverse and eigenvalues, and then get the analytical solution to the state transition matrix $e^{At}$.

$$
A = \begin{bmatrix} -9 & 11 & -21 & 63 & -252 \\ 70 & -69 & 141 & -421 & 1684 \\ -575 & 575 & -1149 & 3451 & -13801 \\ 3891 & -3891 & 7782 & -23345 & 93365 \\ 1024 & -1024 & 2048 & -6144 & 24573 \end{bmatrix}.
$$

(5) Find the basic set of solutions of the following homogeneous equation.

$$
\begin{cases}
6x_1 + x_2 + 4x_3 - 7x_4 - 3x_5 = 0 \\
-2x_1 - 7x_2 - 8x_3 + 6x_4 \quad = 0 \\
-4x_1 + 5x_2 + x_3 - 6x_4 + 8x_5 = 0 \\
-34x_1 + 36x_2 + 9x_3 - 21x_4 + 49x_5 = 0 \\
-26x_1 - 12x_2 - 27x_3 + 27x_4 + 17x_5 = 0.
\end{cases}
$$

(6) Solve the following Lyapunov equation and validate the results.

$$
\begin{bmatrix} 1 & 2 & 3 \\ 4 & 5 & 6 \\ 7 & 8 & 0 \end{bmatrix} X + X \begin{bmatrix} 2 & 3 & 6 \\ 3 & 5 & 2 \\ 3 & 2 & 2 \end{bmatrix} = \begin{bmatrix} 1 & 3 & 2 \\ 3 & 4 & 1 \\ 5 & 2 & 1 \end{bmatrix}.
$$

(7) Find the numerical and analytical solutions to the following Sylvester equation, and validate the results.

$$
\begin{bmatrix} 3 & -6 & -4 & 0 & 5 \\ 1 & 4 & 2 & -2 & 4 \\ -6 & 3 & -6 & 7 & 3 \\ -13 & 10 & 0 & -11 & 0 \\ 0 & 4 & 0 & 3 & 4 \end{bmatrix} X + X \begin{bmatrix} 3 & -2 & 1 \\ -2 & -9 & 2 \\ -2 & -1 & 9 \end{bmatrix} = \begin{bmatrix} -2 & 1 & -1 \\ 4 & 1 & 2 \\ 5 & -6 & 1 \\ 6 & -4 & -4 \\ -6 & 6 & -3 \end{bmatrix}.
$$

(8) Find all the roots to the following algebraic equations

$$
\begin{cases}
x^2 y^2 - zxy - 4x^2 yz^2 = xz^2 \\
xy^3 - 2yz^2 = 3x^3 z^2 + 4xzy^2 \\
y^2 x - 7xy^2 + 3xz^2 = x^4 zy.
\end{cases}
$$

(9) Solve the following nonlinear equations[6] with suitable method

(i) $\begin{cases} xyz = 1 \\ x^2 + 2y^2 + 4z^2 = 7 \\ 2x^2 + y^3 + 6z = 7, \end{cases}$   (ii) $\begin{cases} x^2 + 2\sin(y\pi/2) + z^2 = 0 \\ -2xy + z = 3 \\ x^2 z - y = 7. \end{cases}$

(10) Find all the possible solutions to the following nonlinear matrix equation

$$\begin{bmatrix} 9 & 1 & 0 \\ 8 & 7 & 3 \\ 3 & 0 & 6 \end{bmatrix} \boldsymbol{X}^2 + \boldsymbol{X} \begin{bmatrix} 5 & 6 & 6 \\ 9 & 2 & 2 \\ 6 & 9 & 5 \end{bmatrix} \boldsymbol{X} + \boldsymbol{X} \begin{bmatrix} 7 & 9 & 4 \\ 6 & 7 & 1 \\ 4 & 6 & 4 \end{bmatrix} + \boldsymbol{I}_{3\times 3} = \boldsymbol{0}.$$

(11) Solve the nonlinear matrix equation

$$\boldsymbol{A}\boldsymbol{X}e^{\boldsymbol{B}^2\boldsymbol{X}+\boldsymbol{C}}\boldsymbol{X} + \boldsymbol{X}e^{-\boldsymbol{B}} + \boldsymbol{C} = \boldsymbol{0},$$

where

$$\boldsymbol{A} = \begin{bmatrix} 4 & 4 & 4 \\ 0 & 3 & 9 \\ 4 & 7 & 9 \end{bmatrix}, \quad \boldsymbol{B} = \begin{bmatrix} 1 & 1 & 7 \\ 3 & 5 & 5 \\ 8 & 1 & 0 \end{bmatrix}, \quad \boldsymbol{C} = \begin{bmatrix} 6 & 4 & 7 \\ 1 & 9 & 4 \\ 1 & 3 & 0 \end{bmatrix}.$$

(12) The well-known Lorenz equation is a good example in studying chaotic problems. The mathematical form of Lorenz equation is given by

$$\begin{cases} \dot{x}_1(t) = -\beta x_1(t) + x_2(t)x_3(t) \\ \dot{x}_2(t) = -\sigma x_2(t) + \sigma x_3(t) \\ \dot{x}_3(t) = -x_1(t)x_2(t) + \gamma x_2(t) - x_3(t), \end{cases}$$

where $\beta = 8/3, \sigma = 10, \gamma = 28$, and initial conditions are $x_1(0) = x_2(0) = 0, x_3(0) = 10^{-3}$. Find the numerical solutions and draw three-dimensional phase space trajectory. Also, draw the projections of the trajectory respectively at the $x$–$y$, $x$–$z$ and $y$–$z$ planes.

(13) Solve the following differential equation with MATLAB

$$y^{(3)} + ty\ddot{y} + t^2\dot{y}y^2 = e^{-ty}, \quad y(0) = 2, \ \dot{y}(0) = \ddot{y}(0) = 0,$$

and draw the $y(t)$ plot. Is there analytical solution to the equations?

(14) The mathematical form of Lotka–Volterra predator–prey model is

$$\begin{cases} \dot{x}(t) = 4x(t) - 2x(t)y(t) \\ \dot{y}(t) = x(t)y(t) - 3y(t), \end{cases}$$

with initial states $x(0) = 2, y(0) = 3$. Solve the differential equation and draw the curves.

(15) Find the analytical solutions to the following differential equations and compare the results with their numerical solutions.

(i) $\begin{cases} \ddot{x}(t) = -2x(t) - 3\dot{x}(t) + e^{-5t}, & x(0) = 1, \dot{x}(0) = 2 \\ \ddot{y}(t) = 2x(t) - 3y(t) - 4\dot{x}(t) - 4\dot{y}(t) - \sin t, & y(0) = 3, \dot{y}(0) = 4, \end{cases}$

(ii) $\begin{cases} \ddot{x}(t) + \ddot{y}(t) + x(t) + y(t) = 0, & x(0) = 2, y(0) = 1 \\ 2\ddot{x}(t) - \ddot{y}(t) - x(t) + y(t) = \sin t, & \dot{x}(0) = \dot{y}(0) = -1. \end{cases}$

(16) The mathematical description of the inverted pendulum is

$$\ddot{x} = \frac{u + ml\sin\theta\dot{\theta}^2 - mg\cos\theta\sin\theta}{M + m - m\cos^2\theta},$$

$$\ddot{\theta} = \frac{u\cos\theta - (M + m)g\sin\theta + ml\sin\theta\cos\theta\dot{\theta}}{ml\cos^2\theta - (M + m)l}.$$

If $m = M = 0.5\text{kg}$, $l = 0.3\text{m}$, $g = 9.81\text{m/s}^2$. Find the unit step response of the system, i.e., $u = 1$. Please note that the inverted pendulum is naturally unstable. Control action should be applied to stabilize it.

(17) Solve the following optimization problems.

(i)
$$\min \quad x_1^2 - 2x_1 + x_2,$$
$$\boldsymbol{x} \text{ s.t.} \begin{cases} 4x_1^2 + x_2^2 \leqslant 4 \\ x_1, x_2 \geqslant 0 \end{cases}$$

(ii)
$$\min \quad -(x_1 - 1)^2 - (x_2 - 1)^2.$$
$$\boldsymbol{x} \text{ s.t. } x_1 + x_2 + 5 = 0$$

(18) Consider the following optimization problems with two variables

$$\max \quad -x_1^2 - x_2.$$
$$\boldsymbol{x} \text{ s.t.} \begin{cases} 9 \geqslant x_1^2 + x_2^2 \\ x_1 + x_2 \leqslant 1 \end{cases}$$

Find the solution and validate the results using graphical method.

(19) Solve the following nonlinear programming problem.

$$\min \quad \frac{1}{2\cos x_6}\left[x_1 x_2(1 + x_5) + x_3 x_4\left(1 + \frac{31.5}{x_5}\right)\right].$$

$$\boldsymbol{x} \text{ s.t.} \begin{cases} 0.003079 x_1^3 x_2^3 x_5 - \cos^3 x_6 \geqslant 0 \\ 0.1017 x_3^3 x_4^3 - x_5^2 \cos^3 x_6 \geqslant 0 \\ 0.09939(1 + x_5)x_1^3 x_2^2 - \cos^2 x_6 \geqslant 0 \\ 0.1076(31.5 + x_5)x_3^3 x_4^2 - x_5^2 \cos^2 x_6 \geqslant 0 \\ x_3 x_4(x_5 + 31.5) - x_5[2(x_1 + 5)\cos x_6 + x_1 x_2 x_5] \geqslant 0 \\ 0.2 \leqslant x_1 \leqslant 0.5, 14 < x_2 \leqslant 22, 0.35 \leqslant x_3 \leqslant 0.6 \\ 16 \leqslant x_4 \leqslant 22, 5.8 \leqslant x_5 \leqslant 6.5, 0.14 \leqslant x_6 \leqslant 0.2618 \end{cases}$$

(20) Solve the following benchmark optimization problem [7].

$$\min \quad k.$$

$$q, w, k \text{ s.t.} \begin{cases} q_3 + 9.625 q_1 w + 16 q_2 w + 16 w^2 + 12 - 4 q_1 - q_2 - 78 w = 0 \\ 16 q_1 w + 44 - 19 q_1 - 8 q_2 - q_3 - 24 w = 0 \\ 2.25 - 0.25k \leqslant q_1 \leqslant 2.25 + 0.25k \\ 1.5 - 0.5k \leqslant q_2 \leqslant 1.5 + 0.5k \\ 1.5 - 1.5k \leqslant q_3 \leqslant 1.5 + 1.5k \end{cases}$$

(21) Consider a simple optimization problem with one variable, $f(x) = x\sin(10\pi x) + 2$, $x \in (-1, 2)$. Try to find the maximum value of $f(x)$. It is known that the curve of the function is oscillatory, thus initial search point may affect the final results. Please select randomly 40 initial points in $x \in (-1, 2)$, and search according to the flow chart suggested in Fig. 3-7, and see whether global optimal point can be found. If possible, please extend your function into a global optimal solution search program, for multivariable problems $y = f(\boldsymbol{x})$.

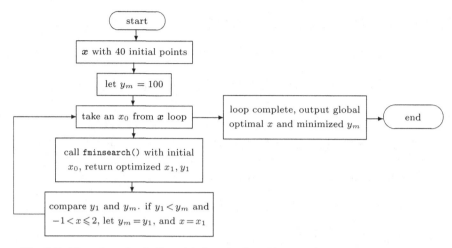

Fig. 3-7   Flow chart for finding global optimal problems with random initial values.

(22) Assume that a set of measured data is given in Table 3-1. If the prototype of the function is $y(x) = ax + bx^2 e^{-cx} + d$, please find the undetermined constants $a, b, c, d$ using least squares method.

Table 3-1   Measured data in Problem (22).

| $x_i$ | 0.1 | 0.2 | 0.3 | 0.4 | 0.5 | 0.6 | 0.7 | 0.8 | 0.9 | 1 |
|---|---|---|---|---|---|---|---|---|---|---|
| $y_i$ | 2.3201 | 2.6470 | 2.9707 | 3.2885 | 3.6008 | 3.9090 | 4.2147 | 4.5191 | 4.8232 | 5.1275 |

(23) Assume that the temperature in a day is measured as shown in Table 3-2. Please fit the data using 3rd and 4th order polynomials and observe the fitting results. If good polynomial fitting is expected, what is the minimum possible order should be used?

Table 3-2   Measured data for Problem (23).

| time | 1 | 2 | 3 | 4 | 5 | 6 | 7 | 8 | 9 | 10 | 11 | 12 |
|---|---|---|---|---|---|---|---|---|---|---|---|---|
| temperature | 14 | 14 | 14 | 14 | 15 | 16 | 18 | 20 | 22 | 23 | 25 | 28 |
| time | 13 | 14 | 15 | 16 | 17 | 18 | 19 | 20 | 21 | 22 | 23 | 24 |
| temperature | 31 | 32 | 31 | 29 | 27 | 25 | 24 | 22 | 20 | 18 | 17 | 16 |

(24) Suppose the step response of a certain linear continuous system is given in Table 3-3, and the prototype of the system response is $y(t) = x_1 + x_2 e^{-x_4 t} + x_3 e^{-x_5 t}$. Please fit the values of $x_i$, with least squares method.

(25) Neural network is an effective model to fit curves. Although detailed information on neural network is not presented, the MATLAB graphical user interface can be used. Please type **nntool** at the MATLAB prompt, and try to fit the above data with neural network.

(26) Find the Laplace transform to the following functions

Table 3-3   Measured data for Problem (24).

| $t$ | $y(t)$ | $t$ | $y(t)$ | $t$ | $y(t)$ | $t$ | $y(t)$ | $t$ | $y(t)$ | $t$ | $y(t)$ |
|-----|--------|-----|--------|-----|--------|-----|--------|-----|--------|-----|--------|
| 0 | 0 | 1.6 | 0.2822 | 3.2 | 0.3024 | 4.8 | 0.3145 | 6.4 | 0.3218 | 8 | 0.3263 |
| 0.1 | 0.08324 | 1.7 | 0.2839 | 3.3 | 0.3034 | 4.9 | 0.315 | 6.5 | 0.3222 | 8.1 | 0.3265 |
| 0.2 | 0.1404 | 1.8 | 0.2855 | 3.4 | 0.3043 | 5 | 0.3156 | 6.6 | 0.3225 | 8.2 | 0.3267 |
| 0.3 | 0.1798 | 1.9 | 0.287 | 3.5 | 0.3051 | 5.1 | 0.3161 | 6.7 | 0.3228 | 8.3 | 0.3269 |
| 0.4 | 0.2072 | 2 | 0.2885 | 3.6 | 0.306 | 5.2 | 0.3166 | 6.8 | 0.3231 | 8.4 | 0.3271 |
| 0.5 | 0.2265 | 2.1 | 0.2899 | 3.7 | 0.3068 | 5.3 | 0.3172 | 6.9 | 0.3235 | 8.5 | 0.3273 |
| 0.6 | 0.2402 | 2.2 | 0.2912 | 3.8 | 0.3076 | 5.4 | 0.3176 | 7 | 0.3238 | 8.6 | 0.3275 |
| 0.7 | 0.2501 | 2.3 | 0.2925 | 3.9 | 0.3084 | 5.5 | 0.3181 | 7.1 | 0.324 | 8.7 | 0.3277 |
| 0.8 | 0.2574 | 2.4 | 0.2937 | 4 | 0.3092 | 5.6 | 0.3186 | 7.2 | 0.3243 | 8.8 | 0.3278 |
| 0.9 | 0.2629 | 2.5 | 0.2949 | 4.1 | 0.3099 | 5.7 | 0.319 | 7.3 | 0.3246 | 8.9 | 0.328 |
| 1 | 0.2673 | 2.6 | 0.2961 | 4.2 | 0.3106 | 5.8 | 0.3195 | 7.4 | 0.3249 | 9 | 0.3282 |
| 1.1 | 0.2708 | 2.7 | 0.2973 | 4.3 | 0.3113 | 5.9 | 0.3199 | 7.5 | 0.3251 | 9.1 | 0.3283 |
| 1.2 | 0.2737 | 2.8 | 0.2983 | 4.4 | 0.312 | 6 | 0.3203 | 7.6 | 0.3254 | 9.2 | 0.3285 |
| 1.3 | 0.2762 | 2.9 | 0.2994 | 4.5 | 0.3126 | 6.1 | 0.3207 | 7.7 | 0.3256 | 9.3 | 0.3286 |
| 1.4 | 0.2784 | 3 | 0.3004 | 4.6 | 0.3133 | 6.2 | 0.3211 | 7.8 | 0.3258 | 9.4 | 0.3288 |
| 1.5 | 0.2804 | 3.1 | 0.3014 | 4.7 | 0.3139 | 6.3 | 0.3214 | 7.9 | 0.3261 | 9.5 | 0.3289 |

(i) $f_1(t) = \dfrac{\sin \alpha t}{t}$,   (ii) $f_2(t) = t^5 \sin \alpha t$,   (iii) $f_3(t) = t^8 \cos \alpha t$,   (iv) $f_4(t) = t^6 e^{\alpha t}$.

(27) Find inverse Laplace transform for the following functions

(i) $F_1(s) = \dfrac{1}{\sqrt{s}\left(s^2 - a^2\right)\left(\sqrt{s} + b\right)}$,   (ii) $F_2(s) = \sqrt{s-a} - \sqrt{s-b}$,

(iii) $F_3(s) = \ln \dfrac{s-a}{s-b}$,   (iv) $F_4(s) = \dfrac{s-a}{\sqrt{s}\left(s^2 - a^2\right)\left(\sqrt{s} + b\right)}$,   (v) $F_5(s) = \dfrac{3a^2}{s^3 + a^3}$,

(vi) $F_6(s) = \dfrac{(s-1)^8}{s^7}$,   (vii) $F_7(s) = \ln \dfrac{s^2 + a^2}{s^2 + b^2}$,

(viii) $F_8(s) = \dfrac{s^2 + 3s + 8}{\prod\limits_{i=1}^{8}(s+i)}$,   (ix) $F_9(s) = \dfrac{1}{2}\dfrac{s+\alpha}{s-\alpha}$.

(28) Find the inverse $z$ transform for the following functions

(i) $F_1(z) = \dfrac{10z}{(z-1)(z-2)}$,   (ii) $F_2(z) = \dfrac{z^2}{(z-0.8)(z-0.1)}$,

(iii) $F_3(z) = \dfrac{z}{(z-a)(z-1)^2}$,   (iv) $F_4(z) = \dfrac{z^{-1}\left(1 - e^{-aT}\right)}{\left(1 - z^{-1}\right)\left(1 - z^{-1}e^{-aT}\right)}$,

(v) $F_e(z) = \dfrac{Az\left[z\cos\beta - \cos(\alpha T - \beta)\right]}{z^2 - 2z\cos\alpha T + 1}$.

(29) If the Laplace transform of a signal is $\dfrac{b}{s^2(s+a)}$, please take the $z$ transform and validate the results.

(30) Please show with a computer that

$$\mathscr{Z}\left\{1 - e^{-akT}\left[\cos bkT + \dfrac{a}{b}\sin bkT\right]\right\} = \dfrac{z(Az + B)}{(z-1)\left(z^2 - 2e^{-aT}\cos bTz + e^{-2aT}\right)},$$

where

$$A = 1 - e^{-aT} \cos bT - \frac{a}{b} e^{-aT} \sin bT, \quad B = e^{-2aT} + \frac{a}{b} e^{-aT} \sin bT - e^{-aT} \cos bT.$$

## Bibliography and References

[1] Xue D Y, Chen Y Q. Solving applied mathematical problems with MATLAB. Boca Raton: CRC Press, 2008

[2] Xue D Y, Chen Y Q. System simulation techniques with MATLAB and Simulink. Chichester: John Wiley and Sons, 2013

[3] Forsythe G E, Malcolm M A, Moler C B. Computer methods for mathematical computations. Englewood Cliffs: Prentice-Hall, 1977

[4] Nelder J A, Mead R. A simplex method for function minimization. Computer Journal, 1965, 7:308–313

[5] D'Errico J. Bound constrained optimization fminsearchbnd, 2005. `http://www.` `mathworks.cn/MATLABcentral/fileexchange/8277-fminsearchbnd`

[6] Yang W Y, Cao W, Chung T S, Morris J. Applied numerical methods using MATLAB. Hoboken, New Jersey: John Wiley & Sons, Inc., 2005

[7] Henrion D. A review of the global optimization toolbox for Maple, 2006

# Chapter 4

# Mathematical Models of
# Linear Control Systems

Mathematical models of control systems are very important in the research of control systems. In order to analyze or simulate a system, the mathematical model of it must be given. The simulation can be performed and the behavior of the system can be assessed. An appropriate controller can then be designed to achieve desired objectives. Thus, mathematical models are fundamental to the analysis and design of control systems.

Most of the analysis and design methods are provided upon the assumptions that the mathematical models of the systems are known. There are, roughly speaking, two ways in obtaining the mathematical models of control systems: One way to obtain models is to derive them from existing physical laws, the other, by model fitting methods from measured data of experiments. The first method is often referred to as physical modeling, while the other, system identification. In actual applications, they both have their own advantages and appropriate field of applications. If the models are established, one should know first how to express it in MATLAB, then the effective analysis and design tasks can be carried out. In this chapter, MATLAB descriptions and conversions to linear control system models are presented. System identification techniques are also introduced.

In control theory courses, linear control systems are often classified as continuous and discrete-time systems. Continuous systems can be modeled as transfer function matrices and state space descriptions, while discrete-time systems can be expressed by discrete-time transfer function matrices and discrete-time state space models. In certain cases, different types of system models may be needed. In fact, different model type may be converted equivalently. For instance, transfer functions and state space models can be converted, continuous systems and discrete-time systems can also be converted. In Section 4.1, MATLAB descriptions of mathematical models of linear continuous control systems are presented, followed by the description of discrete-time model expressions in Section 4.2. They are fundamental to the other materials in the book. Model conversions of different model types are given in Section 4.3. In Section 4.4, complicated models by block diagrams and simplification of the models are presented. In Section 4.5, different model reduction techniques are given. System identification and their MATLAB implementation are presented in Section 4.6.

## 4.1    Linear System Models of Linear Continuous Systems

Linear continuous system can be expressed by transfer functions and state space equations. The former expression is fundamental to classical control systems, while the latter is the so-called "modern" control systems. They are different descriptions of the same system, and are equivalent. Also, zero–pole–gain expression is useful in describing continuous linear systems. In this section, MATLAB expression to these model types are presented, and multivariable system description is also given, with state space or transfer function matrices.

### 4.1.1    *Transfer Function Models*

Continuous dynamical systems can usually be expressed by ordinary differential equations (ODEs), and linear continuous systems can be expressed by linear ODEs. Assuming that the input and output signals are $u(t)$ and $y(t)$, respectively, the ODE can be expressed as

$$
\begin{aligned}
a_1 \frac{\mathrm{d}^n y(t)}{\mathrm{d}t^n} &+ a_2 \frac{\mathrm{d}^{n-1} y(t)}{\mathrm{d}t^{n-1}} + \cdots + a_n \frac{\mathrm{d}y(t)}{\mathrm{d}t} + a_{n+1} y(t) \\
&= b_1 \frac{\mathrm{d}^m u(t)}{\mathrm{d}t^m} + b_2 \frac{\mathrm{d}^{m-1} u(t)}{\mathrm{d}t^{m-1}} + \cdots + b_m \frac{\mathrm{d}u(t)}{\mathrm{d}t} + b_{m+1} u(t),
\end{aligned} \tag{4.1}
$$

where $n$ is referred to as the order of the system.

Since there was no practical tools in solving ODEs centuries ago, integral transforms introduced by Pierre-Simon Laplace (1749–1827, also known as Laplace transform) can be used. Assuming the Laplace transform of output signal $y(t)$ is $Y(s)$, and the initial conditions of $y(t)$ and all its derivatives are zero, the important property $\mathscr{L}[\mathrm{d}^k y(t)/\mathrm{d}t^k] = s^k Y(s)$ can be adopted and the original ODE can be converted into algebraic polynomial equations. The gain of the system, i.e., the ratio of Laplace transforms of output to the input signal, known as the transfer function, can be written as

$$
G(s) = \frac{b_1 s^m + b_2 s^{m-1} + \cdots + b_m s + b_{m+1}}{a_1 s^n + a_2 s^{n-1} + a_3 s^{n-2} + \cdots + a_n s + a_{n+1}}, \tag{4.2}
$$

where $b_i, (i = 1, \cdots, m+1)$ and $a_i, (i = 1, \cdots, n+1)$ are constants, and the system is referred to as linear time invariant (LTI) systems. The denominator polynomial is referred to as the characteristic polynomial of the system. For a physically realizable system, $m \leqslant n$, and such systems are also called proper systems. If $m < n$, the system is strictly proper. The difference $n - m$ is also called the relative order or pole–zero excess of the system.

It can be seen that Laplace transform can convert an ODE into an algebraic equation, which makes the research on control systems easier. Transfer function model is very useful in control theory.

It can be seen from Eqn. (4.2) that transfer function is the ratio of two polynomials. In MATLAB, a polynomial can conventionally be expressed as a numeric vector, containing the coefficients of the polynomial in descending order of $s$. The two polynomials can be expressed first, and `tf()` function in Control System Toolbox can be used to construct a transfer function (TF) object $G$:

$$\text{num} = [b_1, b_2, \cdots, b_m, b_{m+1}]; \quad \text{den} = [a_1, a_2, \cdots, a_n, a_{n+1}];$$
$$G = \text{tf(num,den)};$$

An alternative way of entering transfer function is to express first the Laplace operator $s = \text{tf('s')}$, followed by the MATLAB expression to enter the whole transfer function. In the following examples, the two methods are demonstrated.

**Example 4.1.** Consider the transfer function model

$$G(s) = \frac{12s^3 + 24s^2 + 12s + 20}{2s^4 + 4s^3 + 6s^2 + 2s + 2}.$$

The following MATLAB commands can be used to enter the model into MATLAB workspace as a transfer function object.

```
>> num=[12 24 12 20];
   den=[2 4 6 2 2]; % numerator and denominator polynomials
   G=tf(num,den)   % transfer function model G can be entered
```

If the latter method is used, the transfer function can be entered with the following statements and the results are the same.

```
>> s=tf('s'); % Laplace operator s can be entered first
   G=(12*s^3+24*s^2+12*s+20)/(2*s^4+4*s^3+6*s^2+2*s+2);
```

It can be seen that the input method is quite easy and straightforward. If the transfer function is given in a more complicated form, rather than the expanded one, the latter approach may be easier. The following examples are used to demonstrate the input method.

**Example 4.2.** For the factorized transfer function

$$G(s) = \frac{3(s^2 + 3)}{(s + 2)^3(s^2 + 2s + 1)(s^2 + 5)},$$

the following statements can be given

```
>> s=tf('s'); G=3*(s^2+3)/(s+2)^3/(s^2+2*s+1)/(s^2+5)
   % or G=3*(s^2+3)/((s+2)^3*(s^2+2*s+1)*(s^2+5))
```

and the transfer function can be entered and expanded automatically as

$$G(s) = \frac{3s^2 + 9}{s^7 + 8s^6 + 30s^5 + 78s^4 + 153s^3 + 198s^2 + 140s + 40}.$$

**Example 4.3.** Consider an even more complicated transfer function given by

$$G(s) = \frac{s^3 + 2s^2 + 3s + 4}{s^3(s + 2)[(s + 5)^2 + 5]}.$$

It can be seen that the term $(s + 5)^2 + 5$ comes with complicated operation. It might be very complicated with the first method, however, it can be entered easily and straightforwardly with the second method

```
>> s=tf('s'); G=(s^3+2*s^2+3*s+4)/(s^3*(s+2)*((s+5)^2+5))
```

and it again can be expanded automatically as

$$G(s) = \frac{s^3 + 2s^2 + 3s + 4}{s^6 + 12s^5 + 50s^4 + 60s^3}.$$

In the TF object, many more information (members or properties) are also included. All the members can be displayed with **set** command as (in the new version, **get()** should be used instead)

```
>> set(tf)
          num: Ny-by-Nu cell of row vectors (Nu = no. of inputs)
          den: Ny-by-Nu cell of row vectors (Ny = no. of outputs)
     Variable: [ 's' | 'p' | 'z' | 'z^-1' | 'q' ]
           Ts: Scalar (sample time in seconds)
      ioDelay: Ny-by-Nu array (I/O delays)
   InputDelay: Nu-by-1 vector
  OutputDelay: Ny-by-1 vector
    InputName: Nu-by-1 cell array of strings
   OutputName: Ny-by-1 cell array of strings
   InputGroup: M-by-2 cell array for M input groups
  OutputGroup: P-by-2 cell array for P output groups
        Notes: Array or cell array of strings
     UserData: Arbitrary
```

Apart from the members **num** and **den**, there are other useful members in the transfer function object. For instance, member **Ts** is used for sampling interval, with a default value of 0, for continuous systems. The member **ioDelay** is used to store the time delay constant. Also, the name properties such as **InputName** and **OutputName** can be used to define system model configuration. The modeling of complicated systems will be explored later.

**Example 4.4.** If the time delay constant is $\tau = 3$, i.e., the transfer function is given by $G(s)e^{-3s}$, the following MATLAB commands can be used.

```
>> G.ioDelay=3
```

It can be seen that a transfer function can easily be defined in MATLAB environment. For an existing $G$ object in MATLAB, the numerator and denominator can be retrieved with **tfdata()** function, i.e.,

```
>> [n,d]=tfdata(G,'v')   % where 'v' means to retrieve the values
```

such that $n = [0, 0, 0, 1, 2, 3, 4]$ and $d = [1, 12, 50, 60, 0, 0, 0]$. The numerator and denominator can also be retrieved with the following statements

```
>> num=G.num{1}; den=G.den{1};
```

where {1} should be exactly be expressed as {1,1}, meaning to retrieve component from cells. The pairs {1,1} means the transfer function between the first input and the first output. This approach is suitable for directly describing multivariable systems.

### 4.1.2　State Space Models

State space model is another important way to describe control systems, based on the internally defined state variables. Thus state space models are also addressed as internal models of the systems. In contrast to transfer function models, state space models can be used to describe a much larger variety of control systems, including nonlinear systems. If there are $p$ inputs $u_i(t)$, $(i = 1, \cdots, p)$, and $q$ outputs $y_i(t)$, $(i = 1, \cdots, q)$, and there are $n$ states, a state vector $\boldsymbol{x} = [x_1, x_2, \cdots, x_n]^{\mathrm{T}}$ can be defined, and the state space model can generally written as

$$\begin{cases} \dot{x}_i = f_i(x_1, x_2, \cdots, x_n, u_1, \cdots, u_p), & i = 1, \cdots, n \\ y_i = g_i(x_1, x_2, \cdots, x_n, u_1, \cdots, u_p), & i = 1, \cdots, q, \end{cases} \tag{4.3}$$

where $f_i(\cdot)$ and $g_i(\cdot)$ can either be linear or nonlinear. For linear systems, the state space model can be simplified as

$$\begin{cases} \dot{\boldsymbol{x}}(t) = \boldsymbol{A}(t)\boldsymbol{x}(t) + \boldsymbol{B}(t)\boldsymbol{u}(t) \\ \boldsymbol{y}(t) = \boldsymbol{C}(t)\boldsymbol{x}(t) + \boldsymbol{D}(t)\boldsymbol{u}(t), \end{cases} \tag{4.4}$$

where $\boldsymbol{u} = [u_1, \cdots, u_p]^{\mathrm{T}}$ and $\boldsymbol{y} = [y_1, \cdots, y_q]^{\mathrm{T}}$ are respectively input and output vectors, and the matrices $\boldsymbol{A}(t), \boldsymbol{B}(t), \boldsymbol{C}(t)$ and $\boldsymbol{D}(t)$ are compatible matrices. Here, "compatible" means that the matrix multiplication in the equations exist. More specifically, matrix $\boldsymbol{A}$ is an $n \times n$ square matrix, $\boldsymbol{B}, \boldsymbol{C}$ and $\boldsymbol{D}$ are respectively $n \times p$, $q \times n$, and $q \times p$ matrices. If all the four matrices are time independent, the system is referred to as the LTI system, whose state space model can be written as

$$\begin{cases} \dot{\boldsymbol{x}}(t) = \boldsymbol{A}\boldsymbol{x}(t) + \boldsymbol{B}\boldsymbol{u}(t) \\ \boldsymbol{y}(t) = \boldsymbol{C}\boldsymbol{x}(t) + \boldsymbol{D}\boldsymbol{u}(t). \end{cases} \tag{4.5}$$

Again it is quite easy and straightforward to enter a state space model in MAT-LAB. One may first enter the four matrices, then use `ss()` function to define a state space (SS) object in MATLAB environment $G = \mathtt{ss}(A, B, C, D)$ .

If the matrices are not compatible, the function `ss()` may give error messages to interrupt the execution of the program. Examples below can be used to demonstrate the entering process of state space models.

**Example 4.5.** Multivariable state space models can be entered into MATLAB directly, without the necessity of preprocessing. Now consider a state space model with two inputs and two outputs

$$\begin{cases} \dot{\boldsymbol{x}}(t) = \begin{bmatrix} -12 & -17.2 & -16.8 & -11.9 \\ 6 & 8.6 & 8.4 & 6 \\ 6 & 8.7 & 8.4 & 6 \\ -5.9 & -8.6 & -8.3 & -6 \end{bmatrix} \boldsymbol{x}(t) + \begin{bmatrix} 1.5 & 0.2 \\ 1 & 0.3 \\ 2 & 1 \\ 0 & 0.5 \end{bmatrix} \boldsymbol{u}(t) \\ \boldsymbol{y}(t) = \begin{bmatrix} 2 & 0.5 & 0 & 0.8 \\ 0.3 & 0.3 & 0.2 & 1 \end{bmatrix} \boldsymbol{x}(t). \end{cases}$$

The system model can be specified in MATLAB with the following statements

```
>> A=[-12,-17.2,-16.8,-11.9; 6,8.6,8.4,6;
      6,8.7,8.4,6; -5.9,-8.6,-8.3,-6];
   B=[1.5,0.2; 1,0.3; 2,1; 0,0.5]; C=[2,0.5,0,0.8; 0.3,0.3,0.2,1];
   D=zeros(2,2); G=ss(A,B,C,D)
```

The matrices in an existing SS object $G$ can be retrieved either by ssdata() function, or simply by the commands such as $G.a$ .

A state space models with time delay can be written as

$$\begin{cases} \dot{x}(t) = Ax(t) + Bu(t - \tau_{\mathrm{i}}) \\ z(t) = Cx(t) + Du(t - \tau_{\mathrm{i}}), \quad y(t) = z(t - \tau_{\mathrm{o}}), \end{cases} \tag{4.6}$$

where $\tau_{\mathrm{i}}$ is the input delay, while $\tau_{\mathrm{o}}$ is the output delay. Such a model can be entered into MATLAB workspace as

$$G = \mathtt{ss}(A, B, C, D, \mathtt{'InputDelay'}, \tau_{\mathrm{i}}, \mathtt{'OutputDelay'}, \tau_{\mathrm{o}})$$

In state space models, apart from the delay terms above, an extra property, InternalDelay, can also be used to handle systems with time delay terms inside the system, and more will be given later.

### 4.1.3   *State Space Models with Internal Delays*

Although ordinary state space models already contain delay information, such as input and output delays, the representation may not be sufficient in handling the interconnection problems. In MATLAB, the concept and representation of internal delays are proposed[1].

The ordinary state space model can be extended as shown in Fig. 4-1. The input and output signals of the system can be written as $v(t) = u(t - \tau_{\mathrm{i}})$ and $y(t) = z(t - \tau_{\mathrm{o}})$, respectively. The state space model with internal delays and input output delays can be written as

$$\begin{cases} \dot{x}(t) = Ax(t) + B_1 v(t) + w(t - \tau) \\ z(t) = C_1 x(t) + D_{11} v(t) + D_{12} w(t - \tau) \\ \xi(t) = C_2 x(t) + D_{21} v(t) + D_{22} w(t - \tau), \end{cases} \tag{4.7}$$

and $w_j(t) = \xi_j(t - \tau_j)$, $j = 1, \cdots, k$. The vector $\tau = [\tau_1, \tau_2, \cdots, \tau_k]$ is referred to as internal delays. The MATLAB function getDelayModel() can be used to extract the extended state space model

$$[A, B_1, B_2, C_1, C_2, D_{11}, D_{12}, D_{21}, D_{22}, E, \tau] = \mathtt{getDelayModel}(G, \mathtt{'mat'})$$

### 4.1.4   *Zero–pole–gain Models*

Zero–pole–gain model is an alternative to the conventional transfer function models, where the numerator and denominator polynomials are given in factorized form. The typical form of zero–pole–gain model can be written as

$$G(s) = K \frac{(s - z_1)(s - z_2) \cdots (s - z_m)}{(s - p_1)(s - p_2) \cdots (s - p_n)}, \tag{4.8}$$

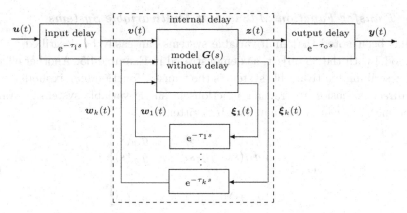

Fig. 4-1 Representation of state space models with delays.

where $K$ is called the gain of the system, and $z_i$, $(i = 1, \cdots, m)$ and $p_i$, $(i = 1, \cdots, n)$ are respectively referred to as zeros and poles of the system. They can either be real, or complex conjugates.

It is also very easy to specify zero–pole–gain model in MATLAB. Vectors can be used to specify the zeros and poles, then, zpk() function can be used to specify ZPK objects, with the following statements

$z = [z_1; \ z_2; \ \cdots; \ z_m];$   $p = [p_1; \ p_2; \ \cdots; \ p_n];$
$G = \text{zpk}(z, \ p, \ K);$

where the two vectors $z$ and $p$ should be column vectors. If they are specified as row vectors, MATLAB can convert them internally into column vectors.

**Example 4.6.** Consider the zero–pole–gain model

$$G(s) = \frac{6(s + 5)(s + 2 + \mathrm{j}2)(s + 2 - \mathrm{j}2)}{(s + 4)(s + 3)(s + 2)(s + 1)}.$$

The following MATLAB commands can be given to enter the ZPK object

```
>> P=[-1;-2;-3;-4]; % Pay attention to the signs
   Z=[-5; -2+2i; -2-2i]; G=zpk(Z,P,6)
```

The model entered can be expressed by

$$G(s) = \frac{6(s + 5)(s^2 + 4s + 8)}{(s + 1)(s + 2)(s + 3)(s + 4)}.$$

Please note that if there are complex zeros or poles, second-order factors with real coefficients are used instead in the display.

The MATLAB command $s = \text{zpk}('s')$ can also be used to define a Laplace operator in factorized form. Thus, zero–pole–gain model can be specified in this way.

```
>> s=zpk('s');
   G=6*(s+5)*(s+2+2i)*(s+2-2i)/((s+1)*(s+2)*(s+3)*(s+4))
```

### 4.1.5   *Transfer Function Matrices of Multivariable Systems*

It has been noted that multivariable systems can easily be described as state space model with the SS object, as demonstrated in Example 4.5. Another effective way of describing multivariable system is the transfer function matrix model, which is the direct extension to transfer functions in single variable systems. Transfer function matrices can mathematically be written as

$$G(s) = \begin{bmatrix} g_{11}(s) & g_{12}(s) & \cdots & g_{1p}(s) \\ g_{21}(s) & g_{22}(s) & \cdots & g_{2p}(s) \\ \vdots & \vdots & \ddots & \vdots \\ g_{q1}(s) & g_{q2}(s) & \cdots & g_{qp}(s) \end{bmatrix}, \tag{4.9}$$

where $g_{ij}(s)$ is defined as the transfer function from the $j$th input to the $i$th output, called the $(i,j)$th sub transfer function. Transfer function matrices can be entered into MATLAB by first specifying sub transfer functions, then the transfer function matrices can be established with matrix input statements.

**Example 4.7.** Consider now a transfer function matrix with time delays [2]

$$G(s) = \begin{bmatrix} \dfrac{0.1134e^{-0.72s}}{1.78s^2 + 4.48s + 1} & \dfrac{0.924}{2.07s + 1} \\ \dfrac{0.3378e^{-0.3s}}{0.361s^2 + 1.09s + 1} & \dfrac{-0.318e^{-1.29s}}{2.93s + 1} \end{bmatrix}.$$

One should first specify all the four sub transfer functions, then compose the transfer function matrix with the following statements

```
>> g11=tf(0.1134,[1.78 4.48 1],'ioDelay',0.72);
   g12=tf(0.924,[2.07 1]);
   g21=tf(0.3378,[0.361 1.09 1],'ioDelay',0.3);
   g22=tf(-0.318,[2.93 1],'ioDelay',1.29);
   G=[g11, g12; g21, g22];
```

The transfer function matrix can also be entered by first specifying the transfer function matrix without delay, then the `ioDelay` member can be updated, such that

```
>> g11=tf(0.1134,[1.78 4.48 1]); g12=tf(0.924,[2.07 1]);
   g21=tf(0.3378,[0.361 1.09 1]); g22=tf(-0.318,[2.93 1]);
   G=[g11, g12; g21, g22]; G.ioDelay=[0.72 0; 0.3, 1.29];
```

Alternatively, multivariable transfer function matrices can be entered in cells. For instance, the above transfer function matrix can be entered with

```
>> G=tf({0.1134,0.924; 0.3378,-0.318},... % numerator expressed in cells
      {[1.78 4.48 1],[2.07 1]; [0.361 1.09 1],[2.93 1]},... % denominator
      'ioDelay',[0.72,0; 0.3,1.29])                         % delay matrix
```

It looks odd because the numerator and denominators are specified in cells, while the delay must be specified in a matrix. However, this is the only acceptable combination supported in the current version.

## 4.2 Mathematical Models of Linear Discrete-time Systems

Discrete systems are often described by difference equations. Single variable discrete-time systems can be expressed by the following difference equations

$$a_1 y[(k+n)T] + a_2 y[(k+n-1)T] + \cdots + a_n y[(k+1)T] + a_{n+1} y(kT)$$
$$= b_0 u[(k+m)T] + b_1 u[(k+m-1)T] + \cdots + b_{m-1} u[(k+1)T] + b_m u(kT), \tag{4.10}$$

where $T$ is the sampling interval of the system.

### 4.2.1 *Discrete-time Transfer Function Models*

Similar to the Laplace transforms in differential equations, $z$ transform can be used to convert a difference equation model into a discrete-time transfer function model, where the important property $\mathscr{Z}\{y[(k+i)T]\} = z^i \mathscr{Z}[y(kT)]$ for zero initial condition problems is used

$$H(z) = \frac{b_0 z^m + b_1 z^{m-1} + \cdots + b_{m-1} z + b_m}{a_1 z^n + a_2 z^{n-1} + \cdots + a_n z + a_{n+1}}. \tag{4.11}$$

Discrete-time transfer function models can be specified in MATLAB in a similar way as in the case of continuous systems. The only difference is that the sampling interval Ts should be specified

```
num = [b_0, b_1, ···, b_{m-1}, b_m];    den = [a_1, a_2, ···, a_n, a_{n+1}];
H = tf(num, den, 'Ts', T);
```

where $T$ should be the positive value for sampling interval of the system. Similar to the case of linear systems, $z = \text{tf}('z', T)$ can be used to define a $z$ operator.

**Example 4.8.** For a discrete-time transfer function model
$$H(z) = \frac{6z^2 - 0.6z - 0.12}{z^4 - z^3 + 0.25z^2 + 0.25z - 0.125},$$
with a sampling interval of $T = 0.1$ s, the following statements can be used
```
>> num=[6 -0.6 -0.12]; den=[1 -1 0.25 0.25 -0.125];
   H=tf(num,den,'Ts',0.1)
```
The same model can alternatively be entered with $z$ operator method
```
>> z=tf('z',0.1);
   H=(6*z^2-0.6*z-0.12)/(z^4-z^3+0.25*z^2+0.25*z-0.125);
```

The expression of discrete-time systems with delay is slightly different from the continuous ones, where

$$H(z) = \frac{b_0 z^m + b_1 z^{m-1} + \cdots + b_{m-1} z + b_m}{a_1 z^n + a_2 z^{n-1} + \cdots + a_n z + a_{n+1}} z^{-d}, \tag{4.12}$$

where the actual delay time is multiples of the sampling interval, i.e., $dT$. To specify such a system, one can set the member ioDelay to $d$, i.e., $H.\text{ioDelay} = d$.

Dividing both numerator and denominator by $z^n$, Eqn. (4.12) can be converted to the following form

$$\widehat{H}\left(z^{-1}\right) = \frac{b_0 + b_1 z^{-1} + \cdots + b_{m-1} z^{m-n+1} + b_m z^{m-n}}{a_1 + a_2 z^{-1} + \cdots + a_n z^{-n+1} + a_{n+1} z^{-n}} z^{-d+m-n}. \tag{4.13}$$

Such a model representation is an alternative form of transfer function model, and it is often used in representing filters. The variable $q$ can also be used to replace $z^{-1}$, and the transfer function can be rewritten as

$$\widehat{H}(q) = \frac{b_0 + b_1 q + \cdots + b_{m-1} q^{n-m-1} + b_m q^{n-m}}{a_1 + a_2 q + \cdots + a_n q^{n-1} + a_{n+1} q^n} q^{d-m+n}. \tag{4.14}$$

Such transfer functions can be entered in a similar way as

```
num = [b_0, b_1, ⋯, b_{m-1}, b_m];     den = [a_1, ⋯, a_{n-1}, a_n, a_{n+1}];
H = tf(num,den,'Ts',T,'Variable','q','ioDelay',d + m − n);
```

Similar to the case in continuous systems, discrete-time zero–pole–gain model can also be entered into MATLAB with zpk() function. Again it should be noted that the sampling interval should be specified.

**Example 4.9.** For a discrete-time zero–pole–gain model

$$H(z) = \frac{(z-1/2)(z-1/2+\mathrm{j}/2)(z-1/2-\mathrm{j}/2)}{120(z+1/2)(z+1/3)(z+1/4)(z+1/5)},$$

and the sampling interval is $T = 0.1\,\text{s}$, the following statements can be used

```
>> z=[1/2; 1/2+1i/2; 1/2-1i/2]; p=[-1/2; -1/3; -1/4; -1/5];
   H=zpk(z,p,1/120,'Ts',0.1)
```

### 4.2.2    *Discrete-time State Space Models*

Discrete-time state space model can be expressed as

$$\begin{cases} \boldsymbol{x}[(k+1)T] = \boldsymbol{F}\boldsymbol{x}(kT) + \boldsymbol{G}\boldsymbol{u}(kT) \\ \boldsymbol{y}(kT) = \boldsymbol{C}\boldsymbol{x}(kT) + \boldsymbol{D}\boldsymbol{u}(kT). \end{cases} \tag{4.15}$$

It can be seen that one can simply enter $\boldsymbol{F}$, $\boldsymbol{G}$, $\boldsymbol{C}$ and $\boldsymbol{D}$ matrices first, then ss() function can be used to compose a state space object.

```
H = ss(F,G,C,D,'Ts',T);
```

Consider a discrete-time state-space model with time delay

$$\begin{cases} \boldsymbol{x}[(k+1)T] = \boldsymbol{F}\boldsymbol{x}(kT) + \boldsymbol{G}\boldsymbol{u}[(k-d)T] \\ \boldsymbol{y}(kT) = \boldsymbol{C}\boldsymbol{x}(kT) + \boldsymbol{D}\boldsymbol{u}[(k-d)T], \end{cases} \tag{4.16}$$

where $dT$ is the time delay. Such a system can be specified into MATLAB

```
H = ss(F,G,C,D,'Ts',T,'ioDelay',d);
```

Discrete-time state space models may also contain internal delays.

## 4.3 Equivalent Conversions of System Models

Various modeling techniques of linear control systems have been presented. In this section, we shall concentrate on how to convert the system model from one type to another. For instance, how to convert a continuous model into a discrete-time one, or how to convert a state space model into a transfer function model. Different forms of state space realization of control systems are also given.

### 4.3.1  *Conversion Between Continuous and Discrete-time Models*

Assume that the state space model is given by Eqn. (4.3), the analytical solution of the state variables can be written as

$$x(t) = e^{A(t-t_0)}x(t_0) + \int_{t_0}^{t} e^{A(t-\tau)}Bu(\tau)d\tau. \tag{4.17}$$

Selecting sampling interval $T$, and set $t_0 = kT$, $t = (k+1)T$, the original solution can be discretized as

$$x[(k+1)T] = e^{AT}x(kT) + \int_{kT}^{(k+1)T} e^{A[(k+1)T-\tau]}Bu(\tau)d\tau. \tag{4.18}$$

If a zero-order hold (ZOH) is used for the input signal $u(t)$, i.e., keeping the input signal fixed within the interval $t \in [kT,(k+1)T]$, the solution can be rewritten as

$$x[(k+1)T] = e^{AT}x(kT) + \int_{0}^{T} e^{A\tau}d\tau\, Bu(kT). \tag{4.19}$$

Comparing Eqns. (4.19) and (4.15), it is found that the discretized state space model can be obtained as the matrices in the discrete-time model can be written as

$$F = e^{AT}, \quad G = \int_{0}^{T} e^{A\tau}d\tau\, B, \tag{4.20}$$

and $C$ and $D$ matrices in the two systems are identical.

If the continuous system is given as a transfer function model, as shown in Eqn. (4.2), one can perform substitution $s = 2(z-1)/[T(z+1)]$ to convert the original model into a discrete-time one. Such a transform is known as Tustin transform, or bilinear transform.

In MATLAB, when there exists an LTI object $G$, it can be transfer function, state space model, or zero–pole–gain model, the discretized version can be obtained with the MATLAB function $G_1 = \text{c2d}(G,T)$ , where $T$ is the sampling interval. Systems with time delays can also be handled. Different discretization algorithms can also be used.

**Example 4.10.** Consider again the multivariable system studied in Example 4.5. Assume that the sampling interval is $T = 0.1\,\text{s}$, the following MATLAB statements can be used to find the discrete-time state space model

```
>> A=[-12,-17.2,-16.8,-11.9; 6,8.6,8.4,6;
      6,8.7,8.4,6; -5.9,-8.6,-8.3,-6];
   B=[1.5,0.2; 1,0.3; 2,1; 0,0.5]; C=[2,0.5,0,0.8; 0.3,0.3,0.2,1];
   D=zeros(2,2); G=ss(A,B,C,D); T=0.1; Gd=c2d(G,T)
```

The discrete state space model obtained is

$$
\begin{cases}
\boldsymbol{x}_{k+1} = \begin{bmatrix} -0.1500 & -1.6481 & -1.6076 & -1.14 \\ 0.5735 & 1.822 & 0.8018 & 0.5735 \\ 0.5765 & 0.8362 & 1.8059 & 0.5765 \\ -0.5665 & -0.8261 & -0.7959 & 0.4236 \end{bmatrix} \boldsymbol{x}_k + \begin{bmatrix} -0.1842 & -0.1272 \\ 0.2668 & 0.1036 \\ 0.3679 & 0.17401 \\ -0.1657 & -0.0233 \end{bmatrix} \boldsymbol{u}_k \\
\boldsymbol{y}_k = \begin{bmatrix} 2 & 0.5 & 0 & 0.8 \\ 0.3 & 0.3 & 0.2 & 1 \end{bmatrix} \boldsymbol{x}_k.
\end{cases}
$$

**Example 4.11.** Consider a time delay system given by $G(s) = \mathrm{e}^{-2s}/(s+2)^3$. Selecting sampling interval $T = 0.1\,\mathrm{s}$, the discretized model under ZOH can be obtained with the following statements

```
>> s=tf('s'); G=1/(s+2)^3; G.ioDelay=2; G1=c2d(G,0.1)
```

The discrete transfer function is

$$
G_{\mathrm{ZOH}}(z) = \frac{0.0001436z^2 + 0.0004946z + 0.0001064}{z^3 - 2.456z^2 + 2.011z - 0.5488} z^{-20}.
$$

If one tries the Tustin approach, the discretized model is obtained

```
>> G2=c2d(G,0.1,'tustin') % Tustin transform
```

The discrete model with Tustin approach is

$$
G_{\mathrm{Tustin}}(z) = \frac{9.391 \times 10^{-5}z^3 + 0.0002817z^2 + 0.0002817z + 9.391 \times 10^{-5}}{z^3 - 2.455z^2 + 2.008z - 0.5477} z^{-20}.
$$

Of course, the properties of the discretized models cannot be assessed by just displaying the above results. In Chapter 4, these models will be compared using simulation methods, for instance, Example 5.22.

In some special applications, one may expect to find the continuous version of a given discrete-time model. If the original system is given by a state space model shown in Eqn. (4.20). The equivalent continuous system can be obtained from[3]

$$
\boldsymbol{A} = \frac{1}{T}\ln \boldsymbol{F}, \quad \boldsymbol{B} = \left( \boldsymbol{F} - \boldsymbol{I} \right)^{-1} \boldsymbol{AG}. \tag{4.21}
$$

If discrete-time transfer function model is given, inverse Tustin transform can be used by substituting $z = (1 + sT/2)/(1 - sT/2)$ into the model.

MATLAB function $G_1 = \mathtt{d2c}(G)$ can be used to perform the conversion. There is no need to specify the sampling interval $T$ in the function call, since the information is already contained in the discrete-time model object $G$. This function is also applicable to the systems with delay.

**Example 4.12.** Consider again the continuous state space model given in Example 4.10. We can first convert it to discrete-time model, when the sampling interval of $T = 0.1\,\mathrm{s}$. Then the MATLAB function $\mathtt{d2c()}$ can be used to convert back to the continuous model.

```
>> A=[-12,-17.2,-16.8,-11.9; 6,8.6,8.4,6;...
      6,8.7,8.4,6; -5.9,-8.6,-8.3,-6];
   B=[1.5,0.2; 1,0.3; 2,1; 0,0.5]; C=[2,0.5,0,0.8; 0.3,0.3,0.2,1];
   D=zeros(2,2); G=ss(A,B,C,D); Gd=c2d(G,0.1); % discretization
   G1=d2c(Gd)   % convert back to continuous model
```

### 4.3.2 Converting to Transfer Function Models

Assume that the state space model is given by

$$\begin{cases} \dot{x}(t) = Ax(t) + Bu(t) \\ y(t) = Cx(t) + Du(t). \end{cases} \tag{4.22}$$

Performing Laplace transform to both sides yields

$$\begin{cases} sIX(s) = AX(s) + BU(s) \\ Y(s) = CX(s) + DU(s), \end{cases} \tag{4.23}$$

where $I$ is an identity matrix, whose size is the same as matrix $A$. It can be found from Eqn. (4.22) that

$$X(s) = \left(sI - A\right)^{-1} BU(s). \tag{4.24}$$

Transfer function matrix can be obtained from

$$G(s) = Y(s)U^{-1}(s) = C\left(sI - A\right)^{-1} B + D. \tag{4.25}$$

It can be seen that the difficulties in the transform lies in evaluating the inverse of $(sI - A)$. Luckily effective algorithms are available, such as Leverier–Fadeev algorithm. Based on the algorithm, an updated `poly()` can be written to increase the accuracy of computation[4].

If the model is given in zero–pole–gain format, the transfer function model can be obtained by simply expanding the numerator and denominator polynomials.

With the use of MATLAB, converting a given LTI model is made much easier. A simple use of the function $G_1 = \text{tf}(G)$ can convert the LTI $G$ into a transfer function object $G_1$. This function is applicable to discrete-time systems as well as multivariable systems. It is also applicable to systems with time delay.

**Example 4.13.** Consider the multivariable state space model given in Example 4.5. The transfer function matrix can be obtained with the following statements

```
>> A=[-12,-17.2,-16.8,-11.9; 6,8.6,8.4,6;
        6,8.7,8.4,6; -5.9,-8.6,-8.3,-6];
    B=[1.5,0.2; 1,0.3; 2,1; 0,0.5]; C=[2,0.5,0,0.8; 0.3,0.3,0.2,1];
    D=zeros(2,2); G=ss(A,B,C,D); G1=tf(G)
```

The following transfer function matrix can be obtained

$$G(s) = \begin{bmatrix} \dfrac{3.5s^3 - 144.1s^2 - 20.69s - 0.8372}{s^4 + s^3 + 0.35s^2 + 0.05s + 0.0024} & \dfrac{0.95s^3 - 64.13s^2 - 9.161s - 0.374}{s^4 + s^3 + 0.35s^2 + 0.05s + 0.0024} \\[3mm] \dfrac{1.15s^3 - 36.32s^2 - 6.225s - 0.1339}{s^4 + s^3 + 0.35s^2 + 0.05s + 0.0024} & \dfrac{0.85s^3 - 15.71s^2 - 2.619s - 0.04559}{s^4 + s^3 + 0.35s^2 + 0.05s + 0.0024} \end{bmatrix}.$$

### 4.3.3  State Space Realization of Control Systems

To convert an LTI model into a state space form is called state space realization of control systems. It should be noted that the equivalent state space model of a transfer function is not unique. Under different selection of state variables, different state space realization can be achieved.

Many state space realization functions are provided in MATLAB Control System Toolbox. The most straightforward one is the ss() function, i.e., $G_1 = \mathtt{ss}(G)$, which converts an LTI object $G$ into state space form $G_1$ in a default way. Apart from the function, other realization forms are also used in control systems. This will be demonstrate in the next chapter.

**Example 4.14.** Consider the delayed transfer function matrix given in Example 4.7. The following statements can be used to perform state space realization

```
>> g11=tf(0.1134,[1.78 4.48 1],'ioDelay',0.72);
   g12=tf(0.924,[2.07 1]);
   g21=tf(0.3378,[0.361 1.09 1],'ioDelay',0.3);
   g22=tf(-0.318,[2.93 1],'ioDelay',1.29);
   G=[g11, g12; g21, g22]; G1=ss(G), G2=tf(G1)
```

The input delay is $\tau_i = [0.3, 0]$, and the state space realization is

$$
\begin{cases}
\dot{x}(t) = \begin{bmatrix}
-2.52 & -0.28 & 0 & 0 & 0 & 0 \\
2 & 0 & 0 & 0 & 0 & 0 \\
0 & 0 & -3.02 & -0.69 & 0 & 0 \\
0 & 0 & 4 & 0 & 0 & 0 \\
0 & 0 & 0 & 0 & -0.48 & 0 \\
0 & 0 & 0 & 0 & 0 & -0.34
\end{bmatrix} x(t) + \begin{bmatrix}
0.25 & 0 \\
0 & 0 \\
0.25 & 0 \\
0 & 0 \\
0 & 1 \\
0 & 0.25
\end{bmatrix} \begin{bmatrix} u_1(t-0.3) \\ u_2(t) \end{bmatrix} \\
z(t) = \begin{bmatrix}
0 & 0.1274 & 0 & 0 & 0.4464 & 0 \\
0 & 0 & 0 & 0.9357 & 0 & -0.4341
\end{bmatrix} x(t),
\end{cases}
$$

with two internal delays $\tau_1 = 0.42$, and $\tau_2 = 1.29$.

From the obtained state space object $G_1$, $G_2 = \mathtt{tf}(G_1)$ command can be used to convert it back to transfer function matrix, which is almost the same as the original one.

### 4.3.4  Balanced Realizations

Balanced realization is another useful realization form of control systems, since the significance of each states can easily found from it. The `balreal()` function provided in the Control System Toolbox can be used directly. The syntax of the function is $[G_b, g, T] = \mathtt{balreal}(G)$, where $G_b$ is the balanced realization of the original system $G$. The returned $T$ matrix is the linear similarity transformation matrix. For stable systems, the controllability and observability Gramians of the balanced realized systems are the same, and they are both diagonal matrices, and the diagonal elements are returned in vector $g$. For stable single variable systems, the absolute values of vector $b$ are the same as the ones in vector $c$.

### 4.3.5 *Minimum Realization of State Space Models*

**Example 4.15.** Before introducing the concept of minimum realization, consider first the transfer function model

$$G(s) = \frac{5s^3 + 50s^2 + 155s + 150}{s^4 + 11s^3 + 41s^2 + 61s + 30}.$$

If no action is performed, we cannot find any further information from it. However, if the zero–pole–gain model is converted with the following statements

```
>> G=tf([5 50 155 150],[1 11 41 61 30]); zpk(G)
```

The zero–pole–gain model of the system is

$$G(s) = \frac{5(s+3)(s+2)(s+5)}{(s+5)(s+3)(s+2)(s+1)}.$$

It can be seen that there are common pole and zero pairs at $s = -2, -3, -5$. Thus, it is safe to cancel them and obtain the simplest form of $G_r(s) = 5/(s+1)$.

The resulting transfer function, after pole–zero cancelation, is called the minimum realization of the system. For single variable systems, it is quite easy to find minimum realization in this way. However, for multivariable systems, finding the minimum realization of the system may be more complicated. MATLAB function $G_m = \texttt{minreal}(G)$ can be used to find the minimum realization directly.

**Example 4.16.** Assume that a multivariable state space mode of a system if given by

$$\begin{cases} \dot{x}(t) = \begin{bmatrix} -6 & -1.5 & 2 & 4 & 9.5 \\ -6 & -2.5 & 2 & 5 & 12.5 \\ -5 & 0.25 & -0.5 & 3.5 & 9.75 \\ -1 & 0.5 & 0 & -1 & 1.5 \\ -2 & -1 & 1 & 2 & 3 \end{bmatrix} x(t) + \begin{bmatrix} 6 & 4 \\ 5 & 5 \\ 3 & 4 \\ 0 & 2 \\ 3 & 1 \end{bmatrix} u(t) \\ y(t) = \begin{bmatrix} 2 & 0.75 & -0.5 & -1.5 & -2.75 \\ 0 & -1.25 & 1.5 & 1.5 & 2.25 \end{bmatrix} x(t). \end{cases}$$

The following statements can be used to find the minimum realization
```
>> A=[-6,-1.5,2,4,9.5; -6,-2.5,2,5,12.5; -5,0.25,-0.5,3.5,9.75;
      -1, 0.5, 0, -1, 1.5;  -2, -1, 1, 2, 3]; % Input A matrix
   B=[6,4; 5,5; 3,4; 0,2; 3,1]; D=zeros(2);
   C=[2,0.75,-0.5,-1.5,-2.75; 0,-1.25,1.5,1.5,2.25];
   G=ss(A,B,C,D); G1=minreal(G)   % find the minimum realization model
```
It is prompted that "2 states removed", the third order minimum realization model is

$$\begin{cases} \dot{\hat{x}}(t) = \begin{bmatrix} -2.4125 & 1.1729 & -0.17022 \\ -0.73946 & 0.12333 & -0.37256 \\ -0.65067 & 1.6766 & -1.7108 \end{bmatrix} \hat{x}(t) + \begin{bmatrix} 6.4843 & 4.0942 \\ 5.1517 & 3.7888 \\ 3.227 & 5.5572 \end{bmatrix} u(t) \\ y(t) = \begin{bmatrix} 0.84235 & 0.073798 & 0.048876 \\ 0.25085 & 0.36129 & 0.46861 \end{bmatrix} \hat{x}(t). \end{cases}$$

It should be noted that the original fifth order model can be reduced to third order model, through internal state transforms, and the original physical meaning of the states are lost.

### 4.3.6  *Conversion between Transfer Functions and Symbolic Expressions*

In the next section in model simplification, symbolic expressions of transfer functions may also be used, and the model thus given is incompatible with the transfer function object in the Control System Toolbox. Two MATLAB functions should be written to convert the model format between them. The listings of the two functions are

```
function G=sym2tf(P)
[n,d]=numden(P); G=tf(sym2poly(n),sym2poly(d));
```

and

```
function P=tf2sym(G)
P=poly2sym(G.num{1},'s')/poly2sym(G.den{1},'s');
```

Please note that the symbolic to transfer function object conversion applies only to the symbolic expressions whose parameters are given numeric, rather than symbolic variables.

## 4.4  Block Diagram Description and Simplification

Generally speaking, the structures in actual control systems are usually complicated. There are very few which can be expressed by a single transfer function or a state space expression. Typically, control systems are composed of several interconnected sub models. In this section, interconnection of sub models are described, and simplification methods to find the overall model are presented. Three typical interconnection structures, i.e., series, parallel and feedback connections, are described first. Internal delay representation of complicated delay loops are explored and modeling methods are demonstrated. Then equivalent transformation and simplification method of complicated systems, in particular with symbolic computation, are presented.

### 4.4.1  *Typical Connections of Control Systems*

If two sub models $G_1(s)$ and $G_2(s)$ are connected in the form as shown in Fig. 4-2 (a), it is referred to as they are in series connection. Under such a connection, the input signal $u(t)$ is fed into block $G_1(s)$, the output of it is used as the input to the second block $G_2(s)$, and the output $y(t)$ of it is the overall output of the whole system. In series connection, the overall model can be written as $G(s) = G_2(s)G_1(s)$. For single variable systems, the two blocks are interchangeable, i.e., $G_1G_2 = G_2G_1$. However, for multivariable systems, they cannot be swapped.

If the two blocks are given by their state space models $G_1(s) = (A_1, B_1, C_1, D_1)$, and $G_2(s) = (A_2, B_2, C_2, D_2)$, the overall model of the system can mathematically

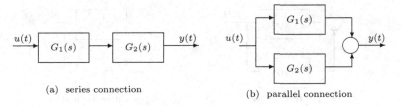

(a) series connection          (b) parallel connection

Fig. 4-2   Series and parallel connection of sub models.

be written as

$$\begin{cases} \begin{bmatrix} \dot{x}_1 \\ \dot{x}_2 \end{bmatrix} = \begin{bmatrix} A_1 & 0 \\ B_2 C_1 & A_2 \end{bmatrix} \begin{bmatrix} x_1 \\ x_2 \end{bmatrix} + \begin{bmatrix} B_1 \\ B_2 D_1 \end{bmatrix} u \\ y = \begin{bmatrix} D_2 C_1, & C_2 \end{bmatrix} \begin{bmatrix} x_1 \\ x_2 \end{bmatrix} + D_2 D_1 u. \end{cases} \tag{4.26}$$

It can be seen from the above formulation that if both sub models are given by transfer functions, or by state space models, the overall model can be retrieved easily with the above formula. However, if one of them is given by transfer function, and the other by state space model, a lot of work should be done to find the overall model, from the above formula. In MATLAB, the overall model can be obtained with $G = G_2 * G_1$ command, no matter what the expressions of $G_1$ and $G_2$ are.

If two sub models $G_1(s)$ and $G_2(s)$ are connected as shown in Fig. 4-2 (b), they are called to be in parallel connection. Both the blocks are excited by the same input, and the outputs of the two blocks are summed up to form the output of the overall system. The overall model for two blocks in parallel connection can be obtained from $G(s) = G_1(s) + G_2(s)$.

If the two blocks are given as state space models $G_1(s) = (A_1, B_1, C_1, D_1)$, and $G_2(s) = (A_2, B_2, C_2, D_2)$, the overall system can be obtained from

$$\begin{cases} \begin{bmatrix} \dot{x}_1 \\ \dot{x}_2 \end{bmatrix} = \begin{bmatrix} A_1 & 0 \\ 0 & A_2 \end{bmatrix} \begin{bmatrix} x_1 \\ x_2 \end{bmatrix} + \begin{bmatrix} B_1 \\ B_2 \end{bmatrix} u \\ y = \begin{bmatrix} C_1, & C_2 \end{bmatrix} \begin{bmatrix} x_1 \\ x_2 \end{bmatrix} + \left( D_1 + D_2 \right) u. \end{cases} \tag{4.27}$$

Under MATLAB, the overall model under parallel connection can easily be obtained with the command $G = G_1 + G_2$.

Two types of feedback connections of two sub models $G_1(s)$ and $G_2(s)$ are shown in Fig. 4-3 (a) and (b). The former one is called positive feedback, while the latter, negative feedback. The overall model can be obtained from

$$\text{positive: } G(s) = \frac{G_1(s)}{1 - G_1(s)G_2(s)}, \quad \text{negative: } G(s) = \frac{G_1(s)}{1 + G_1(s)G_2(s)}. \tag{4.28}$$

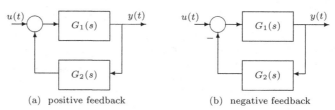

(a)  positive feedback          (b)  negative feedback

Fig. 4-3   Feedback connection structure.

If the two blocks are given by state space models $G_1(s) = (A_1, B_1, C_1, D_1)$, and $G_2(s) = (A_2, B_2, C_2, D_2)$, the overall model can be obtained from

$$\begin{cases} \begin{bmatrix} \dot{x}_1 \\ \dot{x}_2 \end{bmatrix} = \begin{bmatrix} A_1 - B_1 Z D_2 C_1 & -B_1 Z C_2 \\ B_2 Z C_1 & A_2 - B_2 D_1 Z C_2 \end{bmatrix} \begin{bmatrix} x_1 \\ x_2 \end{bmatrix} + \begin{bmatrix} B_1 Z \\ B_2 D_1 Z \end{bmatrix} u \\ y = \begin{bmatrix} Z C_1, & -D_1 Z C_2 \end{bmatrix} \begin{bmatrix} x_1 \\ x_2 \end{bmatrix} + \left( D_1 Z \right) u, \end{cases} \tag{4.29}$$

where $Z = \left( I + D_1 D_2 \right)^{-1}$. If $D_1 = D_2 = 0$, one has $Z = I$, and the overall system can be obtained from

$$\begin{cases} \begin{bmatrix} \dot{x}_1 \\ \dot{x}_2 \end{bmatrix} = \begin{bmatrix} A_1 & -B_1 C_2 \\ B_2 C_1 & A_2 \end{bmatrix} \begin{bmatrix} x_1 \\ x_2 \end{bmatrix} + \begin{bmatrix} B_1 \\ 0 \end{bmatrix} u \\ y = \begin{bmatrix} C_1, & 0 \end{bmatrix} \begin{bmatrix} x_1 \\ x_2 \end{bmatrix}. \end{cases} \tag{4.30}$$

In MATLAB, the statement $G = G_1/(1 + G_1 * G_2)$ can be used to find the overall model of negative feedback systems. The order of the obtained model may be higher than the actual one. MATLAB function `minreal()` can then be used to find the minimum realization form of the system. In MATLAB, `feedback()` function provided in the Control System Toolbox is recommended to be used to evaluate the overall model, with the syntaxes

$G = $ `feedback`$(G_1, G_2)$;        % negative connection
$G = $ `feedback`$(G_1, G_2, 1)$;      % positive connection

In MATLAB, the function `feedback()` can only be used when arguments $G_1$ and $G_2$ are given LTI objects. With certain extension, the following MATLAB function can be written for manipulating symbolic computation tasks. The list of the function is

```
function H=feedbacksym(G1,G2,key)
if nargin==2; key=-1; end
H=G1/(sym(1)-key*G1*G2); H=simple(H);
```

**Example 4.17.** Consider the typical feedback control system shown in Fig. 4-4. Assume that the sub models are given by

$$G(s) = \frac{12s^3 + 24s^2 + 12s + 20}{2s^4 + 4s^3 + 6s^2 + 2s + 2}, \quad G_c(s) = \frac{5s + 3}{s}, \quad H(s) = \frac{1000}{s + 1000}.$$

The overall model can be obtained with the following statements

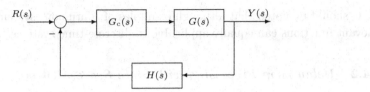

Fig. 4-4   Block diagram of typical feedback connection.

```
>> s=tf('s'); G=(12*s^3+24*s^2+12*s+20)/(2*s^4+4*s^3+6*s^2+2*s+2);
   Gc=(5*s+3)/s; H=1000/(s+1000); GG=feedback(G*Gc,H)
```

The closed-loop model of the system is

$$G_{\rm cl}(s) = \frac{60s^5 + 60156s^4 + 156132s^3 + 132136s^2 + 136060s + 60000}{2s^6 + 2004s^5 + 64006s^4 + 162002s^3 + 134002s^2 + 138000s + 60000}.$$

**Example 4.18.** Consider the feedback system shown in Fig. 4-4. Assume that the multivariable plant model is expressed as state space model

$$\begin{cases} \dot{x}(t) = \begin{bmatrix} -12 & -17.2 & -16.8 & -11.9 \\ 6 & 8.6 & 8.4 & 6 \\ 6 & 8.7 & 8.4 & 6 \\ -5.9 & -8.6 & -8.3 & -6 \end{bmatrix} x(t) + \begin{bmatrix} 1.5 & 0.2 \\ 1 & 0.3 \\ 2 & 1 \\ 0 & 0.5 \end{bmatrix} u(t) \\ y(t) = \begin{bmatrix} 2 & 0.5 & 0 & 0.8 \\ 0.3 & 0.3 & 0.2 & 1 \end{bmatrix} x(t), \end{cases}$$

and the controller is given as a diagonal transfer function matrix where $g_{11}(s) = (2s+1)/s$, $g_{22}(s) = (5s + 2)/s$, the feedback is an identity matrix. The closed-loop system can be obtained with the following statements

```
>> A=[-12,-17.2,-16.8,-11.9; 6,8.6,8.4,6; ...
      6,8.7,8.4,6; -5.9,-8.6,-8.3,-6];
   B=[1.5,0.2; 1,0.3; 2,1; 0,0.5]; C=[2,0.5,0,0.8; 0.3,0.3,0.2,1];
   D=zeros(2,2); G=ss(A,B,C,D);
   s=tf('s'); g11=(2*s+1)/s; g22=(5*s+2)/s; Gc=[g11,0; 0 g22];
   H=eye(2); GG=feedback(G*Gc,H)
```

The state space model of the multivariable system becomes

$$\begin{cases} \dot{x}(t) = \begin{bmatrix} -18.3 & -19 & -17 & -15.3 & 1.5 & 0.4 \\ 1.55 & 7.15 & 8.1 & 2.9 & 1 & 0.6 \\ -3.5 & 5.2 & 7.4 & -2.2 & 2 & 2 \\ -6.65 & -9.35 & -8.8 & -8.5 & 0 & 1 \\ -2 & -0.5 & 0 & -0.8 & 0 & 0 \\ -0.3 & -0.3 & -0.2 & -1 & 0 & 0 \end{bmatrix} x(t) + \begin{bmatrix} 3 & 1 \\ 2 & 1.5 \\ 4 & 5 \\ 0 & 2.5 \\ 1 & 0 \\ 0 & 1 \end{bmatrix} u(t) \\ y(t) = \begin{bmatrix} 2 & 0.5 & 0 & 0.8 & 0 & 0 \\ 0.3 & 0.3 & 0.2 & 1 & 0 & 0 \end{bmatrix} x(t). \end{cases}$$

It can be seen that the MATLAB functions can also be used in dealing with multivariable systems.

It should be noted that although examples of continuous systems are used, the relevant functions can equally applicable to discrete-time systems.

### 4.4.2   Delay Loop Processing with State Space Models

Delay handling in closed-loop systems with traditional LTI objects may be very complicated, if not impossible. Thus, alternative ways of these kind of systems should be explored. For instance, by introducing the representation of "internal delays" in state space models. Before formally introducing the related topics, a simple example below is presented.

**Example 4.19.** Assume that in the typical unity negative feedback structure in Fig. 4-3. The controller is $G_c(s) = 1$, the plant model $G(s) = e^{-2s}/(s+3)$, and it contains a pure time delay of $2$ s. How can we find the closed-loop model of such a system? One obvious way to issue the following MATLAB commands

```
>> G=tf(1,[1 3]); G.ioDelay=2; Gx=feedback(G,1)
```

Surprisingly the following error message will be displayed[1]

```
??? Error using ==> InputOutputModel.feedback at 132
System interconnection gives rise to internal delays and can only be
represented in state space. Convert at least one of the models to
state space using the "ss" command.
```

and it suggested us to use state space representation and use the internal delay concept in solving such a problem. Let us see why the transfer function representation failed. Manually deriving the closed-loop transfer function

$$G_{\mathrm{x}} = \frac{G(s)}{1 + G(s)} = \frac{e^{-2s}/(s+3)}{1 + e^{-2s}/(s+3)} = \frac{e^{-2s}}{s + 3 + e^{-2s}}.$$

It is then found that we are unable to rewrite the closed-loop model in the form of the standard $\widetilde{G}(s)e^{-\tau s}$ form. Thus, the transfer function representation fails in dealing with such kind of problems. Following the above prompt in the error message, we can convert the plant model or other model to state space model, then find the closed-loop model

```
>> G=ss(G); % convert G to SS object, in new versions, command can be omitted
   Gx=feedback(G,1) % recalculate the closed-loop model
```

The closed-loop model can be found

$$A = -4, \; B = C = 1, \; D = 0, \text{ and an internal delay of } 2.$$

**Example 4.20.** Assume that in a computer control feedback system, the plant model is given by continuous form, and the controller is discrete, such that

$$G(s) = \frac{2}{s(s+2)}, \; G_c(z) = \frac{9.1544(z - 0.9802)}{z - 0.8187}, \; T = 0.2\,\text{s}.$$

---

[1]In the new versions of Control System Toolbox, the warning messages are no longer given. The conversion to SS object is performed automatically.

Also, the closed-loop system is a unity negative feedback system. Since the plant model is continuous, while the controller is discrete, conversion must be made to unify them. The commands below get respectively the continuous and discrete closed-loop model

```
>> s=tf('s'); T=0.2; G=2/s/(s+2);
   z=tf('z',T); Gc=9.1544*(z-0.9802)/(z-0.8187);
   G1=feedback(c2d(G,T)*Gc,1), G2=feedback(G*d2c(Gc),1)
```

and the models are

$$G_1(z) = \frac{0.3219z^2 - 0.03376z - 0.2762}{z^3 - 2.167z^2 + 2.004z - 0.8249}, \quad G_2(s) = \frac{18.31s + 2}{s^3 + 3s^2 + 20.31s + 2}.$$

**Example 4.21.** Now consider a multivariable system problem. Assume that the plant model is given by a $2 \times 2$ transfer function matrix in Example 4.7

$$G(s) = \begin{bmatrix} \dfrac{0.1134e^{-0.72s}}{1.78s^2 + 4.48s + 1} & \dfrac{0.924}{2.07s + 1} \\[3mm] \dfrac{0.3378e^{-0.3s}}{0.361s^2 + 1.09s + 1} & \dfrac{-0.318e^{-1.29s}}{2.93s + 1} \end{bmatrix},$$

and the controller is a diagonal PI controller matrix with a pre-compensate matrix

$$G_c(s) = \begin{bmatrix} -0.4136 & 2.6537 \\ 1.1330 & -0.3257 \end{bmatrix} \begin{bmatrix} 3.8582 + 1.0640/s & 0 \\ 0 & 1.1487 + 0.8133/s \end{bmatrix},$$

and the feedback is unity negative feedback given as $H(s) = I_{2\times2}$. Of course we have to convert the plant model into state space form first such that the closed-loop model with internal delays can be constructed. The following statements can be issued

```
>> g11=tf(0.1134,[1.78 4.48 1],'ioDelay',0.72); g12=tf(0.924,[2.07 1]);
   g21=tf(0.3378,[0.361 1.09 1],'ioDelay',0.3);
   g22=tf(-0.318,[2.93 1],'ioDelay',1.29); G=ss([g11, g12; g21, g22]);
   s=tf('s'); H=eye(2); Kp=[-0.4136,2.6537; 1.1330,-0.3257];
   Gc=Kp*[3.8582+1.0640/s, 0; 0, 1.1487+0.8133/s]; Gx=feedback(G*Gc,H)
```

The state space model can be written as

$$A = \begin{bmatrix} -2.5168 & -0.4601 & 0 & -0.7131 & 0.3561 & 0.3308 & -0.11 & 0.2697 \\ 1 & 0 & 0 & 0 & 0 & 0 & 0 & 0 \\ 0 & 0.2033 & -3.0193 & -2.8112 & 0.7123 & 0.6616 & -0.22 & 0.5395 \\ 0 & 0 & 2 & 0 & 0 & 0 & 0 & 0 \\ 0 & -0.5569 & 0 & 0.175 & -2.4343 & -0.0812 & 0.6027 & -0.0662 \\ 0 & -0.2784 & 0 & 0.0875 & -0.9756 & -0.3819 & 0.3013 & -0.0331 \\ 0 & -0.2548 & 0 & 0 & -0.8927 & 0 & 0 & 0 \\ 0 & 0 & 0 & -1.8714 & 0 & 0.8682 & 0 & 0 \end{bmatrix},$$

$$B^T = \begin{bmatrix} -0.3989 & 0 & -0.7978 & 0 & 2.1856 & 1.0928 & 1 & 0 \\ 0.762 & 0 & 1.5241 & 0 & -0.187 & -0.0935 & 0 & 2 \end{bmatrix},$$

$$C = \begin{bmatrix} 0 & 0.2548 & 0 & 0 & 0.8927 & 0 & 0 & 0 \\ 0 & 0 & 0 & 0.9357 & 0 & -0.4341 & 0 & 0 \end{bmatrix},$$

with internal delays of 0.42, 1.29, 0.3. The extended matrices $A$, $B$, $C$ and $D$ can be obtained with the following statements

```
>> H=getDelayModel(Gx)
```

and the matrices of the system are

$$\tilde{A} = \begin{bmatrix} -2.5168 & -0.5617 & 0 & 0 & 0 & 0 & 0 & 0 \\ 1 & 0 & 0 & 0 & 0 & 0 & 0 & 0 \\ 0 & 0 & -3.0193 & -1.385 & 0 & 0 & 0 & 0 \\ 0 & 0 & 2 & 0 & 0 & 0 & 0 & 0 \\ 0 & 0 & 0 & 0.175 & -2.4343 & 0 & 0.6027 & -0.0662 \\ 0 & 0 & 0 & 0.0875 & -0.9756 & -0.3412 & 0.3013 & -0.0331 \\ 0 & 0 & 0 & 0 & -0.8927 & 0 & 0 & 0 \\ 0 & 0 & 0 & -1.8714 & 0 & 0 & 0 & 0 \end{bmatrix},$$

$$\tilde{B} = \begin{bmatrix} 0 & 0 & 0 & 0 & 0.25 \\ 0 & 0 & 0 & 0 & 0 \\ 0 & 0 & 0 & 0 & 0.5 \\ 0 & 0 & 0 & 0 & 0 \\ 2.1856 & -0.187 & -2.1856 & 0.187 & 0 \\ 1.0928 & -0.0935 & -1.0928 & 0.0935 & 0 \\ 1 & 0 & -1 & 0 & 0 \\ 0 & 2 & 0 & -2 & 0 \end{bmatrix}, \quad \tilde{D} = \begin{bmatrix} 0 & 0 & 1 & 0 & 0 \\ 0 & 0 & 0 & 1 & 0 \\ 0 & 0 & 0 & 0 & 0 \\ 0 & 0 & 0 & 0 & 0 \\ -1.6 & 3.05 & 1.6 & -3.05 & 0 \end{bmatrix},$$

$$\tilde{C} = \begin{bmatrix} 0 & 0 & 0 & 0 & 0.8927 & 0 & 0 & 0 \\ 0 & 0 & 0 & 0.9357 & 0 & 0 & 0 & 0 \\ 0 & 0.2548 & 0 & 0 & 0 & 0 & 0 & 0 \\ 0 & 0 & 0 & 0 & 0 & -0.4341 & 0 & 0 \\ 0 & 0 & 0 & -2.8524 & 1.4246 & 0 & -0.44 & 1.0791 \end{bmatrix}.$$

### 4.4.3  *Equivalent Transforms When the Nodes Are Moved*

In dealing with block diagrams of complicated systems, it is often necessary to move the input branch from one node to another. For instance, in the complicated block diagram shown in Fig. 4-5. The difficulty in manipulating the system lies in the loop formed by blocks $G_2(s)$, $G_3(s)$ and $H_2(s)$. The input node of the $H_2(s)$ branch is from within another loop. One should move first the input node from Node A to the output terminal $Y(s)$. Equivalent transforms when nodes are moved should be established.

Two types of node movements shown in Figs. 4-6(a) and (b) are defined, and they are referred to as respectively forward movement and backward movement. In the forward movement shown in Fig. 4-6 (a), if one wants to move the input point of $G_2(s)$ from Node A to B, the new model of the branch should be transformed to $G_2(s)G_1(s)$, with MATLAB representation $G_2 * G_1$. In the backward movement shown in Fig. 4-6(b), If one wants to move $G_2(s)$ from Node B to A, the equivalent new transfer function is $G_2(s)/G_1(s)$, whose MATLAB implementation is $G_2/G_1$ or $G_2 * inv(G_1)$.

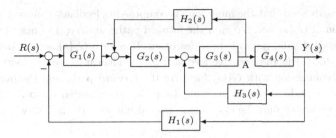

Fig. 4-5   Block diagram of a complicated system.

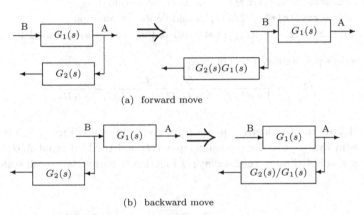

(a)  forward move

(b)  backward move

Fig. 4-6   Equivalent transformation when node moves.

### 4.4.4   *Simplification of Complicated Block Diagrams*

With the above-mentioned equivalent transformation approach, the simplification of complicated block diagrams can easily be achieved. Examples in dealing with the manipulation of complicated block diagrams are given as follows.

**Example 4.22.** Assume that a complicated block diagram is shown in Fig. 4-5. In order to simplify the system model, the input node of branch $H_2(s)$ should be moved from Node A to the output terminal $Y(s)$, as shown in Fig. 4-7.

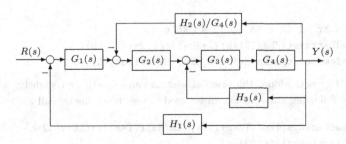

Fig. 4-7   Equivalently transformed block diagram.

Thus, it is easily seen that the inner loop is composed in feedback connection, with the series connection of $G_3(s)$ and $G_4(s)$ in the forward path, and $H_3(s)$ in negative feedback path. The composed sub system is in series connection with $G_2(s)$ as the forward path, and with $H_2(s)/G_4(s)$ in the negative feedback path. Then in the outer loop, the result one is in series connection with $G_1(s)$ for form the forward path, and the overall model can finally be obtained. However, it might be rather complicated to solve the problem by hand. Now we try to find the closed-loop overall model with the following MATLAB statements

```
>> syms G1 G2 G3 G4 H1 H2 H3    % declare symbolic variables
   c1=feedbacksym(G4*G3,H3);    % inner loop evaluation
   c2=feedbacksym(c1*G2,H2/G4); % middle loop evaluation
   G=feedbacksym(c2*G1,H1); pretty(G) % Finding the overall model
```

The closed-loop system can be obtained

$$G(s) = \frac{G_2 G_4 G_3 G_1}{1 + G_4 G_3 H_3 + G_3 G_2 H_2 + G_2 G_4 G_3 G_1 H_1}.$$

**Example 4.23.** Now consider the motor drive system shown in Figs. 4-8. There are two input signals in the system, the set-point input $r(t)$ and the load input $M(t)$. Symbolic computation is adopted using `feedbacksym()` function to derive the overall system model.

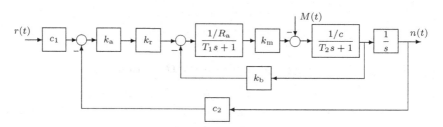

Fig. 4-8   Block diagram of a motor drive system.

Let us consider the case when input signal $r(t)$ acts alone, which means $M(t) = 0$. The following statements can be used to find the overall transfer function, the result will be given later.

```
>> syms Ka Kr c1 c2 c Ra T1 T2 Km Kb s
   Ga=feedbacksym(1/Ra/(T1*s+1)*Km*1/c/(T2*s+1),Kb);
   G1=c1*feedbacksym(Ka*Kr*Ga/s,c2); G1=collect(G1,s)
```

If signal $M(t)$ acts alone, the original system can be adjusted slightly, as shown in Figs. 4-9. The following statements can be used to construct the overall model.

```
>> G2=-feedbacksym(1/c/(T2*s+1)/s, Km/Ra/(T1*s+1)*(Kb*s+c2*Ka*Kr));
   G2=collect(simplify(G2),s)
```

With this commands, the closed-loop model can be obtained as

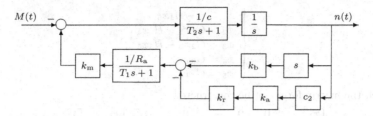

Fig. 4-9   The equivalent block diagram when $M(t)$ acts alone.

$$\boldsymbol{G}^{\mathrm{T}}(s) = \left[ \begin{array}{c} \dfrac{c_1 k_{\mathrm{m}} k_{\mathrm{a}} k_{\mathrm{r}}}{R_{\mathrm{a}} c T_1 T_2 s^3 + (R_{\mathrm{a}} c T_1 + R_{\mathrm{a}} c T_2)s^2 + (k_{\mathrm{m}} k_{\mathrm{b}} + R_{\mathrm{a}} c)s + k_{\mathrm{a}} k_{\mathrm{r}} k_{\mathrm{m}} c_2} \\[4mm] -\dfrac{(T_1 s + 1)R_{\mathrm{a}}}{c R_{\mathrm{a}} T_2 T_1 s^3 + (c R_{\mathrm{a}} T_1 + c R_{\mathrm{a}} T_2)s^2 + (k_{\mathrm{b}} k_{\mathrm{m}} + c R_{\mathrm{a}})s + k_{\mathrm{m}} c_2 k_{\mathrm{a}} k_{\mathrm{r}}} \end{array} \right].$$

### 4.4.5   *Model Simplification Using An Algebraic Approach*

It was pointed out previously that if the loops in the block diagram are complicated, node movement should be made and this method must be done manually. So the procedure might be error-prone. Algebraic equation-based signal flow graph approach should be used. Mason gain formula is a conventional solution to signal flow graph problems[5]. However, for complicated problems, this approach may lead to errors. The connection matrix-based algebraic approach proposed by Professor Huaichen Chen[6] is a practical and effective method in performing simplification to complicated problems. In this section, signal flow graph description is demonstrated, then simplification is performed.

**Example 4.24.** Consider again the block diagram given in Example 4.22. To solve the problem, we must move one of the node first. If there are more loops, node movement might be very complicated and error-prone. An alternative way is to redraw the original system using signal flow graph shown in Fig. 4-10. In the signal flow graph, 5 signal nodes and one input node are defined.

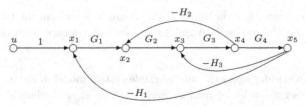

Fig. 4-10   Signal flow graph representation of the system.

For each node, it is not difficult to establish the following node equations

$$\begin{cases} x_1 = u - H_1 x_5 \\ x_2 = G_1 x_1 - H_2 x_4 \\ x_3 = G_2 x_2 - H_3 x_5 \\ x_4 = G_3 x_3 \\ x_5 = G_4 x_4. \end{cases}$$

from which the matrix form can be constructed

$$\begin{bmatrix} x_1 \\ x_2 \\ x_3 \\ x_4 \\ x_5 \end{bmatrix} = \begin{bmatrix} 0 & 0 & 0 & 0 & -H_1 \\ G_1 & 0 & 0 & -H_2 & 0 \\ 0 & G_2 & 0 & 0 & -H_3 \\ 0 & 0 & G_3 & 0 & 0 \\ 0 & 0 & 0 & G_4 & 0 \end{bmatrix} \begin{bmatrix} x_1 \\ x_2 \\ x_3 \\ x_4 \\ x_5 \end{bmatrix} + \begin{bmatrix} 1 \\ 0 \\ 0 \\ 0 \\ 0 \end{bmatrix} u.$$

From the above modeling process, it can be seen that the system can be described in matrix form such that

$$\boldsymbol{X} = \boldsymbol{QX} + \boldsymbol{PU}, \tag{4.31}$$

where $\boldsymbol{Q}$ is called the connection matrix. From the above formula, the transfer function matrix of all $x_i$ signals to the inputs can be obtained[6]

$$\boldsymbol{G} = \frac{\boldsymbol{X}}{\boldsymbol{U}} = (\boldsymbol{I} - \boldsymbol{Q})^{-1} \boldsymbol{P}. \tag{4.32}$$

**Example 4.25.** Consider again the previous example, one can enter the matrices $\boldsymbol{Q}$ and $\boldsymbol{P}$, the transfer function matrix of each node signal to the input signal can be computed directly with the following statements

```
>> syms G1 G2 G3 G4 H1 H2 H3
   Q=[0 0 0 0 -H1; G1 0 0 -H2 0; 0 G2 0 0 -H3; 0 0 G3 0 0; 0 0 0 G4 0];
   P=[1 0 0 0 0]'; inv(eye(5)-Q)*P
```

the transfer function matrix from $u(t)$ to all the states are

$$\begin{bmatrix} X_1/U \\ X_2/U \\ X_3/U \\ X_4/U \\ X_5/U \end{bmatrix} = \begin{bmatrix} (H_3 G_3 G_4 + 1 + G_3 G_2 H_2)/(G_4 G_3 H_3 + G_4 G_3 G_2 G_1 H_1 + 1 + G_3 G_2 H_2) \\ G_1(G_4 G_3 H_3 + 1)/(G_4 G_3 H_3 + G_4 G_3 G_2 G_1 H_1 + 1 + G_3 G_2 H_2) \\ G_2 G_1/(G_4 G_3 H_3 + G_4 G_3 G_2 G_1 H_1 + 1 + G_3 G_2 H_2) \\ G_3 G_2 G_1/(G_4 G_3 H_3 + G_4 G_3 G_2 G_1 H_1 + 1 + G_3 G_2 H_2) \\ G_4 G_3 G_2 G_1/(G_4 G_3 H_3 + G_4 G_3 G_2 G_1 H_1 + 1 + G_3 G_2 H_2) \end{bmatrix}.$$

Since the output signal is $x_5$ in this example, It can be seen from the transfer function matrix that the $X_5/U$ term is identical to the overall transfer function obtained in Example 4.22.

**Example 4.26.** Consider again the multivariable system model in Example 4.23. Again in the previous example, a lot of manual work must be done, including redrawing the original system model. In fact, when connection matrix-based algebraic approach is used, the problem can be solved in a systematic way. Based on the original system structure, the signal flow graph can be draw, as shown in Fig. 4-11.

Five nodal equations can be established from the signal flow chart

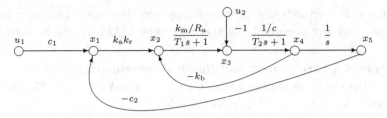

Fig. 4-11   Signal flow graph representation of a multivariable system.

$$\begin{cases} x_1 = c_1 u_1 - c_2 x_5 \\ x_2 = k_a k_r x_1 - k_b x_4 \\ x_3 = \dfrac{k_m/R_a}{T_1 s + 1} x_2 + u_2 \\ x_4 = \dfrac{1/c}{T_2 s + 1} x_3 \\ x_5 = \dfrac{1}{s} x_4, \end{cases}$$

and the matrix form of the equations can also be constructed as follows

$$\begin{bmatrix} x_1 \\ x_2 \\ x_3 \\ x_4 \\ x_5 \end{bmatrix} = \begin{bmatrix} 0 & 0 & 0 & 0 & -c_2 \\ k_a k_r & 0 & 0 & -k_b & 0 \\ 0 & \dfrac{k_m/R_a}{T_1 s + 1} & 0 & 0 & 0 \\ 0 & 0 & \dfrac{1/c}{T_2 s + 1} & 0 & 0 \\ 0 & 0 & 0 & \dfrac{1}{s} & 0 \end{bmatrix} \begin{bmatrix} x_1 \\ x_2 \\ x_3 \\ x_4 \\ x_5 \end{bmatrix} + \begin{bmatrix} c_1 & 0 \\ 0 & 0 \\ 0 & 1 \\ 0 & 0 \\ 0 & 0 \end{bmatrix} \begin{bmatrix} u_1 \\ u_2 \end{bmatrix}.$$

The following statements can be used to simplify the original multivariable system. In the system, node $x_5$ is the output node, whose transfer function to the input nodes $u_1$ and $u_2$ can also be computed. The transfer function matrix obtained is identical to the one obtained in Example 4.23.

```
>> syms Ka Kr c1 c2 c Ra T1 T2 Km Kb s
   Q=[0 0 0 0 -c2; Ka*Kr 0 0 -Kb 0; 0 Km/Ra/(T1*s+1) 0 0 0
      0 0 1/c/(T2*s+1) 0 0; 0 0 0 1/s 0];
   P=[c1 0; 0 0; 0 1; 0 0; 0 0]; W=inv(eye(5)-Q)*P; W(5,:)
```

## 4.5   Model Reduction of Linear Systems

Minimum realization and MATLAB implementation of control systems have been presented in the previous section. With the pole–zero cancelation technique, the order of the original model may be reduced. The reduction is performed using strictly mathematical simplification method. If the order of a high-order system cannot be reduced using minimum realization technique, is their any method to approximate the behavior of the high-order system by a lower-order one? This is the problem to be solved with model reduction techniques.

Model reduction problem was first investigated by Edward J Davison in 1966[7].

Different reduction methods were proposed since then. In this section, several model reduction methods are presented, together with their MATLAB implementations.

### 4.5.1   *Padé Approximations and Routh Approximations*

Assume that the original transfer function is given by Eqn. (4.2). The objective of model reduction is to find a lower order model

$$G_{r/k}(s) = \frac{\beta_1 s^r + \beta_2 s^{r-1} + \cdots + \beta_{r+1}}{\alpha_1 s^k + \alpha_2 s^{k-1} + \cdots + \alpha_k s + \alpha_{k+1}}, \tag{4.33}$$

where $k < n$. For simplicity, assume that $\alpha_{k+1} = 1$.

Assume that the Maclaurin series of $G(s)$ can be written as

$$G(s) = c_0 + c_1 s + c_2 s^2 + \cdots, \tag{4.34}$$

where $c_i$ are referred to as the time moments of the system, which may be obtained recursively with[8]

$$c_0 = b_{k+1}, \text{ and } c_i = b_{k+1-i} - \sum_{j=0}^{i-1} c_j a_{n+1-i+j}, \ i = 1, 2, \cdots. \tag{4.35}$$

If the original system $G(s)$ is given in its state space form, the following formula can be used to calculate the coefficients of Maclaurin series

$$c_i = \frac{1}{i!} \frac{d^i G(s)}{ds^i}\bigg|_{s=0} = -\boldsymbol{C}\boldsymbol{A}^{-(i+1)}\boldsymbol{B}, \ i = 0, 1, \cdots. \tag{4.36}$$

A MATLAB function $c = \texttt{timmomt}(G, k)$ is written for evaluating the first $k$ time moments of the system $G$. The function is

```
function M=timmomt(G,k)
G=ss(G); C=G.c; B=G.b; iA=inv(G.a); iA1=iA; M=zeros(1,k);
for i=1:k, M(i)=-C*iA1*B; iA1=iA*iA1; end
```

If one wants to retain the first $r + k + 1$ time moments $c_i$ $(i = 0, \cdots, r + k)$, one my substitute Eqn. (4.34) into Eqn. (4.33), and compare the coefficients in the equations. The following equations can be obtained[9].

$$\begin{cases} \beta_{r+1} = c_0 \\ \beta_r = c_1 + \alpha_k c_0 \\ \quad \vdots \\ \beta_1 = c_r + \alpha_k c_{r-1} + \cdots + \alpha_{k-r+1} c_0 \\ 0 = c_{r+1} + \alpha_k c_r + \cdots + \alpha_{k-r} c_0 \\ 0 = c_{r+2} + \alpha_k c_{r+1} + \cdots + \alpha_{k-r-1} c_0 \\ \quad \vdots \\ 0 = c_{k+r} + \alpha_k c_{k+r-1} + \cdots + \alpha_2 c_{r+1} + \alpha_1 c_r. \end{cases} \tag{4.37}$$

The following matrix equations can be established from the last $k$ equations that

$$\begin{bmatrix} c_r & c_{r-1} & \cdots & \cdot \\ c_{r+1} & c_r & \cdots & \cdot \\ \vdots & \vdots & \ddots & \vdots \\ c_{k+r-1} & c_{k+r-2} & \cdots & c_r \end{bmatrix} \begin{bmatrix} \alpha_k \\ \alpha_{k-1} \\ \vdots \\ \alpha_1 \end{bmatrix} = -\begin{bmatrix} c_{r+1} \\ c_{r+2} \\ \vdots \\ c_{k+r} \end{bmatrix}. \tag{4.38}$$

It can be seen that if the time moments $c_i$ are known, the denominator coefficients $\alpha_i$ of the reduced order model can be obtained. Then the first $r + 1$ equations of Eqn. (4.37) can be used to evaluate the coefficients $\beta_i$ of the reduced model from

$$
\begin{bmatrix} \beta_{r+1} \\ \beta_r \\ \vdots \\ \beta_1 \end{bmatrix} = \begin{bmatrix} c_0 & 0 & \cdots & 0 \\ c_1 & c_0 & \cdots & 0 \\ \vdots & \vdots & \ddots & \vdots \\ c_r & c_{r-1} & \cdots & c_0 \end{bmatrix} \begin{bmatrix} 1 \\ \alpha_k \\ \vdots \\ \alpha_{k-r+1} \end{bmatrix}. \tag{4.39}
$$

The above algorithm can be implemented in MATLAB to solve Padé approximation problems. The function `pademod()` can be written as follows

```
function Gr=pademod(G,r,k)
c=timmomt(G,r+k+1); Gr=pade_app(c,r,k);
```

where $G$ and $G_r$ are the original and reduced model, respectively, and $r, k$ pairs are the expected numerator and denominator order of the Padé reduced model, with

```
function Gr=pade_app(c,r,k)
w=-c(r+2:r+k+1)'; vv=[c(r+1:-1:1)'; zeros(k-1-r,1)];
W=rot90(hankel(c(r+k:-1:r+1),vv)); V=rot90(hankel(c(r:-1:1)));
x=[1 (W\w)']; dred=x(k+1:-1:1)/x(k+1);
y=[c(1) x(2:r+1)*V'+c(2:r+1)]; nred=y(r+1:-1:1)/x(k+1); Gr=tf(nred,dred);
```

where $c$ stores the time moment vector, $G_r$ returned the Padé approximation.

**Example 4.27.** For the fourth-order model for the given

$$
G(s) = \frac{s^3 + 7s^2 + 11s + 5}{s^4 + 7s^3 + 21s^2 + 37s + 30},
$$

the second-order Padé approximation can be found with the following statements

```
>> G=tf([1,7,11,5],[1,7,21,37,30]); Gr=pademod(G,1,2)
   step(G,Gr,'--'), figure, bode(G,Gr,'--')
```

The Padé reduced model is

$$
G_r(s) = \frac{0.8544s + 0.6957}{s^2 + 1.091s + 4.174}.
$$

The step response and Bode diagram comparisons of the reduced model and the original model are shown in Fig. 4-12(a) and (b), and it can be seen that the reduced model is close to the original model.

**Example 4.28.** Consider a high-order model

$$
G(s) = \frac{0.067s^5 + 0.6s^4 + 1.5s^3 + 2.016s^2 + 1.55s + 0.6}{0.067s^6 + 0.7s^5 + 3s^4 + 6.67s^3 + 7.93s^2 + 4.63s + 1}.
$$

The transfer function $G(s)$ can be entered and the ZPK expression can be obtained

```
>> num=[0.067,0.6,1.5,2.016,1.66,0.6];
   den=[0.067 0.7 3 6.67 7.93 4.63 1]; G=tf(num,den); zpk(G)
```

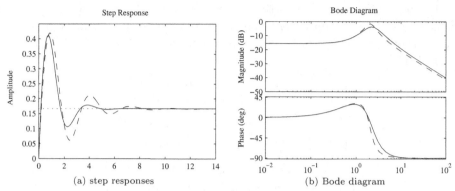

(a) step responses            (b) Bode diagram

Fig. 4-12   Comparison of reduced and original models.

with the ZPK form given by

$$G(s) = \frac{(s+5.92)(s+1.221)(s+0.897)(s^2+0.9171s+1.381)}{(s+2.805)(s+1.856)(s+1.025)(s+0.501)(s^2+4.261s+5.582)}.$$

It is obvious that the original system is stable. With the following statements, a third-order Padé approximation can be obtained.

```
>> Gr=pademod(G,1,3); zpk(Gr)
```

The ZPK model of the reduced system can be written as

$$G_r(s) = \frac{-0.6328(s+0.7695)}{(s-2.598)(s^2+1.108s+0.3123)}.$$

It can be seen that the reduced order model is unstable. It means that Padé approximation approach cannot retain the stability of the original system.

Since Padé approach cannot retain the stability of the original model, a stability-based reduction method was proposed in [10], i.e., using Routh approximation method, to find the stability retaining reduced model. MATLAB implementation of the algorithm is written as

```
function Gr=routhmod(G,nr)
num=G.num{1}; den=G.den{1}; n0=length(den); n1=length(num);
a1=den(end:-1:1); b1=[num(end:-1:1) zeros(1,n0-n1-1)];
for k=1:n0-1,
   k1=k+2; alpha(k)=a1(k)/a1(k+1); beta(k)=b1(k)/a1(k+1);
   for i=k1:2:n0-1,
      a1(i)=a1(i)-alpha(k)*a1(i+1); b1(i)=b1(i)-beta(k)*a1(i+1);
end, end
nn=[]; dd=[1]; nn1=beta(1); dd1=[alpha(1),1]; nred=nn1; dred=dd1;
for i=2:nr,
   nred=[alpha(i)*nn1, beta(i)]; dred=[alpha(i)*dd1, 0];
   n0=length(dd); n1=length(dred); nred=nred+[zeros(1,n1-n0),nn];
   dred=dred+[zeros(1,n1-n0),dd];
   nn=nn1; dd=dd1; nn1=nred; dd1=dred;
end
```

```
Gr=tf(nred(nr:-1:1),dred(end:-1:1));
```

where $G$ and $G_r$ are respectively the original model and the reduced one, and nr is the expected order. It should be noted that the order of the numerator cannot be independently assigned.

**Example 4.29.** Consider again the original transfer function given in Example 4.28, where the Padé approximation method failed. The following MATLAB commands can be issued to find the stable third-order reduced model

```
>> num=[0.067,0.6,1.5,2.016,1.66,0.6];
   den=[0.067 0.7 3 6.67 7.93 4.63 1]; G=tf(num,den);
   Gr=zpk(routhmod(G,3)), step(G,Gr,'--'), figure, bode(G,Gr,'--')
```

With Routh approximation approach, the reduced model is

$$G_r(s) = \frac{0.37792(s^2 + 0.9472s + 0.3423)}{(s + 0.4658)(s^2 + 1.15s + 0.463)}.$$

The step responses and Bode diagrams of the reduced model and the original model are shown in Figs. 4-13(a) and (b), and it can be seen that although the reduced model is stable, the approximation is not satisfactory.

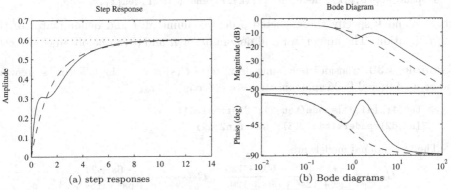

(a) step responses      (b) Bode diagrams

Fig. 4-13   Comparisons of original and reduced models.

Although Routh approach may retain the stability of the original model, it is generally regarded that the time- and frequency-domain fitting quality may not be satisfactory. Other modified reduction such as dominant mode method[11], impulse energy approximation method[12] should usually be used.

### 4.5.2   Padé Approximations to Models with Time Delays

Similar to the Padé approach, Padé approximation techniques can also be used to investigate the reduction problems to systems with time delays. The $k$th order

Padé approximation of time delay $e^{-\tau s}$ term can be written as

$$P_{k,\tau}(s) = \frac{1 - \tau s/2 + p_2(\tau s)^2 - p_3(\tau s)^3 + \cdots + (-1)^{n+1}p_n(\tau s)^k}{1 + \tau s/2 + p_2(\tau s)^2 + p_3(\tau s)^3 + \cdots + p_n(\tau s)^k}, \qquad (4.40)$$

and a MATLAB function $[n,d] = \text{pade}(\tau,k)$ is provided in Control System Toolbox, where $n$ and $d$ return the coefficient vectors of numerator and denominator. Alternatively, if model $G$ has time delay, and $n$th order Padé approximation to the delay term is expected, $G_1 = \text{pade}(G,n)$ can be used directly.

We can now consider the Maclaurin series expansion of the pure time delay term

$$e^{-\tau s} = 1 - \frac{1}{1!}\tau s + \frac{1}{2!}\tau^2 s^2 - \frac{1}{3!}\tau^3 s^3 + \cdots, \qquad (4.41)$$

and it can be seen that the expression is similar to the time moment expression in Eqn. (4.34). Thus, Padé approximation algorithm can be used to find the rational approximation to pure delay terms. A MATLAB function `paderm()` is implemented, which allows the user to select independently the orders of numerator and denominator of the rational approximation.

```
function [n,d]=paderm(tau,r,k)
c(1)=1; for i=2:r+k+1, c(i)=-c(i-1)*tau/(i-1); end
Gr=pade_app(c,r,k); n=Gr.num{1}(k-r+1:end); d=Gr.den{1};
```

where $r$ and $k$ specify the expected orders of numerator and denominator of the approximation. The numerator and denominator $n$ and $d$ can be obtained directly.

**Example 4.30.** Consider pure time delay term $G(s) = e^{-s}$, the following statements can be used to find Padé approximations or different orders

```
>> tau=1; [n1,d1]=pade(tau,3); G1=tf(n1,d1)
   [n2,d2]=paderm(tau,1,3); G2=tf(n2,d2)
```

The two rational models are

$$G_1(s) = \frac{-s^3 + 12s^2 - 60s + 120}{s^3 + 12s^2 + 60s + 120}, \quad G_2(s) = \frac{-6s + 24}{s^3 + 6s^2 + 18s + 24}.$$

**Example 4.31.** Consider the following original model with delays

$$G(s) = \frac{3s + 1}{(s + 1)^3}e^{-2s}.$$

Maclaurin series expansion to the pure time delay term can be obtained, and the time moments for the overall system can be obtained, from which Padé approximation can be obtained

```
>> cd=[1]; tau=2; for i=1:5, cd(i+1)=-tau*cd(i)/i; end; cd
   G=tf([3,1],[1,3,3,1]); c=timmomt(G,5);
   c_hat=conv(c,cd); Gr=zpk(pade_app(c_hat,1,3))
   G.ioDelay=2; Gr1=pade(G,2); step(G,Gr,'--',Gr1,':')
   figure, bode(G,Gr,'--',Gr1,':')
```

The two reduced model are obtained

$$G_{\mathrm{r}}(s) = \frac{0.20122(s + 0.04545)}{(s + 0.04546)(s^2 + 0.4027s + 0.2012)},$$

$$G_{\mathrm{r}1}(s) = \frac{3s^3 - 8s^2 + 6s + 3}{s^5 + 6s^4 + 15s^3 + 19s^2 + 12s + 3}.$$

The step responses and Bode diagrams comparison are shown in Fig. 4-14(a) and (b). It can be seen that it may not be good to approximate delay models with models without time delay. It should be noted that the `pade()` function can only be used in finding the Padé approximation with the same orders of numerator and denominator, while `pade_app()` can freely choose the orders of numerators and denominators.

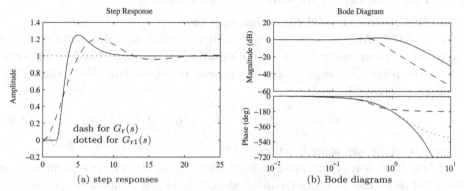

(a) step responses          (b) Bode diagrams

Fig. 4-14   Model comparisons.

### 4.5.3   *Sub-optimal Model Reduction to Models with Time Delays*

To find optimal reduced order models, a suitable objective function should be introduced, and then numerical algorithm should be used to find the optimum parameters of the reduced order models.

**1. Assessment of reduction quality**

To assess the behavior of reduced models, an error signal $e(t)$ is defined in Fig. 4-15. Based on the error signal, certain criteria can be introduced. For instance, one may define the ISE criterion

$$J_{\mathrm{ISE}} = \int_0^\infty e^2(t)\mathrm{d}t.$$

One can then obtain the optimal reduced model using optimization method. Assume that the original model with time delay can be written as

$$G(s)\mathrm{e}^{-Ts} = \frac{b_1 s^{n-1} + \cdots + b_{n-1}s + b_n}{s^n + a_1 s^{n-1} + \cdots + a_{n-1}s + a_n}\mathrm{e}^{-Ts}, \tag{4.42}$$

and the reduced model can be written as

$$G_{r/k}(s)\mathrm{e}^{-\tau s} = \frac{\beta_1 s^r + \cdots + \beta_r s + \beta_{r+1}}{s^k + \alpha_1 s^{k-1} + \cdots + \alpha_{k-1}s + \alpha_k}\mathrm{e}^{-\tau s}. \tag{4.43}$$

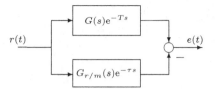

Fig. 4-15   Error signal definition.

The Laplace transform of the error signal can be written as

$$E(s) = \left[ G(s)\mathrm{e}^{-Ts} - G_{r/m}(s)\mathrm{e}^{-\tau s} \right] R(s), \qquad (4.44)$$

where $R(s)$ is the Laplace transform of the input signal $r(t)$.

### 2. Sub-optimal model reduction approach

With MATLAB, it may be quite straightforward to solve optimal model reduction problems using numerical optimization techniques. Based on the error signal $e(t)$ defined earlier, different criteria can be introduced. For instance, the weighted ISE criterion

$$\sigma_h^2 = \int_0^\infty h^2(t)\mathrm{d}t = \int_0^\infty w^2(t)e^2(t)\mathrm{d}t, \qquad (4.45)$$

where $w(t)$ is the weighting function.

When $H(s)$ is a stable rational function, the objective function can also be evaluated using the Åström's recursive algorithm, or the solutions of the relevant Lyapunov equations. If there exists delay terms, the Åström's recursive algorithm cannot be evaluated directly. Padé approximation can be used first to pure delay terms. Thus, the optimization problem is referred to as sub-optimal model reduction method [13]. If there is no delay term, the reduced model is referred to as sub-optimal reduced model.

Defining the decision variable vector $\boldsymbol{\theta} = \left[ \alpha_1, \cdots, \alpha_m, \beta_1, \cdots, \beta_{r+1}, \tau \right]$, the error signal can be rewritten as an explicit function of $\boldsymbol{\theta}$, such that $\widehat{e}(t, \boldsymbol{\theta})$, and the objective function is then defined as[13]

$$J = \min_{\boldsymbol{\theta}} \left[ \int_0^\infty w^2(t)\widehat{e}^2(t, \boldsymbol{\theta})\mathrm{d}t \right]. \qquad (4.46)$$

A MATLAB function opt_app() is written and can be used in sub-optimal reduction to systems with delays

```
function Gr=opt_app(G,r,k,key,G0)
GS=tf(G); num=GS.num{1}; den=GS.den{1};
Td=totaldelay(GS); GS.ioDelay=0; GS.InputDelay=0; GS.OutputDelay=0;
if nargin<5,
    n0=[1,1]; for i=1:k-2, n0=conv(n0,[1,1]); end
    G0=tf(n0,conv([1,1],n0));
end
beta=G0.num{1}(k+1-r:k+1); alph=G0.den{1}; Tau=1.5*Td;
x=[beta(1:r),alph(2:k+1)]; if abs(Tau)<1e-5, Tau=0.5; end
```

```
dc=dcgain(GS); if key==1, x=[x,Tau]; end
y=opt_fun(x,GS,key,r,k,dc);
x=fminsearch(@opt_fun,x,[],GS,key,r,k,dc);
alph=[1,x(r+1:r+k)]; beta=x(1:r+1); if key==0, Td=0; end
beta(r+1)=alph(end)*dc; if key==1, Tau=x(end)+Td; else, Tau=0; end
Gr=tf(beta,alph,'ioDelay',Tau);
```

where $G$ and $G_r$ are respectively the original model and the reduced one, and $r$, $k$ for the expected orders in numerator and denominator. The argument key indicates whether delay term is expected in the reduced order model. An internal function for evaluating objective function is also provided.

```
function y=opt_fun(x,G,key,r,k,dc)
ff0=1e10; a=[1,x(r+1:r+k)]; b=x(1:r+1); b(end)=a(end)*dc; g=tf(b,a);
if key==1, tau=x(end);
    if tau<=0, tau=eps; end, [n,d]=pade(tau,3); gP=tf(n,d);
else, gP=1; end
G_e=G-g*gP; G_e.num{1}=[0,G_e.num{1}(1:end-1)];
[y,ierr]=geth2(G_e); if ierr==1, y=10*ff0; else, ff0=y; end
%  sub function geth2
function [v,ierr]=geth2(G)
G=tf(G); num=G.num{1}; den=G.den{1}; ierr=0; v=0; n=length(den);
if abs(num(1))>eps
    disp('System not strictly proper'); ierr=1; return
else, a1=den; b1=num(2:length(num)); end
for k=1:n-1
    if (a1(k+1)<=eps), ierr=1; return
    else,
        aa=a1(k)/a1(k+1); bb=b1(k)/a1(k+1); v=v+bb*bb/aa; k1=k+2;
        for i=k1:2:n-1, a1(i)=a1(i)-aa*a1(i+1); b1(i)=b1(i)-bb*a1(i+1);
end, end, end
v=sqrt(0.5*v);
```

**Example 4.32.** Consider the original model [14]

$$G(s) = \frac{1 + 8.8818s + 29.9339s^2 + 67.087s^3 + 80.3787s^4 + 68.6131s^5}{1 + 7.6194s + 21.7611s^2 + 28.4472s^3 + 16.5609s^4 + 3.5338s^5 + 0.0462s^6},$$

with the following statements, the reduced order model can be obtained

```
>> num=[68.6131,80.3787,67.087,29.9339,8.8818,1];
   den=[0.0462,3.5338,16.5609,28.4472,21.7611,7.6194,1];
   Gr=zpk(opt_app(tf(num,den),2,3,0))
   step(G,Gr,'--'), figure, bode(G,Gr,'--')
```

the optimal reduced model is

$$G_r(s) = \frac{1523.6536(s^2 + 0.3492s + 0.2482)}{(s + 74.85)(s^2 + 3.871s + 5.052)}.$$

The step responses and Bode diagrams comparisons are shown in Fig. 4-16(a) and (b), and it can be seen that the reduced model is very close to the original model.

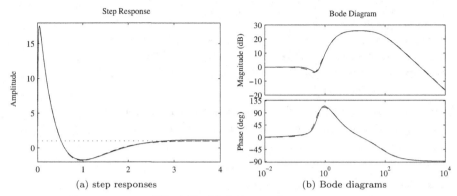

(a) step responses                    (b) Bode diagrams

Fig. 4-16    Model comparisons.

**Example 4.33.** Consider the system model given in [15]

$$G(s) = \frac{432}{(5s+1)(2s+1)(0.7s+1)(s+1)(0.4s+1)},$$

the following MATLAB statements can be used to find the sub-optimal reduced model with a time delay

```
>> den=conv(conv(conv(conv([5 1],[2,1]),[0.7,1]),[1,1]),[0.4,1]);
   G=tf(432,den); Gr=zpk(opt_app(G,0,2,1))
   step(G,Gr,'--'), figure, bode(G,Gr,'--')
```

The reduced model with delay is

$$G_{\mathrm{r}}(s) = \frac{31.4907}{(s+0.3283)(s+0.222)}\mathrm{e}^{-1.5s}.$$

The step responses and Bode diagram comparisons are given in Figs. 4-17(a) and (b), and it can be seen that the fitting is satisfactory.

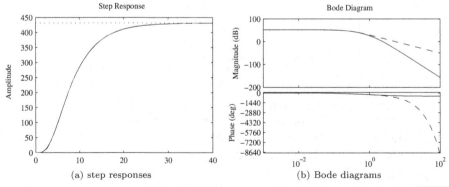

(a) step responses                    (b) Bode diagrams

Fig. 4-17    Model comparisons.

**Example 4.34.** Consider the following non-minimum phase model [13]

$$G(s) = \frac{10s^3 - 60s^2 + 110s + 60}{s^4 + 17s^2 + 82s^2 + 130s + 100}.$$

With sub-optimal reduction method, the following statements can be given

```
>> G=tf([10 -60 110 60],[1 17 82 130 100]);
   Gr=opt_app(G,1,2,1); Gr1=opt_app(G,1,2,0); % with/without delays
   step(G,Gr,'--',Gr1,':'), figure; bode(G,Gr,'--',Gr1,':')
```

The reduced models with and without delays can be obtained as

$$G_r(s) = \frac{2.625s + 1.13}{s^2 + 1.901s + 1.883} e^{-0.698s}, \quad G_{r1}(s) = \frac{0.4701s + 0.8328}{s^2 + 0.5906s + 1.388}.$$

The step responses and Bode diagrams are obtained as shown in Figs. 4-18(a) and (b), and it can be seen that the optimal reduced model with delay neglected the initial oscillation, and in other time period, the fitting is very satisfactory.

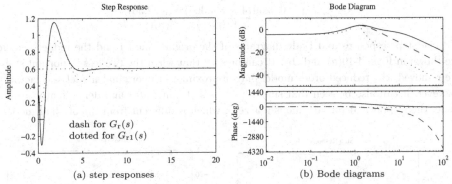

(a) step responses        (b) Bode diagrams

Fig. 4-18   Step response and Bode diagram comparisons.

### 4.5.4   *Reduction Approaches for State Space Models*

#### 1. Balanced realization-based methods

It has been pointed out that the Gramian obtained in balanced realization method may reflect the significance of each state. If the value of a certain Gramian element is much smaller than the rest of the terms, the corresponding state is negligible.

Using matrix partition method, the balanced realization of the original system can be rewritten as

$$\begin{bmatrix} \dot{x}_1 \\ \dot{x}_2 \end{bmatrix} = \begin{bmatrix} A_{11} & A_{12} \\ A_{21} & A_{22} \end{bmatrix} \begin{bmatrix} x_1 \\ x_2 \end{bmatrix} + \begin{bmatrix} B_1 \\ B_2 \end{bmatrix} u, \quad y = \begin{bmatrix} C_1 & C_2 \end{bmatrix} \begin{bmatrix} x_1 \\ x_2 \end{bmatrix} + Du. \quad (4.47)$$

Assuming that the sub state vector $x_2$ is negligible, the original state space model can be rewritten as

$$\begin{cases} \dot{x}_1 = \left( A_{11} - A_{12} A_{22}^{-1} A_{21} \right) x_1 + \left( B_1 - A_{12} A_{22}^{-1} B_2 \right) u \\ y = \left( C_1 - C_2 A_{22}^{-1} A_{21} \right) x_1 + \left( D - C_2 A_{22}^{-1} B_2 \right) u. \end{cases} \quad (4.48)$$

The function `modred()` provided in the Control System Toolbox can be used to solve the reduction problems, and the syntax of the function is

$G_r = \texttt{modred}(G,\texttt{elim})$ , where $G$ is the original model in balance realized form, vector $\texttt{elim}$ is the states to be eliminated, and $G_r$ returns the reduced model.

**Example 4.35.** Consider again the system model in Example 4.27. The following statements can be used to evaluate the Gramian in balanced realization.

```
>> G=tf([1,7,24,24],[1,10,35,50,24]); [G_b,g]=balreal(ss(G))
```

and it is found that $g = [0.5179, 0.0309, 0.0124, 0.0006]^T$. It can be seen that the 3rd and 4th states are negligible. The reduced model can be obtained with the following statements

```
>> G_r=modred(G_b,[3,4]); zpk(G_r)
   step(G,G_r,'--'), figure, bode(G,G_r,'--')
```

with the reduced model

$$G_r(s) = \frac{0.025974(s + 4.307)(s + 22.36)}{(s + 1.078)(s + 2.319)}.$$

The step responses and Bode diagrams of the original model and the reduced model are shown in Figs. 4-19(a) and (b). It can be seen that when the two less important states are removed, the reduced order model may approximate the original model satisfactorily. However, it can also be seen that since the orders of numerator and denominator are the same, the response at initial time is not zero, which is different from the original model.

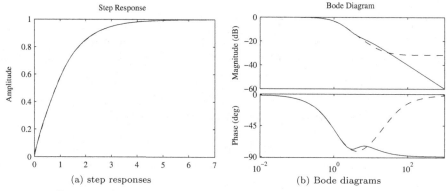

(a) step responses          (b) Bode diagrams

Fig. 4-19   Comparisons of the original model and the reduced model.

## 2. Model reduction with Schur balanced realizations

A Schur balanced realization-based reduction algorithm is implemented in Robust Control Toolbox, with the syntax of $G_r = \texttt{schmr}(G,1,k)$ . The advantages of this function is that it can be used to handle unstable original model $G$.

**Example 4.36.** Consider the original model given in Example 4.32. The Schur reduced model can be obtained with the following statements

```
>> num=[68.6131,80.3787,67.087,29.9339,8.8818,1];
   den=[0.0462,3.5338,16.5609,28.4472,21.7611,7.6194,1];
   G=ss(tf(num,den)); Gh=zpk(schmr(G,1,3))
   step(G,Gh,'--'), figure, bode(G,Gh,'--')
```

with the reduced model

$$G_{\mathrm{r}}(s) = \frac{1485.3076(s^2 + 0.1789s + 0.2601)}{(s + 71.64)(s^2 + 3.881s + 4.188)}.$$

The step response and Bode diagram comparisons are shown in Figs. 4-20(a) and (b), and it can be seen that the fitting is satisfactory, however, they are slightly less accurate, compared with the sub-optimal reduced model.

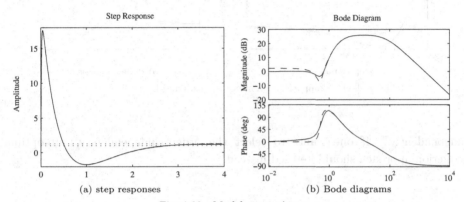

(a) step responses                    (b) Bode diagrams

Fig. 4-20   Model comparisons.

### 3. Optimal Hankel norm reduction approach

A Hankel norm-based optimal reduction is another effective reduction approach[16]. A MATLAB implementation, `ohklmr()`, of such an approach is provided in the Robust Control Toolbox, with the syntax $G_{\mathrm{r}} = \texttt{ohklmr}(G,1,k)$ , where $G$, $G_{\mathrm{r}}$ and $k$ are respectively the original model, reduced model and the expected order of the system.

**Example 4.37.** Consider again the original model given in Example 4.32. A third-order optimal Hankel norm approximation to the system can be obtained with the following statements

```
>> num=[68.6131,80.3787,67.087,29.9339,8.8818,1];
   den=[0.0462,3.5338,16.5609,28.4472,21.7611,7.6194,1];
   G=ss(tf(num,den)); Gh=zpk(ohklmr(G,1,3))
   step(G,Gh,'--'), figure, bode(G,Gh,'--')
```

and the reduced model obtained is

$$G_{\mathrm{r}}(s) = \frac{1527.8048(s^2 + 0.2764s + 0.2892)}{(s + 73.93)(s^2 + 3.855s + 4.585)}.$$

The comparisons of the reduced model and the original one are given in Figs. 4-21(a) and (b), and it can be seen that the quality of the reduced model is close to that of the Schur optimal model.

It can be seen from the examples that the state space reduction method summarized above does not allow the user to choose the order of the numerator

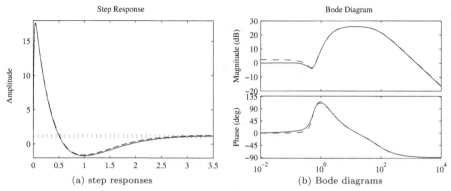

(a) step responses    (b) Bode diagrams

Fig. 4-21    Comparisons of step responses and Bode diagrams.

independently.    If one wants to select the orders independently, sub-optimal reduction approach should be used instead.

### 4.6    Identification of Linear Systems

In the previous sections, it was assumed that the mathematical models are known. In fact, for certain actual systems, the model can be derived with certain physical laws. However, there are also cases where the system models are not known and cannot be derived, not even the structures of the system. In this case, data fitting techniques should be adopted to reconstruct the system models from experimental data. This types of process are also known as system identification.

In actual applications, there are many methods to measure response data from given systems. For instance, one may measure input/output data, or frequency response data. In actual applications, the direct fitting of continuous transfer functions may yield erroneous results due to the non-uniqueness of the fitting results. Alternative methods of fitting discrete-time models can be used instead. Thus, we concentrate on the identification problems of discrete-time systems. One may choose the effective M-sequence to excite the system and acquire data, and to improve the accuracy of identification results.

#### 4.6.1    *Identification of Discrete-time Models*

Similar to the cases described in Section 4.2.1, the discrete-time transfer function can alternatively be written

$$G\left(z^{-1}\right) = \frac{b_1 + b_2 z^{-1} + \cdots + b_m z^{-m+1}}{1 + a_1 z^{-1} + a_2 z^{-2} + \cdots + a_n z^{-n}} z^{-d}, \tag{4.49}$$

and its corresponding difference equation can be written as

$$
\begin{aligned}
y(t) + a_1 y(t-1) + a_2 y(t-2) + \cdots + a_n y(t-n) \\
= b_1 u(t-d) + b_2 u(t-d-1) + \cdots + b_m u(t-d-m+1) + \varepsilon(t),
\end{aligned}
\tag{4.50}
$$

where $\varepsilon(t)$ is the residue signal in identification problems. Here for simplicity, we denote $y(kT)$ by $y(t)$, and $y(t-1)$ represents the output signal $y(t)$ in the last sampling interval. This type of model is also known as the auto-regressive exogenous (ARX) model. Assume that a set of input and output data, $\boldsymbol{u} = \left[ u(1), u(2), \cdots, u(M) \right]^{\mathrm{T}}$, and $\boldsymbol{y} = \left[ y(1), y(2), \cdots, y(M) \right]^{\mathrm{T}}$, are measured. From Eqn. (4.50), it can be seen that

$$
y(1) = -a_1 y(0) - \cdots - a_n y(1-n) + b_1 u(1-d) + \cdots + b_m u(2-m-d) + \varepsilon(1)
$$
$$
y(2) = -a_1 y(1) - \cdots - a_n y(2-n) + b_1 u(2-d) + \cdots + b_m u(3-m-d) + \varepsilon(2)
$$
$$
\vdots
$$
$$
y(M) = -a_1 y(M-1) - \cdots - a_n y(M-n) + b_1 u(M-d)
$$
$$
+ \cdots + b_m u(M+1-m-d) + \varepsilon(M),
$$

where the initial values of $y(t)$ and $u(t)$ are assumed to be zero, for $t \leqslant 0$. Matrix form of the equation can be written as

$$
\boldsymbol{y} = \boldsymbol{\Phi} \boldsymbol{\theta} + \boldsymbol{\varepsilon},
\tag{4.51}
$$

where

$$
\boldsymbol{\Phi} =
\begin{bmatrix}
y(0) & \cdots & y(1-n) & u(1-d) & \cdots & u(2-m-d) \\
y(1) & \cdots & y(2-n) & u(2-d) & \cdots & u(3-m-d) \\
\vdots & & \vdots & \vdots & & \vdots \\
y(M-1) & \cdots & y(M-n) & u(M-d) & \cdots & u(M+1-m-d)
\end{bmatrix},
\tag{4.52}
$$

$$
\boldsymbol{\theta}^{\mathrm{T}} = \left[ -a_1, -a_2, \cdots, -a_n, b_1, \cdots, b_m \right], \quad \boldsymbol{\varepsilon}^{\mathrm{T}} = \left[ \varepsilon(1), \cdots, \varepsilon(M) \right].
\tag{4.53}
$$

In order to minimize the squared values of the residue, i.e., $\min_{\boldsymbol{\theta}} \sum_{i=1}^{M} \varepsilon^2(i)$, the optimum estimation of the determined parameter vector $\boldsymbol{\theta}$ can be written as

$$
\boldsymbol{\theta} = \left[ \boldsymbol{\Phi}^{\mathrm{T}} \boldsymbol{\Phi} \right]^{-1} \boldsymbol{\Phi}^{\mathrm{T}} \boldsymbol{y}.
\tag{4.54}
$$

Since the method minimizes the squared value of the residue, this kind of method is also known as least squares method.

Various MATLAB functions are provided in the System Identification Toolbox, among them, ARX model identification method can be implemented with `arx()` function. For given input data vector $\boldsymbol{u}$ and output vector $\boldsymbol{y}$, if one select the orders of numerator and denominator, and also the delay constant $d$, the function can be called with the syntax $T = \texttt{arx([y,u],[n,m,d])}$, where the identification result can be returned in a variable $T$, whose $T.B$ and $T.A$ members represents the numerator and denominator of the identified system. An illustrative example is given below to show the identification process of the discrete-time systems.

**Example 4.38.** Assume that the measured data of input and output signals are given in Table 4-1. Selecting the orders of numerator and denominator as 3 and 4, the discrete-time model can be obtained

Table 4-1   Measured input and output data.

| $t$ | $u(t)$ | $y(t)$ | $t$ | $u(t)$ | $y(t)$ | $t$ | $u(t)$ | $y(t)$ |
|-----|--------|--------|-----|--------|--------|-----|--------|--------|
| 0 | 1.4601 | 0 | 1.6 | 1.4483 | 16.411 | 3.2 | 1.056 | 11.871 |
| 0.1 | 0.8849 | 0 | 1.7 | 1.4335 | 14.336 | 3.3 | 1.4454 | 13.857 |
| 0.2 | 1.1854 | 8.7606 | 1.8 | 1.0282 | 15.746 | 3.4 | 1.0727 | 14.694 |
| 0.3 | 1.0887 | 13.194 | 1.9 | 1.4149 | 18.118 | 3.5 | 1.0349 | 17.866 |
| 0.4 | 1.413 | 17.41 | 2 | 0.7463 | 17.784 | 3.6 | 1.3769 | 17.654 |
| 0.5 | 1.3096 | 17.636 | 2.1 | 0.9822 | 18.81 | 3.7 | 1.1201 | 16.639 |
| 0.6 | 1.0651 | 18.763 | 2.2 | 1.3505 | 15.309 | 3.8 | 0.8621 | 17.107 |
| 0.7 | 0.7148 | 18.53 | 2.3 | 0.7078 | 13.7 | 3.9 | 1.2377 | 16.537 |
| 0.8 | 1.3571 | 17.041 | 2.4 | 0.8111 | 14.818 | 4 | 1.3704 | 14.643 |
| 0.9 | 1.0557 | 13.415 | 2.5 | 0.8622 | 13.235 | 4.1 | 0.7157 | 15.086 |
| 1 | 1.1923 | 14.454 | 2.6 | 0.8589 | 12.299 | 4.2 | 1.245 | 16.806 |
| 1.1 | 1.3335 | 14.59 | 2.7 | 1.183 | 11.6 | 4.3 | 1.0035 | 14.764 |
| 1.2 | 1.4374 | 16.11 | 2.8 | 0.9177 | 11.607 | 4.4 | 1.3654 | 15.498 |
| 1.3 | 1.2905 | 17.685 | 2.9 | 0.859 | 13.766 | 4.5 | 1.1022 | 14.679 |
| 1.4 | 0.841 | 19.498 | 3 | 0.7122 | 14.195 | 4.6 | 1.2675 | 16.655 |
| 1.5 | 1.0245 | 19.593 | 3.1 | 1.2974 | 13.763 | 4.7 | 1.0431 | 16.63 |

```
>> u=[1.4601,0.8849,1.1854,1.0887,1.413,1.3096,1.0651,0.7148,1.3571,...
      1.0557,1.1923,1.3335,1.4374,1.2905,0.841,1.0245,1.4483,1.4335,...
      1.0282,1.4149,0.7463,0.9822,1.3505,0.7078,0.8111,0.8622,0.8589,...
      1.183,0.9177,0.859,0.7122,1.2974,1.056,1.4454,1.0727,1.0349,...
      1.3769,1.1201,0.8621,1.2377,1.3704,0.7157,1.245,1.0035,1.3654,...
      1.1022,1.2675,1.0431]';
   y=[0,0,8.7606,13.1939,17.41,17.6361,18.7627,18.5296,17.0414,13.4154,...
      14.4539,14.59,16.1104,17.6853,19.4981,19.5935,16.4106,14.3359,...
      15.7463,18.1179,17.784,18.8104,15.3086,13.7004,14.8178,13.2354,...
      12.2993,11.6001,11.6074,13.7662,14.195,13.763,11.8713,13.8566,...
      14.6944,17.8659,17.6543,16.6386,17.1071,16.5373,14.643,15.0862,...
      16.8058,14.7641,15.4976,14.679,16.6552,16.6301]';
   t1=arx([y,u],[4,4,1])
```

The identification results are displayed as

```
Discrete-time IDPOLY model: A(q)y(t) = B(q)u(t) + e(t)
A(q) = 1 - q^-1 + 0.25 q^-2 + 0.25 q^-3 - 0.125 q^-4
B(q) = 4.83e-008 q^-1 + 6 q^-2 - 0.5999 q^-3 - 0.1196 q^-4
Estimated using ARX
Loss function 7.09262e-010 and FPE 9.92966e-010
Sampling interval: 1
```

It can be seen from the above results that

$$G\left(z^{-1}\right) = \frac{4.83 \times 10^{-8}q^{-1} + 6q^{-2} - 0.5999q^{-3} - 0.1196q^{-4}}{1 - q^{-1} + 0.25q^{-2} + 0.25q^{-3} - 0.125q^{-4}},$$

and it can also be equivalently written as

$$H(z) = \frac{4.83 \times 10^{-8}z^3 + 6z^2 - 0.5999z - 0.1196}{z^4 - z^3 + 0.25z^2 + 0.25z - 0.125}.$$

In fact, the measured data was generated from the model given in Example 4.8. It can be seen that the identified model is quire close to the original model. Also, since the information of sampling interval was not specified, the default value of 1 is meaningless. The following statements should be used to identify the model

```
>> U=iddata(y,u,0.1);   % define the sampling interval 0.1
   T=arx(U,[4,4,1]); H=tf(T); G=H(1)   % identification
```

and the result of identification is

$$G(z) = \frac{4.83 \times 10^{-8}z^3 + 6z^2 - 0.5999z - 0.1196}{z^4 - z^3 + 0.25z^2 + 0.25z - 0.125}, \quad \text{with } T_s = 0.1\text{s}.$$

The identified models directly retrieved with tf() function are, in fact, transfer function matrix with two inputs. The first model is the one we expect, while the second one is the transfer function from input signal to the error signal $\varepsilon(k)$. signal, and should be neglected.

The system model can also be identified by low-level commands, based on Eqn. (4.52) and Eqn. (4.54), and almost the same results can be obtained

```
>> Phi=[[0;y(1:end-1)] [0;0;y(1:end-2)],...
       [0;0;0; y(1:end-3)] [0;0;0;0;y(1:end-4)],...
       [0;u(1:end-1)] [0;0;u(1:end-2)],...
       [0;0;0; u(1:end-3)] [0;0;0;0;u(1:end-4)]]; % construct Φ
   T=Phi\y; T' % identification result with Φ\y
   Gd=tf(ans(5:8),[1,-ans(1:4)],'Ts',0.1) % reconstruct the system model
```

The new identification result is

$$G_\mathrm{d}(z) = \frac{-5.824 \times 10^{-7}z^3 + 6z^2 - 0.5999z - 0.1196}{z^4 - z^3 + 0.25z^2 + 0.25z - 0.125}.$$

If the sequence $u$ is used to excite the identified transfer function, with lsim() function provided in Control System Toolbox, the response can be superimposed on the original data, as shown in Fig. 4-22. It can be seen that the identified model is very close to the original data.

```
>> t=0:0.1:4.7; lsim(Gd,u,t); hold on; plot(t,y,'o')
```

A graphical user interface is provided in the System Identification Toolbox, to visualize the identification process. One may enter ident command to invoke the interface. A graphical window shown in Fig. 4-23 is displayed. To identify a system, the measured data should be entered first, by clicking the Time-Domain Data item from Import Data column. The dialog box shown in Fig. 4-24(a) is displayed. One

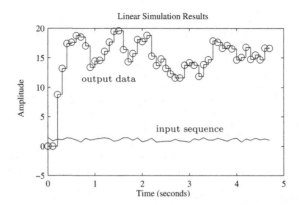

Fig. 4-22  Comparisons of identified model and the original data.

can enter the input and output data in the Input and Output columns respectively, and click Import button to complete data entry process.

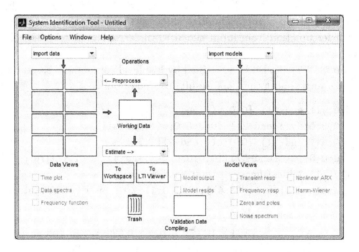

Fig. 4-23  Graphical user interface for system identification.

If one wants to identify the ARX model, the Estimate list box should be clicked, from which the item Parametric Models should be chosen. The dialog box shown in Fig. 4-24(b) can be displayed to allow the user to specify the orders. Then one may click the Estimate button to initiate the identification process, and the same results can be obtained.

### 4.6.2  *Order Selection in Identification*

In the previous examples, the orders of the identified models were assigned. The problem now is how to select the orders of the identified models such that good

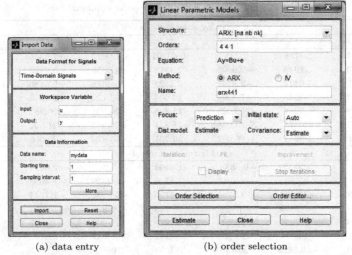

(a) data entry          (b) order selection

Fig. 4-24   Identification parameter setting dialog box.

fitting can be achieved. Akaike's information criterion (AIC) is a practical criterion for order selection, and it is defined as[17, 18]

$$\text{AIC} = \lg \left\{ \det \left[ \frac{1}{M} \sum_{i=1}^{M} \epsilon(i, \boldsymbol{\theta}) \epsilon^T(i, \boldsymbol{\theta}) \right] \right\} + \frac{k}{M}, \tag{4.55}$$

where $M$ is the number of measurement points, $\boldsymbol{\theta}$ is the undetermined parameter vector, and $k$ is the number of parameters to be identified. MATLAB function `v = aic(H)` provided in System Identification Toolbox can be used to evaluate AIC value $v$ from the identified model $H$, which is the IDPOLY object obtained directly from `arx()` function. If the AIC value is small, e.g., it is smaller than $-20$, the order combination $n, m, d$ can be regarded as suitable order selection.

**Example 4.39.** Consider again the identification problem in Example 4.38. It can be seen from Table 4-1 that under the given input signal, the output is nonzero from the 3rd step. Thus, the delay constant $d$ should not exceed 2. Thus, the cases for $d = 0, 1, 2$ should be explored. The following loop structure can be used to calculate AIC values for all possible order combinations, and the AIC values are obtained as shown in Table 4-2.

```
>> U=iddata(y,u,0.1);   % where 0.1 is the sampling interval
   for n=1:7, for m=1:7
       T=arx(U,[n,m,0]); TAic0(n,m)=aic(T);
       T=arx(U,[n,m,1]); TAic1(n,m)=aic(T);
       T=arx(U,[n,m,2]); TAic2(n,m)=aic(T);
   end, end
```

In the table, we used shaded items for those whose AIC values lower than $-20$. It can be seen that the three order combinations, namely, $(4, 5, 0)$, $(4, 4, 1)$ and $(4, 3, 2)$, are suitable ones, and the corresponding models are

$$H_{4,5,0}\left(z^{-1}\right) = \frac{-2.114 \times 10^{-5} + 3.09 \times 10^{-6} z^{-1} + 6z^{-2} - 0.5999z^{-3} - 0.1196z^{-4}}{1 - z^{-1} + 0.25z^{-2} + 0.25z^{-3} - 0.125z^{-4}},$$

Table 4-2    AIC values for different order combinations.

| | | | delay constant $d = 0$ | | | |
|---|---|---|---|---|---|---|
| $n$ | $m = 1$ | 2 | 3 | 4 | 5 | 6 | 7 |
| 1 | 1.3487 | 1.3738 | −0.23458 | −0.63291 | −1.0077 | −1.5346 | −2.61 |
| 2 | 1.2382 | 1.1949 | −2.0995 | −2.3513 | −4.9058 | −5.2429 | −7.4246 |
| 3 | 1.0427 | 1.0427 | −2.8743 | −3.4523 | −5.4678 | −5.6186 | −7.7328 |
| 4 | 1.0223 | 1.0345 | −7.8505 | −10.504 | −20.729 | −20.942 | −20.946 |
| 5 | 1.0079 | 1.0287 | −10.025 | −13.396 | −20.941 | −20.982 | −21.002 |
| 6 | 1.0293 | 1.0575 | −13.658 | −18.931 | −20.944 | −21.002 | −21.125 |
| 7 | 0.98503 | 1.0261 | −16.607 | −20.701 | −20.976 | −20.996 | −21.088 |
| | | | delay constant $d = 1$ | | | |
| 1 | 1.484 | −0.25541 | −0.66303 | −1.0494 | −1.57 | −2.6414 | −3.4085 |
| 2 | 1.346 | −2.1263 | −2.3685 | −4.9326 | −5.2359 | −7.4658 | −7.6678 |
| 3 | 1.0658 | −2.8886 | −3.4758 | −5.4795 | −5.6407 | −7.7744 | −7.9316 |
| 4 | 1.0329 | −7.8839 | −10.53 | −20.733 | −20.973 | −20.984 | −20.9737 |
| 5 | 1.0043 | −10.034 | −13.406 | −20.971 | −21.002 | −21.037 | −21.0356 |
| 6 | 1.023 | −13.694 | −18.965 | −20.982 | −21.037 | −21.148 | −21.1105 |
| 7 | 0.9909 | −16.6423 | −20.7387 | −21.0160 | −21.0324 | −21.1105 | −21.1115 |
| | | | delay constant $d = 2$ | | | |
| 1 | −0.29215 | −0.70464 | −1.0849 | −1.6057 | −2.6827 | −3.415 | −3.5863 |
| 2 | −2.1672 | −2.4101 | −4.9737 | −5.2763 | −7.477 | −7.7083 | −10.2034 |
| 3 | −2.929 | −3.5109 | −5.5163 | −5.6663 | −7.8124 | −7.9722 | −10.5894 |
| 4 | −7.9075 | −10.57 | −20.775 | −21.013 | −21.026 | −21.015 | −20.9850 |
| 5 | −10.07 | −13.438 | −21.011 | −21.036 | −21.079 | −21.077 | −21.0617 |
| 6 | −13.71 | −18.991 | −21.023 | −21.078 | −21.184 | −21.149 | −21.164wee6 |
| 7 | −16.6792 | −20.7794 | −21.0574 | −21.0736 | −21.1488 | −21.1444 | −21.1393 |

$$H_{4,4,1}\left(z^{-1}\right) = \frac{4.83 \times 10^{-8} z^{-1} + 6z^{-2} - 0.5999 z^{-3} - 0.1196 z^{-4}}{1 - z^{-1} + 0.25 z^{-2} + 0.25 z^{-3} - 0.125 z^{-4}},$$

$$H_{4,3,2}\left(z^{-1}\right) = \frac{6z^{-2} - 0.5999 z^{-3} - 0.1196 z^{-4}}{1 - z^{-1} + 0.25 z^{-2} + 0.25 z^{-3} - 0.125 z^{-4}}.$$

If the order combination $(5, 5, 0)$ is selected, the following model can be obtained

$$H_{5,5,0}\left(z^{-1}\right) = \frac{-1.074 \times 10^{-5} - 2.343 \times 10^{-6} z^{-1} + 6z^{-2} - 0.6166 z^{-3} - 0.1182 z^{-4}}{1 - 1.003 z^{-1} + 0.2528 z^{-2} + 0.2492 z^{-3} - 0.1256 z^{-4} + 0.0003231 z^{-5}}.$$

It can be seen from the result that a very small $z^{-5}$ term is introduced, while the other terms are very close to those in $H_{4,5,0}\left(z^{-1}\right)$ model. Thus, it is normally not necessary to choose such high orders. Besides, the AIC values of $H_{5,5,0}\left(z^{-1}\right)$ did not show significant improvement to $H_{4,5,0}\left(z^{-1}\right)$ model, thus a lower order combination should be adopted. In this problem, the order combination of $(4, 4, 1)$ can be regarded as the desired one.

### 4.6.3   *Generation of Signals for Identification*

From the previous example, it can be seen that a set of 48 input point was generated, and the set of data was used to drive the system to find the output data. Then these data can be used to identify the original system model. Sometimes there may exist errors in the identification results.

Pseudo-random binary sequence (PRBS, also known as M-sequence) is a class of effective input signal suitable for the identification of linear control systems. PRBS signal can be generated with the `idinput()` function provided in System Identification Toolbox, with the syntax of $u = $ `idinput(`$k$`,'prbs')` , where the length of the sequence is given by $k = 2^n - 1$, for integer $n$. PRBS signal generation and its use in system identification is demonstrated through examples.

**Example 4.40.** A set of 63 points of PRBS signal can be generated directly with `idinput()` function, and the PRBS sequence can be generated.

```
>> u=idinput(63,'PRBS'); t=[0:.1:6.2]';          % generate PRBS sequence
   stairs(u), set(gca,'XLim',[0,63],'YLim',[-1.1 1.1]) % draw PRBS signal
   figure; crosscorr(u,u)                         % autocorrelation function
```

The PRBS waveform is shown in Fig. 4-25(a). The function `crosscorr(`$x$`,`$y$`)` can be used to draw cross-correlation of the signals $x$ and $y$, and `crosscorr(`$x$`,`$x$`)` can be used to draw the autocorrelation function of the signal $x$. The autocorrelation function of PRBS sequence is obtained as shown in Fig. 4-25(b), and it can be seen that the signal can be regarded as an independent signal.

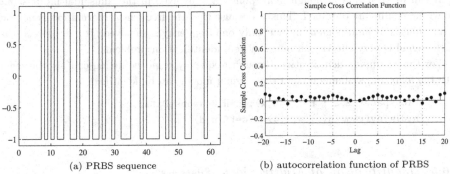

(a) PRBS sequence    (b) autocorrelation function of PRBS

Fig. 4-25   PRBS sequence and its characteristics.

### 4.6.4   *Identification of Continuous Systems*

There are also many methods for the identification of linear continuous systems. For instance, the frequency response-based algorithm by Levy can be used to identify linear continuous, however the result it identified may not be unique, and sometimes it may fail to find correct model[19]. Thus, indirect identification method can be considered, i.e., identify the discrete-time model first, then convert it back to continuous models.

**Example 4.41.** Assume that for the continuous model of

$$G(s) = \frac{s^3 + 7s^2 + 11s + 5}{s^4 + 7s^3 + 21s^2 + 37s + 30}.$$

If one selects the sampling interval of $T = 0.1\,$s, PRBS sequence with 31 points can be generated to excite the original system and the output of the system can be obtained.

With the data, the continuous system can be identified in indirect way, and it is exactly the same as the original model.

```
>> G=tf([1,7,11,5],[1,7,21,37,30]);     % original model
   t=[0:.2:6]'; u=idinput(31,'PRBS');  % generate PRBS signal
   y=lsim(G,u,t);  % compute the output signal with lsim
   U=arx([y u],[4 4 1]);  % identify the discrete-time model
   G1=tf(U); G1=G1(1); G1.Ts=0.2; G2=d2c(G1) % convert to continuous model
```

Now consider to use 81 points of sinusoidal signal to excite the system, the following statements can be used and erroneous identification results can be obtained.

```
>> t=[0:.1:8]'; u=sin(t);   % generate sinusoidal signal
   y=lsim(G,u,t);           % evaluate the output signal
   U=arx([y u],[4 4 1]);    % identify the discrete-time model
   G1=tf(U); G1=G1(1); G1.Ts=0.1; G2=d2c(G1) % conversion to continuous model
```

The identified model is

$$G(s) = \frac{0.01361s^3 - 0.06793s^2 + 9.897s - 2.564}{s^4 + 7s^3 + 21s^2 + 37s + 30}.$$

It can be seen that although more points are involved in the sinusoidal input signal, the wrong results are obtained. This is because that the frequency information is not rich in the sinusoidal input signal, in fact, only one frequency is involved. It can be seen that PRBS signal is very effective in linear system identification problems.

For this example, identification through frequency response fitting can also be made, with the following statements, and the original model can be identified.

```
>> w=logspace(-2,2); H=frd(G,w); h=H.ResponseData;
   [n,d]=invfreqs(h(:),w,4,4); Gd=tf(n,d)
```

### 4.6.5   *Identification of Multivariable Systems*

The MATLAB function arx() can be used directly in the identification of multivariable systems with $q$ inputs and $p$ outputs. The typical difference equation of multivariable models can be expressed as

$$A\left(z^{-1}\right) y(t) = B\left(z^{-1}\right) u(t - d) + \varepsilon(t), \tag{4.56}$$

where $d$ is the delay matrix, $A\left(z^{-1}\right)$ and $B\left(z^{-1}\right)$ are $p \times q$ polynomial matrices

$$\begin{cases} A\left(z^{-1}\right) = I_{p \times q} + A_1 z^{-1} + \cdots + A_{n_a} z^{-n_a} \\ B\left(z^{-1}\right) = I_{p \times q} + B_1 z^{-1} + \cdots + B_{n_b} z^{-n_b}. \end{cases} \tag{4.57}$$

**Example 4.42.** Assume that a discrete-time transfer function matrix is given by

$$G(z) = \begin{bmatrix} \dfrac{0.5234z - 0.1235}{z^2 + 0.8864z + 0.4352} & \dfrac{3z + 0.69}{z^2 + 1.084z + 0.3974} \\ \dfrac{1.2z - 0.54}{z^2 + 1.764z + 0.9804} & \dfrac{3.4z - 1.469}{z^2 + 0.24z + 0.2848} \end{bmatrix}.$$

If the two input channels are excited by two different PRBS sequences, the output signals can be generated. Based on the input, output data, the transfer function matrix can be identified.

```
>> u1=idinput(31,'PRBS'); t=0:.1:3;
   u2=u1(end:-1:1); % generate two sets of PRBS sequences
   g11=tf([0.5234, -0.1235],[1, 0.8864, 0.4352],'Ts',0.1);
   g12=tf([3, 0.69],[1, 1.084, 0.3974],'Ts',0.1);
   g21=tf([1.2, -0.54],[1, 1.764, 0.9804],'Ts',0.1);
   g22=tf([3.4, 1.469],[1, 0.24, 0.2848],'Ts',0.1);
   G=[g11, g12; g21, g22];  % transfer function matrix
   y=lsim(G,[u1 u2],t);       % compute the output sequences
   na=4*ones(2); nb=na; nc=ones(2); U=iddata(y,[u1,u2],0.1);
   T=arx(U,[na nb nc])
```

The $g_{11}(z)$ sub transfer function can be extracted such that

```
>> H=tf(T); g11=H(1,1) % extract sub transfer function g11(z)
```

With the above commands, the sub transfer function is

$$g_{11}(z) = \frac{\begin{array}{l}0.5234z^{11}+1.493z^{10} + 1.847z^9 +1.235z^8 +0.5004z^7 +0.09574z^6 -0.01551z^5 \\ -0.0137z^4 -1.683\times10^{-16}z^3 -3.582\times10^{-17}z^2 -4\times10^{-18}z+5.362\times10^{-19}\end{array}}{z^{12} + 3.974z^{11} + 7.431z^{10} + 8.483z^9 + 6.585z^8 + 3.611z^7 + 1.401z^6}.$$

Minimum realization should be adopted to simplify the identified results. The minimum realized transfer function matrix is very close to the original system.

```
>> G11=minreal(g11,1e-4) % a relatively large tolerance is used
```

### 4.6.6  Least Squares Recursive Identification

The identification methods discussed previously are off-line ones, since the input and output data should be acquired first before identification problems are solved. This kind of methods may not be suitable for real-time control systems. In actual control systems, one may also identify the system model using the current input and output data, using recursive identification methods.

The difference equation of the discrete-time system is

$$y(t) + a_1 y(t-1) + \cdots + a_m y(t-m) = b_1 u(t-d) + b_2 u(t-1-d) + \cdots + b_r u(t-r-d+1), \tag{4.58}$$

and the corresponding transfer function model can be written as

$$G\left(z^{-1}\right) = \frac{b_1 + b_2 z^{-1} + \cdots + b_{r-1}z^{2-r} + b_r z^{1-r}}{1 + a_1 z^{-1} + \cdots + a_{m-1}z^{1-m} + a_m z^{-m}} z^{-d}, \tag{4.59}$$

where $r$ and $m$ are respectively the orders of numerator and denominator of the system, and $d$ is the time delay constant. These values should be selected before the identification process.

From Eqn. (4.59), the original difference equation can be rewritten as

$$
\begin{aligned}
y(t+1) &= -a_1 y(t) - \cdots - a_m y(t-m+1) + b_1 u(t-d+1) \\
&\quad + b_2 u(t-d) + \cdots + b_r u(t-r-d+2) + \varepsilon(t) \\
&= \boldsymbol{\psi}_{n+1}^{\mathrm{T}} \boldsymbol{\theta} + \varepsilon(t),
\end{aligned}
\tag{4.60}
$$

where the parameter vector to identify is

$$
\boldsymbol{\theta}^{\mathrm{T}} = \begin{bmatrix} a_1, a_2, \cdots, a_m, b_1, b_2, \cdots, b_r \end{bmatrix},
\tag{4.61}
$$

and the vector composed of input and output information can be established

$$
\boldsymbol{\psi}_{n+1}^{\mathrm{T}} = \begin{bmatrix} -y(n), \cdots, -y(n-m+1), u(n-d+1), \cdots, u(n-r-d+2) \end{bmatrix}.
\tag{4.62}
$$

The target of system identification is to estimate the coefficients of the system. The procedures of the least squares recursive identification algorithm are:

(1) Let $n = 0$. Select an initial parameter vector $\boldsymbol{\theta}_0$ and an initial weighting matrix $\boldsymbol{P}_0$. Normally, one may select the initial weighting matrix as $\boldsymbol{P}_0 = \alpha^2 \boldsymbol{I}$, where $\alpha$ should be a relatively large constant[20], and $\boldsymbol{I}$ is an identity matrix.

(2) Update the data vector with new input and output data

$$
\boldsymbol{\psi}_{n+1}^{\mathrm{T}} = \begin{bmatrix} -y_n, \cdots, -y_{n-m+1}, u_{n-d}, \cdots, u_{n-d-m+1} \end{bmatrix}.
\tag{4.63}
$$

(3) Update the parameters and intermediate variables recursively from[20]

$$
\boldsymbol{K} = \frac{\boldsymbol{P}_n \boldsymbol{\psi}_{n+1}}{\lambda + \boldsymbol{\psi}_{n+1}^{\mathrm{T}} \boldsymbol{P}_n \boldsymbol{\psi}_{n+1}}
\tag{4.64}
$$

$$
\boldsymbol{P}_{n+1} = \frac{1}{\lambda} \left( \boldsymbol{P}_n - \boldsymbol{K} \boldsymbol{\psi}_{n+1} \boldsymbol{P}_n \right)
\tag{4.65}
$$

$$
\hat{\boldsymbol{\theta}}_{n+1} = \hat{\boldsymbol{\theta}}_n + \boldsymbol{K} \left( y_{n+1} - \boldsymbol{\psi}_{n+1}^{\mathrm{T}} \hat{\boldsymbol{\theta}}_n \right),
\tag{4.66}
$$

where $\boldsymbol{K}$ is the intermediate matrix, $\lambda$ is referred to as the forgetting factor, and $0 \leqslant \lambda \leqslant 1$. If $\lambda = 1$, all the past data should be processed equally.

(4) Let $n = n+1$, then go to step (3), to dynamically identify the system.

The above algorithm can easily be implemented with MATLAB. However, since the algorithm is useful only in on-line control, it is better to implement the algorithm with S-function in Simulink. This will be demonstrated in Chapter 6.

## 4.7  Problems

(1) Enter the following transfer functions into MATLAB workspace

(i) $G(s) = \dfrac{s^2 + 5s + 6}{\left[ (s+1)^2 + 1 \right](s+2)(s+4)}$,

(ii) $H(z) = \dfrac{5(z - 0.2)^2}{z(z - 0.4)(z - 1)(z - 0.9) + 0.6}$, $T = 0.1\,\text{s}$.

(2) Represent the following ordinary differential equations in MATLAB

(i) $y^{(3)}(t) + 10\ddot{y}(t) + 32\dot{y}(t) + 32y(t) = 6u^{(3)}(t) + 4\ddot{u}(t) + 2u(t) + 2\dot{u}(t),$

(ii) $y^{(3)}(t) + 10\ddot{y}(t) + 32\dot{y}(t) + 32y(t) = 6u^{(3)}(t-4) + 4\ddot{u}(t-4) + 2u(t-4) + 2\dot{u}(t-4).$

What are the poles and zeros of the systems? Is it possible to write the transfer functions models directly from the differential equations?

(3) Assume that the system model is described by the following ODE

$$\begin{cases} \dot{x}_1(t) = -x_1(t) + x_2(t) \\ \dot{x}_2(t) = -x_2(t) - 3x_3(t) + u_1(t) \qquad \text{and} \quad y = -x_2(t) + u_1(t) - 5u_2(t), \\ \dot{x}_3(t) = -x_1(t) - 5x_2(t) - 3x_3(t) + u_2(t), \end{cases}$$

where $u_1(t)$ and $u_2(t)$ are input signals. Express such a system in MATLAB workspace and find out the transfer function matrix model.

(4) Express the following difference equations in MATLAB. Assume that the sampling interval is $T = 0.1\,\text{s}$.

(i) $y(k+2) + 1.4y(k+1) + 0.16y(k) = u(k-1) + 2u(k-2),$

(ii) $y(k-2) + 1.4y(k-1) + 0.16y(k) = u(k-1) + 2u(k-2).$

(5) Enter the following zero–pole gain model into MATLAB workspace

(i) $G(s) = \dfrac{8(s+1-j)(s+1+j)}{s^2(s+5)(s+6)(s^2+1)},$

(ii) $H(z^{-1}) = \dfrac{(z^{-1}+3.2)(z^{-1}+2.6)}{z^{-5}(z^{-1}-8.2)}, \quad T = 0.05\,\text{s}.$

(6) Enter the following state space model into MATLAB environment and find the equivalent transfer function model and zero–pole–gain model.

$$\dot{x}(t) = \begin{bmatrix} 1 & 2 & 3 \\ 4 & 5 & 6 \\ 7 & 8 & 0 \end{bmatrix} x(t) + \begin{bmatrix} 4 \\ 3 \\ 2 \end{bmatrix} u, \quad y = [\,1, 2, 3\,] x(t).$$

(7) Find the overall model under the typical feedback control structure. For numeric models, find the state space models and zero–pole–gain models.

(i) $G(s) = \dfrac{211.87s + 317.64}{(s+20)(s+94.34)(s+0.17)}, \quad G_c(s) = \dfrac{169.6s + 400}{s(s+4)}, \quad H(s) = \dfrac{1}{0.01s + 1},$

(ii) $G(z^{-1}) = \dfrac{35786.7z^{-1} + 108444}{(z^{-1}+4)(z^{-1}+20)(z^{-1}+74)}, \quad G_c(z^{-1}) = \dfrac{1}{z^{-1}-1},$

$H(z^{-1}) = \dfrac{1}{0.5z^{-1}-1}.$

(8) Find the closed-loop system model from the typical feedback control system

$$G(s) = \dfrac{K_m J}{Js^2 + Bs + K_r}, \quad G_c(s) = \dfrac{L_q}{L_q s + R_q}, \quad H(s) = sK_v.$$

(9) Assume that the plant and PID controller models are

$$G(s) = \dfrac{10}{(s+1)^3}, \quad G_{\text{PID}}(s) = 0.48\left(1 + \dfrac{1}{1.814s} + 0.4353s\right),$$

under unity negative feedback. Express the system model in MATLAB workspace and find all the closed-loop poles.

(10)  For double input, double output system given by

$$\dot{x}(t) = \begin{bmatrix} 2.25 & -5 & -1.25 & -0.5 \\ 2.25 & -4.25 & -1.25 & -0.25 \\ 0.25 & -0.5 & -1.25 & -1 \\ 1.25 & -1.75 & -0.25 & -0.75 \end{bmatrix} x(t) + \begin{bmatrix} 4 & 6 \\ 2 & 4 \\ 2 & 2 \\ 0 & 2 \end{bmatrix} u(t), \quad y(t) = \begin{bmatrix} 0 & 0 & 0 & 1 \\ 0 & 2 & 0 & 2 \end{bmatrix} x(t).$$

Enter the model into MATLAB workspace, and find the transfer function matrix. If sampling interval $T = 0.1\,$s, find the discrete-time transfer function matrix. Try to convert the model back to its original form and check the accuracy.

(11)  Assume that the multivariable plant and controller are given by

$$G(s) = \begin{bmatrix} \dfrac{-0.252}{(1+3.3s)^3(1+1800s)} & \dfrac{0.43}{(1+12s)(1+1800s)} \\ \dfrac{-0.0435}{(1+25.3s)^3(1+360s)} & \dfrac{0.097}{(1+12s)(1+360s)} \end{bmatrix}, \quad G_c(s) = \begin{bmatrix} -10 & 77.5 \\ 0 & 50 \end{bmatrix}.$$

Enter the model into MATLAB workspace and find the transfer function matrix model under unity negative feedback structure.

(12)  For the multivariable feedback control system with pre-decoupler

$$G(s) = \begin{bmatrix} \dfrac{-0.2e^{-s}}{7s+1} & \dfrac{1.3e^{-0.3s}}{7s+1} \\ \dfrac{-2.8se^{-1.8s}}{9.5s+1} & \dfrac{4.3e^{-0.35s}}{9.2s+1} \end{bmatrix}, \quad Q(s) = \begin{bmatrix} 1 & 6.5 \\ \dfrac{2.8(9.2s+1)e^{-1.45s}}{4.3(9.5s+1)} & e^{-0.7s} \end{bmatrix}.$$

If the multivariable PID controller is[21]

$$G_c(s) = \begin{bmatrix} 0.2612 + \dfrac{0.1339}{s} - 1.8748s & -0.0767 - \dfrac{0.0322}{s} + 0.7804s \\ 0.1540 + \dfrac{0.0872}{s} - 1.1404s & -0.0072 - \dfrac{0.0050}{s} + 0.1264s \end{bmatrix}.$$

and the system is with unity negative feedback structure, please find the closed-loop model.

(13)  Assume that the system structure is shown in Fig. 4-26. Derive the overall model from the input $r(t)$ to the output signal $y(t)$.

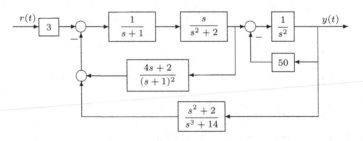

Fig. 4-26   System structure for Problem (13).

(14) Assume that a system model is shown in Fig. 4-27, derive the overall system model from input signal $r(t)$ to output signal $y(t)$.

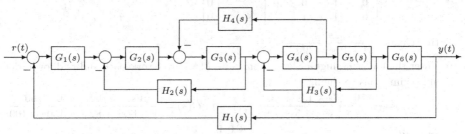

Fig. 4-27 System structure of Problem (14).

(15) A DC motor drive system is shown in Fig. 4-28. Find the overall model and find the equivalent state space model.

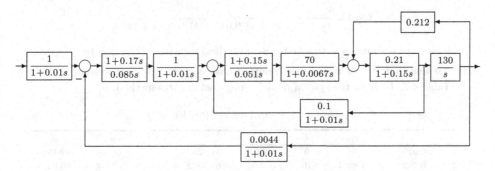

Fig. 4-28 DC motor control system for Problem (15).

(16) Assume that plant, controller models are respectively given by

$$G(s) = \frac{12}{s(s+1)^3}e^{-2s}, \quad G_c(s) = \frac{2s+3}{s},$$

and the system is under unity negative feedback structure. Check whether accurate closed-loop model can be obtained with MATLAB. If not, please find a suitable way to approximate the closed-loop model.

(17) Assume the model is given by

$$G(s) = \frac{(s+1)^2(s^2+2s+400)}{(s+5)^2(s^2+3s+100)(s^2+3s+2500)}.$$

For different sampling intervals, $T = 0.01, 0.1, T = 1\,\mathrm{s}$, discretize the model and compare the step response fitting with MATLAB function step().

(18) Assume that the state space models are given as follows. Check whether the following systems are minimum realized models. If not, please find the minimum realizations of them and explain from transfer function viewpoint why they are not minimum realization models.

(i) $\dot{x}(t) = \begin{bmatrix} -9 & -26 & -24 & 0 \\ 1 & 0 & 0 & 0 \\ 0 & 1 & 0 & 0 \\ 0 & 1 & 1 & -1 \end{bmatrix} x(t) + \begin{bmatrix} 1 \\ 0 \\ 0 \\ 0 \end{bmatrix} u(t), \quad y = [\,0,\,1,\,1,\,2\,]x(t),$

(ii) $G(s) = \dfrac{2s^2 + 18s + 16}{s^4 + 10s^3 + 35s^2 + 50s + 24}.$

(19) Enter the following high-order systems into MATLAB workspace and find low-order approximations to them.

(i) $G(s) = \dfrac{10 + 3s + 13s^2 + 3s^2}{1 + s + 2s^2 + 1.5s^3 + 0.5s^4}$, (ii) $G(s) = \dfrac{10s^3 - 60s^2 + 110s + 60}{s^4 + 17s^2 + 82s^2 + 130s + 100}$,

(iii) $G(s) = \dfrac{1 + 0.4s}{1 + 2.283s + 1.875s^2 + 0.7803s^3 + 0.125s^4 + 0.0083s^5}$,

(iv) $G(z) = \dfrac{24.1467z^3 - 67.7944z^2 + 63.4768z - 19.8209}{z^4 - 3.6193z^3 + 4.9124z^2 - 2.9633z + 0.6703}.$

(20) Assume that the plant model is given by

$$G(s) = \dfrac{1}{(s + 1)(0.2s + 1)(0.04s + 1)(0.008s + 1)}.$$

Please approximate it with a first-order plus dead time model $G_\text{r}(s) = k\mathrm{e}^{-Ls}/(Ts+1)$.

(21) Assume that the measured input, output data of a discrete-time system is given in Table 4-3. Identify the system model using least squares method.

Table 4-3    Measured data of Problem (21).

| $i$ | $u_i$ | $y_i$ | $i$ | $u_i$ | $y_i$ | $i$ | $u_i$ | $y_i$ |
|---|---|---|---|---|---|---|---|---|
| 1 | 0.9103 | 0 | 9 | 0.9910 | 54.5252 | 17 | 0.6316 | 62.1589 |
| 2 | 0.7622 | 18.4984 | 10 | 0.3653 | 65.9972 | 18 | 0.8847 | 63.0000 |
| 3 | 0.2625 | 31.4285 | 11 | 0.2470 | 62.9181 | 19 | 0.2727 | 68.6356 |
| 4 | 0.0475 | 32.3228 | 12 | 0.9826 | 57.5592 | 20 | 0.4364 | 60.8267 |
| 5 | 0.7361 | 28.5690 | 13 | 0.7227 | 67.6080 | 21 | 0.7665 | 57.1745 |
| 6 | 0.3282 | 39.1704 | 14 | 0.7534 | 70.7397 | 22 | 0.4777 | 60.5321 |
| 7 | 0.6326 | 39.8825 | 15 | 0.6515 | 73.7718 | 23 | 0.2378 | 57.3803 |
| 8 | 0.7564 | 46.4963 | 16 | 0.0727 | 74.0165 | 24 | 0.2749 | 49.6011 |

(22) Assume that the measured step response data are given in Table 4-4. It is known that the system is a second-order one whose step response curve is defined as $y(t) = x_1 + x_2\mathrm{e}^{-x_4 t} + x_3\mathrm{e}^{-x_5 t}$. Please find the least squares fitting of the parameters $x_i$ using the method shown in Chapter 3. Then approximate the transfer function model of the system.

## Bibliography and References

[1] MathWorks Inc. Control system toolbox manual
[2] Munro N. Multivariable control 1: the inverse Nyquist array design method. In: Lecture Notes of SERC Vacation School on Control System Design.    UMIST, Manchester, 1989

Table 4-4  Measured data of Problem (22).

| $t$ | $y(t)$ | $t$ | $y(t)$ | $t$ | $y(t)$ | $t$ | $y(t)$ | $t$ | $y(t)$ | $t$ | $y(t)$ |
|---|---|---|---|---|---|---|---|---|---|---|---|
| 0 | 0 | 1.6 | 0.2822 | 3.2 | 0.3024 | 4.8 | 0.3145 | 6.4 | 0.3218 | 8 | 0.3263 |
| 0.1 | 0.08324 | 1.7 | 0.2839 | 3.3 | 0.3034 | 4.9 | 0.315 | 6.5 | 0.3222 | 8.1 | 0.3265 |
| 0.2 | 0.1404 | 1.8 | 0.2855 | 3.4 | 0.3043 | 5 | 0.3156 | 6.6 | 0.3225 | 8.2 | 0.3267 |
| 0.3 | 0.1798 | 1.9 | 0.287 | 3.5 | 0.3051 | 5.1 | 0.3161 | 6.7 | 0.3228 | 8.3 | 0.3269 |
| 0.4 | 0.2072 | 2 | 0.2885 | 3.6 | 0.306 | 5.2 | 0.3166 | 6.8 | 0.3231 | 8.4 | 0.3271 |
| 0.5 | 0.2265 | 2.1 | 0.2899 | 3.7 | 0.3068 | 5.3 | 0.3172 | 6.9 | 0.3235 | 8.5 | 0.3273 |
| 0.6 | 0.2402 | 2.2 | 0.2912 | 3.8 | 0.3076 | 5.4 | 0.3176 | 7 | 0.3238 | 8.6 | 0.3275 |
| 0.7 | 0.2501 | 2.3 | 0.2925 | 3.9 | 0.3084 | 5.5 | 0.3181 | 7.1 | 0.324 | 8.7 | 0.3277 |
| 0.8 | 0.2574 | 2.4 | 0.2937 | 4 | 0.3092 | 5.6 | 0.3186 | 7.2 | 0.3243 | 8.8 | 0.3278 |
| 0.9 | 0.2629 | 2.5 | 0.2949 | 4.1 | 0.3099 | 5.7 | 0.319 | 7.3 | 0.3246 | 8.9 | 0.328 |
| 1 | 0.2673 | 2.6 | 0.2961 | 4.2 | 0.3106 | 5.8 | 0.3195 | 7.4 | 0.3249 | 9 | 0.3282 |
| 1.1 | 0.2708 | 2.7 | 0.2973 | 4.3 | 0.3113 | 5.9 | 0.3199 | 7.5 | 0.3251 | 9.1 | 0.3283 |
| 1.2 | 0.2737 | 2.8 | 0.2983 | 4.4 | 0.312 | 6 | 0.3203 | 7.6 | 0.3254 | 9.2 | 0.3285 |
| 1.3 | 0.2762 | 2.9 | 0.2994 | 4.5 | 0.3126 | 6.1 | 0.3207 | 7.7 | 0.3256 | 9.3 | 0.3286 |
| 1.4 | 0.2784 | 3 | 0.3004 | 4.6 | 0.3133 | 6.2 | 0.3211 | 7.8 | 0.3258 | 9.4 | 0.3288 |
| 1.5 | 0.2804 | 3.1 | 0.3014 | 4.7 | 0.3139 | 6.3 | 0.3214 | 7.9 | 0.3261 | 9.5 | 0.3289 |

[3] Sun Z Q, Yuan Z R. Computer-aided design of control systems. Beijing: Tsinghua University Press, 1988. (In Chinese)

[4] Xue D Y, Chen Y Q. System simulation techniques with MATLAB and Simulink. Chichester: John Wiley and Sons, 2013

[5] D'Azzo J J, Houpis C H. Linear control system analysis and design: conventional and modern. New York: McGraw-Hill, 4th edition, 1995

[6] Chen H C. MATLAB and its applications in electronic information courses. Beijing: Publishing House of Electronics Industry, 2002

[7] Davison E J. A method for simplifying linear dynamic systems. IEEE Transaction on Automatic Control, 1966, AC-11:93–101

[8] Chen C F, Shieh L S. A novel approach to linear model simplification. International Journal of Control, 1968, 8:561–570

[9] Bultheel A, van Barel M. Padé techniques for model reduction in linear system theory: a survey. Journal of Computational and Applied Mathematics, 1986, 14:401–438

[10] Hutton M F. Routh approximation for high-order linear systems. Proceedings of 9th Allerton Conference, 1971, 160–169

[11] Shamash Y. Linear system reduction using Padé approximation to allow retention of dominant modes. International Journal of Control, 1975, 21:257–272

[12] Lucas T N. Some further observations on the differential method of model reduction. IEEE Transaction on Automatic Control, 1992, AC-37:1389–1391

[13] Xue D Y, Atherton D P. A suboptimal reduction algorithm for linear systems with a time delay. International Journal of Control, 1994, 60(2):181–196

[14] Hu X H. FF-Padé method of model reduction in frequency domain. IEEE Transaction on Automatic Control, 1987, AC-32:243–246

[15] Gruca A, Bertrand P. Approximation of high-order systems by low-order models with delays. International Journal of Control, 1978, 28:953–965

[16] Glover K. All optimal Hankel-norm approximations of linear multivariable systems and their $L^\infty$-error bounds. International Journal of Control, 1984, 39:1115–1193

[17] Akaike H. A new look at the statistical model identification. IEEE Transactions on Automatic Control, 1974, AC-19(6):716–723

[18] Ljung L. System identification — theory for the user. Upper Saddle River, N J: PTR Prentice Hall, 2nd edition, 1999

[19] Xue D Y. Simulation and computer-aided design of control systems. Beijing: China Machine Press, 2005. (In Chinese)

[20] Han Z J. Adaptive control. Beijing: Tsinghua University Press, 1995. (In Chinese)

[21] Wang Q G, Ye Z, Cai W J, Hang C C. PID control for multivariable processes. Berlin: Springer, 2008

# Chapter 5

# Computer-Aided Analysis of Linear Control Systems

If the mathematical models of systems are established, properties of the systems can be analyzed. For linear control systems, stability is the most important property. In the early stages of the development of control theory, most of the theoretical achievements were on the stability of the systems. Due to the limitations of mathematics then, it was regarded that it was not possible to find all the roots of polynomial equations. Various indirect methods such as Routh table, Hurwitz matrix method and Jury criterion were used to assess the stability of linear systems. In fact, with the use of computer and advanced software such as MATLAB, the evaluation of eigenvalues of the systems is an extremely easy task. In this book, the direct method is used to assess the stability of linear systems. In Section 5.1, other properties such as controllability and observability are presented and canonical realization of systems are addressed. The norm measures in robust control are also presented. In Section 5.2, analytical solutions to linear system responses are presented for transfer function models and state space models. In Section 5.3, numerical time response analysis in linear continuous and discrete-time systems are presented. The time responses to various input signals can be evaluated, and methods are given to evaluate for systems with nonzero initial conditions. Root locus analysis of systems is illustrated in Section 5.4, and an interactive method for finding the critical gain is demonstrated. Interactive method in control system design using root locus is explored. In Section 5.5, frequency domain analysis of systems is presented, and Bode diagram, Nyquist plots and Nichols charts are illustrated for single variable systems. For multivariable systems, inverse Nyquist array approach is presented. With the use of the materials in this chapter, the users are equipped with the capability for linear control systems, and these capabilities are essential in the design of control systems.

## 5.1 Properties of Linear Control Systems

Among the properties of control systems, stability is of course the most important one. If a system is unstable, it cannot be applied, controllers are then required to stabilize. If the system is stable, other properties of the systems can further be analyzed. There are many approaches to assess the stability of control systems. In this book, direct assessment to stability of linear systems are presented. Then the properties such as controllability, observability as well as norm measures are presented.

### 5.1.1   *Stability of Linear Systems*

It has been presented earlier that the typical mathematical descriptions to linear continuous systems are transfer functions and state space expressions. With the properly chosen state variables, the state space models can be constructed from transfer functions. The function `ss()` provided in MATLAB Control System Toolbox can be used to find the state space realizations from the LTI objects.

Consider the state space model of a linear continuous system written as

$$\begin{cases} \dot{x}(t) = Ax(t) + Bu(t) \\ y(t) = Cx(t) + Du(t). \end{cases} \tag{5.1}$$

With the given input signal $u(t)$, the analytical solutions of the state variables can be evaluated from

$$x(t) = e^{A(t-t_0)}x(t_0) + \int_{t_0}^{t} e^{A(t-\tau)}Bu(\tau)d\tau. \tag{5.2}$$

It can be seen that if the input signal $u(t)$ is a bounded signal, the states $x(t)$ are also bounded if the state transition matrix $e^{At}$ is bounded, i.e., the eigenvalues of the matrix $A$ all have negative real parts. It can then be concluded that the conditions for the stability of linear state space equations are that all the eigenvalues of matrix $A$ have negative real parts. It is also known in control theory that the eigenvalues of matrix $A$ are the same as the poles of the system. Thus, if the poles can all be obtained, the stability of the systems can be assessed.

In the early stages in the development of control theory, since computer aids were not available, it was recognized that the solutions of high-order polynomial equations very difficult, if not impossible. Indirect methods were then used to assess the stability of linear systems, for instance, the Routh criterion, Hurwitz criterion and Lyapunov Theorem. Since the rapid development of computers and software like MATLAB, the evaluation of the characteristic roots of a polynomial equation is a very simple task. Thus, for linear systems, there is no longer any need to use indirect approaches for the assessment of stabilities.

In MATLAB Control System Toolbox, the poles of an LTI object $G$ can be evaluated with `p = eig(G)`, where $p$ vector returns all the poles. This function is applicable for all LTI objects, whether they are transfer functions, state space models or zero–pole–gain models, or whether they are single variable and multivariable systems. This makes the stability assessment of linear systems a very simple job. Besides, the function `pzmap(G)` can be used to display the poles and zeros on the $s$-plane. If all the poles are located on the left-hand-side of the $s$-plane, the continuous system is stable.

If a mathematical model of a linear system is represented in MATLAB as $G$, the functions `pole(G)` and `zero(G)` can also be used to find respectively the poles and zeros of the system.

Consider the discrete-time state space model

$$\begin{cases} \boldsymbol{x}[(k+1)T] = \boldsymbol{F}\boldsymbol{x}(kT) + \boldsymbol{G}\boldsymbol{u}(kT) \\ \boldsymbol{y}(kT) = \boldsymbol{C}\boldsymbol{x}(kT) + \boldsymbol{D}\boldsymbol{u}(kT), \end{cases} \tag{5.3}$$

the analytical solutions of the state variables can be written as

$$\boldsymbol{x}(kT) = \boldsymbol{F}^k \boldsymbol{x}(0) + \sum_{i=0}^{k-1} \boldsymbol{F}^{k-i-1} \boldsymbol{G}\boldsymbol{u}(iT). \tag{5.4}$$

It can be seen that if the states $\boldsymbol{x}(kT)$ are bounded, the matrix $\boldsymbol{F}^k$ must be bounded, i.e., the modules of the eigenvalues of the matrix $\boldsymbol{F}$ must be smaller than 1. It can be concluded that a discrete-time system is stable, if the magnitudes of all the eigenvalues of matrix $\boldsymbol{F}$ are smaller than 1, or if all the eigenvalues are located within a unit circle.

Before the popular use of MATLAB and other tools, it was very difficult to find the eigenvalues of a given matrices and polynomials. Jury tables should be used to assess indirectly the stability of discrete-time systems. The Jury table construction is much more complicated than the Routh table. With the powerful MATLAB, the eigenvalues of the system can be obtained directly and the stability can be assessed by checking where there exists poles outside the unit circles. The function `pzmap(G)` can also be used to show graphically the poles and zero positions of the system $G$. It is not necessary then to assess the stability with indirect methods.

Even more simply, stability of linear system can be assessed directly with the function `key = isstable(G)`. If the returned variable `key` is 1, the system is stable. The model $G$ can be continuous or discrete, single variable or multivariable, however, it cannot be used to deal with systems with internal delays.

**Example 5.1.** Assume that the open-loop transfer function is given by

$$G(s) = \frac{10s^4 + 50s^3 + 100s^2 + 100s + 40}{s^7 + 21s^6 + 184s^5 + 870s^4 + 2384s^3 + 3664s^2 + 2496s},$$

the following MATLAB statements can be used to assess the stability of the closed-loop with unity negative feedback structure.

```
>> num=[10,50,100,100,40]; den=[1,21,184,870,2384,3664,2496,0];
   G=tf(num,den); GG=feedback(G,1); % construct the closed-loop model
   pzmap(GG), eig(GG), isstable(GG) % show the zero and pole positions
```

The closed-loop poles are $-6.9223, -3.6502 \pm \text{j}2.302, -2.0633 \pm \text{j}1.7923, -2.6349,$ $-0.015765$. Since all the poles are located in the left-hand-side of the $s$ plane, the closed-loop system is stable. The pole positions in Fig. 5-1 validated the above conclusion.

Alternatively, the zero–pole–gain model can also be obtained with `zpk(GG)`

$$G(s) = \frac{10(s+2)(s+1)(s^2 + 2s + 2)}{(s + 6.922)(s + 2.635)(s + 0.01577)(s^2 + 4.127s + 7.47)(s^2 + 7.3s + 18.62)}.$$

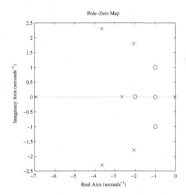

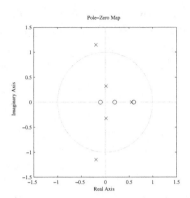

Fig. 5-1   Pole–zero of continuous system.     Fig. 5-2   Zero–pole of the discrete system.

**Example 5.2.** Assume that an open-loop discrete-time plant and controller are given by

$$H(z) = \frac{6z^2 - 0.6z - 0.12}{z^4 - z^3 + 0.25z^2 + 0.25z - 0.125}, \quad G_c(z) = 0.3\frac{z - 0.6}{z + 0.8},$$

with a sampling interval of $T = 0.1\,$s, and the closed-loop system is with unity negative feedback. The closed-loop eigenvalues and their magnitudes can be obtained with the following MATLAB statements

```
>> num=[6 -0.6 -0.12]; den=[1 -1 0.25 0.25 -0.125];
   H=tf(num,den,'Ts',0.1);                    % discrete-time plant model
   z=tf('z','Ts',0.1); Gc=0.3*(z-0.6)/(z+0.8); % controller model
   GG=feedback(H*Gc,1);                        % closed-loop model
   pzmap(GG), abs(eig(GG)), isstable(GG)       % the three methods
```

The magnitudes of the poles are 1.1644, 1.1644, 0.5536, 0.3232, 0.3232, with the first two larger than 1. The closed-loop system is unstable. The positions of the poles and zeros of the closed-loop system can also be obtained with **pzmap(GG)**, as shown in Fig. 5-2. It can be seen that there are two poles located outside of the unit circle, which indicates that the closed-loop system is unstable.

With the **zpk(GG)** command, the original system can also be written as

$$G(z) = \frac{1.8(z - 0.6)(z - 0.2)(z + 0.1)}{(z - 0.5536)(z^2 - 0.03727z + 0.1045)(z^2 + 0.3908z + 1.356)}.$$

In the last term in the denominator, the constant 1.356 is larger than 1, and it is the product of a pair of complex conjugates, thus the system is unstable.

If indirect stability assessment methods are used instead, Routh and Jury tables should be constructed first for continuous and discrete-time systems. The indirect methods can only be used to check whether the system is stable, no other information can be obtained. With the direct methods, the approximate behavior of the systems may also be obtained. For instance, for continuous systems, if there is a real pole located very close to the imaginary axis compared with others, the behavior of the system is close to a first-order system. If there is a pair of dominant complex poles very close to the imaginary axis, there may be strong oscillation.

These conclusions cannot be drawn with indirect methods. It can be seen that the direct method is much superior to the indirect methods, presented mainly in control textbooks.

### 5.1.2 *Internal Stability of Feedback Control Systems*

In the analysis and practical applications of feedback control systems, the stability, i.e., input–output stability, is not adequate, since the internal signals may be unbounded with finite external input signals. In this case, although the system is theoretically input–output stable, the internal unbounded signal may damage the hardware structure of the practical system. Thus, the internal stability problems should also be investigated.

Consider the feedback control system with disturbances shown in Fig. 5-3, which is an extension to the typical feedback system. Under such a system structure, $d(t)$ is the external disturbance, while $n(t)$ is the measurement noise.

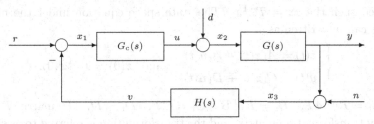

Fig. 5-3  Feedback system with disturbances.

In Fig. 5-3, if the nine transfer functions from input signals $(r, d, n)$ to the output signals $(x_1, x_2, x_3)$ are all stable, the system is referred to as internally stable.

A transfer function matrix can be composed with the nine transfer function as

$$\begin{bmatrix} x_1 \\ x_2 \\ x_3 \end{bmatrix} = \frac{1}{1 + G(s)G_c(s)H(s)} \begin{bmatrix} 1 & -G(s)H(s) & -H(s) \\ G_c(s) & 1 & -G_c(s)H(s) \\ G(s)G_c(s) & G(s) & 1 \end{bmatrix} \begin{bmatrix} r \\ d \\ n \end{bmatrix}. \quad (5.5)$$

It is very complicated and tedious to judge the stability of the transfer functions one by one. The simple assessment methods for internal stability include the following

(1) The transfer function has no right-hand-side zeros;

(2) The product $H(s)G(s)G_c(s)$ has no pole–zero cancelation for $\mathscr{R}[s] \geqslant 0$.

Condition (1) checks, in fact, the input–output stability while (2) is essential in checking the internal stability of the system. This assessment approach can also be extended to the cases in multivariable systems and discrete-time systems. Based on the above approach, a MATLAB function `intstable()` can be written for the assessment of internal stability of the typical feedback control systems.

```
function key=intstable(G,Gc,H)
GG=minreal(feedback(G*Gc,H)); Go=H*G*Gc; Go1=minreal(Go); p=eig(GG);
```

```
z0=eig(Go); z1=eig(Go1); zz=setdiff(z0,z1); % find pole--zero pairs
if (G.Ts>0), % discrete-time system assessment
    key=any(abs(p)>1); if key==0, key=2*any(abs(zz)>1); end
else,          % continuous system assessment
    key=any(real(p)>0); if key==0, key=2*any(real(zz)>0); end
end
```

If the closed-loop system is input–output unstable, the returned key is 1. If it is internally unstable, key returns 2, otherwise key=0. This function also works for multivariable and discrete-time systems.

### 5.1.3  *Similarity Transformation of Linear Control Systems*

It has been pointed out that when the state variables are selected differently, the state space realization is also different. The relationship among these state space equations will be studied in this section.

Assume that there exists a nonsingular matrix $T$, a new state variable $z$ can be defined such that $z = T^{-1}x$. The state space equation under the new state variables can be written as

$$\begin{cases} \dot{z}(t) = A_t z(t) + B_t u(t) \\ y(t) = C_t z(t) + D_t u(t), \end{cases} \quad \text{and} \quad z(0) = T^{-1}x(0), \tag{5.6}$$

where $A_t = T^{-1}AT$, $B_t = T^{-1}B$, $C_t = CT$, $D_t = D$. The matrix $T$ is called similarity transformation matrix, and the transformation is referred to as similarity transformation of the system.

In the MATLAB Control System Toolbox, the function ss2ss() can be used to perform similarity transformation, with the syntax $G_1 = \text{ss2ss}(G,T)$, where $G$ is the original state space model, and $T$ is the transformation matrix. The similarity transformed system is returned in $G_1$.

**Example 5.3.** In practical applications, the transformation matrix $T$ can be arbitrarily chosen, as long as it is a nonsingular square matrix. Assume that the original state space model of a system is given by

$$\begin{cases} \dot{x}(t) = \begin{bmatrix} 0 & 1 & 0 & 0 \\ 0 & 0 & 1 & 0 \\ 0 & 0 & 0 & 1 \\ -24 & -50 & -35 & -10 \end{bmatrix} x(t) + \begin{bmatrix} 0 \\ 0 \\ 0 \\ 1 \end{bmatrix} u(t) \\ y(t) = \begin{bmatrix} 24 & 24 & 7 & 1 \end{bmatrix} x(t). \end{cases}$$

and we can select a transformation matrix as a backward diagonal matrix, with its elements in backward diagonal all set to 1, the new state space equation can be obtained with the following MATLAB commands

```
>> A=[0 1 0 0; 0 0 1 0; 0 0 0 1; -24 -50 -35 -10];
   G1=ss(A,[0;0;0;1],[24 24 7 1],0);   % state space model
   T=fliplr(eye(4)); G2=ss2ss(G1,T)    % similarity transform results
```

The transformed state space model is

$$
\begin{cases}
\dot{z}(t) = \begin{bmatrix} -10 & -35 & -50 & -24 \\ 1 & 0 & 0 & 0 \\ 0 & 1 & 0 & 0 \\ 0 & 0 & 1 & 0 \end{bmatrix} z(t) + \begin{bmatrix} 1 \\ 0 \\ 0 \\ 0 \end{bmatrix} u(t) \\
y(t) = \begin{bmatrix} 1 & 7 & 24 & 24 \end{bmatrix} z(t).
\end{cases}
$$

This is the controllable canonical form of the state space models in textbooks [1].

### 5.1.4 *Controllability of Linear Systems*

Controllability and observability of linear systems are fundamental to the state space-based control theory. This concept was proposed by Kalman in 1960[2]. The properties establish the basis for the design of state feedback controllers and observers. Assume that the state space equation can be expressed as $\left( A, B, C, D \right)$, and for any initial time $t_0$, the state $x_i(t)$ can be controlled from initial state $x_i(t_0)$ to any preassigned state $x_i(t_f)$ for any finite time $t_f$ with the bounded input signal $u(t)$, the $i$th state is called controllable. If all the states in a system are controllable, the original system is referred to as a controllable system.

The controllability of the system indicates whether the internal states of the system can be accessed by external input signals. For linear time invariant control systems, if a state is controllable, it can be controlled arbitrarily with certain external input signals.

#### 1. Controllability assessment for linear systems

A controllability matrix is defined as

$$ T_c = \begin{bmatrix} B, AB, A^2 B, \cdots, A^{n-1} B \end{bmatrix}. \tag{5.7} $$

If matrix $T_c$ is a full-rank matrix, the system is controllable. If it is not, the rank of the matrix is the number of controllable states. The rank of a matrix can easily be evaluated with MATLAB, with `rank(T)`. The controllability of the system can then be assessed.

The controllability matrix $T_c$ can easily be constructed with the MATLAB function `Tc = ctrb(A,B)`. Low-level MATLAB commands can also be used to construct the matrix. The method presented above applies both for continuous systems and discrete-time systems. Examples below can be used to demonstrate the solution to the controllability assessment problems.

**Example 5.4.** For the following state space model of a discrete-time system

$$
x[(k+1)T] = \begin{bmatrix} -2.2 & -0.7 & 1.5 & -1 \\ 0.2 & -6.3 & 6 & -1.5 \\ 0.6 & -0.9 & -2 & -0.5 \\ 1.4 & -0.1 & -1 & -3.5 \end{bmatrix} x(kT) + \begin{bmatrix} 6 & 9 \\ 4 & 6 \\ 4 & 4 \\ 8 & 4 \end{bmatrix} u(kT),
$$

the following statements can be used to enter the matrices $A$, $B$, to construct the controllability matrix, and to assess the controllability of the system.

```
>> A=[-2.2,-0.7,1.5,-1; 0.2,-6.3,6,-1.5; ...
      0.6,-0.9,-2,-0.5; 1.4,-0.1,-1,-3.5];
   B=[6,9; 4,6; 4,4; 8,4]; Tc=ctrb(A,B), rank(Tc)
```

The controllability matrix is

$$T_c = \begin{bmatrix} 6 & 9 & -18 & -22 & 54 & 52 & -162 & -118 \\ 4 & 6 & -12 & -18 & 36 & 58 & -108 & -202 \\ 4 & 4 & -12 & -10 & 36 & 26 & -108 & -74 \\ 8 & 4 & -24 & -6 & 72 & 2 & -216 & 34 \end{bmatrix},$$

and it can be seen that the rank of it is 3, the system is not controllable.

An alternative assessment method for controllability is to use the controllability Gramian method. The controllability Gramian is defined as

$$L_c = \int_0^\infty e^{-At} BB^T e^{-A^T t} dt. \tag{5.8}$$

If the controllability Gramian is nonsingular, the system is controllable. Also, please note that only control systems have controllability Gramians.

The controllability Gramian is a symmetrical matrix, and it is a solution to the following Lyapunov equation

$$AL_c + L_c A^T = -BB^T. \tag{5.9}$$

In MATLAB Control System Toolbox, $L_c = \texttt{lyap}(A, B*B')$ can be used to solve directly the Lyapunov equation. If the solution cannot be obtained, the system is not controllable. The controllability Gramian can be obtained with the MATLAB function $G_c = \texttt{gram}(G, 'c')$ . For discrete-time systems, two functions can still be used, however, the definitions of them are different

$$L_c = \sum_{k=0}^\infty A^k BB^T (A^T)^k, \quad AXA^T - X + BB^T = 0. \tag{5.10}$$

**Example 5.5.** Consider the discrete-time model

$$H(z) = \frac{6z^2 - 0.6z - 0.12}{z^4 - z^3 + 0.25z^2 + 0.25z - 0.125},$$

with a sampling interval of $T = 0.1\,\text{s}$. The following MATLAB statements can be used to compute the controllability Gramian.

```
>> num=[6 -0.6 -0.12]; den=[1 -1 0.25 0.25 -0.125];
   H=tf(num,den,'Ts',0.1)    % enter and display the transfer function
   Lc=gram(ss(H),'c')        % compute the controllability Gramian
```

The controllability Gramian for the system is

$$L_c = \begin{bmatrix} 10.765 & 15.754 & 7.3518 & 0 \\ 15.754 & 43.061 & 31.508 & 3.6759 \\ 7.3518 & 31.508 & 43.061 & 7.8769 \\ 0 & 3.6759 & 7.8769 & 2.6913 \end{bmatrix}.$$

## 2. Controllable staircase decomposition

For partially controllable systems, staircase decomposition can be applied such that a nonsingular matrix $T$ can be constructed such that the original system $(A, B, C, D)$ can be decomposed as

$$A_c = \begin{bmatrix} \widehat{A}_{\bar{c}} & 0 \\ \widehat{A}_{21} & \widehat{A}_c \end{bmatrix}, \quad B_c = \begin{bmatrix} 0 \\ \widehat{B}_c \end{bmatrix}, \quad C_c = \begin{bmatrix} \widehat{C}_{\bar{c}}, \widehat{C}_c \end{bmatrix}, \tag{5.11}$$

and such a case is referred to as the controllable staircase form, and the uncontrollable space $\left( \widehat{A}_{\bar{c}}, 0, \widehat{C}_{\bar{c}} \right)$ can be separated directly from the controllable subspace $\left( \widehat{A}_c, \widehat{B}_c, \widehat{C}_c \right)$. It is complicated to construct such a transformation matrix, and the function ctrbf() can be used directly to get the staircase form and the transformation matrix $T_c$

   [Ac,Bc,Cc,Tc] = ctrbf(A,B,C)

If the original state space system is controllable, no decomposition is made.

**Example 5.6.** Consider the uncontrollable system studied in Example 5.4. The following statements can be used to find the controllable staircase form

```
>> A=[-2.2,-0.7,1.5,-1; 0.2,-6.3,6,-1.5;...
      0.6,-0.9,-2,-0.5; 1.4,-0.1,-1,-3.5];
   B=[6,9; 4,6; 4,4; 8,4]; C=[1 2 3 4]; [Ac,Bc,Cc,Tc]=ctrbf(A,B,C);
```

The transformed state space model is

$$\hat{x}[(k+1)T] = \begin{bmatrix} -4 & 0 & 0 & 0 \\ \hline -4.638 & -3.823 & -0.5145 & -0.127 \\ -3.637 & 0.1827 & -3.492 & -0.1215 \\ -4.114 & -1.888 & 1.275 & -2.685 \end{bmatrix} \hat{x}(kT) + \begin{bmatrix} 0 & 0 \\ \hline 0 & 0 \\ 2.754 & -2.575 \\ -11.15 & -11.93 \end{bmatrix} u(kT),$$

$$y(kT) = \begin{bmatrix} -1.098, 1.379, -2.363, 4.616 \end{bmatrix} x(kT),$$

with the transformation matrix

$$T_c = \begin{bmatrix} 0.091 & 0.32 & -0.914 & 0.228 \\ -0.588 & 0.781 & 0.202 & -0.05 \\ 0.467 & 0.311 & -0.05 & -0.825 \\ 0.653 & 0.435 & 0.346 & 0.513 \end{bmatrix}.$$

### 5.1.5   *Observability of Linear Systems*

Assume again that the state space model is given by $\left( A, B, C, D \right)$. For any initial time $t_0$, if the state $x_i(t)$ at a finite time $t_f$, $x_i(t_f)$ can be exactly determined with the input and output signal in the interval $t \in \left[ t_0, t_f \right]$, the state is referred to as observable. If all the states are observable, the system is called a observable system.

Similar to the controllability problem, the observability of a system is the property which indicates whether the internal states can be reconstructed from the external input and output signals. For linear time invariant systems, if a state is observable, it can be reconstructed with a device called observers.

Again, an observability matrix can be constructed

$$T_{\mathrm{o}} = \begin{bmatrix} C \\ CA \\ CA^2 \\ \vdots \\ CA^{n-1} \end{bmatrix}, \tag{5.12}$$

such that if it is full-rank, the system is observable.

It is known from control theory that the controllability and observability problems are dual. If one wants to study the observability of the system $\left(A, C\right)$, he can alternatively study the controllability of the system $\left(A^{\mathrm{T}}, C^{\mathrm{T}}\right)$. The controllability methods presented earlier can be extended to the assessment of observability problems.

Of course in MATLAB Control System Toolbox, functions `obsv()` and `obsvf()` can also be used to construct the observability matrix and find the observability staircase form of the systems. Also, the function `gram(G,'o')` can be used to calculate the observability Gramian defined as

$$L_{\mathrm{o}} = \int_0^\infty \mathrm{e}^{-A^{\mathrm{T}}t} C^{\mathrm{T}} C \mathrm{e}^{-At} \mathrm{d}t, \tag{5.13}$$

and it satisfies the Lyapunov equation

$$A^{\mathrm{T}} L_{\mathrm{o}} + L_{\mathrm{o}} A = -C^{\mathrm{T}} C. \tag{5.14}$$

For discrete-time systems, the above two equations are

$$L_{\mathrm{o}} = \sum_{k=0}^\infty \left(A^{\mathrm{T}}\right)^k C^{\mathrm{T}} C A^k, \quad A^{\mathrm{T}} L_{\mathrm{o}} A - L_{\mathrm{o}} + C^{\mathrm{T}} C = 0. \tag{5.15}$$

### 5.1.6  *Canonical Kalman Decompositions*

It can be seen from the previous presentation that controllable staircase decomposition can be used to separate controllable and uncontrollable subspaces. Also, observable staircase form can be used to separate observable and unobservable subspaces. Thus, four subspaces are involved. Controllable staircase transformation can be applied first, followed by the observable staircase transformation. The canonical form can finally be written as

$$\begin{cases} \dot{z}(t) = \begin{bmatrix} \widehat{A}_{\bar{\mathrm{c}},\bar{\mathrm{o}}} & \widehat{A}_{1,2} & 0 & 0 \\ 0 & \widehat{A}_{\bar{\mathrm{c}},\mathrm{o}} & 0 & 0 \\ \widehat{A}_{3,1} & \widehat{A}_{3,2} & \widehat{A}_{\mathrm{c},\bar{\mathrm{o}}} & \widehat{A}_{3,4} \\ 0 & \widehat{A}_{4,2} & 0 & \widehat{A}_{\mathrm{c},\mathrm{o}} \end{bmatrix} z(t) + \begin{bmatrix} 0 \\ 0 \\ \widehat{B}_{\mathrm{c},\bar{\mathrm{o}}} \\ \widehat{B}_{\mathrm{c},\mathrm{o}} \end{bmatrix} u(t) \\ y(t) = \begin{bmatrix} 0 & \widehat{C}_{\bar{\mathrm{c}},\mathrm{o}} & 0 & \widehat{C}_{\mathrm{c},\mathrm{o}} \end{bmatrix} z(t), \end{cases} \tag{5.16}$$

where the $\left( \widehat{A}_{\bar{c},\bar{o}}, 0, 0 \right)$ is the uncontrollable, unobservable subspace, $\left( \widehat{A}_{\bar{c},o}, 0, \widehat{C}_{c,\bar{o}} \right)$ is the uncontrollable, but observable subspace, $\left( \widehat{A}_{c,\bar{o}}, \widehat{B}_{c,\bar{o}}, 0 \right)$ and $\left( \widehat{A}_{c,o}, \widehat{B}_{c,o}, \widehat{C}_{c,o} \right)$ are respectively controllable, unobservable subspace, and controllable, observable subspace. Such a canonical form is referred to as Kalman decomposition of the system. Normally, we are interested in the controllable and observable subspace. Such a subspace is, in fact, the minimum realization of the system.

### 5.1.7 MATLAB Solutions to Canonical State Space Models

In state space descriptions of systems, the canonical forms such as controllable, observable and Jordanian are often needed. Also, for multivariable systems, Luenberger canonical form is also very useful. In this section, these canonical forms are studied.

**1. Canonical forms of single variable systems**
The commonly used canonical forms include controllable, observable and Jordanian canonical forms for single variable systems. If the transfer function is

$$G(s) = \frac{b_1 s^{n-1} + b_2 s^{n-2} + \cdots + b_{n-1} s + b_n}{s^n + a_1 s^{n-1} + a_2 s^{n-2} + \cdots + a_{n-1} s + a_n}, \qquad (5.17)$$

the controllable canonical form is written by

$$\begin{cases} \dot{x} = A_c x + B_c u \\ y = C_c x + D_c u \end{cases} \implies \begin{cases} \dot{x} = \begin{bmatrix} 0 & 1 & \cdots & 0 \\ 0 & 0 & \cdots & 0 \\ \vdots & \vdots & \ddots & \vdots \\ 0 & 0 & \cdots & 1 \\ -a_n & -a_{n-1} & \cdots & -a_1 \end{bmatrix} x + \begin{bmatrix} 0 \\ 0 \\ \vdots \\ 0 \\ 1 \end{bmatrix} u \\ y = \begin{bmatrix} b_n, & b_{n-1}, & \cdots, & b_1 \end{bmatrix} x, \end{cases} \qquad (5.18)$$

and the observable canonical form is written by

$$\begin{cases} \dot{x} = A_o x + B_o u \\ y = C_o x + D_o u \end{cases} \implies \begin{cases} \dot{x} = \begin{bmatrix} 0 & 0 & \cdots & 0 & -a_n \\ 1 & 0 & \cdots & 0 & -a_{n-1} \\ 0 & 1 & \cdots & 0 & -a_{n-2} \\ \vdots & \vdots & \ddots & \vdots & \vdots \\ 0 & 0 & \cdots & 1 & -a_1 \end{bmatrix} x + \begin{bmatrix} b_n \\ b_{n-1} \\ b_{n-2} \\ \vdots \\ b_1 \end{bmatrix} u \\ y = \begin{bmatrix} 0, & 0, & \cdots, & 1 \end{bmatrix} x. \end{cases} \qquad (5.19)$$

It can be seen that the two canonical forms are dual, i.e.,

$$A_c = A_o^{\mathrm{T}}, \quad B_c = C_o^{\mathrm{T}}, \quad C_c = B_o^{\mathrm{T}}, \quad D_c = D_o^{\mathrm{T}}, \qquad (5.20)$$

and the dual state space model can be obtained with $G_c = G_o{}'$.

The Jordanian canonical form can be written if the eigenvalues of matrix $A$ are obtained as $\lambda_1, \lambda_2, \cdots, \lambda_n$, where the $i$th eigenvalue $\lambda_i$ correspond to the eigenvector $v_i$ such that

$$A v_i = \lambda_i v_i, \quad i = 1, 2, \cdots, n, \qquad (5.21)$$

and the modal matrix $\Lambda$ of matrix $A$ is

$$
\Lambda = T^{-1}AT = \begin{bmatrix} J_1 & & & \\ & J_2 & & \\ & & \ddots & \\ & & & J_k \end{bmatrix}, \tag{5.22}
$$

where $J_i$ is the Jordanian matrix. The two canonical forms can be obtained directly with the sscanform() function

```
function [Gs,T]=sscanform(G,type)
switch type
   case 'ctrl'
      G=tf(G); Gs=[];
      d=G.den{1}(1); G.num{1}=G.num{1}/d; % monic transformation
      G.den{1}=G.den{1}/d; d=G.num{1}(1);
      G1=G; G1.ioDelay=0; G1=G1-d;    % get the strictly proper model
      num=G1.num1; den=G1.den1; n=length(G.den{1})-1;
      A=[zeros(n-1,1) eye(n-1); -den(end:-1:2)];
      B=[zeros(n-1,1);1]; C=num(end:-1:2); D=d;
      Gs=ss(A,B,C,D,'Ts',G.Ts,'ioDelay',G.ioDelay);
   case 'obsv', Gs=sscanform(G,'ctrl').';
   case 'jordan',
      G1=ss(G); [T a]=jordan(G1.a); T=inv(T); Gs=ss2ss(G1,T);
   otherwise, error('The option is not applicable.')
end
```

With such a function, the above-mentioned canonical forms of the single variable state space model can be obtained with the syntaxes

$$G_s = \texttt{sscanform}(G,\texttt{'ctrl'}) \qquad \text{\% controllable canonical form}$$
$$G_s = \texttt{sscanform}(G,\texttt{'obsv'}) \qquad \text{\% observable canonical form}$$
$$[G_s,T] = \texttt{sscanform}(G,\texttt{'jordan'}) \quad \text{\% Jordanian canonical form}$$

Some of the canonical forms can alternatively be obtained with the MATLAB function canon(), with the syntaxes

$$[G_s,T] = \texttt{canon}(G,\texttt{'modal'}) \qquad \text{\% Jordanian canonical form}$$
$$[G_s,T] = \texttt{canon}(G,\texttt{'companion'}) \quad \text{\% companion canonical form}$$

However, it should be noted that if the system has repeated eigenvalues, the canon() function may give wrong results. If the original model $G$ is an SS object, transformation matrix $T$ can also be generated.

**Example 5.7.** The controllable canonical form of

$$G(s) = \frac{6s^4 + 2s^2 + 8s + 10}{2s^4 + 6s^2 + 4s + 8}$$

can be obtained with the direct call to the sscanform() function

>> num=[6 0 2 8 10]; den=[2 0 6 4 8]; % the numerator and denominator arrays
   G=tf(num,den); Gs=sscanform(G,'ctrl') % controllable canonical form

The controllable canonical form of the system is

$$
\begin{cases}
\dot{z}(t) = \begin{bmatrix} 0 & 1 & 0 & 0 \\ 0 & 0 & 1 & 0 \\ 0 & 0 & 0 & 1 \\ -4 & -2 & -3 & 0 \end{bmatrix} z(t) + \begin{bmatrix} 0 \\ 0 \\ 0 \\ 1 \end{bmatrix} u(t) \\
y(t) = \begin{bmatrix} -7 & -2 & -8 & 0 \end{bmatrix} z(t) + 3u(t).
\end{cases}
$$

Note that since the orders of numerator and denominator are the same, some work must be done first to rewrite it to the form of $d + \widetilde{G}(s)$, where $\widetilde{G}(s)$ is strictly proper. Similarly, other canonical forms can also be obtained with sscanform() function.

The companion form can be obtained with the following statement

>> [G1,T]=canon(Gs,'companion')

The canonical form and transformation matrix are

$$
\begin{cases}
\dot{z}(t) = \begin{bmatrix} 0 & 0 & 0 & -4 \\ 1 & 0 & 0 & -2 \\ 0 & 1 & 0 & -3 \\ 0 & 0 & 1 & 0 \end{bmatrix} z(t) + \begin{bmatrix} 1 \\ 0 \\ 0 \\ 0 \end{bmatrix} u(t) \quad T = \begin{bmatrix} 2 & 3 & 0 & 1 \\ 3 & 0 & 1 & 0 \\ 0 & 1 & 0 & 0 \\ 1 & 0 & 0 & 0 \end{bmatrix}.
\\
y(t) = \begin{bmatrix} 0 & -8 & -2 & 17 \end{bmatrix} z(t) + 3u(t),
\end{cases}
$$

**Example 5.8.** Consider the transfer function with repeated poles

$$
G(s) = \frac{s^3 + 4s + 2}{(s+1)^3(s+2)}.
$$

There are repeated poles at $s = -1$. The following statements can be used to obtain the Jordanian forms, and the results by canon() function is wrong.

>> s=zpk('s'); G=(s^3+4*s+2)/(s+1)^3/(s+2);
   G1=sscanform(G,'jordan'), G2=canon(G,'modal')

The Jordanian form of the system is obtained as

$$
\begin{cases}
\dot{z}(t) = \begin{bmatrix} -2 & 0 & 0 & 0 \\ 0 & -1 & 1 & 0 \\ 0 & 0 & -1 & 1 \\ 0 & 0 & 0 & -1 \end{bmatrix} z(t) + \begin{bmatrix} 2 \\ 0.21808 \\ -0.5394 \\ 1.2425 \end{bmatrix} u(t) \\
y(t) = \begin{bmatrix} 7 & -2.4144 & 7 & -7 \end{bmatrix} z(t).
\end{cases}
$$

## 2. Luenberger canonical form for multivariable systems

Luenberger canonical form is one of the important controllable canonical forms for multivariable systems. The following procedures can be used to construct a matrix $S$[3]

$$
S = \begin{bmatrix} b_1, Ab_1, \cdots, A^{\sigma_1-1}b_1, b_2, \cdots, A^{\sigma_2-1}b_2, \cdots, A^{\sigma_p-1}b_p \end{bmatrix}, \tag{5.23}
$$

where $\sigma_i$ is the maximum number such that the proceeding columns are linearly independent. The first $n$ columns in such a matrix can be selected to establish an

$n \times n$ square matrix $\boldsymbol{L}$. If the number of columns of the thus constructed matrix is smaller than $n$, i.e., the system is not completely controllable, random numbers can be appended such that $\boldsymbol{L}$ is a full-rank matrix with $n$ columns. Taking inverse to $\boldsymbol{L}$, the following methods can be used to extract the corresponding rows

$$
\boldsymbol{L}^{-1} = \begin{bmatrix} \boldsymbol{l}_1^{\mathrm{T}} \\ \vdots \\ \boldsymbol{l}_{\sigma_1}^{\mathrm{T}} \\ \vdots \\ \boldsymbol{l}_{\sigma_1+\sigma_2}^{\mathrm{T}} \\ \vdots \end{bmatrix} \begin{array}{l} \\ \\ \leftarrow \text{extract this row} \\ \\ \leftarrow \text{extract this row} \\ \\ \end{array} \tag{5.24}
$$

and the transformation matrix $\boldsymbol{T}^{-1}$ can be constructed as

$$
\boldsymbol{T}^{-1} = \begin{bmatrix} \boldsymbol{l}_{\sigma_1}^{\mathrm{T}} \\ \vdots \\ \boldsymbol{l}_{\sigma_1}^{\mathrm{T}} \boldsymbol{A}^{\sigma_1-1} \\ \vdots \\ \boldsymbol{l}_{\sigma_1+\sigma_2}^{\mathrm{T}} \boldsymbol{A}^{\sigma_2-1} \\ \vdots \end{bmatrix}. \tag{5.25}
$$

With matrix $\boldsymbol{T}$, similarity transformation can be applied to get the Luenberger canonical form for multivariable systems. MATLAB implementation of the above algorithm can be written as follows to construct matrix $\boldsymbol{T}$, and the transformed model can be obtained with ss2ss() function.

```
function T=luenberger(A,B)
n=size(A,1); p=size(B,2); S=[]; sigmas=[]; k=1;
for i=1:p
   for j=0:n-1
      S=[S,A^j*B(:,i)];
      if rank(S)==k, k=k+1;
      else, sigmas(i)=j-1; S=S(:,1:end-1); break; end
   end
   if k>n, break; end
end
k=k-1; % if not completely controllable, random numbers are used
if k<n
   while rank(S)~=n, S(:,k+1:n)=rand(n,n-k); end
end
L=inv(S); iT=[];
for i=1:p, for j=0:sigmas(i)
   iT=[iT; L(i+sum(sigmas(1:i)),:)*A^j];
end, end
if k<n, iT(k+1:n,:)=L(k+1:end,:); end   %n full-rank matrix generation
T=inv(iT);   % transformation matrix construction
```

The following MATLAB functions can be used to get the Luenberger transformation matrix $T = \texttt{luenberger}(A,B)$, then the function $G_s = \texttt{ss2ss}(G,T)$ can be used to get the Luenberger canonical form $G_s$.

**Example 5.9.** For the state space system given by

$$\dot{x}(t) = \begin{bmatrix} 15 & 6 & -12 & 9 \\ 4 & 14 & 8 & -4 \\ 2 & 4 & 10 & -2 \\ 9 & 6 & -12 & 15 \end{bmatrix} x(t) + \begin{bmatrix} 3 & 3 \\ 2 & 2 \\ -2 & -2 \\ 3 & 9 \end{bmatrix} u(t),$$

function `luenberger()` can be used to construct a transformation matrix such that the Luenberger canonical form can be obtained

```
>> A=[15,6,-12,9; 4,14,8,-4; 2,4,10,-2; 9,6,-12,15];
   B=[3,3; 2,2; -2,-2; 3,9]; T=luenberger(A,B) % transformation matrix
   A1=inv(T)*A*T, B1=inv(T)*B  % get Luenberger canonical form
```

The transformation matrix and the transformed system are

$$T = \begin{bmatrix} 18 & 3 & 61.2 & 3 \\ -48 & 2 & -79.2 & 2 \\ 48 & -2 & 43.2 & -2 \\ 18 & 3 & -46.8 & 9 \end{bmatrix}, \quad \dot{z}(t) = \begin{bmatrix} 0 & 1 & 0 & 0 \\ -144 & 30 & -57.6 & 9.6 \\ 0 & 0 & 0 & 1 \\ 0 & 0 & -108 & 24 \end{bmatrix} z(t) + \begin{bmatrix} 0 & 0 \\ 1 & 0 \\ 0 & 0 \\ 0 & 1 \end{bmatrix} u(t).$$

### 5.1.8  Norms of Linear Systems

Similar to the norms of a matrix, norm measures to linear systems are also very important. The commonly used norms of linear systems, $\mathcal{H}_2$ and $\mathcal{H}_\infty$ are defined respectively as

$$\|G(s)\|_2 = \sqrt{\frac{1}{2\pi} \int_{-\infty}^{\infty} \sum_{i=1}^{p} \sigma_i \big[ G^{\mathrm{H}}(\mathrm{j}\omega) G(\mathrm{j}\omega) \big] \mathrm{d}\omega}, \quad \|G(s)\|_\infty = \sup_{\omega} \overline{\sigma} \big[ G(\mathrm{j}\omega) \big], \quad (5.26)$$

where $\sigma_i(\cdot)$ is the $i$th singular value of the matrix, while $\overline{\sigma}(\cdot)$ is the upper bound of the singular values. In the above $\mathcal{H}_2$ norm formula, the sum can also be written as the trace of the matrix.

It can be seen from Eqn. (5.26) that $\mathcal{H}_\infty$ norm is the peak value of the magnitude of frequency response. For discrete-time systems, the norms are defined as

$$\|G(z)\|_2 = \sqrt{\frac{1}{2\pi} \int_{-\pi}^{\pi} \sum_{i=1}^{p} \sigma_i \big[ G^{\mathrm{H}}(\mathrm{e}^{\mathrm{j}\omega}) G(\mathrm{e}^{\mathrm{j}\omega}) \big] \mathrm{d}\omega}, \quad \|G(z)\|_\infty = \sup_{\omega} \overline{\sigma} \big[ G(\mathrm{e}^{\mathrm{j}\omega}) \big]. \quad (5.27)$$

If an LTI object of a system is given by $G$, the $\|G(s)\|_2$ and $\|G(s)\|_\infty$ norms of it can be computed directly with MATLAB functions `norm(G)` and `norm(G,inf)`. The norms of discrete-time systems can also be calculated with the function. Norms of the systems can be used in robust controller design, or as objective functions in optimal controller design.

**Example 5.10.** The norms of the multivariable system in Example 5.4 can be obtained directly with the following statements, and the norms of the unstable discrete system are respectively $\|\boldsymbol{G}(s)\|_2 = \infty$, $\|\boldsymbol{G}(s)\|_\infty = 45.5817$.

```
>> A=[-2.2,-0.7,1.5,-1; 0.2,-6.3,6,-1.5; ...
      0.6,-0.9,-2,-0.5; 1.4,-0.1,-1,-3.5];
   B=[6,9; 4,6; 4,4; 8,4]; C=[1 2 3 4]; G=ss(A,B,C,[0 0],'Ts',0.1);
   norm(G,2), norm(G,inf)
```

## 5.2    Analytical Time Domain Responses of Linear Systems

It has been pointed out earlier that the mathematical foundation of linear systems are ordinary differential equations and difference equations, and the analytical solutions to them can be obtained in some cases. In this section, three analytical methods are presented. Then the universal analytical solution to a typical second-order system is presented and some of the specifications such as overshoot, settling time are presented.

### 5.2.1    *Analytical Solutions with Direct Integration Method*

For the state space model $(\boldsymbol{A}, \boldsymbol{B}, \boldsymbol{C}, \boldsymbol{D})$, with initial state vector of $\boldsymbol{x}(t_0)$ and input $\boldsymbol{u}(t)$, the analytical solution can be expressed in Eqn. (5.2) as rewritten here:

$$\boldsymbol{x}(t) = e^{\boldsymbol{A}(t-t_0)}\boldsymbol{x}(t_0) + \int_{t_0}^{t} e^{\boldsymbol{A}(t-\tau)}\boldsymbol{B}\boldsymbol{u}(\tau)\mathrm{d}\tau. \tag{5.28}$$

With the symbolic computation facilities provided in MATLAB and Symbolic Math Toolbox, the analytical solution of the problem can be obtained with

$$y = C * (\text{expm}(A * (t - t_0)) * x_0 + \dots$$
$$\text{expm}(A * t) * \text{int}(\text{expm}(-A * \tau) * B * \text{subs}(u, t, \tau), \tau, t_0, t))$$

where `subs()` function can be used in variable substitution, since the original input is a function of $t$, while here the function of $\tau$ is used. When the analytical solution is found, `simple()` function can usually be used to simplify the results.

**Example 5.11.** Assume that the state space model is given by

$$\begin{cases} \dot{\boldsymbol{x}}(t) = \begin{bmatrix} -19 & -16 & -16 & -19 \\ 21 & 16 & 17 & 19 \\ 20 & 17 & 16 & 20 \\ -20 & -16 & -16 & -19 \end{bmatrix} \boldsymbol{x}(t) + \begin{bmatrix} 1 \\ 0 \\ 1 \\ 2 \end{bmatrix} u(t) \\ y(t) = \begin{bmatrix} 2, 1, 0, 0 \end{bmatrix} \boldsymbol{x}(t). \end{cases}$$

with initial state vector of $\boldsymbol{x}^{\mathrm{T}}(0) = \begin{bmatrix} 0, 1, 1, 2 \end{bmatrix}$. The input signal is $u(t) = 2 + 2e^{-3t}\sin 2t$. With the following statements, the analytical solution of the system can be obtained

```
>> syms t tau; u=2+2*exp(-3*t)*sin(2*t);
   A=[-19,-16,-16,-19; 21,16,17,19; 20,17,16,20; -20,-16,-16,-19];
   B=[1; 0; 1; 2]; C=[2 1 0 0]; D=0;   x0=[0; 1; 1; 2];
```

```
y=C*(expm(A*t)*x0+...
    expm(A*t)*int(expm(-A*tau)*B*subs(u,t,tau),tau,0,t))
y=simple(y)
```

The analytical solution of the output signal is

$$y(t) = -54 + \frac{127}{4}te^{-t} + 57e^{-3t} + \frac{119}{8}e^{-t} + 4t^2e^{-t} - \frac{135}{8}e^{-3t}\cos 2t + \frac{77}{4}e^{-3t}\sin 2t.$$

**Example 5.12.** Now let us consider the system model in Example 5.9. If the output is $x_1(t)$, and the two inputs are respectively $u_1(t) = 2 + 2e^{-3t}\sin(2t)$, and $u_2(t) = e^t$, the direct integration method can be used such that the analytical solution can be obtained

```
>> A=[15,6,-12,9; 4,14,8,-4; 2,4,10,-2; 9,6,-12,15];
   B=[3,3; 2,2; -2,-2; 3,9]; C=[1 0 0 0]; syms t tau;
   x0=[0; 1; 1; 2]; u=[2+2*exp(-3*t)*sin(2*t); t*exp(t)];
   y=simple(C*(expm(A*t)*x0+...
       int(expm(A*(t-tau))*B*subs(u,t,tau),tau,0,t)))
```

The analytical solution of the system is

$$y(t) = \frac{3438}{62305}e^{-3t}\sin 2t + \frac{4164}{62305}e^{-3t}\cos 2t + \frac{5238169}{4653084}e^{24t} + \frac{15}{23}e^t t - \frac{83}{51}e^{6t} + \frac{489}{2645}e^t + \frac{1}{4}.$$

### 5.2.2 Analytical Solutions with State Augmentation Method

It can be seen that due to the input term, an integral must be evaluated and it might be difficult. If the external signal $u(t)$ does not exist, the analytical solution is much easier. Here state augmentation method is applied to a class of typical input signals, so that the analytical solutions can be found[4].

Consider first the unit step signal $u(t) = 1(t)$. If an additional state is introduced such that $x_{n+1}(t) = u(t)$, the derivative of the signal can be written as $\dot{x}_{n+1}(t) = 0$. Thus, the original state space model can be rewritten as

$$\begin{bmatrix} \dot{\boldsymbol{x}}(t) \\ \hline \dot{x}_{n+1}(t) \end{bmatrix} = \begin{bmatrix} \boldsymbol{A} & \boldsymbol{B} \\ \hline \boldsymbol{0} & \boldsymbol{0} \end{bmatrix} \begin{bmatrix} \boldsymbol{x}(t) \\ \hline x_{n+1}(t) \end{bmatrix}. \tag{5.29}$$

It can be seen that the original system can be converted to

$$\begin{cases} \dot{\tilde{\boldsymbol{x}}}(t) = \tilde{\boldsymbol{A}}\tilde{\boldsymbol{x}}(t) \\ \tilde{\boldsymbol{y}}(t) = \tilde{\boldsymbol{C}}\tilde{\boldsymbol{x}}(t), \end{cases} \tag{5.30}$$

where

$$\tilde{\boldsymbol{A}} = \begin{bmatrix} \boldsymbol{A} & \boldsymbol{B} \\ \hline \boldsymbol{0} & \boldsymbol{0} \end{bmatrix}, \quad \tilde{\boldsymbol{x}}(t) = \begin{bmatrix} \boldsymbol{x}(t) \\ \hline x_{n+1}(t) \end{bmatrix}, \quad \tilde{\boldsymbol{x}}(0) = \begin{bmatrix} \boldsymbol{x}(0) \\ \hline 1 \end{bmatrix}, \tag{5.31}$$

The analytical solution can be obtained from

$$\tilde{\boldsymbol{x}}(t) = e^{\tilde{\boldsymbol{A}}t}\tilde{\boldsymbol{x}}(0). \tag{5.32}$$

For a class of input signals defined as

$$u(t) = u_1(t) + u_2(t) = \sum_{i=0}^{m} c_i t^i + e^{d_1 t}\left[ d_2 \cos d_4 t + d_3 \sin d_4 t \right], \qquad (5.33)$$

the additional states $x_{n+1} = e^{d_1 t} \cos d_4 t$, $x_{n+2} = e^{d_1 t} \sin d_4 t$, $x_{n+3} = u_1(t), \cdots$ $x_{n+m+3} = u_1^{(m-1)}(t)$ can be introduced such that the augmented system in Eqn. (5.30) can be established where

$$\widetilde{A} = \begin{bmatrix} A & d_2 B & d_3 B & B & 0 & \cdots & 0 \\ & d_1 & -d_4 & & & & \\ 0 & d_4 & d_1 & & 0 & & \\ & & & 0 & 1 & \cdots & 0 \\ & & & 0 & 0 & \cdots & 0 \\ 0 & & 0 & \vdots & \vdots & \ddots & \vdots \\ & & & 0 & 0 & \cdots & 0 \end{bmatrix}, \widetilde{x}(t) = \begin{bmatrix} x(t) \\ \hline x_{n+1}(t) \\ x_{n+2}(t) \\ \hline x_{n+3}(t) \\ x_{n+4}(t) \\ \vdots \\ x_{n+m+3}(t) \end{bmatrix}, \widetilde{x}(0) = \begin{bmatrix} x(0) \\ \hline 1 \\ 0 \\ \hline c_0 \\ c_1 \\ \vdots \\ c_m m! \end{bmatrix}, \quad (5.34)$$

whose analytical solution can still be obtained from Eqn. (5.32).

A MATLAB function ss_augment() is written to establish the augmented state space model for single input systems

```
function [Ga,Xa]=ss_augment(G,cc,dd,X)
G=ss(G); Aa=G.a; Ca=G.c; Xa=X; Ba=G.b; D=G.d;
if (length(dd)>0 & sum(abs(dd))>1e-5),
   if (abs(dd(4))>1e-5),
      Aa=[Aa dd(2)*Ba, dd(3)*Ba; ...
       zeros(2,length(Aa)), [dd(1),-dd(4); dd(4),dd(1)]];
      Ca=[Ca dd(2)*D dd(3)*D]; Xa=[Xa; 1; 0]; Ba=[Ba; 0; 0];
   else,
      Aa=[Aa dd(2)*B; zeros(1,length(Aa)) dd(1)];
      Ca=[Ca dd(2)*D]; Xa=[Xa; 1]; Ba=[B;0];
end, end
if (length(cc)>0 & sum(abs(cc))>1e-5), M=length(cc);
   Aa=[Aa Ba zeros(length(Aa),M-1); zeros(M-1,length(Aa)+1) ...
         eye(M-1); zeros(1,length(Aa)+M)];
   Ca=[Ca D zeros(1,M-1)]; Xa=[Xa; cc(1)]; ii=1;
   for i=2:M, ii=ii*i; Xa(length(Aa)+i)=cc(i)*ii; end
end
Ga=ss(Aa,zeros(size(Ca')),Ca,D);
```

where $cc = [c_0, c_1, \cdots, c_m]$, and $dd = [d_1, d_2, d_3, d_4]$. Symbolic Math Toolbox can then be used to find the analytical solutions of the augmented system.

**Example 5.13.** Consider again the problem shown in Example 5.11. The ss_augment() can be used to get the augmented system, and the analytical solution is exactly the same as the one obtained earlier in Example 5.11.

```
>> cc=[2]; dd=[-3,0,2,2]; x0=[0; 1; 1; 2];
   A=[-19,-16,-16,-19; 21,16,17,19; 20,17,16,20; -20,-16,-16,-19];
   B=[1; 0; 1; 2]; C=[2 1 0 0]; D=0; G=ss(A,B,C,D);
   [Ga,xx0]=ss_augment(G,cc,dd,x0); Ga.a, xx0'
   syms t; y=Ga.c*expm(Ga.a*t)*xx0
```

The mathematical model of the augmented system is

$$\dot{\tilde{x}}(t) = \begin{bmatrix} -19 & -16 & -16 & -19 & 0 & 2 & 1 \\ 21 & 16 & 17 & 19 & 0 & 0 & 0 \\ 20 & 17 & 16 & 20 & 0 & 2 & 1 \\ -20 & -16 & -16 & -19 & 0 & 4 & 2 \\ 0 & 0 & 0 & 0 & -3 & -2 & 0 \\ 0 & 0 & 0 & 0 & 2 & -3 & 0 \\ 0 & 0 & 0 & 0 & 0 & 0 & 0 \end{bmatrix} \tilde{x}(t), \quad \tilde{x}(0) = \begin{bmatrix} 0 \\ 1 \\ 1 \\ 2 \\ 1 \\ 0 \\ 2 \end{bmatrix}.$$

### 5.2.3 Analytical Solutions with Laplace and z Transforms

#### 1. Continuous systems

Assume that the transfer function of the system is given by

$$G(s) = \frac{b_1 s^m + b_2 s^{m-1} + \cdots + b_m s + b_{m+1}}{s^n + a_1 s^{n-1} + a_2 s^{n-2} + \cdots + a_{n-1} s + a_n}, \tag{5.35}$$

and the Laplace transform of the input signal is $U(s)$, then the Laplace transform of the output signal is obtained from $Y(s) = G(s)U(s)$. Inverse Laplace transform can be used to find the analytical solution of the output signal $y(t)$. In MATLAB Symbolic Math Toolbox, Laplace transform and its inverse can be obtained with respectively the functions `laplace()` and `ilaplace()`.

**Example 5.14.** Consider the transfer function model

$$G(s) = \frac{s^3 + 7s^2 + 3s + 4}{s^4 + 7s^3 + 17s^2 + 17s + 6}.$$

If the input is a unit step signal, the analytical solution of the output signal can be obtained with the following statements

```
>> syms s G=(s^3+7*s^2+3*s+4)/(s^4+7*s^3+17*s^2+17*s+6);
   y=ilaplace(G*laplace(sym(1)))
```

The analytical solution of the system is

$$y(t) = \frac{2}{3} - 9e^{-2t} + \frac{31}{12}e^{-3t} - \frac{1}{4}e^{-t}\big(-23 + 14t\big).$$

**Example 5.15.** If the transfer function contains complex poles

$$G(s) = \frac{s+3}{s^4 + 2s^3 + 11s^2 + 18s + 18},$$

the following statements can be used to evaluate the analytical solutions

```
>> syms s; G=(s+3)/(s^4+2*s^3+11*s^2+18*s+18);
   y=ilaplace(G*laplace(sym(1)))
```

The analytical solution of the system is

$$y(t) = \frac{1}{6} + \frac{1}{255}\cos 3t - \frac{13}{255}\sin 3t - \frac{1}{170}e^{-t}\Big(29\cos t + 3\sin t\Big).$$

## 2. Discrete-time systems

For a discrete-time transfer function $F(z)$, if the $z$ transform of the input signal is $U(z)$, the output signal can be written as $Y(z) = G(z)U(z)$. With inverse $z$ transform, the analytical solution of the output signal can be obtained. MATLAB Symbolic Math Toolbox can be used to evaluate the $z$ transform and its inverse with ztrans(), and iztrans().

**Example 5.16.** Consider a discrete-time transfer function

$$G(z) = \frac{(z-1/3)}{(z-1/2)(z-1/4)(z+1/5)}.$$

If the input signal is a unit step input, the following statements can be used to find the analytical solutions to the system

```
>> syms z; G=(z-1/3)/(z-1/2)/(z-1/4)/(z+1/5);
   y=iztrans(G*ztrans(sym(1)))
```

The analytical solution of the system is

$$y(n) = -\frac{80}{81}\left(\frac{1}{4}\right)^n + \frac{800}{567}\left(-\frac{1}{5}\right)^n - \frac{40}{21}\left(\frac{1}{2}\right)^n + \frac{40}{27}.$$

**Example 5.17.** If the discrete-time transfer function is with repeated poles

$$G(z) = \frac{5z-2}{(z-1/2)^3(z-1/3)},$$

the unit step response can be obtained with the following MATLAB commands

```
>> syms z; G=(5*z-2)/(z-1/2)^3/(z-1/3);
   y=iztrans(G*ztrans(sym(1)))
```

The analytical solution of the system is

$$y(n) = -108\left(\frac{1}{3}\right)^n + 72\left(\frac{1}{2}\right)^n - 60\left(\frac{1}{2}\right)^n n - 12\left(\frac{1}{2}\right)^n n^2 + 36.$$

## 3. Systems with time delays

If the system to be studied contains pure time delays, i.e., the transfer functions are $G(s)e^{-Ls}$ and $H(z)z^{-k}$ for continuous and discrete-time models, the output functions can be evaluated analytically first to the systems with no time delay. Then the variables $t$ and $n$ can be replaced by $t - L$ and $n - k$ such that the analytical solutions to the systems with delays can be obtained.

**Example 5.18.** Consider the transfer function $G(s)$ in Example 5.14. If the system has 2 s of delay, the analytical solution can be obtained by direct variable substitution

```
>> syms s t; G=(s^3+7*s^2+3*s+4)/(s^4+7*s^3+17*s^2+17*s+6);
   Y=G/s; y=ilaplace(Y); y=subs(y,t,t-2)
```

The analytical solution of the system can be written as

$$y = \frac{2}{3} - 9e^{-2t+4} + \frac{31}{12}e^{-3t+6} - \frac{1}{4}e^{-t+2}\left(14t - 51\right).$$

More strictly speaking, the analytical solution can be written as

$$y = \begin{cases} 0, & t \leqslant 2 \\ 2/3 - 9e^{-2(t-2)} + 31e^{-3(t-2)}/12 - e^{-(t-2)}\left(14(t-2) - 23\right)/4, & t > 2. \end{cases}$$

or alternatively

$$y(t) = \left\{\frac{2}{3} - 9e^{-2(t-2)} + \frac{31}{12}e^{-3(t-2)} - \frac{1}{4}e^{-(t-2)}\left[14(t-2) - 23\right]\right\} \times 1(t-2),$$

where $1(\cdot)$ is Heaviside function. The step response of the system can be obtained with the following statements, as shown in Fig. 5-4.

```
>> ezplot(y*heaviside(t-2),[0,10])
```

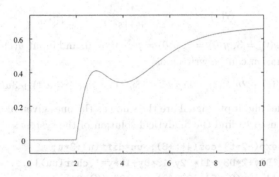

Fig. 5-4   Step response of the delay system.

**Example 5.19.** Consider again the transfer function

$$G(z)z^{-5} = \frac{5z - 2}{(z - 1/2)^3(z - 1/3)}z^{-5}.$$

It can be seen that the system without delay is exactly the same as the one studied in Example 5.17. The following MATLAB statements can be used to find the solution, by substituting $n$ with $n - 5$

```
>> syms z n; G=(5*z-2)/(z-1/2)^3/(z-1/3);
   y=iztrans(G*ztrans(sym(1))); y=subs(y,n,n-5)
```

and the analytical solution to the delay system can be written as

$$y(n) = -108\left(\frac{1}{3}\right)^{n-5} + 72\left(\frac{1}{2}\right)^{n-5} - 60\left(\frac{1}{2}\right)^{n-5}(n-5) - 12\left(\frac{1}{2}\right)^{n-5}(n-5)^2 + 36.$$

More exactly, the analytical solution can be written as

$$y(n) = \begin{cases} 0, & n \leqslant 5 \\ -108\,(1/3)^{n-5} + (-12n^2 + 60n + 72)\,(1/2)^{n-5} + 36, & n > 5. \end{cases}$$

Although the following statements can be directly used in solving the original problem, the readability of the result is not quite satisfactory.

```
>> syms z; G=(5*z-2)/(z-1/2)^3/(z-1/3)*z^(-5); R=z/(z-1); y=iztrans(G*R)
```

### 5.2.4    *Time Responses of Systems with Nonzero Initial Conditions*

In the definitions of transfer functions, zero initial conditions are assumed. If the initial output signals and their derivatives are not zero, extensions to the original transfer functions should be introduced, such that the initial outputs can be considered. The `dsolve()` function in Section 3.3.4 is recommended, since from the transfer function model, linear time invariant ordinary differential equations can be reestablished.

**Example 5.20.** Consider again the transfer function in Example 5.15

$$G(s) = \frac{s+3}{s^4 + 2s^3 + 11s^2 + 18s + 18},$$

with initial values $y(0) = 3$, $\dot{y}(0) = 5$, $\ddot{y}(0) = y^{(3)}(0) = 0$, and input $u(t) = e^{-2t}\cos(4t+6)$, the differential equation can be written as

$$y^{(4)}(t) + 2y^{(3)}(t) + 11\ddot{y}(t) + 18\dot{y}(t) + 18y(t) = \dot{u}(t) + 3u(t),$$

and the initial values and input signal are the same as the ones given above. The following statements can be used to find the analytical solution of the system

```
>> syms t; u=exp(-2*t)*cos(4*t+6); uu=diff(u)+3*u;
   y=dsolve(['D4y+2*D3y+11*D2y+18*Dy+18*y=',char(uu)],...
       'y(0)=3','Dy(0)=5','D2y(0)=0','D3y(0)=0')
```

The right-and-side of the equation is calculated first, and the result is converted to a string with `char()` function. The square brackets are used to join the left-hand-side and right-hand-side of the original equation together to form a complete string. The analytical solution to the system can be written as

$$y(t) = \left( \frac{2032\cos 6}{67575} + \frac{668\sin 6}{22525} + \frac{218}{255} \right) \sin 3t - \left( \frac{233\cos 6}{22525} - \frac{524\sin 6}{22525} + \frac{132}{85} \right) \cos 3t$$

$$- e^{-t}\cos t \left( \frac{31\cos 6}{11050} + \frac{176\sin t}{5525} - \frac{387}{85} \right) - e^{-t}\sin t \left( \frac{1117\cos 6}{11050} + \frac{282\sin 6}{5525} - \frac{594}{85} \right)$$

$$+ \frac{e^{-2t}\cos 3t}{135150} \Big[ 2703\cos(t+6) - 3604\sin(t+6) - 1305\cos(7t+6) + 460\sin(7t+6) \Big]$$

$$- \frac{e^{-2t}\sin 3t}{135150} \Big[ 3604\cos(t+6) + 2703\sin(t+6) + 460\cos(7t+6) + 1305\sin(7t+6) \Big]$$

$$- \frac{e^{-2t}\cos t}{22100} \Big[ 533\cos(3t+6) - 595\cos(5t+6) - 1469\sin(3t+6) + 765\sin(5t+6) \Big]$$

$$+ \frac{e^{-2t}\sin t}{22100} \Big[ 1469\cos(3t+6) + 765\cos(5t+6) + 533\sin(3t+6) + 595\sin(5t+6) \Big].$$

### 5.2.5 *Time Response Specifications of Second-order Systems*

Assume that the open-loop model is $G_o(s) = \omega_n^2/s(s + 2\zeta\omega_n)$, and the feedback system is constructed with unity negative feedback, The variable $\zeta$ is referred to as the damping ratio, and $\omega_n$ is the natural frequency. The closed-loop model can be obtained as

$$G(s) = \frac{\omega_n^2}{s^2 + 2\zeta\omega_n s + \omega_n^2}. \tag{5.36}$$

With unit step input, it can easily be found with MATLAB Symbolic Math Toolbox function that the analytical solution of $y(t)$ can be expressed as

$$y(t) = 1 - \omega_n e^{-\zeta\omega_n t} \left[ \frac{\cosh(\omega_d t)}{\omega_n} + \frac{\zeta \sinh(\omega_d t)}{\omega_d} \right], \tag{5.37}$$

where $\omega_d = \sqrt{\zeta^2 - 1}\,\omega_n$. The above unified form can be shown with the following statements

```
>> syms z wn s; G=wn^2/(s^2+2*z*wn*s+wn^2);
   y=ilaplace(G*laplace(sym(1)))
```

Alternatively from control textbooks, for different values of $\zeta$, the analytical solutions of the system can be expressed as

(1) If $\zeta = 0$, the step response is simplified as $y(t) = 1 - \cos(\omega_n t)$, and referred to as zero damping oscillation.

(2) If $0 < \zeta < 1$, the system response is referred to as under-damping oscillation, where

$$y(t) = 1 - e^{-\zeta\omega_n t} \frac{1}{\sqrt{1 - \zeta^2}} \sin\left(\omega_n\sqrt{1 - \zeta^2}\,t + \tan^{-1}\sqrt{1 - \zeta^2}/\zeta\right).$$

(3) If $\zeta = 1$, $y(t) = 1 - (1 + \omega_n t)e^{-\omega_n t}$ is referred to as critical damping response.

(4) If $\zeta > 1$, the over-damping response can be written as

$$y(t) = 1 - \frac{\omega_n}{2\sqrt{\zeta^2 - 1}} \left[ \frac{e^{\left(-\zeta - \sqrt{\zeta^2 - 1}\right)\omega_n t}}{-\zeta - \sqrt{\zeta^2 - 1}} - \frac{e^{\left(-\zeta + \sqrt{\zeta^2 - 1}\right)\omega_n t}}{-\zeta + \sqrt{\zeta^2 - 1}} \right].$$

If $\omega_n = 1\,\text{rad/s}$, and for different damping ratios $\zeta$'s, the step responses can be obtained as shown in Fig. 5-5(a), where when $\zeta = 1$, Eqn. (5.37) cannot be used directly, since the denominator is zero. In this case, it should be replaced by $1 + \epsilon$.

```
wn=1; yy=[]; t=0:.1:12; zet=[0:0.1:0.9, 1+eps,2,3,5];
for z=zet
   if z==1, z=1+eps; end, wd=sqrt(z^2-1)*wn;
   y=1-wn*exp(-z*wn*t).*[cosh(wd*t)/wn+z*sinh(wd*t)/wd]; yy=[yy; y];
end
plot(t,yy)
```

It can be seen that when $\zeta$ is small, the oscillation is strong, and if $\zeta = 0$, there is zero damping oscillation. If $\zeta \geqslant 1$, there is no longer damping in the output, and the speed of responses is becoming lower.

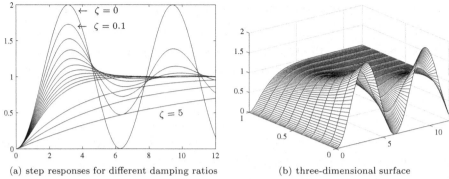

(a) step responses for different damping ratios     (b) three-dimensional surface

Fig. 5-5     Step responses for different damping ratios.

Three-dimensional surface plot can also be obtained with the following MATLAB statements and the surface is shown in Fig. 5-5(b).

```
>> i=find(zet<=1);     % remove the step responses for ζ > 1
   z1=zet(i); y1=yy(i,:);   % extract relevant data
   surf(t,z1,y1), set(gca,'YDir','reverse')   % set direction in y axis
```

A typical step response of a linear system is shown in Fig. 5-6, and the interested specifications in step responses are

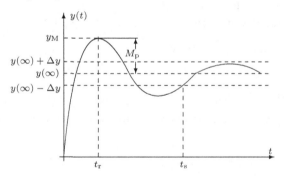

Fig. 5-6     Typical waveform of the step response.

(1) **Steady-state value** $y(\infty)$. The value of system response when the output settled down after a long period of time. For unstable systems, the steady-state value is infinity. Final value theorem in Laplace transform can be used to find the steady-state value of the step response

$$y(\infty) = \lim_{s \to 0} s\, G(s)\frac{1}{s} = G(0) = \frac{b_m}{a_n}, \tag{5.38}$$

i.e., the ratio of constant terms in the numerator and denominator of the system. If the system model is $G$, the steady-state value can also be obtained directly with the function `dcgain(G)`.

(2) **Percent overshoot** $\sigma$. Assume that the peak value is given by $y_\mathrm{p}$, the

percent overshoot is defined as

$$\sigma = \frac{y_{\mathrm{p}} - y(\infty)}{y(\infty)} \times 100\%. \tag{5.39}$$

(3) **Rise time** $t_{\mathrm{r}}$. The rise time is usually defined as the time period required such that the output changes from 10% to 90% of its steady-state value.

(4) **Settling time** $t_{\mathrm{s}}$. The time when the output signal enters and remains in the specific error band around the steady-state value. The width of the error band is usually selected as 2% or 5% of the steady-state value.

For a well-designed servo system, the steady-state error and overshoot should be small or zero. Also, the rise time and settling time should be small. These specifications are usually considered in the controller design.

## 5.3 Numerical Solutions of Time Domain Responses

Analytical solutions to linear systems have been studied. Strictly speaking, there is usually no analytical solution approach for system orders higher than four. Due to Abel theorem, there is no analytical solution method for a polynomial equation. In the previous presentation, analytical and numerical solution approaches are combined to find the solution with high precision.

In practical applications, analytical solutions are not necessary, step response plotting is adequate. In this case, numerical solution techniques to ordinary differential equations can be used to evaluate system responses and the plots can also be obtained.

In this section, step and impulses of linear systems are presented, and time responses for arbitrary inputs can also be evaluated. Multivariable time responses are also studied in this section.

### 5.3.1 *Step Responses and Impulse Responses*

Step responses of an LTI system can be obtained immediately with the function `step()` provided in the Control System Toolbox. Impulse responses can be drawn with function `impulse()`. For systems with arbitrary input signals, the function `lsim()` can be used directly. For systems containing nonlinear elements, the facilities of the powerful Simulink can be used, which will be fully presented in the next chapter. The function `step()` can be called with the following syntaxes

```
step(G)           % if no returned argument, plot automatically
[y,t] = step(G)   % returns response data, without plots
[y,t] = step(G,t_f) % set a terminate time t_f, without plots
y = step(G,t)     % select a time vector t, without plots
```

where $G$ can be any LTI model. It can be transfer function, state space or zero–

pole–gain model, and it can either be continuous or discrete-time model, single variable or multivariable model, with or without time delays. If no returned arguments is used in the function call, step response of the system can be drawn automatically. If the step responses of several systems are expected, the following syntax can be used, where the options are exactly drawn, and the options are the same as the ones in `plot()` function. For instance, with the command `step(`$G_1$`,'-',`$G_2$`,'-.b',`$G_3$`,':r')` , a solid line is used to show the step response of $G_1$, blue dash dot line for $G_2$, and red dotted line for $G_3$.

**Example 5.21.** Assume that a continuous model with time delay is

$$G(s) = \frac{10s + 20}{10s^4 + 23s^3 + 26s^2 + 23s + 10}e^{-s}.$$

The model can be entered first, and the step response of the system can then be obtained as shown in Fig. 5-7(a).

```
>> G=tf([10 20],[10 23 26 23 10],'ioDelay',1); % system model
   step(G,30); % draw step response with terminate time 30
```

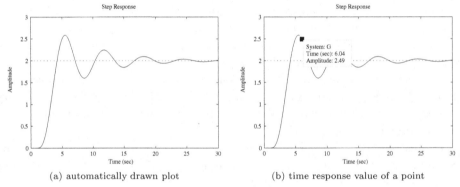

(a) automatically drawn plot      (b) time response value of a point

Fig. 5-7   Step response of a linear system.

If one clicks at a point with the left mouse button on the curve, the information regarding the point can be obtained as shown in Fig. 5-7(b). The step response can further be analyzed with this facility.

The quantitative specifications such as overshoot and settling time can be obtained with the items in the shortcut menu as shown in Fig. 5-8(a), displayed by clicking the right mouse button. The menu items in Characteristics can be used to show these specifications, as shown in Fig. 5-8(b). If further information is required, one can move mouse button to the dot on the plot.

The analytical solution to the step response of the system can also be found

```
>> syms s t; G1=poly2sym(G.num{1},s)/poly2sym(G.den{1},s);
   y=ilaplace(G1/s), y1=subs(y,t,t-1)
```

The analytical of the system can be obtained

$$y(t) = 2 - \frac{10}{17}e^{-t+1}(t+2) - \frac{4}{17}e^{-3(t-1)/20}\left[\cos\frac{\sqrt{391}}{20}(t-1) + \frac{103\sqrt{391}}{391}\sin\frac{\sqrt{391}}{20}(t-1)\right].$$

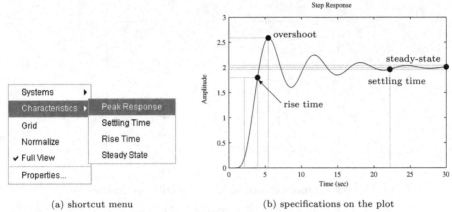

| (a) shortcut menu | (b) specifications on the plot |
|---|---|

Fig. 5-8    Step response specifications.

**Example 5.22.** Different discretization methods have been presented in Chapter 4, and here we shall study the influence of sampling interval to the discretization behaviors. Assume that the continuous model is given by

$$G(s) = \frac{1}{s^2 + 0.2s + 1} e^{-s}.$$

Select the sampling intervals $T = 0.01, 0.1, 0.5, 1.2\,\text{s}$, the following statements can be used to find the discretized models, and draw the step responses as shown in Fig. 5-9. It can be seen that if the sampling interval selected is too large, the characteristics of the original system cannot be retained.

```
>> G=tf(1,[1 0.2 1],'ioDelay',1);   % input the continuous model
   G1=c2d(G,0.01,'zoh'); G2=c2d(G,0.1); G3=c2d(G,0.5);
   G4=c2d(G,1.2); % Tustin transform, sometimes with complex coefficients
   step(G,'-',G2,'--',G3,':',G4,'-.',10)   % compare step responses
```

The discretized models can be obtained

$$G_1(z) = \frac{4.997 \times 10^{-5} z + 4.993 \times 10^{-5}}{z^2 - 1.998z + 0.998} z^{-100}, \quad G_2(z) = \frac{0.004963z + 0.00493}{z^2 - 1.97z + 0.9802} z^{-10},$$

$$G_3(z) = \frac{0.1185z + 0.1145}{z^2 - 1.672z + 0.9048} z^{-2}, \quad G_4(z) = \frac{0.01967z^2 + 0.7277z + 0.3865}{z^3 - 0.6527z^2 + 0.7866z}.$$

It should be noted that the step responses of discrete-time models obtained with **step()** function are drawn as staircase form, as if a zero-order hold was used. Also, the shortcut menu with right mouse button click is also supported for discrete-time systems.

**Example 5.23.** Consider the two-input, two-output system shown in Example 4.7, rewritten as

$$G(s) = \begin{bmatrix} \dfrac{0.1134 e^{-0.72s}}{1.78s^2 + 4.48s + 1} & \dfrac{0.924}{2.07s + 1} \\ \dfrac{0.3378 e^{-0.3s}}{0.361s^2 + 1.09s + 1} & \dfrac{-0.318 e^{-1.29s}}{2.93s + 1} \end{bmatrix}.$$

The following statements can be entered and the step responses of the multivariable system can be obtained as shown in Fig. 5-10(a).

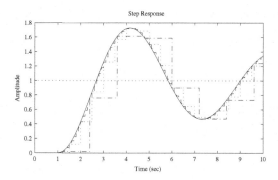

Fig. 5-9   Comparisons of continuous system and discretized models.

```
>> g11=tf(0.1134,[1.78 4.48 1],'ioDelay',0.72); g12=tf(0.924,[2.07 1]);
   g21=tf(0.3378,[0.361 1.09 1],'ioDelay',0.3);
   g22=tf(-0.318,[2.93 1],'ioDelay',1.29);
   G=[g11, g12; g21, g22]; % transfer function matrix
   step(G)                 % step responses of the multivariable systems
```

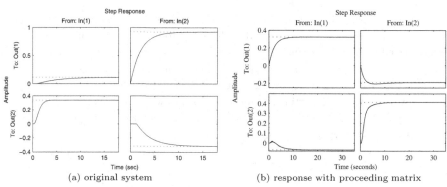

(a) original system          (b) response with proceeding matrix

Fig. 5-10   Step responses of the multivariable systems.

It should be noted that the step responses of a multivariable system is obtained by each input is active alone. From the step responses obtained, it can be seen that when $u_1(t)$ is active alone, the size of $y_2(t)$ is relatively large. This phenomenon is referred to as coupling of multivariable systems. To design controllers for multivariable systems, decoupling approaches are normally used. If the coupling is not very strong, the controller for the channels can be designed separately. Consider the static pre-compensator $\boldsymbol{K}_{\mathrm{p}}$

$$\boldsymbol{K}_{\mathrm{p}} = \begin{bmatrix} 0.1134 & 0.924 \\ 0.3378 & -0.318 \end{bmatrix},$$

the new transfer function matrix can be written as $\boldsymbol{G}(s)\boldsymbol{K}_{\mathrm{p}}$. With manual manipulation, it is easily found that for instance, the upper left term in the transfer function matrix can be expressed as

$$0.1134\frac{0.1134e^{-0.72s}}{1.78s^2 + 4.48s + 1} + 0.924\frac{0.3378e^{-0.3s}}{0.361s^2 + 1.09s + 1}.$$

Since the delay constant of the two terms are different, the result cannot be written in the form of $g(s)e^{-\tau s}$. Thus, the overload functions for the operators of $+$, $-$, $*$, and feedback() may fail for the transfer function matrices with different delays. In this case, two methods can be used instead to solve the problems. One is to use Padé approximation to the delay terms to approximate the transfer function matrices by rational transfer functions, and the other, is to use state space model with internal delays.

The following statements involving state space models with internal delays can be used to draw the step responses

```
>> Kp=[0.1134,0.924; 0.3378,-0.318]; step(ss(G)*Kp)
```

Alternatively, for instance, 0/2 Padé approximation can be used below and the following statements can be used to draw the step response of the compensated system $G(s)K_p$, as shown in Fig. 5-10(b).

```
>> [n1,d1]=paderm(0.72,0,2); g11.ioDelay=0; g11=tf(n1,d1)*g11;
   [n1,d1]=paderm(0.30,0,2); g21.ioDelay=0; g21=tf(n1,d1)*g21;
   [n1,d1]=paderm(1.29,0,2); g22.ioDelay=0; g22=tf(n1,d1)*g22;
   G=[g11, g12; g21, g22]; hold on; step(G*Kp)
```

It can be seen that with such a static compensator, the behavior of coupling is significantly improved, such that it might be possible to design controllers individually for each channels.

Of course, the approximate result should be validated. One way is to replace the delay terms with Padé approximation with different orders to see whether consistent results can be obtained. Alternatively, numerical simulation with Simulink can be used to get exact results. This topic will be presented in Chapter 6.

The impulse responses of an LTI object can be obtained with MATLAB Control System Toolbox function impulse(), and the syntaxes of the function are exactly the same as those for step() function. For instance, the impulse response of the system in Example 5.21 can be obtained with the following statements, as shown in Fig. 5-11.

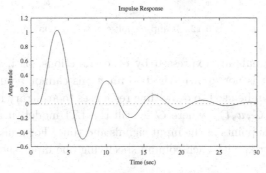

Fig. 5-11    Impulse response of the system.

```
>> G=tf([10 20],[10 23 26 23 10],'ioDelay',1); % system model
   impulse(G, 30); % impulse response of the system when terminate time is 30s
```

### 5.3.2 Time Domain Responses for Arbitrary Inputs

Step responses and impulse responses are the two mostly used time responses, and they can be evaluated with the functions `step()` and `impulse()`.

If the Laplace transform of the input signal is $R(s)$, which can be written as a rational function, the output signal can be written as $Y(s) = G(s)R(s)$. The time response $Y(s)$ of the system can be directly obtained with the `impulse()` function.

**Example 5.24.** For the delayed system

$$G(s) = \frac{10s + 20}{10s^4 + 23s^3 + 26s^2 + 23s + 10}e^{-s},$$

the unit ramp response of the system can be obtained with the following existing `step()` or `impulse()` functions.

The Laplace transform of a unit ramp function is $1/s^2$. Thus, the ramp response of the system $G(s)$ is the same as the step response of system $G(s)/s$, or the impulse response of the system $G(s)/s^2$. The following MATLAB statements can be used to obtain the ramp response of the system, as shown in Fig. 5-12.

```
>> G=tf([10 20],[10 23 26 23 10],'ioDelay',1); % system model
   s=tf('s'); step(G/s); % it can alternatively be obtained with impulse(G/s^2)
```

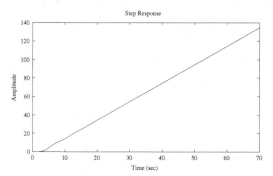

Fig. 5-12   Ramp response of the system.

If the input signals are expressed by other functions, or if the mathematical model of the input is not known, the two functions cannot be used. In this case, `lsim()` function can be used to draw time responses to arbitrary input signals, with the syntax $\mathtt{lsim}(\boldsymbol{G},\boldsymbol{u},\boldsymbol{t})$ , where $\boldsymbol{G}$ is still the LTI model, $\boldsymbol{u}$ and $\boldsymbol{t}$ are used to describe the sample points in the input signals and time. For multivariable systems, $\boldsymbol{u}$ should be a matrix, with each column specifying one input signal.

**Example 5.25.** Consider again the multivariable system in Example 4.7. If the two input signals are $u_1(t) = 1 - e^{-t}\sin(3t + 1)$ and $u_2(t) = \sin(t)\cos(t + 2)$, respectively, the following statements can be used to draw the time responses driven by the two signals simultaneously with the function lsim(), and the results are shown in Fig. 5-13.

```
>> g11=tf(0.1134,[1.78 4.48 1],'ioDelay',0.72);
   g12=tf(0.924,[2.07 1]); g22=tf(-0.318,[2.93 1],'ioDelay',1.29);
   g21=tf(0.3378,[0.361 1.09 1],'ioDelay',0.3);
   G=[g11, g12; g21, g22]; % transfer function matrix
   t=[0:.1:15]'; u=[1-exp(-t).*sin(3*t+1),sin(t).*cos(t+2)]; % two inputs
   lsim(G,u,t);   % draw automatically the system responses
```

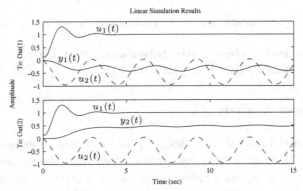

Fig. 5-13   Time responses of the multivariable system.

### 5.3.3 *Responses for Systems with Nonzero Initial Conditions*

The above-mentioned time response evaluating functions such as step(), lsim() are all based on the assumptions that the initial conditions of the systems are zeros. If the initial conditions are not zeros, the initial() function should be used. The syntax of the function is $[y,t] = \text{initial}(G,x_0,t_f)$ , where $t_f$ is the terminating simulation time. If superposition theorem is used, the response obtained can be added to the results obtained with lsim().

**Example 5.26.** Consider the system in Example 5.11. Analytical solution to the system response was obtained. Here, the time domain response for systems with nonzero initial conditions can be obtained as shown in Fig. 5-14.

```
>> A=[-19,-16,-16,-19; 21,16,17,19; 20,17,16,20; -20,-16,-16,-19];
   B=[1; 0; 1; 2]; C=[2 1 0 0]; G=ss(A,B,C,0);
   x0=[0; 1; 1; 2]; [y1,t]=initial(G,x0,10);
   u=2+2*exp(-3*t).*sin(2*t); y2=lsim(G,u,t); plot(t,y1+y2)
```

The analytical solution can be obtained, and the time response of the system is exactly the same as the one obtained in Fig. 5-14.

```
>> syms t tau; u=2+2*exp(-3*t)*sin(2*t);
   y=C*(expm(A*t)*x0+...
```

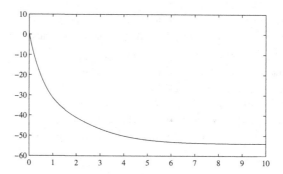

Fig. 5-14   Time domain response for systems with nonzero initial conditions.

```
expm(A*t)*int(expm(-A*tau)*B*subs(u,t,tau),tau,0,t));
hold on; ezplot(y,[0,10]), ylim([-60 0])
```

## 5.4   Root Locus Analysis

Root locus-based analysis and design is an important technique in automatic control theory. Root locus of a system originated from the research on stability of linear systems, and it was a milestone in the early stages of the development of control theory. It continues to be a useful and practical method.

The basic idea of loot locus technique assumes that the open-loop model of a single variable system is $G(s)$, the proportional controller is given by $K$, and the closed-loop is assumed to be constructed as a unity negative feedback. The closed-loop system model can be obtained as $G_c(s) = KG(s)/(1 + KG(s))$. The characteristic equation of the closed-loop system is then

$$1 + KG(s) = 0. \tag{5.40}$$

For a specific value of $K$, the above equation can alternatively be written as a polynomial equation, and the roots of it can immediately be obtained. If the value of $K$ changes, another set of roots can be found. For different values of $K$, the trajectories of each root can be obtained. The trajectories are referred to as root locus of the system.

The function `rlocus()` in MATLAB Control System Toolbox can be used to draw the root locus of the system. The syntaxes of the function are quite simple, and similar to `step()`, where

```
rlocus(G)          % if no returned argument, plot root locus automatically
rlocus(G,K)            % for the given K, draw root locus
[R,K] =rlocus(G)   % R is the root locus data, no plot drawn
rlocus(G₁,'-',G₂,'-.b',G₃,':r') % draw root loci of several systems
```

The function can only be used for single variable systems. In continuous systems, the systems with time delays cannot be handled, since the characteristic equations are no longer polynomial equations. For discrete-time systems, there is no such restriction.

One can click the left mouse button on a certain point of the root locus and the relevant information, such as the gain, positions of the poles, possible damping ratio and overshoot, will be displayed.

With the root locus obtained, the `grid` command can be used to show the iso-damping and natural frequency contours, and these information are useful in controller design.

**Example 5.27.** Assume that the open-loop model is given by

$$G(s) = \frac{s^2 + 4s + 8}{s^5 + 18s^4 + 120.3s^3 + 357.5s^2 + 478.5s + 306}.$$

If computers are not used, the method in control theory courses cannot be used, since the open-loop poles and zeros are not known, which means that the starting and terminating points of the root locus branches are difficult to get, not to mention the exact root locus sketching. With the use of MATLAB, a simple `rlocus()` function can be used and the root locus can be obtained immediately, as shown in Fig. 5-15(a).

```
>> num=[1 4 8]; den=[1,18,120.3,357.5,478.5,306];
   G=tf(num,den); rlocus(G) % input system model and draw root locus
```

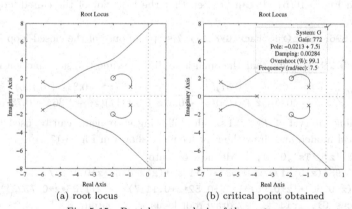

(a) root locus          (b) critical point obtained

Fig. 5-15   Root locus analysis of the system.

By clicking a point on the root locus, the relevant information can be displayed. For instance, if we click the point intersecting the imaginary axis, the information displayed will be shown in Fig. 5-15(b), where the critical gain is 772. Thus, if the gain $K > 772$, the closed-loop system becomes unstable.

**Example 5.28.** Consider the open-loop model

$$G(s) = \frac{10}{s(s+3)(s^2 + 2s + 4)}.$$

The following statements can be used to specify the system model and draw the root locus, as shown in Fig. 5-16(a). The contours are also obtained on the root locus.

```
>> s=tf('s'); G=10/(s*(s+3)*(s^2+3*s+4));
   rlocus(G), grid    % draw the root locus with contours
```

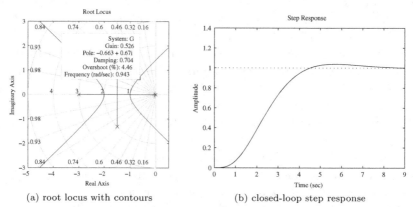

| (a) root locus with contours | (b) closed-loop step response |
| --- | --- |

Fig. 5-16   Root locus and step response.

In practical control, if the damping ratio $\zeta$ is around 0.707, the behavior of the system is recommended. The intersection of the root locus with iso-damping ratio of 0.707 can be clicked and the information are displayed as shown in Fig. 5-16(a), where $K = 0.526$. Such a gain can be used and the step response of the closed-loop system can be obtained as shown in Fig. 5-16(b). It can be seen that the behavior of the closed-loop system is satisfactory.

```
>> K=0.526; step(feedback(G*K,1)) % step response of the closed-loop system
```

**Example 5.29.** Assume that the open-loop discrete-time transfer function is given

$$G(z) = \frac{-0.95(z+0.51)(z+0.68)(z+1.3)(z^2-0.84z+0.196)}{(z+0.66)(z+0.96)(z^2-0.52z+0.1117)(z^2+1.36z+0.7328)},$$

with sampling interval of $T = 0.1\,\mathrm{s}$. The following statements can be used to enter the mathematical model, and draw the root locus, as shown in Fig. 5-17.

```
>> z=tf('z','Ts',0.1);   % define z operator
   G=-0.95*(z+0.51)*(z+0.68)*(z+1.3)*(z^2-0.84*z+0.196)/...
     ((z+0.66)*(z+0.96)*(z^2-0.52*z+0.1117)*(z^2+1.36*z+0.7328));
   rlocus(G), grid        % draw root locus with contours
```

**Example 5.30.** Consider the open-loop discrete-time model

$$G(z) = \frac{0.52(z-0.49)(z^2+1.28z+0.4385)}{(z-0.78)(z+0.29)(z^2+0.7z+0.1586)},$$

with sampling interval of $T = 0.1\,\mathrm{s}$. The following statements can be used to enter the open-loop model into MATLAB workspace, and draw directly the root locus, as shown in Fig. 5-18(a).

```
>> z=tf('z','Ts',0.1);
   G=0.52*(z-0.49)*(z^2+1.28*z+0.4385)/...
     ((z-0.78)*(z+0.29)*(z^2+0.7*z+0.1586));
   rlocus(G)  % draw root locus
```

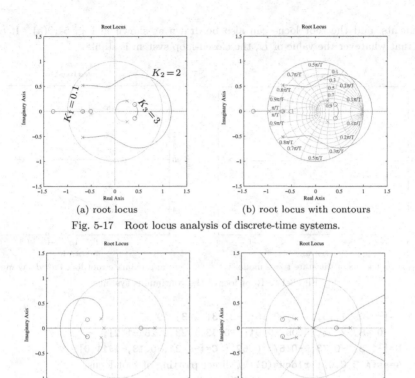

(a) root locus        (b) root locus with contours

Fig. 5-17   Root locus analysis of discrete-time systems.

(a) root locus        (b) root locus with delays

Fig. 5-18   Root loci for discrete-time systems.

Again with the **grid** command, the iso-damping contours and natural frequency contours can be displayed automatically. It can also be seen that by clicking the intersection of the root locus with the unit circle, the critical gain can be obtained as 2.83, i.e., if $K > 2.83$, the closed-loop system becomes unstable.

Consider the system with a six-step delay. The new model can be entered into MAT-LAB workspace, and the exact root locus of it can be obtained as shown in Fig. 5-18(b). It can be seen that the critical gain in this case is $K < 1.16$, otherwise the closed-loop system is unstable. It can be seen that if there is delay in the plant model, the stability range is reduced.

```
>> G.ioDelay=6; rlocus(G), grid,    % root locus for system with delay
```

**Example 5.31.** Consider the continuous open-loop model with delay

$$\begin{cases} \dot{x}(t) = \begin{bmatrix} -0.99 & 1.16 & 1.76 & -0.16 \\ -2.03 & -2.3 & 2.9 & -2.45 \\ -0.48 & -3.96 & -2.05 & -0.91 \\ -0.43 & 1.23 & 2.26 & -1.2 \end{bmatrix} x(t) + \begin{bmatrix} -1.3 \\ -0.73 \\ -0.57 \\ 0.62 \end{bmatrix} u(t-1) \\ y(t) = \begin{bmatrix} -1.34 & -0.13 & -1.11 & 0 \end{bmatrix} x(t). \end{cases}$$

The state space model without delay can be entered easily with the following statements, and the root locus can also be drawn as shown in Fig. 5-19(a). It can be seen that whatever the value of $K$, the closed-loop system is stable.

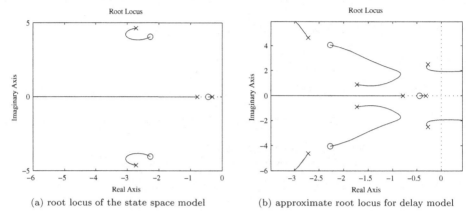

(a) root locus of the state space model        (b) approximate root locus for delay model

Fig. 5-19   Root loci of the continuous systems.

```
>> A=[-0.99,1.16,1.76,-0.16; -2.03,-2.3,2.9,-2.45;
      -0.48,-3.96,-2.05,-0.91; -0.43,1.23,2.26,-1.2];
   B=[-1.3; -0.73; -0.57; 0.62]; C=[-1.34,-0.13,-1.11,0];
   G=ss(A,B,C,0); rlocus(G)   % direct plotting of root locus
```

The **rlocus()** function cannot be used to draw root loci for continuous systems with delays, since the characteristic equations are no longer polynomial equations. In this case, Padé approximation can be used for the delay term, and the root locus for such an approximate system can be drawn instead, as shown in Fig. 5-19(b). It can be seen that the critical gain for the new system is $K \leqslant 0.88$.

```
>> [n,d]=paderm(1,0,4); rlocus(tf(n,d)*G)
```

**Example 5.32.** Consider the plant model with time delay

$$G(s) = \frac{6s + 4}{s(s^2 + 3s + 1)}e^{-2s}.$$

The following MATLAB statements can be used to draw approximate root locus with 2nd order Padé approximation, as shown in Fig. 5-20(a), from which the critical gain obtained is 0.185.

```
>> s=tf('s'); G=(6*s+4)/s/(s^2+3*s+1); G.ioDelay=2;
   rlocus(pade(G,2)) % root locus with 2nd order Padé approximation
```

By further increasing the order of Padé approximation, e.g., with 4th order Padé approximation, the root locus can be obtained as shown in Fig. 5-20(b), from which the critical gain is about 0.185. If the order of Padé approximation is further increased, the critical gain obtained may still be similar.

The root loci drawn in the previous examples are all for negative feedback structures. For positive feedback structures, the command `rlocus(-G)` can be used to directly drawing the root loci.

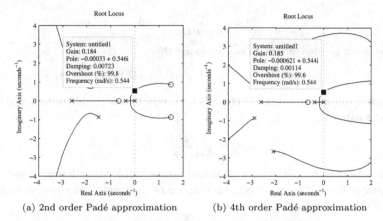

(a) 2nd order Padé approximation   (b) 4th order Padé approximation

Fig. 5-20   Approximate root locus for delay system.

**Example 5.33.** Assume that the open-loop model is given by

$$G(s) = \frac{s^2 + 5s + 6}{s^5 + 13s^4 + 65s^3 + 157s^2 + 184s + 80}.$$

The following statements can be used to draw the root locus for the positive feedback structure, as shown in Fig. 5-21. The critical gain of the system can be found such that when $K > 13.6$, the closed-loop system is not stable.

```
>> G=tf([1 5 6],[1 13 65 157 184 80]); rlocus(-G)
```

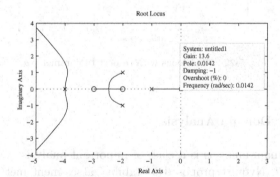

Fig. 5-21   Root locus of the positive feedback system.

The root locus analysis so far illustrated are the loci for open-loop gains. It can also be extended to other parameters in the system.

**Example 5.34.** Consider the plant model

$$G(s) = \frac{5(s+5)(s^2 + 6s + 12)}{(s+a)(s^3 + 4s^2 + 3s + 2)},$$

with tunable parameter $a$. Denote $N_1(s) = 5(s+5)(s^2 + 6s + 12)$, $D_1(s) = s^3 + 4s^2 + 3s + 2$, the characteristic equation can be written as

$$1 + \frac{N_1(s)}{(s+a)D_1(s)} = 0.$$

Through simple derivations, it can be found that

$$N_1(s) + (s+a)D_1(s) = 0, \quad \Rightarrow \quad \left[N_1(s) + sD_1(s)\right] + aD_1(s) = 0,$$

from which it can be seen that the characteristic equation is converted to $1 + a\widetilde{G}(s) = 0$, with $\widetilde{G}(s)$ written as

$$\widetilde{G}(s) = \frac{D_1(s)}{N_1(s) + sD_1(s)}.$$

The following statements can be given to draw the root locus with respect to parameter $a$, as shown in Fig. 5-22. It can be seen that for this example, the closed-loop system is stable, for any value of $a \geqslant 0$.

```
>> s=tf('s'); N1=5*(s+5)*(s^2+6*s+12); D1=s^3+4*s^2+3*s+2;
   G1=D1/(N1+s*D1); rlocus(G1)
```

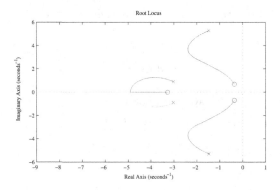

Fig. 5-22   Root locus with respect to parameter $a$.

## 5.5   Frequency Domain Analysis

Frequency domain analysis is a class of important analysis methods in control systems. In 1932, Nyquist proposed a stability assessment method later known as Nyquist theorem[5]. Another method proposed by Bode is an alternative frequency domain analysis approach, and the relationship among the frequency, magnitude and phase is studied. The method is later known as Bode diagram approach[6]. Nichols redefined the existing Bode diagram, and proposed another method, studying the relationship between the magnitude and phase of the transfer function. The plot drawn is later referred to as Nichols chart[7]. These methods were the most important frequency domain approaches in single variable systems, and these plots are useful in control systems design. Since there exists coupling among the signals in multivariable systems, it might be not a good way to design controllers directly, decoupling should be carried out first.

In this section, Nyquist theorem-based frequency domain analysis for single variable systems is presented first. Inverse Nyquist array and the concept of diagonal dominant for multivariable systems are then presented in the next section.

### 5.5.1 *Frequency Domain Analysis of Single Variable Systems*

For the transfer function model $G(s)$, if the frequency variable $j\omega$ is used for the variable $s$, the gain $G(j\omega)$ can be represented by a complex quantity, and it is a function of $\omega$. There are several ways to express such a complex quantity, and different frequency response plots can be defined.

(1) The complex quantity can be expressed as real and imaginary parts

$$G(j\omega) = P(\omega) + jQ(\omega), \tag{5.41}$$

and $P(\cdot)$ and $Q(\cdot)$ are respectively the real and imaginary parts, and they are the functions of the frequency $\omega$. If horizontal and vertical axes are used to represent respectively the real and imaginary parts, the plot of the complex gain $G(j\omega)$ can be obtained, and the plot is referred to as the Nyquist plots. Nyquist plots is an effective method in indirectly assessing the stability. Unfortunately, conventional Nyquist plots do not have information on the frequency, and the information is essential in controller design.

A MATLAB function `nyquist()` is provided in Control System Toolbox, with the following typical syntaxes

```
nyquist(G)          % automatically draw Nyquist plot
nyquist(G,{ωm,ωM})    % draw Nyquist plot over given frequency range
nyquist(G,ω)         % draw Nyquist plot for given vector ω
[R,I,ω]=nyquist(G)   % compute Nyquist response data, no plots
nyquist(G1,'-',G2,'-.b',G3,':r')  % draw Nyquist for several systems
```

One can click a point on the Nyquist plot such that the gain and frequency can be displayed. MATLAB facilitates new characteristics to conventional Nyquist plots. The overload `grid` command can be used to superimpose on the Nyquist plot with M-circles.

(2) Complex quantity $G(j\omega)$ can be expressed in magnitude and phase form

$$G(j\omega) = A(\omega)e^{-j\phi(\omega)}. \tag{5.42}$$

The frequency $\omega$ can be used as the horizontal axis, magnitude $A(\omega)$ and phase $\phi(\omega)$ can respectively be used as the vertical axes, such that the new plots can be constructed. If the scales for the axes are defined as follows: the frequency axis can be set to logarithmic scale with the unit of rad/s, the value of the magnitude can be assigned to decibels (dBs) with the transformation $M(\omega) = 20\lg|A(\omega)|$, and the phase can be expressed in degrees, the plots thus defined are referred to as Bode diagrams of the system.

The `bode()` function provided in the Control System Toolbox of MATLAB can be used to show directly Bode diagrams, and the commonly used syntaxes are

```
bode(G)        % automatically draw Bode diagram
bode(G,{ωm,ωM})      % Bode diagram for specific frequency range
bode(G,ω)        % Bode diagram for specified frequency vector ω
[A,φ,ω] = bode(G)    % compute Bode diagram data
bode(G1,'-',G2,'-.b',G3,':r')    % Bode for several systems
```

The difference between Bode diagram and Nyquist plot are that the relationship of the $G(j\omega)$ with respect to frequency $\omega$ can be shown explicitly on the plots.

(3) If the magnitude and phase representation of the complex quantity $G(j\omega)$ is used, while the horizontal and vertical axes are assigned to phase and magnitude respectively, the new plots can be drawn. The new plots are referred to as Nichols chart of the system.

The function `nichols()` can be used to draw Nichols chart and the syntaxes are exactly the same as the `bode()` function. The command `grid` can be used to superimpose M-circles to the resulted plots.

For discrete-time system $H(z)$, the complex variable $z = e^{j\omega T}$ is used in the transfer function model, and again complex quantity of the gain can be expressed as $\widehat{H}(j\omega)$. The functions `bode()`, `nyquist()` and `nichols()` can also be used for discrete-time systems, and the syntaxes are the same.

**Example 5.35.** Consider linear continuous open-loop system

$$G(s) = \frac{s+8}{s(s^2 + 0.2s + 4)(s+1)(s+3)},$$

the following MATLAB statements can be used to draw the Nyquist plot of the system, and superimposed with M-circles.

```
>> s=tf('s'); G=(s+8)/(s*(s^2+0.2*s+4)*(s+1)*(s+3));
   nyquist(G), grid    % Nyquist plot superimposed with M-circles
   ylim([-1.5 1.5])    % set the range of y-axis manually
```

Since there is a pole located at $s = 0$, when the value of $\omega$ is small, the magnitude of the gain may be very large, far away from the origin and the critical point $(-1, j0)$. Details of the Nyquist plot around the unit circle cannot be seen clearly. Zoomed Nyquist plot can be obtained with `ylim()` function, as shown in Fig. 5-23(a).

On the traditional Nyquist plots, the frequency information of a certain point is missing. With the Nyquist plot drawn in MATLAB, the information on frequency, magnitude, phase and possible overshoot can be obtained by mouse clicking on the interested point on the curve, as shown in Fig. 5-23(b). The new facilities are useful in the frequency domain analysis and design of control systems.

With the following MATLAB statements, Bode diagram and Nyquist plot of the system can be obtained as shown in Fig. 5-24. It can be seen that the facilities provided in MATLAB can be used to perform frequency domain analysis easily.

```
>> bode(G);            % draw automatically Bode diagram
```

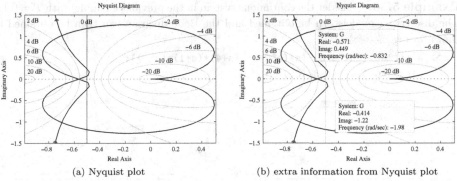

(a) Nyquist plot          (b) extra information from Nyquist plot

Fig. 5-23   Frequency domain analysis.

```
figure; nichols(G), grid  % draw Nichols chart with M-contours
```

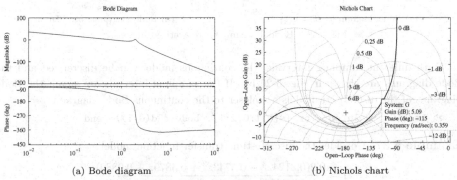

(a) Bode diagram          (b) Nichols chart

Fig. 5-24   Frequency domain analysis plots.

The MATLAB functions have dedicated facilities to frequency domain analysis of linear control systems. For instance, the shortcut menu Characteristics displayed in Fig. 5-25(a) can be used to assess stability of the closed-loop system, the Bode diagram shown in Fig. 5-25(b) is presented with stability information. The functions `nyquist()` and `nichols()` have their own Characteristics menus. If mouse pointer is moved on top of a point on the plot, more information will be displayed.

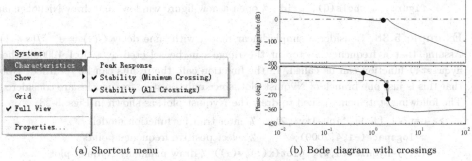

(a) Shortcut menu          (b) Bode diagram with crossings

Fig. 5-25   Frequency response and specifications.

**Example 5.36.** Consider the continuous system in the previous example, with $T = 0.1$ s. The discretized models can be obtained and the Bode diagram can then be obtained as shown in Fig. 5-26(a).

```
>> s=tf('s'); G=(s+8)/(s*(s^2+0.2*s+4)*(s+1)*(s+3));
   G1=c2d(G,0.1); bode(G1)
```

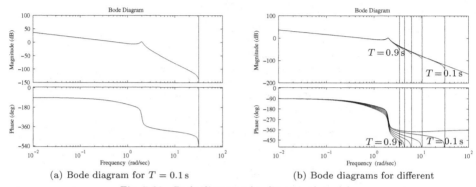

(a) Bode diagram for $T = 0.1$ s          (b) Bode diagrams for different

Fig. 5-26     Bode diagrams for discretized models.

With different sampling intervals, the continuous model can be discretized and the Bode diagrams are shown in Fig. 5-26(b). If the sampling intervals are small, the Bode diagrams of the discretized models are closer to the continuous Bode diagram.

```
>> bode(G), hold on; for T=[0.1:0.2:1], bode(c2d(G,T)); end
```

**Example 5.37.** Consider the discrete-time transfer function model

$$G(z) = \frac{0.2(0.3124z^3 - 0.5743z^2 + 0.3879z - 0.0889)}{z^4 - 3.233z^3 + 3.9869z^2 - 2.2209z + 0.4723},$$

with a sampling interval of $T = 0.1$ s. The following commands can be used to enter the model into MATLAB workspace, and draw the Nyquist plot and Nichols chart can be obtained as shown in Fig. 5-27. From this example, it can be seen that frequency domain analysis of discrete-time systems is very simple and straightforward.

```
>> num=0.2*[0.3124 -0.5743 0.3879 -0.0889];
   den=[1 -3.233 3.9869 -2.2209 0.4723];
   G=tf(num,den,'Ts',0.1);    % enter the system model
   nyquist(G); grid          % draw Nyquist plot, with M-circles
   figure, nichols(G), grid  % open a new figure window, and draw Nichols chart
```

**Example 5.38.** Consider a simple linear model with time delay $G(s) = \mathrm{e}^{-2s}/(s+1)$. Assume that a frequency vector in the range can be selected $\omega \in [0.1, 10000]$, then nyquist() function can be called. In the function call, the results can be returned. Note that this is just one branch of Nyquist plot, since only positive frequencies are considered. The following statements issued to draw the Nyquist plot, as shown in Figs. 5-28.

```
>> G=tf(1,[1 1],'ioDelay',2);   % enter transfer function model
   w=logspace(-1,4,2000);       % select positive frequency points
   [x,y]=nyquist(G,w); plot(x(:),y(:)) % draw manually Nyquist plot
```

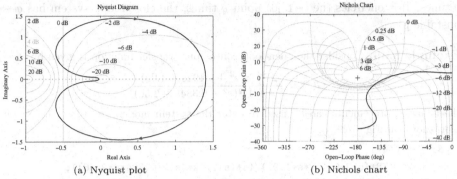

(a) Nyquist plot                    (b) Nichols chart

Fig. 5-27   Frequency domain analysis of discrete-time systems.

In the Nyquist plot obtained, `grid` command can no longer be used to draw the M-circles, since the plot is not drawn with `nyquist()` function. This Nyquist plot is the typical Nyquist plot with time delay.

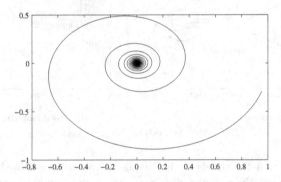

Fig. 5-28   Nyquist plot with time delay.

### 5.5.2   *Stability Assessment of Feedback Systems*

The early application of frequency domain analysis is in the stability assessment of closed-loop systems, with open-loop models. The theoretical foundation in stability analysis is the Nyquist theorem, which states that if the open-loop model has $m$ unstable poles, the closed-loop system is stable if and only if the open-loop Nyquist plot encircle $m$ circles in counterclockwise direction the point $(-1, j0)$.

Nyquist theorem can further be explained in the following two cases:

(1) If the open-loop transfer function $G(s)H(s)$ is stable, the closed-loop system is stable, if and only if the Nyquist plot $G(s)H(s)$ does not encircle the $(-1, j0)$ point. If the Nyquist encircles the $(-1, j0)$ point $p$ times, the closed-loop system has $p$ unstable poles.

(2) If the open-loop $G(s)H(s)$ has $p$ unstable poles, the closed-loop system is stable, if and only if the Nyquist plot of the $G(s)H(s)$ encircles the $(-1, j0)$ point

$p$ times. If it encircles the $(-1, \mathrm{j}0)$ point $q$ times, the closed-loop system has $q - p$ unstable poles.

**Example 5.39.** Consider the open-loop continuous transfer function is given by

$$G(s) = \frac{2.7778(s^2 + 0.192s + 1.92)}{s(s + 1)^2(s^2 + 0.384s + 2.56)},$$

the following statements can be used to enter the system model, and draw the Nyquist plot, shown in Fig. 5-29(a).

```
>> s=tf('s');
   G=2.7778*(s^2+0.192*s+1.92)/(s*(s+1)^2*(s^2+0.384*s+2.56));
   nyquist(G); axis([-2.5,0,-1.5,1.5]); grid   % draw Nyquist plot
```

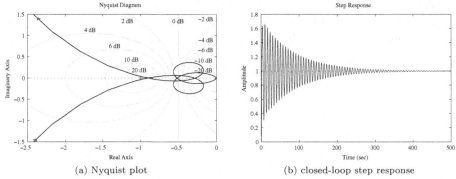

(a) Nyquist plot                  (b) closed-loop step response

Fig. 5-29   Analysis of the given system.

It can be seen that the trends in the Nyquist is rather complicated. However, it can be seen that the total Nyquist plot does not encircle the $(-1, \mathrm{j}0)$ point, and there is no unstable poles in the open-loop model, the closed-loop system is stable. Step response of the closed-loop system can be obtained as shown in Fig. 5-29(b).

```
>> step(feedback(G,1))    % closed-loop step response
```

It can also be seen that although the closed-loop system is stable, there exists very strong oscillation in the step response. Thus, the behavior is not satisfactory. Also, a slight disturbance may make the system unstable. A controller is expected to improve the behavior of the system.

### 5.5.3    Gain Margins and Phase Margins

It can be seen from the previous example that although the stability of the system is very important, it is not the only criterion in describing the behavior of the system. Sometimes, although the closed-loop system is stable, it may also be useless, due to the strong oscillation in the system responses. Besides, if there exists slight change in the gain of the open-loop system, i.e., the Nyquist plot may be stretched, the new Nyquist plot may encircle the $(-1, \mathrm{j}0)$ point, the closed-loop system may become unstable. Quantitative studies on the frequency responses, i.e., the margins, are useful approaches for this kind of problems.

The gain and phase margins are interpreted on the Nyquist plot and Nichols chart shown in Fig. 5-30 (a) and (b). In Bode diagrams, the margins can also be explained.

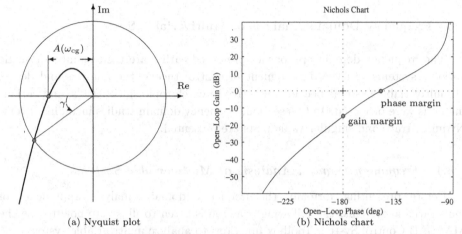

(a) Nyquist plot      (b) Nichols chart

Fig. 5-30   Illustration of the gain and phase margins.

If the Nyquist plot intersects the negative real axis at frequency $\omega_{\rm cg}$, the reciprocal of the gain, $G_{\rm m} = 1/A(\omega_{\rm cg})$, is defined as the gain margin of the system. If the Nyquist plot intersects at frequency $\omega_{\rm cp}$ with the unit circle, the phase margin is defined as $\gamma = \phi(\omega_{\rm cp}) - 180°$.

It can be seen that the larger the gain margin $G_{\rm m}$, or the larger the value of the phase margin, the stronger its capability in the resistance to disturbances. If $G_{\rm m} < 1$ or $\gamma < 0$, the closed-loop system is unstable. The following cases are considered:

(1) If the Nyquist plot does not intersect with the negative real axis, the gain margin is infinite, while the frequency is NaN.

(2) If the Nyquist plot has several intersections between the points $(-1, {\rm j}0)$ and $(0, {\rm j}0)$, the nearest point to $(-1, {\rm j}0)$ is selected as the gain margin.

(3) If the Nyquist plot does not intersect the unit circle, the phase margin is infinite, and the frequency is NaN.

(4) If there are many intersections in the Nyquist plot with the unit circle in the third quadrant, the angle nearest to the negative real axis is used.

The function `margin()` can be used in the Control System Toolbox to directly compute the gain and phase margins, with $[G_{\rm m}, \gamma, \omega_{\rm cg}, \omega_{\rm cp}] = {\rm margin}(G)$ .

In the results, if any margin is infinite, `Inf`, the corresponding frequency is NaN.

**Example 5.40.** Consider the open-loop model shown in Example 5.39. The following statements can be used to enter the system model, and find the gain and phase margin of the system, whether the gain margin is 1.105 at frequency 0.96209rad/s, and phase margin 2.0985°, at 0.92607rad/s. Since the gain and phase margins are very small, the closed-loop system is with strong oscillation.

```
>> s=tf('s'); G=2.7778*(s^2+0.192*s+1.92)/(s*(s+1)^2*(s^2+0.384*s+2.56));
   [gm,pm,wg,wp]=margin(G) % compute the margins
```

## 5.6　Frequency Domain Analysis of Multivariable Systems

The frequency domain approaches presented earlier are used mainly for single variable systems. In the development of control theory, the analysis and design of multivariable systems became an active research topic since 1970's, and various methods were proposed. In this section, frequency domain studies including inverse Nyquist arrays and singular value plots are presented.

### 5.6.1　*Frequency Domain Analysis of Multivariable Systems*

Before presenting formally the frequency domain analysis approaches of multivariable systems, the following example is given to illustrate how to use the MATLAB Control System Toolbox functions to analyze multivariable systems.

**Example 5.41.** Consider the multivariable model [8]

$$
G(s) = \begin{bmatrix} \dfrac{0.806s + 0.264}{s^2 + 1.15s + 0.202} & \dfrac{-15s - 1.42}{s^3 + 12.8s^2 + 13.6s + 2.36} \\ \dfrac{1.95s^2 + 2.12s + 0.49}{s^3 + 9.15s^2 + 9.39s + 1.62} & \dfrac{7.15s^2 + 25.8s + 9.35}{s^4 + 20.8s^3 + 116.4s^2 + 111.6s + 18.8} \end{bmatrix}.
$$

The following MATLAB commands can be used to enter first the transfer function matrix into MATLAB environment, then to draw directly the Nyquist plots with nyquist() function, as shown in Fig. 5-31.

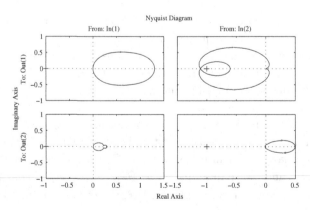

Fig. 5-31　Nyquist plots for the multivariable system.

```
>> g11=tf([0.806 0.264],[1 1.15 0.202]);
   g12=tf([-15 -1.42],[1 12.8 13.6 2.36]);
   g21=tf([1.95 2.12 0.49],[1 9.15 9.39 1.62]);
   g22=tf([7.15 25.8 9.35],[1 20.8 116.4 111.6 18.8]);
   G=[g11, g12; g21, g22]; nyquist(G), % draw Nyquist plots
```

Since the Nyquist plots obtained are the ones for each of the subsystem, the most important property for multivariable systems — the interaction among the input and output channels — are not presented at all, they are not very helpful in control design.

The above-mentioned `nyquist()` function is not suitable for the frequency domain analysis of multivariable systems, since it is not the same as the mainstream analysis methods for multivariable systems. For frequency domain analysis and design of multivariable systems, the British school led by Professors Howard H Rosenbrock[9], Alistair G J MacFralane[10] is very influential. The inverse Nyquist array (INA) is used instead in the graphical representation of multivariable systems.

The Multivariable Frequency Design Toolbox (MFD) developed by Boyel and Maciejowski[11] is suitable for the analysis and design of multivariable systems. A series of functions can be used directly for multivariable systems. In the MFD toolbox, the common denominator and the numerator polynomial matrix should be entered. This is rather complicated, we can use an alternative function, `mvss2tf()`, to find them directly from state space models. The syntax of the function is $[N,d] = \text{mvss2tf}(A,B,C,D)$ , where $d$ is the common denominator polynomial, and $N$ is the numerator matrix, and the state space model can be extracted directly with the function `ss()`.

**Example 5.42.** Consider the transfer function matrix of two-input, two-output system

$$G(s) = \begin{bmatrix} \dfrac{s+4}{(s+1)(s+5)} & \dfrac{1}{5s+1} \\ \dfrac{s+1}{s^2+10s+100} & \dfrac{2}{2s+1} \end{bmatrix}.$$

It is difficult to describe the system in common denominator form. The following statements can be used to calculate the common denominator $d(s)$ and the numerator polynomial matrix

```
>> s=tf('s');
   G=[(s+4)/((s+1)*(s+5)), 1/(5*s+1); (s+1)/(s^2+10*s+100), 2/(2*s+1)];
   G1=ss(G); [N,d]=mvss2tf(G1.a,G1.b,G1.c,G1.d)
```

where the common denominator is

$$d(s) = s^6 + 16.7s^5 + 176.3s^4 + 767.1s^3 + 971.5s^2 + 415s + 50,$$

and the numerator polynomial matrix $N(s)$ is

$$\begin{bmatrix} s^5+14.7s^4+149.9s^3+499.4s^2+294s+40 & 0.2s^5+3.3s^4+34.6s^3+146.5s^2+165s+50 \\ s^5+7.7s^4+16s^3+13.4s^2+4.6s+0.5 & s^5+16.2s^4+168.2s^3+683s^2+630s+100 \end{bmatrix}.$$

Please note that the conversion method given here is not suitable to handle models with delays. If a transfer function matrix has delay terms, the delay-free model should be expressed first, and delay constants should be modeled through a separate matrix. Alternatively, we shall write a MATLAB function to solve the problem based on simple Control System Toolbox functions, in frequency domain, and the modeling problem is bypassed.

### 5.6.2  *Diagonal Dominance Analysis*

Assume that the transfer function matrix of the forward path is $\boldsymbol{Q}(s)$ and the feedback path transfer function matrix $\boldsymbol{H}(s)$, the closed-loop transfer function matrix can then be written as

$$G(s) = \left[ I + Q(s)H(s) \right]^{-1} Q(s), \tag{5.43}$$

where $\boldsymbol{I} + \boldsymbol{Q}(s)\boldsymbol{H}(s)$ is referred to as the return difference matrix. In the return difference matrix, the frequency domain analysis becomes more convenient with inverse Nyquist array (INA) approaches[9].

Similar to single variable system, Nyquist plot encircles the $(-1, j0)$ point, while for multivariable systems, the number of encirclements of the INA of difference matrix around the $(0, j0)$ point are counted.

Gershgorin theorem is the foundation of the inverse Nyquist array in the design of multivariable design approaches. For complex matrix

$$C = \begin{bmatrix} c_{11} & \cdots & c_{1k} & \cdots & c_{1n} \\ \vdots & \ddots & \vdots & \ddots & \vdots \\ c_{k1} & \cdots & c_{kk} & \cdots & c_{kn} \\ \vdots & \ddots & \vdots & \ddots & \vdots \\ c_{n1} & \cdots & c_{nk} & \cdots & c_{nn} \end{bmatrix}, \tag{5.44}$$

the eigenvalue $\lambda$ satisfies

$$\mid \lambda - c_{kk} \mid \leqslant \sum_{j \neq k} \mid c_{kj} \mid, \text{ and } \mid \lambda - c_{kk} \mid \leqslant \sum_{j \neq k} \mid c_{jk} \mid. \tag{5.45}$$

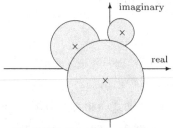

Fig. 5-32  Gershgorin theorem.

As illustrated in Fig. 5-32, all the eigenvalues of the matrix are located inside these circles. In other words, a class of circles centered on the $c_{kk}$ and radius of the sum of the absolute values of the rest of the elements in the row or column. These circles are Gershgorin circles. Besides, the two inequalities are referred to as column and row Gershgorin circles.

In fact, a smaller radius can be obtained with

$$| \lambda - c_{kk} | \leqslant \min \left( \sum_{j \neq k} | c_{kj} |, \ \sum_{j \neq k} | c_{jk} | \right). \tag{5.46}$$

Assume that at a frequency $\omega$, the INA in the forward path is

$$\hat{Q}(j\omega) = \begin{bmatrix} \hat{q}_{11}(j\omega) & \cdots & \hat{q}_{1p}(j\omega) \\ \vdots & \ddots & \vdots \\ \hat{q}_{q1}(j\omega) & \cdots & \hat{q}_{qp}(j\omega) \end{bmatrix}, \tag{5.47}$$

where $\hat{q}_{ij}(j\omega)$ is a complex quantity. For frequency response data, the envelope of a series of Gershgorin circles form the Gershgorin band. If all the Gershgorin bands for the frequencies do not encircle the origin, the system is referred to as a diagonal dominant system. It is easily seen that the eigenvalues of the diagonal dominant matrix are not located at the origin, and the closed-loop system under negative feedback structure is stable.

For the selected frequency vector $w$, and the multivariable model is known, the function mv2fr() in the MFD Toolbox can be used in evaluating the frequency response data for the frequency points, with the syntaxes

$H = \text{mv2fr}(N, d, w)$      % for multivariable transfer function matrix
$H = \text{mv2fr}(A, B, C, D, w)$      % for state space model

where the returned variable $H$ is a matrix composed of frequency response data, and it is essential data type in the MFD Toolbox. The functions plotnyq() and fgersh() in the MFD Toolbox can be used to draw Nyquist plot and Gershgorin circles. However, the syntaxes of the procedures are quite complicated. For the systems with equal input and output channels, a new function inagersh($H$) can be written, which can be used to draw inverse Nyquist plot with Gershgorin bands, and the contents of the function are

```
function inagersh(H,nij)
t=[0:.1:2*pi,2*pi]'; [nr,nc]=size(H); nw=nr/nc; ii0=1:nc;
if nargin==1, ii=1:nc; jj=1:nc;
else, ii=nij(1); jj=nij(2); end
for i=1:nc, circles{i}=[]; end
for k=1:nw  % evaluate inverse Nyquist array for the frequencies
    Ginv=inv(H((k-1)*nc+1:k*nc,:)); nyq(:,:,k)=Ginv;
    for j=1:nc
        ij=find(ii0~=j);
        v=min([sum(abs(Ginv(ij,j))),sum(abs(Ginv(j,ij)))]);
        x0=real(Ginv(j,j)); y0=imag(Ginv(j,j));
        r=sum(abs(v)); % compute Gershgorin circles radius
        circles{j}=[circles{j}, x0+r*cos(t)+sqrt(-1)*(y0+r*sin(t))];
end, end
for i=ii, for j=jj
```

```
if nargin==1, subplot(nc,nc,(i-1)*nc+j); end
for k=1:nw, NN(k)=nyq(i,j,k); end
if i==j, % diagonal plots with Gershgorin circles
    plot(real(NN),imag(NN),real(circles{i}),imag(circles{i}));
else      % non-diagonal elements
    plot(real(NN),imag(NN))
end, end, end
```

There are two input arguments in the function, the first is with the frequency data $H$, while the other $n_{ij}$ indicates the Nyquist plot of the $(i,j)$th pair, and can be omitted. Compared with the `plotnyq()` function in the MFD Toolbox, the `inagersh()` function is much simpler. Besides, the minimum radius obtained by row and column Gershgorin circles is used.

**Example 5.43.** Consider the multivariable system studied in Example 5.41. The following statements can be used to draw inverse Nyquist plot, as shown in Fig. 5-33(a).

```
>> g11=tf([0.806 0.264],[1 1.15 0.202]);
   g12=tf([-15 -1.42],[1 12.8 13.6 2.36]);
   g21=tf([1.95 2.12 0.49],[1 9.15 9.39 1.62]);
   g22=tf([7.15 25.8 9.35],[1 20.8 116.4 111.6 18.8]);
   G=[g11, g12; g21, g22]; w=logspace(-2,1.5);
   G=ss(G); H=mv2fr(G.a,G.b,G.c,G.d,w); inagersh(H);  % INA plot
```

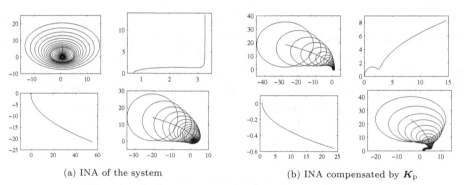

       (a) INA of the system                  (b) INA compensated by $K_{\mathrm{p}}$

Fig. 5-33    Inverse Nyquist arrays for multivariable systems.

It can be seen from the results that the Gershgorin bands are too wide and the origin is encircled, the system is not a diagonal dominant one, so it might be rather complicated in controller design.

To solve the problem, a pre-compensator matrix

$$K_{\mathrm{p}} = \begin{bmatrix} 0.3610 & 0.4500 \\ -1.1300 & 1.0000 \end{bmatrix}$$

can be introduced, and the following MATLAB statements can be used to draw the inverse Nyquist array with Gershgorin bands for the compensated system, as shown in Fig. 5-33(b). It can be seen that the Gershgorin bands are much narrower, and do not encircle the origin, which indicates that the compensated system is diagonal dominant, and is suitable for further controller design.

```
>> Kp=[0.3610,0.4500; -1.1300,1.0000];
   G=ss(G*Kp); H=mv2fr(G.a,G.b,G.c,G.d,w); inagersh(H);  % INA curves
```

In Multivariable Frequency Domain Toolbox, low-level functions can be used to calculate frequency domain response data for plots with different connections. For instance, the frequency response of two blocks $G_1(s)$ and $G_2(s)$ in series connection can be evaluated with the function $H = \mathtt{fmulf}(w, H_2, H_1)$. If a matrix $K$ is multiplied by the transfer function matrix, the function $H = \mathtt{fmul}(w, H_1, K)$ or $H = \mathtt{fmul}(w, K, H_1)$ can be used. The function $H = \mathtt{faddf}(w, H_1, H_2)$ can be used to evaluate the two transfer function matrices $G_1(s)$ and $G_2(s)$ in parallel connections. The function $H = \mathtt{faddf}(w, K, H_1)$ can be used to add matrix $K$ to the frequency response of a transfer function matrix. The function $H = \mathtt{fdly}(w, H_1, D)$ can be used to evaluate the system responses with delay matrix $D$. With the MFD Toolbox, the function $H = \mathtt{finv}(w, H_1)$ can be used to evaluate the inverse Nyquist responses[1].

It can be seen from the above functions that if the system structures are complicated, finding frequency responses is rather a complicated task. To simplify this process, a new MATLAB function mfrd() is designed, with $H = \mathtt{mfrd}(G, w)$. In this function, $G$ can be any LTI object, and it may even be the multivariable models with internal delays. For complicated model structures, $G$ can be calculated first, with the sophisticated interconnection functions provided in the Control System Toolbox. The listings of the new function are

```
function H1=mfrd(G,w)
H=frd(G,w); h=H.ResponseData; H1=[];
for i=1:length(w); H1=[H1; h(:,:,i)]; end
```

**Example 5.44.** Consider the multivariable system with delay [8]

$$
G(s) = \begin{bmatrix} \dfrac{0.1134e^{-0.72s}}{1.78s^2 + 4.48s + 1} & \dfrac{0.924}{2.07s + 1} \\[2ex] \dfrac{0.3378e^{-0.3s}}{0.361s^2 + 1.09s + 1} & \dfrac{-0.318e^{-1.29s}}{2.93s + 1} \end{bmatrix}.
$$

The following statements can be used to draw inverse Nyquist array plots shown in Fig. 5-34(a). It is obvious that the system is not a diagonal dominant system.

```
>> G=[tf(0.1134,[1.78 4.48 1]), tf([0.924],[2.07,1]);
      tf(0.3378,[0.361,1.09,1]), tf(-0.318,[2.93 1])];
   G=ss(G); D=[0.72 0; 0.3 1.29]; w=logspace(0,1);
   H=mv2fr(G.a,G.b,G.c,G.d,w);
   H1=fdly(w,H,D); inagersh(H1); % INA plot with Gershgorin bands
```

---

[1] Please note that the name of the finv() function is the same as the one in Statistics Toolbox. If the two toolboxes are both present in MATLAB, the orders of them should be readjusted in the MATLAB path settings.

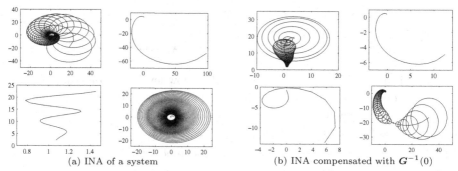

(a) INA of a system        (b) INA compensated with $\boldsymbol{G}^{-1}(0)$

Fig. 5-34    Inverse Nyquist arrays with Gershgorin bands.

In the frequency domain design theory for multivariable systems, the matrix $\boldsymbol{K}_\mathrm{p} = \boldsymbol{G}^{-1}(0)$ can be used to multiply the transfer function matrix to compensate the system, and to achieve the goal of diagonal dominance[9]. The following statements can be used and the compensated inverse Nyquist plot is obtained as shown in Fig. 5-34(b). It can be seen that the thus compensated system improved the property of diagonal dominance of the original system. Later, the design of multivariable systems will be explored.

```
>> H0=mv2fr(G.a,G.b,G.c,G.d,0);              % calculate Kp = G^{-1}(0)
   Kp=inv(H0); H2=fmul(w,H1,Kp); inagersh(H2); % draw INA curves
```

With the new `mfrd()` function, the above statements can be simplified to

```
>> G.ioDelay=D; G1=G*Kp; H2=mfrd(G1,w); inagersh(H2)
```

If a multivariable system is compensated as a diagonal dominant one, the system is said to be decoupled well, and controllers can be designed separately, without affecting too much to the behavior of other channels. Thus, the compensation process of the original system is very important, and various methods can be used for the decoupling of multivariable systems[8]. It should be noted that inverse Nyquist array-based representation can be adopted.

### 5.6.3    *Singular Value Plots for Multivariable Systems*

Bode diagrams can be used to describe the behaviors of single variable systems, however, they are not suitable for multivariable systems. Singular value representation should be used instead. Assume that for frequency $\omega$, the singular value of it can be obtained as $\sigma_1(\omega)$, $\sigma_2(\omega)$, $\cdots$, $\sigma_m(\omega)$, the curves of them versus $\omega$ are referred to as the singular value plots for multivariable systems. Singular value plots can be regarded as an extension of Bode diagrams to multivariable systems. Singular value plots are useful in addressing robust control of multivariable systems, and will be presented in Chapter 9.

A function `sigmaplot()` is provided in Control System Toolbox[12] to draw singular value plots, and the syntaxes of it are the same as the `bode()` function. In old versions of Control System Toolbox, the function name is `sigma()`.

**Example 5.45.** Consider again the multivariable system studied in Example 5.44

$$G(s) = \begin{bmatrix} \dfrac{0.1134e^{-0.72s}}{1.78s^2 + 4.48s + 1} & \dfrac{0.924}{2.07s + 1} \\ \dfrac{0.3378e^{-0.3s}}{0.361s^2 + 1.09s + 1} & \dfrac{-0.318e^{-1.29s}}{2.93s + 1} \end{bmatrix}.$$

The singular value plots can easily be drawn with the following statements, and the curves are as shown in Fig. 5-35.

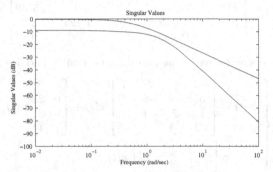

Fig. 5-35  Singular value plots of the multivariable system.

```
>> g11=tf(0.1134,[1.78 4.48 1],'ioDelay',0.72);
   g12=tf(0.924,[2.07 1]);
   g21=tf(0.3378,[0.361 1.09 1],'ioDelay',0.3);
   g22=tf(-0.318,[2.93 1],'ioDelay',1.29);
   G=[g11, g12; g21, g22]; sigmaplot(G)
```

## 5.7  Problems

(1) Assess the stability of the following models

   (i) $\dfrac{1}{s^3 + 2s^2 + s + 2}$,  (ii) $\dfrac{1}{6s^4 + 3s^3 + 2s^2 + s + 1}$,  (iii) $\dfrac{1}{s^4 + s^3 - 3s^2 - s + 2}$,

   (iv) $\dfrac{3s + 1}{s^2(300s^2 + 600s + 50) + 3s + 1}$,  (v) $\dfrac{0.2(s + 2)}{s(s + 0.5)(s + 0.8)(s + 3) + 0.2(s + 2)}$.

(2) Assess the stability of the following discrete-time systems

   (i) $H(z) = \dfrac{-3z + 2}{z^3 - 0.2z^2 - 0.25z + 0.05}$,

   (ii) $H(z) = \dfrac{3z^2 - 0.39z - 0.09}{z^4 - 1.7z^3 + 1.04z^2 + 0.268z + 0.024}$,

   (iii) $H(z) = \dfrac{z^2 + 3z - 0.13}{z^5 + 1.352z^4 + 0.4481z^3 + 0.0153z^2 - 0.01109z - 0.001043}$,

   (iv) $H(z^{-1}) = \dfrac{2.12z^{-2} + 11.76z^{-1} + 15.91}{z^{-5} - 7.368z^{-4} - 20.15z^{-3} + 102.4z^{-2} + 80.39z^{-1} - 340}$.

(3) For the following state space equations, assess the stability

(i) $\dot{x}(t) = \begin{bmatrix} -0.2 & 0.5 & 0 & 0 & 0 \\ 0 & -0.5 & 1.6 & 0 & 0 \\ 0 & 0 & -14.3 & 85.8 & 0 \\ 0 & 0 & 0 & -33.3 & 100 \\ 0 & 0 & 0 & 0 & -10 \end{bmatrix} x(t) + \begin{bmatrix} 0 \\ 0 \\ 0 \\ 0 \\ 30 \end{bmatrix} u(t),$

(ii) $x[(k+1)T] = \begin{bmatrix} 17 & 24.54 & 1 & 8 & 15 \\ 23.54 & 5 & 7 & 14 & 16 \\ 4 & 6 & 13.75 & 20 & 22.5889 \\ 10.8689 & 1.2900 & 19.099 & 21.896 & 3 \\ 11 & 18.0898 & 25 & 2.356 & 9 \end{bmatrix} x(kT) + \begin{bmatrix} 1 \\ 2 \\ 3 \\ 4 \\ 5 \end{bmatrix} u(kT).$

(4) Find all the poles and zeros of the multivariable system and assess the stability.

$$\begin{cases} \dot{x}(t) = \begin{bmatrix} -3 & 1 & 2 & 1 \\ 0 & -4 & -2 & -1 \\ 1 & 2 & -1 & 1 \\ -1 & -1 & 1 & -2 \end{bmatrix} x(t) + \begin{bmatrix} 1 & 0 \\ 0 & 2 \\ 0 & 3 \\ 1 & 1 \end{bmatrix} u(t) \\ y(t) = \begin{bmatrix} 1 & 2 & 2 & -1 \\ 2 & 1 & -1 & 2 \end{bmatrix} x(t). \end{cases}$$

Note that the concepts of the zeros in multivariable system are different from the single variable systems. The function `tzero()` can be used to find the transmission zeros of the systems. Also, `pzmap()` can still be used for multivariable systems.

(5) Consider the transfer function model of the system

$$G(s) = \frac{0.2(s+2)}{s(s+0.5)(s+0.8)(s+3) + 0.2(s+2)},$$

write the controllable, observable canonical form of the system.

(6) Assess the controllability, observability of the following systems, and write out the canonical forms, Luenberger form, and find the $\mathcal{H}_2$ norm and $\mathcal{H}_\infty$ norm.

(i) $A = \begin{bmatrix} 0 & 1 & 1 & 1 \\ 0 & 0 & 0 & 1 \\ 0 & 1 & 0 & 0 \\ 0 & 0 & 1 & 1 \end{bmatrix}$, $B = \begin{bmatrix} 1 & 0 \\ 0 & 0 \\ 0 & 1 \\ 1 & 0 \end{bmatrix}$, $C = \begin{bmatrix} 1 & 0 & 0 & 0 \\ 0 & 1 & 0 & 0 \end{bmatrix}$,

(ii) $A = \begin{bmatrix} 0 & 2 & 0 & 0 \\ 0 & 1 & -2 & 0 \\ 0 & 0 & 3 & 1 \\ 1 & 0 & 0 & 0 \end{bmatrix}$, $B = \begin{bmatrix} 2 & 0 \\ 1 & 2 \\ 0 & 1 \\ 0 & 0 \end{bmatrix}$, $C = \begin{bmatrix} 0 & 1 & 0 & 0 \\ 0 & 0 & 1 & 0 \end{bmatrix}.$

(7) Find out the minimum realization of the following state space models

$$\dot{x}(t) = \begin{bmatrix} 0 & -3 & 0 & 0 \\ 1 & -4 & 0 & 0 \\ 0 & 0 & 0 & 0 \\ 0 & 0 & 1 & -2 \end{bmatrix} x(t) + \begin{bmatrix} 3 & 2 \\ 1 & 2 \\ 1 & 1 \\ 1 & 1 \end{bmatrix} u(t), \quad y(t) = \begin{bmatrix} 0 & 1 & 0 & 0 \\ 0 & 0 & 0 & 1 \end{bmatrix} x(t).$$

(8) Find the analytical solution of the following system

$$\dot{x}(t) = \begin{bmatrix} -5 & 2 & 0 & 0 \\ 0 & -4 & 0 & 0 \\ -3 & 2 & -4 & -1 \\ -3 & 2 & 0 & -4 \end{bmatrix} x(t), \quad x(0) = \begin{bmatrix} 1 \\ 2 \\ 0 \\ 1 \end{bmatrix},$$

and compare with the numerical methods.

(9) For the eighth-order model $G(s)$

$$\frac{18s^7 + 514s^6 + 5982s^5 + 36380s^4 + 122664s^3 + 222088s^2 + 185760s + 40320}{s^8 + 36s^7 + 546s^6 + 4536s^5 + 22449s^4 + 67284s^3 + 118124s^2 + 109584s + 40320},$$

if the system has initial states, write out the analytical solutions to step and impulse responses. If the input signal is $u(t) = \sin(3t + 5)$, find the analytical solution of the system response and compare graphically the results with numerical ones.

(10) Assume that PI and PID controllers can be written as

$$G_{PI}(s) = K_p + \frac{K_i}{s}, \quad G_{PID}(s) = K_p + \frac{K_i}{s} + K_d s.$$

Please explain why PI and PID controllers can eliminate the steady-state errors in step responses. Can we eliminate steady-state error with PI or PID controllers for unstable plants? Why?

(11) Draw the unit step response of the following state space model

$$\dot{x}(t) = \begin{bmatrix} -0.2 & 0.5 & 0 & 0 & 0 \\ 0 & -0.5 & 1.6 & 0 & 0 \\ 0 & 0 & -14.3 & 85.8 & 0 \\ 0 & 0 & 0 & -33.3 & 100 \\ 0 & 0 & 0 & 0 & -10 \end{bmatrix} x(t) + \begin{bmatrix} 0 \\ 0 \\ 0 \\ 0 \\ 30 \end{bmatrix} u(t), \quad y(t) = \begin{bmatrix} 1, 0, 0, 0, 0 \end{bmatrix} x(t).$$

Draw all the states. Selecting different sampling intervals $T$, discretize the system and show the step responses. Compare with the continuous system and observe the variations in the specifications of overshoot and settling time in step responses.

(12) Assume that for the continuous transfer function

$$G(s) = \frac{-2s^2 + 3s - 4}{s^3 + 3.2s^2 + 1.61s + 3.03},$$

select different sampling intervals $T = 0.01, 0.1, 1\,\mathrm{s}$ to discretize the system, and compare step responses with the continuous system.

(13) For the following open-loop systems, draw the root loci and find the critical gains $K$ which make the closed-loop systems unstable.

(i) $G(s) = \dfrac{K(s+6)(s-6)}{s(s+3)(s+4-4\mathrm{j})(s+4-4\mathrm{j})}$,  (ii) $G(s) = K\dfrac{s^2 + 2s + 2}{s^4 + s^3 + 14s^2 + 8s}$,

(iii) $G(s) = \dfrac{1}{s(s^2/2600 + s/26 + 1)}$,  (iv) $G(s) = \dfrac{800(s+1)}{s^2(s+10)(s^2 + 10s + 50)}$.

(14) Draw the root locus for the following state space model, and find the critical gain $K$.

$$\dot{x}(t) = \begin{bmatrix} -1.5 & -13.5 & -13 & 0 \\ 1 & 0 & 0 & 0 \\ 0 & 1 & 0 & 0 \\ 0 & 0 & 1 & 0 \end{bmatrix} x(t) + \begin{bmatrix} 1 \\ 0 \\ 0 \\ 0 \end{bmatrix} u(t), \quad y(t) = \begin{bmatrix} 0, 0, 0, 1 \end{bmatrix} x(t).$$

(15) Assume that a continuous system with delay is given by

$$G(s) = \frac{K(s-1)e^{-2s}}{(s+1)^5},$$

draw the root locus with unity negative feedback and find the critical gain $K$.

(16) For the open-loop transfer function

$$G(s) = \frac{K}{s(s+10)(s+20)(s+40)},$$

and assume the system with unity negative feedback. Draw the root locus and find the gain $K$ which makes the damping ratio approximately equals to $\zeta = 0.707$.

(17) For the given discrete-time plant model

$$H(z) = K\frac{1}{(z+0.8)(z-0.8)(z-0.99)(z-0.368)},$$

draw the root locus and find the critical gain $K$ which makes the unity negative feedback system stable. Select any gain $K$ which makes the system stable, and draw the closed-loop step response, and find the overshoot and settling time.

(18) For the above system, if there exists a pure delay, such that $\widetilde{H}(z) = H(z)z^{-8}$, repeat the above process.

(19) For the open-loop model

$$G(s) = \frac{0.3(s+2)(s^2+2.1s+2.23)}{s^2(s^2+3s+4.32)(s+a)},$$

draw the root locus for the variable $a$ and find the critical value of $a$ such that the closed-loop system with unity negative feedback is stable.

(20) Analyze the following open-loop models in frequency domain and draw the Bode diagrams, Nyquist plots and Nichols charts. Evaluate the magnitude and phase margins and label them on the plots. Assume that the closed-loop systems are constructed as unity negative feedbacks, analyze the stability of the closed-loop system frequency domain responses and validate the results with step response curves.

(i) $G(s) = \dfrac{8(s+1)}{s^2(s+15)(s^2+6s+10)}$,     (ii) $G(s) = \dfrac{4(s/3+1)}{s(0.02s+1)(0.05s+1)(0.1s+1)}$,

(iii) $\dot{x}(t) = \begin{bmatrix} 0 & 2 & 1 \\ -3 & -2 & 0 \\ 1 & 3 & 4 \end{bmatrix} x(t) + \begin{bmatrix} 4 \\ 3 \\ 2 \end{bmatrix} u(t),\ y(t) = \begin{bmatrix} 1,2,3 \end{bmatrix} x(t),$

(iv) $H(z) = 0.45\dfrac{(z+1.31)(z+0.054)(z-0.957)}{z(z-1)(z-0.368)(z-0.99)},$

(v) $G(s) = \dfrac{6(-s+4)}{s^2(0.5s+1)(0.1s+1)}$,     (vi) $G(s) = \dfrac{10s^3 - 60s^2 + 110s + 60}{s^4 + 17s^3 + 82s^2 + 130s + 100}.$

(21) Assume that the typical feedback system is given by

$$G(s) = \frac{2}{s[(s^4+5.5s^3+21.5s^2+s+2)+20(s+1)]},$$

$$G_c(s) = K\frac{1+0.1s}{1+s}, H(s) = 1,$$

and $K = 1$. Draw the Bode diagram, Nyquist plot and Nichols chart and assess the performance from the frequency responses. Draw the closed-loop step response of the system, and predict how to modify the value of $K$ to improve the system responses.

(22) Perform frequency domain analysis to the delayed systems, draw the frequency response curves, and calculate the margins. Assess the stability of the closed-loop systems and validate the results through time domain responses.

(i) $G(s) = \dfrac{(-2s + 1)e^{-3s}}{s^2(s^2 + 3s + 3)(s + 5)(s^2 + 2s + 6)}$,

(ii) $H(z) = \dfrac{z^2 + 0.568}{(z - 1)(z^2 - 0.2z + 0.99)} z^{-5}$, $T = 0.05\,\mathrm{s}$.

(23) Assume that the plant model $G(s) = 1/s^2$, and an optimal controller is written as

$$G_c(s) = \frac{5620.82s^3 + 199320.76s^2 + 76856.97s + 7253.94}{s^4 + 77.40s^3 + 2887.90s^2 + 28463.88s + 2817.59},$$

and the closed-loop system is unity negative feedback structure. Draw the Nyquist plots and Nichols charts with M-circles.

(24) Assume that the open-loop model and controller are given by

$$G(s) = \frac{100(1 + s/2.5)}{s(1 + s/0.5)(1 + s/50)}, \quad G_c(s) = \frac{1000(s + 1)(s + 2.5)}{(s + 0.5)(s + 50)},$$

assess the step response of the system with frequency domain approach and validate the assessment with simulation methods.

(25) Assume that a transfer function matrix with delays is given by

$$G(s) = \begin{bmatrix} \dfrac{0.06371}{s^2 + 2.517s + 0.5618}e^{-0.72s} & \dfrac{0.4464}{s + 0.4831} \\ \dfrac{0.9357}{s^2 + 3.019s + 2.77}e^{-0.3s} & \dfrac{-0.1085}{s + 0.3413}e^{-1.29s} \end{bmatrix}.$$

Draw the inverse Nyquist array with Gershgorin bands, and check whether the system is a diagonal dominant one. Draw the open-loop step responses curves and see whether the above conclusion is correct or not.

(26) For the two-input, two-output system

$$G(s) = \begin{bmatrix} \dfrac{0.806s + 0.264}{s^2 + 1.15s + 0.202} & \dfrac{-(15s + 1.42)}{s^3 + 12.8s^2 + 13.6s + 2.36} \\ \dfrac{1.95s^2 + 2.12s + 4.90}{s^3 + 9.15s^2 + 9.39s + 1.62} & \dfrac{7.14s^2 + 25.8s + 9.35}{s^4 + 20.8s^3 + 116.4s^2 + 111.6s + 188} \end{bmatrix},$$

draw the inverse Nyquist plot with Gershgorin bands, and locate the eigenvalues on the plot at different frequencies to validate Gershgorin theorem. Draw the step response and see whether the system is well decoupled.

(27) In practical frequency domain analysis of multivariable systems, Gershgorin band is rather conservative. The radius of the circles should be reduced. If the feedback vector $F = [f_1, \cdots, f_n]$ is introduced, Ostrowski bands can be drawn, with the new radius defined as $r_i(s) = \phi_i(s)d_i(s)$, where $d_i(s)$ is the radius of the Gershgorin circles. The shrink factor is defined as

$$\phi_i(s) = \max_{j,j \neq i} \frac{d_j(s)}{f_j + \hat{q}_{jj}(s)}.$$

Modify the inagersh.m file such that Ostrowski band can be calculated.

(28) Bode magnitude plot describes the relationship between the gain of $G(s)$ and the frequencies, i.e., the relationship between $|G(j\omega)|$ and $s = j\omega$. With MATLAB's powerful three-dimensional graphics facilities, three-dimensional surface plot can be constructed, such that $s = x + jy$. Please draw three-dimensional surface plots for

(i) $G(s) = \dfrac{3s + 1}{s^2(300s^2 + 600s + 50) + 3s + 1}$,

(ii) $G(s) = \dfrac{(-2s + 1)e^{-3s}}{s^2(s^2 + 3s + 3)(s + 5)(s^2 + 2s + 6)}$.

## Bibliography and References

[1] Kailath T. Linear systems. Englewood Cliffs: Prentice-Hall, 1980

[2] Kalman R E. On the theory of control systems. Proceedings of 1st IFAC Congress, 1960. Moscow

[3] Zheng D Z. Linear systems theory. Beijing: Tsinghua University Press, 1980. (In Chinese)

[4] Xue D Y, Ren X Q. Simulation and analytical methods for continuous systems. Automatica Sinica, 1992, 19(6):694–702. (In Chinese)

[5] Nyquist H. Regeneration theory. Bell Systems Technical Journal, 1932, 11:126–147

[6] Bode H. Network analysis and feedback amplifier design. New York: D Van Nostrand, 1945

[7] James H M, Nichols N B, Phillips R S. Theory of servomechanisms. In: MIT Radiation Laboratory Series, Volumn 25. New York: McGraw-Hill, 1947

[8] Munro N. Multivariable control 1: the inverse Nyquist array design method. In: Lecture Notes of SERC Vacation School on Control System Design. UMIST, Manchester, 1989

[9] Rosenbrock H H. Computer-aided control system design. New York: Academic Press, 1974

[10] MacFarlane A G J, Postlethwaite I. The generalized Nyquist stability criterion and multivariable root loci. International Journal of Control, 1977, 25:81–127

[11] Boyel J M, Ford M P, Maciejowski J M. A multivariable toolbox for use with MAT-LAB. IEEE Control Systems Magazine, 1989, 9:59–65

[12] MathWorks Inc. Control system toolbox manual

# Chapter 6

# Simulink and Simulation of Nonlinear Systems

In the previous chapters, linear systems were mainly modeled and analyzed. Nonlinear systems were not considered. In real world, all the systems by nature are nonlinear. The nonlinearities in some of the systems are not significant, thus they can be neglected, and the systems can be simplified with linear ones. With the linear system modeling and analysis methods, these systems can be handled directly. However, in some systems, the nonlinear effects are so significant that they cannot be neglected, and the linear system theory is no longer applicable. Modeling and simulation methods should be used for these systems.

Computer simulation of control systems mainly investigates the behavior of the system when driven by certain input signals, and draws conclusion from the results. For linear systems, the methods in Chapters 4 and 5 can be used, and relevant functions in the MATLAB Control System Toolbox can be used directly to assess the properties of them. To investigate nonlinear systems, the numerical solution approaches for nonlinear differential equations presented in Chapter 3 can be adopted instead.

For even more complicated systems, the above approaches may fail. For instance, for systems with complicated structures, it is usually extremely difficult to write out an ordinary differential equation model of the systems, if not impossible. With a block diagram modeling technique, the problems can then be solved easily and straightforwardly. Simulink environment is an ideal tool for this purpose[1]. Various blocks are provided in Simulink, and with them, systems of arbitrary complexity can be modeled and simulated. Simulink is now an essential component to MATLAB, where the necessary blocks for linear, nonlinear and other advanced elements are provided. For instance, in SimPowerSystems blockset, motor blocks are provided, while in SimMechanics blockset, rigid bodies and joints are provided. These blocksets enable the users to build complicated systems easily and reliably.

In Section 6.1, a brief introduction to Simulink and commonly used groups and blocks are presented, to familiarize the readers with Simulink model library. This will establish a good foundation for Simulink modeling. In Section 6.2, modeling and simulation methods are provided and illustrative examples are given to show the model construction, linking, and simulation procedures on the simulation models. In

Section 6.3, Simulink modeling and simulation analysis of various control systems, including multivariable systems, computer control systems, time varying systems, switching systems and stochastic systems are presented. In Section 6.4, various static nonlinearities are presented in Simulink, and describing function analysis and linearization are also presented. In Section 6.5, advanced Simulink modeling techniques such as subsystem modeling and masking are presented. In Section Section 6.6, S-function programming and application are presented. Theoretically, systems with arbitrary complexity can be modeled and analyzed easily.

## 6.1    Fundamentals of Simulink Modeling

### 6.1.1    *Introduction to Simulink*

Simulink was released by MathWorks Inc around 1990's, with an original name of SimuLAB, and it was renamed to Simulink in 1992. There is a two-folder meaning in the name, "simu" and "link", while the former stands for simulation and the latter for linking block diagrams. Simulink can be used to establish simulation model graphically using building blocks. It can be used in the modeling and simulation of control systems, as well as other systems. Besides, many engineering blocks such as motors, mechanisms can be used directly to construct and simulate complicated systems.

The Simulink block library shown in Fig.6-1 can be opened with the command

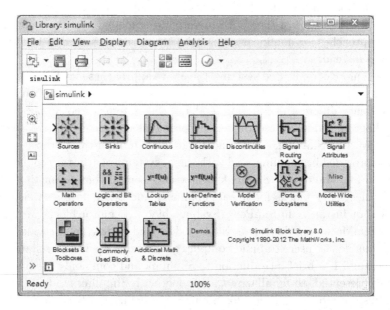

Fig. 6-1    Simulink block library.

`open_system(simulink)`. There are lower-level libraries and groups such as Continuous and Discrete in the main library. The lower-level libraries and groups can be opened by double clicking the icons. The model library shown here is with Simulink version 8.0, under MATLAB R2012b.

Click the Simulink icon ▤ in the toolbar in MATLAB command window, the model library browser is opened as shown in Fig. 6-2. The users can alternatively use this browser in system modeling. The one shown in Fig. 6-1 is more suitable for presentation, thus it will be used throughout the book.

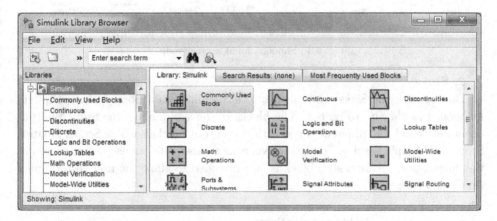

Fig. 6-2   Simulink library browser.

### 6.1.2   *Commonly Used Blocks in Simulink*

It can be seen from the main library shown in Fig. 6-1 that there are lower-level groups and libraries under each icon, and there may further be other lower-level ones under each icons. With the use of the blocks in the library, complicated Simulink models can be constructed. Here, a very brief description to those libraries and groups are presented so that the readers may acquaint with the current block libraries, since this is the foundation for complicated system modeling.

**1. Sources**

Double click the icon labeled Sources in the Simulink main library, the contents in the group will be opened as shown in Fig. 6-3[1]. In this group, the signal sources such as Step, Clock, Signal Generator, From File, From Workspace, Sine Wave, Ramp, Pulse Generator are provided. Also, periodic signals can be generated with Repeating Sequence, and white noise stochastic signals can be generated with Band-Limited White Noise block. An input port can be represented with In block. Moreover, the Signal Builder allows user to graphically design the input waveform.

---

[1]In order to better show the contents in the groups, the layout of the blocks in each group were rearranged manually.

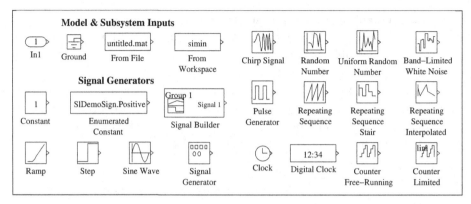

Fig. 6-3    Simulink input source group.

## 2. Sinks

Double click the Sinks group icon in the Simulink main library, the group will be opened as shown in Fig. 6-4. The blocks in the group allow the user to output simulation results in different ways, with the output blocks such as Scope, Floating Scope, X-Y Graph, Display, To File, To Workspace. Also, one can use Out to represent the output port. A Stop stop block is also provided to allow the user to terminate simulation process.

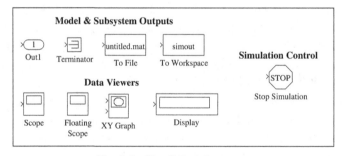

Fig. 6-4    Simulink sinks group.

## 3. Continuous

Double click the Continuous icon in the Simulink main library, the continuous blocks shown in Fig. 6-5 will be opened. The commonly used linear continuous models such as Transfer Fcn, State Space and Zero–Pole are provided. Also, different kinds of delay blocks, Transport Delay, Variable Transport Delay and Variable Time Delay, are provided. Integrator blocks with different options, and Derivative block are provided in the group. Two PID controllers with different variations are provided in the group and they can be used to simulate PID control systems.

In fact, there are limitations in these linear continuous blocks. One is that the transfer function blocks are assumed to be with zero initial conditions. Another one is that the multivariable transfer function matrices cannot be modeled directly.

For systems with nonzero conditions, the blocks in Simulink Extras group in

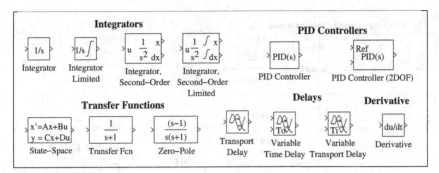

Fig. 6-5   Simulink continuous blocks group.

Toolboxes and Blocksets can be opened.  Double click the Additional Linear icon
in the group, the blocks in Fig. 6-6(a) will be opened, where transfer functions
with nonzero initial conditions can alternatively be used. To model multivariable
transfer functions, or use directly other LTI object in MATLAB workspace, the
Control System Toolbox Blockset can be used as shown in Fig. 6-6(b). The LTI
System block can be used to represent LTI objects in MATLAB workspace. This
block now can handle LTI blocks with internal delays directly.

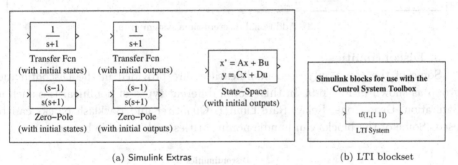

(a) Simulink Extras                         (b) LTI blockset
Fig. 6-6   Other groups for linear system models.

## 4. Discrete

Linear discrete-time blocks are contained in the Discrete group as shown in
Fig. 6-7, where Zero-order Hold, First-order Hold blocks are available. Discrete-time
linear blocks such as Discrete Transfer Fcn, Discrete State-Space, Discrete Zero–Pole,
Discrete Filter are also provided, where the filter model is given in Eqn. (4.14).
Different time delay blocks such as Unit Delay, and Discrete Integrator are provided
also in the group. The block Memory is used to store the signal in the previous
sampling interval. Also, the two discrete-time PID controllers are also provided.

Again the above transfer function model cannot handle blocks with nonzero
initial conditions. The Additional Discrete subgroup in Simulink Extras group can be
used as shown in Fig. 6-8. The Control System Toolbox block LTI System can also
be used for discrete-time systems.

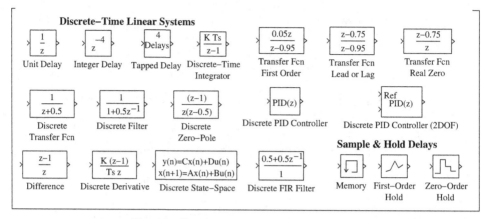

Fig. 6-7    Simulink discrete-time blocks group.

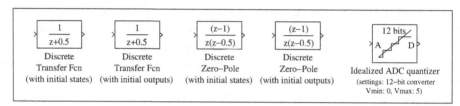

Fig. 6-8    Additional discrete-time system group.

## 5. Discontinuities

Some of the commonly used nonlinearities are provided in the Discontinuities group as shown in Fig. 6-9. In this group, different types of nonlinearities such as Saturation, Dead Zone, Relay, Rate Limiter, Quantizer and Backlash blocks can be used. Some of the blocks can handle nonlinearities with variable boundaries.

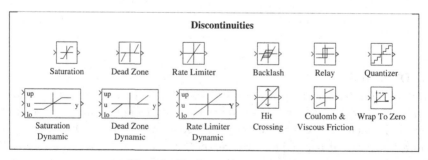

Fig. 6-9    Nonlinear element group.

## 6. Math operations

Mathematical function blocks are provided in Math group shown in Fig. 6-10, including the Sum, Product, Gain, Combinational Logic, Math Function, Abs, Sign, Trigonometric Function blocks. Also, the Algebraic Constraint can be used to solve algebraic equations.

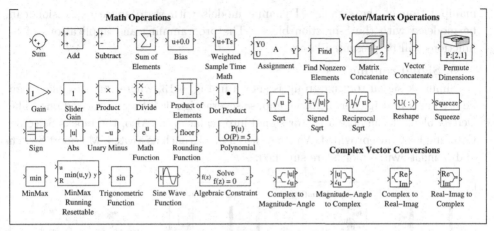

Fig. 6-10   Mathematical function group.

## 7. Look-up tables

Look-Up Table group is shown in Fig. 6-11, where the blocks Look Up Table, Look Up Table (2-D), Look Up Table (n-D) are provided. Later, arbitrary piecewise linear nonlinearities will be presented. The Look-up Table Dynamic block allows the user to assign data with signals so that dynamic tables can be established.

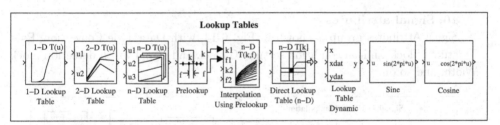

Fig. 6-11   Lookup table group.

## 8. User-defined functions

More complicated functions can be modeled with the blocks in the User-Defined Function group shown in Fig. 6-12. The Fcn block can be used for the

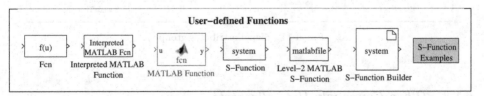

Fig. 6-12   User-defined functions group.

simple manipulation of signals, and MATLAB Fcn and Embedded MATLAB Function blocks can be used to accept user-defined MATLAB functions to perform static manipulation of the signals. Dynamic models with state space expression can be modeled with the S-function block. The programming and applications of S-functions will be presented later.

**9. Signal routing**

Simulink signal routing group is shown in Fig. 6-13, where the Mux block can be used as a multiplexer, i.e., to compose several signals into a vectorized one. The Demux block decompose a vector signal into scalar ones. Also, the blocks Selector, Goto and From are provided. Various switch blocks such as Switch, Multiport Switch and Manual Switch blocks are supplied.

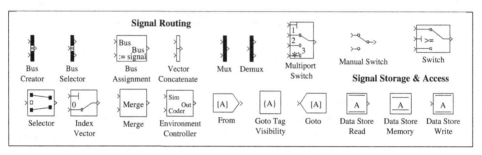

Fig. 6-13    Signal routing group.

**10. Signal attributes**

Signal Attributes group is shown in Fig. 6-14, with Data Type Conversion, Rate Transition blocks, initial condition setting IC block and signal width detection block Width, and so on.

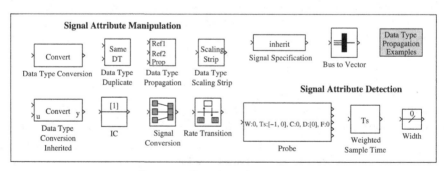

Fig. 6-14    Signal attributes group.

### 6.1.3  *Other Commonly Used Blocksets*

Apart from the above standard block groups presented, there are other blocksets related to MATLAB toolboxes as shown in Fig. 6-15.

The blocksets related to control systems are Control System Toolbox, System

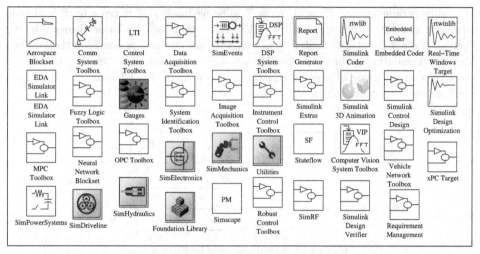

Fig. 6-15   Simulink blocksets and toolboxes.

Identification Toolbox, Fuzzy Logic Toolbox, model predict control MPC Toolbox, Neural Network Blockset, Simulink Control Design, Simulink Design Optimization and DSP System Toolbox. The blocksets related to real-time control are Data Acquisition Toolbox, Instrument Control Toolbox, SimRF, xPC Target, Read-Time Windows Target and so on. Also included are the multi-domain physical system modeling blocksets Simscape, SimDriveline, SimPowerSystems, SimMechanics, SimElectronics, Computer Vision System Toolbox, etc. These blocksets can be used in professional simulation models of various kinds. Since these blocksets are developed and maintained by well-known scholars and professional in the related fields, the simulation results obtained are reliable.

## 6.2   Simulink Modeling and Simulation

### 6.2.1   *Introduction to Simulink Modeling Methodology*

Block diagram modeling with Simulink is quite simple and straightforward. There is no need for the user to write programs, graphical manipulation of the blocks are necessary in constricting complicated block diagrams. Then simulation can be invoked to study the behavior of the Simulink model with menus, and the results can be displayed directly on scopes. Equipped with the powerful Simulink facilities, the capabilities of the user can be enhanced significantly. A simple example is given below to illustrate the Simulink modeling procedures, and to show the simulation methods and skills.

**Example 6.1.** Consider the typical nonlinear feedback control system shown in Fig. 6-16, where the plant model is a second-order transfer function, and there is a PI controller, $G_c(s) = (K_p s + K_i)/s$, followed by an actuator saturation with width $\Delta = 2$, the controller parameters are $K_p = 3$, $K_i = 2$. The feedback loop is given by a dead zone nonlinear element with a width of $\delta = 0.1$. Since there are nonlinear elements in the system, it is not possible to analyze it exactly with the methods presented in the previous chapters, simulation is the only plausible way for the system. It is also very difficult to solve the corresponding differential equation with the method in Chapter 2, since a slight carelessness in modeling may lead to serious errors.

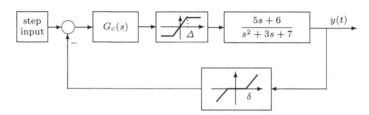

Fig. 6-16   A typical nonlinear feedback system.

Simulink is an effective tool in performing simulation analysis for the nonlinear system. The following procedures can be used in constructing the simulation model.

(1) **Open a blank model window.** A block model window can be opened with the File → New → Model menu in Simulink menu bar, or by clicking the ⬚ icon in the Simulink model window toolbar.

(2) **Copy relevant blocks to the window.** Copy the necessary blocks from their original groups to the model window by mouse dragging. For instance, drag the Step block from the Sources group to the model window, and drag the Sum block from the Math group to the model window, and so on. The necessary blocks in the model window are now shown in Fig. 6-17.

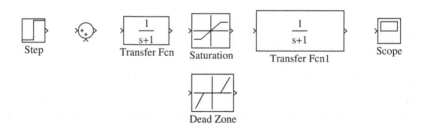

Fig. 6-17   Model editing window (model file: c5mblk1.mdl).

(3) **Modify the parameters of the blocks.** With observation, it is found that the parameters in some of the blocks are different from the ones in the original system shown in Fig. 6-16(a). For instance, the plant model, controller model and the Sum block are all different. Double click the Sum block, the parameter dialog box shown in Fig. 6-18 will be displayed, the List of Signs edit box shows the signs of the input channels, and | indicates no input channel at the corresponding port. It can be seen that if the string |+- is used instead, the subtracter required in negative feedback loop can be defined.

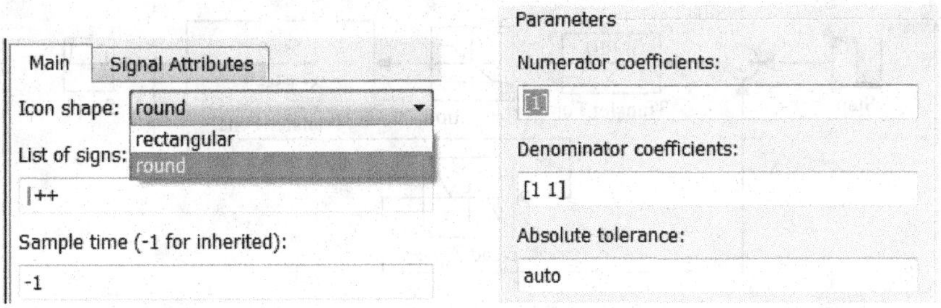

| Main | Signal Attributes | | Parameters |
|---|---|---|---|
| Icon shape: | round ▼ | | Numerator coefficients: |
| List of signs: | rectangular<br>round | | [1] |
| |++ | | | Denominator coefficients: |
| | | | [1 1] |
| Sample time (-1 for inherited): | | | Absolute tolerance: |
| -1 | | | auto |

(a) dialog box of Sum                    (b) dialog box of Transfer Fcn

Fig. 6-18   Parameter dialog boxes for Sum and Transfer Fcn.

If there are too many input channels, the default round icon is no longer suitable, the rectangular item from the Icon shape listbox should be selected instead. A rectangular sum block can then be defined. In the Sample time ($-1$ for inherited) edit box, the sampling interval of the signal should be specified. Usually, 0 can be used for continuous system, and if it is set to $-1$, the sampling interval of the block inherits that of its input signal.

Similarly, transfer function block can also be redefined. Double click the controller block, the dialog box shown in Fig. 6-18(b) will be opened, where the numerator and denominator polynomials of the expected transfer function should be specified respectively in the Numerator and Denominator edit boxes. The polynomials can still be expressed as coefficient vectors in the descending order of $s$, as in the Control System Toolbox. For instance, the parameters of the PI controller can be assigned respectively to [3,2] and [1,0], and those for the plant model can be set to [5,6] and [1,3,7]. The icons of the transfer function blocks can be changed accordingly.

The parameters in other blocks should be modified as: In the Step signal block, the Step time parameter should be changed to 0, from its default value of 1; In the Saturation block, the Upper limit and Lower limit parameters should be set to 2 and $-2$; In the Dead Zone block, the Start of dead zone and End of dead zone parameters should be set to $-0.1$ and 0.1, respectively.

(4) **Connect the blocks to complete the simulation system.** The blocks in the model editing windows should be connected now, according to the given one required in Fig. 6-16. One can click the output port of one block, drag the mouse button to the input port of the other block, and release the mouse button to connect the two blocks. An alternative way is to click the source block, hold on the Ctrl key and click at the target block. The connection can be established automatically. The connected system block diagram is shown in Fig. 6-19.

Unfortunately, the layout of the feedback path is not satisfactory. The block rotating and flipping facilities in Simulink can be used to modify the feedback loop. One can click the Dead Zone block, then click it with right mouse button, the Format → Rotate & Flip submenu in the shortcut menu shown in Fig. 6-20, allowing the user to rotate, flip and add shadows to the block as shown respectively in Figs. 6-21(a), (b) and (c).

Alternatively, if one connects the output signal to the negative feedback port of Sum block directly, then one can move the Dead Zone block on top of the connection line and release the mouse button. The block will be embedded in the feedback path, and perform flip action automatically, if necessary. The finalized Simulink block diagram is

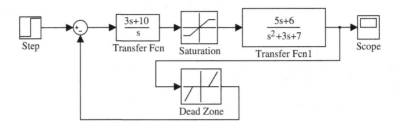

Fig. 6-19   Block diagram after connection (file name: c5mblk2.mdl).

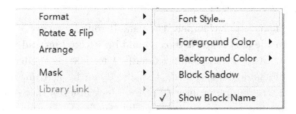

Fig. 6-20   **Format** and **Rotate & Flip** submenus.

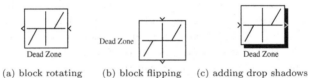

(a) block rotating     (b) block flipping     (c) adding drop shadows

Fig. 6-21   Simple manipulations of the block.

then obtained as shown in Fig. 6-22. It can be seen that the new Simulink model looks much better than the one obtained earlier.

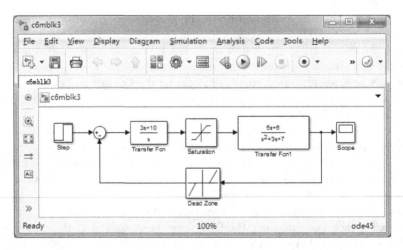

Fig. 6-22   Finalized simulation model (file name: c5mblk3.mdl).

(5) **Invoke simulation session.** When the Simulink model is established, simulation session can be invoked, either by clicking the simulation icon ▶ in the toolbar, or by selecting the menu item Simulation → Run (in earlier versions, menu Simulation → Start). Simulation process can be started, and one can double click the Scope icon to get the result shown in Fig. 6-23(a).

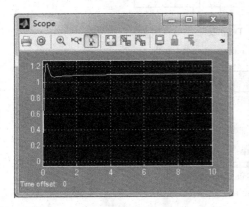 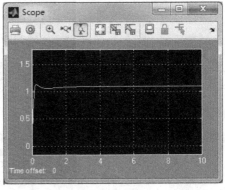

(a) direct simulation result        (b) result when controller is modified

Fig. 6-23　Scope output of the simulation results.

It can be seen that the tracking speed is rather slow in the system. With the knowledge on PI controllers, the value of $K_p$ should be increased. One can set the value of $K_p$ to 10, such that the system output is obtained as shown in Fig. 6-23(b).

A Slider Gain block in the Math group can be used to allow the user to adjust $K_p$ with a scroll bar. The new Simulink model with such a block can be established as shown in Fig. 6-24(a). By double clicking the Kp block, the dialog box can be obtained as shown in Fig. 6-24(b). In simulation, a scroll bar can be used to adjust the value of $K_p$.

### 6.2.2　*Simulation Algorithms and Simulation Parameter Selections*

Select the Simulation menu item in the model as shown in Fig. 6-25, the menu item Configuration Parameters can be used to open a simulation parameter setting dialog box shown in Fig. 6-26. On the left-hand-side of the dialog box, there are many panes, where the Solver pane is the one with most of the relevant simulation control parameters:

(1) Simulation time provides two edit boxes, allows the user to specify the Start time and Stop time for the simulation session.

(2) Type group in Solver options column has two options, and enables the user to select Variable-step and Fixed step, and in the Solver listbox, various algorithms such as ode45 (Dormand–Prince), ode15s (stiff/NDF) are provided.

(3) Simulation precision can be controlled by Relative Tolerance and Absolute Tolerance options. For different algorithms, there are further options. The default setting of Relative Tolerance parameter is 1e-3 and it is too large. It is suggested to

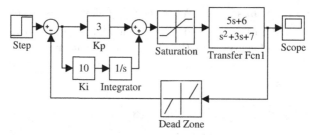

(a) new model (file name: c5mblk4.mdl)

(b) Slider Gain dialog box

Fig. 6-24    An alternative simulation model with a scroll bar.

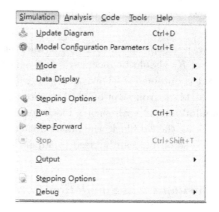

Fig. 6-25    Simulation menu.

set the option to 1e-6 or 1e-7. It is worth mentioning that although error tolerance is set to an extremely small value in variable-step algorithm, the computation load may increase much.

(4) Maximum and minimum allowed steps are allowed to be set with Max step size and Min step size. If the actual step size exceeds the boundaries in simulation, warning dialog box will be given.

(5) The levels of some of error or warning messages can be specified in the Diagnostics pane in the dialog box, they will not be presented in the book.

Having specified the control parameters, the Simulation → Run menu item (in the earlier versions, the Simulation → Start menu) or the ▶ button in the toolbar can

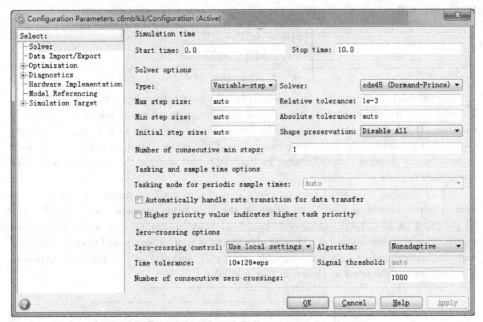

Fig. 6-26   Simulation control parameters dialog box.

be used to start simulation process. After simulation, an automatically generated vector `tout` will be returned to MATLAB workspace. If output ports (Outport blocks) are used in the model, the variable `yout` will also be returned to MATLAB workspace. The commands such as `plot(tout,yout)` can also be used to draw simulation results.

Apart from the Simulation menu to start the simulation process, function `sim()` can also be used, with $[t, x, y] = \text{sim}(model, \text{tspan}, options)$, where *model* is the model name of the Simulink file, with extension name .slx (in earlier versions, .mdl). The returned variable $t$ and $y$ returns the time and output signals of simulation. Variable $x$ returns the state matrix.

Simulation control parameters *options* can be specified with `simset()` function, with $options = \text{simset}(parameter\ 1, value\ 1, parameter\ 2, value\ 2, \cdots)$, where *parameter*'s are the names of the parameters to be controlled (should be quoted with single quotation marks), and *value*'s are relevant values of the parameters. Control parameter names can be listed with the `help simset` command. For instance, if we want to change the `'RelTol'` property to $10^{-7}$, the command `options = simset('RelTol',1e-7)` or `options.RelTol = 1e-7` can be used.

### 6.2.3   *An Illustrative Example of Simulink Modeling*

The well-known Rössler differential equation is used as an example to demonstrate the modeling and simulation procedures in Simulink.

**Example 6.2.** Consider the Rössler equation given in Example 3.13, with

$$\begin{cases} \dot{x}(t) = -y(t) - z(t) \\ \dot{y}(t) = x(t) + ay(t) \\ \dot{z}(t) = b + [x(t) - c]z(t). \end{cases}$$

The parameters are $a = b = 0.2$, $c = 5.7$, and the initial states are $x(0) = y(0) = z(0) = 0$. To model a differential equation, the systematical way is to assign an integrator to a state variable. If we define the output of the integrator as the state signal, then the input terminal is by nature the first-order derivative of the state. Thus, it is not too difficult to construct a Simulink model shown in Fig. 6-27, and assume the initial values of the integrators to zero.

Before starting the simulation process, let the terminate of simulation be 100, and relative error tolerance be $10^{-7}$. Starting the simulation process, two variables will be returned to MATLAB workspace, **tout** and **yout**, where **tout** is a column vector, representing the time instances. The variable **yout** is a matrix, composed of three columns, each one corresponding to a state variable, $x(t)$, $y(t)$, and $z(t)$. Thus, the time responses of the states are obtained as shown in Fig. 6-28(a).

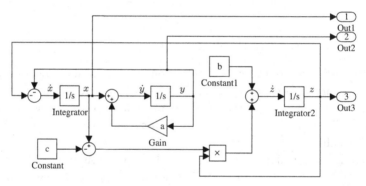

Fig. 6-27   Simulink model of Rössler differential equation   (file name: c6mrossler.mdl).

```
>> plot(tout,yout)     % draw time responses of the states
```

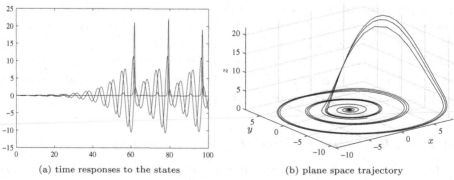

(a) time responses to the states          (b) plane space trajectory

Fig. 6-28   Simulation results of Rössler equation.

If $x(t)$, $y(t)$ and $z(t)$ are defined as axes, the three-dimensional trajectory can be drawn as shown in Fig. 6-28(b). Function comet3() can be used to show dynamically the phase space trajectory.

```
>> comet3(yout(:,1),yout(:,2),yout(:,3)), grid  % phase space trajectory
```

Many blocks, such as the Integrator block, in Simulink support vector inputs. Several individual input signals can be grouped into a vector signal with Mux block. With Demux block, the grouped vector signal can be separated into scalar signals again. With Mux block and the vectorized Integrator block, Simulink model for Rössler differential equation can be reconstructed as shown in Fig. 6-29(a). Fcn block is used to describe the complicated mathematical operations, rather than the low-level block construction. By default, the input to the Fcn block is denoted as u, and if u is a vector input, u[$i$] represents its $i$th component. It can be seen that the thus constructed Simulink model is far much simpler than the low-level one in Fig. 6-27. The new model is easier to debug and maintain.

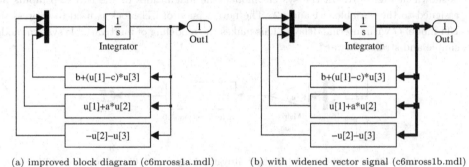

(a) improved block diagram (c6mross1a.mdl)   (b) with widened vector signal (c6mross1b.mdl)

Fig. 6-29   Another Simulink model for Rössler equation.

Simulink models allow the decoration of vectorized blocks. For instance, the Format → Wide nonscalar lines menu item can be selected to represent the vector signals in thick lines as shown in Fig. 6-29(b). If the menu item Format → Signal dimensions is selected, the signal lines will be labeled the dimensions of the signals. For instance, since there are three states, the vector signal is marked with 3 as shown in Fig. 6-30(a). Also, the Format → Port data types menu allows to mark the data type on the signals as shown in Fig. 6-30(b). In this way, the Simulink model will be made more readable.

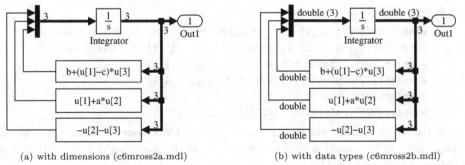

(a) with dimensions (c6mross2a.mdl)   (b) with data types (c6mross2b.mdl)

Fig. 6-30   Decorations of vector block and signals.

## 6.3   Simulink Modeling of Various Control Systems

In this section, the Simulink modeling various control systems such as multivariable systems, computer control systems, time varying systems, multi-rate systems, switching systems and stochastic systems will be given. Through Simulink, we can easily analyze the corresponding systems.

**Example 6.3. Modeling of multivariable systems with delays.** In Example 5.23, step responses of a multivariable system with internal delays is given, using Control System Toolbox. Since there exists time delay in the system, state space models with internal delays were used, or as in Example 5.23, Padé approximation was used to perform approximate simulation. Equipped with the powerful Simulink, the same system can be represented easily, and accurate simulation results can be obtained. A constructed model is shown in Fig. 6-31. In the system model, the magnitudes of the two step inputs are assigned to the variables u1 and u2. The new version of LTI block is used to express the LTI model $G$ with internal delays. This makes the modeling of multivariable system model simple and straightforward.

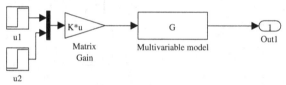

Fig. 6-31   Simulink model of the multivariable system   (file: c6mmimon.mdl).

Recall the results obtained in Example 5.23, where `step()` function was used, and the outputs for each step input were evaluated

```
>> g11=tf(0.1134,[1.78 4.48 1],'ioDelay',0.72);
   g21=tf(0.3378,[0.361 1.09 1],'ioDelay',0.3);
   g12=tf(0.924,[2.07 1]); g22=tf(-0.318,[2.93 1],'ioDelay',1.29);
   G=[g11, g12; g21, g22]; G=ss(G);   % convert to SS with internal delays
   Kp=[0.1134,0.924; 0.3378,-0.318]; step(G*Kp,15);
```

With the Simulink model, the output signals driven individually by the two inputs can also be obtained. The results by Simulink and by `step()` function can be drawn together in Fig. 6-32, and it can be seen that the two results are the same. They cannot be distinguished from the curves.

```
>> u1=1; u2=0; [t1,a,y1]=sim('c6mmimo',15); % first input acts alone
   u1=0; u2=1; [t2,a,y2]=sim('c6mmimo',15); [y,t]=step(G*Kp,15);
   subplot(221), plot(t,y(:,1,1),':',t1,y1(:,1))
   subplot(222), plot(t,y(:,1,2),':',t2,y2(:,1))
   subplot(223), plot(t,y(:,2,1),':',t1,y1(:,2))
   subplot(224), plot(t,y(:,2,2),':',t2,y2(:,2))
```

If the old versions of Simulink are used, the LTI block does not allow $G$ to contain delay terms. In this case, low-level representations of the multivariable systems should be made as shown in Fig. 6-33.

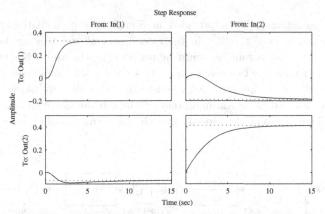

Fig. 6-32 Comparisons of step responses of the multivariable system.

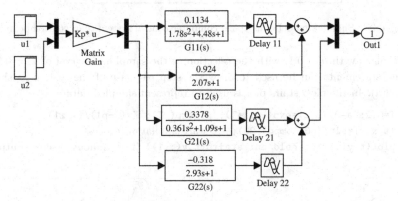

Fig. 6-33 Simulink model of the multivariable system (file: c6mmimo.mdl).

**Example 6.4. Computer control system.** Consider the typical computer control system shown in Fig. 6-34[2]. In the system, the controller is discrete followed by zero-

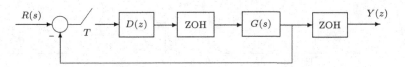

Fig. 6-34 Computer control system.

order hold (ZOH), and sampling interval of $T$, while the plant is continuous. Assume that the plant and controller are given by

$$G(s) = \frac{a}{s(s+1)}, \quad D(z) = \frac{1 - e^{-T}}{1 - e^{-0.1T}} \frac{z - e^{-0.1T}}{z - e^{-T}},$$

where $a = 0.1$. For such a system, it is not easy to write the whole system with a single differential equation set, thus one is not likely able to simulate computer control systems with functions like ode45(). Block diagram is a feasible way to handle this kind of problems.

With the modeling facilities provided in Simulink, the simulation model can be established as shown in Fig. 6-35. In the model, several variables are used, $a$, $T$, $z_1$, $p_1$, and $K$, the first two parameters must be provided by the user, while the other three can be calculated from the two given parameters. In the first zero-order hold ZOH, the sampling interval can be specified to $T$, and in the other discrete blocks, the sampling interval can be specified as $-1$, meaning they will inherit the sampling interval from their input blocks. There is no need to specify in each block with sampling interval of $T$.

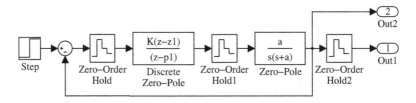

Fig. 6-35    Simulink model of a typical computer control system (file: c6mcompc.mdl).

In a plant with $a = 0.1$, with the selection of the sampling interval of $T = 0.2\,$s, the following statements can be used to draw the step response of the system as shown in Fig. 6-36(a). In the plot, stairs plot is used to represent sampled data.

```
>> T=0.2; a=0.1; z1=exp(-0.1*T); p1=exp(-T); K=(1-p1)/(1-z1);
   [t,x,y]=sim('c6mcompc',20);   % start simulation process
   plot(t,y(:,2)); hold on; stairs(t,y(:,1)) % continuous/discrete output
```

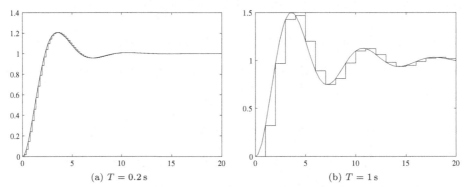

(a) $T = 0.2\,$s                    (b) $T = 1\,$s

Fig. 6-36    System responses for different values of sampling intervals.

Consider the larger sampling interval $T = 1\,$s. The following statements can be used to draw step response as shown in Fig. 6-36(b). It can be seen that when the sampling interval is too large, there exist large differences between the continuous and sampling signals.

```
>> T=1; z1=exp(-0.1*T); p1=exp(-T); K=(1-p1)/(1-z1); % input parameters
   [t,x,y]=sim('c6mcompc',20); plot(t,y(:,2));       % simulation
   hold on; stairs(t,y(:,1))                          % draw stairs
```

In fact, using the conversion approach given in Chapter 4, the equivalent continuous or discrete transfer function under sampling interval $T$ can be obtained, and step responses can be obtained with the following MATLAB statement

```
>> T=0.2; z1=exp(-0.1*T); p1=exp(-T); K=(1-p1)/(1-z1);
   Dz=zpk(z1,p1,K,'Ts',T);            % controller model
   G=zpk([],[0;-a],a); Gz=c2d(G,T);   % discrete plant
   GG=zpk(feedback(Gz*Dz,1)), step(GG) % step response
```

The transfer function of the discrete controller is

$$G_c(z) = \frac{0.32187(z - 0.9802)(z + 0.8753)}{(z - 0.9817)(z^2 - 1.185z + 0.8403)}.$$

The commands may get the same results as in the Simulink model, and the analysis process is simpler. However, if the loop contains any nonlinear elements, the command line form may not work.

In fact, the zero-order hold following controller $D(z)$ is redundant and can be omitted. The ZOH connected to the output is also redundant, since the output of the plant is continuous. They can be deleted from the model, and the new model is simplified as shown in Fig. 6-37.

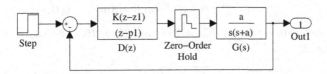

Fig. 6-37  Simplified computer control system model  (file name: c6mcomc1.mdl).

Of course, the simulation model may further be simplified, by deleting the ZOH as shown in Fig. 6-38. Also, the simplified model is not quite complete in the concept of control, it works perfectly in simulation. Since in the simulation process, the default output of the discrete controller remains at the same value within each sampling interval, just as if there is a zero-order hold is following it.

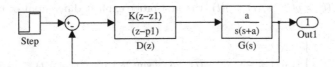

Fig. 6-38  Simulink model with further simplification  (file name: c6mcomc2.mdl).

From the Simulink model, it can be seen that since some of the parameters in the model are given by variable names, the variables must be assigned values each time the model is opened. This may be very complicated and tedious. In practical system modeling, the File $\rightarrow$ Model properties menu can be selected, and by selecting its Callback pane, the dialog box shown in Fig. 6-39 will be displayed. The model parameters can be assigned in the PreLoadFcn edit box. In this way, when the model opens every time, the data will be loaded into MATLAB workspace automatically.

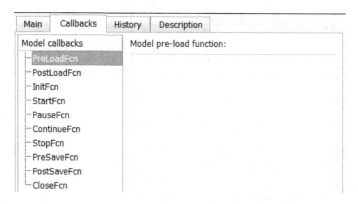

Fig. 6-39   Dialog box of model property setting.

**Example 6.5. Modeling of time varying system.** Consider a PI control system shown in Fig. 6-40, where the plant model is given by a time varying differential equation

$$\ddot{y}(t) + e^{-0.2t}\dot{y}(t) + e^{-5t}\sin(2t+6)y(t) = u(t),$$

and the controller parameters are $K_p = 200$, and $K_i = 10$. The width of the actuator saturation is $\delta = 2$.

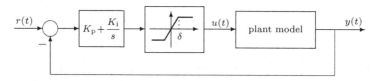

Fig. 6-40   PI control of a time varying plant.

It can be seen that apart from the time varying plant model, the modeling of other components in the loop is quite simple and straightforward. For the time varying plant model, let $x_1(t) = y(t)$, $x_2(t) = \dot{y}(t)$, the first-order explicit differential equation can be rewritten as

$$\begin{cases} \dot{x}_1(t) = x_2(t) \\ \dot{x}_2(t) = -e^{-0.2t}x_2(t) - e^{-5t}\sin(2t+6)x_1(t) + u(t). \end{cases}$$

Using the modeling strategy in Example 6.2, one integrator can be assigned to each state variable. The simulation model of the closed-loop system can be established as shown in Fig. 6-41.

With the simulation model, the following statements can be issued to draw the step response of the time varying system as shown in Fig. 6-42.

```
>> opt=simset('RelTol',1e-8);    % set the relative tolerance
   Kp=200; Ki=10;                % set controller parameters
   [t,x,y]=sim('c6mtimv',10,opt); plot(t,y)   % simulation results
```

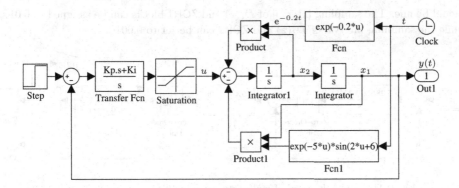

Fig. 6-41   Simulink model of the time varying systems   (file name: c6mtimv.mdl).

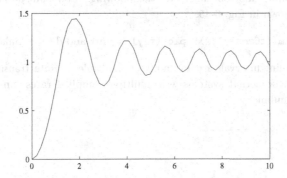

Fig. 6-42   Step response of the time varying system.

**Example 6.6. Modeling of multi-rate system.** Assume that in the double-loop motor drive system shown in Fig. 6-43, the sampling interval of the inner current loop and outer speed loop are $T_1 = 0.001$ s, and $T_2 = 0.01$ s. The models of the two controllers are

$$D_1(z) = \frac{0.0967z - 0.0965}{z - 1}, \quad D_2(z) = \frac{5.2812z - 5.2725}{z - 1}.$$

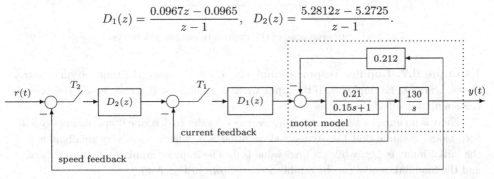

Fig. 6-43   Block diagram of multi-rate system.

With the given control structure, the Simulink model can be constructed as shown in Fig. 6-44. Since $T_2$ is the integer multiples of $T_1$, the direct use of the discrete blocks should be fine. The sampling interval of $D_1(z)$ and **ZOH1** blocks can be assigned to 0.01 s, while the sampling interval of $D_2(z)$ and **ZOH2** can be set to 0.001 s.

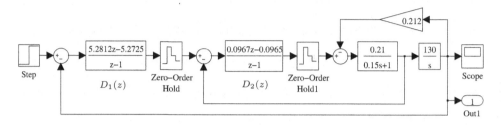

Fig. 6-44    Simulink model of multi-rate system    (file name: c6mmulr.mdl).

Simulation results can be obtained with the following statements, and the step response of the system is shown in Fig. 6-45.

```
>> [t,x,y]=sim('c6mmulr',2); plot(t,y) % start and draw simulation process
```

If the two sampling intervals are not in integer multiples, a **Rate Transition** block should be used. It can be seen that systems with multiple sampling rates can be modeled and simulated with Simulink.

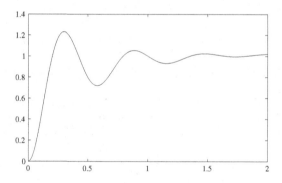

Fig. 6-45    Step response of the multi-rate sampling data system.

**Example 6.7. Impulse response analysis.** Consider again the time varying control system shown in Example 6.5. If the input signal is an impulse function, how can we create the Simulink model?

There is no impulse signal generator, we may consider to describe it approximately with **Step** block. Assume that the step signal duration is $a$, where $a$ is a very small value and the initial input is $1/a$, while its final value is 0. The impulse input can be approximated and the Simulink model can be established as shown in Fig. 6-46.

Theoretically speaking, if $a \to 0$, the input signal is the unit impulse input. In simulation practice, larger values of $a$'s are also acceptable. For instance, when $a = 0.001$, the simulation results are the same as the case with smaller values of $a$'s, as shown in Fig. 6-47.

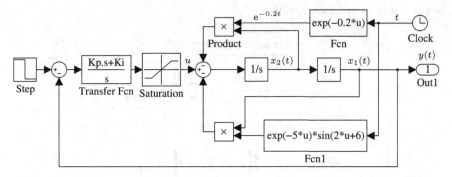

Fig. 6-46 Impulse response of a time varying system (file name: c6mtimva.mdl).

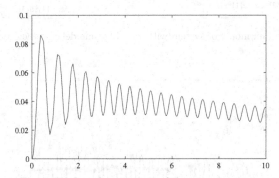

Fig. 6-47 Impulse response of time varying system.

```
>> opt=simset('RelTol',1e-8);    % set relative tolerance
   Kp=200; Ki=10; a=0.001;       % set controller parameters
   [t,x,y]=sim('c6mtimva',10,opt); plot(t,y)   % simulation
```

In fact, it can be seen from the example, although the value of $a$ selected is relatively large, for instance, $a = 0.1$, the simulation results are still satisfactory.

**Example 6.8. System with variable time delay.** The mathematical model is

$$
\begin{cases}
\dot{x}_1(t) = -2x_2(t) - 3x_1(t - 0.2|\sin t|) \\
\dot{x}_2(t) = -0.05x_1(t)x_3(t) - 2x_2(t - 0.8) \\
\dot{x}_3(t) = 0.3x_1(t)x_2(t)x_3(t) + \cos(x_1(t)x_2(t)) + 2\sin 0.1t^2,
\end{cases}
$$

and the initial state vector is $x(0) = [1, 1, 1]^T$. It is easily seen that there exists signal of $x_1$ at time $t - 0.2|\sin t|$, thus the delay is also time varying. Simulink should be used to solve the problem. The Variable Time Delay block in the Continuous group can be used to model the delay term.

Like other block diagram modeling, three integrators are needed to define the signals $x_1$, $x_2$ and $x_3$ and the input ports of these integrators are $\dot{x}_1$, $\dot{x}_2$ and $\dot{x}_3$, as shown in Fig. 6-48. Please note that Variable Time Delay block is used to model the delay term, with its second input port given by $0.2|\sin t|$. The results of simulating such a system are shown in Fig. 6-49. Different simulation control options can be tested to validate the correctness of the simulation results.

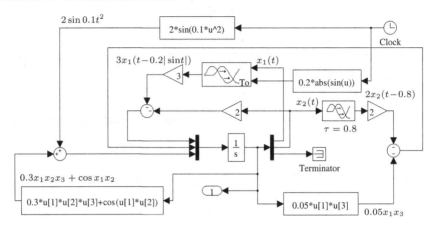

Fig. 6-48　Simulink model of system with variable time delay　(file: c6mdde3.mdl).

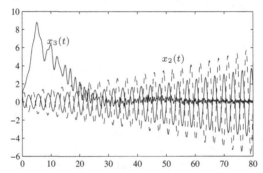

Fig. 6-49　Numerical solutions to system with variable time delay.

**Example 6.9. Modeling of switching system**. Assume that there are two subsystems $\dot{x} = A_i x$, where

$$A_1 = \begin{bmatrix} 0.1 & -1 \\ 2 & 0.1 \end{bmatrix}, \quad A_2 = \begin{bmatrix} 0.1 & -2 \\ 1 & 0.1 \end{bmatrix}.$$

Please note that both the two subsystems are unstable. If there is a switch, it switches the subsystem $A_1$ when $x_1 x_2 < 0$, i.e., on the quadrants II and IV of the $x_1$–$x_2$ plane, and switches to subsystem $A_2$ when the $x_1 x_2 \geqslant 0$, i.e., on the quadrants I and III. The Simulink model of the switching system can be constructed as shown in Fig. 6-50(a), with the dialog box of the Switch block as shown in Fig. 6-50(b). In order to implement the switching condition, the threshold of the switch block can be set to 0. Besides, in order to get accurate simulation results, the Enable zero-crossing detection checkbox should be checked.

The simulation results can be drawn with the following statements as shown in Fig. 6-51. Please note that although the two subsystems are unstable, under the given switching conditions, the whole system is stable.

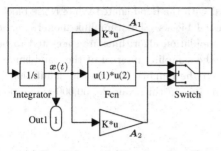

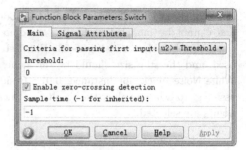

(a) Simulink model (file: c6mswi1.mdl)          (b) dialog box of Switch block

Fig. 6-50   Simulink model of the switching system.

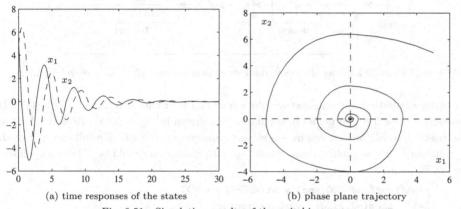

(a) time responses of the states          (b) phase plane trajectory

Fig. 6-51   Simulation results of the switching system.

```
>> plot(tout,yout), figure; plot(yout(:,1),yout(:,2))
```

**Example 6.10. Nonlinear feedback system with stochastic input**. Assume that the nonlinear model is shown in Fig. 6-52, where plant $G(s)$ is linear and nonlinear element is a saturation

$$G(s) = \frac{s^3 + 7s^2 + 24s + 24}{s^4 + 10s^3 + 35s^2 + 50s + 24}, \text{ nonlinearity } \mathcal{N}(e) = \begin{cases} 2\,\text{sign}(e), & |e| > 1 \\ 2e, & |e| \leqslant 1. \end{cases}$$

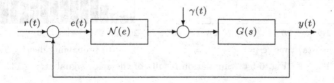

Fig. 6-52   Nonlinear system with stochastic inputs.

The stochastic disturbance signal $\delta(t)$ is Gaussian white noise with zero mean, and a variance of 3. The deterministic signal is $r(t) = 0$. It should be noted that in continuous systems, the stochastic signal should be modeled with the Band-limited White Noise block, and cannot be modeled with other random signal blocks. The Simulink model can be constructed as shown in Fig. 6-53. Fixed-step simulation algorithms are suggested to be used, and the step size should be the same as the sampling interval of the Band-limited White Noise block, for instance, 0.01. Besides, if the number of points in simulation is assigned to a large value, the results are meaningful. In this example, 30,000 simulation points are selected.

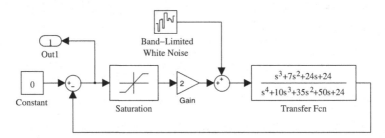

Fig. 6-53    Simulink model of the nonlinear stochastic system    (file name: c6mnlrsys.mdl).

After simulation, the returned variables `tout` and `yout` can be returned into MATLAB workspace. The last 500 points in simulation are drawn in Fig. 6-54(a). However, for the stochastic system, the time response is almost meaningless. Statistical results are expected. For instance, the probability density function with histogram should be obtained as shown in Fig. 6-54(b).

```
>> plot(tout(end-500:end),yout(end-500:end))
   c=linspace(-2,2,20); y1=hist(yout,c);
   figure; bar(c,y1/(length(tout)*(c(2)-c(1))))
```

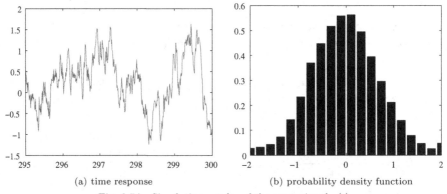

(a) time response                     (b) probability density function
Fig. 6-54    Simulation results of the error signal $e(t)$.

In real applications, any form of input signals can be constructed with Simulink. Periodic signals can also be constructed by the Repeating Sequence in the Sources group. Sometimes, if low-level block diagram construction of input signals are complicated, MATLAB programs can be written, with the form of S-functions. This will be illustrated later through examples.

## 6.4 Analysis and Simulation of Nonlinear Systems

Before the popularity of the powerful simulation languages and environments such as CSMP, ACSL, and MATLAB/Simulink, the analysis of nonlinear systems was restricted to a small category of nonlinear feedback control systems, usually with fixed system structures. Approximate approaches such as describing function methods[3] and phase plane trajectory were usually used. In this section, piecewise nonlinearity construction will be illustrated. Then limit cycles and linearization techniques will be presented, with Simulink.

### 6.4.1 *Modeling of Piecewise Nonlinearities*

The blocks of the Discontinuities group shown in Fig. 6-9 may be misleading, due to the limited forms of nonlinearities in Simulink model library. In fact, with the use of Simulink blocks, piecewise nonlinearities of any complexity can be modeled with a couple of Simulink blocks. Besides, any nonlinear components can be expressed easily with S-function modeling. In this part, the modeling strategy of piecewise linear nonlinearities, single-valued or multi-valued, will be illustrated.

Single-valued static piecewise nonlinearities can be represented easily with the 1-D Lookup Table block in the Lookup Tables group. Consider the piecewise nonlinearity shown in Fig. 6-55(a). The turning points of the nonlinearity are $(x_1, y_1)$, $(x_2, y_2)$, $\cdots$, $(x_{N-1}, y_{N-1})$, $(x_N, y_N)$. If the lookup table block is to be used in modeling the piecewise nonlinearity, a point $x_0$ less than $x_1$ should be selected and the corresponding $y_0$ can be evaluated. Similarly, a point $x_{N+1}$ larger than $x_N$ should be assigned too, and the value $y_{N+1}$ should be calculated. Two vectors xx and yy can then be constructed, such that

$$\mathbf{xx} = [x_0, x_1, x_2, \cdots, x_N, x_{N+1}]; \quad \mathbf{yy} = [y_0, y_1, y_2, \cdots, y_N, y_{N+1}];$$

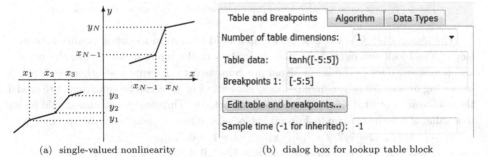

(a) single-valued nonlinearity  (b) dialog box for lookup table block

Fig. 6-55  Construction of single-valued nonlinearity.

Double clicking the 1-D Lookup Table, block, the dialog box shown in Fig. 6-55(b) can be displayed. In the Vector of input values and Vector of output values edit boxes, the vectors of turning points xx and yy and can be entered. Then the piecewise nonlinearity can be successfully constructed.

The modeling of multi-valued nonlinearities is slightly more difficult. Examples will be given to show the modeling of double-valued static nonlinearities.

**Example 6.11.** It is shown through the above example that any single-valued nonlinearity can be modeled or approximated by lookup table blocks. If there are loops in the nonlinearity, switches should be used as well.

Consider the two double-valued nonlinearities with loops shown in Figs. 6-56(a) and (b). Suppose we want to model the nonlinearity in Fig. 6-56(a). In the loop, when the input is increasing, one single-valued branch is used, while if the input signal is decreasing, another single-valued branch may be taken. Thus, the loop nonlinearity can be separated into two single-valued branches shown in Fig.6-57. Of course, the single-valued functions are conditional, it must find out whether the input signal is increasing or not first.

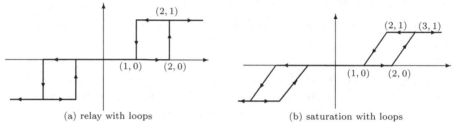

(a) relay with loops                    (b) saturation with loops

Fig. 6-56    Examples of nonlinearities with loops.

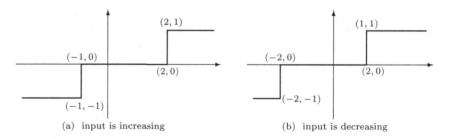

(a) input is increasing                    (b) input is decreasing

Fig. 6-57    Nonlinearity with loops can be separated with single-valued branches.

The Memory block in the Discrete group should be used in modeling nonlinearity with loops. The block will output the previous values of the input signal. Thus, the current and previous values of the input signal are compared to determine whether the input is increasing or not. Thus, a Simulink model shown in Fig. 6-58 can be constructed to model the nonlinearity of Fig.6-56(a). In the switch block, the Threshold parameter should be set to a value of 0.5. In the two lookup table blocks, the turning points can be specified by

$$x_1 = [-3, -1, -1 + \epsilon, 2, 2 + \epsilon, 3], \quad y_1 = [-1, -1, 0, 0, 1, 1],$$
$$x_2 = [-3, -2, -2 + \epsilon, 1, 1 + \epsilon, 3], \quad y_2 = [-1, -1, 0, 0, 1, 1],$$

where $\epsilon$ should a very small number, for instance, the MATLAB constant eps.

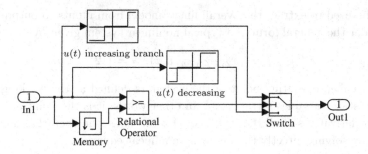

Fig. 6-58   Simulink description of the nonlinearity with loops   (file name: c6mloop.mdl).

Consider again the loop nonlinearity shown in Fig. 6-56(b). The same Simulink model can be used, where the following quantities can be entered in the two lookup table blocks, and the new model can be constructed as shown in Fig. 6-59.

$x_1 = [-3, -2, -1, 2, 3, 4]$, $y_1 = [-1, -1, 0, 0, 1, 1]$,
$x_2 = [-4, -3, -2, 1, 2, 3]$, $y_2 = [-1, -1, 0, 0, 1, 1]$,

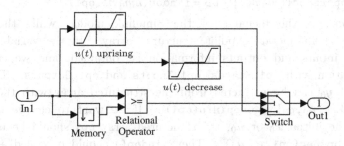

Fig. 6-59   New Simulink model with loops   (c6mloopa.mdl).

From the above analysis, it can be seen that any static nonlinear element, single-valued or multi-valued, can be constructed in a similar manner, and the models can be used directly in simulation.

### 6.4.2   *Linearization of Nonlinear Systems*

Compared with nonlinear systems, linear systems have certain advantages, since they can be analyzed and designed easily and in a systematic way. In actual applications, nonlinear behaviors exist everywhere. Strictly speaking, all models should be nonlinear. Sometimes, we can use linear models to approximate nonlinear ones. The linearization technique extracts the approximate linear behavior from nonlinear systems, thus it is an effective way in dealing with nonlinear systems. The linearized model extracted may fit the behavior of the original nonlinear system within a region of the operating point. On the other hand, if the original system is linear, and the structure of the system is complicated, the linearization technique can also be used to extract the overall linear model from inputs to outputs.

Consider the general form of a typical nonlinear system given by

$$\dot{x}_i(t) = f_i(x_1, x_2, \cdots, x_n, \boldsymbol{u}, t), \quad i = 1, 2, \cdots, n. \tag{6.1}$$

The so-called operating point of the system is defined as the working point at which the state variables settle down. In other words, it is the point at which the first-order derivatives of all the states equal zero. Thus, the operating point can be obtained by solving directly the following nonlinear equation.

$$f_i(x_1, x_2, \cdots, x_n, \boldsymbol{u}, t) = 0, \quad i = 1, 2, \cdots, n. \tag{6.2}$$

Numerical methods can be used for solving nonlinear equations. A MATLAB function `findop()` is provided to find the operating point from a given Simulink model, but before that we have to use another function `operspec()` to get the input, state and output information.

The syntaxes of these functions are

`op1 = operspec(mname);   op = findop(mname,op1)`

where *mname* is the filename of the Simulink model, while the returned variable `op` is an operating point structured array. In the variable `op1`, all the states, inputs and outputs information is contained, and we can extract the information with `op1.States`, `op1.Inputs` and `op1.Outputs`. The vectors $x_0$, $u_0$ and $y_0$ can be extracted from the structured array with the following function, `[x0,u0,y0] = getopinfo(op1)`. If we want to change the default setting of the initial $x_0$ or $u_0$, the structured array `op1` should be modified to `op2 = initopspec(op1,x0,u0)`. Then `findop()` should be called again. The function `[x0,u0] = getopinfo(op)` can also be used to find the finalized steady-state states $x_0$ and inputs $u_0$.

```
function [x0,u0,y0]=getopinfo(op)
x=op.States; u=op.Inputs; x0=[]; u0=[]; y0=[];
for i=1:length(x); x0=[x0; x(i).x]; end
for i=1:length(u); u0=[u0; u(i).u]; end
if nargout==3, y=op.Outputs; for i=1:length(y); y0=[y0;y(i).y]; end, end
```

In earlier versions of Simulink, operating point extraction can be made with function `trim()`, with the syntax $[x,u,y,x_{\rm d}] = {\tt trim}(mname,x_0,u_0)$.

Within the neighborhood of the operating point $(\boldsymbol{u}_0, \boldsymbol{x}_0)$, the nonlinear dynamic system can be linearized such that

$$\Delta\dot{x}_i = \sum_{j=1}^{n} \left.\frac{\partial f_i(\boldsymbol{x}, \boldsymbol{u})}{\partial x_j}\right|_{\boldsymbol{x}_0, \boldsymbol{u}_0} \Delta x_j + \sum_{j=1}^{p} \left.\frac{\partial f_i(\boldsymbol{x}, \boldsymbol{u})}{\partial u_j}\right|_{\boldsymbol{x}_0, \boldsymbol{u}_0} \Delta u_j, \tag{6.3}$$

and the model can be written as

$$\Delta\dot{\boldsymbol{x}}(t) = \boldsymbol{A}_{\rm l}\Delta\boldsymbol{x}(t) + \boldsymbol{B}_{\rm l}\Delta\boldsymbol{u}(t). \tag{6.4}$$

Selecting new state and input vectors as $z(t) = \Delta x(t)$ and $v(t) = \Delta u(t)$, the linearized state space model is written as

$$\dot{z}(t) = A_1 z(t) + B_1 v(t), \tag{6.5}$$

where the Jacobian matrix is defined as

$$A_1 = \begin{bmatrix} \partial f_1/\partial x_1 & \cdots & \partial f_1/\partial x_n \\ \vdots & \ddots & \vdots \\ \partial f_n/\partial x_1 & \cdots & \partial f_n/\partial x_n \end{bmatrix}, \quad B_1 = \begin{bmatrix} \partial f_1/\partial u_1 & \cdots & \partial f_1/\partial u_p \\ \vdots & \ddots & \vdots \\ \partial f_n/\partial u_1 & \cdots & \partial f_n/\partial u_p \end{bmatrix}. \tag{6.6}$$

Having obtained the operating point, the function `linearize()` can be used to extract the linearized model, with $G = \text{linearize}(mname, \text{op})$, where op is the operating point structured array. The linearized continuous state space model is returned in a state space object $G$. If the variable op is not specified, the default operating point will be used. In fact, if a Simulink model consists only of linear elements, the operating point object is not necessary. The overall linear model can still be extracted from the Simulink model.

In earlier versions of MATLAB, the linearization process can be carried out with the following functions

$$[A, B, C, D] = \text{linmod2}(mname, x_0, u_0) \qquad \% \text{ linearization}$$
$$[A, B, C, D] = \text{linmod}(mname, x_0, u_0) \qquad \% \text{ continuous with delays}$$
$$[A, B, C, D] = \text{dlinmod}(mname, x_0, u_0) \qquad \% \text{ with discrete terms}$$

where $x_0$, $u_0$ is the operating point. For linear Simulink models, these two arguments can be omitted. Functions `linmod()` and `linmod2()` are similar, the former can be used to handle systems with delays with Padé approximation algorithms.

**Example 6.12.** Consider the computer control system studied in Example 6.4, where a Simulink model was established. If linearization is expected, the input and output of the Simulink model should be indicated with Inport and Outport blocks. The modified Simulink model is given in Fig. 6-60,

```
>> T=0.2; a=0.1; z1=exp(-0.1*T); p1=exp(-T); K=(1-p1)/(1-z1);
   G=zpk(linearize('c6mcomp2'))
```

and the linearized discrete system can be obtained

$$G(z) = \frac{0.32187(z - 0.9802)(z + 0.8753)}{(z - 0.9817)(z^2 - 1.185z + 0.8403)},$$

which is exactly the same as the one obtained in Example 6.4.

If earlier versions of MATLAB are used, the following statement can be used and the same results can be obtained.

```
>> [A,B,C,D]=dlinmod('c6mcomp2'); zpk(ss(A,B,C,D,'Ts',0.2))
```

**Example 6.13.** Consider the multivariable system in Example 6.3. If the model is to be linearized, the input and output ports should be replaced by the In1 and Out1 blocks as shown in Fig. 6-61.

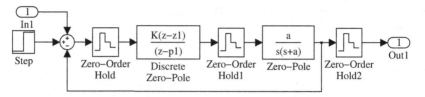

Fig. 6-60   A variation of the computer control system     (file name: c6mcomp2.mdl).

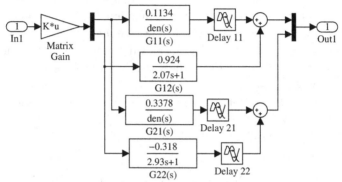

Fig. 6-61   The modified Simulink model    (file name: c6mmdly1.mdl).

The following commands can be used to carry out linearization process to the Simulink model. The step responses of the multivariable system can be obtained as shown in Fig. 6-62. and the results are very close to the exact simulation results.

```
>> Kp=[0.1134,0.924; 0.3378,-0.318]; G=linearize('c6mmdly1');
   % or in earlier versions of MATLAB, use [A,B,C,D]=linmod('c6mmdly1')
   step(ss(A,B,C,D)) % note in the above command, linmod2() cannot be used
```

The linearized state space model is

$$
A = \begin{bmatrix}
-8.33 & -23.15 & 0 & 0 & 0 & 0 & 0 & 0 & 0.06 & 0 & 0 & 0 \\
1 & 0 & 0 & 0 & 0 & 0 & 0 & 0 & 0 & 0 & 0 & 0 \\
0 & 0 & -0.48 & 0 & 0 & 0 & 0 & 0 & 0 & 0 & 0 & 0 \\
0 & 0 & 0 & -20 & -133.33 & 0 & 0 & 0 & 0 & 0 & 0.94 & 0 \\
0 & 0 & 0 & 1 & 0 & 0 & 0 & 0 & 0 & 0 & 0 & 0 \\
0 & 0 & 0 & 0 & 0 & -4.65 & -7.21 & 0 & 0 & 0 & 0 & -0.11 \\
0 & 0 & 0 & 0 & 0 & 1 & 0 & 0 & 0 & 0 & 0 & 0 \\
0 & 0 & 0 & 0 & 0 & 0 & 0 & -2.52 & -0.56 & 0 & 0 & 0 \\
0 & 0 & 0 & 0 & 0 & 0 & 0 & 1 & 0 & 0 & 0 & 0 \\
0 & 0 & 0 & 0 & 0 & 0 & 0 & 0 & 0 & -3.02 & -2.77 & 0 \\
0 & 0 & 0 & 0 & 0 & 0 & 0 & 0 & 0 & 1 & 0 & 0 \\
0 & 0 & 0 & 0 & 0 & 0 & 0 & 0 & 0 & 0 & 0 & -0.34
\end{bmatrix},
$$

$$
B^{\mathrm{T}} = \begin{bmatrix}
0 & 0 & 0.3378 & 0 & 0 & 0 & 0 & 0.1134 & 0 & 0.1134 & 0 & 0.3378 \\
0 & 0 & -0.318 & 0 & 0 & 0 & 0 & 0.924 & 0 & 0.924 & 0 & -0.318
\end{bmatrix},
$$

$$
C = \begin{bmatrix}
-16.667 & 0 & 0.4464 & 0 & 0 & 0 & 0 & 0 & 0.0637 & 0 & 0 & 0 \\
0 & 0 & 0 & -40 & 0 & -9.3023 & 0 & 0 & 0 & 0 & 0.9357 & -0.1085
\end{bmatrix}.
$$

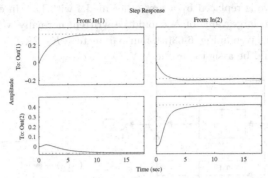

Fig. 6-62   Comparisons of step responses of exact and linearized models.

## 6.5   Subsystem and Model Masking Methods

In the modeling and simulation of control systems, sometimes complicated control structures are to be handled. Normally, it would be very complicated to represent the whole system with a single Simulink model. A good approach is to divide the whole system into several several subsystems. Moreover, some of the subsystems can be masked into reusable independent blocks, and the user's own block library or blockset can be constructed. In this section, the topics of the construction and application of subsystems and the masking procedures will be presented.

### 6.5.1   *Subsystem Creation*

To create a subsystem, the input and output terminals should be assigned. The input port In1 can be copied into the model window block from the Sources group, and output port, Out1 can be copied from Sinks group. Between the input and output ports, the internal structure can be constructed.

Of course, if there is an established block diagram, and part of the block diagram is needed to compose into a subsystem, left click the lower left corner, drag the mouse to the upper right corner and release the mouse button, all the blocks and connections in the region will be selected. The Edit → Create Subsystem menu (or Diagram → Subsystem & Model Reference → Create subsystem from selection menu in the new version) can be selected to create the subsystem. The signals entering the region are regarded as input ports, and those that flow out of the region are regarded as output ports. The subsystem is then established.

**Example 6.14.** PID controller is a commonly used block in automatic control applications. The mathematical model of the industrial PID controller is

$$U(s) = K_{\mathrm{p}} \left( 1 + \frac{1}{T_i s} + \frac{s T_{\mathrm{d}}}{1 + s T_{\mathrm{d}}/N} \right) E(s), \qquad (6.7)$$

where pure derivative is replaced by a first-order model with lag. In order to have first-order approximation, large value of $N$ should be written, normally with $N \geqslant 10$. In the PID controller model given in Fig. 6-63(a), four parameters, $K_p$, $T_i$, $T_d$ and $N$ are assigned. These variables should be assigned in the MATLAB workspace.

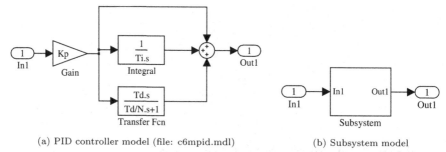

(a) PID controller model (file: c6mpid.mdl)          (b) Subsystem model

Fig. 6-63   Simulink description of the PID controller.

The Edit → Select All menu can be used to select all the blocks in the current model window. When the Ctrl is held, clicking a certain block may deselect it. Once all the necessary blocks are selected, Edit → Create Subsystem menu may construct a subsystem in Fig. 6-63(b). By double clicking the subsystem model, the internal structure of the model can be opened as shown in Fig. 6-63(a).

Apart from regular subsystems, other types of subsystems such as enabled subsystems, triggered subsystems can also be modeled, details can be found in [1,4].

### 6.5.2   Subsystem Masking

Suppose that in a double-loop control system, there are two PID controllers. If the PID controllers are both modeled by a subsystem, the parameters of the two controllers are the same. This will cause problems. In order to make the PID controllers mutually independent, masking techniques should be used. To mask a subsystem means to hide the internal structure of the subsystem, and when the block is double clicked, a parameter setting dialog box will be given instead, allowing the users to specify the parameters of the masked block. In fact, most of the blocks provided in Simulink are masked from low-level models. For instance, in a transfer function block, the internal structure is not accessible to users. Only numerator and denominator polynomials can be assigned to the block. Also, consider the PID controller subsystem; it can be masked such that the four parameters can be entered with dialog boxes.

To mask a user-designed model, the first thing to do is to convert the whole block diagram of the Simulink model into a subsystem. Select the subsystem icon, and then, using the Edit → Mask Subsystem menu, the dialog box of the model mask editor interface shown in Fig. 6-64 can be opened. The user can use this interface to design the mask block properties.

In the PID controller described earlier, four parameters should be masked, and a dialog box is needed to accept the four parameters from the users. If one wants to mask a model, the model should be created as a subsystem first. Select the subsystem icon, use Edit → Mask Subsystem menu, a dialog box shown in Fig. 6-64 will be displayed.

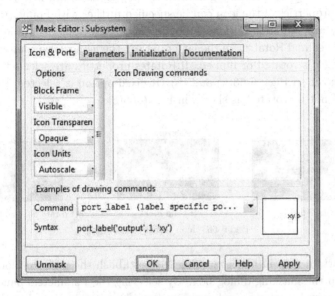

Fig. 6-64    Masking dialog box.

In the masking dialog box, the following information should be specified

(1) Drawing commands pane allows three ways of representing icons of the masked block. The MATLAB commands plot() can be used to draw curves, disp() can be used to write text and image() allows you to display images.

If a circle shown in Fig.6-65(a) is needed to be displayed as the icon, one should specify in the Drawing commands edit box the MATLAB command plot(cos(0:.1:2*pi),sin(0:.1:2*pi)).

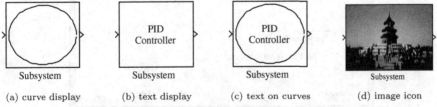

(a) curve display     (b) text display     (c) text on curves     (d) image icon

Fig. 6-65    Examples of different forms of icon design.

If the command disp('PID\nController') is used in the Drawing commands edit box, the icon shown in Fig. 6-65(b) will be made, where \n will indicate carriage return in the string. If the plot() is used followed by the `disp('PID\nController')` command, the text will be superimposed on the plot as shown in Fig. 6-65(c).

If the command `image(imread('tiantan.jpg'))` is used in the edit box, the icon with the image of tiantan.jpg file will be created as shown in Fig. 6-65(d).

(2) The properties of the icon can be specified further with Frame (with options Transparency and Rotation options). For instance, the Rotation property has two options — Fixed and Rotates. In the latter option, the icon is also rotated or flipped when the block is rotated or flipped. If Rotates properties are selected, the results will be as shown in Figs. 6-66(a) and (b). If Fixed option is selected, the image in the icon will not be rotated as shown in Fig. 6-66(c).

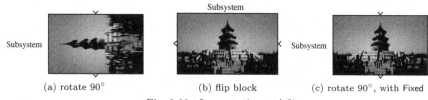

(a) rotate 90°          (b) flip block          (c) rotate 90°, with Fixed

Fig. 6-66    Icon rotation and flip.

An important step in block masking is to establish the internal block variables with those in the masking dialog box. By selecting the Parameters pane, as shown in Fig. 6-67, variable names can be specified and they can be linked to the variables in the block directly.

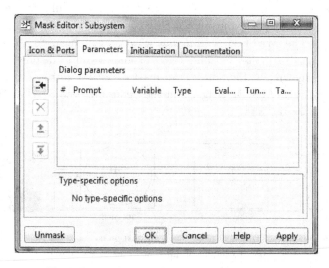

Fig. 6-67    Parameter dialog box in block masking.

The buttons ⊒⁺ and ✕ are used to assign and delete variable names. For instance, in the PID controller block, click the ⊒⁺ button four times, and four data entries are prepared. Clicking for the first time gives the dialog box as shown in Fig. 6-68. In the Prompt, prompt information can be entered. For instance, the message Proportional Kp can be specified. In the Variable edit box, the variable name can be entered as Kp. Note that the variable names should be the same as the ones in the block diagram.

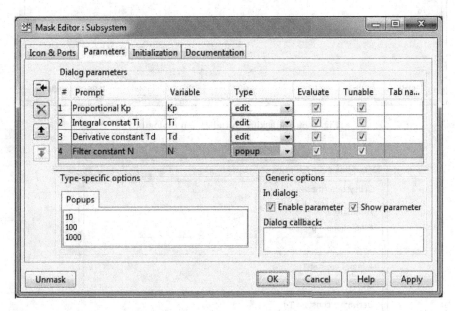

Fig. 6-68　Variable editing in the list box.

The following method can be adopted to set up connections with the variables in the masked subsystems. In the edit box Type, the default option is edit, meaning that the edit box should accept data. For instance, $N$ can be used to allow it to be selected from a few values, and the other available options are in popup. The Popup string string can be entered as 10 | 100 | 1000.

The positions of the variables can be arranged, and the ± and ∓ buttons can be used to move the item up and down respectively. The user may further select the Documentation pane to arrange the help information. The subsystem can be masked in this way. Double click the mask box, and the dialog box shown in Fig. 6-70 is displayed, allowing the user to enter the parameters of the PID controller. Note that the value of the filter constant $N$ can be assigned in the listbox, and as it is expressed, the allowed options are 10, 100 or 1000.

Click the right mouse button to display the shortcut menu, select the Look under mask item, and the internal structure of the masked model will be opened as shown in Fig. 6-71(a). We can modify the names of the input and output ports. For instance, the input port can be renamed as error, and the output port can be renamed as control; the new masked block is changed automatically to the form

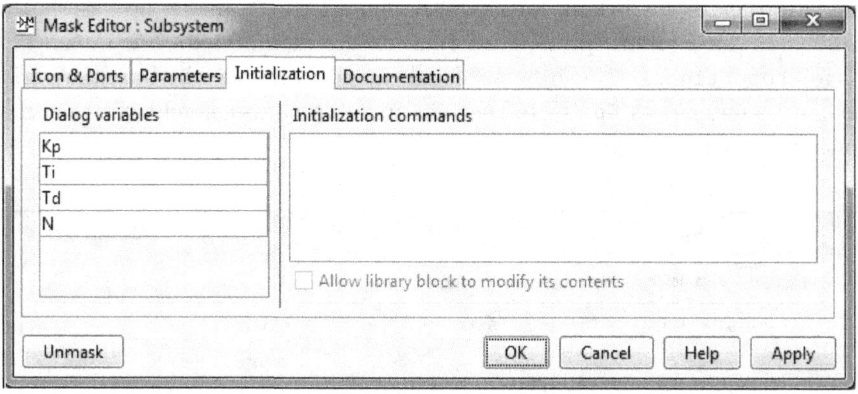

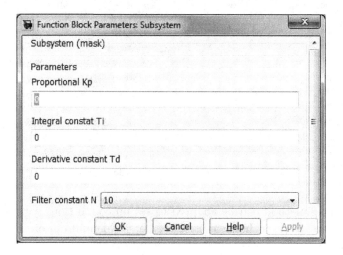

Fig. 6-69    Masking initialization dialog box.

Fig. 6-70    Dialog box of the masked block.

shown in Fig. 6-71(b). Note that to display the names of the ports properly, the option Icon transparency in the masking dialog box should be changed to Transparent.

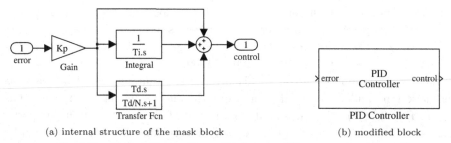

(a) internal structure of the mask block      (b) modified block

Fig. 6-71   Masked block with modified ports    (file name: c6mpidm.mdl).

**Example 6.15.** Consider again the static piecewise nonlinearity. The Simulink model in Fig. 6-59 can be regarded as the internal structure of the general description. Single-valued nonlinearity can also be represented in this form, where the increasing and decreasing branches are the same. The parameters of the two lookup table blocks can be assigned to (xu, yu) and (xd,yd), respectively. The model can be made into a subsystem and masked.

In the parameter dialog of the block, the two variables xx and yy are expected in Fig. 6-72. In practical applications, if the nonlinearity is single-value nonlinearity, the turning points of the nonlinearity can be specified, just the same as in lookup table block. If double-valued nonlinearity is to be described, the turning points should be described by two row matrices, with the first row denoting the turning points in the increase branch, while the second row the decreasing branch.

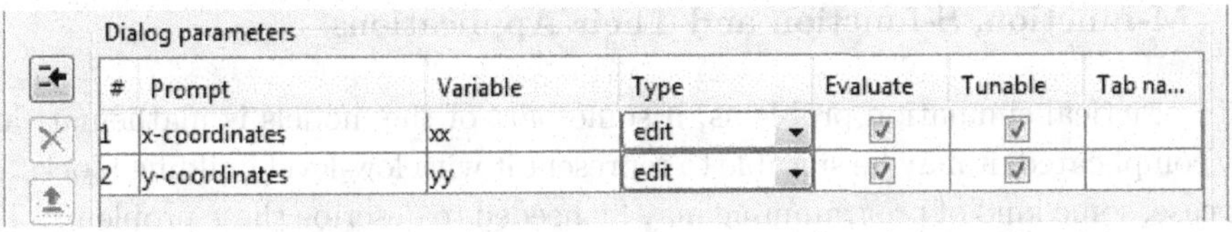

| Dialog parameters | | | | | | |
|---|---|---|---|---|---|---|
| # | Prompt | Variable | Type | Evaluate | Tunable | Tab na... |
| 1 | x-coordinates | xx | edit ▾ | ☑ | ☑ | |
| 2 | y-coordinates | yy | edit ▾ | ☑ | ☑ | |

Fig. 6-72    Dialog box of model mask initialization.

It is obvious the variable names are different from the ones in the model, since the model parameter pairs (xu, yu) and (xd,yd) are to be assigned. This can be done in the Initialization column, and the following statements should be specified.

```
if size(yy,1)==1, xx=[xx; xx]; yy=[yy; yy]; end;
yu=yy(1,:); yd=yy(2,:); xu=xx(1,:); xd=xx(2,:);
```

Thus, the variables can be automatically assigned at the initialization stage. In the icon design column, the command plot(xx',yy') can be used, and the icon model can be drawn directly, once the data are specified. Please refer to the one given in file c6mmsk2.mdl. The parameters of the double-valued nonlinearity in Example 6.11 are given in the model.

### 6.5.3    *Constructing Users' Own Block Library*

If the user has already created a set of Simulink blocks, and wants to create a new block library for them, the following procedures are taken:

(1) The menu File → New → Library in the Simulink model can be used to open a blank window. The model window should be saved. For instance, if a PID controller block group is to be created, the model library may be saved to pidblock.mdl.

(2) Copy the user blocks to this block library. Similarly, in the block library, the user may create lower-level block libraries, if necessary.

(3) Confirm the blocks included in the block library are independent of their own model windows. This can be checked by right clicking each block, and to see whether the Link options menu items are grey. Make sure that such menu items are greyed.

(4) If the new block library needs to appear in Simulink model browser, a file

slblocks.m should be created in MATLAB search path. This can be done by copy a file with the same name from other blocksets into your folder. Then modify the following statements as follows:

```
blkStruct.Name = sprintf('PID Control\n& Simulation\nBlockset');
blkStruct.OpenFcn = 'pidblock';  % point to your own block library
blkStruct.MaskDisplay = 'disp(''PID\nBlockset'')';  % model display
```

The new block library, or blockset, can be established. The block library will be shown in the Simulink model browser.

## 6.6    M-function, S-function and Their Applications

In practical simulation problems, if some part of the models is mathematically very complicated, it may be suitable to represent it with low-level building blocks. In this case, some kind of programming may be needed to describe these problems. The programming can be in M- and S-functions, and their application fields are different. M-functions can be used to describe the static relationship between the input and output signals, while S-functions can be used to describe dynamic relationships, i.e., the relationship by continuous and discrete state space equations. In control systems, complicated controller algorithms can be implemented by S-functions, and S-functions can be embedded in blocks. If M- and S-functions programming are applied, theoretically speaking, systems with any complicity can be modeled in Simulink.

S-functions have their own fixed structures. MATLAB can be used to write S-functions. Also, the programming languages such as C, C++, Fortran and Ada can be used to write S-functions. In this section, MATLAB programming in S-functions will be presented, and illustrative examples will be shown in M- and S-function programming.

### 6.6.1    *Basic Structure of M-function Blocks*

M-function blocks can be used to describe static nonlinear functions between the input and output signals. Suppose we want to use a new block to describe saturation nonlinearity, with a width of 3, and an amplitude of 2, the following M-function can be written as

```
function y=satur_non(x)
if abs(x)>=3, y=2*sign(x); else, y=2/3*x; end
```

The MATLAB Fcn block (in new version, the Interpreted MATLAB Function block) in the User-Defined Functions group can be used to describe the static nonlinearity. Unfortunately, nonlinear functions with additional parameters are not supported.

## 6.6.2 Basic Structures of S-functions

It has been presented earlier that M-functions can be used to describe the static relationship between input and output signals. The input signals can be used to solely calculate the output signals. However, if dynamic signals are involved, for instance, continuous and discrete state space equations, S-functions, i.e., system functions, are needed.

S-functions have a fixed structure. The structures of S-functions with MAT-LAB and C are different. Here, only the structure in MATLAB is presented. The introductory statements of S-function are

> function $[\text{sys},x_0,\text{str},\text{ts}]$ = $fun(t,x,u,\text{flag},p_1,p_2,\cdots)$

where *fun* is the name of the S-function, $t$, $x$, $u$ are respectively the time, states and inputs of the block, respectively. The argument flag is used to control the execution of the S-function.

(1) If flag is zero, the initialization process of S-function is executed. A function mdlInitializeSizes() should be written to describe the structure of the block, for instance, the numbers of continuous and discrete states, the numbers of the input and output ports, and so on. Also, the information regarding the sampling interval and initial state vector $x_0$ should be returned. The function sizes = simsizes is called to get default S-function structured data sizes, with the following members

NumContStates represents the number of continuous states in the S-function;

NumDiscStates represents the number of discrete states;

NumInputs and NumOutputs represent the number of inputs and outputs;

DirFeedthrough reflects whether the input signals are used in the outputs;

NumSampleTimes describes the number of sampling intervals.

The structured data sizes can be assigned to the returned variable sys with sys = simsizes(sizes) . Apart from sys, the initial state vector $x_0$, the help string str and sampling interval ts are returned, where ts should be a double column matrix, the first column stores the sampling intervals, and the second the offsets, with $[t_1, t_2]$.

(2) If flag is 1, the continuous states should be updated with the user function mdlDerivatives(), and the derivative of the continuous states should be returned in variable sys.

(3) When flag is 2, the discrete states are updated with the user function mdlUpdate(), and the discrete states should be returned with sys.

(4) If flag is 3, the output signal is calculated with the user function mdlOutputs(), and the output of the block is returned in the variable sys.

(5) If flag is 4, the user function mdlGetTimeOfNextVarHit() is called. This facility is useful in describing discrete-event systems.

(6) If flag is 9, the S-function is terminated, with the user function mdlTerminate(). In this case, no arguments are returned.

No other values of flag are currently supported, when the S-function is written, it can be embedded in a Simulink block. An S-function can be executed in a Simulink model in the following way. At the beginning of the whole simulation process, the `flag` variable is set to 0 automatically, and the initialization function is called. Then in each simulation step, the `flag` value is set to 3 first, to compute the output signal of the block. Then it is set to 1 and 2, to allow the updates of the continuous and discrete-time state variables, respectively. In the next simulation step, the value of the `flag` is set to 3→1→2 sequentially, to repeat the above procedure until the end of the simulation process.

### 6.6.3  *Examples of MATLAB S-function Programming*

In S-function programming, the following problems should be pointed out. In the initialization function programming, the user should know what are the inputs and outputs of the system. Also, the numbers of input, output, continuous and discrete states, and the information on sampling interval should be learnt before the program is written. The continuous and state space equations should be given. The evaluation of the output signals should be given. Bearing these in mind, the S-functions can be written. Here, a few illustrative examples are given in S-function programming.

**Example 6.16.** The S-function programming of a tracker–differentiator. The discrete state space model of the tracker–differentiator is given by [5]

$$\begin{cases} x_1(k+1) = x_1(k) + Tx_2(k) \\ x_2(k+1) = x_2(k) + T\mathrm{fst}(x_1(k), x_2(k), u(k), r, h), \end{cases} \tag{6.8}$$

where $T$ is the sampling interval, $u(k)$ is the input at time $k$. The additional arguments are $r$, $h$, and $T$ for the S-function block, where $r$ determines the tracking speed, $h$ determines the behavior in filtering of the tracker–differentiator. $T$ is the sampling interval of the system. Function $\mathrm{fst}(\cdot)$ can be calculated from

$$\delta = rh, \quad \delta_0 = \delta h, \quad b = x_1 - u + hx_2, \quad a_0 = \sqrt{\delta^2 + 8r|b|}, \tag{6.9}$$

$$a = \begin{cases} x_2 + b/h, & |b| \leqslant \delta_0 \\ x_2 + 0.5(a_0 - \delta)\mathrm{sign}(b), & |b| > \delta_0, \end{cases} \tag{6.10}$$

$$\mathrm{fst} = \begin{cases} -ra/\delta, & |a| \leqslant \delta \\ -r\mathrm{sign}(a), & |a| > \delta. \end{cases} \tag{6.11}$$

It can be seen that the related mathematical description is rather complicated to express in Simulink with low-level block diagram construction. Thus, it is necessary to use S-function to represent the input–output relationship. From Eqn. (6.8), the discrete state space equation is given, and it can be seen that there are two discrete states, $x_1(k)$ and $x_2(k)$, but with no continuous states. There is one input signal $u(k)$. For the tracker–differentiator block, the outputs are, in fact, the states, where $y_1(k) = x_1(k)$ traces the input, and the other $y_2(k) = x_2(k)$, constructs the derivative of the input. Thus, there are two output signals. The sampling interval is $T$. Since the output equation is $y(k) = x(k)$, the input signal $u(k)$ is not explicitly involved, the `DirectFeedthrough` member should be set to 0. Based on the above considerations, the following S-function can be implemented.

```
function [sys,x0,str,ts]=han_td(t,x,u,flag,r,h,T)
switch flag,
case 0 % calling the initialization function, to be written by the user
    [sys,x0,str,ts] = mdlInitializeSizes(T);
case 2 % calling function to update the discrete states
    sys = mdlUpdates(x,u,r,h,T);
case 3 % calculate the output signals
    sys = mdlOutputs(x);
case {1, 4, 9} % currently unused flag values
    sys = [];
otherwise % error handling
    error(['Unhandled flag = ',num2str(flag)]);
end
% when flag is 0, initialization process is modeled
function [sys,x0,str,ts] = mdlInitializeSizes(T)
% simsizes function is called to define default template of S-function. The members
% in the variable sizes should be assigned
sizes = simsizes;               % load the default template
sizes.NumContStates = 0;        % no continuous states
sizes.NumDiscStates = 2;        % with two discrete states
sizes.NumOutputs = 2;           % with two output signals --- tracing and derivative
sizes.NumInputs = 1;            % one input channel
sizes.DirFeedthrough = 0;       % input signal is not explicitly involved in output
sizes.NumSampleTimes = 1;       % single sampling interval
sys = simsizes(sizes);          % initialize the block with above settings
x0 = [0; 0];                    % set initial states to zeros
str = [];                       % set str empty string
ts = [T 0];                     % set sampling interval to T
% function for flag = 2, to update discrete states
function sys = mdlUpdates(x,u,r,h,T)
sys(1,1)=x(1)+T*x(2);
sys(2,1)=x(2)+T*fst2(x,u,r,h);
% function for flag= 3, to calculate outputs
function sys = mdlOutputs(x)
sys=x;
% user-defined sub function fst2
function f=fst2(x,u,r,h)
delta=r*h; delta0=delta*h; b=x(1)-u+h*x(2);
a0=sqrt(delta*delta+8*r*abs(b));
a=x(2)+b/h*(abs(b)<=delta0)+0.5*(a0-delta)*sign(b)*(abs(b)>delta0);
f=-r*a/delta*(abs(a)<=delta)-r*sign(a)*(abs(a)>delta);
```

The above S-function can be embedded into a block, and an example of Simulink model using the block is shown in Fig. 6-73(a). The S-function block is driven by a signal generator, and the S-function block han_td is connected to a **Scope** block to display the waveform of the tracker–differentiator block. Double click the S-function block, the parameters dialog box is opened as shown in Fig. 6-73(b). In the dialog box, the additional parameters are set to $r = 30$, $h = 0.01$ and $T = 0.001$. If sinusoidal signal is generated by the signal generator block, the outputs of the system can be obtained as shown in Fig. 6-74.

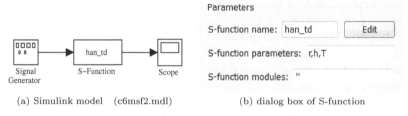

(a) Simulink model  (c6msf2.mdl)          (b) dialog box of S-function

Fig. 6-73   Tracker–differentiator model.

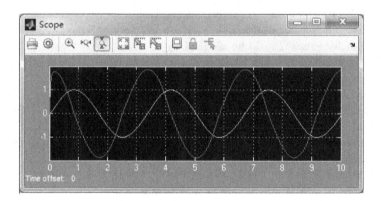

Fig. 6-74   Outputs of the tracker–differentiator system.

**Example 6.17.** Consider the recursive least squares identification method presented earlier in Section 4.6.6. We use the identification approach to implement it using S-function.

To identify a system model, the input signal $u(t)$ and output signal $y(t)$ should be used, and the identification results are the parameters of the system. Thus, the input signal for the S-function can be denoted by $\boldsymbol{u}(t) = [u(t), y(t)]^{\mathrm{T}}$, while the output of the S-function should be $\hat{\boldsymbol{\theta}}(t)$, which are the parameters of the system.

In order to get a sequence of signal $u(t)$ at different instances, a variable delay block is used to represent $u(t - d)$. Also, delay blocks are used to generate signals $u_{N-d}, \cdots, u_{N-d-5}, y_N, \cdots, y_{N-5}$. The restriction is that the maximum order of the system is 5 which would be sufficient for most of the applications. With these signals, it can be seen that the input to the S-function block can be defined as $\boldsymbol{U}(t) =$

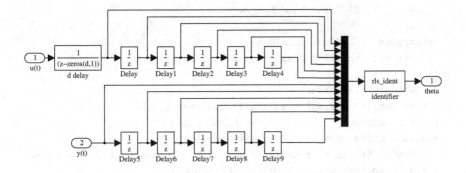

Fig. 6-75 Simulink model for recursive least squares identification.

$[u_{N-d}, \cdots, u_{N-d-5}, y_N, \cdots, y_{N-5}]^{\mathrm{T}}$, i.e., the number of inputs is 12. The parameters to be identified are $\boldsymbol{\theta}^{\mathrm{T}} = [a_1, a_2, \cdots, a_m, b_1, b_2, \cdots, b_{r+1}]$, and it can be seen the number of outputs is $m + r + 1$.

Since the block has no continuous states in the S-function, there is no need to write a function to evaluate the derivative of the states. From Eqn. (4.64)–Eqn. (4.66), the discrete state update formulae are given, and they are rewritten here

$$K = \frac{P_N \psi_{N+1}}{\lambda + \psi_{N+1}^{\mathrm{T}} P_N \psi_{N+1}}, \tag{6.12}$$

$$P_{N+1} = \frac{1}{\lambda}\Big( P_N - K \psi_{N+1}^{\mathrm{T}} P_N \Big), \tag{6.13}$$

$$\hat{\boldsymbol{\theta}}_{N+1} = \hat{\boldsymbol{\theta}}_N + K\Big( y_{N+1} - \psi_{N+1}^{\mathrm{T}} \hat{\boldsymbol{\theta}}_N \Big), \tag{6.14}$$

where

$$\psi_{N+1}^{\mathrm{T}} = \Big[ -y(N), \cdots, -y(N-m+1), u(N-d+1), \cdots, u(N-r-d+2) \Big]. \tag{6.15}$$

From the above equations, it can be seen that $K$ is a gain matrix, it is not a state variable, while matrices $P_{N+1}$ and $\hat{\boldsymbol{\theta}}_{N+1}$ are states, since their values at time $N+1$ are dependant upon the values at time $N$. Equations (6.13) and (6.14) are state space equations. However, their original form are in matrices, and in S-function, only one state vector is needed. They need to be converted to a state vector. Let $x_1 = \hat{\boldsymbol{\theta}}_{N+1}$ and $x_2 = P_{N+1}$, there are $(r+m+1)(r+m+2)$ states, and the state vector is $x^{\mathrm{T}} = [x_1^{\mathrm{T}}, x_2^{\mathrm{T}}]$. The following S-function can be written to describe the recursive identification algorithm.

```
function [sys,x0,str,ts]=rls_ident(t,x,u,flag,r,m,P0,lam)
switch flag,
    case 0 % initialization
        [sys,x0,str,ts] = mdlInitializeSizes(r,m,P0);
    case 2 % update discrete states
        sys=mdlUpdate(t,x,u,r,m,lam);
    case 3 % compute the output, i.e., the identified parameters of the system
        sys = mdlOutputs(t,x,u,r+m+1);
```

```
    case {1, 4, 9} % undefined flag 's
        sys = [];
    otherwise        % error handling
        error(['Unhandled flag = ',num2str(flag)]);
end
% the initialization function
function [sys,x0,str,ts] = mdlInitializeSizes(r,m,P0)
sizes = simsizes;               % get the default template
sizes.NumContStates = 0;  % no continuous states
sizes.NumDiscStates = (r+m+1)*(r+m+2); % set the number of discrete states
sizes.NumOutputs=r+m+1;     % number of outputs
sizes.NumInputs = 12;       % number of input is 12
sizes.DirFeedthrough = 0; % the input signal is not directly used in the output
sizes.NumSampleTimes = 1; % single sampling interval
sys = simsizes(sizes);      % confirm the S-function setting
x0 = [zeros(r+m+1,1); P0(:)]; % initial state are assumes to be random numbers
str = []; ts = [-1 0];       % -1 means to inherit the sampling interval of the input
function sys = mdlUpdate(t,x,u,r,m,lam)     % update discrete states
psi=[-u(8:m+7); u(2:2+r)]'; PN=reshape(x(r+m+2:end),r+m+1,r+m+1);
K=PN*psi'/(lam+psi*PN*psi'); PN1=(PN-K*psi*PN)/lam;
sys=[x(1:r+m+1)+K*(u(7)-psi*x(1:r+m+1)); PN1(:)];
function sys = mdlOutputs(t,x,u,M)     % compute the output
sys=x(1:M);     % the outputs are the first M = r + m + 1 states, i.e., the vector θ̂
```

An identification example is given in Fig. 6-76(a), and the parameters of the model can be obtained as shown in Fig. 6-76(b). It can be seen that the on-line identification results agree well with the parameters of the model.

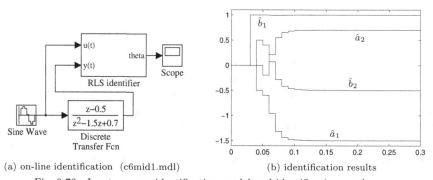

(a) on-line identification  (c6mid1.mdl)          (b) identification results

Fig. 6-76    Least squares identification model and identification results.

**Example 6.18.** To establish a staircase signal generator block, the key time instances are $t_1, t_2, \cdots, t_N$, and the corresponding output levels are $r_1, r_2, \cdots, r_N$. It might be quite complicated to model it using existing the low-level Simulink blocks, and the M-function block does not allow the use of additional parameters $t_i$ and $y_i$. Thus, the S-function is the only choice for modeling such a signal generator with one block.

From this application, the block obviously has no input port, and has only one output port. There are no state signals since it is static. Two additional vectors, tTime = $[t_1, t_2, \cdots, t_N]$ and yStep = $[r_1, r_2, \cdots, r_N]$ can be used to describe the staircase required. The following MATLAB function can be written to describe such a block.

```
function [sys,x0,str,ts]=multi_step(t,x,u,flag,tTime,yStep)
switch flag,
case 0                                           % initialization
    sizes = simsizes;                            % read the template
    sizes.NumContStates=0; sizes.NumDiscStates=0;  % no state required
    sizes.NumOutputs=1; sizes.NumInputs=0;       % number of I/O
    sizes.DirFeedthrough=0; sizes.NumSampleTimes=1;
    sys=simsizes(sizes); x0=[]; str=[]; ts=[0 0];
case 3, i=find(tTime<=t); sys=yStep(i(end));     % evaluate output
case {1,2,4,9},   sys = [];                      % unused flags
otherwise, error(['Unhandled flag=',num2str(flag)]); % error handling
end
```

### 6.6.4  *Mask an S-Function Block*

The direct use of S-function block by other users may not be an easy task, since the additional parameters must be same with those in S-function definition statements, without any prompts. Using the masking technique presented earlier, the prompts can be assigned to the additional parameters in dialog boxes. This makes the block much easier to use.

Masking S-function is an easy task. Right mouse button can be used, and the Mask S-function item from the shortcut menu can be selected to mask S-function blocks.

**Example 6.19.** Consider the S-function of staircase waveform in Example 6.18. The S-function can be masked, with the additional arguments tTime and yStep. These two variables should be inserted into the Parameters pane, in the mask edit box shown in Fig. 6-67. In the Initialization pane, the following code should be given

```
n=length(tTime);
if length(tTime)==length(yStep)
    xx(1:2:2*n)=tTime; xx(2:2:2*n)=tTime+eps;
    xx(2*n+1)=2*tTime(end)-tTime(end-1);
    yy(2:2:2*n)=yStep; yy(3:2:2*n+1)=yStep;
else, errordlg('Error in Data'), end
```

while in the Icon pane, we can simply write plot(xx,yy). A masked Simulink block staircase_wave.mdl can be created for later use.

## 6.7   Problems

(1) In the standard Simulink model library, the existing blocks are relatively well organized in groups. Please study the groups and their components, and get familiar with the commonly used blocks, so that when Simulink modeling task is needed, the relevant blocks can be found easily.

(2) Consider the simple linear differential equation

$$y^{(4)} + 5y^{(3)} + 63\ddot{y} + 4\dot{y} + 2y = e^{-3t} + e^{-5t}\sin(4t + \pi/3),$$

with initial values $y(0) = 1, \dot{y}(0) = \ddot{y}(0) = 1/2, y^{(3)}(0) = 0.2$. Model the differential equation with Simulink, and draw the solution curve. It is known from Chapter 3, differential equations can be solved numerically and analytically and such results could be compared with simulation results.

(3) Consider the time varying differential equation

$$y^{(4)} + 5ty^{(3)} + 6t^2\ddot{y} + 4\dot{y} + 2e^{-2t}y = e^{-3t} + e^{-5t}\sin(4t + \pi/3),$$

with initial values $y(0) = 1, \dot{y}(0) = \ddot{y}(0) = 1/2, y^{(3)}(0) = 0.2$. Model the differential equation with Simulink and draw the simulation results. In fact, time varying differential equations can be solved numerically with MATLAB functions, and the results could be compared.

(4) Assume the trajectory $(x, y)$ of the Apollo satellite satisfies

$$\ddot{x} = 2\dot{y} + x - \frac{\mu^*(x + \mu)}{r_1^3} - \frac{\mu(x - \mu^*)}{r_2^3}, \quad \ddot{y} = -2\dot{x} + y - \frac{\mu^*y}{r_1^3} - \frac{\mu y}{r_2^3},$$

where

$$\mu = 1/82.45, \quad \mu^* = 1 - \mu, \quad r_1 = \sqrt{(x + \mu)^2 + y^2}, \quad r_2 = \sqrt{(x - \mu^*)^2 + y^2},$$

and assume the initial values are $x(0) = 1.2$, $\dot{x}(0) = 0$, $y(0) = 0$, $\dot{y}(0) = -1.04935751$. Establish a Simulink and draw the trajectory $(x, y)$.

(5) Establish a Simulink model for the well-known Van der Pol nonlinear equation

$$\ddot{y} + \mu(y^2 - 1)\dot{y} + y = 0.$$

Perform simulation and draw the results.

(6) For the two-input, two-output system given by

$$\dot{x} = \begin{bmatrix} 2.25 & -5 & -1.25 & -0.5 \\ 2.25 & -4.25 & -1.25 & -0.25 \\ 0.25 & -0.5 & -1.25 & -1 \\ 1.25 & -1.75 & -0.25 & -0.75 \end{bmatrix} x + \begin{bmatrix} 4 & 6 \\ 2 & 4 \\ 2 & 2 \\ 0 & 2 \end{bmatrix} u, \quad y = \begin{bmatrix} 0 & 0 & 0 & 1 \\ 0 & 2 & 0 & 2 \end{bmatrix} x,$$

and assume the two inputs are $\sin t$ and $\cos t$. Use Simulink to construct the system model, and draw simulation results.

(7) For the $4 \times 4$ transfer function matrix of a multivariable system [6]

$$G(s) = \begin{bmatrix} 1/(1+4s) & 0.7/(1+5s) & 0.3/(1+5s) & 0.2/(1+5s) \\ 0.6/(1+5s) & 1/(1+4s) & 0.4/(1+5s) & 0.35/(1+5s) \\ 0.35/(1+5s) & 0.4/(1+5s) & 1/(1+4s) & 0.6/(1+5s) \\ 0.2/(1+5s) & 0.3/(1+5s) & 0.7/(1+5s) & 1/(1+4s) \end{bmatrix}.$$

Represent the simulation model in Simulink, and perform simulation. The `step()` function in Chapter 5 can also be used to simulate the system. Compare the two results.

(8) For the implicit differential equation given by

$$\begin{cases} \sin x_1 \dot{x}_1 + \cos x_2 \dot{x}_2 + x_1 = 1 \\ -\cos x_2 \dot{x}_1 + \sin x_1 \dot{x}_2 + x_2 = 0, \end{cases}$$

with $x_1(0) = x_2(0) = 0$. Find the simulation results of the equations.

(9) Establish the Simulink model given in Fig. 6-77 [7] and observe the simulation results under step input.

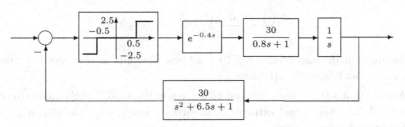

Fig. 6-77   Block diagram of Problem (9).

(10) Establish the Simulink model for the nonlinear system shown in Fig. 6-78 [8]. Assume that the magnitude of the input step signal is 1.1, observe the system responses for the output and error signals. Find the operating point of the system, and get the linearized model. Compare with simulation and approximate results. Besides, there is a series connection of two nonlinear elements, are they exchangeable?

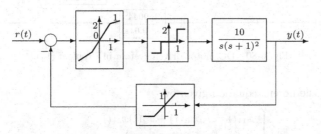

Fig. 6-78   Block diagram of a nonlinear system of Problem (10).

(11) For the Simulink model given in Fig. 6-79, please write its mathematical equations.
(12) Establish a Simulink model for the model below and draw the step response.

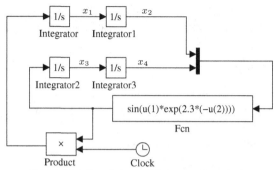

Fig. 6-79   Simulink model for Problem (11).

$$G(s) = \frac{1 + \dfrac{3e^{-s}}{s+1}}{s+1}.$$

(13)  Consider the delay differential equation

$$\frac{dy(t)}{dt} = \frac{0.2y(t-30)}{1 + y^{10}(t-30)} - 0.1y(t),$$

assume that the initial value is $y(0) = 0.1$, use Simulink to represent the differential equation and draw the $y(t)$ curve.

(14)  Assume that a DC motor drive system is given in Fig. 6-80. Use Simulink to construct a simulation model, and extracts its linearized model. Draw the step response and frequency response curves.

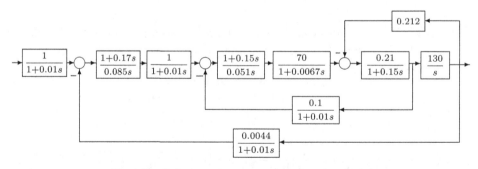

Fig. 6-80   DC motor driven system in Problem (14).

(15)  Consider the Lorenz equation given by

$$\begin{cases} \dot{x}_1(t) = -\beta x_1(t) + x_2(t)x_3(t) \\ \dot{x}_2(t) = -\rho x_2(t) + \rho x_3(t) \\ \dot{x}_3(t) = -x_1(t)x_2(t) + \sigma x_2(t) - x_3(t). \end{cases}$$

The model has no input signals, and has three continuous states $x_i(t)$. They can also be regarded as the output signals. The variables $\beta, \sigma, \rho$ and initial state vector

$x_i(0)$ can be used as additional parameters. Mask the system and draw solutions of the differential equations for different values of additional parameters.

(16) Assume the for the error signal $e(t)$, different integral criteria can be defined as

$$J_{\text{ISE}} = \int_0^\infty e^2(t)\mathrm{d}t, \quad J_{\text{ITAE}} = \int_0^\infty t|e(t)|\mathrm{d}t, \quad J_{\text{ISTE}} = \int_0^\infty t^2 e^2(t)\mathrm{d}t.$$

Please mask a block evaluating the ITAE, ISE, ISTE criteria. The requirements are, the error signal $e(t)$ is the input signal to the block; double click the block, a dialog box is displayed; one can select the criteria from the listbox in the dialog box, and the selected criterion will be the output signal of the block.

(17) For piecewise linear nonlinearities described by $y(x) = k_i x + b_i$, in the $i$th interval $e_i \leqslant x < e_{i+1}$, if the key points $e_1, e_2, \cdots, e_{N+1}$, and the known values $k_1, b_1, k_2, b_2, \cdots, k_N, b_N$ are the additional parameters to the block, try to mask an S-function block to describe the piecewise nonlinearity.

(18) Assume that in a programmable logic device (PLD), there are 6 inputs, $A$, $B$, $W_1$, $W_2$, $W_3$, $W_4$, where $W_i$ are encoding signals. Their values will determine the output signal $Y$, with the logic relationship as shown in Table 6-1 [9]. Please write an M-function block to implement the PLD.

Table 6-1   The logic relations for Problem (18).

| $W_1$ | $W_2$ | $W_3$ | $W_4$ | $Y$ | $W_1$ | $W_2$ | $W_3$ | $W_4$ | $Y$ |
|---|---|---|---|---|---|---|---|---|---|
| 0 | 0 | 0 | 0 | 0 | 1 | 0 | 0 | 0 | $A\overline{B}$ |
| 0 | 0 | 0 | 1 | $AB$ | 1 | 0 | 0 | 1 | $A$ |
| 0 | 0 | 1 | 0 | $\overline{A+B}$ | 1 | 0 | 1 | 0 | $\overline{B}$ |
| 0 | 0 | 1 | 1 | $AB + \overline{AB} = A \odot B$ | 1 | 0 | 1 | 1 | $A + \overline{B}$ |
| 0 | 1 | 0 | 0 | $\overline{A}B$ | 1 | 1 | 0 | 0 | $\overline{A}B + A\overline{B} = A \oplus B$ |
| 0 | 1 | 0 | 1 | $B$ | 1 | 1 | 0 | 1 | $A + B$ |
| 0 | 1 | 1 | 0 | $\overline{A}$ | 1 | 1 | 1 | 0 | $\overline{A} + \overline{B} = \overline{AB}$ |
| 0 | 1 | 1 | 1 | $\overline{A} + B$ | 1 | 1 | 1 | 1 | 1 |

(19) In Example 6.16, S-function was used to implement the complicated tracker–differentiator model. The complicated part is the static fst($\cdot$), and this function can be modeled by M- or S-functions. Then low-level block can be constructed to implement tracker–differentiator block to compare the results with those in Example 6.16.

## Bibliography and References

[1] The MathWorks Inc. Simulink user's guide, 2005
[2] Franklin G F, Powell J D, Workman M. Digital control of dynamic systems. Reading MA: Addison Wesley, 3rd edition, 1988
[3] Atherton D P. Nonlinear control engineering — describing function analysis and design. London: Van Nostrand Reinhold, 1975
[4] Xue D Y, Chen Y Q. System simulation techniques with MATLAB and Simulink. Chichester: John Wiley and Sons, 2013

[5] Han J Q, Yuan L L. Discrete form of tracking–differentiators. System Science and Mathematics, 1999, 19(3):268–273. (In Chinese)

[6] Rosenbrock H H. Computer-aided control system design. New York: Academic Press, 1974

[7] Liu D G, Fei J G. Digital simulation algorithms of dynamic systems. Beijing: Science Publishers, 2001. (In Chinese)

[8] Wang W L. Automatic control principles. Beijing: Science Publishers, 2001. (In Chinese)

[9] Peng R X. Fundamentals of digital electronics. Wuhan: Wuhan University of Technology Press, 2001. (In Chinese)

# Chapter 7

# Classical Design Approaches of Control Systems

The earlier presentation focuses on the solutions of modeling and simulation problems of control systems. From this chapter on, the design problems for control systems will be addressed. In fact, controller design problems can be regarded as the inverse problems of system analysis, since in systems analysis, the controllers are assumed to be known, while in controller design problems, the target is to find suitable controllers and control strategies for given plant models. In this case, the probing of controllers are to be discussed.

With the rapid development of computer technology, the study on computer-aided design of control systems made great achievement not only on the tools, but also on theory and on algorithms. The difficult controller design problems can easily be solved using new approaches and tools. Trial-and-error methods were used in the earlier stages of control systems, however, with the popularity of new tools, the design algorithms can easily be achieved under modern computers and software. Under many circumstances, what the designer does is to inform what kind of conditions are known, and the controllers, together with simulation results, can be obtained directly with suitable CACSD tools.

In Section 7.1, lead–lag type of compensators are introduced, and the concept and properties are summarized. A phase margin and crossover frequency-based controller design approach is given and implemented in MATLAB. In Section 7.2, classical state feedback controller design methods and their solutions in MATLAB are presented, including linear quadratic optimal control and pole placement methods. The concept and design of observers are presented, and observer-based controller and regulator are introduced. Section 7.3 presents the ideas of optimal control, and implementation of optimal controller design in MATLAB is presented. In particular, the OCD interface developed by the authors is demonstrated. In Section 7.4, the controller design interface in Control System Toolbox is illustrated, root locus and Bode diagram-based interactive design method is demonstrated. Examples are given to illustrate automatic tuning of controller parameters. In Section 7.5, frequency domain design for multivariable systems is presented, including inverse Nyquist array design, pseudo-diagonalization method and parameter optimization methods. In Section 7.6, dynamic decoupling methods are given, and the concept of standard transfer function is presented. Based on it, two decoupling design methods are illustrated.

## 7.1 Design of Phase Lead–lag Compensators

Series control shown in Fig. 7-1 is a widely used structure. In the control system, $r(t)$ and $y(t)$ are the input and output of the control system. If the target of control is to let the output follow the input signal, the control is usually referred to as servo control. In this control structure, the signals $e(t)$ and $u(t)$ are also very important. They are often referred to as the error signal and the control signal respectively. In the servo control systems, we often expect the error signal $e(t)$ as small as possible. Meanwhile in many control systems, the control signal $u(t)$ is related to the energy. Thus, from an energy saving point of view, we often expect the control effort as small as possible.

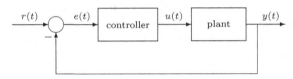

Fig. 7-1   Series control structure.

Widely used series controllers are the lead–lag type of controllers and PID type of controllers. In this section, basic properties of lead–lag controllers and a design algorithm will be given.

### 7.1.1 *Lead–leg Compensators*

Lead–lag compensator is a common form of series control, and the control structure is simple and easy to adjust. In this subsection, the properties of lead compensator, lag compensator, and lead–lag compensator are given.

**1. Phase lead compensator**

The mathematical model of phase lead compensator is

$$G_c(s) = K\frac{\alpha T s + 1}{T s + 1}, \tag{7.1}$$

where $\alpha > 1$, and its pole–zero locations are shown in Fig. 7-2(a). The typical Bode diagram of this type of controller is shown in Fig. 7-2(b). It can be seen that with this kind of compensator with positive phase, the phase of the forward path will be increased, i.e., lead the phase of the plant. Thus, it is usually referred to as phase lead, or simply lead, compensator. This compensator will have the maximum phase at frequency $\omega = T$. A properly designed compensator is to increase the crossover frequency and phase margin, which means to make the closed-loop system with smaller overshoot and fast respond speed.

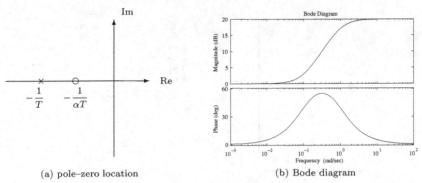

(a) pole–zero location        (b) Bode diagram

Fig. 7-2   Characteristics of lead compensator.

## 2. Phase lag compensator

The mathematical model of the phase lag compensator is

$$G_c(s) = K\frac{Ts+1}{\alpha Ts+1},\tag{7.2}$$

where $\alpha > 1$. The pole–zero locations are shown in Fig. 7-3(a), and the Bode diagram is shown in Fig. 7-3(b). The Bode diagram of the compensator is to have the phase at minimum negative value at frequency $\omega = T$. If the compensator is well designed, the crossover frequency is decreased, while the phase margin increased. This also means to reduce the response speed, while decreasing the overshoot of the system.

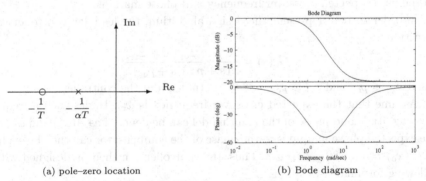

(a) pole–zero location        (b) Bode diagram

Fig. 7-3   Phase lag compensator.

## 3. Lead–lag compensator

The mathematical model of a phase lead–lag compensator is

$$G_c(s) = K\frac{(\alpha T_1 s+1)(T_2 s+1)}{(T_1+1)(\beta T_2 s+1)},\tag{7.3}$$

where $\alpha > 1$ for phase lead, while $\beta > 1$ for phase lag. Thus, it has both properties of phase lead and phase lag. The pole–zero locations of lead–lag compensator is given in Fig. 7-4(a), while the typical Bode diagram is shown in Fig. 7-4(b).

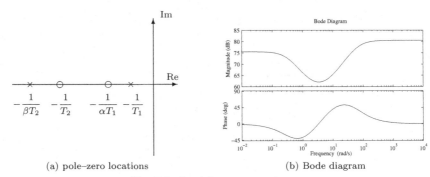

(a) pole–zero locations                    (b) Bode diagram

Fig. 7-4   Lead–lag compensator.

This type of compensator may increase the response speed and reduce the overshoot, if the compensator is well designed. Since there are two more degrees of-freedom than the lead compensator, the control behavior is better than the lead compensator, and the adjustment of this type of compensator is more complicated than the lead compensator.

### 7.1.2   *A Design Algorithm for Lead–lag Compensator*

Trial and error methods can be used in controller design, however, these kinds of tasks are quite time consuming. Sometimes, good results may not be obtained. The algorithm given below can be used to design lead–lag type of controllers, based on the user expected crossover frequency and phase margins.

In order to better present the design algorithm, the lead–lag controller can be rewritten as

$$G_c(s) = \frac{K_c(s + z_{c_1})(s + z_{c_2})}{(s + p_{c_1})(s + p_{c_2})}, \tag{7.4}$$

where $z_{c_1} \leqslant p_{c_1}$ and $z_{c_2} \geqslant p_{c_2}$, and $K_c$ is the gain of the controller.

Assume that the expected crossover frequency is $\omega_c$. Under such a frequency, the magnitude and phase of the plant model can be denoted as $A(\omega_c)$ and $\phi_1(\omega_c)$. If the expected phase margin is $\gamma$, the phase of the compensator can then be evaluated as $\phi_c(\omega_c) = \gamma - 180° - \phi_1(\omega_c)$. Thus, the controller can then be designed with the following formula:

(1) If $\phi_c(\omega_c) > 0$, lead controller is needed, and can be designed with

$$\alpha = \frac{z_{c_1}}{p_{c_1}} = \frac{1 - \sin \phi_c(\omega_c)}{1 + \sin \phi_c(\omega_c)}, \tag{7.5}$$

where

$$z_{c_1} = \sqrt{\alpha}\,\omega_c, \quad p_{c_1} = \frac{z_{c_1}}{p_{c_1}} = \frac{\omega_c}{\sqrt{\alpha}}, \quad K_c = \frac{\sqrt{\omega_c^2 + p_{c_1}^2}}{\sqrt{\omega_c^2 + z_{c_1}^2}\,A(\omega_c)}. \tag{7.6}$$

Thus, the static error tolerance can be calculated

$$K_1 = \lim_{s \to 0} s^v G_o(s) = \frac{b_m}{a_{n-v}} \frac{K_c z_{c_1}}{p_{c_1}}, \tag{7.7}$$

where $v$ is the multiples of the poles of $G(s)$ at $s = 0$. $G_o(s)$ is the open-loop transfer function under the controller.

If $K_1 \geqslant K_v$, where $K_v$ is the static error tolerance gain, the lead compensator is sufficient. Otherwise, phase-lag compensator is needed. Besides, if the plant model does not contain integrator, a relatively large value of $K_v$ should be selected. Other types of controllers, such as PID controller, introduce integral action, and these controllers eliminate static errors.

(2) Lead–lag compensator can further be designed with

$$z_{c_2} = \frac{\omega_c}{10}, \quad p_{c_2} = \frac{K_1 z_{c_2}}{K_v}. \tag{7.8}$$

(3) If $\phi_c(\omega_c) < 0$, lag compensator is needed and designed as

$$K_1 = \frac{b_m K_c}{a_{n-v}}, \quad K_c = \frac{1}{A(\omega_c)}, \quad z_{c_2} = \frac{\omega_c}{10}, \quad p_{c_2} = \frac{K_1 z_{c_2}}{K_v}. \tag{7.9}$$

Based on the above algorithm, the following MATLAB function can be implemented. The listings of the function `leadlagc()` are as follows[1]

```
function Gc=leadlagc(G,Wc,Gam_c,Kv,key)
G=tf(G); [Gai,Pha]=bode(G,Wc); Phi_c=sin((Gam_c-Pha-180)*pi/180);
den=G.den{1}; a=den(end:-1:1);
ii=find(abs(a)<=0); num=G.num{1}; G_n=num(end);
if length(ii)>0, a=a(ii(1)+1); else, a=a(1); end;
alpha=sqrt((1-Phi_c)/(1+Phi_c)); Zc=alpha*Wc; Pc=Wc/alpha;
Kc=sqrt((Wc*Wc+Pc*Pc)/(Wc*Wc+Zc*Zc))/Gai; K1=G_n*Kc*alpha/a;
if nargin==4, key=1;
    if Phi_c<0, key=2; else, if K1<Kv, key=3; end, end
end
switch key
case 1, Gc=tf([1 Zc]*Kc,[1 Pc]);
case 2
    Kc=1/Gai; K1=G_n*Kc/a; Gc=tf([1 0.1*Wc],[1 K1*Gcn(2)/Kv]);
case 3
    Zc2=Wc*0.1; Pc2=K1*Zc2/Kv; Gcn=Kc*conv([1 Zc],[1,Zc2]);
    Gcd=conv([1 Pc],[1,Pc2]); Gc=tf(Gcn,Gcd);
end
```

The syntax of the function is $G_c = \mathtt{leadlagc}(G, \omega_c, \gamma, K_v, \mathtt{key})$, where key is the identifier to indicate the type of controller, with 1 for lead controller, 2 for lag controller, and 3 for lead–lag controller. If key is not given, automatic selection of control type is used instead. The parameters $\omega_c$ and $\gamma$ are expected crossover frequency and phase margin of the system, and the static gain tolerance is $K_v$.

**Example 7.1.** Assume that the plant model is

$$G(s) = \frac{4(s+1)(s+0.5)}{s(s+0.1)(s+2)(s+10)(s+20)}.$$

Selecting the expected crossover frequency of $\omega_c = 20\,\text{rad/s}$, and different expected phase margins can be tried with the loop structure. For instance, the expected phase margins are $\gamma = 20°, 30°, \cdots, 90°$, the lead–lag compensators can be designed with the following statements. The closed-loop step responses and the open-loop Bode diagrams are obtained as shown in Figs. 7-5(a) and (b).

```
>> s=tf('s'); G=4*(s+1)*(s+0.5)/s/(s+0.1)/(s+2)/(s+10)/(s+20)
   wc=20; f1=figure; f2=figure;   % open two figure models
   for gam=20:10:90
       Gc=leadlagc(G,wc,gam,1000,3);
       figure(f1); step(feedback(G*Gc,1),1); hold on
       figure(f2); bode(Gc*G); hold on;
   end
```

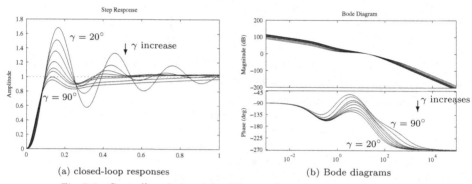

(a) closed-loop responses          (b) Bode diagrams

Fig. 7-5   Controllers designed for different phase margin specifications.

It can be seen that when the expected phase margin increases, the overshoot of the closed-loop responses will decrease. For this example, when the expected phase margin reaches 60°, the overshoot is relatively small. If $\gamma$ is selected too large, the response is not satisfactory. Normally, we should select $\gamma$ in the range 40°–60°. If the crossover frequency $\omega_c$ is fixed, the response speed is similar.

If we select $\omega_c = 20 \, \text{rad/s}$ and $\gamma = 60°$, the following statements can be used to design the controller

$$G_{c_1}(s) = \frac{27283.5668(s + 2.326)(s + 2)}{(s + 172)(s + 0.3173)}, \quad G_{c_2}(s) = \frac{27283.5668(s + 2.326)}{s + 172}.$$

```
>> Gc1=zpk(leadlagc(G,20,60,1000,3))   % design phase lead--lag controller
   Gc2=zpk(leadlagc(G,20,60,1000,1))   % design a lead controller
   figure; step(feedback(G*Gc1,1),'-',feedback(G*Gc2,1),':',1)
```

With the above statements, the closed-loop step response under the controller can also be drawn as shown in Fig. 7-6. For the given plant model, the control behavior is satisfactory.

If the expected phase margin is fixed at 60°, and if we try different values of the crossover frequency $\omega_c$, the following statements can be used to get the closed-loop step responses and open-loop Bode diagrams as shown in Figs. 7-7(a) and (b).

```
>> gam=60; f1=figure; f2=figure;   % open two figure windows
   for wc=5:5:30
```

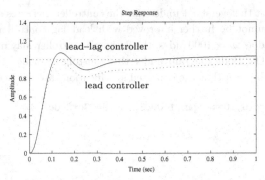

Fig. 7-6    Step response with phase margin designed controller.

```
Gc=leadlagc(G,wc,gam,1000,3); [a,b,c,d]=margin(Gc*G);
figure(f1); step(feedback(G*Gc,1),3); hold on
figure(f2); bode(Gc*G); hold on;
end
```

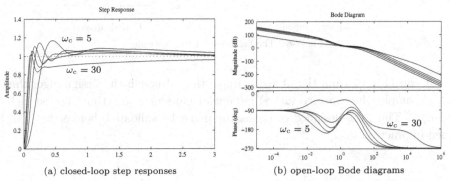

(a) closed-loop step responses          (b) open-loop Bode diagrams

Fig. 7-7    The control behavior under different expected crossover frequencies.

It can be seen that the response speed increases when the expected $\omega_c$ increases. However, when the expected crossover frequency $\omega_c$ increases to a certain value, the closed-loop system may become unstable. Besides, in the design algorithm, the size of control signal is not restricted. Sometimes, extremely large control signals may result. Thus, this kind of controller may not be actually usable. For instance, when $\omega_c = 30$ rad/s, the control signal can be drawn with the following statements, and it can be seen that the initial control signal may reach $1.4557 \times 10^5$ at initial stage, thus this controller is not applicable.

```
>> Gc=leadlagc(G,30,60,1000,3); y=step(feedback(Gc,G)); max(y)
```

Assume that the expected $\gamma = 60°$ and $\omega_c = 100$ rad/s, the following statements can be used to design the controller, and the closed-loop step response can be obtained as shown in Fig. 7-8(a).

```
>> gam=60; wc=100; figure;
   Gc=leadlagc(G,wc,gam,1000,3); step(feedback(G*Gc,1),0.5);
```

It is obvious that the overshoot under this the controller increases a lot such that good control behavior cannot be further improved with lead–lag controllers. If the crossover frequency is selected as $\omega_c = 1000\,\text{rad/s}$, the designed controller may make the closed-loop system unstable. The Bode diagram under this controller can be obtained as shown in Fig. 7-8(b). It can be seen that the expected specifications are not achieved.

```
>> Gc1=leadlagc(G,10*wc,gam,1000,3); bode(Gc*G,Gc1*G)
```

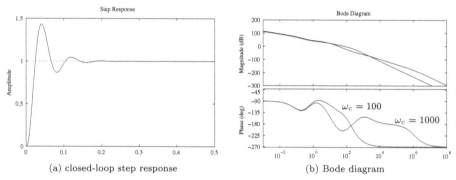

(a) closed-loop step response               (b) Bode diagram

Fig. 7-8    The behaviors of the controllers.

It can be seen from the above example that although the design algorithm is rather simple, the expected $(\omega_c, \gamma)$ parameter pairs may sometimes be too high to achieve. Thus, the designed compensators must be validated, before they can be used in practice.

## 7.2    State Space-based Controller Design Strategies

State space system theory was established in the 1960's, and was once referred to as modern control theory. State space analysis of control systems has been presented earlier. In this section, we shall concentrate on the concept of state feedback, and two state space-based strategies, i.e., the linear quadratic optimal regulator and pole placement method, are introduced. The concept of observers is introduced, and observer-based feedback control will be presented.

### 7.2.1    *State Feedback Control*

The system structure with state feedback control is shown in Fig. 7-9(a). More detailed internal structure of state feedback control system is given in Fig. 7-9(b). In the system, the control signal $u(t) = v(t) - Kx(t)$ can be substituted into the open-loop state space model, and the closed-loop state space model under state feedback matrix $K$ is

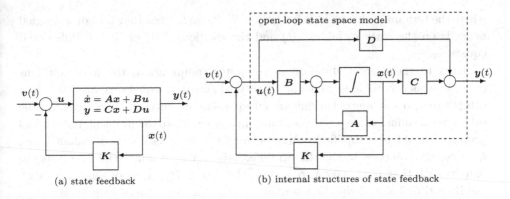

(a) state feedback   (b) internal structures of state feedback

Fig. 7-9   State feedback control structure.

$$\begin{cases} \dot{x}(t) = (A - BK)x(t) + Bv(t) \\ y(t) = (C - DK)x(t) + Dv(t). \end{cases} \tag{7.10}$$

It can be shown that if the plant $(A, B)$ is fully controllable with suitable choices of the matrix $K$, the poles of the closed-loop system $A - BK$ can be placed to any pre-assigned locations.

### 7.2.2   *Linear Quadratic Optimal Regulators*

Assume the linear time invariant state space model is given by

$$\begin{cases} \dot{x}(t) = Ax(t) + Bu(t) \\ y(t) = Cx(t) + Du(t). \end{cases} \tag{7.11}$$

A performance index, or optimization criterion, is introduced to design an input signal $u(t)$, such that

$$J = \frac{1}{2}x^{\mathrm{T}}(t_{\mathrm{f}})Sx(t_{\mathrm{f}}) + \frac{1}{2}\int_{t_0}^{t_{\mathrm{f}}}\left[x^{\mathrm{T}}(t)Q(t)x(t) + u^{\mathrm{T}}(t)R(t)u(t)\right]\mathrm{d}t \tag{7.12}$$

is minimized, where $Q$ and $R$ are weighting matrices for the states and inputs, respectively. The variable $t_{\mathrm{f}}$ is the terminate time. The matrix $S$ is introduced to describe some kind of constraints on the terminal values. This kind of control is often referred to as linear quadratic (LQ) optimal control problems.

It is known from linear quadratic optimal control theory that[2], if the criterion $J$ is to be minimized, the control signal can be selected as

$$u^{*}(t) = -R^{-1}B^{\mathrm{T}}P(t)x(t), \tag{7.13}$$

where $P(t)$ is a symmetrical matrix, satisfying Riccati differential equation

$$\dot{P}(t) = -P(t)A - A^{\mathrm{T}}P(t) + P(t)BR^{-1}B^{\mathrm{T}}P(t) - Q, \tag{7.14}$$

where the terminal value of $P(t)$ is $P(t_f) = S$. It can be seen that the control signal depends on the state variables $x(t)$ and the solutions $P(t)$ of Riccati differential equations.

Even to the current standard of computer computation, the joint solutions of state space equations and the Riccati differential equations are still very complicated, since some of the differential equations are initial value problems, while others are terminal value problems. Thus, in order to solve the problem, the original problem should be simplified. Assume that the terminate time is infinite, i.e., $t_f \to \infty$, the solutions to the Riccati differential equation must tend to a constant matrix, such that $\dot{P}(t) = 0$. Also, assume the matrix $P(t)$ is a constant matrix $P$, the Riccati differential equation is reduced to an algebraic Riccati equation

$$PA + A^{\mathrm{T}}P - PBR^{-1}B^{\mathrm{T}}P + Q = 0. \tag{7.15}$$

The control problem is then referred to as linear quadratic regulator (LQR) problem. Assume that $u^*(t) = -Kx(t)$, where $K = R^{-1}B^{\mathrm{T}}P$. The closed-loop state space equations under state feedback is converted to Eqn. (7.10).

Function lqr() is provided in the Control System Toolbox to solve linear quadratic optimal regulator problems, with syntax $[K,P] = \mathrm{lqr}(A,B,Q,R)$, where $(A, B)$ is the open-loop model of the plant, $K$ is the state feedback matrix, and $P$ is the solution of Riccati algebraic equation, where Schur decomposition is used in solving the Riccati algebraic equation. The Riccati equation can also be solved with are() and care() functions.

For discrete systems, linear quadratic criterion can be written as

$$J = \frac{1}{2}x^{\mathrm{T}}(N)Sx(N) + +\frac{1}{2}\sum_{k=0}^{N}\left[x^{\mathrm{T}}(k)Qx(k) + u^{\mathrm{T}}(k)Ru(k)\right], \tag{7.16}$$

and the corresponding dynamic Riccati equation can be written as[3]

$$P(k) = F^{\mathrm{T}}\left[P(k+1) - P(k+1)GR^{-1}G^{\mathrm{T}}P(k+1)\right]F + Q, \tag{7.17}$$

where $P(N) = S$, $N$ is the terminal time. $(F, G)$ is the discrete state space model. For optimal linear quadratic regulator problems, $P$ is a constant matrix, satisfying discrete Riccati algebraic equation

$$P = F^{\mathrm{T}}\left(P - PGR^{-1}G^{\mathrm{T}}P\right)F + Q. \tag{7.18}$$

Thus, the optimal control signal is

$$K = \left(R + G^{\mathrm{T}}PG\right)^{-1}B^{\mathrm{T}}PF. \tag{7.19}$$

Discrete Riccati algebraic equation can be solved with dare() function, and the control problem can be solved directly with function dlqr(), with the syntax $[K,P] = \mathrm{dlqr}(F,G,Q,R)$.

It can be seen from the control law that the optimality depends heavily on the selections of the weighting matrices $Q$ and $R$. So far, there is no well accepted weighting matrix selection algorithm. The optimality is some-what artificial. If the matrices $Q$ and $R$ are not well chosen, although the "optimal" solution can be obtained, however, this kind of optimal is meaningless, sometimes misleading conclusions may be obtained.

Generally speaking, if we want to restrict the size of input signals, large weighting matrix $R$ should be selected to force the input signal to be small. For multivariable systems, if we want the size of the $i$th input small, large values in the $i$th column of $R$ should be selected. Similarly, if the $j$th state is expected to be small, the $j$th column in $Q$ matrix should be selected large. These guidelines are just quantitative ones, and there is no widely accepted algorithms to date, in selecting the matrices.

**Example 7.2.** Assume that the continuous state space model is given by

$$A = \begin{bmatrix} 2 & 0 & 4 & 1 & 2 \\ 1 & -2 & -4 & 0 & 1 \\ 1 & 4 & 3 & 0 & 2 \\ 2 & -2 & 2 & 3 & 3 \\ 1 & 4 & 6 & 2 & 1 \end{bmatrix}, \quad B = \begin{bmatrix} 1 & 2 \\ 0 & 1 \\ 0 & 0 \\ 0 & 0 \\ 0 & 0 \end{bmatrix}.$$

Selecting the weighting matrices $Q = \text{diag}(1000, 0, 1000, 500, 500)$, and $R = I_2$, the following statements can be given, and the state feedback matrix and Riccati algebraic equation solution can be obtained

```
>> A=[2,0,4,1,2; 1,-2,-4,0,1; 1,4,3,0,2; 2,-2,2,3,3; 1,4,6,2,1];
   B=[1,2; 0,1; 0,0; 0,0; 0,0]; Q=diag([1000 0 1000 500 500]);
   R=eye(2); [K,P]=lqr(A,B,Q,R) % state feedback matrix and ARE solution
   eig(A-B*K)    % closed-loop pole positions
```

The state feedback matrix and Riccati equation solution can be found

$$K^{\mathrm{T}} = \begin{bmatrix} 21.978 & 24.09 \\ -19.867 & 27.463 \\ -17.195 & 82.937 \\ 15.978 & 75.931 \\ -7.1739 & 67.526 \end{bmatrix}, \quad P = \begin{bmatrix} 21.978 & -19.867 & -17.195 & 15.978 & -7.1739 \\ -19.867 & 67.198 & 117.33 & 43.975 & 81.874 \\ -17.195 & 117.33 & 503.52 & 345.84 & 237.17 \\ 15.978 & 43.975 & 345.84 & 661.53 & 379.92 \\ -7.1739 & 81.874 & 237.17 & 379.92 & 374 \end{bmatrix},$$

and under the state feedback, the closed-loop poles are located at $-70.9010$, $-5.9113$, $-2.1770$, $-5.8155 \pm \mathrm{j}6.2961$.

### 7.2.3 Pole Placement Controller Design

If the state space model of the plant is given, various controllers can be introduced. For instance, with state feedback, the poles of the closed-loop system can be placed to the pre-assigned locations. If the pole positions of the closed-loop system are selected reasonably, the dynamic behavior of the closed-loop system may be desired. The method to place closed-loop locations is called pole placement method.

In this section, pole placement algorithms will be presented. Assume that the open-loop state space expression of the system is given by

$$\begin{cases} \dot{x}(t) = Ax(t) + Bu(t) \\ y(t) = Cx(t) + Du(t), \end{cases} \qquad (7.20)$$

where the sizes of the $A, B, C, D$ matrices are compatible. A state feedback matrix $K$ can be introduced such that $u(t) = r(t) - Kx(t)$, with $r(t)$ as the external input signal to the system. The closed-loop state space model can be written as

$$\begin{cases} \dot{x}(t) = (A - BK)x(t) + Br(t) \\ y(t) = (C - DK)x(t) + Dr(t). \end{cases} \qquad (7.21)$$

Assume that the expected closed-loop poles are $\mu_i, i = 1, 2, \cdots, n,$ and the characteristic equation of the closed-loop system $\alpha(s)$ can be expressed as

$$\alpha(s) = \prod_{i=1}^{n}(s - \mu_i) = s^n + \alpha_1 s^{n-1} + \alpha_2 s^{n-2} + \cdots + \alpha_{n-1}s + \alpha_n. \qquad (7.22)$$

For open-loop state space model $(A, B, C, D)$, under state feedback vector $K$, the closed-loop state space model can be written as $(A-BK, B, C-DK, D)$. If the closed-loop poles are to be placed to the desired locations, pole placement techniques can be used. Here, several algorithms and their MATLAB implementation will be introduced.

### 1. Bass–Gura algorithm
Assume that the open-loop characteristic polynomial $a(s)$ can be written as

$$a(s) = \det(sI - A) = s^n + a_1 s^{n-1} + a_2 s^{n-2} + \cdots + a_{n-1}s + a_n. \qquad (7.23)$$

If the plant model is fully controllable, the state feedback vector $K$ can be obtained with[4]

$$K = \gamma^{\mathrm{T}} \Gamma^{-1} T_{\mathrm{c}}^{-1}, \qquad (7.24)$$

where $\gamma^{\mathrm{T}} = \left[ (a_n - \alpha_n), \cdots, (a_1 - \alpha_1) \right], T_{\mathrm{c}} = \left[ B, AB, \cdots, A^{n-1}B \right]$ are controllable judgement matrix, and

$$\Gamma = \begin{bmatrix} a_{n-1} & a_{n-2} & \cdots & a_1 & 1 \\ a_{n-2} & a_{n-3} & \cdots & 1 & \\ \vdots & \vdots & \ddots & & \\ a_1 & 1 & & & \\ 1 & & & & \end{bmatrix}. \qquad (7.25)$$

It can be seen that since $\Gamma$ is a nonsingular Hankel matrix, the matrix is invertible. If system is fully controllable, matrix $T_{\mathrm{c}}$ for single variable system is also convertible. The state feedback vector $K$ can be selected to place all the closed-loop poles to the pre-assigned locations. Based on the algorithm, the following MATLAB function bass_pp() can be written as

```
function K=bass_pp(A,B,p)
a1=poly(p); a=poly(A); % determines the characteristic polynomials of original and
L=hankel(a(end-1:-1:1)); C=ctrb(A,B); % desired closed-loop system
K=(a1(end:-1:2)-a(end:-1:2))*inv(L)*inv(C); % find the state feedback vector
```

In the function call, $(A, B)$ is the open-loop state space model, and variable $p$ is a vector which stores the desired closed-loop pole positions. The returned variable $K$ is the state feedback vector.

### 2. Ackermann algorithm

Pole placement problems of single variable system can also be solved using another algorithm. In the algorithm, the state feedback vector $K$ can be obtained directly with

$$K = -\begin{bmatrix} 0,0,\cdots,0,1 \end{bmatrix} T_c^{-1} \alpha(A), \qquad (7.26)$$

where $\alpha(A)$ is the polynomial matrix, which substitutes $A$ into Eqn. (7.22). This matrix can be obtained with `polyvalm()` function. If the system is controllable, the matrix $T_c$ is a full-rank matrix. For single variable systems, $T_c^{-1}$ exists. Thus, this algorithm can be used to design pole placement controllers. The algorithm is referred to as Ackermann algorithm.

In Control System Toolbox, function `acker()` is provided to implement the Ackermann algorithm, and the syntax of the function is exactly the same as the one for `bass_pp()` function, $K = \text{acker}(A,B,p)$ . It should be noted that in single variable systems the state feedback vector $K$ is unique, thus, the two algorithms yield the same result.

### 3. Robust placement algorithm

For multivariable systems, the state feedback matrix $K$ is not unique, thus it is possible to get robust solutions. In Control System Toolbox, `place()` function is provided based on robust pole placement algorithm[5], and the state feedback matrix $K$ can be returned, with the same syntax $K = \text{place}(A,B,p)$ .

It should be pointed out that `place()` function cannot be used to solve problems with repeated desired pole positions. The functions `acker()` and `base_pp()`, however, can be used to solve multiple poles problems for single variable systems.

**Example 7.3.** Assume that the state space equation of the system is

$$\dot{x}(t) = \begin{bmatrix} 0 & 2 & 0 & 0 & -2 & 0 \\ 1 & 0 & 0 & 0 & 0 & -1 \\ 0 & 1 & 0 & 0 & 0 & 0 \\ 0 & 0 & 0 & 3 & 0 & 0 \\ 2 & 0 & 0 & 1 & 0 & 0 \\ 0 & 0 & -1 & 0 & 1 & 0 \end{bmatrix} x(t) + \begin{bmatrix} 1 & 2 \\ 0 & 0 \\ 0 & 1 \\ 0 & -1 \\ 0 & 1 \\ 0 & 0 \end{bmatrix} u(t).$$

If we want to place the closed-loop poles to $-1, -2, -3, -4, -1 \pm j$, with state feedback, the following statements should be used

```
>> A=[0,2,0,0,-2,0; 1,0,0,0,0,-1; 0,1,0,0,0,0;
      0,0,0,3,0,0; 2,0,0,1,0,0; 0,0,-1,0,1,0];
```

```
B=[1,2; 0,0; 0,1; 0,-1; 0,1; 0,0];
p=[-1 -2 -3 -4 -1+1i -1-1i]; % desired closed-loop poles
K=place(A,B,p),                % pole placement for multivariable systems
p1=eig(A-B*K)'                 % closed-loop pole position verifications
```

It can be seen that the state feedback matrix $K$ obtained, and the closed-loop poles are indeed, placed to the desired positions. Besides, since the plant model is a multivariable system, the functions acker() and base_pp() cannot be used.

$$K = \begin{bmatrix} 7.9333 & -18.553 & -19.134 & 20.65 & 18.698 & 22.126 \\ -0.36944 & -2.0412 & -2.3166 & -9.5475 & 0.57469 & 1.5013 \end{bmatrix}.$$

**Example 7.4.** Consider the discrete model in Example 5.4 is given by

$$\boldsymbol{x}[(k+1)T] = \begin{bmatrix} 0 & 1 & 0 & 0 \\ 0 & 0 & -1 & 0 \\ 0 & 0 & 0 & 1 \\ 0 & 0 & 5 & 0 \end{bmatrix} \boldsymbol{x}(kT) + \begin{bmatrix} 0 & 1 \\ 0 & -1 \\ 0 & 0 \\ 0 & 0 \end{bmatrix} \boldsymbol{u}(kT).$$

If the desired poles are $-0.1, -0.2, -0.5 \pm 0.2$j, the following statements can be given to design state feedback matrix

```
>> A=[0 1 0 0 ; 0 0 -1 0; 0 0 0 1; 0 0 5 0]; % enter A matrix
   B=[0 1 ; 0 -1; 0 0 ; 0 0];                % enter B matrix
   p=[-0.1; -0.2; -0.5+0.2i; -0.5-0.2i];     % assign the desired poles
   K=place(A,B,p)                            % design state feedback controller
```

However, the message "??? Error using ==> place, Can't place eigenvalues there" will be displayed, indicating that the pole placement cannot be completed. With the function rank(ctrb($A,B$)), it can be seen that the rank of the controllability judgement matrix is 2, thus the system is not fully controllable. Thus, the closed-loop poles cannot be arbitrarily placed. In this case, partial pole placement should be made[6].

### 7.2.4 *Observer Design and Observer-based Regulators*

In real applications, not all the states can be measured, since the states are the internal signals in the system. Thus, direct state feedback may not be possible. It is obvious that we can make artificially the same state space model $A, B, C, D$ like in the plant model, and measure the states of the artificial system, and to run state feedback based on the artificial states. In this way, the states of the plant can be reconstructed. However, the artificial states may not be exactly the same as the ones in the original plants, since we are not able to construct the artificial model exactly the same as in the original plant, which may be subject to disturbances to the model parameters and even structures. Thus, the outputs and inputs of the original systems should be used to reconstruct the states of the plant. The reconstruction of states can be implemented through observers.

The typical structure of the observer is shown in Fig. 7-10. If the original model

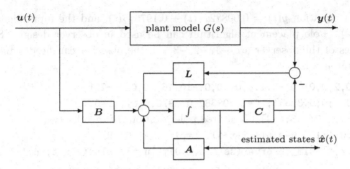

Fig. 7-10   Typical structure of state observers.

$(A, C)$ is fully observable, the state space model of the observer can be written as

$$\dot{\hat{x}}(t) = A\hat{x}(t) + Bu(t) - L\big[C\hat{x}(t) + Du(t) - y(t)\big] \\ = (A - LC)\hat{x}(t) + (B - LD)u(t) + Ly(t), \tag{7.27}$$

where $L$ is a column vector, such that $(A - LC)$ is stabilized. From Eqn. (7.27), it can be found that

$$\dot{\hat{x}}(t) - \dot{x}(t) = (A - LC)\hat{x}(t) + (B - LD)u(t) + Ly(t) - Ax(t) - Bu(t) \\ = (A - LC)\big[\hat{x}(t) - x(t)\big]. \tag{7.28}$$

The analytical solution of the equation is

$$\hat{x}(t) - x(t) = e^{(A-LC)(t-t_0)}\big[\hat{x}(t_0) - x(t_0)\big]. \tag{7.29}$$

Since $(A - LC)$ is stable, it can be seen that

$$\lim_{t \to \infty} \big[\hat{x}(t) - x(t)\big] = 0. \tag{7.30}$$

The observed states can approximate the states of the original system.

A MATLAB function sim_observer() is written, which is an extension to the one given in [1], to simulate the states and observed states of the system for arbitrary input $u(t)$. The listing of the function is

```
function [xh,x]=sim_observer(G,L,u,t)
G=ss(G); [y,t,x]=lsim(G,u,t); A=G.a; B=G.b; C=G.c; D=G.d;
[y1,t,xh1]=lsim(ss((A-L*C),(B-L*D),C,D),u,t);
[y2,t,xh2]=lsim(ss((A-L*C),L,C,D),y,t); xh=xh1+xh2;
```

The syntax of the function is $[\hat{x}, x] = \text{sim\_observer}(G, L, u, t)$, where $G$ is the state space model of the plant, $L$ is the observer vector. The vectors $u$ and $t$ are the samples of the input signal. The reconstructed time response of the states are returned in $\hat{x}$, while the actual states of the original plant are given in $x$.

**Example 7.5.** Assume that the state space model of the plant is

$$\dot{x}(t) = \begin{bmatrix} 0 & 2 & 0 & 0 \\ 0 & -0.1 & 8 & 0 \\ 0 & 0 & -10 & 16 \\ 0 & 0 & 0 & -20 \end{bmatrix} x(t) + \begin{bmatrix} 0 \\ 0 \\ 0 \\ 0.3953 \end{bmatrix} u(t),$$

with output equation $y(t) = 0.09882x_1(t) + 0.1976x_2(t)$, and the input signal is $u(t) = \sin(1.2t + 2)$. Pole placement algorithm can be used in observer design. Suppose the desired poles of the observer are $-1, -2, -3, -4$, the observer can be designed, with the following statements

```
>> A=[0,2,0,0; 0,-0.1,8,0; 0,0,-10,16; 0,0,0,-20];
   B=[0;0;0;0.3953]; C=[0.09882,0.1976,0,0]; D=0;
   P=[-1; -2; -3; -4]; % desired pole positions of the observer
   t=0:0.1:10; u=sin(1.2*t+1); L=place(A',C',P)';
   [xh,x,t]=sim_observer(ss(A,B,C,D),L,u,t); plot(t,x,t,xh,':');
```

The observer vector designed is $\boldsymbol{L} = [10.1215, -106.7824, 288.4644, -193.5749]^{\mathrm{T}}$. With this observer, the time responses of the states of the original system and the reconstructed ones with observers can be obtained as shown in Fig. 7-11(a), and the errors of the states are shown in Fig. 7-11(b). It can be seen that the reconstructed states are satisfactory.

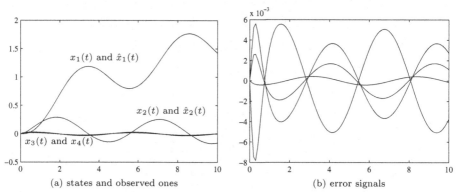

(a) states and observed ones                    (b) error signals

Fig. 7-11   Comparisons of the states and observed states.

When the state observer is designed, the state feedback with observer, i.e., the states are, in fact, the reconstructed states from the observer, is constructed as shown in Fig. 7-12.

Consider the feedback structure in Fig. 7-10, according to Eqn. (7.27), the state feedback can be expressed into two subsystems, $\boldsymbol{G}_1(s)$ and $\boldsymbol{G}_2(s)$, the inputs for the two subsystems are $\boldsymbol{u}(t)$ and $\boldsymbol{y}(t)$. The subsystem $\boldsymbol{G}_1(s)$ can be written as

$$\begin{cases} \dot{\hat{\boldsymbol{x}}}_1(t) = \left( \boldsymbol{A} - \boldsymbol{LC} \right)\hat{\boldsymbol{x}}_1(t) + \left( \boldsymbol{B} - \boldsymbol{LD} \right)\boldsymbol{u}(t) \\ \boldsymbol{y}_1(t) = \boldsymbol{K}\hat{\boldsymbol{x}}_1(t), \end{cases} \tag{7.31}$$

while subsystem $\boldsymbol{G}_2(s)$ is written as

$$\begin{cases} \dot{\hat{\boldsymbol{x}}}_2(t) = \left( \boldsymbol{A} - \boldsymbol{LC} \right)\hat{\boldsymbol{x}}_2(t) + \boldsymbol{L}\boldsymbol{y}(t) \\ \boldsymbol{y}_2(t) = \boldsymbol{K}\hat{\boldsymbol{x}}_2(t). \end{cases} \tag{7.32}$$

The closed-loop system can be written in Fig. 7-13(a). With slight modifications, the typical feedback system structure in Fig. 7-13(b) can be constructed. In the

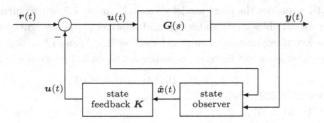

Fig. 7-12 State feedback structure with observer.

system, the equivalent blocks are

$$G_c(s) = \left[I + G_1(s)\right]^{-1}, \quad H(s) = G_2(s). \tag{7.33}$$

It can be shown that in the typical feedback structure, the controller model $G_c(s)$ can be further written as

$$G_c(s) = I - K\left(sI - A + BK + LC - LDK\right)^{-1}B. \tag{7.34}$$

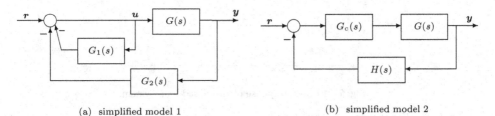

(a) simplified model 1           (b) simplified model 2

Fig. 7-13 Observer-based state feedback control.

The state space realization of $G_c(s)$ can be written as

$$\begin{cases} \dot{x}(t) = \left(A - BK - LC + LDK\right)x(t) + Bu(t) \\ y(t) = -Kx(t) + u(t). \end{cases} \tag{7.35}$$

Since the observer is implied in the feedback structure, the control structure is often referred to as observer-based controller structure. With state feedback matrix $K$ and observer matrix $L$, the controller and feedback models can be obtained with the following MATLAB function, with the syntax $[G_c, H] = \mathtt{obsvsf}(G, K, L)$ .

```
function [Gc,H]=obsvsf(G,K,L)
H=ss(G.a-L*G.c,L,K,0); Gc=ss(G.a-G.b*K-L*G.c+L*G.d*K,G.b,-K,1);
```

If the reference input is $r(t) = 0$, the controller $G_c(s)$ is referred as observer-based regulator, and it can further be simplified as

$$\begin{cases} \dot{x}(t) = \left(A - BK - LC + LDK\right)x(t) + Lu(t) \\ y(t) = Kx(t). \end{cases} \tag{7.36}$$

The regulator can also be obtained with $G_c = \mathtt{reg}(G, K, L)$ .

**Example 7.6.** Consider the plant model given in Example 7.5, where smaller weights can be made on state variables $x_1(t)$ and $x_2(t)$, and relatively larger weights on the other two variables. The weighting matrices can be selected as $R = 1$, and $Q = \mathrm{diag}(0.01, 0.01, 2, 3)$. The following statements can be used to design optimum LQ controller

```
>> A=[0,2,0,0; 0,-0.1,8,0; 0,0,-10,16; 0,0,0,-20];
   B=[0;0;0;0.3953]; C=[0.09882,0.1976,0,0]; D=0;
   Q=diag([0.01,0.01,2,3]); R=1;          % weighting matrices
   K=lqr(A,B,Q,R), step(ss(A-B*K,B,C,D)) % design direct state feedback LQ
```

It can be seen that the state feedback vector obtained is $K = [0.1000, 0.9429, 0.7663, 0.6387]$. Under such a state feedback vector, the step response of the closed-loop system can be obtained as shown in Fig. 7-14.

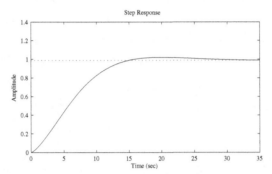

Fig. 7-14    Step response of the closed-loop system.

Assume that the states cannot be measured, an observer can be designed to reconstruct the states, and then the feedback act on the reconstructed feedback can be implemented. Pole placement algorithm can be used in controller design, with the poles of the observer set as $-5$. The step response of the observer-based controller obtained is the same as the one obtained in Fig. 7-14.

```
>> P=[-5;-5;-5;-5]; G=ss(A,B,C,D); L=acker(A',C', P)'; % observer design
   [Gc,H]=obsvsf(G,K,L);                    % observer-based controllers
   step(ss(A-B*K,B,C,D),feedback(G*Gc,H)) % compare step responses
```

The following statements can be used to perform minimum realization to the closed-loop model of the observer-based controller. Eight pairs of poles and zeros will be canceled. The minimum realized model is a 4th order model, very close to the one with state feedback.

```
>> zpk(minreal(feedback(G*Gc,H))) % minimum realization
   zpk(minreal(ss(A-B*K,B,C,D)))   % the direct state feedback model
```

The minimum realization model of the observer-based controller is

$$G_1(s) = \frac{-1.1466 \times 10^{-15}(s + 9.338 \times 10^7)(s - 9.338 \times 10^7)(s + 1)}{(s + 20.01)(s + 10.01)(s^2 + 0.3341s + 0.05052)},$$

and it can finally be simplified to

$$G_1^*(s) = \frac{9.9982(s + 1)}{(s + 20.01)(s + 10.01)(s^2 + 0.3341s + 0.05052)}.$$

## 7.3 Optimal Controller Design

### 7.3.1 *Introduction to Optimal Control*

"Optimal control" is so-called because it refers to achieving certain objectives under particular conditions or constraints; the aim is to to define the control action such that a given criterion is minimized or maximized. Here, the criterion is the same as the objective function in optimization problems in Section 3.4. In optimal control, the commonly used objectives can be assigned to integrals of error signals. For some small-scale problems, analytical solutions may be found. Some constrained optimal control problems can be solved using Pontryagin's maximum principle. Since in the early days computers and powerful software were not widely available, indirect ways of solving optimal control problems were explored. Among these, linear quadratic optimal control problems received much attention in the control community where two weighting matrices $Q$ and $R$ were introduced and some beautiful mathematical formulae for the problem were derived. However, there is no widely accepted method for assigning these two weighting matrices. This makes the optimal criterion superficial, if not meaningless and even misleading.

Suitable criteria for servo control systems are integral-type ones for the tracking error signals defined as

$$J_{\text{IAE}} = \int_0^\infty |e(t)| dt, \quad J_{\text{ITAE}} = \int_0^\infty t|e(t)| dt. \tag{7.37}$$

With the powerful tools such as MATLAB, many optimal control problems can be converted to numerical optimization problems. Although the solutions may not have perfect mathematical formula, the results are more practical. Here, examples will be given to demonstrate optimal control problems.

**Example 7.7.** Assume that the plant model is

$$G(s) = \frac{10(s+1)(s+0.5)}{s(s+0.1)(s+2)(s+10)(s+20)}.$$

In Example 7.1, lead–lag controllers were designed. In this example, optimal design of controllers will be presented.

Suppose that ITAE criterion is selected, the Simulink model in Fig. 7-15(a) can be constructed. In the system model, the ITAE integral is returned in the output port. If the system response settles down at the steady-state value, the ITAE integral settles down at the infinite ITAE integral.

In order to minimize the ITAE criterion, the following MATLAB function is written to describe the objective function for optimization

```
function y=c7optm1(x)
assignin('base','Z1',x(1)); assignin('base','P1',x(2));
assignin('base','Z2',x(3)); assignin('base','P2',x(4));
assignin('base','K',x(5));       % assign variables in MATLAB workspace
[t,a,yy]=sim('c7moptm1.mdl',3); y=yy(end); % objective function evaluation
```

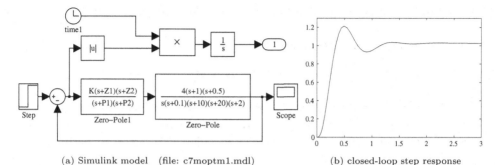

(a) Simulink model   (file: c7moptm1.mdl)                  (b) closed-loop step response

Fig. 7-15   Step response with optimal lead–lag compensator.

In the objective function, **assignin()** function is used to assign the components of $x$ into MATLAB workspace, so that the Simulink model can use these values directly. The following statements can be used to solve the optimization problem.

```
>> options=optimset('Display','iter','Jacobian','off','LargeScale','off');
   x0=[5:-1:1]; v=fminsearch(@c7optm1,x0,options)
```

The optimal lead–lag controller is

$$G_c(s) = 243.77\frac{(s+53)(s+66.58)}{(s+38.28)(s+62.09)}.$$

Under such a controller, the step response of the system is obtained as shown in Fig. 7-15(b). It can be seen that with optimization involved, the settling time is significantly reduced. However, the overshoot is rather large.

In practical optimization process, it is found that since the zeros of the system may settle down at extremely small values, which makes the simulation process very slow. To solve the problem, constraints should be introduced. For instance, the lower bounds for the five decision variables should be set to 0.01. In this case, the following statements can be used to design the controller.

```
>> v=fmincon(@c7optm1,x0,[],[],[],[],0.01*ones(5,1),[],[],options)
```

Another advantage by numerical optimization technique is that constraints can be introduced deliberately. For instance, if the user thinks the 21% of overshoot is too large, a constraints on overshoot can be introduced. The Simulink model in Fig. 7-16(a) can be constructed, and a constraint can then be set to $\sigma \leqslant 3\%$. The objective function can be rewritten as follows. If the constraints are not satisfied, the objective function should be set to a very large number

```
function y=c7optm2(x)
assignin('base','Z1',x(1)); assignin('base','P1',x(2));
assignin('base','Z2',x(3)); assignin('base','P2',x(4));
assignin('base','K',x(5));    % assign MATLAB workspace variables
[t,a,yy]=sim('c7moptm2.mdl',3); y=yy(end,1);   % evaluate criterion
if max(yy(:,2))>1.03, y=1.2*y; end % when overshoot is too large
```

With the following statements, the optimal lead–lag controller can be designed, and the closed-loop response is obtained as shown in Fig. 7-16(b).

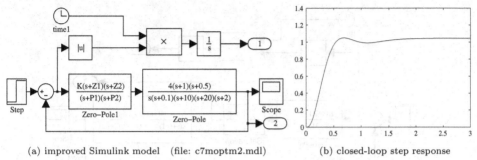

(a) improved Simulink model   (file: c7moptm2.mdl)       (b) closed-loop step response

Fig. 7-16   System model and response with overshoot constraints.

```
>> v=fmincon(@c6optm2,x0,[],[],[],[],0.01*ones(5,1),[],[],options)
```

The optimal controller is

$$G_{c_2}(s) = 161.4965 \frac{(s + 43.1203)(s + 55.7344)}{(s + 28.4746)(s + 61.0652)}.$$

In fact, the above design process neglected one important problem, the size of control signal. It can be found that the control signal obtained may reach large values such as 200. This will sometimes cause problems to the hardware of the real-time systems. To solve the problems in real applications, actuator saturation is appended to the linear controller to force the control signal keep within a certain range. With theoretical methods, this case cannot be solved easily. With numerical optimization techniques, this kind of problem can be solved easily, with almost no extra computation efforts.

**Example 7.8.** Consider again the previous example. If the controller is followed by actuator saturation, which makes the size of control signal smaller than 20, the new Simulink model can be constructed as shown in Fig. 7-17. The objective function is rewritten as

```
function y=c7optm3(x)
assignin('base','Z1',x(1)); assignin('base','P1',x(2));
assignin('base','Z2',x(3)); assignin('base','P2',x(4));
assignin('base','K',x(5));   % assign MATLAB workspace variables
[t,a,yy]=sim('c7moptm2.mdl',15); y=yy(end,1);   % evaluate criterion
if max(yy(:,2))>1.03, y=1.4*y; end % if overshoot too large
```

With the following MATLAB statements, the optimal controller can be designed as

$$G_c(s) = 37.1595 \frac{(s + 142.6051)(s + 62.6172)}{(s + 20.3824)(s + 27.6579)}.$$

```
>> v=fmincon(@c7optm3,x0,[],[],[],[],0.01*ones(5,1),[],[],options)
```

The step response of the closed-loop system can be obtained as shown in Fig. 7-18. It can be seen that although actuator saturation is introduced in the controller, the control behavior is still satisfactory.

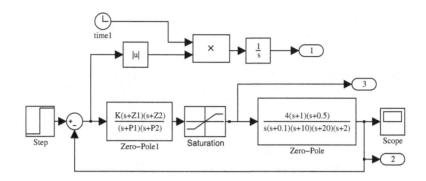

Fig. 7-17    Simulink model with actuator saturations    (file name: c7optm3.mdl).

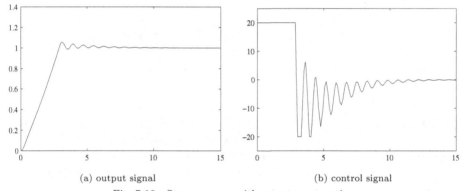

(a) output signal                          (b) control signal

Fig. 7-18    Step response with actuator saturation.

### 7.3.2  *An Optimal Controller Design Interface*

It is known from the demonstration given earlier that the optimal controller design problems based on numerical optimization techniques are no longer restricted to the traditional forms, since arbitrary objective functions can be defined, thus the optimization-based optimal controller design techniques have much better future perspectives in control engineering.

The authors summarized the typical form of servo control systems, and developed an optimal controller design interface based on error integral criteria. MATLAB and Simulink are used to design meaningful optimal controllers. In the interface, the users are allowed to describe the control system structure with Simulink. The controller can be in any form and any structure, with variables to be optimized. We named the interface OCD, for optimal controller designer.

The procedures of using OCD interface are summarized below:

(1) Type `ocd` at the MATLAB prompt, the interface shown in Fig. 7-19 is displayed. The interface can be used to design optimal controllers with the facilities provided in MATLAB and Simulink.

(2) A Simulink model should be constructed first. Two important issues are the

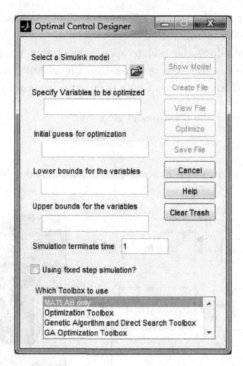

Fig. 7-19　Graphical user interface for the optimal controller design program.

error signal criterion and the variables in the controller. For instance, the variables Kp and Ki are used to describe the PI controller.

(3) In the edit box labeled Select a Simulink model, enter the name of the Simulink file. Before the use of OCD, the user should have already established a Simulink model, defining the error criterion.

(4) Fill in the edit box labeled Specify Variables to be optimized the names of variables to be optimized, and the variable names are separated by commas.

(5) Fill in an estimated time to terminate simulation. Theoretically, the terminating time is infinity, however, it is not proper in numerical simulation. A fairly large terminating time should be entered in the edit box labeled by Simulation terminate time. It should be noted that the parameter may affect the optimization results. It was pointed out that if the ITAE curve settles down at time $\hat{t}_f$, the terminate time $t_f$ is selected in the interval $(\hat{t}_f, 2\hat{t}_f)$, the parameters of the controller designed may not change much[7].

(6) Clicking the Create File button to write automatically the objective function in MATLAB, with the file name opt_*.m automatically assigned. The Clear Trash button can be clicked to delete the temporary files.

(7) Click Optimize button will invoke the optimal controller design process. The optimal parameters are returned in the variable ctrl_pars. If the controller is not satisfactory, the button can be clicked again. In the actual problem, the functions

`fminsearch()`, `fmincon()` or `nonlin()` can be called automatically by the interface to design the optimal controllers.

(8) The interface allows the user to specify the lower, upper bounds and initial values of the decision variables, optimization algorithms, simulation algorithms. These can be done through relevant edit boxes and listboxes.

**Example 7.9.** Consider the plant model given by

$$G(s) = \frac{1}{s(s+1)^4}.$$

If an optimal PID controller is expected, the Simulink model shown in Fig. 7-20(a) can be established.

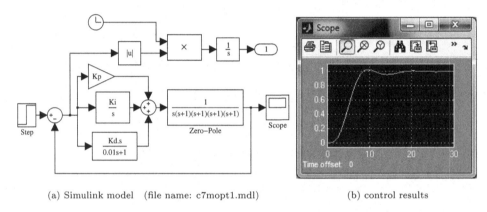

(a) Simulink model   (file name: c7mopt1.mdl)          (b) control results

Fig. 7-20   Simulink model and control result with optimal PID controller.

In MATLAB command window, type **ocd** command, the interface shown in Fig. 7-19 is opened. Specify **c7mopt1** in the edit box labeled Select a Simulink model, and in the Specify Variables to be optimized edit box, write **Kp,Ki,Kd**, and in Simulation terminate time edit box specify 30. Click the Create File button. The objective function will be generated automatically

```
function y=optfun_2(x)
assignin('base','Kp',x(1));
assignin('base','Ki',x(2));
assignin('base','Kd',x(3));
try
    [t_time,x_state,y_out]=sim('c7mopt1',[0,30.000000]);
catch
    y_out=1e10;
end
y=y_out(end,1);
```

where the decision variables are assigned to the variables $K_p, K_i, K_d$ in MATLAB workspace. Then perform simulation and set the ITAE criterion to the output variable $y$, i.e., the objective function. The **try** and **catch** structure allows the user to bypass ill-conditioned situations by pressing Ctrl+C keys at any time, without terminating the optimization processes.

Click the Optimize button to invoke optimization process. Meanwhile, if the scope in Simulink model is opened, the optimization process can be visualized. Through optimization process, the optimal controller can be found

$$G_c(s) = 0.2583 + \frac{0.0001}{s} + \frac{0.7159s}{0.01s+1}.$$

Since the weight to the integrator is extremely small, PD controller can be used. Under the controller, the step response of the closed-loop system can be obtained as shown in Fig. 7-20(b). It can be seen that the control results are satisfactory.

**Example 7.10.** OCD interface is not restricted to design simple problems such as optimal PID controllers design. It can be used to other problems with complicated control structures. For instance, the cascade PI controller design problem shown in Fig. 7-21 can be solved simply with OCD.

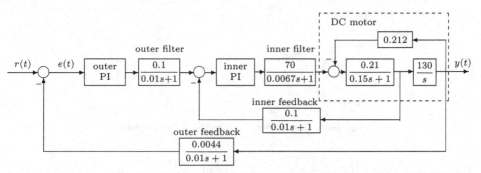

Fig. 7-21   DC motor drive system with double loops.

In order to solve this problem, the Simulink model shown in Fig. 7-22 should be constructed first. In this model, there are four parameters to be optimized, Kp1, Ki1, Kp2, and Ki2. ITAE integral signal is generated and connected to the first output port.

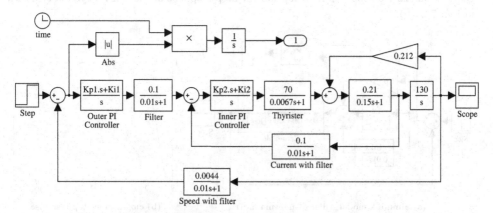

Fig. 7-22   Simulink model of cascade PI control system   (file name: c7model2.mdl).

When OCD interface is executed, c7model2 can be entered in the edit box labeled Select a Simulink model, and in the edit box labeled Specify Variables to be optimized, specify Kp1,Ki1,Kp2,Ki2. In Simulation terminate time edit box, fill in 0.6. Once all these are done, click Create File button to generate objective function, and then click the Optimize button to initiate the optimal controller design process. The optimal controller parameters obtained are $K_{p_1} = 37.9118$, $K_{i_1} = 12.1855$, $K_{p_2} = 10.8489$, and $K_{i_2} = 0.9591$. Thus, the optimal cascade PI cobtrollers can be obtained

$$G_{c_1}(s) = 37.9118 + \frac{12.1855}{s}, \quad G_{c_2}(s) = 10.8489 + \frac{0.9591}{s}.$$

The step response of the system is shown in Fig. 7-23 and it can be seen that the control results are satisfactory.

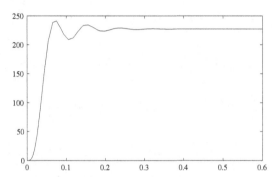

Fig. 7-23   Step response of the motor drive system.

**Example 7.11.** In the previous examples, the ITAE criterion was used. The question now is why ITAE is used, rather than the ISE criterion appears in most literature, while the computation of ISE is much simpler. Consider again the plant model studied in Example 7.9. If ISE criterion is used, the Simulink model shown in Fig. 7-24(a) should be constructed first. Through the optimization process, the optimal PID controller is $G_c(s) = 0.2722 + 0.0054/s + 1.6954s$, and the step response of the control system is shown in Fig. 7-24(b).

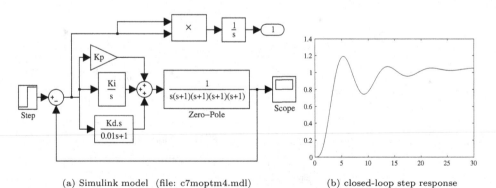

(a) Simulink model  (file: c7moptm4.mdl)              (b) closed-loop step response

Fig. 7-24   Optimal PID controller design with ISE criterion.

Comparing the control results with the one obtained with ITAE criterion, it can be seen that the result under ISE criterion is not as good. The reason is that ISE criterion treats the error at any time instances equally, thus it may still lead to oscillations when $t$ is relatively large. ITAE criterion, however, imposes heavy penalty to the error signal when $t$ gets larger. This may force the system to settle down as soon as possible to steady-state value, i.e., to make the error signal approach to zero as soon as possible. Thus, ITAE criterion is suitable for use when servo control is involved.

### 7.3.3 *Other Applications of OCD Interface*

OCD interface applies not only to controller design problems, it works well in other situations when the integral error can be defined in Simulink. For instance, in the case of model reduction, Simulink is used to express the responses of the original model and the reduced model when subjected to the same input signal. The error between them can be used to generate the integrals through ISE or other criteria. The OCD interface can be used directly in finding the optimal reduced models.

**Example 7.12.** Suppose the original model is given by $G(s) = 1/(s+1)^6$, and a first-order delay model is expected in the form $G_r(s) = e^{-Ls}/(Ts+1)$. The target is to find the parameters $L$ and $T$. A Simulink model defining the ITAE integral can be established as shown in Fig. 7-25. With OCD, the optimal reduced model can easily be found as

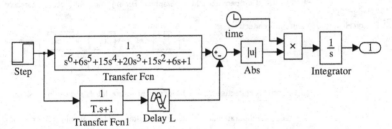

Fig. 7-25   Simulink model for model reduction   (file name: c7mmr.mdl).

Invoke OCD interface, fill in the relevant edit boxes with c7mmr.mdl, L,T, and 10 for terminate time. Click **Create File** to generate objective function, and then click **Optimize** button to start the optimization process. The optimal parameters are $L = 3.66$, $T = 2.6665$, i.e., the optimal reduced model is $G^*(s) = e^{-3.66s}/(2.6665s + 1)$.

OCD interface can be used in many other situations. For instance, nonlinear controller is considered as an extremely difficult task for more design approaches. However, since OCD is supported by Simulink, the systems with nonlinearities can be solved equally, and the users may not notice the difference, whether there are nonlinear problems involved or not. In the next sections, the applications of using OCD interface in multivariable control systems are explored.

## 7.4   Controller Design Interfaces in Control System Toolbox

Several controller design interfaces are provided in the Control System Toolbox. The single variable control system interface (SISO Tool) and PID design interface (PID Tool) are interactive interfaces. In this section, SISO Tool is discussed and demonstrated.

### 7.4.1   *Introduction to MATLAB Controller Design Interface*

An interactive controller design interface, `sisotool()` is provided in the Control System Toolbox with the syntax  `sisotool(`$G$`,`$G_c$`)` , where $G$ is the plant model, $G_c$ is the controller model. An interactive controller design interface is opened as shown in Fig. 7-26. Click the **Control Architecture** button, the dialog box in Fig. 7-27 is displayed which allows the user to select or modify control structures. The lower-level interfaces allow the user to add poles and zeros and adjust the gain to design controller models. An example is given to demonstrate the use of SISO Tool.

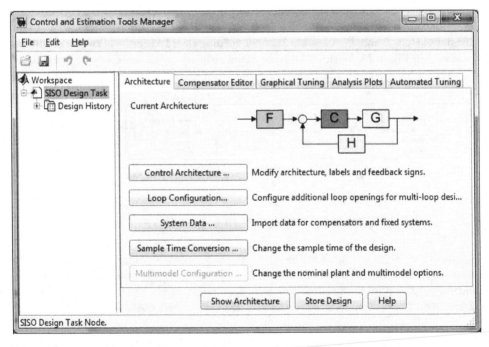

Fig. 7-26   Main interface in controller design.

**Example 7.13.** Assume that the plant model is given by

$$G(s) = \frac{10(s+1)(s+0.5)}{s(s+0.1)(s+2)(s+10)(s+20)},$$

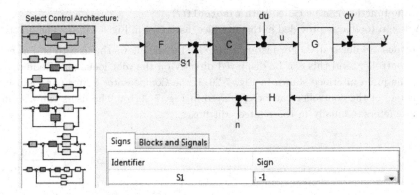

Fig. 7-27  Dialog box for control structure settings.

the following statements can be used to initiate `sisotool()` function, and the interface in Fig. 7-28 is displayed for controller design. On the left-hand-side is the root locus of $G$, and Bode diagrams is given on the right.

```
>> s=tf('s'); G=4*(s+1)*(s+0.5)/s/(s+0.1)/(s+2)/(s+10)/(s+20)
   Gc1=27283.5668*(s+2.326)*(s+2)/(s+172)/(s+0.3173);
   sisotool(G,Gc1)      % start the SISO Tool interface
```

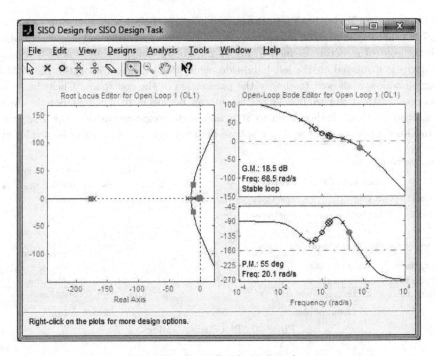

Fig. 7-28  Controller design interface.

In the above command, $G_{c_1}$ is the initial controller model. If initial controller is not

given, the function can be called with `sisotool(G)`.

A design toolbar is provided in the interface, as shown in Fig. 7-29(a). The functions of the buttons are illustrated. For instance, the ✕ button allows the user to add a real pole in the controller, and this can be displayed directly on the root locus and Bode diagram.

In the main interface shown in Fig. 7-26, if the Compensator Editor pane is used, the parameters of the controller can be displayed in Fig. 7-29(b). The users can also modify the parameters manually in the related edit boxes.

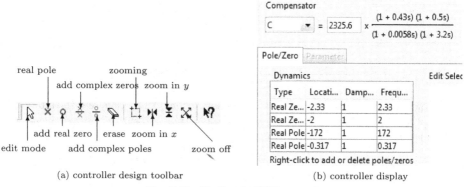

(a) controller design toolbar                    (b) controller display

Fig. 7-29   Toolbar in SISO control.

The Graphical Tuning button in the main window is clicked, and a window as shown in Fig. 7-30(a) is displayed. The interactive controller parameter adjusting layout is displayed, with the control structure defined in Fig. 7-28. For instance, under default setting, the root locus is displayed on the left-hand-side, while Bode diagram is on the right. Mouse dragging action is allowed to change the parameters of the controller. Click the Analysis Plots pane in the main window, plots layout can be specified. For instance, in the Plot Type listbox, if Plot 1 listbox is set to Step, and in the Responses listbox, the first group is set to Closed Loop: r to y, the step response between signals $r$ and $y$ will be displayed.

**Design plots configuration**

| Plot | Available Open/Closed l | Plot Type |
|---|---|---|
| Plot 1 | Open Loop 1 ▼ | Root Locus ▼ |
| Plot 2 | Open Loop 1 ▼ | Open-Loo... ▼ |
| Plot 3 | Open Loop 1 ▼ | None ▼ |

Summary of available Open/Closed loops to tune:

| Loop Name | Loop Description |
|---|---|
| Open Loop 1 | Open Loop L |
| Closed Loop 1 | Closed Loop - From r to y |

**Analysis Plots**

|  | Plot 1 | Plot 2 | Plot 3 |
|---|---|---|---|
| Plot Type | None ▼ | None ▼ | None ▼ | N |

Contents of Plots

| Plots | | | | | | | Responses |
|---|---|---|---|---|---|---|---|
| 1 | 2 | 3 | 4 | 5 | 6 | All | |
| ☐ | ☐ | ☐ | ☐ | ☐ | ☐ | ☑ | Closed Loop r to y |
| ☐ | ☐ | ☐ | ☐ | ☐ | ☐ | ☑ | Closed Loop r to u |
| ☐ | ☐ | ☐ | ☐ | ☐ | ☐ | ☑ | Input Sensitivity |
| ☐ | ☐ | ☐ | ☐ | ☐ | ☐ | ☑ | Output Sensitivity |

(a) layout of plots                    (b) layout setting

Fig. 7-30   Plot display settings.

If Analysis Plots pane is selected, a dialog box shown in Fig. 7-30(b) is displayed from which the user may select the plots to be displayed.

Step response of the system under current controller can be displayed with the

Analysis → Response to Step Command menu, as shown in Fig. 7-31(a). The Real-Time Update checkbox should be checked. If the controller is changed, the step responses will be immediately changed. Thus, interactive modification to controller parameters is allowed.

For instance, if a lead–lag controller is expected, an extra real pole and zero can be added, on top of the current lead controller. The pole can be placed to the left of zero. The pole zero locations and gain can be modified interactively to get desired response, as shown in Fig. 7-31(b). This may probably be the best possible controller tuned manually. The controller obtained can be displayed as

$$G_c(s) = 434 \frac{(1+0.049s)(1+0.035s)}{(1+0.0086s)(1+0.015s)}.$$

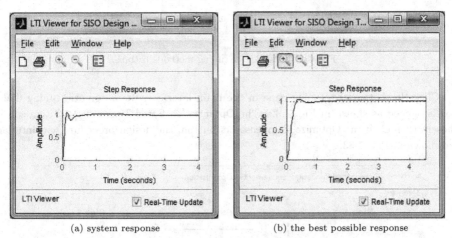

(a) system response        (b) the best possible response

Fig. 7-31   Closed-loop step responses.

### 7.4.2   An Example of Parameter Automatic Tuning for Single Variable Systems

With the Automated Tuning pane in the main interface selected, automatic tuning of controller parameters can be invoked. The parameter tuning interface shown in Fig. 7-32 can be displayed. In the Design method listbox, several tuning algorithms such as Optimization Based Tuning, PID Tuning, Internal Model Control (IMC) Tuning, LQG Synthesis and Loop Shaping approaches are implemented. Here, the Optimization Based Tuning method is introduced.

**Example 7.14.** Consider again the plant model in the above example. If a lead–lag controller is expected, a controller prototype should be established in MATLAB first. For instance, let $G_c(s) = (s+1)(s+2)/[(s+3)(s+4)]$. Thus, the following statements can be used to start the SISO Tool interface.

```
>> s=tf('s'); G=4*(s+1)*(s+0.5)/s/(s+0.1)/(s+2)/(s+10)/(s+20);
   Gc=(s+1)*(s+2)/(s+3)/(s+4); sisotool(G,Gc)
```

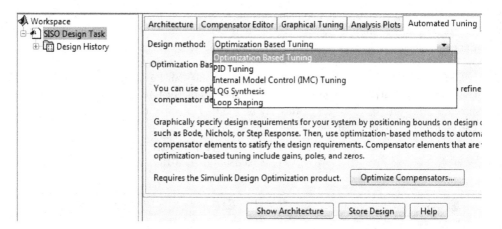

Fig. 7-32   Parameter tuning methods listbox.

Click the **Automated Tuning** pane in the main interface, the automatic tuning dialog box is opened as shown in Fig. 7-32. The **Optimization Based Tuning** listbox item can be chosen, then click the **Optimize Compensators** button, the design procedure and interface are shown in Fig. 7-33.

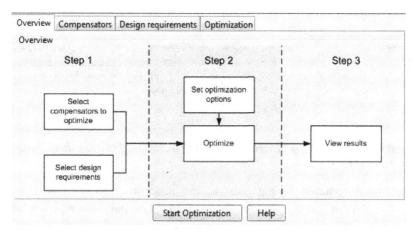

Fig. 7-33   Parameter automatic tuning procedures and settings.

It can be seen from the procedures that the user should first select the control structure and the parameters to be optimized, then specify the design requirements, and finally start the optimization process. The following illustrate the controller design procedures step by step.

(1) **Selection of parameters to be optimized**. Click the **Compensators** pane, the interface shown in Fig. 7-34 is opened. The user can select the parameters from the list. In this example, there are five parameters to be optimized. They are the gain, and poles and zeros of the lead–lag controller.

(2) **Design requirements specification**. Click the **Design requirements** pane, the

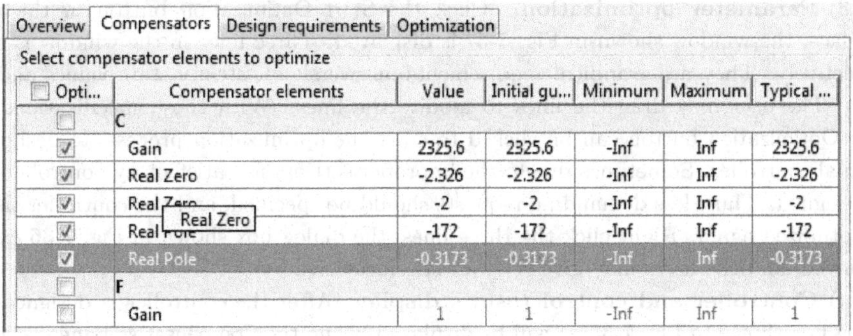

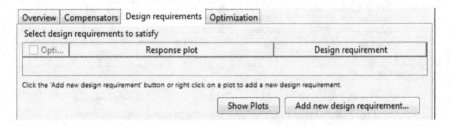

Fig. 7-34  Selecting the parameters to be optimized.

interface shown in Fig. 7-35 will be displayed. In the default case, no design requirements are specified. The user may add his own requirements. Click the Add new design requirement button, the dialog box shown in Fig. 7-36 is displayed. The design requirements can be specified in it, including the settings on overshoot and settling time.

Fig. 7-35  Design requirements specification interface.

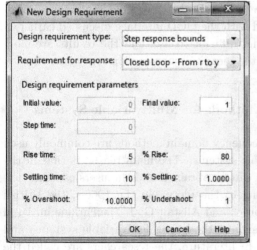

Fig. 7-36  Design requirement dialog box.

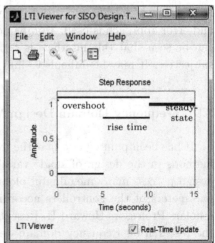

Fig. 7-37  Graphical representation.

(3) **Parameter optimization.** Click the Start Optimization button in the main interface, the window shown in Fig. 7-37 is displayed. Three lines in the window is given respectively. They are graphical requirements on overshoot, steady-state values and rise time. The user may drag the lines to modify the lines. With these specifications, the Start Optimization button can be clicked to start the optimization process, to design the optimal controller. Sometimes due to the improper setting, no satisfactory controllers can be designed. Thus, less demanding requests should be specified, and the controller should be optimized again. Right click the three lines, the dialog box shown in Fig. 7-36 can be displayed, and the users may give relevant specifications.

(4) **Controller and control results display.** After the controller is designed, the dialog box shown in Fig. 7-38(a) will be displayed, when the Compensators pane is clicked. The parameters in the controller are displayed. The control results are shown in Fig. 7-38(b). It can be seen that the designed controller is far more efficient than the one manually tuned in Example 7.13.

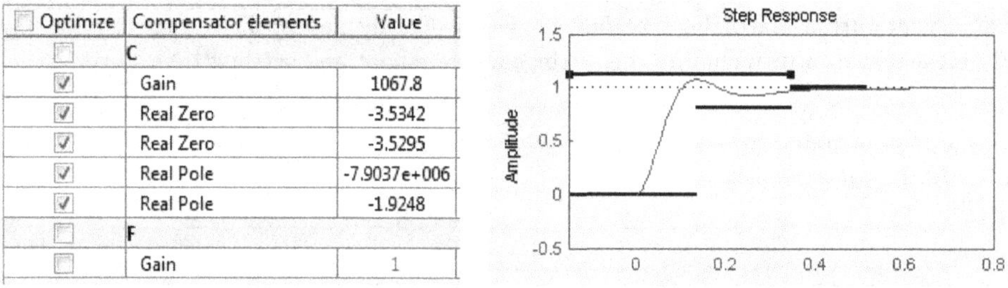

| Optimize | Compensator elements | Value |
|---|---|---|
| ☐ | C | |
| ☑ | Gain | 1067.8 |
| ☑ | Real Zero | -3.5342 |
| ☑ | Real Zero | -3.5295 |
| ☑ | Real Pole | -7.9037e+006 |
| ☑ | Real Pole | -1.9248 |
| ☐ | F | |
| ☐ | Gain | 1 |

(a) controller designed          (b) step response

Fig. 7-38   Control results with the directly designed controller.

In fact, the designed controller is an acceptable controller, rather than optimal controller. If the three lines are properly chosen, good controllers can be designed. However, it is not an easy task to select properly the three lines. Sometimes, trial-and-error approach is used. Compared with the OCD interface discussed earlier, it can be seen that this interface is rather difficult to use, and the results are more subjective. It may be difficult to find the meaningful controller.

## 7.5   Frequency Domain Design Methods for Multivariable Systems

It has been pointed out that the frequency domain methods are commonly used methods in the design of single variable systems. The main reason is that in the design process many meaningful plots can be obtained and the users can tune the parameters of the controllers according to the plots. In the 1960's, the British scholars Professors Howard H. Rosenbrock and Alistair G. J. MacFarlane initiated the research on frequency domain design methods on multivariable systems, and a series of achievements were made. In literature, the researchers are called the British School.

Since there is coupling among the input–output pairs in multivariable systems, most work is on finding good decoupling approaches, so that the design tasks can be converted to single variable design problems. The main frequency domain methods including inverse Nyquist array (INA) methods[8], characteristic locus method[9], reversed-frame normalisation (RFN)[10], sequential loop closing[11], and parameters optimization method[12].

In this section, the pseudo-diagonalization method in multivariable systems is given, then the inverse Nyquist array decoupling method is presented. Parameter optimization method is also illustrated, and finally the use of OCD is tested in multivariable controller design.

### 7.5.1 *Diagonal Dominant and Pseudo-diagonalization*

In the frequency domain analysis of multivariable systems, the transfer function matrices are usually assessed for whether they are diagonal dominant or not. If the systems are diagonal dominant, the controller of individual loops are made, and this may not have too much impact on other loops. Diagonal dominance of transfer function matrices are assessed with the help of Gershgorin Theorem, as discussed in Section 5.5.

If the transfer function matrix studied is not diagonal dominant, some kind of compensation methods should be introduced, so that it can be converted to diagonal dominant matrices. Then individual loop single variable design method can be used, regardless of the coupling. The typical block diagram of Nyquist-type methods is shown in Fig. 7-39, where $K_p(s)$ is the pre-compensating matrix such that $G(s)K_p(s)$ is a diagonal dominant matrix. Matrix $K_d(s)$ can be used to introduce further dynamic compensation to diagonal dominant matrices.

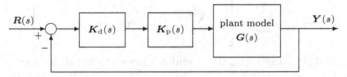

Fig. 7-39   Typical block diagram of multivariable systems.

In multivariable systems design, the design of $K_p(s)$ matrix is a crucial step. It may affect the final design results. In practical applications, this matrix is usually designed as a simple constant matrix. The users may select a constant matrix with their own experience, the matrix may introduce elementary matrix transformation, such that the compensated matrix is diagonal dominant. Matrix $K_p(s)$ can be chosen with the trial-and-error method, where normally $K_p(s)$ can first be selected as $K_p(s) = G^{-1}(0)$, such that at least $G(s)K_p(s)$ is an identity matrix at frequency 0.

Trial-and-error methods are not quite suitable in computer-aided design process.

Thus, many researchers proposed different methods to perform diagonal dominant transformations. In this section, pseudo-diagonalization method[13] is presented to select the pre-composition matrix $K_\mathrm{p}$. Assume that at frequency $\mathrm{j}\omega_0$, the inverse Nyquist array of its transfer function matrix can be expressed as

$$\hat{g}_{ik}(\mathrm{j}\omega_0) = \alpha_{ik} + \mathrm{j}\beta_{ik}, \quad i, k = 1, 2, \cdots, m, \tag{7.38}$$

where $m$ is the number of outputs, and we have to assume that the numbers of inputs and outputs are the same. In order to obtain an optimal compensation matrix $K_\mathrm{p}$, the following procedures are taken

(1) Select a frequency $\mathrm{j}\omega_0$, find the inverse Nyquist array $\hat{g}_{ik}(\mathrm{j}\omega_0)$.

(2) For each $q$ $(q = 1, 2, \cdots, m)$, create a matrix $A_q$, where

$$a_{il,q} = \sum_{k=1 \text{ and } k\neq q}^{m} \left[ \alpha_{ik}\alpha_{lk} + \beta_{ik}\beta_{lk} \right], \quad i, l = 1, 2, \cdots, m. \tag{7.39}$$

(3) Find the eigenvalues and eigenvectors of matrix $A_q$, and denote its eigenvector of its smallest eigenvalue by $k_q$.

(4) For each $q$, the minimum eigenvector can be spanned into a compensation matrix $K_\mathrm{p}$.

$$K_\mathrm{p}^{-1} = \begin{bmatrix} k_1, & k_2, & \cdots, & k_m \end{bmatrix}^\mathrm{T}. \tag{7.40}$$

The above pseudo-diagonalization is introduced about a certain frequency, and the frequency itself still needs trial-and-error method to find. Alternatively, several frequency points in a frequency range can be used to implement weighted pseudo-diagonalization method. Select $N$ frequency points, $\omega_1, \omega_2, \cdots, \omega_N$, and assume its $r$th frequency point weighted by $\psi_r$, the following method can be used to construct $A_q$ matrix

$$A_{il,q} = \sum_{r=1}^{N} \psi_r \left[ \sum_{k=1 \text{ and } k\neq q}^{m} (\alpha_{ik,r}\alpha_{lk,r} + \beta_{ik,r}\beta_{lk,r}) \right], \tag{7.41}$$

where $\alpha_{:,:,r}$ and $\beta_{:,:,r}$ represent the $\alpha$ and $\beta$ values at the $r$th frequency. Thus, step (3) in the pseudo-diagonalization algorithm can be used to establish the matrix $K_\mathrm{p}$.

According to the above algorithm, a MATLAB function `pseudiag()` can be written to implement the pseudo-diagonalization matrix. The inverse Nyquist array for the certain frequency points is expressed in variable $G_1$, and $R$ is the weighting vector composed of $\psi_i$'s, with default values of 1's. Matrix $K_\mathrm{p}$ can be returned and the listing of the function is

```
function Kp=psuediag(G1,R)
A=real(G1); B=imag(G1); [n,m]=size(G1); N=n/m; Kp=[];
if nargin==1, R=ones(N,1); end
for q=1:m, L=1:m; L(q)=[];
    for i=1:m, for l=1:m, a=0;
        for r=1:N, k=(r-1)*m;
```

```
        a=a+R(r)*sum(A(k+i,L).*A(k+1,L)+B(k+i,L).*B(k+1,L));
      end,
      Ap(i,l)=a;
    end, end
    [x,d]=eig(Ap); [xm,ii]=min(diag(d)); Kp=[Kp; x(:, ii)'];
  end
```

**Example 7.15.** Consider the four-input, four-output model[8]

$$\boldsymbol{G}(s) = \begin{bmatrix} 1/(1+4s) & 0.7/(1+5s) & 0.3/(1+5s) & 0.2/(1+5s) \\ 0.6/(1+5s) & 1/(1+4s) & 0.4/(1+5s) & 0.35/(1+5s) \\ 0.35/(1+5s) & 0.4/(1+5s) & 1/(1+4s) & 0.6/(1+5s) \\ 0.2/(1+5s) & 0.3/(1+5s) & 0.7/(1+5s) & 1/(1+4s) \end{bmatrix}.$$

The following statements can be used to draw inverse Nyquist array plots with Gershgorin circles, as shown in Fig. 7-40(a).

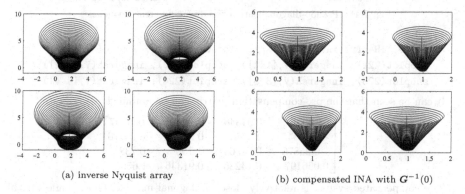

(a) inverse Nyquist array         (b) compensated INA with $\boldsymbol{G}^{-1}(0)$

Fig. 7-40   Inverse Nyquist array plots with Gershgorin circles.

```
>> s=tf('s'); w=logspace(-1,0);
   G=[1/(1+4*s), 0.7/(1+5*s), 0.3/(1+5*s), 0.2/(1+5*s);
      0.6/(1+5*s), 1/(1+4*s), 0.4/(1+5*s), 0.35/(1+5*s);
      0.35/(1+5*s), 0.4/(1+5*s), 1/(1+4*s), 0.6/(1+5*s);
      0.2/(1+5*s),0.3/(1+5*s),0.7/(1+5*s),1/(1+4*s)]; H=mfrd(G,w);
   subplot(221), inagersh(H,[1 1]), subplot(222), inagersh(H,[2 2])
   subplot(223), inagersh(H,[3 3]), subplot(224), inagersh(H,[4 4])
```

It can be seen from the plots that the original system is not diagonal dominant. Select a pre-compensation matrix $\boldsymbol{K} = \boldsymbol{G}^{-1}(0)$, the following statements can be used to draw the compensated inverse Nyquist array plots as shown in Fig. 7-40(b). It can be seen that the diagonal dominance property is improved. However, since the Gershgorin bands are too wide, this model is not suitable for use in direct controller design.

```
>> K=inv(mfrd(G,0)); W=mfrd(G*K,w);
   subplot(221), inagersh(W,[1 1]), subplot(222), inagersh(W,[2 2])
   subplot(223), inagersh(W,[3 3]), subplot(224), inagersh(W,[4 4])
```

Now let us consider the pseudo-diagonalization function **pseudiag()** for frequency point $\omega_0 = 0.9\,\mathrm{rad/s}$. The inverse Nyquist array plots can be obtained as shown in Fig. 7-41(a).

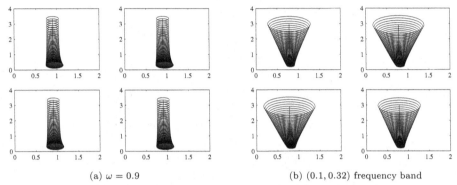

(a) $\omega = 0.9$            (b) $(0.1, 0.32)$ frequency band

Fig. 7-41    Pseudo-diagonalization results for different frequencies.

```
>> v=0.9; iH=mfrd(inv(G),v); Kp=inv(pseudiag(iH)), V=mfrd(G*Kp,w);
   subplot(221), inagersh(V,[1 1]), subplot(222), inagersh(V,[2 2])
   subplot(223), inagersh(V,[3 3]), subplot(224), inagersh(V,[4 4])
```

It can be seen that the pre-compensation matrix can be obtained

$$
\boldsymbol{K}_{\mathrm{p}} = \begin{bmatrix}
1.6595 & -0.91346 & -0.14286 & 0.056197 \\
-0.73847 & 1.755 & -0.24064 & -0.25876 \\
-0.25876 & -0.24064 & 1.755 & -0.73847 \\
0.056197 & -0.14286 & -0.91346 & 1.6595
\end{bmatrix}.
$$

The compensated system is relatively close to diagonal matrix. Thus, single variable design methods can be used for each individual loops, regardless its impact to other loops. If frequencies in an interval $(0.01, 0.4)$ are used, the following statements are issued

```
>> v=logspace(-2,log10(0.4)); iH=mfrd(inv(G),v);
   Kp=inv(pseudiag(iH)), Q=mfrd(G*Kp,w);
   subplot(221), inagersh(Q,[1 1]), subplot(222), inagersh(Q,[2 2])
   subplot(223), inagersh(Q,[3 3]), subplot(224), inagersh(Q,[4 4])
```

the inverse Nyquist array plots can be obtained as shown in Fig. 7-41(b), and the compensation matrix becomes

$$
\boldsymbol{K}_{\mathrm{p}} = \begin{bmatrix}
2.036 & -1.3304 & -0.18838 & 0.14936 \\
-1.0707 & 2.1785 & -0.27704 & -0.35538 \\
-0.35538 & -0.27704 & 2.1785 & -1.0707 \\
0.14936 & -0.18838 & -1.3304 & 2.036
\end{bmatrix}.
$$

In [14], similar pseudo-diagonalization algorithms are used to construct dynamic compensation matrices $\boldsymbol{K}_{\mathrm{p}}(s)$. The readers are advised to reference the literature if necessary.

The limitation of inverse Nyquist array approach is that the transfer function matrix of the original system must be a square matrix, i.e., the numbers of inputs and outputs are the same, such that the inverse Nyquist matrix exists. If the system matrix is not square, the inverse Nyquist array methods cannot be used, direct Nyquist array approaches can be used instead.

**Example 7.16.** Consider the multivariable system with delays studied in Example 5.44

$$
G(s) = \begin{bmatrix} \dfrac{0.1134e^{-0.72s}}{1.78s^2 + 4.48s + 1} & \dfrac{0.924}{2.07s + 1} \\ \dfrac{0.3378e^{-0.3s}}{0.361s^2 + 1.09s + 1} & \dfrac{-0.318e^{-1.29s}}{2.93s + 1} \end{bmatrix}.
$$

The system is not a diagonal dominant one. With the $K_{p_1} = G^{-1}(0)$ compensation, the $g_{22}(s)$ term is not very obvious. Another matrix $K_{p_2}^{-1} = [1, 0; 0.5, 1]$ can be introduced to further compensate the system. The compensated inverse Nyquist array is shown in Fig. 7-42(a), and it can be seen that the new compensated system is diagonal dominant.

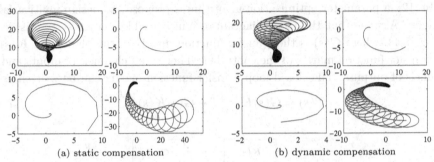

(a) static compensation      (b) dynamic compensation

Fig. 7-42 Inverse Nyquist arrays after compensation.

```
>> G=[tf(0.1134,[1.78 4.48 1]), tf([0.924],[2.07,1]);
      tf(0.3378,[0.361,1.09,1]), tf(-0.318,[2.93 1])];
   G1=G; G1.ioDelay=[0.72 0; 0.3 1.29];
   w=logspace(0,1); Kp1=inv(mfrd(G,0));
   Kp2=inv([1 0; 0.5 1]); H3=mfrd(G1*Kp1*Kp2,w); inagersh(H3)
```

It has been pointed out that the diagonal dominant system can be designed individually for each control loops. For instance, the dynamic compensation matrix can be introduced

$$
K_d(s) = \begin{bmatrix} 1 & 0 \\ 0 & (0.3s + 1)/(0.05s + 1) \end{bmatrix}, \text{ i.e., } K_d^{-1}(s) = \begin{bmatrix} 1 & 0 \\ 0 & (0.05s + 1)/(0.3s + 1) \end{bmatrix}.
$$

The inverse Nyquist array plots of $Q^{-1}(s) = K_d^{-1}(s)K_{p_2}^{-1}K_{p_1}^{-1}G^{-1}(s)$ is shown in Fig. 7-42(b), it can be seen that the compensated system is strongly diagonal dominant.

```
>> s=tf('s'); Kd=[1 0; 0 (0.3*s+1)/(0.05*s+1)];
   inagersh(mfrd(G1*Kp1*Kp2*Kd,w))
```

The following statements can be used to draw step responses of the closed-loop system, as shown in Fig. 7-43.

```
>> step(feedback(ss(G1)*Kp1*Kp2*Kd,eye(2)),15)
```

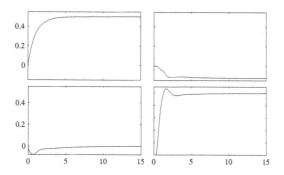

Fig. 7-43    Closed-loop step responses.

### 7.5.2    *Parameter Optimization Design for Multivariable Systems*

In [12], a parameter optimization algorithm is proposed to design multivariable systems. Assume that the block diagram of multivariable control system is given in Fig. 7-44, where $G(s)$ is the transfer function matrix of the plant, and $K(s)$ is the transfer function matrix of the controller. There are $l$ channels of inputs and $m$ channels of outputs. The closed-loop transfer function matrix can be written as

$$T(s) = G(s)K(s)\big[I + G(s)K(s)\big]^{-1}. \tag{7.42}$$

Fig. 7-44    Structure of multivariable control system.

If the closed-loop transfer function matrix approaches to a pre-assigned target transfer function matrix $T_t(s)$ within a specific frequency range, parameter optimization method can be used to design suitable controllers[12]. The corresponding target controller $K_t(s)$ satisfies $G(s)K_t(s) = T_t(s)\big[I - T_t(s)\big]^{-1}$. An error function $E(s) = T_t(s) - T(s)$ can be defined, and it is shown through simple conversion that

$$E(s) = \big[I - T(s)\big]\big[G(s)K(s) - G(s)K_t(s)\big]\big[I - T_t(s)\big]. \tag{7.43}$$

If $\|E(s)\|$ is small enough, $K(s)$ approaches $K_t(s)$ close enough, thus

$$\begin{aligned}
E(s) &= \big[I - T_t(s)\big]\big[G(s)K(s) - G(s)K_t(s)\big]\big[I - T_t(s)\big] + o\big(\|E(s)\|^2\big) \\
&\approx \big[I - T_t(s)\big]\big[G(s)K(s) - G(s)K_t(s)\big]\big[I - T_t(s)\big].
\end{aligned} \tag{7.44}$$

Denote $K(s) = N(s)/d(s)$, where $d(s)$ is the common denominator polynomial chosen by the user, and $N(s)$ is the polynomial matrix with known order, and the coefficients are undetermined. Let $B(s) = I - T_t(s)$, $A(s) = B(s)G(s)/d(s)$, and

$$Y(s) = B(s)G(s)K_t(s)B(s). \tag{7.45}$$

Eqn. (7.44) can be written as

$$Y(s) \approx A(s)N(s)B(s) + E(s). \tag{7.46}$$

In order to find the optimal parameters in polynomial matrix $N(s)$, the following optimization criterion is introduced

$$\|E\|_2^2 = \min_{N(s)} \int_{-\infty}^{\infty} \text{tr}\Big[E^{\text{T}}(-\text{j}\omega)E(\text{j}\omega)\Big]\text{d}\omega, \tag{7.47}$$

where $Y(s) = \big[y_1(s), y_2(s), \cdots, y_m(s)\big]$, $N(s) = \big[n_1(s), n_2(s), \cdots, n_m(s)\big]$, $E(s) = \big[e_1(s), e_2(s), \cdots, e_m(s)\big]$. The following equation can be established

$$\begin{bmatrix} y_1(s) \\ y_2(s) \\ \vdots \\ y_m(s) \end{bmatrix} \approx \Big[B^{\text{T}}(s) \otimes A(s)\Big] \begin{bmatrix} n_1(s) \\ n_2(s) \\ \vdots \\ n_m(s) \end{bmatrix} + \begin{bmatrix} e_1(s) \\ e_2(s) \\ \vdots \\ e_m(s) \end{bmatrix}, \tag{7.48}$$

where $\otimes$ is the Kronecker product. The controller numerator polynomial $n_i(s)$ can be written as $n_i(s) = \big[n_{1i}(s), n_{2i}(s), \cdots, n_{li}(s)\big]^{\text{T}}$. Assume that

$$n_{ij}(s) = v_{ij}^0 s^p + v_{ij}^1 s^{p-1} + \cdots + v_{ij}^{p-1} s + v_{ij}^p, \tag{7.49}$$

where for $n_i(s)$, $p$ is a positive integer, then polynomial matrix can be used to describe numerator coefficients. For sub-polynomials of lower orders, the $p$th order form can still be used. In this case, the coefficients of higher order terms are assumes to be 0's. The following matrix can be established

$$\Sigma(s) = \begin{bmatrix} s^p & s^{p-1} & \cdots & 1 & & & & & \\ & & & & s^p & s^{p-1} & \cdots & 1 & \\ & & & & & & & \ddots & \\ & & & & & & s^p & s^{p-1} & \cdots & 1 \end{bmatrix}, \tag{7.50}$$

with

$$\begin{bmatrix} n_1(s) \\ n_2(s) \\ \vdots \\ n_m(s) \end{bmatrix} = \Sigma v, \quad \text{and} \quad v = \big[v_{11}^0, v_{11}^1, \cdots, v_{ml}^p\big]^{\text{T}}. \tag{7.51}$$

Let $X(s) = \Big[B^{\text{T}}(s) \otimes A(s)\Big]\Sigma(s)$, $\eta(s) = \big[y_1^{\text{T}}(s), y_2^{\text{T}}(s), \cdots, y_m^{\text{T}}(s)\big]^{\text{T}}$, $\varepsilon(s) = \big[e_1^{\text{T}}(s), e_2^{\text{T}}(s), \cdots, e_m^{\text{T}}(s)\big]^{\text{T}}$, the standard least squares form of Eqn. (7.48) can be written as

$$\eta(s) = X(s)v + \varepsilon(s). \tag{7.52}$$

In order to get $\boldsymbol{\eta}$ and $\boldsymbol{X}$ matrices, frequency analysis methods can be used. A group of frequencies $\{\omega_i\}, i = 1, 2, \cdots, M$ can be chosen, and matrices $\boldsymbol{X}(\mathrm{j}\omega_i)$ and $\boldsymbol{\eta}(\mathrm{j}\omega_i)$ can be approximated and matrices $\boldsymbol{X}(\mathrm{j}\omega)$ and $\boldsymbol{\eta}(\mathrm{j}\omega)$ can be constructed

$$\boldsymbol{X}(\mathrm{j}\omega) = \begin{bmatrix} \boldsymbol{X}(\mathrm{j}\omega_1) \\ \boldsymbol{X}(\mathrm{j}\omega_2) \\ \vdots \\ \boldsymbol{X}(\mathrm{j}\omega_M) \end{bmatrix}, \quad \boldsymbol{\eta}(\mathrm{j}\omega) = \begin{bmatrix} \boldsymbol{\eta}(\mathrm{j}\omega_1) \\ \boldsymbol{\eta}(\mathrm{j}\omega_2) \\ \vdots \\ \boldsymbol{\eta}(\mathrm{j}\omega_M) \end{bmatrix}. \tag{7.53}$$

It is easily found from Eqn. (7.52) that the least squares solutions of the controller parameters can be obtained

$$\hat{\boldsymbol{v}}(\mathrm{j}\omega) = \left[ \boldsymbol{X}^{\mathrm{T}}(-\mathrm{j}\omega)\boldsymbol{X}(\mathrm{j}\omega) \right]^{-1} \boldsymbol{X}^{\mathrm{T}}(-\mathrm{j}\omega)\boldsymbol{\eta}(\mathrm{j}\omega). \tag{7.54}$$

From the above presentation, it is found that the $\hat{\boldsymbol{v}}$ parameters may contain complex values, such that the controllers may not be implemented. Numerical tricks are used to ensure $\boldsymbol{v}(\mathrm{j}\omega)$ are real[12]

$$\hat{\boldsymbol{v}}(\mathrm{j}\omega) = \mathscr{R}\left[ \boldsymbol{X}^{\mathrm{T}}(-\mathrm{j}\omega)\boldsymbol{X}(\mathrm{j}\omega) \right]^{-1} \mathscr{R}\left[ \boldsymbol{X}^{\mathrm{T}}(-\mathrm{j}\omega)\boldsymbol{\eta}(\mathrm{j}\omega) \right], \tag{7.55}$$

where $\mathscr{R}(\cdot)$ extracts the real part.

MFD Toolbox provides a function `fedmunds()` to implement the parameter optimization algorithm. The traditional algorithm is extended, since the common denominator $d(s)$ is no longer needed. Each of the components in controller matrix can be set independently. The syntax of the function is $N = $ `fedmunds`$(\boldsymbol{w}, \boldsymbol{H}, \boldsymbol{H}_{\mathrm{t}}, \boldsymbol{N}_0, \boldsymbol{D})$ , where $\boldsymbol{w}$ is a vector of selected frequencies, $\boldsymbol{H}$ and $\boldsymbol{H}_{\mathrm{t}}$ are the frequency responses of the plant $\boldsymbol{G}(s)$ and target system $\boldsymbol{T}(s)$, respectively. $\boldsymbol{D}$ is the polynomial matrix of the denominator, while $\boldsymbol{N}_0$ represents the structure of the polynomial matrix of numerator. If a component in matrix $\boldsymbol{N}_0$ is zero, it means that this component need not be optimized, thus the whole parameter optimization process is simplified. Matrix $\boldsymbol{N}$ returns the numerator coefficients optimized, as demonstrated in the next example.

**Example 7.17.** Consider the state space plant model [15]

$$A = \begin{bmatrix} 0 & 0 & 1.1320 & 0 & -1 \\ 0 & -0.0538 & -0.1712 & 0 & 0.0705 \\ 0 & 0 & 0 & 1 & 0 \\ 0 & 0.0485 & 0 & -0.8556 & -1.013 \\ 0 & -0.2909 & 0 & 1.0532 & -0.6859 \end{bmatrix}, \quad B = \begin{bmatrix} 0 & 0 & 0 \\ -0.120 & 1 & 0 \\ 0 & 0 & 0 \\ 4.419 & 0 & -1.665 \\ 1.575 & 0 & -0.0732 \end{bmatrix},$$

and $C = \begin{bmatrix} I_3 & \mathbf{0}_{3\times2} \end{bmatrix}$. It can be seen that the system has three inputs and three outputs. The following statements can be used to enter the system and its frequency response data.

```
>> A=[0,0,1.1320,0,-1;  0,-0.0538,-0.1712,0,0.0705;  0,0,0,1,0;
      0,0.0485,0,-0.8556,-1.013;0,-0.2909,0,1.0532,-0.6859];
   B=[0,0,0;  -0.120,1,0;  0,0,0;  4.419,0,-1.665;  1.575,0,-0.0732];
   C=eye(3,5);  G=ss(A,B,C,0);  w=logspace(-3,2);  Hg=mfrd(G,w);
```

If the target closed-loop transfer function matrix is selected

$$T_t(s) = \mathrm{diag}\left[\frac{3^2}{(s+3)^2}, \frac{3^2}{(s+3)^2}, \frac{10^2}{(s+10)^2}\right],$$

the model and its frequency response data can be obtained with

```
>> s=tf('s'); g=3^2/(s+3)^2;
   T=[g,0,0; 0,g,0; 0,0,10^2/(s+10)^2]; Ht=mfrd(T,w);
```

The target controller can be written as $K_t = G^{-1} T_t \left( I - T_t \right)^{-1}$. Bode magnitude plots can be obtained for each of its components as shown in Fig. 7-45. Loop structures are used, and in the loops, low-level commands are used to replace **bodemag**$(K_t, w)$ function calls, since the default plots obtained with **bodemag()** are not quite informative.

```
>> I=eye(3); Kt=inv(G)*T*inv(I-T); Hk=mfrd(Kt,w);
   for i=1:3, for j=1:3,
       subplot(3,3,3*(i-1)+j); G0=fget(w,Hk,[i,j]);
       semilogx(w,20*log10(abs(G0))), xlim([0.001,100])
   end, end
```

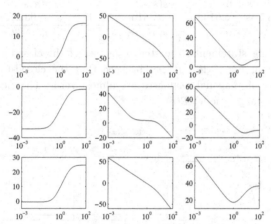

Fig. 7-45   Bode magnitude plots of the target controller.

It can be seen from the plots that there is no need to introduce integrators in the first column elements, since the initial magnitudes are flat. While in the other two columns, integrators are needed. For the first input, a pole at $s = -6$ should be selected due to the downward turning point, and to the second and third columns, the poles at $s = -6$ and $s = -30$ should be selected respectively. Thus, the following structure should be assigned to the target controller

$$k_{i1}(s) = \frac{v_{i1}^0 s + v_{i1}^1}{s + 6}, \quad k_{i2}(s) = \frac{v_{i2}^0 s^2 + v_{i2}^1 s + v_{i2}^2}{s(s+6)}, \quad k_{i3}(s) = \frac{v_{i3}^0 s^2 + v_{i3}^1 s + v_{i3}^2}{s(s+30)}.$$

It can be seen that the maximum order of the controller is 2. Besides, since $k_{i1}(s)$ are selected as first-order models, it is better to unify them as second-order models as $k_{i1}(s) = (0s^2 + v_{i1}^0 s + v_{i1}^1)/(0s^2 + s + 6)$, with the first values of both numerator and denominator assigned to 0's. Thus, the denominator and numerator matrices are

$$\boldsymbol{D} = \begin{bmatrix} 0 & 1 & 6 & 1 & 6 & 0 & 1 & 30 & 0 \\ 0 & 1 & 6 & 1 & 6 & 0 & 1 & 30 & 0 \\ 0 & 1 & 6 & 1 & 6 & 0 & 1 & 30 & 0 \end{bmatrix}, \boldsymbol{N}_0 = \begin{bmatrix} 0 & 1 & 1 & 1 & 1 & 1 & 1 & 1 & 1 \\ 0 & 1 & 1 & 1 & 1 & 1 & 1 & 1 & 1 \\ 0 & 1 & 1 & 1 & 1 & 1 & 1 & 1 & 1 \end{bmatrix},$$

where matrix $\boldsymbol{N}_0$ is used to indicate which component in the matrix needs to be optimized. The two matrices can be entered, and then the optimal controller can be designed

```
>> d=[0 1 6 1 6 0 1 30 0]; den=[d; d; d]; % three rows are the same
   num=[zeros(3,1) ones(3,8)]; % construct the numerator matrix
   N=fedmunds(w,Hg,Ht,num,den) % direct design of the optimal controller
```

The optimized numerator matrix $\boldsymbol{N}$ can be obtained as

$$\boldsymbol{N} = \begin{bmatrix} 0 & -6.5183 & -4.1806 & 0 & 0 & 1.9101 & -5.2977 & 6.3218 & 77.927 \\ 0 & -0.7822 & 0.1328 & 0 & 9 & 0.7134 & -0.6161 & 0.6246 & 22.991 \\ 0 & -17.3 & -5.6199 & 0 & 0 & 5.3316 & -99.857 & -63.275 & 104.83 \end{bmatrix}.$$

Thus, the transfer function matrix of the controller $\boldsymbol{K}(s)$ can be written as

$$\boldsymbol{K}(s) = \begin{bmatrix} \dfrac{-6.5183s - 4.1806}{s+6} & \dfrac{1.9101}{s(s+6)} & \dfrac{-5.2977s^2 + 6.3218s + 77.927}{s(s+30)} \\ \dfrac{-0.7822s + 0.1328}{s+6} & \dfrac{9s + 0.7134}{s(s+6)} & \dfrac{-0.6161s^2 + 0.6246s + 22.991}{s(s+30)} \\ \dfrac{-17.3s - 5.6199}{s+6} & \dfrac{5.3316}{s(s+6)} & \dfrac{-99.857s^2 - 63.275s + 104.83}{s(s+30)} \end{bmatrix}.$$

With the following statements, the step responses of the closed-loop system can be obtained, as shown in Fig. 7-46. It can be seen that the closed-loop system is fully decoupled, since the off-diagonal responses are almost zero. The closed-loop responses are very close to the target model $\boldsymbol{T}(s)$.

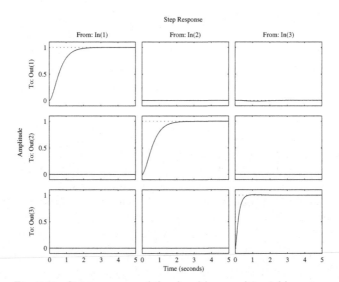

Fig. 7-46    Step responses of the closed-loop multivariable system.

```
>> d1=[1,6]; d2=[1 6 0]; d3=[1 30 0];
```

```
K11=tf(N(1,2:3),d1); K12=tf(N(1,6),d2); K13=tf(N(1,7:9),d3);
K21=tf(N(2,2:3),d1); K22=tf(N(2,5:6),d2); K23=tf(N(2,7:9),d3);
K31=tf(N(3,2:3),d1); K32=tf(N(3,6),d2); K33=tf(N(3,7:9),d3);
K=[K11 K12 K13; K21 K22 K23; K31 K32 K33]; Hk1=mfrd(K,w);
Gc=feedback(G*K,I); step(Gc,T,'--',5), figure;
for i=1:3, for j=1:3, subplot(3,3,3*(i-1)+j);
    G1=abs(fget(w,Hk,[i,j])); G2=abs(fget(w,Hk1,[i,j]));
    semilogx(w,20*log10(G1),w,20*log10(G2),'--'), xlim([1e-3,100])
end, end
```

The Bode magnitude plots of the actual controller and the target controller are shown in Fig. 7-47. It can be seen that most of the sub transfer functions agree very well. Although slight differences can be found in other sub transfer functions, especially in the third column, the global matching quality is satisfactory.

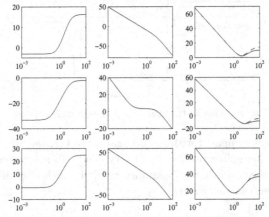

Fig. 7-47    Bode magnitude plots of the controller and the target controllers.

It can be seen from the above design that if diagonal target transfer function matrix $T(s)$ and suitable denominator $D$ are selected, perfect decoupling can be obtained. Assume that the same target matrix is used, while the $D$ matrix is not properly chosen, say $d_1(s) = s + 40$, $d_2(s) = s(s + 20)$, and $d_3(s) = s(s + 40)$, the following statements can be used to design optimal decoupling controller. The step responses of the closed-loop system can be obtained as shown in Fig. 7-48.

```
>> d1=[1,40]; d2=[1 20 0]; d3=[1 60 0];
   den=[0 d1,d2,d3]; den=[den; den; den];
   N0=[zeros(3,1) ones(3,8)]; N=fedmunds(w,Hg,Ht,N0,den)
   K11=tf(N(1,2:3),d1); K12=tf(N(1,4:6),d2); K13=tf(N(1,7:9),d3);
   K21=tf(N(2,2:3),d1); K22=tf(N(2,4:6),d2); K23=tf(N(2,7:9),d3);
   K31=tf(N(3,2:3),d1); K32=tf(N(3,4:6),d2); K33=tf(N(3,7:9),d3);
   K=[K11 K12 K13; K21 K22 K23; K31 K32 K33];
   Gc=feedback(G*K,I); step(Gc,T,'--',5),
```

with the coefficient matrix of the new controller

$$N = \begin{bmatrix} 0 & -31.81 & -37.137 & 0.1893 & -0.916 & 6.6776 & -11.711 & 16.984 & 152.83 \\ 0 & -3.858 & -2.1672 & -1.805 & 26.887 & 2.4319 & -1.339 & 1.4999 & 45.302 \\ 0 & -87.48 & -51.757 & 0.4892 & -2.697 & 17.362 & -192.63 & -121.07 & 205.77 \end{bmatrix}.$$

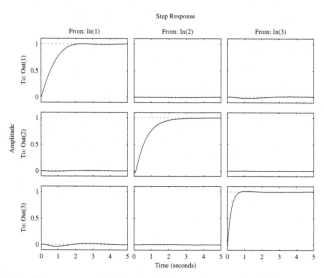

Fig. 7-48    Step response of the closed-loop system under the new controller.

It can be seen that compared with the original controller, the new controller is not as good, although the decoupling results is still very good. To get better results, the Bode magnitude plots in Fig. 7-45 should be studied carefully, such that suitable poles can be selected for the target controller $K_t(s)$.

### 7.5.3    *Optimal Controller Design with OCD Interface*

It can be seen earlier that the optimal controller design problems for single variable systems are solved with OCD interface. We are now trying to explore the use of OCD in the design of multivariable systems. Assume that after the static pre-compensator, the system possesses some diagonal dominance, individual loop control can be performed. Assume the $i$th input is used to excite the system alone, the global error signal is composed by weighting each channel of error together. The weighted ITAE criterion is established

$$J = \int_0^\infty t\Big[a_1|e_1(t)| + a_2|e_2(t)| + \cdots + a_m|e_m(t)|\Big]\mathrm{d}t. \qquad (7.56)$$

Now controller design for each individual loop is considered. It should be noted that when the $i$th input acts alone its weight can be selected as $a_i = 1$, while other weights should be selected as large values so as to reduce the disturbances from other loops. For instance, set $a_j = 10$.

**Example 7.18.** Consider again the multivariable delay system studied in Example 5.44. Weighted ITAE criterion can be used to design optimal PI controllers for the system. The Simulink model shown in Fig. 7-49 can be established, where $\boldsymbol{K}_\mathrm{p}$ is the static compensation matrix given in the example. The following statements can be used can be used to specify the models

```
>> a1=1; a2=10; u1=1; u2=0; um=1.5; Kp2=1; Ki2=1;
   Kp=[-0.41357,2.6537; 1.133,-0.32569];
```

OCD interface can be used to design $K_{\mathrm{p}_1}$ and $K_{\mathrm{i}_1}$ parameters, such that the controller can be found, with $K_{\mathrm{p}_1} = 3.8582$, and $K_{\mathrm{i}_1} = 1.0640$.

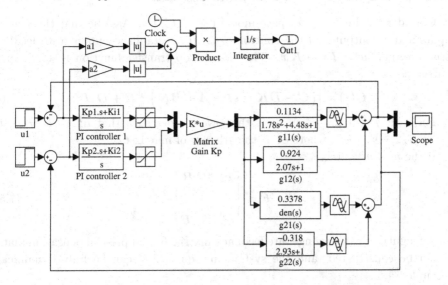

Fig. 7-49   Simulink model for the multivariable system   (file name: c7mmopt.mdl).

If the parameters can be modified to $\mathtt{a1} = 10$; $\mathtt{a2} = 1$; $\mathtt{u1} = 0$; $\mathtt{u2} = 1$, OCD interface can be used to design optimal PI controller for the second channel. The controller designed is $K_{\mathrm{p}_2} = 1.1487$, and $K_{\mathrm{i}_2} = 0.8133$. The step responses of the closed-loop system can be obtained as shown in Fig. 7-50. It can be seen that the control results are satisfactory.

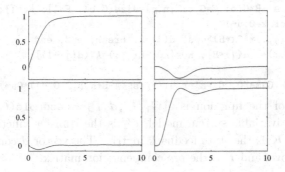

Fig. 7-50   Step responses of multivariable systems.

## 7.6   Decoupling Control of Multivariable Systems

In the analysis and design of multivariable systems, the coupling problems are the most difficult problems. Decoupling of multivariable systems is the major topic in system research. In the previous presentation, decoupling problems were already considered in some of the algorithms, while in others, decoupling was not considered. In this section, decoupling problem will be further explored.

### 7.6.1   *Decoupling Control with State Feedback*

Consider the linear state space model $(A, B, C, D)$. Assume that there are $m$ inputs and $m$ outputs. If the control signal $u$ is established upon state feedback structure, i.e., $u = \boldsymbol{\Gamma} r - K x$. The closed-loop transfer function matrix can be written as

$$G(s) = \left[ \left( C - DK \right) \left( sI - A + BK \right)^{-1} B + D \right] \boldsymbol{\Gamma}. \qquad (7.57)$$

For each $j = 1, 2, \cdots, m$, $d_j$ is the lowest order such that $c_j^T A^{d_j} B \neq 0$, for $d_j = 0, 1, 2, \cdots, n - 1$, where $c_j^T$ is the $j$th row of matrix $C$.

If the $m \times m$ matrix

$$F = \begin{bmatrix} c_1^T A^{d_1} B \\ \vdots \\ c_m^T A^{d_m} B \end{bmatrix} \qquad (7.58)$$

is nonsingular, the following state feedback matrix $K$ and pre-compensation matrix $\boldsymbol{\Gamma}$ can be constructed, and the system in Eqn. (7.57) can be fully dynamically decoupled[4].

$$\boldsymbol{\Gamma} = F^{-1}, \quad K = \boldsymbol{\Gamma} \begin{bmatrix} c_1^T A^{d_1+1} \\ \vdots \\ c_m^T A^{d_m+1} \end{bmatrix}. \qquad (7.59)$$

Based on the algorithm, the following MATLAB function can be written as

```
function [G1,K,d,Gam]=decouple(G)
G=ss(G); A=G.a; B=G.b; C=G.c; [n,m]=size(G.b); F=[]; KO=[];
for j=1:m, for k=0:n-1
    if norm(C(j,:)*A^k*B)>eps, d(j)=k; break; end, end
    F=[F; C(j,:)*A^d(j)*B]; KO=[KO; C(j,:)*A^(d(j)+1)];
end
Gam=inv(F); K=Gam*KO; G1=minreal(tf(ss(A-B*K,B,C,G.d))*Gam);
```

The syntax of the function is $[G_1, K, d, \boldsymbol{\Gamma}] = \text{decouple}(G)$, where $G$ is the original multivariable system model, $G_1$ is the transfer function matrix after decoupling, and $K$ is the state feedback matrix. The vector $d$ contains the values of $d_j$ defined above, and $\boldsymbol{\Gamma}$ is the pre-compensation matrix.

**Example 7.19.** Consider the two-input, two-output system given below

$$\begin{cases} \dot{x} = \begin{bmatrix} 2.25 & -5 & -1.25 & -0.5 \\ 2.25 & -4.25 & -1.25 & -0.25 \\ 0.25 & -0.5 & -1.25 & -1 \\ 1.25 & -1.75 & -0.25 & -0.75 \end{bmatrix} x + \begin{bmatrix} 4 & 6 \\ 2 & 4 \\ 2 & 2 \\ 0 & 2 \end{bmatrix} u \\[4mm] y = \begin{bmatrix} 0 & 0 & 0 & 1 \\ 0 & 2 & 0 & 2 \end{bmatrix} x. \end{cases}$$

The following commands can be used to design decoupling matrices when the system model is entered into MATLAB workspace

```
>> Athen =[2.25, -5, -1.25, -0.5;  2.25, -4.25, -1.25, -0.25;
     0.25, -0.5, -1.25,-1;  1.25, -1.75, -0.25, -0.75];
   B=[4, 6; 2, 4; 2, 2; 0, 2]; C=[0, 0, 0, 1; 0, 2, 0, 2];
   G=ss(A,B,C,0); [G1,K,d,Gam]=decouple(G)
```

The state feedback matrix $K$ and matrix $\Gamma$ are obtained, and it can be seen that the off-diagonal components in transfer function matrix $G_1(s)$ is extremely small, and can be neglected. The system can be regarded completely decoupled.

$$G_1(s) = \begin{bmatrix} 1/s & 0 \\ -8.9 \times 10^{-16}/s & 1/s \end{bmatrix}, \quad K = \frac{1}{8}\begin{bmatrix} -1 & -3 & -3 & 5 \\ 5 & -7 & -1 & -3 \end{bmatrix}, \quad \Gamma = \begin{bmatrix} -1.5 & 0.25 \\ 0.5 & 0 \end{bmatrix}.$$

With the state feedback matrix $K$ and pre-compensation matrix $\Gamma$, the system is fully decoupled. The decoupled transfer function matrix can be expressed as

$$G_1 = \text{diag}\left(\left[1/s^{d_1+1}, \cdots, 1/s^{d_m+1}\right]\right). \tag{7.60}$$

With decoupling matrices $(K, \Gamma)$, the closed-loop structure can be constructed as shown in Fig. 7-51. The part within the box is fully decoupled, and the outer loop controller $G_c(s)$ can be designed with individual channel methods.

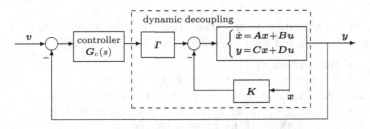

Fig. 7-51   Decoupling state feedback control structure.

## 7.6.2   *Decoupling of State Feedback with Pole Placement*

The dynamical decoupling algorithm can only be used to decouple the system into diagonal integrator type transfer function matrix, and the design for integrator type of system are usually very complicated. If state feedback decoupling strategy is still used, with $u = \Gamma r - Kx$, the diagonal components of decoupled system may be transformed into the following form

$$
G_{K,\Gamma}(s) = \begin{bmatrix} \dfrac{1}{s^{d_1+1}+a_{1,1}s^{d_1}+\cdots+a_{1,d_1+1}} & & \\ & \ddots & \\ & & \dfrac{1}{s^{d_m+1}+a_{m,1}s^{d_m}+\cdots+a_{m,d_m+1}} \end{bmatrix}, \quad (7.61)
$$

where the definitions of $d_i$, $i = 1, 2, \cdots, m$ are exactly the same as given earlier, and each polynomial coefficients $s^{d_i+1} + a_{i,1}s^{d_i} + \cdots + a_{i,d_i+1}$ can be designed with pole placement methods.

The standard transfer functions can be used to construct the expected transfer function models. The $n$th order standard transfer function can be constructed as[16, 17]

$$
T(s) = \frac{a_n}{s^n + a_1 s^{n-1} + a_2 s^{n-2} + \cdots + a_{n-1}s + a_n}, \quad (7.62)
$$

where the optimal denominator polynomial coefficients $a_i$ of $T(s)$ under ITAE criterion are given in Table. 7.6.2.

Table 7-1  Optimal denominator coefficients of standard transfer functions.

| $n$ | overshoot | $\omega_n t_s$ | monic denominator polynomials |
|---|---|---|---|
| 1 | | | $s + \omega_n$ |
| 2 | 4.6% | 6.0 | $s^2+1.41\omega_n s+\omega_n^2$ |
| 3 | 2% | 7.6 | $s^3+1.75\omega_n s^2+2.15\omega_n^2 s+\omega_n^3$ |
| 4 | 1.9% | 5.4 | $s^4+2.1\omega_n s^3+3.4\omega_n^2 s^2+ 2.7\omega_n^3 s+\omega_n^4$ |
| 5 | 2.1% | 6.6 | $s^5+2.8\omega_n s^4+5.0\omega_n^2 s^3+5.5\omega_n^3 s^2+3.4\omega_n^4 s+\omega_n^5$ |
| 6 | 5% | 7.8 | $s^6+3.25\omega_n s^5+6.6\omega_n^2 s^4+8.6\omega_n^3 s^3+7.45\omega_n^4 s^2+3.95\omega_n^5 s+\omega_n^6$ |
| 7 | 10.9% | 10.0 | $s^7+4.475\omega_n s^6+10.42\omega_n^2 s^5+15.08\omega_n^3 s^4+15.54\omega_n^4 s^3+10.64\omega_n^5 s^2+4.58\omega_n^6 s+\omega_n^7$ |

Based on the algorithm given earlier, the $n$th order standard transfer function model can be constructed with the following MATLAB function

```
function G=std_tf(wn,n)
M=[1,1,0,0,0,0,0 0; 1,1.41,1,0,0,0,0 0;
   1,1.75,2.15,1,0,0,0 0; 1,2.1,3.4,2.7,1,0,0 0;
   1,2.8,5.0,5.5,3.4,1,0 0; 1,3.25,6.6,8.6,7.45,3.95,1,0;
   1,4.475,10.42,15.08,15.54,10.64,4.58,1];
G=tf(wn^n,M(n,1:n+1).*(wn.^[0:n]));
```

The syntax of the function is $T = \mathtt{std\_tf}(\omega_n, n)$ , with $\omega_n$ the natural frequency, and $n$ is the expected order. The returned variable $T$ is the standard transfer function.

Define a matrix $E$ such that each row can be written as $e_i^{\mathrm{T}} = c_i^{\mathrm{T}}A^{d_i}B$, while each row $f_i^{\mathrm{T}}$ of the other matrix $F$ are defined as

$$
f_i^{\mathrm{T}} = c_i^{\mathrm{T}}\Big( A^{d_i+1} + a_{i,1}A^{d_i} + \cdots + a_{i,d_i+1}I \Big). \quad (7.63)
$$

Thus, the state feedback matrix $K$ and the pre-compensation matrix $\Gamma$ can be written as

$$\Gamma = E^{-1}, \quad K = \Gamma F. \tag{7.64}$$

Based on this algorithm, incorporate with the standard transfer functions, the dynamic decoupling algorithm with pole placement can be written as

```
function [G1,K,d,Gam]=decouple_pp(G,wn)
G=ss(G); A=G.a; B=G.b; C=G.c; [n,m]=size(G.b); E=[]; F=[];
for i=1:m, for j=0:n-1,
    if norm(C(i,:)*A^j*B)>eps, d(i)=j; break, end, end
    g1=std_tf(wn,d(i)+1); [n1,d1]=tfdata(g1,'v');
    F=[F; C(i,:)*polyvalm(d1,A)]; E=[E; C(i,:)*A^d(i)*B];
end
Gam=inv(E); K=Gam*F; G1=minreal(tf(ss(A-B*K,B,C,G.d))*Gam);
```

The syntax of the function is $[G_1, K, d, \Gamma] = \text{decouple\_pp}(G, \omega_n)$ , where $\omega_n$ is the natural frequency expected. Other arguments are the same as those in `decouple()`.

**Example 7.20.** Consider the multivariable control system in Example 7.19. Select the natural frequency $\omega_n = 5$, the following statements can be used to enter the system model, then function `decouple_pp()` can be used to design the decoupling controller

```
>> A=[2.25, -5, -1.25, -0.5; 2.25, -4.25, -1.25, -0.25;
      0.25, -0.5, -1.25,-1; 1.25, -1.75, -0.25, -0.75];
   B=[4, 6; 2, 4; 2, 2; 0, 2]; C=[0, 0, 0, 1; 0, 2, 0, 2];
   G=ss(A,B,C,0); [G1,K,d,Gam]=decouple_pp(G,5)
```

The feedback matrix $K$, pre-compensation matrix and decoupled system can be obtained

$$K = \frac{1}{8}\begin{bmatrix} -1 & 17 & -3 & -35 \\ 5 & -7 & -1 & 17 \end{bmatrix}, \quad \Gamma = \begin{bmatrix} -1.5 & 0.25 \\ 0.5 & 0 \end{bmatrix}, \quad G_1(s) = \begin{bmatrix} 1/(s+5) & 0 \\ \epsilon & 1/(s+5) \end{bmatrix},$$

where $\epsilon$ is a transfer function with coefficient of $10^{-14}$.

**Example 7.21.** Consider the $3 \times 3$ state space model studied in Example 7.17. Select a natural frequency of $\omega_n = 3$, the following statements can be used to design dynamic decoupling system

```
>> A=[0,0,1.1320,0,-1; 0,-0.0538,-0.1712,0,0.0705; 0,0,0,1,0;
      0,0.0485,0,-0.8556,-1.013;0,-0.2909,0,1.0532,-0.6859];
   B=[0,0,0; -0.120,1,0; 0,0,0; 4.419,0,-1.665; 1.575,0,-0.0732];
   C=eye(3,5); G=ss(A,B,C,0);
   [G1,K,d,Gam]=decouple_pp(G,3), step(G1,10)
```

The decoupling matrices are

$$K = \begin{bmatrix} -6.5183 & -0.2122 & -3.7546 & -0.1645 & 2.5991 \\ -0.7822 & 2.9207 & -0.6218 & -0.0197 & 0.3824 \\ -17.3 & -0.5924 & -15.37 & -2.4633 & 7.5066 \end{bmatrix}, \quad \Gamma = \begin{bmatrix} -0.7243 & 0 & -0.0318 \\ -0.0869 & 1 & -0.0038 \\ -1.9222 & 0 & -0.6851 \end{bmatrix}.$$

The decoupled system is very close to the diagonal matrix

$$G_1 = \text{diag} \left( \frac{1}{s^2 + 4.23s + 9}, \frac{1}{s + 3}, \frac{1}{s^2 + 4.23s + 9} \right).$$

The closed-loop step response is obtained as shown in Fig. 7-52. It can be seen that the decoupling results are satisfactory.

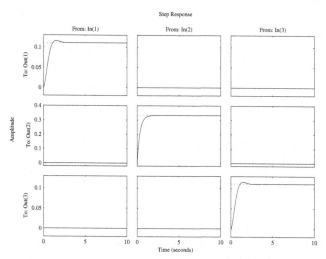

Fig. 7-52   Step responses of multivariable system.

If the states of the systems cannot be directly measured, observers can be designed to reconstruct the states and the decoupling controllers can be used on the reconstructed states.

## 7.7   Problems

(1) Assume that the plant and a controller model are given by

$$G(s) = \frac{210(s + 1.5)}{(s + 1.75)(s + 16)(s + 1.5 \pm \text{j}3)}, \quad G_c(s) = \frac{52.5(s + 1.5)}{s + 14.86}.$$

Please observe the dynamic behavior of the system under the controller. Find the gain and phase margins of the compensated system. If the control behavior is not satisfactory, please give suggestions to improve the dynamic behaviors of the system.

(2) For the following plant models

(i)  $G(s) = \dfrac{16}{s(s + 1)(s + 2)(s + 8)}$,   (ii)  $G(s) = \dfrac{2(s + 1)}{s(47.5s + 1)(0.0625s + 1)^2}$,

please design lead–lag compensator, and validate whether the expected phase margins and crossover frequencies can be reached. Try different phase margins and crossover frequencies to improve the behavior of the closed-loop system, and verify the results with the controllers.

(3) Assume that the state space model of a linear system is given by

$$\dot{x}(t) = \begin{bmatrix} 0 & 1 & 0 & 0 \\ 0 & 0 & 1 & 0 \\ -3 & 1 & 2 & 3 \\ 2 & 1 & 0 & 0 \end{bmatrix} x(t) + \begin{bmatrix} 1 & 0 \\ 2 & 1 \\ 3 & 2 \\ 4 & 3 \end{bmatrix} u(t).$$

Select weighting matrices $Q = \text{diag}(1, 2, 3, 4)$ and $R = I_2$. Design an optimal linear quadratic regulator. Find the close-loop pole positions, and draw the step responses to the states.

(4) Consider the system model in Example 7.2, where a controller $K$ was designed. It is known that there are many solutions to the corresponding Riccati equation and the controller was designed by one of them. Try to get other controllers and compare the results.

(5) A two-input two-output system is given by

$$\dot{x}(t) = \begin{bmatrix} 2.25 & -5 & -1.25 & -0.5 \\ 2.25 & -4.25 & -1.25 & -0.25 \\ 0.25 & -0.5 & -1.25 & -1 \\ 1.25 & -1.75 & -0.25 & -0.75 \end{bmatrix} x(t) + \begin{bmatrix} 4 & 6 \\ 2 & 4 \\ 2 & 2 \\ 0 & 2 \end{bmatrix} u(t), y(t) = \begin{bmatrix} 0 & 0 & 0 & 1 \\ 0 & 2 & 0 & 2 \end{bmatrix} x(t).$$

Assume that the weighting matrices $Q = \text{diag}([1, 4, 3, 2])$ and $R = I_2$, design an optimal quadratic regulator and draw the step responses of the system. In order to improve the behavior of the closed-loop systems, how should the weighting matrix $Q$ be modified?

(6) Assume that the state space model is given by

$$\dot{x}(t) = \begin{bmatrix} -0.2 & 0.5 & 0 & 0 & 0 \\ 0 & -0.5 & 1.6 & 0 & 0 \\ 0 & 0 & -14.3 & 85.8 & 0 \\ 0 & 0 & 0 & -33.3 & 100 \\ 0 & 0 & 0 & 0 & -10 \end{bmatrix} x(t) + \begin{bmatrix} 0 \\ 0 \\ 0 \\ 0 \\ 30 \end{bmatrix} u(t), \ y(t) = [1, 0, 0, 0, 0] x(t).$$

Please find all the open-loop poles and zeros. If one wants to place the poles to $P = [-1, -2, -3, -4, -5]$, please design the pole placement controller. Further, please find the closed-loop step response of the closed-loop system. If you want to further improve the dynamic responses, please modify the positions of the expected poles and then design the controller again. Please also construct the observer-based controller, and compare the responses.

(7) For the given plant model

$$\dot{x}(t) = \begin{bmatrix} 2 & 1 & 0 & 0 \\ 0 & 2 & 0 & 0 \\ 0 & 0 & -1 & 0 \\ 0 & 0 & 0 & -1 \end{bmatrix} x(t) + \begin{bmatrix} 0 \\ 1 \\ 1 \\ 1 \end{bmatrix} u(t), \ y(t) = [1, 0, 1, 0] x(t).$$

Please design a state feedback vector $k$, such that the closed-loop poles can be placed at $(-2, -2, -1, -1)$. Is it possible to place all the closed-loop poles to move to $-2$? Please explain the reasons.

(8) Please design state observers to the following plant model

$$\dot{x}(t) = \begin{bmatrix} 0 & 0 & 1 & 0 & 0 \\ 1 & 0 & 0 & 0 & 0 \\ 0 & 1 & 0 & 1 & -1 \\ 0 & 1 & 1 & 1 & 0 \\ 0 & 0 & 1 & 0 & 0 \end{bmatrix} x(t) + \begin{bmatrix} 1 \\ 2 \\ 1 \\ 0 \\ 1 \end{bmatrix} u(t), \quad y(t) = [0,0,0,1,1]x(t).$$

Please analyze the observer designed, and see whether the observer is successful. If not, please redesign the observer until satisfactory results are obtained.

(9) The mathematical model of an inverted pendulum is

$$\ddot{x} = \frac{u + ml \sin \theta \dot{\theta}^2 - mg \cos \theta \sin \theta}{M + m - m \cos^2 \theta},$$

$$\ddot{\theta} = \frac{u \cos \theta - (M + m)g \sin \theta + ml \sin \theta \cos \theta \dot{\theta}}{ml \cos^2 \theta - (M + m)l},$$

where $m = M = 0.5$kg, g= 9.81m/s$^2$, $l = 0.3$m. Please design a controller to generate proper input signal $u(t)$, such that the inverted pendulum remains at upright position, i.e., $\theta = 90°$.

(10) Consider the transfer function matrix of a two-input, two-output system

$$G(s) = \begin{bmatrix} \dfrac{s+4}{(s+1)(s+5)} & \dfrac{1}{5s+1} \\ \dfrac{s+1}{s^2+10s+100} & \dfrac{2}{2s+1} \end{bmatrix}.$$

Please design a pre-compensation matrix to implement good decoupling results. Select reasonable target model and design decoupling controllers using parameter optimization method.

(11) Since there exists coupling in multivariable systems, PID controllers cannot normally be designed for individual loops. Pre-compensation should be used first. Consider the diagonal dominant method used in the model in Example 5.43. Assume the plant model is given by

$$G(s) = \begin{bmatrix} \dfrac{0.806s + 0.264}{s^2 + 1.15s + 0.202} & \dfrac{-15s - 1.42}{s^3 + 12.8s^2 + 13.6s + 2.36} \\ [3mm] \dfrac{1.95s^2 + 2.12s + 0.49}{s^3 + 9.15s^2 + 9.39s + 1.62} & \dfrac{7.15s^2 + 25.8s + 9.35}{s^4 + 20.8s^3 + 116.4s^2 + 111.6s + 18.8} \end{bmatrix},$$

and assume the pre-compensation matrix is

$$K_{\mathrm{p}} = \begin{bmatrix} 0.3610 & 0.4500 \\ -1.1300 & 1.0000 \end{bmatrix},$$

with the use of individual loop PID controllers, and observe the control results.

(12) Consider the 3 × 3 model in Example 7.17. The design method seems to be rather complicated, since a target model should be selected, and the structures of the target controller should be specified by analyzing the Bode plots. Please use optimal PID controller design method and compare the control results.

(13) Design optimal PID controllers for the following multivariable plants [18]

$$\text{(i)} \quad G_1(s) = \begin{bmatrix} \dfrac{12.8e^{-s}}{16.7s+1} & \dfrac{-18.9e^{-3s}}{21s+1} \\ \dfrac{6.6e^{-7s}}{10.9s+1} & \dfrac{-19.6e^{-3s}}{14.4s+1} \end{bmatrix}, \quad \text{(ii)} \quad G_2(s) = \begin{bmatrix} \dfrac{-0.2e^{-s}}{7s+1} & \dfrac{1.3e^{-0.3s}}{7s+1} \\ \dfrac{-2.8se^{-1.8s}}{9.5s+1} & \dfrac{4.3e^{-0.35s}}{9.2s+1} \end{bmatrix},$$

$$\text{(iii)} \quad G_3(s) = \begin{bmatrix} \dfrac{-1e^{-s}}{6s+1} & \dfrac{1.5e^{-s}}{15s+1} & \dfrac{0.5e^{-s}}{10s+1} \\ \dfrac{0.5e^{-2s}}{s^2+4s+1} & \dfrac{0.5e^{-3s}}{s^2+4s+1} & \dfrac{0.513e^{-s}}{s+1} \\ \dfrac{0.375e^{-3s}}{10s+1} & \dfrac{-2e^{-2s}}{10s+1} & \dfrac{-2e^{-3s}}{3s+1} \end{bmatrix}.$$

(14) Consider the following two-input, two-output systems [19]

$$\text{(i)} \quad A = \begin{bmatrix} -1 & 1 & 1 & 1 \\ 6 & 0 & -3 & 1 \\ -1 & 1 & 1 & 2 \\ 2 & -2 & -2 & 0 \end{bmatrix}, B = \begin{bmatrix} 0 & 0 \\ 1 & 0 \\ 0 & 0 \\ 0 & 1 \end{bmatrix}, C = \begin{bmatrix} 2 & 0 & -1 & 0 \\ -1 & 0 & 1 & 0 \end{bmatrix},$$

$$\text{(ii)} \quad A = \begin{bmatrix} 3 & 1 & 0 \\ 0 & 0 & -1 \\ 0 & 1 & -1 \end{bmatrix}, B = \begin{bmatrix} 0 & 0 \\ 1 & 0 \\ 0 & 1 \end{bmatrix}, C = \begin{bmatrix} 2 & -1 & 1 \\ 0 & 2 & 1 \end{bmatrix},$$

$$\text{(iii)} \quad G(s) = \begin{bmatrix} \dfrac{3}{s^2+2} & \dfrac{2}{s^2+s+1} \\ \dfrac{4s+1}{s^2+2s+1} & \dfrac{1}{s} \end{bmatrix}.$$

Please design dynamic decoupling controllers using state feedback method. Also, design pole placement decoupling methods and comments on the impact of natural frequency selection on control results.

## Bibliography and References

[1] Xue D Y. Design and analysis of feedback control systems with MATLAB. Beijing: Tsinghua University Press, 2000. (In Chinese)

[2] Anderson B D O, Moore J B. Linear optimal control. Englewood Cliffs: Prentice-Hall, 1971

[3] Franklin G F, Powell J D, Workman M. Digital control of dynamic systems. Reading MA: Addison Wesley, 3rd edition, 1988

[4] Balasubramanian R. Continuous time controller design. In: IEE Control Engineering Series, Volume 39. London: Peter Peregrinus Ltd, 1989

[5] Kautskey J, Nichols N K, Van Dooren P. Robust pole-assignment in linear state feedback. International Journal of Control, 1985, 41(5):1129–1155

[6] Saad Y. Projection and deflation methods for partial pole assignment in linear state feedback control. IEEE Transaction on Automatic Control, 1988, AC-33:290–297

[7] Xue D Y, Chen Y Q. MATLAB solutions to mathematical problems in control. Beijing: Tsinghua University Press, 2007. (In Chinese)

[8] Rosenbrock H H. Computer-aided control system design. New York: Academic Press, 1974

[9] MacFarlane A G J, Kouvaritakis B. A design technique for linear multivariable feedback systems. International Journal of Control, 1977, 25:837–874

[10] Hung Y S, MacFarlane A G J. Multivariable feedback: a quasi-classical approach. In: Lecture Notes in Control and Information Sciences, Volume 40. New York: Springer-Verlag, 1982

[11] Mayne D Q. Sequential design of linear multivariable systems. Proceedings of IEE, Part D, 1979, 126:568–572

[12] Edmunds J M. Control system design and analysis using closed-loop Nyquist and Bode arrays. International Journal of Control, 1979, 30:773–802

[13] Hawkins D J. Pseudodiagonalisation and the inverse Nyquist array method. Proceedings of IEE, Part D, 1972, 119:337–342

[14] Ford M P, Daly K C. Dominance improvement by pseudodecoupling. Proceedings of IEE, Part D, 1979, 126:1316–1320

[15] Maciejowski J M. Multivariable feedback design. Wokingham: Addison-Wesley, 1989

[16] Graham F D, Lathrop R C. The synthesis of "optimum" transient repsponses — criteria and standard forms. AIEE Transactions, 1953, 73:273–288. Zurich, Switzerland

[17] Dorf R C, Bishop R H. Modern Control Systems. Upper Saddle River, NJ: Prentice-Hall, 9th edition, 2001

[18] Johnson M A, Moradi M H. PID control — new identification and design methods. London: Springer, 2005

[19] Zheng D Z. Linear systems theory. Beijing: Tsinghua University Press, 1980. (In Chinese)

# Chapter 8

# Parameter Tuning of PID Controllers

PID control is one of the earliest developed control strategies[1]. Since the design methods and control structures are simple and straightforward, it is quite suitable for industrial applications. Besides, as the design of PID controllers does not require precise plant models, and the control results are usually satisfactory, it becomes the most widely used controller type in industry. Over the recent 30 years, theoretical research and applications of PID controllers recalled the attention of academic researchers. The automatic tuning of PID controllers proposed by Karl Åström exhibited advanced behaviors[2], and this kind of strategy isalso supplied by hardware manufacturers such that they are widely used in industrial control[3–5].

There are large varieties of PID controllers, such as continuous, discrete, with different structures. They can either be designed in MATLAB with new functions in Control System Toolbox or by the blocks provided in Simulink. They can also be established with low-level blocks.

In Section 8.1, the mathematical representations of PID controllers are given, and various PID controller structures are presented. The MATLAB representations of PID controllers are provided. Since a large variety of PID controller tuning algorithms are based on first-order plus dead-time (FOPDT) plant models, the FOPDT model approximation are given in Section 8.2, and this can be regarded as the basis for PID controller tuning algorithms. In Section 8.3, some classical PID controller tuning algorithms based on FOPDT plants are presented, including Ziegler–Nichols method and its variations, Coon–Cohen parameter tuning method, Chien–Hrones–Reswick algorithm. In Section 8.4, a FOPDT plant-based PID controller tuning interface, PID Tuner, is described, and different tuning algorithms can be compared in the interface. In Section 8.5, some of the PID controller tuning algorithms for other types of plant models are presented, and interactive MATLAB interface for PID controller design is illustrated. In Section 8.6, an optimal PID controller interface, OptimPID, developed by the authors is presented. If the plant model can be described by Simulink, the optimal PID controller can be designed directly with the interface.

## 8.1    Introduction to PID Controller Design

### 8.1.1    *Continuous PID Controllers*

PID controller is a commonly used series controller. In practice, the output signal of the PID controller is followed by the nonlinearity of actuator saturation, and the PID controlled system structure is given in Fig. 8-1. In control systems, their may exist various disturbance signals, such as load disturbances, parameters changes in the plants. These disturbances are classified into the disturbance signal. Besides, in practical control systems, the sensors are inevitable and are subjected to noises, usually high-frequency noises. These noises are classified into the measurement noise.

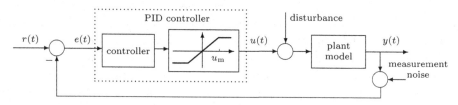

Fig. 8-1    Basic structure of PID control.

### 1. Parallel PID controllers
The typical form of continuous PID controller is

$$u(t) = K_\mathrm{p}e(t) + K_\mathrm{i} \int_0^t e(\tau)\mathrm{d}\tau + K_\mathrm{d}\frac{\mathrm{d}e(t)}{\mathrm{d}t}, \tag{8.1}$$

where $K_\mathrm{p}$, $K_\mathrm{i}$ and $K_\mathrm{d}$ are respectively the weights to the error signal $e(t)$, the integral and the derivative of $e(t)$. The weighted sum of these signals is used to drive the plant model. If the controller is well designed, the control signal may adjust the actuating signal $u(t)$ to the plant model and achieve good results.

The system in Fig. 8-1 is, in fact, a nonlinear system. In approximate linear system analysis method, the limit parameter of saturation is $\infty$, i.e., nonlinear part of saturation is neglected.

The PID control structure is simple where the three weighting coefficients $K_\mathrm{p}$, $K_\mathrm{i}$ and $K_\mathrm{d}$ have significant physical meanings. The proportional part acts on the current error signal. If an error signal occurs, the controller reacts to it to reduce the error. Normally speaking, when the value of $K_\mathrm{p}$ is large, the error will be small and the sensitivity to load disturbance will be reduced. However, it is more sensitive when $K_\mathrm{p}$ continues to increase and the closed-loop system will go unstable. The integral portion acts on the past values of the error signal, and the static error will be removed with integral controller. When the value of $K_\mathrm{i}$ is increased, it likely leads to an increase in the overshoot, and causes oscillation in the system output. If $K_\mathrm{i}$ is selected as small values, the speed of the system to approach steady-state value will decrease. The derivative portion in the controller acts on the derivative, or the change rate of the error signal. It is to some extent related to the future values of the error signal. The increase in the values of $K_d$ will speed up the system responses, and reduce settling time. However, if the value of $K_d$ is too large, problems may occur when subjected to system noises or large time delays.

The Laplace transform of continuous PID controller can be written as

$$G_c(s) = K_p + \frac{K_i}{s} + K_d s. \tag{8.2}$$

The pure derivative actions cannot be used in the controller in practice. The one with first-order lag should be used to approximate the derivative action

$$G_c(s) = K_p + \frac{K_i}{s} + \frac{K_d s}{T_f s + 1}, \tag{8.3}$$

where $T_f$ is the filter constant. This type of PID controller can be described by the `pid()` function in the Control System Toolbox, and can be used to directly enter the parallel PID controller, with $G_c = \mathtt{pid}(K_p, K_i, K_d, T_f)$ . Other types of PID controller can also be expressed with the function. For instance, if $K_d$ is zero, PI controller can be specified.

## 2. Standard PID controllers

In many process control literatures, PID controllers are often described by

$$u(t) = K_p \left[ e(t) + \frac{1}{T_i} \int_0^t e(\tau) d\tau + T_d \frac{de(t)}{dt} \right], \tag{8.4}$$

and this kind of controller is also known as the standard PID controller. Comparing Eqns. (8.1) and (8.4), it is easily found that $K_i = K_p/T_i$, $K_d = K_p T_d$. Thus, the two kinds of controllers are equivalent. In Control System Toolbox, this types of PID controller can be entered with $G_c = \mathtt{pidstd}(K_p, T_i, T_d, N)$ .

Laplace transformation to Eqn. (8.4) may derive the transfer function model of the controller

$$G_c(s) = K_p \left( 1 + \frac{1}{T_i s} + T_d s \right). \tag{8.5}$$

In order to avoid pure derivative action, the transfer function with first-order lag should be used to approximate pure derivative action. Thus, the PID controller can be written as

$$G_c(s) = K_p \left( 1 + \frac{1}{T_i s} + \frac{T_d s}{T_d/N s + 1} \right), \tag{8.6}$$

where $N \to \infty$ represents pure derivative operation. In practical applications, it is not necessary to select extremely large values for $N$, normally $N$ as 10 may well approximate the pure derivative action[6].

Although Eqns. (8.2) and (8.6) can be used to represent PID controllers, their applications are different. In literatures, the latter one is mainly used, while in optimization processes, the former one is more suitable.

### 8.1.2   Discrete PID Controllers

If the value of the sampling interval $T$ is small, the derivative and integral of the error signal at time $kT$ can be approximated with the backward formula

$$\frac{de(t)}{dt} \approx \frac{e(kT) - e[(k-1)T]}{T}, \tag{8.7}$$

$$\int_0^{kT} e(t)dt \approx T \sum_{i=0}^{k} e(iT) = \int_0^{(k-1)T} e(t)dt + Te(kT). \tag{8.8}$$

Substituting them into Eqn. (8.1), the discrete form of the PID controller is

$$u(kT) = K_p e(kT) + K_i T \sum_{m=0}^{k} e(mT) + \frac{K_d}{T} \Big[ e(kT) - e[(k-1)T] \Big]. \tag{8.9}$$

The brief notation of the controller can be denoted by

$$u_k = K_p e_k + K_i T \sum_{m=0}^{k} e_m + \frac{K_d}{T}(e_k - e_{k-1}). \tag{8.10}$$

This controller is referred to as backward Euler discrete-time PID controller. Similarly, forward Euler discrete PID controller can be expressed by

$$u_k = K_p e_k + K_i T \sum_{m=0}^{k+1} e_m + \frac{K_d}{T}(e_{k+1} - e_k). \tag{8.11}$$

With the backward Euler algorithm, the discrete-time PID controller is

$$G_c(z) = K_p + \frac{K_i T z}{z-1} + \frac{K_d(z-1)}{Tz}, \tag{8.12}$$

while the forward Euler discrete-time PID controller is

$$G_c(z) = K_p + \frac{K_i T}{z-1} + \frac{K_d(z-1)}{T}. \tag{8.13}$$

Discrete PID controllers can be represented in MATLAB, with the Control System Toolbox functions `pid()` and `pidstd()`, where the sampling interval $T$ can be assigned, with $G_c = \mathtt{pidstd}(K_p, T_i, T_d, N, T)$ . Besides, discrete algorithm such as forward and backward should also be specified.

**Example 8.1.** Consider the following PID controllers

$$C_1(s) = 1.5 + \frac{5.2}{s} + 3.5s, \quad C_2(s) = 1.5 \left( 1 + \frac{3.5s}{1 + 0.035s} \right),$$

$$C_3(z) = 1.5 + \frac{5.2}{z-1} + 3.5(z-1), \quad C_4(z) = 1.5 \left( 1 + \frac{z}{5.2(z-1)} + \frac{3.5(z-1)}{z} \right),$$

where the sampling interval is assumed to be $T = 0.1$ s. Analyzing the above controllers, it can be seen that $C_1(s)$ is an ideal parallel PID controller, with filter constant $T_f$ as zero. Controller $C_2(s)$ is a standard PD controller, with integral constant $T_i = \infty$, and $N = 100$. $C_3(z)$ is an ideal discrete parallel PID controller, with $T_f = 0$. Controller $C_4(z)$ is an ideal standard discrete-time PID controller, with backward integral, and $N = \infty$. These controllers can be entered into MATLAB with

```
>> C1=pid(1.5,5.2,3.5,0); C2=pidstd(1.5,inf,3.5,100);
   C3=pid(1.5,52,0.35,0,0.1);
   C4=pidstd(1.5,52,0.35,inf,0.1,'IFormula','backward');
```

### 8.1.3  *Variations of PID Controllers*

Apart from the classical PID controllers, different variations of PID controllers are used in practice. Some of the commonly variations are

#### 1. PID controllers with integral separation

The purpose of the integral action in PID control is that it may eliminate steady-state errors. However, the side effect of integral action may contribute to the increase of overshoot. Thus, in practical control systems, a straightforward solution is that at the starting stage of control if the steady-state error is large, the integral action can be turned off to speed up the response. When the steady-state error is small enough, integral action is turned on to eliminate steady-state errors. This type of PID controller is referred to as PID controllers with integral separation. If this kind of control structure is used, the control system may not be analyzed with linear control systems approaches.

#### 2. Discrete-time incremental PID controllers

Consider the discrete-time PID controller in Eqn. (8.9). The integral part depends on all the error values in the past. Thus, it might be complicated to implement the integral part, since all the past values should be memorized. A better way is to compute the increment of the controller $\Delta u_k = u_k - u_{k-1}$

$$u_k - u_{k-1} = K_p\Big(e_k - e_{k-1}\Big) + K_i T e_k + \frac{K_d}{T}\Big(e_k + e_{k-2} - 2e_{k-1}\Big). \qquad (8.14)$$

The control signal can be calculated with $u_k = u_{k-1} + \Delta u_k$. Thus, the current control signal is generated by adding up its signal at last time instance and the increment $\Delta u_k$. This type of controller is also known as incremental PID controller. The Simulink implementation of the controller is shown in Fig. 8-2.

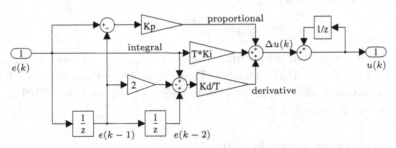

Fig. 8-2   Simulink model of the incremental PID controller   (file name: c8mdpid1.mdl).

#### 3. PID controllers with anti-windup

When the set-point of the signal changes, since the error signal is large, and the integral of the error signal is aggregating to a certain value. When the output signal of the system reaches the set-point, and error is changed to negative value, due to the existing large value in the integral action, the control signal may remain at its upper limit, such that the output signal of the system would continue to increase to cancel off the large integral until a certain time. This phenomenon is referred to as integral windup[3]. To overcome the problem, various anti-windup PID controllers are proposed. In Fig. 8-3, Simulink model of an anti-windup PID controller is given.

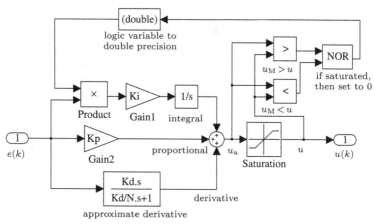

Fig. 8-3   Simulink model of an anti-windup PID controller   (file: c8mantiw.mdl).

Besides, powerful PID controller blocks are provided in Simulink, and various PID controllers and their variations can be described by the blocks easily. These blocks are suggested to be used directly in PID control system analysis and design.

## 8.2   First-order Delay Model Approximation to Plant Models

Many of the classical PID tuning algorithms are proposed based on the assumption that the process plant is given by first-order plus dead-time (FOPDT) model. The FOPDT model is given by

$$G(s) = \frac{k}{Ts+1}e^{-Ls}. \qquad (8.15)$$

The main reason for this is that the step responses of most processes are very similar to the FOPDT models. Thus, it is usually necessary to find the FOPDT approximations to the process models. In this section, FOPDT model approximation is presented.

### 8.2.1   *FOPDT Model by Step Responses*

The general shape of the step response of typical process plants is shown in Fig. 8-4(a). For these responses, FOPDT model can be used, and on the plot the straight lines can be drawn. From them, the parameters $k$, $L$ and $T$ can be obtained. Sometimes the drawing of the three lines may be subjective, or not accurate.

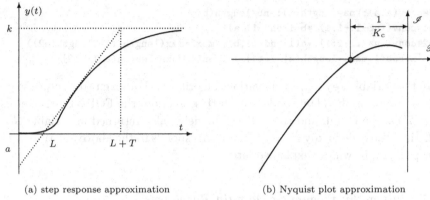

(a) step response approximation          (b) Nyquist plot approximation

Fig. 8-4   First-order plus dead-time model approximation.

These parameters can also be identified numerically. The corresponding step response of the system can be written as

$$\hat{y}(t) = \begin{cases} k\left[1 - e^{-(t-L)/T}\right], & t > L \\ 0, & t \leqslant L. \end{cases} \tag{8.16}$$

Thus, the least squares curve fitting method in Chapter 3 can be used to fit the parameters. The getfopdt() developed by the authors can be used to extract the key parameters of FOPDT model. The listing of the function is given by

```
function [K,L,T,G1]=getfopdt(key,G)
switch key
case 1, [y,t]=step(G);
    fun=@(x,t)x(1)*(1-exp(-(t-x(2))/x(3))).*(t>x(2));
    x=lsqcurvefit(fun,[1 1 1],t,y); K=x(1); L=x(2); T=x(3);
case 2, [Kc,Pm,wc,wcp]=margin(G);
    ikey=0; L=1.6*pi/(3*wc); K=dcgain(G); T=0.5*Kc*K*L;
    if isfinite(Kc), x0=[L;T];
        while ikey==0, u=wc*x0(1); v=wc*x0(2);
            FF=[K*Kc*(cos(u)-v*sin(u))+1+v^2; sin(u)+v*cos(u)];
    J=[-K*Kc*wc*sin(u)-K*Kc*wc*v*cos(u),-K*Kc*wc*sin(u)+2*wc*v;
        wc*cos(u)-wc*v*sin(u), wc*cos(u)]; x1=x0-inv(J)*FF;
        if norm(x1-x0)<1e-8, ikey=1; else, x0=x1; end, end
    L=x0(1); T=x0(2);   end
case 3, [n1,d1]=tfderv(G.num{1},G.den{1});
    [n2,d2]=tfderv(n1,d1); K1=dcgain(n1,d1); K2=dcgain(n2,d2);
    K=dcgain(G); Tar=-K1/K; T=sqrt(K2/K-Tar^2); L=Tar-T;
case 4
    Gr=opt_app(G,0,1,1); L=Gr.ioDelay;
    T=Gr.den{1}(1)/Gr.den{1}(2); K=Gr.num{1}(end)/Gr.den{1}(2);
end
G1=tf(K,[T 1],'iodelay',L);
function [e,f]=tfderv(b,a)
```

```
f=conv(a,a); na=length(a); nb=length(b);
e1=conv((nb-1:-1:1).*b(1:end-1),a);
e2=conv((na-1:-1:1).*a(1:end-1),b); maxL=max(length(e1),length(e2));
e=[zeros(1,maxL-length(e1)) e1]-[zeros(1,maxL-length(e2)) e2];
```

where the variable **key** represents various algorithms. For given step response data, key $= 1$, and $G$ is the plant model. With this function, the FOPDT parameters $k$, $L$ and $T$ can be found, and the FOPDT model is also returned in variable $G_1$. In the listing, the code in key $= 1$ paragraph corresponds to the above algorithm, while other paragraphs will be explained later.

### 8.2.2   *Fitting by Frequency Domain Responses*

Nyquist plot is another representation of FOPDT model. The frequency $\omega_c$ at the intersection of Nyquist plot with the negative real axis, and the value of ultimate gain $K_c$ shown in Fig. 8-4(b) are useful in describing the FOPDT model. These two parameters are, in fact, the gain margin and its frequency, and they can be obtained directly with function **margin()**.

Consider the frequency response of the following first-order model

$$G(j\omega) = \frac{k}{Ts+1}e^{-Ls}\bigg|_{s=j\omega} = \frac{k}{Tj\omega+1}e^{-j\omega L}. \tag{8.17}$$

It is known that at crossover frequency $\omega_c$, the ultimate gain $K_c$ is the first intersection with the negative real axis. They satisfy the following equations

$$\begin{cases} \dfrac{k\left(\cos\omega_c L - \omega_c T \sin\omega_c L\right)}{1+\omega_c^2 T^2} = -\dfrac{1}{K_c} \\ \sin\omega_c L + \omega_c T \cos\omega_c L = 0. \end{cases} \tag{8.18}$$

Besides, since $k$ is the steady-state value of the plant, it can be obtained directly from the plant model, for instance with **dcgain()**. two variables $x_1 = L$ and $x_2 = T$ are defined, and the two equations can also be established

$$\begin{cases} f_1(x_1,x_2) = kK_c\left(\cos\omega_c x_1 - \omega_c x_2 \sin\omega_c x_1\right) + 1 + \omega_c^2 x_2^2 = 0 \\ f_2(x_1,x_2) = \sin\omega_c x_1 + \omega_c x_2 \cos\omega_c x_1 = 0. \end{cases} \tag{8.19}$$

Jacobian matrix can be derived

$$J = \begin{bmatrix} -kK_c\omega_c \sin\omega_c x_1 - kK_c\omega_c^2 x_2 \cos\omega_c x_1 & -kK_c\omega_c \sin\omega_c x_1 + 2\omega_c^2 x_2 \\ \omega_c \cos\omega_c x_1 - \omega_c^2 x_2 \sin\omega_c x_1 & \omega_c \cos\omega_c x_1 \end{bmatrix}. \tag{8.20}$$

Thus, the two parameters $(x_1,x_2)$ can be obtained with quasi-Newton algorithm. In function **getfopdt()**, the paragraph for key $= 2$ implements the algorithm.

### 8.2.3 *Transfer Function-based Identification*

Consider the FOPDT model $G_n(s) = ke^{-Ls}/(1 + Ts)$. Take the first- and second-order derivative of $G_n(s)$ with respect to $s$, then

$$\frac{G_n'(s)}{G_n(s)} = -L - \frac{T}{1+Ts}, \quad \frac{G_n''(s)}{G_n(s)} - \left(\frac{G_n'(s)}{G_n(s)}\right)^2 = \frac{T^2}{(1+Ts)^2}.$$

The derivatives at $s = 0$ are

$$T_{ar} = -\frac{G_n'(0)}{G_n(0)} = L + T, \quad T^2 = \frac{G_n''(0)}{G_n(0)} - T_{ar}^2, \tag{8.21}$$

where $T_{ar}$ is referred to as the average residence time. It can be seen that $L = T_{ar} - T$. The gain of the system can be obtained from $k = G_n(0)$. In the getfopdt() function, the paragraph in key $= 3$ implements the algorithm.

### 8.2.4 *Sub-optimal Reduction Method*

The sub-optimal model reduction approach in [7] can be used to solve the three key parameters directly, and the MATLAB implementation of the algorithm is presented in Section 4.5. In the getfopdt() function, the paragraph in key $= 4$ implements the algorithm.

**Example 8.2.** Assume that the transfer function of plant model is $G(s) = 1/(s + 1)^5$, the following statements can be used to extract the FOPDT models, and the step response results are compared in Fig. 8-5.

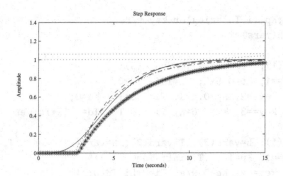

Fig. 8-5 Comparisons of different FOPDT's.

```
>> s=tf('s'); G=1/(s+1)^5;          % the plant model
   [K1,L1,T1,G1]=getfopdt(1,G),  [K2,L2,T2,G2]=getfopdt(2,G)
   [K3,L3,T3,G3]=getfopdt(3,G),  [K4,L4,T4,G4]=getfopdt(4,G)
   step(G,'-',G1,':',G2,'*',G3,'--',G4,'-.',15) % comparisons
```

The approximate models are listed below. It can be seen that the sub-optimal reduction algorithm yields the best fitting quality of all the four models.

$$G_1(s) = \frac{1.053 \mathrm{e}^{-2.45s}}{3.14s+1}, \quad G_2(s) = \frac{\mathrm{e}^{-2.65s}}{3.725s+1}, \quad G_3(s) = \frac{\mathrm{e}^{-2.76s}}{2.236s+1}, \quad G_4(s) = \frac{\mathrm{e}^{-2.59s}}{2.624s+1}.$$

## 8.3    Parameter Tuning of PID Controllers for FOPDT Plants

### 8.3.1    *Ziegler–Nichols Empirical Formula*

In 1942, Ziegler and Nichols published the well-known empirical formula[8]. It is a feasible solution to practical controller tuning problems in process control. This method is later known as Ziegler–Nichols tuning formula. This method and its variations are still used in process control.

Assume that the key parameters $k$, $L$ and $T$ of FOPDT model are obtained, an intermediate parameter can be defined as $a = kL/T$. Thus, the parameters of P, PI, or PID controllers can be designed from Table 8-1. Based on the formula, a MATLAB function `ziegler()` is written[6]. With the function, the PID-type controller can be designed directly.

Table 8-1    Ziegler–Nichols tuning rules.

| controller | with step responses | | | with frequency domain responses | | |
|---|---|---|---|---|---|---|
| type | $K_{\mathrm{p}}$ | $T_{\mathrm{i}}$ | $T_{\mathrm{d}}$ | $K_{\mathrm{p}}$ | $T_{\mathrm{i}}$ | $T_{\mathrm{d}}$ |
| P | $1/a$ | | | $0.5K_{\mathrm{c}}$ | | |
| PI | $0.9/a$ | $3L$ | | $0.4K_{\mathrm{c}}$ | $0.8T_{\mathrm{c}}$ | |
| PID | $1.2/a$ | $2L$ | $L/2$ | $0.6K_{\mathrm{c}}$ | $0.5T_{\mathrm{c}}$ | $0.12T_{\mathrm{c}}$ |

```
function [Gc,Kp,Ti,Td]=ziegler(key,vars)
switch length(vars)
   case 3,
      K=vars(1); Tc=vars(2); N=vars(3);
      if key==1, Kp=0.5*K; Ti=inf; Td=0;
      elseif key==2, Kp=0.4*K; Ti=0.8*Tc; Td=0;
      elseif key==3, Kp=0.6*K; Ti=0.5*Tc; Td=0.12*Tc; end
   case 4
      K=vars(1); L=vars(2); T=vars(3); N=vars(4); a=K*L/T;
      if key==1, Kp=1/a; Ti=inf; Td=0;
      elseif key==2, Kp=0.9/a; Ti=3*L; Td=0;
      elseif key==3, Kp=1.2/a; Ti=2*L; Td=L/2; end
   case 5,
      K=vars(1); Tc=vars(2); rb=vars(3); N=vars(5);
      pb=pi*vars(4)/180; Kp=K*rb*cos(pb);
      if key==2, Ti=-Tc/(2*pi*tan(pb)); Td=0;
      elseif key==3, Ti=Tc*(1+sin(pb))/(pi*cos(pb)); Td=Ti/4;
   end, end
   Gc=pidstd(Kp,Ti,Td,N);
```

where key $= 1, 2, 3$ corresponds respectively to P, PI, PID controllers. The user can use it to select controller type. The other argument is vars = $[k, L, T, N]$. With this function, the selected controller can be designed. Since the length of vars is 4, the "case 4" paragraph of the function is called. Other lengths of vars will be explained later.

If frequency domain response data are given, the ultimate gain $K_c$ and its crossover frequency $\omega_c$ can be used, and a new variable can be defined, $T_c = 2\pi/\omega_c$. Then the controller parameters can be designed with Table 8-1. The ziegler() mentioned earlier can be used to design the controllers, with vars = $[K_c, T_c, N]$. The algorithm is implemented in the "case 3" paragraph.

**Example 8.3.** Assume that a fifth order plant model is given by $G(s) = 1/(s+1)^5$. With the conclusion from Example 8.2, the parameters of a well-fitting FOPDT approximation are given by $k = 1, T = 2.2624, L = 2.59$. The PI and PID controller can be designed with the formula in Table 8-1.

```
>> s=tf('s'); G=1/(s+1)^5; N=10;          % plant model entering
   k=1; T=2.2624; L=2.59; a=k*L/T;         % FOPDT fitting
   Kp=0.9/a; Ti=3*L; G1=Kp*(1+tf(1,[Ti 0]));  % PI controller design
   Kp=1.2/a; Ti=2*L; Td=0.5*L; p=[Kp,Ti,Td]   % PID controller design
```

It can be seen that the designed PI and PID controllers are

$$G_1(s) = 0.7862\left(1 + \frac{1}{7.77s}\right), \quad G_2(s) = 1.0482\left(1 + \frac{1}{5.18s} + \frac{1.295s}{0.1295s+1}\right),$$

and the above PID controller can also be designed with $G_2 = $ ziegler(3, $[k, L, T, N]$). With the controllers, the step responses can be obtained, as shown in Fig. 8-6(a). Unfortunately, the controllers designed are not satisfactory.

```
>> G2=Kp*(1+tf(1,[Ti,0])+tf([Td 0],[Td/N 1])); % construct PID controller
   step(feedback(G*G1,1),'-',feedback(G*G2,1),'--')
```

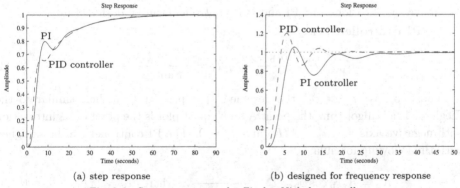

(a) step response        (b) designed for frequency response

Fig. 8-6    Step responses under Ziegler–Nichols controllers.

With the frequency response obtained with margin() function, the new PI and PID controllers can be designed, using the Ziegler–Nichols formula in Table 8-1. The closed-loop responses with the new controllers are shown in Fig. 8-6(b). For this example, the quality of control is improved.

```
>> [Kc,b,wc,d]=margin(G); Tc=2*pi/wc;  % extract frequency response data
   Kp=0.4*Kc; Ti=0.8*Tc; [Kp,Ti]; G1=Kp*(1+tf(1,[Ti 0])); % PI controller
   Kp=0.6*Kc; Ti=0.5*Tc; Td=0.12*Tc;   % PID controller
   G2=Kp*(1+tf(1,[Ti,0])+tf([Td 0],1));
   step(feedback(G*G1,1),'-',feedback(G*G2,1),'--')
```

### 8.3.2  *Improved Ziegler–Nichols Algorithm*

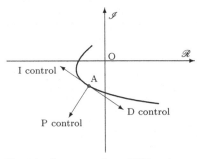

Fig. 8-7   Interpretation of PID actions.

The frequency domain response interpretation of PID controller is given in Fig. 8-7. Consider a point A on the Nyquist plot of the plant model. If proportional action is imposed, the parameter $K_p$ stretches or compresses the point along the OA line. Derivative and integral actions stretch the point along its perpendicular directions, as shown in the plot. Thus, through properly chosen controller parameters, a certain point A on the Nyquist plot can be moved to any specified point.

Suppose a gain $G(j\omega_0) = r_a e^{j(\pi+\phi_a)}$ is selected as point A, and it is expected to move the point to point $A_1$ with a proper PID controller. The gain at point $A_1$ is assumed to be $G_1(j\omega_0) = r_b e^{j(\pi+\phi_b)}$. Further assume that at frequency $\omega_0$, the PID controller can be written as $G_c(s) = r_c e^{j\phi_c}$, then

$$r_b e^{j(\pi+\phi_b)} = r_a r_c e^{j(\pi+\phi_a+\phi_c)}. \tag{8.22}$$

A controller can then be selected, such that $r_c = r_b/r_a$, and $\phi_c = \phi_b - \phi_a$. From the above specifications, the PI and PID controllers can be designed by

(1) **PI controller.** Select

$$K_p = \frac{r_b \cos(\phi_b - \phi_a)}{r_a}, \; T_i = \frac{1}{\omega_0 \tan(\phi_a - \phi_b)}. \tag{8.23}$$

Thus, to have $\phi_a > \phi_b$, the designed $T_i$ is positive. Further, similar to the Ziegler–Nichols algorithm, the point A on Nyquist plot is the point of its interaction with negative axis, i.e., $r_a = 1/K_c$ and $\phi_a = 0$. The PI controller can be designed with the following formula

$$K_p = K_c r_b \cos\phi_b, \; T_i = -\frac{T_c}{2\pi\tan\phi_b}, \; \text{where } T_c = 2\pi/\omega_c. \tag{8.24}$$

(2) **PID controller.** It can be denoted by

$$K_p = \frac{r_b \cos(\phi_b - \phi_a)}{r_a}, \; \omega_0 T_d - \frac{1}{\omega_0 T_i} = \tan(\phi_b - \phi_a). \tag{8.25}$$

It can be seen that there are infinite number of solutions $T_i$ and $T_d$ satisfying Eqn. (8.25). A constant $\alpha$ can be specified such that $T_d = \alpha T_i$. Thus, the unique solution of $T_i$ and $T_d$ can be found

$$T_i = \frac{1}{2\alpha\omega_0}\left[\tan(\phi_b - \phi_a) + \sqrt{4\alpha + \tan^2(\phi_b - \phi_a)}\right], \; T_d = \alpha T_i. \quad (8.26)$$

It can be shown that in the Ziegler–Nichols tuning algorithm, $\alpha$ is selected as $\alpha = 1/4$. If further, still assume that point A is the intersection of Nyquist plot with the negative real axis, i.e., $r_a = 1/K_c$ and $\phi_a = 0$, the PID controller can be designed as, with $\alpha = 1/4$

$$K_p = K_c r_b \cos\phi_b, \; T_i = \frac{T_c}{\pi}\left(\frac{1 + \sin\phi_b}{\cos\phi_b}\right), \; T_d = \frac{T_c}{4\pi}\left(\frac{1 + \sin\phi_b}{\cos\phi_b}\right). \quad (8.27)$$

It can be seen that through proper $r_b$ and $\phi_b$, PI and PID controllers can be designed. The algorithm is implemented in function `ziegler()`, where vars $= [K_c, T_c, r_b, \phi_b, N]$, corresponding to the "**case 5**" paragraph in the listing.

**Example 8.4.** Consider again the plant model $G(s) = 1/(s + 1)^6$ in Example 8.3. Selecting $r_b = 0.8$, and for the different values of $\phi_b$, a loop structure can be used to draw the step responses as shown in Fig. 8-8(a).

```
>> s=tf('s'); G=1/(s+1)^5; % plant model input
   [Kc,b,wc,a]=margin(G); Tc=2*pi/wc; rb=0.8;
   for phi_b=[10:10:80],    % use loop to try different phase margins
       [Gc,Kp,Ti,Td]=ziegler(3,[Kc,Tc,rb,phi_b,10]);
       step(feedback(G*Gc,1),20), hold on
   end
```

From the step responses for different values $\phi_b$, it can be found that when $\phi_b$ is small, the overshoot may be very large. Thus, relatively large value of $\phi_b$ should be selected. However, the increase of $\phi_b$ will make the response speed slower and slower. Some trade-off on the selection of $\phi_b$ and response speed should be made.

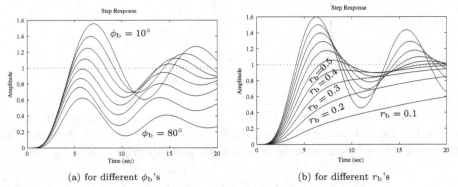

(a) for different $\phi_b$'s          (b) for different $r_b$'s

Fig. 8-8   Step responses for the improved Ziegler–Nichols approach.

For the same plant, if we fix $\phi_b = 20°$, and try different values of $r_b$'s, the step responses can be obtained as shown in Fig. 8-8(b).

```
>> phi_b=20;              % fix phase margin
   for rb=0.1:0.1:1,     % try different magnitude in loop structure
      [Gc,Kp,Ti,Td]=ziegler(3,[Kc,Tc,rb,phi_b,10]);
      step(feedback(G*Gc,1),20), hold on
   end
```

It can be seen that when $r_b = 0.5$, and $\phi_b = 20°$ are selected, relatively good step responses can be obtained. The controller under this selection can be designed again

```
>> [Gc,Kp,Ti,Td]=ziegler(3,[Kc,Tc,0.5,20,10])
```

The controller obtained is

$$G_c(s) = 1.3557 \left( 1 + \frac{1}{3.9314s} + \frac{0.9828s}{1 + 0.09828s} \right).$$

### 8.3.3  *Improved PID Control Structure and Algorithms*

Apart from the standard PID control structure, there are different variations. For instance, the derivative action can be placed in the feedback path. Also, the refined PID controller is another option. In this section, some of the variations are presented.

**1. PID controller with derivative in feedback path**

It is found that the step input may lead to a jump to the error signal at initial time. If pure derivative action is used, an extremely large control signal will appear, thus it might better to move the derivative action to relatively smooth changing signals, such as the output signal. In the control structure in Fig. 8-9, the derivative action is placed in the feedback path. However, the response speed may be lower than the classical PID controllers.

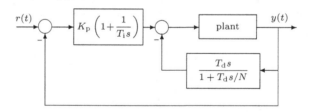

Fig. 8-9    Derivative in the feedback path.

Compared with the typical feedback structure shown in Fig. 4-4, the system shown in Figs. 8-9 can be converted easily to the typical feedback structure. The transfer functions of the forward and feedback path are respectively

$$G_c(s) = K_p \left( 1 + \frac{1}{T_i s} \right), \tag{8.28}$$

$$H(s) = \frac{(1 + K_p/N)T_i T_d s^2 + K_p(T_i + T_d/N) + K_p}{K_p(T_i s + 1)(T_d s/N + 1)}. \tag{8.29}$$

### 2. Refined Ziegler–Nichols controller

The typical PID controller with Ziegler–Nichols tuning rule normally introduces strong oscillation in set-point control and usually with large overshoot. It is necessary to convert the control structure, and the refined Ziegler–Nichols tuning rule can be used[9]. The mathematical model of the refined PID controller is

$$u(t) = K_{\mathrm{p}} \left[ (\beta u_{\mathrm{c}} - y) + \frac{1}{T_{\mathrm{i}}} \int e \, \mathrm{d}t - T_{\mathrm{d}} \frac{\mathrm{d}y}{\mathrm{d}t} \right], \tag{8.30}$$

where the derivative action is taken on the output signal. Part of the input signal is also added to the control signal. Normally, we select $\beta < 1$, and the controller can further be written as

$$u(t) = K_{\mathrm{p}} \left( \beta e + \frac{1}{T_{\mathrm{i}}} \int e \, \mathrm{d}t \right) - K_{\mathrm{p}} \left[ (1 - \beta)y + T_{\mathrm{d}} \frac{\mathrm{d}y}{\mathrm{d}t} \right]. \tag{8.31}$$

The block diagram representation of the control structure is shown in Fig. 8-10. The control structure can also be converted to the typical feedback control structure shown in Fig. 4-4, with the forward and feedback models given by

$$G_{\mathrm{c}}(s) = K_{\mathrm{p}} \left( \beta + \frac{1}{T_{\mathrm{i}} s} \right), \tag{8.32}$$

$$H(s) = \frac{T_{\mathrm{i}} T_{\mathrm{d}} \beta (N + 2 - \beta) s^2 / N + (T_{\mathrm{i}} + T_{\mathrm{d}}/N)s + 1}{(T_{\mathrm{i}} \beta s + 1)(T_{\mathrm{d}} s / N + 1)}. \tag{8.33}$$

Consider the refined PID structure shown in Fig. 8-10, a normalized delay $\tau$ and first-order constant $\kappa$ can be introduced, with $\kappa = K_{\mathrm{c}} k$, and $\tau = L/T$. Based on the values of $\tau$ and $\kappa$, the following tuning rule can be used to design the PID controller

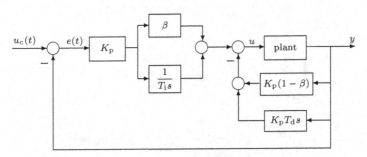

Fig. 8-10    Refined PID control structure.

(1) If $2.25 < \kappa < 15$ or $0.16 < \tau < 0.57$, the original Ziegler–Nichols parameters should be used. In order to keep the overshoot no more than 10% or 20%, the value of $\beta$ should be respectively $\beta = (15 - \kappa)/(15 + \kappa)$ or $\beta = 36/(27 + 5\kappa)$.

(2) If $1.5 < \kappa < 2.25$ or $0.57 < \tau < 0.96$, the $T_{\mathrm{i}}$ parameter in Ziegler–Nichols controller should be changed to $T_{\mathrm{i}} = 0.5\mu T_{\mathrm{c}}$, with $\mu = 4\kappa/9$, and $\beta = 8(\mu - 1)/17$.

(3) If $1.2 < \kappa < 1.5$, in order to keep the overshoot smaller than 10%, the parameters of the PID controller should be refined to

$$K_{\mathrm{p}} = \frac{5}{6}\left(\frac{12+\kappa}{15+14\kappa}\right), \quad T_{\mathrm{i}} = \frac{1}{5}\left(\frac{4}{15}\kappa+1\right). \tag{8.34}$$

A MATLAB function `rziegler()` is written to implement the algorithm, to design a refined Ziegler–Nichols PID controller[6], with $\mathrm{vars} = [k, L, T, N, K_{\mathrm{c}}, T_{\mathrm{c}}]$.

```
function [Gc,Kp,Ti,Td,b,H]=rziegler(vars)
K=vars(1); L=vars(2); T=vars(3); N=vars(4); a=K*L/T; Kp=1.2/a;
Ti=2*L; Td=L/2; Kc=vars(5); Tc=vars(6); kappa=Kc*K; tau=L/T; H=[];
if (kappa>2.25 & kappa<15) | (tau>0.16 & tau<0.57)
   b=(15-kappa)/(15+kappa);
elseif (kappa<2.25 & kappa>1.5) | (tau<0.96 & tau>0.57)
   mu=4*jappa/9; b=8*(mu-1)/17; Ti=0.5*mu*Tc;
elseif (kappa>1.2 & kappa<1.5),
   Kp=5*(12+kappa)/(6*(15+14*kappa)); Ti=0.2*(4*kappa/15+1); b=1;
end
Gc=tf(Kp*[b*Ti,1],[Ti,0]); nH=[Ti*Td*b*(N+2-b)/N,Ti+Td/N,1];
dH=conv([Ti*b,1],[Td/N,1]); H=tf(nH,dH);
```

**Example 8.5.** Consider again the plant model $G(s) = 1/(s+1)^5$ studied in Example 8.3. The following statements can be used to design the refined PID controller, and the closed-loop step response is shown in Fig. 8-11. Unfortunately, the result of the refined PID controller is not satisfactory either, for this example.

```
>> s=tf('s'); G=1/(s+1)^5; [K,L,T]=getfopdt(4,G);
   [Kc,p,wc,m]=margin(G); Tc=2*pi/wc;     % extract the key variables
   [Gc,Kp,Ti,Td,beta,H]=rziegler([K,L,T,10,Kc,Tc]);
   G_c=feedback(G*Gc,H); step(G_c);       % closed-loop step response
```

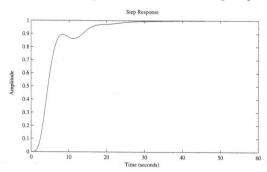

Fig. 8-11   Step response of the refined PID controller.

### 3. A variation of PID controller

A variation of PID controller is given in [10], with the following structure.

$$G_{\mathrm{c}}(s) = K_{\mathrm{p}}\left(1+\frac{1}{T_{\mathrm{i}}s}\right)\frac{1+T_{\mathrm{d}}s}{1+T_{\mathrm{d}}s/N}. \tag{8.35}$$

Many different tuning rules are summarized in the book [10], and the readers are advised to reference the book for the controller tuning algorithms.

### 8.3.4  *Chien–Hrones–Reswick Parameter Tuning Algorithm*

In practical applications, there are a lot of variations to the traditional Ziegler–Nichols algorithm. The Chien–Hrones–Reswick (CHR) algorithm is one of them. The empirical formula for PID controller design is given in Table 8-2. In the criteria provided in the algorithm, it allows 0% overshoot and fast response with 20% of overshoot. Compared with the traditional Ziegler–Nichols tuning algorithm, the time constant $T$ is directly used in the CHR algorithm.

Table 8-2   CHR tuning formula for set-point control.

| controller | with 0% overshoot | | | with 20% overshoot | | |
|---|---|---|---|---|---|---|
| type | $K_p$ | $T_i$ | $T_d$ | $K_d$ | $T_i$ | $T_d$ |
| P | $0.3/a$ | | | $0.7/a$ | | |
| PI | $0.35/a$ | $1.2T$ | | $0.6/a$ | $T$ | |
| PID | $0.6/a$ | $T$ | $0.5L$ | $0.95/a$ | $1.4T$ | $0.47L$ |

Based on the algorithm, a MATLAB function `chrpid()` is written

```
function [Gc,Kp,Ti,Td]=chrpid(key,vars)
K=vars(1); L=vars(2); T=vars(3); N=vars(4); ov=vars(5)+1;
a=K*L/T; KK=[0.3,0.35,1.2,0.6,1,0.5; 0.7,0.6,1,0.95,1.4,0.47];
if key==1, Kp=KK(ov,1)/a; Ti=inf; Td=0;
elseif key==2, Kp=KK(ov,2)/a; Ti=KK(ov,3)*T; Td=0;
else, Kp=KK(ov,4)/a; Ti=KK(ov,5)*T; Td=KK(ov,6)*L; end
Gc=pidstd(Kp,Ti,Td,N);
```

The syntax of the function is $[G, K_p, T_i, T_d] = \texttt{chrpid(key,vars)}$ , where the returned variables are the same as the `ziegler()` function, and key $= 1,2,3$ is for P, PI and PID controllers. The variable vars $= [k, L, T, N, O_s]$, where $O_s = 0$ for no overshoot, and 1 for 20% of overshoot.

**Example 8.6.** Consider again the plant model in Example 8.3. The following statements can be used to design Ziegler–Nichols PID controllers and CHR controllers under the two criteria

```
>> s=tf('s'); G=1/(s+1)^5; [k,L,T]=getfopdt(4,G); N=10;
   [Gc1,Kp,Ti,Td]=ziegler(3,[k,L,T,N])
   [Gc2,Kp,Ti,Td]=chrpid(3,[k,L,T,N,0])
   [Gc3,Kp,Ti,Td]=chrpid(3,[k,L,T,N,1])
```

The controllers obtained are

$$G_{c2}(s) = 0.6085 \left(1 + \frac{1}{2.6236s} + \frac{1.2935s}{0.12935s+1}\right),$$

$$G_{c3}(s) = 0.9635 \left( 1 + \frac{1}{3.6731s} + \frac{1.2159s}{0.12159s+1} \right).$$

The step responses of the closed-loop systems under the three controllers can be obtained as shown in Fig. 8-12. It can be seen that although the one with 0% overshoot is slow, the control behavior is acceptable, at least it is better than the traditional Ziegler–Nichols controller.

```
>> step(feedback(G*Gc1,1),'-',feedback(G*Gc2,1),'--',...
        feedback(G*Gc3,1),':',50)
```

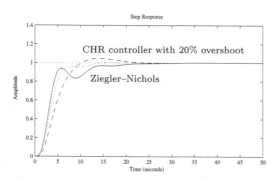

Fig. 8-12    Step responses comparison under different controllers.

### 8.3.5    *Optimal PID Controller Tuning Rule*

Consider the key parameters $k$, $L$ and $T$ of the FOPDT plant model. Numerical optimization techniques can be performed for a certain optimization criterion, and a set of parameters $K_p$, $T_i$ and $T_d$ can be obtained. When the parameters of the plant model are changed, another set of controller parameters can be obtained. With curve fitting methods, the empirical formula can be established. Many tuning formula are summarized in this way.

There are various selections in optimization criteria, for instance, the time weighted criteria can be defined as

$$J_n = \int_0^\infty t^{2n} e^2(t)\mathrm{d}t, \tag{8.36}$$

where $n = 0$ is the ISE criterion, and the criteria for $n = 1$ and $n = 2$ are referred to as ISTE and IST$^2$E criteria[11]. Besides, the commonly used criteria are IAE and ITAE, defined respectively as

$$J_{\mathrm{IAE}} = \int_0^\infty |e(t)|\mathrm{d}t, \quad J_{\mathrm{ITAE}} = \int_0^\infty t|e(t)|\mathrm{d}t. \tag{8.37}$$

Zhuang and Atherton proposed the optimal PID controller tuning empirical formula based on Eqn. (8.36)[11]

$$K_{\mathrm{p}} = \frac{a_1}{k}\left(\frac{L}{T}\right)^{b_1}, \quad T_{\mathrm{i}} = \frac{T}{a_2 + b_2(L/T)}, \quad T_{\mathrm{d}} = a_3 T\left(\frac{L}{T}\right)^{b_3}. \tag{8.38}$$

For different ranges of $L/T$, the parameter pairs $(a, b)$ can be found directly from Table 8-3. If the FOPDT fitting of the original plant can be obtained, the $a_i, b_i$ parameters can be obtained, thus the controller parameters can be evaluated from the above formula to construct the optimal PID controller

Table 8-3　Optimal PID parameters for set-point control.

| range of $L/T$ | 0.1 ~ 1 | | | 1.1 ~ 2 | | |
|---|---|---|---|---|---|---|
| criteria | ISE | ISTE | IST$^2$E | ISE | ISTE | IST$^2$E |
| $a_1$ | 1.048 | 1.042 | 0.968 | 1.154 | 1.142 | 1.061 |
| $b_1$ | −0.897 | −0.897 | −0.904 | −0.567 | −0.579 | −0.583 |
| $a_2$ | 1.195 | 0.987 | 0.977 | 1.047 | 0.919 | 0.892 |
| $b_2$ | −0.368 | −0.238 | −0.253 | −0.220 | −0.172 | −0.165 |
| $a_3$ | 0.489 | 0.385 | 0.316 | 0.490 | 0.384 | 0.315 |
| $b_3$ | 0.888 | 0.906 | 0.892 | 0.708 | 0.839 | 0.832 |

The limitation of the formula is that only the $0.1 \leqslant L/T \leqslant 2$ range is supported. It is not suitable for plants with large time delay terms.

Murrill[10, 12] proposed IAE optimal PID controller algorithm

$$K_\text{p} = \frac{1.435}{K}\left(\frac{T}{L}\right)^{0.921}, T_\text{i} = \frac{T}{0.878}\left(\frac{T}{L}\right)^{0.749}, T_\text{d} = 0.482T\left(\frac{T}{L}\right)^{-1.137}, \qquad (8.39)$$

which is suitable for the range $0.1 < L/T < 1$. For ordinary plant models, it is pointed out that[13] if the value of 1.435 in the $K_\text{p}$ equation is changed to 3, the algorithm can be extended into other $L/T$ ranges.

With ITAE criterion, the following PID tuning empirical formula can be used[10, 12].

$$K_\text{p} = \frac{1.357}{K}\left(\frac{T}{L}\right)^{0.947}, T_\text{i} = \frac{T}{0.842}\left(\frac{T}{L}\right)^{0.738}, T_\text{d} = 0.318T\left(\frac{T}{L}\right)^{-0.995}. \qquad (8.40)$$

The suitable range is still $0.1 < L/T < 1$. For the range $0.05 \leqslant L/T \leqslant 6$, another ITAE optimal PID controller is proposed[14]

$$K_\text{p} = \frac{(0.7303 + 0.5307T/L)(T + 0.5L)}{K(T + L)}, \ T_\text{i} = T + 0.5L, \ T_\text{d} = \frac{0.5LT}{T + 0.5L}. \qquad (8.41)$$

**Example 8.7.** Consider again the plant model $G(s) = 1/(s + 1)^6$ in Example 8.3. The optimal FOPDT fitting of the model is $G(s) = e^{-3.37s}/(2.883s + 1)$, i.e., $k = 1$, $L = 3.37$ and $T = 2.883$. The following statements can be used to design the PID controllers

```
>> s=tf('s'); G=1/(s+1)^5;    % input plant model
   K=1; L=2.59; T=2.624;      % get approximate FOPDT model
   Kp1=1.142*(L/T)^(-0.579); Ti1=T/(0.919-0.172*(L/T));
   Td1=0.384*T*(L/T)^0.839; [Kp1,Ti1,Td1] % Zhuang & Atherton ISTE
```

The optimal controller designed as

$$G_1(s) = 1.1507\left(1 + \frac{1}{3.5023s} + \frac{0.9967s}{0.09967s + 1}\right).$$

With the algorithm given in Eqn. (8.41), the PID controller can be designed

```
>> Ti2=T+0.5*L; Kp2=(0.7303+0.5307*T/L)*Ti2/(K*(T+L));
   Td2=(0.5*L*T)/(T+0.5*L); [Kp2,Ti2,Td2] % ITAE optimal PID controller
```

and the new controller is

$$G_2(s) = 0.9530 \left( 1 + \frac{1}{3.9190s} + \frac{0.8671s}{0.08671s + 1} \right).$$

The step responses of the system with the two controllers are obtained as shown in Fig.8-13. It can be seen that the controllers are satisfactory.

```
>> Gc1=Kp1*(1+tf(1,[Ti1,0])+tf([Td1,0],[Td1/10 1]));
   Gc2=Kp2*(1+tf(1,[Ti2,0])+tf([Td2,0],[Td2/10 1]));
   step(feedback(Gc1*G,1),'-',feedback(Gc2*G,1),'--')
```

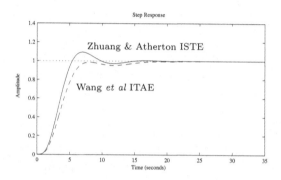

Fig. 8-13    Step responses of the two PID controllers.

## 8.4    PID Tuner — A PID Controller Design Interface

Hundreds of PID parameter tuning algorithms based on the FOPDT plant model are presented in [15]. Some of the algorithms were presented in the previous section. In this section, the PID Tuner interface developed by the authors is presented. In the interface, all the algorithms in [15] are implemented, and the facilities such as FOPDT approximation, PID controller design and simulation are supported in the user-friendly manner. Different PID controllers designed can be compared with the interface.

The following procedures can be used in PID Tuner interface:

(1) Type `pid_tuner` command at MATLAB prompt, the interface shown in Fig. 8-14 can be displayed. The blank area to be discussed later at the bottom of the interface is reserved for system responses display.

(2) Click the Plant model button, a dialog box will be displayed to allow the user to enter the transfer function of the block model into the interface. The numerator, denominator and delay constance can be entered in the dialog box. The button Modify Plant Model can be clicked to modify the plant model.

(3) Having entered the plant model, the Get FOPDT parameters button can be clicked to extract the FOPDT model, and the key parameters $k$, $L$ and $T$ can

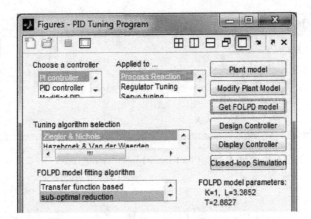

Fig. 8-14   PID Tuner interface   (upper part).

be obtained and displayed. Different algorithms are allowed to extract the key parameters, and the algorithm can be selected from the FOPDT model parameters fitting listbox. The sub-optimal optimal reduction method is recommended.

(4) With the $k$, $L$ and $T$ parameters, the PID controllers can be designed. Different PID controller structures, design algorithms can be selected from the listboxes. For instance, in the top left listbox, P, PI, PID controller, and its variation in Eqn. (8.35) can be selected. In the Apply to listbox, the purpose of controllers can be selected, such as for servo control, disturbance rejection controllers can be specified. When the items in the two listboxes are specified, the Tuning algorithm selection listbox will be generated, according to the algorithms in [10].

(5) The Design Controller button can be clicked to design automatically the PID controller, with the selected algorithm, and the results are displayed.

(6) Closed-loop step response of the system under the designed controller can be displayed if the Closed-loop Simulation button is clicked.

Various tuning algorithms in [10] are designed, and the list can be further augmented with simple program structure. An example is used to illustrate the use of the interface.

**Example 8.8.** Consider the plant model $G(s) = 1/(s+1)^6$. Type pid_tuner command at MATLAB prompt to start the interface, as shown in Fig. 8-14. Click Plant model button to open a dialog box, shown in Fig. 8-15. In the dialog box, the numerator, denominator coefficients and delay constant can be specified. Then click Apply button to load the plant model into the interface.

If we want to design PID controllers, FOPDT parameters should be extracted. A suitable algorithm in the FOPDT model parameters fitting listbox should be selected, with sub optimal reduction item recommended. Then click Get FOPDT model button to get the FOPDT parameters. The users can select a design algorithm from the relevant listboxes, and by clicking the Design Controller button, the PID controller can be obtained. For instance, the Minimum IAE (Wang et al) item can be chosen, and the controller can be

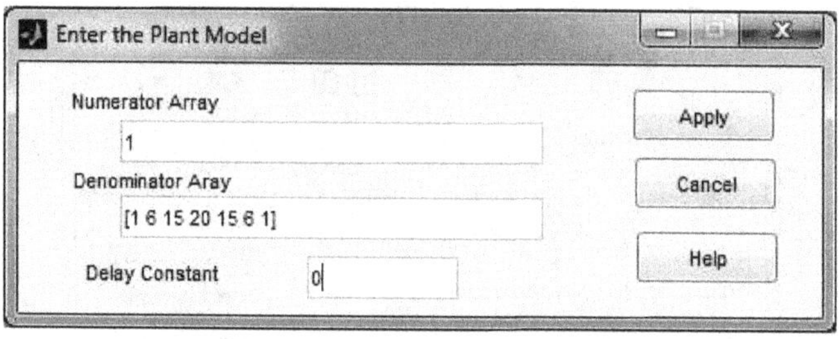

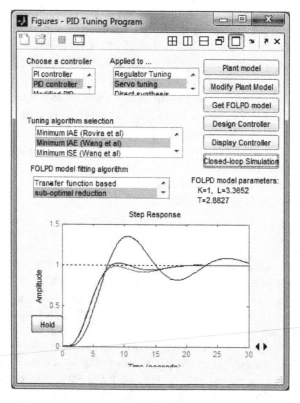

Fig. 8-15    Plant model input dialog box.

designed as

$$G_c(s) = 0.936172 \left( 1 + \frac{1}{4.565340s} + 1.062467s \right).$$

Click Closed-loop Simulation button, the closed-loop step response under such a controller can be obtained and displayed in the interface, as shown in Fig. 8-16. The Hold button can be used to preserve the plot axis, so that the step responses under different controllers can be shown together.

Fig. 8-16    PID Tuner interface and results display.

## 8.5 PID Parameters Tuning for Other Plant Types

So far, most of the PID tuning algorithms presented are based on FOPDT models. In practice, many plant models cannot be well approximated by FOPDT ones, thus the tuning algorithms presented earlier cannot be used. In [10], a lot of reference models and algorithms are presented, and the readers are advised to refer to that for more details. Here, only a few representative will be presented, and their MATLAB implementations are given.

### 8.5.1 *PD and PID Parameter Tuning for IPD Plants*

Many plant models can be approximated by delay models followed by an integrator, i.e., $G(s) = Ke^{-Ls}/s$. This type of models are usually referred to as integrator plus delay (IPD) models. This type of model cannot be approximated by FOPDT ones.

Since the plant model already contains integral action, it is not necessary to design controllers with integrators. Sometimes PD controllers are adequate for these models, since the large overshoot induced by integrators can be avoided. The typical forms of PD and PID controllers are

$$G_{\text{PD}}(s) = K_{\text{p}}(1 + T_{\text{d}}s), \quad G_{\text{PID}}(s) = K_{\text{p}}\left(1 + \frac{1}{T_{\text{i}}s} + T_{\text{d}}s\right). \tag{8.42}$$

In [16], different criteria are used, and the parameters of the controllers can be obtained with

$$
\begin{aligned}
&\text{PD controller } K_{\text{p}} = \frac{a_1}{KL}, \quad T_{\text{d}} = a_2 L \\
&\text{PID controller } K_{\text{p}} = \frac{a_3}{KL}, \quad T_{\text{i}} = a_4 L, \quad T_{\text{d}} = a_5 L,
\end{aligned}
\tag{8.43}
$$

where
  for ISE criterion, select $a_1 = 1.03$, $a_2 = 0.49$, or $a_3 = 1.37$, $a_4 = 1.49$, $a_5 = 0.59$;
  for ITSE, select $a_1 = 0.96$, $a_2 = 0.45$, or $a_3 = 1.36$, $a_4 = 1.66$, $a_5 = 0.53$;
  for ISTSE, select $a_1 = 0.9$, $a_2 = 0.45$, or $a_3 = 1.34$, $a_4 = 1.83$, $a_5 = 0.49$.

The above algorithm can be implemented in the function below to design the expected PD or PID controllers

```
function [Gc,Kp,Ti,Td]=ipdctrl(key,key1,K,L,N)
a=[1.03,0.49,1.37,1.49,0.59; 0.96,0.45,1.36,1.66,0.53;
   0.9,0.45,1.34,1.83,0.49];
if key==1
   Kp=a(key1,1)/K/L; Td=a(key1,2)*L; Ti=inf;
else
   Kp=a(key1,3)/K/L; Ti=a(key1,4)*L; Td=a(key1,5)*L;
end
Gc=pidstd(Kp,Ti,Td,N);
```

### 8.5.2   *PD and PID Parameter Tuning for FOLIPD Plants*

Another commonly used plant models is expressed as $G(s) = Ke^{-Ls}/[s(Ts + 1)]$. This type of model is referred to as first-order lag and integrator plus delay (FOLIPD) model.

Since the integral action already exists in the plant model, the steady-state error can be eliminated even if there is no integral action in the controllers. Thus, PD controllers are usually adequate for this type of plants. A PD tuning algorithm is provided in [10].

$$K_p = \frac{2}{3KL}, \quad T_d = T. \tag{8.44}$$

PID controller design algorithm is also given in [10].

$$K_p = \frac{1.111T}{KL^2} \frac{1}{\left[1 + (T/L)^{0.65}\right]^2}, \quad T_i = 2L\left[1 + \left(\frac{T}{L}\right)^{0.65}\right], \quad T_d = \frac{T_i}{4}. \tag{8.45}$$

Based on these two tuning algorithms, a MATLAB function `folipd()` can be written for PD and PID controllers design. The argument `key` is used to specify controller type, with 1 for PD controller, otherwise a PID controller is designed. If the parameters $k$, $L$, $T$ and $N$ are given, the controllers can be designed.

```
function [Gc,Kp,Ti,Td]=folipd(key,K,L,T,N)
if key==1, Kp=2/3/K/L; Td=T; Ti=inf;
else, a=(T/L)^0.65;
    Kp=1.111*T/(K*L^2)/(1+a)^2; Ti=2*L*(1+a); Td=Ti/4;
end
Gc=pidstd(Kp,Ti,Td,N);
```

**Example 8.9.** Consider the plant model given by $G(s) = 1/(s(s + 1)^4)$. Since there is integral action in the plant model, it cannot be approximated by FOPDT models. FOLIPD models can be used instead. Let us keep the integrator and approximate the rest by a FOPDT model, the whole model is, in fact, the expected FOLIPD model. Based on it, PD and PID controllers can be designed. The closed-loop step responses can be obtained as shown in Fig. 8-17.

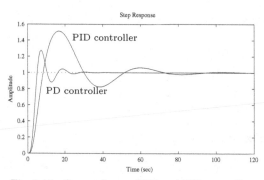

Fig. 8-17   Comparisons of PD and PID controllers.

```
>> s=tf('s'); G1=1/(s+1)^4; G=G1/s; Gr=opt_app(G1,0,1,1);
   K=Gr.num{1}(2)/Gr.den{1}(2); L=Gr.ioDelay; T=1/Gr.den{1}(2);
   [Gc1,Kp1,Ti1,Td1]=folipd(1,K,L,T,10); % PD controller desigm
   [Gc2,Kp2,Ti2,Td2]=folipd(2,K,L,T,10); % PID controller design
   step(feedback(G*Gc1,1),feedback(G*Gc2,1))
```

The controllers are

$$G_{\text{PD}}(s)=0.3631\left(1+\frac{2.3334s}{1+0.2333s}\right), \quad G_{\text{PID}}(s)=0.1635\left(1+\frac{1}{7.9638s}+\frac{1.9910s}{1+0.1991s}\right).$$

It can be seen from the simulation results that for this plant model, the PD controller is better than the PID controller. Since there is already an integral term in the plant model, an extra integral component may increase the overshoot and reduce the speed of the responses.

### 8.5.3 PD and PID Parameter Tuning for Unstable FOPDT Plants

In practical control, the plant model can sometimes by approximated with unstable FOPDT models, i.e., $G(s) = Ke^{-Ls}/(Ts - 1)$. The following algorithms can be used to design PID controllers[16].

$$K_{\text{p}} = \frac{a_1}{K}A^{b_1}, \quad T_{\text{i}} = a_2TA^{b_2}, \quad T_{\text{d}} = a_3T\left[1 - b_3A^{-0.02}\right]A^{\gamma}, \qquad (8.46)$$

where $A = L/T$, $a_i$, $b_i$ and $\gamma$ parameters can be selected directly from Table 8-4. A MATLAB function can be written in the design of PID controllers for unstable FOPDT models.

Table 8-4    Parameters for unstable plants.

| criterion | $a_1$ | $b_1$ | $a_2$ | $b_2$ | $a_3$ | $b_4$ | $\gamma$ |
|-----------|-------|-------|-------|-------|-------|-------|----------|
| ISE | 1.32 | 0.92 | 4 | 0.47 | 3.78 | 0.84 | 0.95 |
| ITAE | 1.38 | 0.9 | 4.12 | 0.9 | 3.62 | 0.85 | 0.93 |
| ISTSE | 1.35 | 0.95 | 4.52 | 1.13 | 3.7 | 0.86 | 0.97 |

```
function [Gc,Kp,Ti,Td]=ufopdt(key,K,L,T,N)
par=[1.32,0.92,4,0.47,3.78,0.84,0.95;
     1.38,0.9,4.12,0.9,3.62,0.85,0.93;
     1.35,0.95,4.52,1.13,3.7,0.86,0.97];
a1=par(key,1); b1=par(key,2); a2=par(key,3); b2=par(key,4);
a3=par(key,5); b3=par(key,6); gam=par(key,7);
A=L/T, Kp=a1*A^b1/K; Ti=a2*T*A^b2;
Td=a3*T*(1-b3*A^(-0.02))*A^gam; Gc=pidstd(Kp,Ti,Td,N);
```

**Example 8.10.** Consider the unstable plant model $G(s) = e^{-s}/(s - 1)$. It can be seen that the key parameters are $k = 1, T = 1, L = 1$. The following statements can be used to design PID controllers, and the closed-loop step responses are shown in Fig. 8-18. It can be seen that although the controllers can stabilize the closed-loop system, the control results are very poor. Better design methods will be given later.

```
>> k=1; T=1; L=1; G=tf(k,[T -1],'ioDelay',L); N=100;
   G1=ufopdt(1,k,L,T,N), G2=ufopdt(2,k,L,T,N), G3=ufopdt(3,k,L,T,N)
   step(feedback(G*G1,1),feedback(G*G2,1),'--',feedback(G*G3,1),':')
```

The three PID controllers designed are

$$G_1(s) = 1.32\left(1 + \frac{1}{4s} + \frac{0.605s}{0.00605s+1}\right), \; G_2(s) = 1.38\left(1 + \frac{1}{4.12s} + \frac{0.543s}{0.00543s+1}\right),$$

$$G_3(s) = 1.35\left(1 + \frac{1}{4.52s} + \frac{0.518s}{0.00518s+1}\right).$$

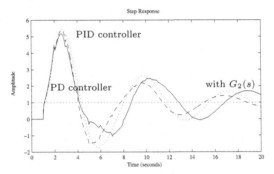

Fig. 8-18   Comparisons of different PID controllers.

### 8.5.4   *Interactive PID Controller Tuning Interface*

### 1. PID controller design function

In the new versions of MATLAB Control System Toolbox, several PID controller design tools are provided, such as `pidtune()`, `pidtool()`. These functions can be used directly in PID controller design. The supported PID-type controllers are listed in Table 8-5.

With $G_c = \texttt{pidtune}(G,\texttt{type})$ function, controller $G_c$ can be designed for plant model $G$, and the controller type is specified with `type`.

**Example 8.11.** Suppose the plant model is given by $G(s) = \mathrm{e}^{-2s}/[s(s+1)^4]$. This model cannot be described by FOPDT model, special algorithms can be used to design controllers. For instance, the following statements can be used, and the PI, PD and PID controllers can be designed, and the closed-loop system responses are shown in Fig. 8-19. It can be seen that these controllers are acceptable. Besides, since there is no derivative action in PI controller, the response speed is slow.

```
>> s=tf('s'); G=exp(-2*s)/s/(s+1)^4;
   Gc1=pidtune(G,'pd'), Gc2=pidtune(G,'pid'), Gc3=pidtune(G,'pi')
   step(feedback(G*Gc1,1),'-',feedback(G*Gc2,1),':',...
       feedback(G*Gc3,1),'--',60)
```

The three controllers are

$$G_{c1}(s) = 0.134 + 0.284s, \; G_{c2}(s) = 0.134 + \frac{0.00031}{s} + 0.302s, \; G_{c3}(s) = 0.0846 + \frac{0.00012}{s}.$$

Table 8-5　PID-type controllers supported by Control System Toolbox.

| keyword type | controller type | continuous model | discrete model |
|---|---|---|---|
| 'p' | proportional | $K_p$ | $K_p$ |
| 'i' | integral | $\dfrac{K_i}{s}$ | $K_i \dfrac{T}{z-1}$ |
| 'pi' | PI controller | $K_p + \dfrac{K_i}{s}$ | $K_p + K_i \dfrac{T}{z-1}$ |
| 'pd' | PD controller | $K_p + K_d s$ | $K_p + K_d \dfrac{z-1}{T}$ |
| 'pdf' | PD with filter | $K_p + K_d \dfrac{s}{T_f s + 1}$ | $K_p + K_d \dfrac{1}{T_f + \dfrac{T}{z-1}}$ |
| 'pid' | PID controller | $K_p + \dfrac{K_i}{s} + K_d s$ | $K_p + K_i \dfrac{T}{z-1} + K_d \dfrac{z-1}{T}$ |
| 'pidf' | PID with filter | $K_p + \dfrac{K_i}{s} + K_d \dfrac{s}{T_f s + 1}$ | $K_p + K_i \dfrac{T}{z-1} + K_d \dfrac{1}{T_f + \dfrac{T}{z-1}}$ |

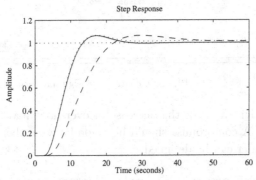

Fig. 8-19　Step responses of closed-loop system under various controllers.

## 2. An interactive PID controller design interface

The new `pidtool()` function is provided in the new Control System Toolbox, and it is an interactive interface for designing PID-type controllers. The syntax of the function is $G_c = \texttt{pidtool}(G, \texttt{type})$. For instance, in the previous example, if a parallel PID controller is expected, the statement `pidtool(G,'pid')` can be used. The initial interface is shown in Fig. 8-20. The closed-loop step response of the system can be obtained directly. If the Interactive tuning horizontal bar is adjusted, then the interactive method can be used to tune the parameters of the controller, and the control response can be shown while adjusting the parameters.

In the interface shown in Fig. 8-20, when the horizonal bar is dragged to 15.1 s, the overshoot is similar to the one in Fig. 8-20, but the respond speed is increased. The ⮕ button in the Show parameters pane can be used, and the controller parameters and closed-loop step response can be obtained as shown in Fig. 8-21. Meanwhile, other specifications for the controller are given as well. In

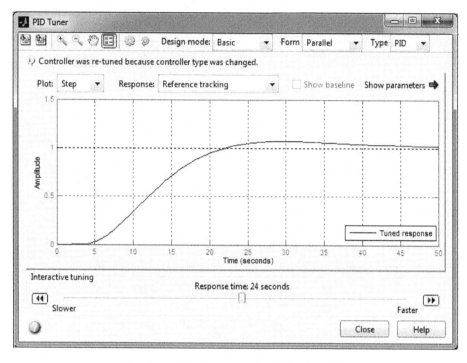

Fig. 8-20    PID-type controller design interface.

the interactive design method, the decrease of overshoot may lead to a decrease in response speed. A compromise should be made between those specifications, so that a good controller can be designed.

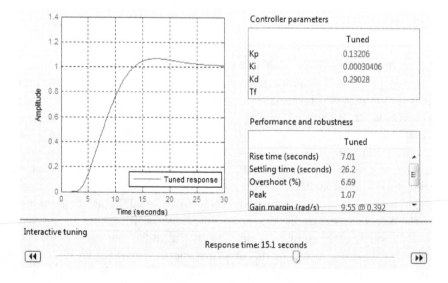

Fig. 8-21    The controller and step response.

The default selection in **Design mode** listbox is **Basic**. Under this mode, the response time can be adjusted, to design the parameters of the controller. If the **Extended** mode is selected from the listbox, the interactive horizontal bars are shown in Fig. 8-22. Two parameters, **Bandwidth** and **Phase margin** can be adjusted. To increase bandwidth means to increase the speed of response, meanwhile the overshoot may also be increased. To increase phase margin means ro reduce the overshoot, while when the phase margin is set to a very large value, the response may not be satisfactory.

Under such tuning methods, the two parameters should be compromised, so as to improve the responses. For instance, by selecting bandwidth to $0.159\,\mathrm{rad/s}$, and phase margin to $66°$, the step response can be shown in Fig. 8-23, along with the controller parameters and important response specifications.

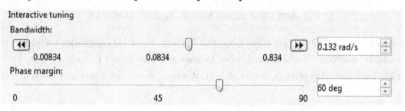

Fig. 8-22   Interactive horizontal bar.

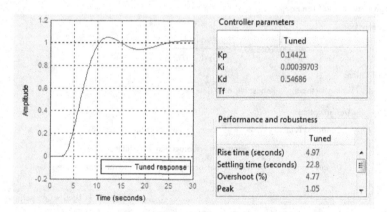

Fig. 8-23   The new PID controller and step response.

When the PID controller is designed, the ▦ button in the toolbar can be selected to save the plant and controller models into MATLAB workspace. With the ▦ button, controller model can be read from MATLAB workspace.

### 8.5.5   *PID Controller Design and Tuning*

Recall the single variable design interface SISO Tool, the interface can also be used in PID controller design and interactive tuning. An example is illustrated below to show the PID controller design process.

**Example 8.12.** Consider again the plant model studied in Example 8.11. The following command can be used to start the design interface. Selecting the Automated Tuning pane, the interface shown in Fig. 8-24 can be displayed.

```
>> s=tf('s'); G=exp(-2*s)/s/(s+1)^4; sisotool(G)
```

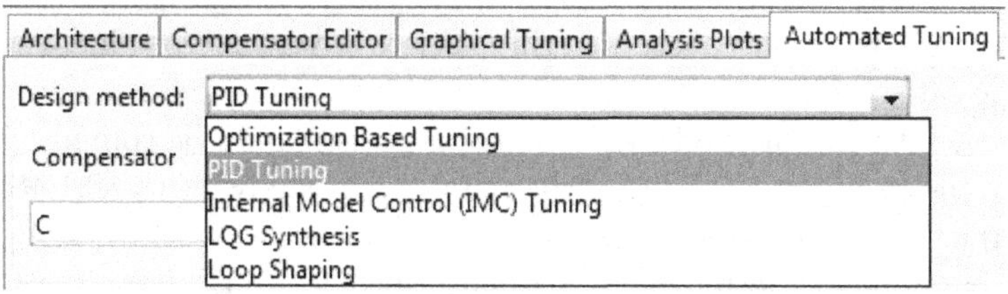

Fig. 8-24   Parameter tuning algorithm selection.

By selecting the PID Tuning item from the listbox, the PID controller parameter tuning process can be started. Various controller types can be selected from it. Then, by clicking the Update Compensator button, a suitable controller can be designed as shown in Fig. 8-25.

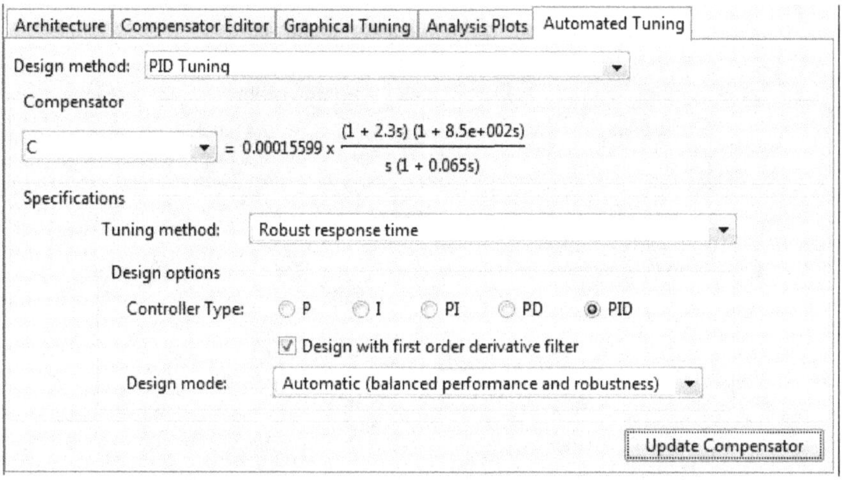

Fig. 8-25   Automatic tuning PID controller algorithm selection.

In Tuning method listbox, two types of parameter tuning approaches, i.e., Robust response time and Classical design formula are available as shown in Fig. 8-26(a). When Robust response time is selected, the contents of the Formula listbox are as shown in Fig. 8-26(b). A default algorithm and interactive tuning method can be used to design the controllers.

If the Classical design formula item is selected, the contents in the Formula listbox are as shown in Fig. 8-27(a), where the loop shaping methods such as MIGO algorithm, approximate MIGO algorithm[17] are supported. MIGO algorithm is more suitable for the parameter tuning problems for multiple plants with the same PID controller. If a certain

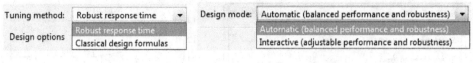

(a) two types of tuning algorithms     (b) robust tuning approach

Fig. 8-26   Robust parameter tuning selections.

algorithm and control structure are selected, the **Update Compensator** button can be used to design the suitable controller as shown in Fig. 8-27(b).

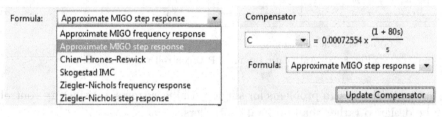

(a) classical algorithms     (b) results of A-MIGO algorithm

Fig. 8-27   Classical design and results.

It should be noted that not all the controller types can be actually designed. For instance, although the controller type is set to **PID**, and **Approximate MIGO step response** algorithm is selected, PI controller can be designed, rather than the expected PID controller. This is because in that algorithm, PI controller is regarded sufficient for the plant model. Besides, all the classical tuning algorithms apply only to stable plant models. If the plant model is not stable, or contains nonlinearity, the interface cannot be used, and the controller design problem too cannot be used.

When the design processes is completed, the **File → Export** menu item can be selected to transfer the controller to MATLAB workspace. The dialog box shown in Fig. 8-28(a) will be opened from which the users may select the model name to return to MATLAB workspace. If more than one model is to be returned, **Ctrl** key can be held down while clicking the variable names. The selected models can be returned to MATLAB workspace by clicking the **Export to Workspace** button. The button **Export to Disk** can be used to save the models into files. For instance, the controller can be returned in variable $C_1$ with $C_1 = 0.132 + 0.000304/s + 0.29s$. The following MATLAB statements can be used to draw the system response as shown in Fig. 8-28(b).

```
>> step(feedback(G*C1,1))
```

It can be seen that the control result is relatively satisfactory. Unfortunately, there exist steady-state error, although its value is very small.

It can be seen from the above example that with the PID controller tuning interface provided in Control System Toolbox, interactive methods or other existing algorithms can be used to design PID controllers. However, there are obvious limitations using the interfaces. For instance, only linear plant models can be treated. If there are nonlinearities in the plants or in the controllers, the problem cannot be solved with the interface. Also, if the plant model is unstable, or even non-minimal phase, a feasible controller cannot be normally found. Besides, similar

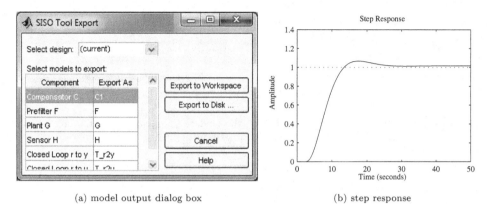

(a) model output dialog box          (b) step response

Fig. 8-28   Automatic tuning of PID controller and the results.

to the controller design problems for single variable systems, satisfactory controller can be designed rather than optimal controllers.

### 8.5.6   *Automatic Tuning Tool based on MATLAB and Simulink*

It has been pointed out that simple commands or interfaces cannot be used in the controller design problems, especially when there exist nonlinearities in the plant model, or with other complicated control structures. In this case, Simulink should be used to model exactly the plant. However, in the interface provided in MATLAB, although the original plant can be expressed in Simulink, linearization process is used.

**Example 8.13.** Consider the time varying plant model

$$\ddot{y}(t) + e^{-0.2t}\dot{y}(t) + e^{-5t}\sin(2t + 6)y(t) = u(t),$$

and the PID controller has actuator saturation, with $|u(t)| \leqslant 2$. This linear model cannot be expressed with LTI object in MATLAB. Simulink should be used to express the PID control system model, shown in Fig. 8-29. In the Simulink model, the menu commands can be used to assign the input and output ports. Specifically, right click the error signal $e(t)$, the shortcut menu is displayed, where **Linearization Points** submenu is shown in Fig. 8-30. In the PID block, the limits of the actuator saturation are assigned to $\pm 2$. Besides, an **Input Point** mark ⅋ can be added to the error signal $e(t)$. Also, an **Output Point** mark ⅋ should be added to the output signal $u(t)$.

Double click the PID control button, the PID controller tuning interface will be displayed. Click the **Tune** button in the interface to start the PID controller tuning process. Linearization facilities will be initiated first, the interactive facilities for controller design process is performed based on the linearized model. For the plant model given in the example, the controller design interface is shown in Fig. 8-31.

It is worth mentioning that since the time varying and nonlinear characteristics are neglected in the design process, although the interactive tool can be used, the control results may be very poor. For instance, the controller designed are $K_{\mathrm{p}} = 0.3265$, $K_{\mathrm{i}} =$

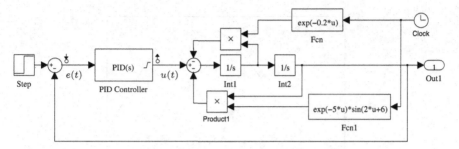

Fig. 8-29 Block diagram of PID control (file: c8foptpid.mdl).

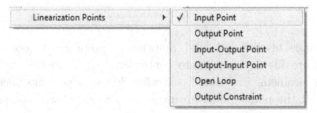

Fig. 8-30 Simulink menu.

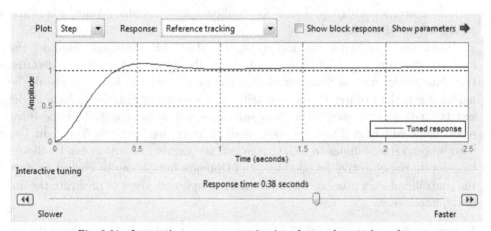

Fig. 8-31 Interactive parameter tuning interface and control results.

0.1169, and $K_d = -0.0047$. The output of the system, when the controller is applied to the original model in Simulink, is shown in Fig. 8-32. It can be seen that the control result is much poor, the result is even worth than the one designed on the linearized model, shown in Fig. 8-31. Thus, it can be concluded that the current MATLAB interface is not applicable to plants with nonlinearities.

## 8.6  OptimPID — An Optimal PID Controller Design Interface

The OCD interface presented in the last chapter converted successfully the optimal controller design problems into numerical optimization problem. The

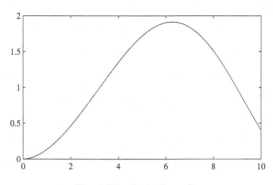

Fig. 8-32    Control results.

powerful facilities of Simulink and numerical optimization tool are combined together, and provide new ideas into controller design. In this chapter, focused on the specific problems in optimal controller design, a new interface, OptimPID, is developed. If the plant model of any kind is modeled with Simulink, optimal PID controller can be designed. Compared with the interfaces provided in Control System Toolbox, the interface is much more powerful, and it can be used in the optimal controller design problems for nonlinear and unstable plants, where the MATLAB interfaces fail.

When the user types `optimpid` in the MATLAB command window, the interface shown in Fig. 8-33 is displayed. What the users need to do is to describe the plant model with a Simulink file. If the plant model is linear, it should be modeled with LTI object $G$ and a possible delay constant tau, the default model `mod_lti.mdl` can be used. The Simulink name should be specified in the Plant model name edit box. Then, the user should specify the Terminate Time edit box with proper value. Similar to OCD controller, the Create File button can be clicked to generate the objective function file, and Optimize button can be clicked to start the controller design process. The following examples are given to illustrate the use of the interface.

**Example 8.14.** Consider the linear plant model in Example 8.11. The following statements can be used first to enter it in MATLAB workspace.

```
>> s=tf('s'); G=1/s/(s+1)^4; tau=2;
```

In the OptimPID toolbox, an existing mod_lti.mdl model file is used to express linear SISO model. Start the OptimPID with command `optimpid`, the main interface will be displayed as shown in Fig. 8-33. In the Plant model name edit box, fill in mod_lti. In the Terminate Time edit box, fill in 40. Then click the Create File button, the objected function will be generated automatically. The Optimize button can be clicked to start the optimization process. The scope shown in Fig. 8-34(a) will be opened automatically, such that the optimization process is visualized. The parameters of the optimized PID controller is returned in the Tuned Controller edit box. It should be noted that in order to reduce the computation load, the maximum allowed iteration number is set to a small

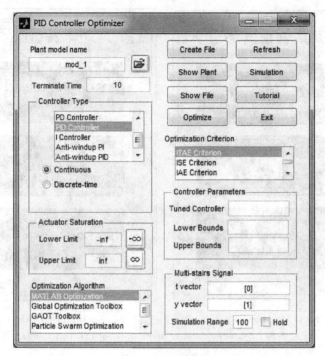

Fig. 8-33   OptimPID interface.

value. Sometimes Optimize button may be clicked several times to complete the design task.

Apart from the default design parameters, other facilities are supported in the interface:

(1) **Controller type selection**. The controller type can be selected from the Controller Type listbox. P, PI, PD, PID and variations of PID controller, such as PID with anti-windup can be selected. Discrete controllers can also be selected with the checkbox.

(2) **Actuator saturation**. If there is actuator saturation in the controller, the Upper limit and Lower limit edit boxes can be specified. Selecting and designing PID controller with actuator saturation may not add much computation burden.

(3) **Optimization algorithm selection**. The currently supported optimization algorithms include the function provided in MATLAB and its Optimization Toolbox and Global Optimization Toolbox. Besides, the third-party free toolboxes are also supported such as Genetic Algorithm Optimization Toolbox (GAOT) and Particle Swarm Optimization Toolbox (PSOt). These free toolboxes are more likely to find global optimized results. The related functions are called directly by the interface, and it is not necessary for the readers to master these optimization algorithms.

(4) **Objective function declaration**. The Optimization Criterion listbox can be used to specify the objective function, with the default ITAE criterion. If ISE Criterion is selected, the responses in Fig. 8-34(b) can be obtained. It is obvious that ITAE criterion is better than ISE for this example.

(5) **Staircase excitation and simulation**. When the controller is designed, the staircase signal can be selected by specifying in the Staircase Waveform edit boxes the

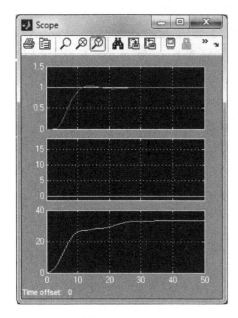 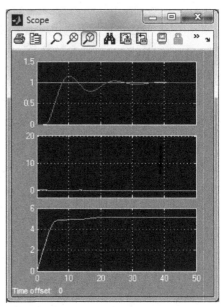

(a) ITAE criterion                                    (b) ISE criterion

Fig. 8-34   System responses under optimal PID controllers.

vectors which describe the turning points of the staircase waveform. The terminate time in simulation can be specified in the **Simulation Range** edit box. Clicking **Simulation** button will start the simulation process. If **Hold** checkbox is selected, the staircase waveform will be used as the input to design controller again, such that the total error criterion in the servo control is minimized.

**Example 8.15.** Assume that the plant is an unstable linear model

$$G(s) = \frac{s+2}{s^4 + 8s^3 + 4s^2 - s + 0.4},$$

and the actuator saturation exists, with its boundaries at $\Delta = \pm 5$. In this case, the `pidtune()` and `sisotool()` interface in the Control System Toolbox cannot be used to design controllers. With OptimPID interface, the plant model should be entered first into MATLAB workspace.

```
>> s=tf('s'); G=(s+2)/(s^4+8*s^3+4*s^2-s+0.4); tau=0;
```

Start the OptimPID interface, and fill in mod_lti and 6 respectively into the **Plant Model** and **Terminate Time** edit boxes, then click **Create File** and **Optimize** buttons, the output and control signal under the optimal controller are shown in Figs. 8-35(a) and (b). It can be seen that the control results are satisfactory.

**Example 8.16.** Consider the time varying plant in Example 8.13

$$\ddot{y}(t) + e^{-0.2t}\dot{y}(t) + e^{-5t}\sin(2t+6)y(t) = u(t).$$

In the original example, the interactive PID control interface was used to design directly the PID controller. Unfortunately, the controller behavior was rather poor. Now consider

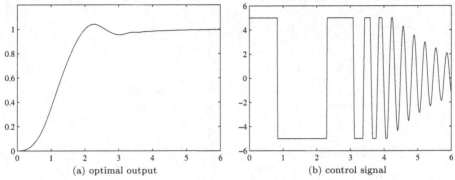

(a) optimal output        (b) control signal

Fig. 8-35   Optimal PID design for unstable plant model.

using OptimPID interface to design directly the optimal PID controller. The input–output relationship of the time varying plant can be expressed with the Simulink model shown in Fig. 8-36(a). Assume that the control signal is bounded with $|u(t)| \leqslant 2$, and select the terminate time to 5, the optimal control results are obtained as shown in Fig. 8-36(b). The control result is satisfactory.

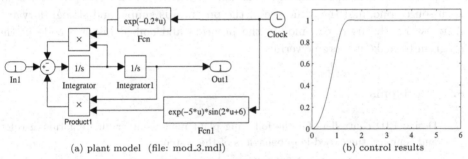

(a) plant model   (file: mod_3.mdl)       (b) control results

Fig. 8-36   Optimal PID controller design and results.

Now let us use staircase waveform to excite the system. The staircase waveform can be expressed by the vectors $t = [0, 10, 22, 35, 50]$ and $y = [1, 6, 3, 2, 5]$. The vectors can be specified in the Staircase Waveform edit boxes. The terminate time can be selected to 70. Click Simulation button, the system response can be obtained as shown in Fig. 8-37(a). It can be seen that although the controller may yield perfect unit step response, the responses to the staircase input is very poor. The controller for the staircase waveform should be redesigned.

If the Hold checkbox is selected, then click the Create File button, the objective function will be created for the staircase signal responses. The Optimize button can be clicked, and the optimal PID controller can be optimized again, and the control results in Fig. 8-37(b) can be obtained.

In OptimPID interface, the user need only to provide the Simulink model of the nonlinear plant, or simply specify the model object $G$ and tau for linear plant. Then the interface can be used in controller design. The plant model can be of

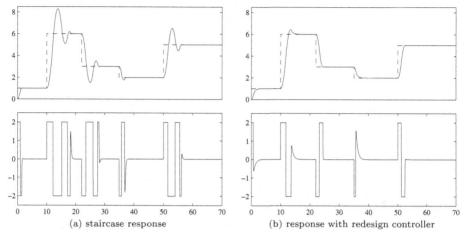

(a) staircase response          (b) response with redesign controller

Fig. 8-37   System response for staircase input signal.

any complexity, as long as it can be described by SISO Simulink model. If there exist difficulties in finding the optimal controller, the additional genetic algorithm and particle swarm optimization tools can be used instead. The program is an open-source one, and the structure of the program is simple and straightforward. If necessary, the users can modify the program and embed his own code in the program to make it more powerful.

## 8.7   Problems

(1) Design PID controllers for the following plant models under different tuning rules, and compare the closed-loop behaviors of the systems.

(i) $G_a(s) = \dfrac{1}{(s+1)^3}$,   (ii) $G_b(s) = \dfrac{1}{(s+1)^5}$,   (iii) $G_c(s) = \dfrac{-1.5s+1}{(s+1)^3}$.

If discrete PID controllers are used, please compare the control results of continuous and discrete PID controllers with the same parameters.

(2) Please use the interactive PID controller design interface and other tools in MATLAB to design controllers for the following plants [5]

(i) $G_1(s) = \dfrac{1}{(s+1)^6}$,   (ii) $G_2(s) = \dfrac{12.8e^{-s}}{16.8s+1}$,   (iii) $G_3(s) = \dfrac{37.7e^{-10s}}{(2s+1)(7200s+1)}$,

(iv) $G_4(s) = \dfrac{(10s-1)e^{-s}}{(2s+1)(4s+1)}$,   (v) $G_5(s) = \dfrac{5.526e^{-2.5s}}{s^2+0.6s+2.5}$,

(vi) $G_6(s) = \dfrac{10.078e^{-10s}}{s^2+0.14s+0.49}$,   (vii) $G_7(s) = \dfrac{3.3}{(1+0.1s)(1+0.2s)(1+0.7s)}$.

(3) Approximate the following plant models with first-order delay models, and compare in time and frequency domain the approximation results.

(i) $G(s) = \dfrac{12(s^2-3s+6)}{(s+1)(s+5)(s^2+3s+6)(s^2+s+2)}$,   (ii) $G(s) = \dfrac{-5s+2}{(s+1)^2(s+3)^3}e^{-0.5s}$.

(4) For the following plants with pure time delay, design optimal PID controller under

the ITAE, IAE, and ISE criteria and compare the results.

(i)  $G_\mathrm{a}(s) = \dfrac{1}{(s+1)(2s+1)} e^{-s}$,  (ii)  $G_\mathrm{b}(s) = \dfrac{1}{(17s+1)(6s+1)} e^{-30s}$.

(5) Assume that the plant model is given by delay differential equation

$$\frac{dy(t)}{dt} = \frac{0.2y(t-1)}{1+y^{10}(t-1)} - 0.1y(t) + u(t).$$

If PI controller is used, please convert the optimal controller design problem into numerical optimization problem, and get the optimal PI parameters. Please draw the closed-loop step response. If we want to reduce the overshoot, please introduce constraints and convert the controller design problem into constrained optimization problem, and find the optimal controller.

(6) For the time varying plant model

$$\ddot{y}(t) + e^{-0.2t}\dot{y}(t) + e^{-5t}\sin(2t+6)y(t) = u(t),$$

design an optimal PI controller that can minimize the ITAE criterion. Please use finite time ITAE criterion to approximate infinite integral. Compare the impact of the terminate time on the control results. If IAE or ISE criteria are used, what are the optimal PI controllers and the control results?

(7) Consider the plant model with large time delay $G(s) = e^{-20s}/(s+1)^3$. Design PID controllers with MATLAB function pidtune() and other tools and compare control behaviors.

(8) Since there exist coupling among the inputs and outputs of the multivariable systems, it may be difficult to design good PID controllers individually for each input–output pairs. Consider the diagonal dominance compensation method in Example 5.43, to the multivariable model

$$G(s) = \begin{bmatrix} \dfrac{0.806s + 0.264}{s^2 + 1.15s + 0.202} & \dfrac{-15s - 1.42}{s^3 + 12.8s^2 + 13.6s + 2.36} \\ \dfrac{1.95s^2 + 2.12s + 0.49}{s^3 + 9.15s^2 + 9.39s + 1.62} & \dfrac{7.15s^2 + 25.8s + 9.35}{s^4 + 20.8s^3 + 116.4s^2 + 111.6s + 18.8} \end{bmatrix},$$

with static pre-compensation matrix of

$$K_\mathrm{p} = \begin{bmatrix} 0.3610 & 0.4500 \\ -1.1300 & 1.0000 \end{bmatrix}.$$

Try to design PID controllers independently for the two loops, and evaluate the control results.

(9) Find good first-order plus dead-time approximations to the following models, and compare the accuracy of the approximate models in time and frequency domain.

(i)  $G(s) = \dfrac{12(s^2 - 3s + 6)}{(s+1)(s+5)(s^2+3s+6)(s^2+s+2)}$,  (ii)  $G(s) = \dfrac{-5s+2}{(s+1)^2(s+3)^3} e^{-0.5s}$.

(10) For the plant models with pure time delay, please design optimal PID controllers under the ITAE, IAE and ISE criteria, and compare control results.

(i)  $G_1(s) = \dfrac{1}{(s+1)(2s+1)} e^{-s}$,  (ii)  $G_2(s) = \dfrac{1}{(17s+1)(6s+1)} e^{-30s}$.

(11) Design optimal continuous and discrete PID controllers for the following discrete plant models [18]

(i) $H(z) = \dfrac{7}{z^4 - 1.31z^3 + 1.21z^2 - 0.287z - 0.0178}$, $T = 0.01\,\text{s}$,

(ii) $H(z) = \dfrac{3z^2 - 1}{z^5 - 0.6z^4 + 0.13z^3 - 0.364z^2 + 0.1416z - 0.288}$, $T = 0.01\,\text{s}$.

(12) Design an optimal PID controller for the plant [19]

$$G(s) = \frac{1 + 3e^{-s}/(s+1)}{s+1}.$$

## Bibliography and References

[1] Bennett S. Development of the PID controllers. IEEE Control Systems Magazine, 1993, 13(6):58–65

[2] Åström K J, Hang C C, Persson P, Ho W K. Towards intellegient PID control. Automatica, 1992, 28(1):1–9

[3] Åström K J, Hägglund T. PID controllers: theory, design and tuning. Research Triangle Park, Instrument Society of America, 1995

[4] Tao Y H, Yin Y X, Ge L S. New types of PIDcontrol and applications. Beijing: Machanical Industry Press, 2001. (In Chinese)

[5] Johnson M A, Moradi M H. PID control — new identification and design methods. London: Springer, 2005

[6] Xue D Y. Design and analysis of feedback control systems with MATLAB. Beijing: Tsinghua University Press, 2000. (In Chinese)

[7] Xue D Y, Atherton D P. A suboptimal reduction algorithm for linear systems with a time delay. International Journal of Control, 1994, 60(2):181–196

[8] Ziegler J G, Nichols N B. Optimum settings for automatic controllers. Transaction of ASME, 1944, 64:759–768

[9] Hang C C, Åström K J, Ho W K. Refinement of the Ziegler-Nichols tuning formula. Proceedings of IEE, Part D, 1991, 138:111–118

[10] O'Dwyer A. Handbook of PI and PID controller tuning rules. London: Imperial College Press, 2003

[11] Zhuang M, Atherton D P. Automatic tuning of optimum PID controllers. Proceedings of IEE, Part D, 1993, 140:216–224

[12] Murrill P W. Automatic control of processes. International Textbook Co, 1967

[13] Cheng G S, Hung J C. A least-squares based self-tuning of PID controller. Proceedings of the IEEE South East Conference, 1985, 325–332. Raleigh, North Carolina, USA

[14] Wang F S, Juang W S, Chan C T. Optimal tuning of PID controllers for single and cascade control loops. Chemical Engineering Communications, 1995, 132:15–34

[15] O'Dwyer A. PI and PID controller tuning rules for time delay processes: a summary. Proceedings of the Irish Signals and Systems Conference, 1999

[16] Visioli A. Optimal tuning of PID controllers for integral and unstable processes. Proceedings of IEE, Part D, 2001, 148(2):180–184

[17] Åström K J, Hägglund T. Revisiting the Ziegler-Nichols step response method for PID control. Journal of Process Control, 2004, 14:635–650

[18] Hellerstein J L, Diao Y, Parekh S, Tilbury D M. Feedback control of computing systems. Hoboken, New Jersey: IEEE Press and John Wiley & Sons Inc, 2004

[19] Brosilow C, Joseph B. Techniques of model-based control. Englewood Cliffs: Prentice Hall, 2002

# Chapter 9

# Robust Control and
# Robust Controller Design

Many controller design algorithms are introduced in the previous two chapters. Some of the algorithms may yield good controllers with small overshoot and fast respond speed. However, there are changes in the parameters of the plant model, or if the system is subjected to noises and disturbances, the behavior of the system may become very poor, or even, the closed-loop systems may become unstable. This indicates that the "robustness" of the system is not good. In this case, robust controllers are needed. Generally speaking, the robustness of PID-type controllers is usually very high.

In the state space control theory, linear quadratic optimal regulators are usually the most well-studied controller design problem. It is based on the assumption that all the states can be exactly reconstructed with observers. In real applications, in the sensors, measurement noises are unavoidable. Combined with the Kalman filter technique for stochastic signals, linear quadratic Gaussian (LQG) problems appeared[1]. In the earlier researches, optimal control and optimal filtering problems were usually considered separately. Later, it was pointed out that[2] the phase margin of the control system thus designed may be very small, and loop transfer recovery techniques were introduced to overcome the problems. In Section 9.1, linear quadratic Gaussian problems and loop transfer recovery techniques are presented, and the LQG/LTR controller design approaches are explored. Norm-based robust control is another attractive field. In 1979, George Zames pioneered the robust control theory based on the minimization of the norms in Hardy space[3]. John Doyle and collaborators proposed state space-based numerical solution framework for robust controller design in 1991[4]. The $\mathcal{H}_\infty$ control strategy developed since 1980's become more systematic. Although the computation required are quite complicated, the problems can be handled easily and directly by MATLAB and relevant toolboxes. In Section 9.2, norm-based robust control problem formulation is presented, and the problem formulation in MATLAB is also illustrated. In Section 9.3, norm-based robust controller design algorithms, such as optimal $\mathcal{H}_2$ and $\mathcal{H}_\infty$ controllers are introduced. Examples are given to show the impact of weighting functions to the control results. Loop shaping robust control is demonstrated. Linear matrix inequality (LMI) can be used to convert optimal control problems into the well-developed linear algebra problem, and the design methods are presented in Section 9.4. In Section 9.5, quantitative feedback theory (QFT)-based robust controller design method will be demonstrated, in the control of uncertain systems.

## 9.1　Linear Quadratic Gaussian Control

Linear quadratic optimal control problems and MATLAB solutions are illustrated in Chapter 7. If there are stochastic input disturbances, or measurement noises, the original optimal regulator further extended linear quadratic Gaussian (LQG) problems. In this section, LQG problems are formulated and loop transfer recovery techniques are presented.

### 9.1.1　*LQG Problems*

Assume that the state space representation of the plant is

$$\begin{cases} \dot{\boldsymbol{x}}(t) = \boldsymbol{A}\boldsymbol{x}(t) + \boldsymbol{B}\boldsymbol{u}(t) + \boldsymbol{\Gamma}\boldsymbol{w}(t) \\ \boldsymbol{y}(t) = \boldsymbol{C}\boldsymbol{x}(t) + \boldsymbol{D}\boldsymbol{u}(t) + \boldsymbol{v}(t), \end{cases} \tag{9.1}$$

where $\boldsymbol{w}(t)$ and $\boldsymbol{v}(t)$ are white noise signals, representing respectively the uncertainties and measurement noises. Assume that these signals are Gaussian processes, with zero mean, and covariance matrices of

$$\mathrm{E}\big[\boldsymbol{w}(t)\boldsymbol{w}^{\mathrm{T}}(t)\big] = \boldsymbol{\Xi} \geqslant \boldsymbol{0}, \quad \mathrm{E}\big[\boldsymbol{v}(t)\boldsymbol{v}^{\mathrm{T}}(t)\big] = \boldsymbol{\Theta} > \boldsymbol{0}, \tag{9.2}$$

where $\mathrm{E}[\boldsymbol{x}]$ is the mean (or mathematical expectation) of vector $\boldsymbol{x}$, and $\mathrm{E}[\boldsymbol{x}\boldsymbol{x}^{\mathrm{T}}]$ is the covariance matrix of Gaussian signal $\boldsymbol{x}$ with zero mean. Further assume that $\boldsymbol{w}(t)$ and $\boldsymbol{v}(t)$ signals are mutually independent, i.e., $\mathrm{E}[\boldsymbol{w}(t)\boldsymbol{v}^{\mathrm{T}}(t)] = \boldsymbol{0}$. The optimal control criterion can be defined as

$$J = \mathrm{E}\left\{\int_0^\infty \big[\boldsymbol{z}^{\mathrm{T}}(t)\boldsymbol{Q}\boldsymbol{z}(t) + \boldsymbol{u}^{\mathrm{T}}(t)\boldsymbol{R}\boldsymbol{u}(t)\big]\mathrm{d}t\right\}, \tag{9.3}$$

where $\boldsymbol{z}(t) = \boldsymbol{M}\boldsymbol{x}(t)$ is a linear transformation of the state variable vector $\boldsymbol{x}(t)$, and the weighting matrix $\boldsymbol{Q}$ is a symmetrical semi-positive definite matrix, while $\boldsymbol{R}$ is a symmetrical positive definite matrix. The mathematical descriptions are $\boldsymbol{Q} = \boldsymbol{Q}^{\mathrm{T}} \geqslant \boldsymbol{0}$, $\boldsymbol{R} = \boldsymbol{R}^{\mathrm{T}} > \boldsymbol{0}$. For single variable systems, $\boldsymbol{R}$ is a scalar. The definitions of these matrices are the same as the ones defined in Chapter 7.

Thus, typical LQG problems can be divided into two subsystems, one is for LQ optimal control problem, and the other, the state estimation problems with disturbances.

### 9.1.2　*Solving LQG Problems with MATLAB*

#### 1. LQG structure with Kalman filters

In practical applications, there are random measurement noises. Thus, the states if the system cannot be reconstructed using the simple state observers presented in

Chapter 7. The Kalman filters in Eqn. (9.1) should be used instead to estimate the states.

The optimal state estimate $\hat{x}(t)$ is defined to minimize the covariance matrix

$$\min_{\hat{x}(t)} \mathrm{E}\left\{ \left[ x(t) - \hat{x}(t) \right] \left[ x(t) - \hat{x}(t) \right]^{\mathrm{T}} \right\}. \tag{9.4}$$

The estimated states $\hat{x}(t)$ can be used to replace the state variables $x(t)$ in state feedback control. The system structure shown in Fig. 9-1 can be constructed to implement the Kalman filter, where the gain matrix is

$$K_{\mathrm{f}} = P_{\mathrm{f}} C^{\mathrm{T}} \Theta^{-1}, \tag{9.5}$$

and $P_{\mathrm{f}}$ satisfies the following Riccati algebraic equation

$$P_{\mathrm{f}} A^{\mathrm{T}} + A P_{\mathrm{f}} - P_{\mathrm{f}} C^{\mathrm{T}} \Theta^{-1} C P_{\mathrm{f}} + \Gamma \Xi \Gamma^{\mathrm{T}} = 0, \tag{9.6}$$

where $P_{\mathrm{f}}$ is a symmetrical semi-positive definite matrix, i.e., $P_{\mathrm{f}} = P_{\mathrm{f}}^{\mathrm{T}} \geqslant 0$.

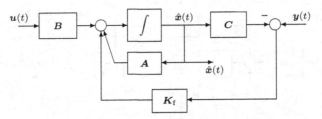

Fig. 9-1   Block diagram representation of Kalman filter.

The function `kalman()` is provided in the Control System Toolbox to design the Kalman filter matrix $K_{\mathrm{f}}$ with $[G_{\mathrm{k}}, K_{\mathrm{f}}, P_{\mathrm{f}}] = \mathtt{kalman}(G, \Xi, \Theta)$, where $G$ is the state space equation $(A, \tilde{B}, C, \tilde{D})$ of Gaussian disturbance. There are two inputs, with $\tilde{B} = \begin{bmatrix} B, & \Gamma \end{bmatrix}$, $\tilde{D} = \begin{bmatrix} D, & D \end{bmatrix}$. In the returned arguments, $G_{\mathrm{k}}$ is the Kalman state estimator, and $P_{\mathrm{f}}$ is the solutions of the Riccati algebraic equation.

**Example 9.1.** For the follow system model

$$\dot{x}(t) = \begin{bmatrix} -0.02 & 0.005 & 2.4 & -32 \\ -0.14 & 0.44 & -1.3 & -30 \\ 0 & 0.018 & -1.6 & 1.2 \\ 0 & 0 & 1 & 0 \end{bmatrix} x(t) + \begin{bmatrix} 0.14 \\ 0.36 \\ 0.35 \\ 0 \end{bmatrix} u(t) + \begin{bmatrix} -0.12 \\ -0.86 \\ 0.009 \\ 0 \end{bmatrix} \xi(t), \; y(t) = x_2 + v(t),$$

with $\Xi = 10^{-3}$, $\Theta = 10^{-7}$. The following MATLAB statements can be used to design the Kalman filter

```
>> A=[-0.02,0.005,2.4,-32; -0.14,0.44,-1.3,-30; ...
      0,0.018,-1.6,1.2; 0,0,1,0];
   B=[0.14; 0.36; 0.35; 0]; G=[-0.12; -0.86; 0.009; 0];
   C=[0,1,0,0]; G=ss(A,[B,G],C,[0,0]);
   Xi=1e-3; Theta=1e-7; [Gk,Kf,Pf]=kalman(G,Xi,Theta)
```

The solutions of Riccati equation is

$$P_f = \begin{bmatrix} 0.0044357 & 2.1533 \times 10^{-5} & -3.6456 \times 10^{-5} & -7.7729 \times 10^{-5} \\ 2.1533 \times 10^{-5} & 8.7371 \times 10^{-6} & -2.5369 \times 10^{-7} & -3.5741 \times 10^{-7} \\ -3.6456 \times 10^{-5} & -2.5369 \times 10^{-7} & 3.0037 \times 10^{-7} & 6.3871 \times 10^{-7} \\ -7.7729 \times 10^{-5} & -3.5741 \times 10^{-7} & 6.3871 \times 10^{-7} & 1.3623 \times 10^{-6} \end{bmatrix},$$

with the filter gain vector $K_f = [215.33, 87.371, -2.5369, -3.5741]^T$.

## 2. Separation principles in LQG controller design

If the optimal estimated signal $\hat{x}(t)$ is obtained, the LQG control structure shown in Fig. 9-2 can be established. The optimal control signal $u^*(t)$ satisfies $u^*(t) = -K_c\hat{x}(t)$. The optimal state feedback matrix $K_c$ can be obtained from $K_c = R^{-1}B^T P_c$, and matrix $P_c$ satisfies the following Riccati algebraic equation

$$A^T P_c + P_c A - P_c B R^{-1} B^T P_c + M^T Q M = 0, \tag{9.7}$$

where $P_c$ is a semi-positive definite matrix, i.e., $P_c = P_c^T \geqslant 0$.

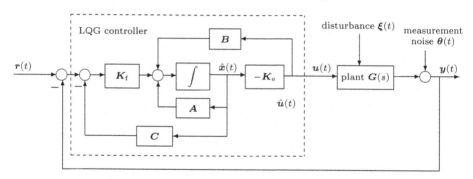

Fig. 9-2    LQG control structure.

It can be seen that the LQG problem is divided into two separate problems — the optimal estimation problem and the optimal control problem. The optimal solution of the problem is based on the optimal solutions of the two sub problems, This method is known as the separation principle of LQG control problem.

## 3. Design of observer-based LQG regulators

The state space model of the plant is

$$\begin{cases} \dot{x}(t) = Ax(t) + Bu(t) + \xi(t) \\ y(t) = Cx(t) + Du(t) + \theta(t), \end{cases} \tag{9.8}$$

and the optimal criterion is written as

$$J = \lim_{t_f \to \infty} E\left\{ \int_0^{t_f} [x^T, u^T] \begin{bmatrix} Q & N_c \\ N_c^T & R \end{bmatrix} \begin{bmatrix} x \\ u \end{bmatrix} dt \right\}, \tag{9.9}$$

where $N_c$ is normally a zero vector.

Kalman filter-based LQG regulator structure is shown in Fig. 9-3. Assume that the state feedback matrix $K_c$ and Kalman filter matrix $K_f$ are given, through separation principle the Kalman filter model can be constructed

$$\dot{\hat{x}}(t) = A\hat{x}(t) + Bu(t) + K_f\left[y(t) - C\hat{x}(t) - Du(t)\right]. \tag{9.10}$$

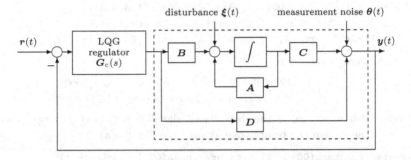

Fig. 9-3   Structure of Kalman filter-based LQG regulator.

The Kalman filter-based LQG regulator can be written as

$$G_c(s) = \left[\begin{array}{c|c} A - K_fC - BK_c + K_fDK_c & K_f \\ \hline K_c & 0 \end{array}\right]. \tag{9.11}$$

Please note that the matrix $G_c(s)$ is not an ordinary matrix. It is, in fact, the shorthand notation of state space model, represented in the partitioned matrix form. Function $\texttt{lqg()}$ provided in the Robust Control Toolbox can be used to construct estimator-based LQG regulator, with the syntax $G_f = \texttt{lqg}(G, W, V)$, where the returned variable $G_f$ is the state space model of the LQG regulator, and the matrices $W$ and $V$ can be evaluated from

$$W = \begin{bmatrix} Q & N_c \\ N_c^{\mathrm{T}} & R \end{bmatrix}, \quad V = \begin{bmatrix} \varXi & N_f \\ N_f^{\mathrm{T}} & \varTheta \end{bmatrix}, \tag{9.12}$$

with $\varXi$ and $\varTheta$ the covariance matrix of the disturbance signal $\xi(t)$ and the measurement noise signal $\theta(t)$, and $N_c$ and $N_f$ are usually assumed to be zero vectors. It can be seen that matrix $V$ is, in fact, the cross-correlation function of the signals $\xi(t)$ and $\theta$, i.e.

$$\mathrm{E}\left\{\begin{bmatrix} \xi(t) \\ \theta(\tau) \end{bmatrix}\left[\xi(t)\ \theta(\tau)\right]^{\mathrm{T}}\right\} = \begin{bmatrix} \varXi & N_f \\ N_f^{\mathrm{T}} & \varTheta \end{bmatrix}\delta(t - \tau). \tag{9.13}$$

Please note that $\varXi$ is the covariance matrix of $\xi(t)$ signal. If the plant model in Eqn. (9.1) is used, it is equivalent to $\varXi = \varGamma\varXi\varGamma^{\mathrm{T}}$.

**Example 9.2.** Consider the following state space model of the plant

$$\dot{x}(t) = \begin{bmatrix} 0 & 1 & 0 & 0 \\ -5000 & -100/3 & 500 & 100/3 \\ 0 & -1 & 0 & 1 \\ 0 & 100/3 & -4 & -60 \end{bmatrix}x(t) + \begin{bmatrix} 0 \\ 25/3 \\ 0 \\ -1 \end{bmatrix}u(t) + \begin{bmatrix} -1 \\ 0 \\ 0 \\ 0 \end{bmatrix}\xi(t),$$

where $y(t) = [0, 0, 1, 0]\boldsymbol{x}(t) + \theta(t)$, and $\varXi = 7 \times 10^{-4}$, $\varTheta = 10^{-8}$. Selecting the matrices $\boldsymbol{Q} = \mathrm{diag}(5000, 0, 50000, 1)$, and $R = 0.001$, the following statements can be used to solve the LQG problem

```
>> A=[0,1,0,0; -5000,-100/3,500,100/3; 0,-1,0,1; 0,100/3,-4,-60];
   B=[0; 25/3; 0; -1]; C=[0,0,1,0]; D=0; G0=ss(A,B,C,D);
   Q=diag([5000,0,50000,1]); R=0.001; G0=ss(A,B,C,D);
   Xi=7e-4; Theta=1e-8; W=[Q,zeros(4,1); zeros(1,4),R];
   V=[Xi*G*G',zeros(4,1); zeros(1,4),Theta]; Gc=zpk(lqg(G0,W,V))
```

The designed controller is

$$G_c(s) = \frac{1231049.0702(s + 40.47)(s^2 + 105.5s + 5000)}{(s^2 + 39.17s + 868.2)(s^2 + 493.9s + 1.234\times 10^5)}.$$

Under such a system, if the disturbance signal is neglected, the closed-loop step response of the system can be obtained as shown in Fig. 9-4(a).

```
>> step(feedback(G0*Gc,1)), figure; bode(G0,'-',G*Gc,'--')
```

The open-loop Bode diagrams of the original model and the compensated model are shown in Fig. 9-4(b). It can be seen that when the LQG controller is used, the open-loop characteristics is significantly improved. The phase margin of the system is $\gamma = 43°$.

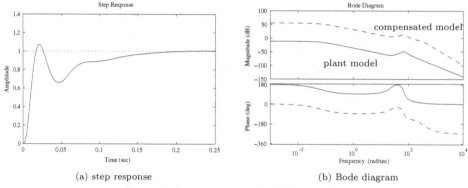

(a) step response             (b) Bode diagram

Fig. 9-4   System responses in LQG control.

### 9.1.3   *LQG Control with Loop Transfer Recovery*

#### 1. LQG/LTR controller design algorithm

It can be seen from the Kalman filter-based optimal LQG controller design algorithm that the controller design problem can be separated into the solutions of two Riccati equations, and the equations can be solved easily with MATLAB.

In fact, things are not always this simple. It is pointed out that the stability margin of the system thus designed may be very poor[2]. A small disturbance to the system may result in the instability problem in the whole system.

In the solution algorithms of LQG problems, the dynamic characteristics of the filter is usually selected much faster than that of the system itself. In practical applications, this selection is proven wrong. The LQG controller thus designed may significantly reduce the stability margins.

With direct state feedback, the open-loop transfer function can be written as $G_{\mathrm{LQSF}}(s) = K_c\big(sI - A\big)^{-1}B$, while under LQG controller, the open-loop transfer function becomes

$$G_{\mathrm{L,LQG}}(s) = K_c\big(sI - A + BK + LC\big)^{-1}LC\big(sI - A\big)^{-1}B. \qquad (9.14)$$

**Example 9.3.** Consider the transfer function model

$$G(s) = \frac{-(948.12s^3 + 30325s^2 + 56482s + 1215.3)}{s^6 + 64.554s^5 + 1167s^4 + 3728.6s^3 - 5495.4s^2 + 1102s + 708.1}.$$

With the following MATLAB statements, the state space model of the system can be written as

```
>> n=-[948.12, 30325, 56482, 1215.3];
   d=[1,64.554,1167,3728.6,-5495.4,1102,708.1]; G=ss(tf(n,d));
```

Selecting weighting matrices $Q = C^{\mathrm{T}}C$, and $R = 1$, the following MATLAB statements, and the optimal LQG controller can be designed if there exists Gaussian disturbances, and assuming $\Gamma$ vector defined as $\Gamma = B$. Assume also $\Xi = 10^{-4}$, and $\Theta = 10^{-5}$, the following MATLAB statements can be used to design the Kalman filter. The Nyquist plots and Bode diagrams under the two controllers are obtained as shown in Fig. 9-5. It can be seen that the Kalman filter-based feedback control system has significant differences with the direct feedback structure.

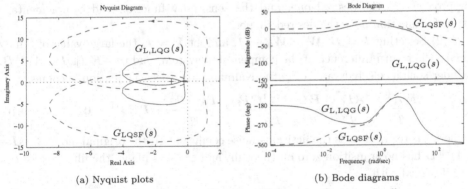

(a) Nyquist plots  (b) Bode diagrams

Fig. 9-5 Open-loop frequency domain analysis under the two controllers.

```
>> Q=G.c'*G.c; R=1; [Kc,P]=lqr(G.a,G.b,Q,R); G0=ss(G.a,G.b,Kc,0);
   Xi=1e-4; Theta=1e-5; G1=ss(G.a,[G.b, G.b],G.c,[G.d,G.d]);
   [K_Sys,L,P2]=kalman(G1,Xi,Theta); a1=G.a-G.b*Kc-L*G.c;
   Gc=ss(a1,L,Kc,0); nyquist(G*Gc,'-',G0,'--');
   figure; bode(G*Gc,'-',G0,'--');
```

Model $G_{\mathrm{L,LQG}}(s)$ is the series connection of the two subsystems $\big(A - BK - LC, L, K, 0\big)$ and $\big(A, B, C, 0\big)$. The Nyquist plots of $G_{\mathrm{L,LQG}}(s)$ and $G_{\mathrm{LQSF}}(s)$ are also obtained, and it can be seen that the two plots are different.

It can be seen that if the weighting matrices are not properly chosen, extremely very large differences exist in the open-loop transfer functions of the two control structures. One effective solution to the problem is to introduce the loop transfer recovery (LTR) technique. With such technique, the open-loop transfer function under LQG controller approaches the direct state feedback as close as possible.

Selecting $\Xi_1 = q\Xi$, it can be shown that when $q \to \infty$, the open-loop transfer function with LQG controller designed under $\Xi_1$ will approach the open-loop transfer function with direct state feedback, i.e.,

$$\lim_{q \to \infty} K_c\Big(sI - A + BK + LC\Big)^{-1} LC\Big(sI - A\Big)^{-1} B = K_c\Big(sI - A\Big)^{-1}B. \quad (9.15)$$

It can be seen that the key point in LQG/LTR controller design is to select a suitable value of $q$. This value should be selected as a very large number, although it not necessary to really select it as an infinite number.

For the selected weighting matrices, state feedback matrix should be designed first. The LTR technique should then be used to design a Kalman filter, such that the open-loop transfer function approaches to the one by direct state feedback as close as possible. The following two steps should be used:

(1) Design optimal LQ controller under the selected weighting matrices $Q$ and $R$, and then adjust the weighting matrices $Q$ and $R$, such that the open-loop transfer function $-K_c\Big(sI - A\Big)^{-1}B$ reaches satisfactory results. Then select $Q = C^T C$, and change the value of $R$, such that the open-loop transfer function approaches to the desired one, and the sensitivity function and complementary transfer function have the desired shape.

(2) Selecting $\Gamma = B$, $W = W_0 + qI$, and let $V = I$, the large value of $q$ may make the return difference of the compensated system tend to $-K_c(j\omega I - A)^{-1}B$. Under such a selected value of $q$, the Kalman filter Riccati equation becomes

$$\frac{P_f A^T}{q} + \frac{AP_f}{q} - \frac{P_f C^T V^{-1} C P_f}{q} + \frac{\Gamma W_0 \Gamma^T}{q} + \Gamma \Theta \Gamma^T = 0, \quad (9.16)$$

where $q$ is referred to as the fictitious-noise coefficient. If the original model $C(sI - A)^{-1}B$ has no transition zero on the right half of the $s$ plane, the filter vector can be designed with

$$K_f \to q^{1/2} B V^{-1/2}, \quad \text{when } q \to \infty. \quad (9.17)$$

In practical applications, the value of $q$ should not be selected to an extremely large value, otherwise truncation error may be introduced to affect the robustness of the control system. Normally, the value can be selected as $q = 10^{10}$.

**Example 9.4.** Consider again the system in Example 9.3. If LTR technique is used, the following statements can be used to draw Nyquist plots of the open-loop transfer function for different values of $q$'s can be obtained as shown in Fig. 9-6(a).

```
>> num=-[948.12, 30325, 56482, 1215.3];
   den=[1, 64.554, 1167, 3728.6, -5495.4, 1102, 708.1];
```

```
G=ss(tf(num,den)); Xi=1e-4; Theta=1e-5; Q=G.c'*G.c; R=1;
[Kc,P]=lqr(G.a,G.b,Q,R); nyquist(ss(G.a,G.b,Kc,0)), hold on
for q=[1,1e4,1e6,1e8,1e10,1e12,1e14]
    G1=ss(G.a,[G.b, G.b],G.c,[G.d,G.d]);
    [K_Sys,L,P2]=kalman(G1,q*Xi,Theta);
    a1=G.a-G.b*Kc-L*G.c; G_o=G*ss(a1,L,Kc,0); nyquist(G_o)
end
```

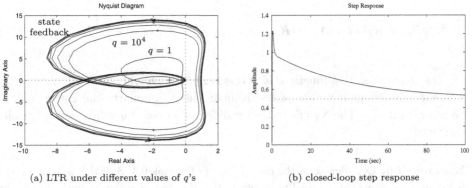

(a) LTR under different values of $q$'s          (b) closed-loop step response

Fig. 9-6   LQG/LTR control results.

It can be seen that when $q$ is selected as $10^{10}$, the loop transfer function can be restored to the one with direct state feedback. Under such a selection $q$, the closed-loop step response can be obtained as shown in Fig. 9-6(b).

```
>> q=1e10; [K_Sys,L,P2]=kalman(G1,q*Xi,Theta); a1=G.a-G.b*Kc-L*G.c;
   G_o=G*ss(a1,L,Kc,0); figure; step(feedback(G_o,1),100), zpk(Gc)
```

and the controller designed is

$$G_c(s) = \frac{-1152907209704.35(s+44.2)(s+9.278)(s+0.7933)(s^2+56.31s+1430)}{(s+3.114\times10^4)(s+6.541)(s+1.785)(s-2.804)(s^2+3.107\times10^4 s+9.649\times10^8)}.$$

Although the closed-loop system is stable, the controller itself is unstable, thus the system is not applicable in practice. For the given plant model, there is no internally stable LQG controller.

## 2. LQG/LTR problem solutions in MATLAB

Function ltrsyn() is provided in the Robust Control Toolbox, and it allows the user to design LTR controllers at input or output terminal of the system. In earlier versions, functions ltru() and ltry() can be used instead.

(1) **LTR at input terminal.** If the LTR is performed at the input of the system, then

$$\lim_{q\to\infty} \mathit{\Gamma} K_c\Big(sI - A + BK_c + K_fC\Big)^{-1}K_f = K_c\Big(sI - A\Big)^{-1}B, \qquad (9.18)$$

and the syntax of the function is $G_{\mathrm{c}} = \mathtt{ltrsyn}(G, K_{\mathrm{c}}, \Xi, \Theta, q, \omega, \mathtt{'input'})$ , where $G$ is the plant model, $K_{\mathrm{c}}$ is the expected state feedback matrix, $q$ is a vector with different selected values of $q$. The vector $\omega$ contains the sample frequencies. The returned argument $G_{\mathrm{c}}$ is the state space model of the LQG/LTR controller. In the function, the Nyquist plots for different values of $q$ will be automatically displayed.

(2) **LTR at output terminal**. If the LTR is performed at the output terminal of the system, then

$$\lim_{q \to \infty} \boldsymbol{\Gamma} \boldsymbol{K}_{\mathrm{c}}\Big( s\boldsymbol{I} - \boldsymbol{A} + \boldsymbol{B}\boldsymbol{K}_{\mathrm{c}} + \boldsymbol{K}_{\mathrm{f}}\boldsymbol{C} \Big)^{-1} \boldsymbol{K}_{\mathrm{f}} = \boldsymbol{C}\Big( s\boldsymbol{I} - \boldsymbol{A} \Big)^{-1} \boldsymbol{K}_{\mathrm{f}}. \qquad (9.19)$$

The syntax of the function is $G_{\mathrm{c}} = \mathtt{ltrsyn}(G, K_{\mathrm{f}}, Q, R, q, \omega, \mathtt{'output'})$ , where $K_{\mathrm{f}}$ is the gain vector of the Kalman filter. Similarly the controller can be returned in $G_{\mathrm{c}}$. The Nyquist plots for different values of $q$ will be automatically displayed.

**Example 9.5.** Consider again the plant model in Example 9.3. Selecting a $q$ vector, the following statements can be used to design LTR controllers, and the Nyquist plots of the open-loop transfer functions for different value of $q$'s can be obtained, and the results are very close to the ones shown in Fig. 9-6(a).

```
>> q0=[1,1e4,1e6,1e8,1e10,1e12,1e14];
   num=-[948.12, 30325, 56482, 1215.3];
   den=[1, 64.554, 1167, 3728.6, -5495.4, 1102, 708.1];
   G=ss(tf(num,den)); Xi=1e-4; Theta=1e-5; Q=G.c'*G.c;
   R=1; [Kc,P]=lqr(G.a,G.b,Q,R); w=logspace(-2,2,200);
   Gc=ltrsyn(G,Kc,Xi,Theta,q0,w,'input');
```

It can be seen that when the value of $q$ selected is large enough, for instance $q > 10^{10}$, the loop transfer function at the input terminal is relatively close to the one with direct state feedback. The closed-loop step response under the LQG/LTR controller is displayed, and it is very close to the one obtained in Example 9.4.

```
>> q=1e10; Gc=ltrsyn(G,Kc,Xi,Theta,q,w,'input');
   step(feedback(G*Gc,1),100); zpk(Gc)
```

The designed controller is

$$G_{\mathrm{c}}(s) = \frac{-219546319.0288(s + 30.22)(s + 29.71)(s + 6.758)(s + 1.314)(s + 0.01257)}{(s + 3114)(s + 30)(s + 1.963)(s + 0.02177)(s^2 + 3107s + 9.672 \times 10^6)}.$$

It can be seen that the controller is stable, thus the feedback system is internally stable. The internally unstable phenomenon in Example 9.4 is avoided.

## 9.2 General Descriptions to Robust Control Problems

### 9.2.1 *Small Gain Theorem*

The general structure of robust control system is shown in Fig. 9-7(a), where $P(s)$ is the augmented plant model, and $F(s)$ is the controller model. The transfer function from input $u_1(t)$ to output $y_1(t)$ can be denoted as $T_{y_1 u_1}(t)$. Small gain theorem is the theoretical basis in robust control. The small gain theorem is described below:

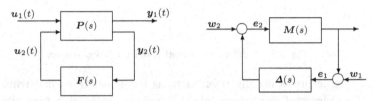

(a) standard feedback control structure　　(b) illustration of small gain theorem

Fig. 9-7　General structure of $\mathcal{H}_2$ and $\mathcal{H}_\infty$ control.

Assume that $M(s)$ is stable, the closed-loop system in Fig. 9-7(b) is well-posed and stable for all the stable $\boldsymbol{\Delta}(s)$, if and only if the following small gain condition is satisfied.

$$||M(s)||_\infty ||\boldsymbol{\Delta}(s)||_\infty < 1. \tag{9.20}$$

In fact, for linear systems, the small gain theorem can be understood as follows. If for any disturbance model $\boldsymbol{\Delta}(s)$, the norm of the open-loop transfer function is smaller than one, the open-loop Nyquist plot will never encircle the $(-1, j0)$ point. Thus, the closed-loop system will be always stable, no matter what the stable model $\boldsymbol{\Delta}(s)$ is. This stability is also known as robust stability. In fact, small gain theorem can generally be applied to nonlinear systems.

### 9.2.2 *Structures of Robust Controllers*

In the closed-loop system structure shown in Fig. 9-7(a), augmented plant model is introduced. The augmented plant model can be generally written as

$$P(s) = \begin{bmatrix} P_{11}(s) & P_{12}(s) \\ P_{21}(s) & P_{22}(s) \end{bmatrix} = \left[ \begin{array}{c|cc} A & B_1 & B_2 \\ \hline C_1 & D_{11} & D_{12} \\ C_2 & D_{21} & D_{22} \end{array} \right], \tag{9.21}$$

and the corresponding augmented state space equation is

$$\dot{x}(t) = Ax + \begin{bmatrix} B_1 & B_2 \end{bmatrix} \begin{bmatrix} u_1 \\ u_2 \end{bmatrix}, \quad \begin{bmatrix} y_1 \\ y_2 \end{bmatrix} = \begin{bmatrix} C_1 \\ C_2 \end{bmatrix} x + \begin{bmatrix} D_{11} & D_{12} \\ D_{21} & D_{22} \end{bmatrix} \begin{bmatrix} u_1 \\ u_2 \end{bmatrix}. \tag{9.22}$$

The closed-loop system can be sketched as shown in Fig. 9-8[5]. The closed-loop transfer function from external input $u_1(t)$ to the external output $y_1(t)$ can be written as

$$T_{y_1 u_1}(s) = P_{11}(s) + P_{12}(s)\big[I - F(s)P_{22}(s)\big]^{-1} F(s)P_{21}(s). \qquad (9.23)$$

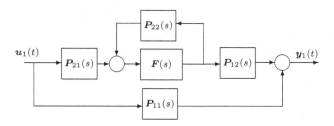

Fig. 9-8    A different description of closed-loop system.

Such a structure is usually referred to as the linear fractional transformation model. The target of robust control is to design a stabilizing controller $u_2(s) = F(s)y_2(s)$, such that the norm of the closed-loop system $T_{y_1 u_1}(s)$ takes a value less than 1, i.e., $\|T_{y_1 u_1}(s)\| < 1$. It can be seen from Eqn. (9.23) that typically the following three kind of robust control problems can be formulated:

(1) $\mathcal{H}_2$ **optimal control problem.** The problem to solve is

$$\min_{F(s)} \|T_{y_1 u_1}(s)\|_2. \qquad (9.24)$$

(2) $\mathcal{H}_\infty$ **optimal control problem.** The problem to solve is

$$\min_{F(s)} \|T_{y_1 u_1}(s)\|_\infty. \qquad (9.25)$$

(3) **Standard** $\mathcal{H}_\infty$ **control problem.** Any controller $F(s)$ satisfying the following inequality can be regarded as a solution to the problem.

$$\|T_{y_1 u_1}(s)\|_\infty < 1. \qquad (9.26)$$

The weighted controller structure is shown in Fig. 9-9(a), where $W_1(s)$, $W_2(s)$ and $W_3(s)$ are weighting functions. These functions are selected such that $G(s)$, $W_1(s)$ and $W_3(s)G(s)$ are proper. In other words, these transfer functions are bounded when $s \to \infty$. It can be seen that the condition did not require $W_3(s)$ itself to be proper. If the block diagram in Fig. 9-9(a) is changed slightly, the control structure in Fig. 9-9(b) can be constructed. The system structure is the same as the one in standard robust control structure in Fig. 9-7(a).

Assume that the state space model of the plant is $\big(A, B, C, D\big)$, and the state space models for the weighting functions for $W_1(s)$, and $W_2(s)$ are respectively $\big(A_{W_1}, B_{W_1}, C_{W_1}, D_{W_1}\big)$, $\big(A_{W_2}, B_{W_2}, C_{W_2}, D_{W_2}\big)$. $W_3(s)$ model can be expressed by the improper model

$$W_3(s) = C_{W_3}\big(sI - A_{W_3}\big)^{-1} B_{W_3} + P_m s^m + \cdots + P_1 s + P_0. \qquad (9.27)$$

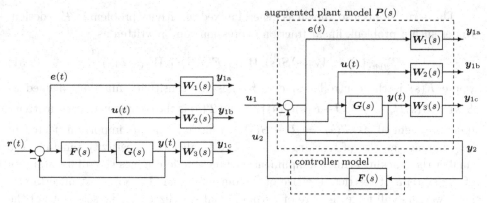

(a) general weighted sensitivity functions      (b) block structure of two-port system

Fig. 9-9    Block diagram representation of weighted sensitivity problem.

Equation (9.22) can be written as

$$P(s) = \left[\begin{array}{ccccc|cc} A & 0 & 0 & 0 & 0 & B \\ -B_{W_1}C & A_{W_1} & 0 & 0 & B_{W_1} & -B_{W_1}D \\ 0 & 0 & A_{W_2} & 0 & 0 & B_{W_2} \\ B_{W_3}C & 0 & 0 & A_{W_3} & 0 & B_{W_3}D \\ \hline -D_{W_1}C & C_{W_1} & 0 & 0 & D_{W_1} & -D_{W_1}D \\ 0 & 0 & C_{W_2} & 0 & 0 & D_{W_2} \\ \widetilde{C}+S_{W_3}C & 0 & 0 & C_{W_3} & 0 & \widetilde{D}+D_{W_3}D \\ \hline -C & 0 & 0 & 0 & I & -D \end{array}\right], \quad (9.28)$$

where

$$\widetilde{C} = P_0 C + P_1 CA + \cdots + P_m CA^{m-1},$$
$$\widetilde{D} = P_0 D + P_1 CB + \cdots + P_m CA^{m-2}B. \quad (9.29)$$

In the augmented model, any weighting function can be an empty one, and can be described in MATLAB as $W_i(s) = []$. The robust control problem can be solved according to the following three cases:

(1) **Sensitivity problem.** In the problem, $W_2(s)$ and $W_3(s)$ are empty;

(2) **Mixed sensitivity and performance problem.** In the problem, $W_2(s)$ is empty, or to a very small value;

(3) **General mixed sensitivity problem.** All the three weighting functions should be provided.

Under general cases, the augmented plant model can be written as

$$P(s) = \left[\begin{array}{c|c} W_1(s) & -W_1(s)G(s) \\ 0 & W_2(s) \\ 0 & W_3(s)G(s) \\ \hline I & -G(s) \end{array}\right]. \quad (9.30)$$

This structure is also known as general mixed sensitivity problem in $\mathcal{H}_\infty$ design. Under such a problem, linear fraction expression can be written as

$$T_{y_1 u_1}(s) = \left[ \boldsymbol{W}_1(s)\boldsymbol{S}(s), \boldsymbol{W}_2(s)\boldsymbol{F}(s)\boldsymbol{S}(s), \boldsymbol{W}_3(s)\boldsymbol{T}(s) \right]^{\mathrm{T}}, \tag{9.31}$$

where $\boldsymbol{F}(s)$ is the controller model, $\boldsymbol{S}(s)$ is the sensitivity function, defined as $\boldsymbol{S}(s) = \boldsymbol{E}(s)\boldsymbol{R}^{-1}(s) = \left[ \boldsymbol{I} + \boldsymbol{F}(s)\boldsymbol{G}(s) \right]^{-1}$, and $\boldsymbol{T}(s)$ is the complementary sensitivity function, defined as $\boldsymbol{T}(s) = \boldsymbol{I} - \boldsymbol{S}(s)$. Sensitivity is an important factor in determining the size of tracking errors. The smaller the sensitivity function, the smaller the tracking error. Complimentary function determines the robust stability of the system. It restricts the size of the output signal. If there exist uncertainty, large weights will force the size of output signal stabilized[6]. The selections of the weighting functions in sensitivity and complementary are sometimes contradictory. Compromises between them must be made. It is pointed out that robust controller design is the art of weighting functions selection[7].

### 9.2.3   *Description of Loop Shaping Techniques*

It can be seen from the open-loop frequency response in Chapter 5 that the magnitude response determines the performance of closed-loop systems. Thus, if the shape of the open-loop magnitude plot is assigned intentionally, and used as the model of $\boldsymbol{W}_1(s)$, with the help of the robust controller design method, the optimal $\mathcal{H}_\infty$ controller can be designed, and force the open-loop magnitude to follow the shape of $\boldsymbol{W}_1(s)$ so as to achieve satisfactory closed-loop behavior. This is the basic consideration of loop shaping techniques.

Assume that the mathematical model of the forward path is $\boldsymbol{L}(s)$. From typical feedback control structure, $\boldsymbol{L}(s) = \boldsymbol{G}(s)\boldsymbol{F}(s)$, and the sensitivity function $\boldsymbol{S}(s)$, controller to input transfer function $\boldsymbol{R}(s)$ and complementary sensitivity transfer function $\boldsymbol{T}(s)$ can be written as

$$\begin{cases} \boldsymbol{S}(s) = \left[ \boldsymbol{I} + \boldsymbol{L}(s) \right]^{-1} \\ \boldsymbol{R}(s) = \boldsymbol{F}(s) \left[ \boldsymbol{I} + \boldsymbol{L}(s) \right]^{-1} \\ \boldsymbol{T}(s) = \boldsymbol{G}(s)\boldsymbol{F}(s) \left[ \boldsymbol{I} + \boldsymbol{L}(s) \right]^{-1}. \end{cases} \tag{9.32}$$

The relationship between typical loop shaping and weighting function selections are illustrated in Fig. 9-10. The expected magnitude response curve $\boldsymbol{L}(s)$ can be selected. Since the design for uncertain systems are usually performed, the upper bound $\overline{\sigma}(\boldsymbol{L})$ and lower bound $\underline{\sigma}(\boldsymbol{L})$ should be selected according to the actual situations. Then based on the curves, the weighting functions $\boldsymbol{W}_1(s)$ and $\boldsymbol{W}_3(s)$ can be selected. With these weighting functions, robust controllers can be designed.

In practical robust controller design, we should select

$$\overline{\sigma}[\boldsymbol{S}(\mathrm{j}\omega)] \leqslant |\boldsymbol{W}_1^{-1}(s)|, \quad \overline{\sigma}[\boldsymbol{R}(\mathrm{j}\omega)] \leqslant |\boldsymbol{W}_2^{-1}(s)|, \quad \overline{\sigma}[\boldsymbol{T}(\mathrm{j}\omega)] \leqslant |\boldsymbol{W}_3^{-1}(s)|. \tag{9.33}$$

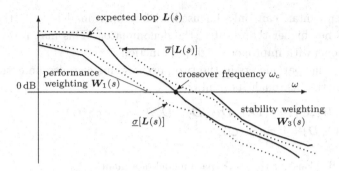

Fig. 9-10   Illustrations of weighting functions and loop shaping.

If $\underline{\sigma}[L(s)] \gg 1$, then $S(s) \approx L^{-1}(s)$, and when $\overline{\sigma}[L(s)] \ll 1$, then $T(s) \approx L(s)$. Thus, with proper chosen weighting functions, loop shaping design can be ensured.

From the conditions given earlier, the weighting functions $W_1(s)$ and $W_3(s)$ can be selected to ensure the magnitude plot of the open-loop system. Then, considering a suitable weighting function $W_2(s)$ to restrict the size of the control signal, robust controllers can be directly designed. The example in controller design will be demonstrated in the next section.

### 9.2.4   *MATLAB Description of Robust Control Systems*

In earlier versions of MATLAB, there were three dedicated toolboxes, Robust Control Toolbox[8], $\mu$ Analysis and Synthesis Toolbox[9] and Linear Matrix Inequality Toolbox[10] to solve robust controller design problems. The descriptions to control problems were different in the three toolboxes. Now the three toolboxes are combined into the new Robust Control Toolbox. The system models can either be described by the LTI objects in Control System Toolbox, or with the uncertain system representation in the Robust Control Toolbox. In this section, different description methods are given.

**1. System description methods with Robust Control Toolbox**

With the function mksys() provided in the Robust Control Toolbox, the two-port augmented plant model can be established, with the typical syntax

$S = \mathtt{mksys}(A, B_1, B_2, C_1, C_2, D_{11}, D_{12}, D_{21}, D_{22}, \mathtt{'tss'})$

where 'tss' indicates the use of the two-port state space equation in Eqn. (9.21). If the user does not want to use this definition, the TF or SS objects in the Control System Toolbox can also be used. From unified framework point of view, the LTI object descriptions are suggested.

When the plant model and weighting function models are established, the augmented system can be described by augtf() and augw() functions, provided in Robust Control Toolbox, with the syntaxes

$S_{\mathrm{tss}} = \mathtt{augtf}(S, W_1, W_2, W_3), \qquad S_{\mathrm{tss}} = \mathtt{augw}(S, W_1, W_2, W_3)$

The latter syntax can only be used with proper models, i.e., the order of numerator is not higher than that of the denominator. This may raise difficulties for the problems with improper weighting functions.

The particular parameters in the two-port systems can also be extracted with branch() function, through the syntaxes

$$[A,B_1,B_2,C_1,C_2,D_{11},D_{12},D_{21},D_{22}] = \text{branch}(G)$$
$$[A,B,C,D] = \text{branch}(G)$$

**Example 9.6.** Consider the state space model of a plant

$$\dot{x}(t) = \begin{bmatrix} 0 & 1 & 0 & 0 \\ -5000 & -100/3 & 500 & 100/3 \\ 0 & -1 & 0 & 1 \\ 0 & 100/3 & -4 & -60 \end{bmatrix} x(t) + \begin{bmatrix} 0 \\ 25/3 \\ 0 \\ -1 \end{bmatrix} u(t), \quad y(t) = [0,0,1,0]x(t).$$

If the weighting functions $W_1(s) = 100/(s+1)$, $W_3(s) = s/1000$ are selected, the following statements can be used to create the model of the augmented plant model with

```
>> A=[0,1,0,0; -5000,-100/3,500,100/3; 0,-1,0,1; 0,100/3,-4,-60];
   B=[0; 25/3; 0; -1];  C=[0,0,1,0]; D=0; G=ss(A,B,C,D);
   s=tf('s'); W1=100/(s+1); W3=s/1000; W2=1e-5;
   T_ss=augtf(G,W1,W2,W3);  % two-port augmented plant
```

Note that since there is no $W_2(s)$ weighting function, it can be set to a small positive value, for instance, $10^{-5}$, otherwise the $D_{12}$ sub matrix in Eqn. (9.28) is a singular matrix, such that the problem has no solution. The augmented model is

$$P(s) = \begin{bmatrix} 0 & 1 & 0 & 0 & 0 & 0 & 0 \\ -5000 & -33.333 & 500 & 33.333 & 0 & 0 & 8.3333 \\ 0 & -1 & 0 & 1 & 0 & 0 & 0 \\ 0 & 33.333 & -4 & -60 & 0 & 0 & -1 \\ 0 & 0 & -1 & 0 & -1 & 1 & 0 \\ 0 & 0 & 0 & 0 & 100 & 0 & 0 \\ 0 & 0 & 0 & 0 & 0 & 0 & 10^{-5} \\ 0 & -0.001 & 0 & 0.001 & 0 & 0 & 0 \\ 0 & 0 & -1 & 0 & 0 & 1 & 0 \end{bmatrix}.$$

## 2. System matrix description

The state space model $(A,B,C,D)$ can also be expressed as a system matrix $P$ in the form

$$P = \left[ \begin{array}{cc|c} A & B & n \\ C & D & \vdots \\ \hline & & 0 \\ \hline 0 & & -\infty \end{array} \right]. \tag{9.34}$$

If the augmented system $G$ is expressed in state space form, the system matrix $P$ can also be obtained with the function $P = \text{sys2smat}(G)$, where $G$ can be an

LTI model, or a two-port augmented model. The listing of the function is

```
function P=sys2smat(G)
G=ss(G); P=[G.a G.b; G.c G.d]; P([1,end+1],end+1)=[length(G.a),-inf];
```

To retrieve the state space model $G$ from the system matrix $P$, the following MATLAB function can be written with the syntax $G = \text{smat2ss}(P)$ .

```
function G=smat2ss(P), n=P(1,end);
G=ss(P(1:n,1:n),P(1:n,n+1:end-1),P(n+1:end-1,1:n),P(n+1:end-1,n+1:end-1));
```

**Example 9.7.** Consider again the plane model and weighting functions in Example 9.6. The following statements can be issued to establish the system matrix $P$ for the augmented system

```
>> A=[0,1,0,0; -5000,-100/3,500,100/3; 0,-1,0,1; 0,100/3,-4,-60];
   B=[0; 25/3; 0; -1];  C=[0,0,1,0]; D=0; G=ss(A,B,C,D);
   W1=[0,100; 1,1]; W2=1e-5; W3=[1,0; 0,1000];
   S_tss=augtf(G,W1,W2,W3); P=sys2smat(S_tss) % convert to system matrix
```

and the system matrix of augmented model obtained is

$$
P = \left[
\begin{array}{cccc:cc:c:c}
0 & 1 & 0 & 0 & 0 & 0 & 0 & 5 \\
-5000 & -33.333 & 500 & 33.333 & 0 & 0 & 8.3333 & 0 \\
0 & -1 & 0 & 1 & 0 & 0 & 0 & 0 \\
0 & 33.333 & -4 & -60 & 0 & 0 & -1 & 0 \\
0 & 0 & -1 & 0 & -1 & 1 & 0 & 0 \\
\hdashline
0 & 0 & 0 & 0 & 100 & 0 & 0 & 0 \\
\hdashline
0 & 0 & 0 & 0 & 0 & 0 & 10^{-5} & 0 \\
0 & -0.001 & 0 & 0.001 & 0 & 0 & 0 & 0 \\
0 & 0 & -1 & 0 & 0 & 1 & 0 & 0 \\
\hdashline
0 & 0 & 0 & 0 & 0 & 0 & 0 & -\infty
\end{array}
\right].
$$

It should be noted that if the plant and weighting functions contain improper subsystems, the system matrix form cannot be established. Function augtf() is the only way to express the model.

### 3. Descriptions of uncertain systems

A new class ureal is defined in the Robust Control Toolbox. It can be used to describe an uncertain variable within an interval. The syntaxes of the function are

$p = \text{ureal}('p',p_0,'Range',[p_m,p_M])$ % variable in interval $p \in [p_m,p_M]$

$p = \text{ureal}('p',p_0,'PlusMinus',\delta)$ % variable with bias $p = p_0 \pm \delta$

$p = \text{ureal}('p',p_0,'Percentage',A)$ % percentage bias $p = p_0(1 \pm 0.01A)$

where $p_0$ is referred to as its nominal value, and its range of variations can be defined in the function. With such an uncertain variable, the functions tf() and ss() can be used to establish uncertain transfer functions and state space models. If the uncertain model $G$ is established, the function $G_1 = \text{usample}(G,N)$ can be used to generate $N$ samples randomly in $G_1$. The system analysis functions in Chapter 5 such as bode() and step() can also be used in the analysis of uncertain systems.

**Example 9.8.** Consider the typical second-order uncertain transfer function

$$G(s) = \frac{\omega_n^2}{s(s + 2\zeta\omega_n)}, \text{ with } \zeta \in (0.2, 0.9), \text{ and, } \omega_n \in (2, 10).$$

The nominal values are $\zeta_0 = 0.7$, and $\omega_0 = 5$. The following statements can be used to construct the uncertain model, and the open-loop Bode diagrams and closed-loop step responses of the uncertain system can be obtained as shown in Fig. 9-11. It should be noted that the samples generated each time by usample() are different.

```
>> z=ureal('z',0.7,'Range',[0.2,0.9]); wn=ureal('wn',5,'Range',[2,10]);
   Go=tf(wn^2,[1 2*z*wn 0]); Go1=usample(Go,10);
   bode(Go1); figure; step(feedback(Go1,1))
```

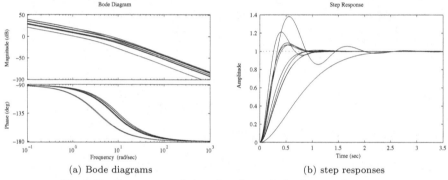

(a) Bode diagrams                    (b) step responses

Fig. 9-11   Frequency and time domain analysis of uncertain systems.

The block diagram of control system with uncertain parameters is shown in Fig. 9-12, where the uncertain model is composed of two parts — additive uncertainty $\boldsymbol{\Delta}_a(s)$ and multiplicative uncertainty $\boldsymbol{\Delta}_m(s)$. With the uncertain model description, the uncertain plant model can be described, and simulation analysis of uncertain system under robust controllers can be performed. However, unfortunately, in the current version of Simulink, the uncertain model block is not supported.

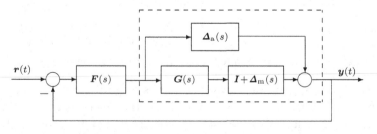

Fig. 9-12   Block diagram of uncertain control system.

For the additive uncertainty, the weighting function should be selected

$$\overline{\sigma}[\Delta_a(j\omega)] = \frac{1}{\overline{\sigma}[R(j\omega)]} \geqslant |W_2(j\omega)|, \tag{9.35}$$

and for multiplicative uncertainty, the weighting function should be

$$\overline{\sigma}[\Delta_m(j\omega)] = \frac{1}{\overline{\sigma}[T(j\omega)]} \geqslant |W_3(j\omega)|. \tag{9.36}$$

When the weighting functions $W_2(s)$ and $W_3(s)$ are selected, which ensure rejection of the disturbances and uncertainty, the weighting function $W_1(s)$ can be selected with loop shaping technique, such that the dynamic behavior of the system reaches the expected requirements.

## 9.3 Norm-based Robust Controller Design

The new Robust Control Toolbox combines the original Robust Control Toolbox, $\mu$ Analysis and Synthesis Toolbox and the LMI Toolbox[11], and all the functions are rewritten. Although the functions of the original three toolboxes can still be used, the new toolbox designed has some new functions and syntaxes. The function names are formalized, and it is simple to use and more flexible.

### 9.3.1 *Design of $\mathcal{H}_\infty$ and $\mathcal{H}_2$ Robust Controllers*

Consider the two-port state space plant model structure shown in Fig. 9-7(a). The target of $\mathcal{H}_\infty$ controller design is to find a controller $F(s)$, such that the $\mathcal{H}_\infty$ normal of the loop transfer function is restricted to a small number $\gamma$, such that $\|T_{y_1 u_1}(s)\|_\infty < \gamma$. The state space model of the controller can be expressed as

$$\dot{x}(t) = A_f x(t) - ZLu(t), \quad y(t) = Kx(t), \tag{9.37}$$

where

$$A_f = A + \gamma^{-2} B_1 B_1^T X + B_2 K + ZLC_2 \tag{9.38}$$
$$K = -B_2^T X, \quad L = -YC_2^T, \quad Z = \left(I - \gamma^{-2} YX\right)^{-1},$$

and $X$ are $Y$ are the solutions of the following two algebraic Riccati equations

$$A^T X + XA + X\left(\gamma^{-2} B_1 B_1^T - B_2 B_2^T\right)X + C_1 C_1^T = 0 \tag{9.39}$$
$$AY + YA^T + Y\left(\gamma^{-2} C_1^T C_1 - C_2^T C_2\right)Y + B_1^T B_1 = 0.$$

The prerequisite conditions of the existence of $\mathcal{H}_\infty$ controller are:

(1) $D_{11}$ is small enough, such that $D_{11} < \gamma$;
(2) The solution $X$ of the controller Riccati equation is a positive definite matrix
(3) The solution $Y$ of the observer Riccati equation is a positive definite matrix
(4) $\lambda_{\max}(XY) < \gamma^2$, i.e., the eigenvalues of the product of the two matrices, which are the solutions of the Riccati equations, are all smaller than $\gamma^2$.

Under the above prerequisite conditions, a minimization problem for $\gamma$ can be posed, and this is the optimal $\mathcal{H}_\infty$ controller design problem.

For the two-port model $G_{\mathrm{tss}}$, the relevant functions in the new Robust Control Toolbox can be used in robust controller design. The syntaxes of the functions are

$[G_{\mathrm{c}}, G_{\mathrm{cl}}] = \mathtt{h2syn}(G_{\mathrm{tss}})$     % optimal $\mathcal{H}_2$ controller design

$[G_{\mathrm{c}}, G_{\mathrm{cl}}, \gamma] = \mathtt{hinfsyn}(G_{\mathrm{tss}})$     % optimal $\mathcal{H}_\infty$ controller design

where the returned variables $G_{\mathrm{c}}$ and $G_{\mathrm{cl}}$ are the controller and closed-loop state space models, with the latter given by two-port state space model. The function `branch()` can be used to extract the parameters of the state space equations. The returned variable $\gamma$ is the minimized value in optimal $\mathcal{H}_\infty$ control.

**Example 9.9.** Consider the augmented system model studied in Example 9.6. The following statements can be used to design the optimal $\mathcal{H}_2$ and optimal $\mathcal{H}_\infty$ controllers

```
>> A=[0,1,0,0; -5000,-100/3,500,100/3; 0,-1,0,1; 0,100/3,-4,-60];
   B=[0; 25/3; 0; -1]; C=[0,0,1,0]; G=ss(A,B,C,0); s=tf('s');
   W1=100/(s+1); W2=1e-5; W3=s/1000; G1=augtf(G,W1,W2,W3);
   Gc1=zpk(h2syn(G1)), [Gc2,a,g]=hinfsyn(G1); Gc2=zpk(Gc2), g
```

The optimal value $\gamma = 0.3726$, and the optimal controllers are

$$G_{\mathrm{c1}}(s) = \frac{-9945947.5203(s + 67.4)(s + 0.06391)(s^2 + 25.87s + 4643)}{(s + 1)(s^2 + 23.81s + 535.7)(s^2 + 1370s + 5.045 \times 10^5)},$$

$$G_{\mathrm{c2}}(s) = \frac{-587116783.7874(s + 67.4)(s + 0.06391)(s^2 + 25.87s + 4643)}{(s + 1.573e004)(s + 1303)(s + 1)(s^2 + 23.79s + 535.7)}.$$

The open-loop Bode diagrams and the closed-loop step responses under the two controllers can be obtained as shown in Figs. 9-13(a) and (b). For this example, the behavior of optimal $\mathcal{H}_\infty$ controller is slightly better than the optimal $\mathcal{H}_2$ controller.

```
>> bode(G*Gc1,'-',G*Gc2,'--'), figure;
   step(feedback(G*Gc1,1),'-',feedback(G*Gc2,1),'--')
```

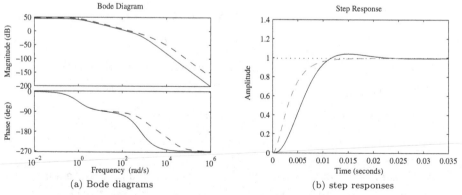

(a) Bode diagrams                    (b) step responses

Fig. 9-13   Comparisons of different controllers.

**Example 9.10.** Consider again the multivariable model studied in Example 5.41

$$G(s) = \begin{bmatrix} \dfrac{0.806s + 0.264}{s^2 + 1.15s + 0.202} & \dfrac{-15s - 1.42}{s^3 + 12.8s^2 + 13.6s + 2.36} \\ \dfrac{1.95s^2 + 2.12s + 0.49}{s^3 + 9.15s^2 + 9.39s + 1.62} & \dfrac{7.15s^2 + 25.8s + 9.35}{s^4 + 20.8s^3 + 116.4s^2 + 111.6s + 18.8} \end{bmatrix}.$$

The model can be entered to MATLAB workspace directly. Now let us consider the mixed sensitivity problem, with weighting functions

$$\boldsymbol{W}_1(s) = \begin{bmatrix} \dfrac{100}{s + 0.5} & 0 \\ 0 & 100 \\ & s+1 \end{bmatrix}, \quad \boldsymbol{W}_3(s) = \begin{bmatrix} \dfrac{s}{100} & 0 \\ 0 & \dfrac{200}{s} \end{bmatrix}. \tag{9.40}$$

Similar to the examples given earlier, we can select the small weight $\boldsymbol{W}_2(s) = \mathrm{diag}([10^{-5}, 10^{-5}])$. The two-port augmented model can be constructed, and the optimal $\mathcal{H}_\infty$ controller can be designed directly. The closed-loop step response and the open-loop singular value plot can be obtained, as shown in Fig. 9-14.

```
>> g11=tf([0.806 0.264],[1 1.15 0.202]); s=tf('s');
   g12=tf([-15 -1.42],[1 12.8 13.6 2.36]);
   g21=tf([1.95 2.12 0.49],[1 9.15 9.39 1.62]);
   g22=tf([7.15 25.8 9.35],[1 20.8 116.4 111.6 18.8]);
   G=[g11, g12; g21, g22]; w2=tf(1); W2=1e-5*[w2,0; 0,w2];
   W1=[100/(s+0.5), 0; 0, 100/(s+1)]; W3=[s/1000, 0; 0 s/200];
   Tss=augtf(G,W1,W2,W3); [Gc,a,g]=hinfsyn(Tss); zpk(Gc(1,2));
   step(feedback(G*Gc,eye(2)),0.1), figure; sigma(G*Gc)
```

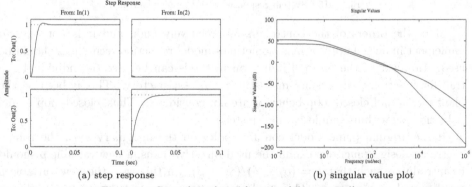

(a) step response          (b) singular value plot

Fig. 9-14   Control results with optimal $\mathcal{H}_\infty$ controller.

The result is $\gamma = 0.7087$. It can be seen that for the unsolved multivariable problem in Chapter 5, the solutions here are satisfactory. When the first input acts along, the first output $y_1(t)$ is quite good, while the second output $y_2(t)$ is almost zero. Similar thing happens when the second input acts alone. However, the order of the controller is extremely high. For instance, the 14th order model $g_{12}(s)$ can be obtained

$$g_{12}(s) = \frac{\begin{array}{c} 935095.7364(s + 1223)(s + 761.6)(s + 11.54)(s + 8.096)(s + 8.002) \\ (s + 0.9354)(s + 0.9336)(s + 0.9306)(s + 0.5)(s + 0.2175) \\ (s + 0.2164)(s + 0.2147)(s + 0.09511) \end{array}}{\begin{array}{c} (s + 1.312\times 10^4)(s + 1678)(s + 657)(s + 11.55)(s + 8.1)(s + 1.052) \\ (s + 1)(s + 0.9331)(s + 0.9218)(s + 0.5)(s + 0.3369) \\ (s + 0.2467)(s + 0.2263)(s + 0.2167) \end{array}}.$$

It can be seen that the response speed of $y_{22}(t)$ is relatively slower than $y_{11}(t)$. The weight $w_{1,22}(s)$ in $\boldsymbol{W}_1(s)$ should be increased. Let $w_{1,22}(s) = 1000/(s+1)$, and design the optimal $\mathcal{H}_\infty$ controller again, the closed-loop step responses and open-loop singular value plots can be obtained, as shown in Fig. 9-15. It can be seen that $y_{22}(t)$ is significantly improved, with $\gamma = 2.2354$.

```
>> W1=[100/(s+0.5) 0; 0 1000/(s+1)]; Tss=augtf(G,W1,W2,W3);
   [Gc1,a,g]=hinfsyn(Tss); step(feedback(G*Gc1,eye(2)),0.1);
   figure; sigma(G*Gc1)
```

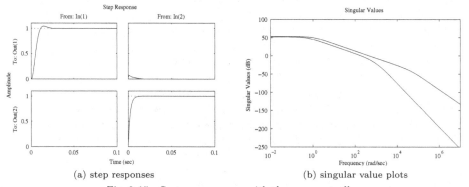

(a) step responses           (b) singular value plots

Fig. 9-15   System responses with the new controller.

Since the orders of the controllers are relatively high, and it is not easy to implement in actual applications, sometimes model reduction techniques should be used. However, if the optimal reduction methods can be used on individual sub transfer functions, the results may still not be satisfactory. This is because the plant model and closed-loop behavior are not considered. Thus, closed-loop model reduction algorithms should be used instead[12, 13].

If the original plant model contains poles on the imaginary axis, the robust controller design functions cannot be used directly. Thus, a new variable $p$ should be introduced such that $s = (\alpha p + \delta)/(\gamma p + \beta)$. In this way, the new variable $p$ can be used to replace $s$. This kind of transformation is referred to as bilinear transformation.

Under bilinear transformation, the poles on the imaginary axis can be moved to other places. The robust controller can be designed for the new model. Assume that the controller designed is $\boldsymbol{F}(p)$, inverse transform $p = (-\beta s + \delta)/(\gamma s + \alpha)$ should be used to transform the variable $p$ back to $s$. In this case, the new controller $\boldsymbol{G}_c(s)$ can be designed.

Function `bilin()` provided in the Robust Control Toolbox can be used to perform bilinear transformations, with $S_1 = \texttt{bilin}(G,\texttt{vers},\texttt{method},\texttt{aug})$ , where $G$ is the original model, $S_1$ is the transformed model. The variable `vers` is used to indicate the direction of the bilinear transformation. When `vers` $= 1$, the default $s$ to $p$ transform is taken, while $-1$ means the transform from $p$ to $s$. The variable `method` is used to indicate the algorithm of transformation, with options `'Tustin'` the default one, representing Tustin transformation. Another commonly used transform is $p = s + \lambda$, with $\lambda < 0$. The transform converts the plant model $(A, B, C, D)$ to $\left(A - \lambda I, B, C, D\right)$. When the controller is designed, inverse transform can be used to transform $\left(A_{\mathrm{F}}, B_{\mathrm{F}}, C_{\mathrm{F}}, D_{\mathrm{F}}\right)$ back into $\left(A_{\mathrm{F}} + \lambda I, B_{\mathrm{F}}, C_{\mathrm{F}}, D_{\mathrm{F}}\right)$.

**Example 9.11.** Consider the non-minimal phase plant with double integrators. The following weighting functions are selected

$$G(s) = \frac{5(-s+3)}{s^2(s+6)(s+10)}, \quad w_1(s) = \frac{300}{s+1}, \quad w_3(s) = 100s^2, \quad w_2(s) = 10^{-5}.$$

If the shift value is selected as $p_1 = 0.2$, the augmented plant model is shifted, and the robust $\mathcal{H}_\infty$ controller is designed. The closed-loop step response can be obtained as shown in Fig. 9-16(a).

```
>> p1=0.2; s=tf('s'); G=5*(-s+3)/s^2/(s+6)/(s+10);
   [a b c d]=ssdata(ss(G)); a1=a+p1*eye(size(a)); G0=ss(a1,b,c,d);
   w1=300/(s+1); w2=1e-5; w3=100*s^2; G1=augtf(G0,w1,w2,w3);
   [Gc,a,g]=hinfsyn(G1); [a b c d]=ssdata(Gc);
   a1=a-p1*eye(size(a)); Gc1=zpk(ss(a1,b,c,d)),
   step(feedback(G*Gc1,1),30); figure; step(feedback(Gc1,G),30)
```

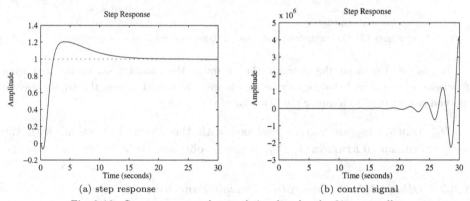

Fig. 9-16   Step response and control signal under the $\mathcal{H}_\infty$ controller.

The controller designed is

$$G_{\mathrm{c}_1}(s) = \frac{92367281430851.58(s + 0.1852)(s + 1.033)(s + 5.987)(s + 10.01)}{(s + 5 \times 10^7)(s + 2.324 \times 10^6)(s + 1.2)(s^2 + 6.165s + 16.57)}.$$

It can be seen that the control signal $u(t)$ can also be obtained, as shown in Fig. 9-16(b). It can be seen that although under the $\mathcal{H}_\infty$ controller, the closed-loop behavior is satisfactory, and the control signal is too large, thus the controller designed is not applicable. The reason for the large control signal is that since the weight $w_2$ on control signal is too small, it was set to $10^5$ in the previous design, which means that there is almost no restriction on the control signal. Now, if the weight $w_2$ is increased to a scale similar to those in $w_1$ and $w_3$, for instance, $w_2 = 100$, the new controller can be designed, and the closed-loop response and control signal can be obtained as shown in Fig. 9-17.

```
>> w2=100; G1=augtf(G0,w1,w2,w3); [Gc2,a,g]=hinfsyn(G1);
   [a b c d]=ssdata(Gc2); a1=a-p1*eye(size(a)); Gc2=zpk(ss(a1,b,c,d))
   step(feedback(G*Gc2,1),30); figure; step(feedback(Gc2,G),30)
```

The new optimal $\mathcal{H}_\infty$ controller becomes

$$G_{c_2}(s) = \frac{210694.4853(s+10)(s+6)(s+1.113)(s+0.1653)}{(s+3.464 \times 10^4)(s+12.04)(s+1.2)(s^2+6.748s+14.15)}.$$

It can be seen that although the control performance is slightly decreased, the scale of the control signal is significantly reduced. Thus, the new controller is more applicable.

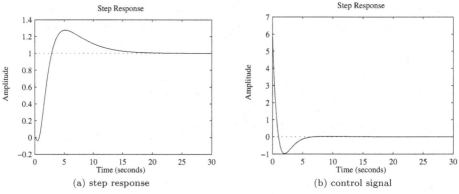

(a) step response                    (b) control signal

Fig. 9-17   Step response and control signal under the new controller.

It can be seen from the example that through the modification of the weighting functions, the system behavior can be significantly improved, Thus, the trial-and-error method can be used to improve the behavior of the system.

$\mathcal{H}_\infty$ controllers can also be designed with the **dhinf()** function, with the syntaxes similar to **hinfsyn()**. Details can be obtained with the **help** commands.

### 9.3.2   *Other Robust Controller Design Functions*

Various robust controller design functions such as mixed sensitivity $\mathcal{H}_\infty$ controller design function **mixsyn()**, and loop shaping function **hinfsyn()** are obtained in Robust Control Toolbox.

### 1. Mixed sensitivity design function

For proper weighting functions, **mixsyn()** function can be used to design optimal $\mathcal{H}_\infty$ controller, with the syntax $[G_c, G_{cl}, \gamma] = \text{mixsyn}(G, W_1, W_2, W_3)$ . In the function call, the weighting functions $\boldsymbol{W}_i$ can be expressed with transfer functions or transfer function matrices. Improper transfer function $\boldsymbol{W}_3(s)$ is not supported in the function. If improper function is needed, proper approximations with far away poles can be used. Also, $\boldsymbol{D}_{12}$ matrix must be a nonsingular matrix.

**Example 9.12.** Consider again the plant model in Example 9.6. Select the weights

$$W_1(s) = \frac{10000}{s+1}, \ W_{30}(s) = \frac{s}{10}, \ W_2(s) = 0.01.$$

Since $W_{30}(s)$ is an improper transfer function, the new weight $W_3(s) = s/(0.001s+10)$ can be used to approximate it. Thus, the following statements can be used to design optimal $\mathcal{H}_\infty$ controller

```
>> A=[0,1,0,0; -5000,-100/3,500,100/3; 0,-1,0,1; 0,100/3,-4,-60];
   B=[0; 25/3; 0; -1]; C=[0,0,1,0]; D=0; G=ss(A,B,C,D);
   s=tf('s'); W1=10000/(s+1); W2=1e-2; W30=s/10; W3=s/(0.001*s+10);
   Gc=mixsyn(G,W1,W2,W3); Gc=zpk(Gc)
   G1=augtf(G,W1,W2,W30); Gc1=hinfsyn(G1); Gc1=zpk(minreal(Gc1))
   bode(G*Gc,G*Gc1,'--'), figure
   step(feedback(G*Gc,1),'-',feedback(G*Gc,1),'--',0.1)
```

The designed controller model is

$$G_c(s) = \frac{-7639033578.46(s+999.96)(s+67.4)(s+0.06391)(s^2+25.87s+4643)}{(s+1.191\times10^6)(s+1000)(s+386.3)(s+1)(s^2+23.3s+536.1)},$$

$$G_{c1}(s) = \frac{-20253599367.1624(s+67.4)(s+0.06391)(s^2+25.87s+4643)}{(s+3.157\times10^6)(s+386.3)(s+1)(s^2+23.3s+536.1)}.$$

Bode diagram of the system is shown in Fig. 9-18(a), closed-loop step response can be obtained as shown in Fig. 9-18(b). It can be seen that the control behavior is satisfactory. Besides, $W_3(s)$ is approximated with a proper $W_{30}(s)$, and the quality of the controller designed is not affected. Apart from the far away poles and zeros, the two controllers are almost identical.

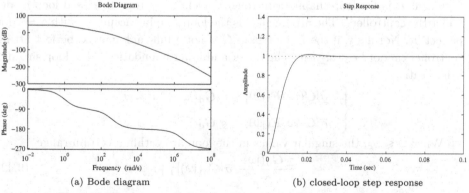

(a) Bode diagram        (b) closed-loop step response

Fig. 9-18 Frequency and time domain analysis of the nominal systems.

Assume that the uncertain model is multiplicative form, and it is known that $\Delta_m(s) =$

$p_1/(s + p_2)$. The uncertain ranges are $p_1 \in (-0.1, 2)$, and $p_2 \in (-2, 8)$. It can be seen that the uncertainty dynamics may change around stable and unstable samples, and the gain also has a very large range. Under such uncertainties, the open-loop Bode diagrams and closed-loop step responses under the same $\mathcal{H}_\infty$ controller can be obtained, as shown in Figs. 9-19(a) and (b). It can be seen that although there are significant changes in the plant model, the closed-loop step responses are almost the same.

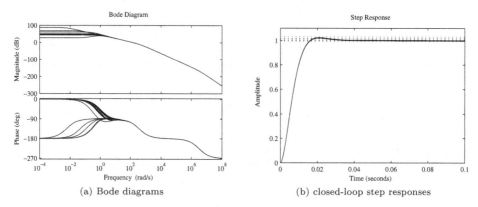

(a) Bode diagrams          (b) closed-loop step responses

Fig. 9-19   Frequency and time domain analysis of uncertain system.

```
>> p1=ureal('p1',1,'PlusMinus',[-0.1,2]);
   p2=ureal('p2',1,'PlusMinus',[-2,8]);
   Gm=tf(p1,[1 p2]); G1=G*(1+Gm); % construct uncertain plant model
   bode(G1*Gc); figure; step(feedback(G1*Gc,1),0.1)
```

## 2. Loop shaping-based design function

Sensitivity problem can be solved directly with `loopsyn()` function, with $\mathcal{H}_\infty$ loop shaping algorithm, with the syntax $[F, C, \gamma] = \texttt{loopsyn}(G, G_d)$ , where $G$ is the plant model, $G_d$ is the expected loop transfer function, and the returned argument $F$ is the loop shaping controller model. $C$ returns the closed-loop model under the controllers. The argument $\gamma$ is the loop shaping accuracy, with $\gamma = 1$ for perfect fit. Normally, if the $D$ matrix in $G$ is not a full-rank matrix, perfect fitting controller cannot be designed. The upper and lower boundaries of the loop singular values satisfy

$$\begin{cases} \gamma \underline{\sigma}[G(j\omega)F(j\omega)] \leqslant \overline{\sigma}[G_d(j\omega)], & \omega \leqslant \omega_c \\ \gamma \overline{\sigma}[G(j\omega)F(j\omega)] \leqslant \underline{\sigma}[G_d(j\omega)], & \omega \geqslant \omega_c. \end{cases} \quad (9.41)$$

When $\omega \leqslant \omega_c$, the singular values in the loop are within a certain range.

$$\left( \frac{\underline{\sigma}[G_d(j\omega)]}{\gamma}, \overline{\sigma}[G_d(j\omega)]\gamma \right). \quad (9.42)$$

**Example 9.13.** Consider again the multivariable model is Example 5.41. The two loop transfer functions can be selected as $G_d(s) = 500/(s + 1)$. The following statements can be used in designing the loop shaping controller.

```
>> g11=tf([0.806 0.264],[1 1.15 0.202]);
   g12=tf([-15 -1.42],[1 12.8 13.6 2.36]);
   g21=tf([1.95 2.12 0.49],[1 9.15 9.39 1.62]);
   g22=tf([7.15 25.8 9.35],[1 20.8 116.4 111.6 18.8]);
   G=[g11, g12; g21, g22]; s=tf('s'); Gd=500/(s+1);
   [F,a,g]=loopsyn(G,Gd); zpk(F), g
```

where the design precision is $\gamma = 1.62$. Under the designed controller, the loop singular value plots and closed-loop step responses can be obtained as shown in Fig. 9-20. It can be seen that the control results are satisfactory.

```
>> sigma(G*F,'-',Gd/g,':',Gd*g,':')        % the boundaries of singular values
   figure; step(feedback(G*F,eye(2)),0.1)  % closed-loop step response
```

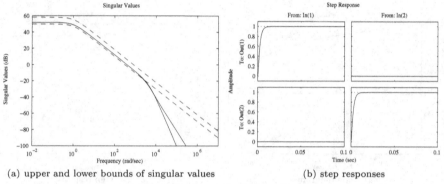

(a) upper and lower bounds of singular values          (b) step responses

Fig. 9-20  Loop shaping results.

Besides, it can be seen from Fig. 9-20(a) that when the frequency is high, the singular values obtained lie outside the upper and lower boundaries. In fact, the Bode diagram is semi-logarithmic plot ($-20\,$dB is about 0.1, very small value). Also, the order of the controller may be very high, for this example, 18th order controller can be obtained, and it is difficult to implement in real-time applications.

### 3. Robust controller design with $\mu$ analysis and synthesis tools

A $\mu$ analysis and synthesis-based function `hinfsyn()`[14] provided in Robust Control Toolbox can be used in robust controller design. An alternative version of the function can be called with $K = \text{hinfsyn}(P, p, q, \gamma_\text{m}, \gamma_\text{M}, \epsilon)$ , where $P$ is the system matrix description of the augmented plant model, and $p, q$ are the numbers of inputs and outputs of the system. Bisection algorithm is used to calculate the optimal value of $\gamma$. The interval $(\gamma_\text{m}, \gamma_\text{M})$ should be specified in the function call, and the convergent error tolerance is specified in $\epsilon$. These arguments cannot be omitted in the function call. The controller model $K$ can be returned, also in system matrix format.

**Example 9.14.** Consider again the augmented plant model as given in Example 9.6. The $\mu$ analysis and synthesis function `hinfsyn()` can be used to design directly the optimal $\mathcal{H}_\infty$ controller

```
>> A=[0,1,0,0; -5000,-100/3,500,100/3; 0,-1,0,1; 0,100/3,-4,-60];
   B=[0; 25/3; 0; -1]; C=[0,0,1,0]; D=0; G=ss(A,B,C,D); s=tf('s');
   W1=100/(s+1); W2=1e-5; W3=s/1000; G1=augtf(G,W1,W2,W3);
   P=sys2smat(G1); [G3,a,g1]=hinfsyn(G1,1,1,0.1,10,1e-3)
   [Gc1,a,g2]=hinfsyn(G1); bode(G*Gc1,'-',G*G3,'--');
   figure; step(feedback(G*Gc1,1),'-',feedback(G*G3,1),'--')
```

The controller obtained is

$$G_{c_3}(s) = \frac{-6127048154.952(s + 67.4)(s + 0.06391)(s^2 + 25.87s + 4643)}{(s + 1.658 \times 10^5)(s + 1279)(s + 1)(s^2 + 23.79s + 535.7)}.$$

Under the control of the two controllers, the open-loop Bode diagrams and closed-loop step responses are obtained as shown in Figs. 9-21(a) and (b). It can be seen that the behavior of these controllers are very close.

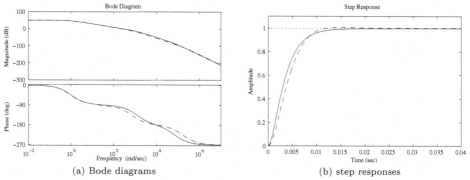

(a) Bode diagrams            (b) step responses

Fig. 9-21   Comparisons of controllers by different algorithms.

It can be seen that the control effect of the controllers are fully dependent upon the selection of weighting matrices. However, there are no universally accepted methods in choosing the weighting functions. Usually, trial-and-error method should be used to achieve satisfactory control results.

### 9.3.3   *Youla Parameterization*

Suppose the plant model $P(s)$ is stable, all the stabilizing controllers can be constructed

$$F(s) = \left\{ \frac{P(s)Q(s)}{1 - P(s)Q(s)} \right\}, \tag{9.43}$$

where $Q(s)$ is arbitrary stable transfer function. This result is known as Youla parameterization[15, 16], also known as Youla–Kačera parameterization. For single variable systems, the plant model can be written as $P(s) = N(s)/D(s)$, where $N(s)$ and $D(s)$ are stable polynomials. One stabilizing controller $C(s) = X(s)/Y(s)$ can be obtained from the following Bezout identity

$$N(s)X(s) + M(s)Y(s) = 1. \tag{9.44}$$

All the stabilizing controllers can be constructed, for any stable $Q(s)$, as

$$F(s) = \left\{ \frac{X(s) + M(s)Q(s)}{Y(s) - N(s)Q(s)} \right\}. \tag{9.45}$$

## 9.4 Linear Matrix Inequality Theory and Solutions

The theory and application of linear matrix inequalities (LMI) is an area that has received attention from the control community during the last thirty years[17]. The concept of linear matrix inequality and its applications in control systems was proposed by Willems[18]. This method can be used to convert many optimal control problems into linear programming problems. With the well-established solution to linear programming problems, some optimal control design problems can be solved directly.

In this section, the fundamental concept and typical forms of linear matrix inequality problems are presented. Necessary transformation methods are addressed, and the numerical solutions are given. Finally, the applications of LMIs in controller design are presented.

### 9.4.1  *General Descriptions of Linear Matrix Inequalities*

The typical form of linear matrix inequality is

$$\boldsymbol{F}(\boldsymbol{x}) = \boldsymbol{F}_0 + x_1\boldsymbol{F}_1 + \cdots + x_m\boldsymbol{F}_m < 0, \tag{9.46}$$

where $\boldsymbol{x} = [x_1, x_2, \cdots, x_m]^\mathrm{T}$ is the decision variable. Matrix $\boldsymbol{F}_i$ is a complex Hermitian matrix or real symmetrical matrix. The whole matrix inequality $\boldsymbol{F}(\boldsymbol{x})$ is a negative definite matrix. The solutions $\boldsymbol{x}$ to the inequality is a convex set, i.e.,

$$\boldsymbol{F}\left[\alpha\boldsymbol{x}_1 + (1 - \alpha)\boldsymbol{x}_2\right] = \alpha\boldsymbol{F}(\boldsymbol{x}_1) + (1 - \alpha)\boldsymbol{F}(\boldsymbol{x}_2) < 0, \tag{9.47}$$

where $\alpha > 0, 1 - \alpha > 0$. The solution is also known as the feasibility solution. The linear matrix inequalities are sometimes the constraints in optimization problems. Assume that for two linear matrix inequalities $\boldsymbol{F}_1(\boldsymbol{x}) < 0$ and $\boldsymbol{F}_2(\boldsymbol{x}) < 0$, a single linear matrix inequality can be constructed

$$\begin{bmatrix} \boldsymbol{F}_1(\boldsymbol{x}) & 0 \\ 0 & \boldsymbol{F}_2(\boldsymbol{x}) \end{bmatrix} < 0. \tag{9.48}$$

More generally, many linear matrix inequalities $\boldsymbol{F}_i(\boldsymbol{x}) < 0$, $(i = 1, 2, \cdots, k)$ can be composed into a single linear matrix inequality $\boldsymbol{F}(\boldsymbol{x}) < 0$, where

$$\boldsymbol{F}(\boldsymbol{x}) = \begin{bmatrix} \boldsymbol{F}_1(\boldsymbol{x}) & & & \\ & \boldsymbol{F}_2(\boldsymbol{x}) & & \\ & & \ddots & \\ & & & \boldsymbol{F}_k(\boldsymbol{x}) \end{bmatrix} < 0. \tag{9.49}$$

Linear matrix inequality problems are usually classified into three type of problems: feasibility problems, linear objective function problems, and generalized eigenvalue problems.

### 1. Feasibility problems

Feasibility problems are, in fact, the constraint conditions in ordinary optimization problems. For the inequality

$$F(x) < 0, \tag{9.50}$$

a feasible solution can be found. The feasibility problem is to find a solution to $F(x) < t_{min}I$, where $t_{min}$ is the minimal value obtained with numerical algorithms. If such a $t_{min} < 0$ is found, the feasibility solution can be constructed, otherwise a warning message is given, when no feasible solution is found.

To demonstrate the relationship of ordinary control problems with linear matrix inequalities, let us first consider the Lyapunov stability judgement problem, which says that in linear systems, if for any given positive definite matrix $Q$, the solution of the Lyapunov equation

$$A^{T}X + XA = -Q \tag{9.51}$$

has positive definite solution $X$, the system is stable, i.e., all the eigenvalues of the matrix are located in the left-hand-side of the complex plane. The previous equation can also be converted into a Lyapunov inequality.

$$A^{T}X + XA < 0. \tag{9.52}$$

Since $X$ is a symmetrical matrix, a vector $x$ containing the $n(n+1)/2$ elements can be used to describe the original matrix such that

$$x_i = X_{i,1}, i = 1, 2, \cdots, n, x_{n+i} = X_{i,2}, i = 2, 3, \cdots, n, \cdots, \tag{9.53}$$

and it can further be written that

$$x_{(2n-j+2)(j-1)/2+i} = X_{i,j}, \; j = 1, 2, \cdots, n, i = j, j+1, \cdots, n, \tag{9.54}$$

and then from the subscripts in $x$, the double subscripts in matrix $X$ can be calculated. Based on the representation, a MATLAB function `lyap2lmi()` is created for the above conversion

```
function F=lyap2lmi(A0)
if prod(size(A0))==1, n=A0;
   for i=1:n, for j=1:n,
      i1=int2str(i);j1=int2str(j); eval(['syms a' i1 j1]),
      eval(['A(' i1 ',' j1 ')=a' i1 j1,';'])
   end, end
else, n=size(A0,1); A=A0; end
vec=0;    for i=1:n, vec(i+1)=vec(i)+n-i+1; end
for k=1:n*(n+1)/2,  X=zeros(n);
   i=find(vec>=k); i=i(1)-1; j=i+k-vec(i)-1;
   X(i,j)=1; X(j,i)=1; F(:,:,k)=A.'*X+X*A;
end
```

Function $F=\texttt{lyap2lmi}(A)$ returns a three-dimensional array $F$ for the given matrix $A$, with $F(:,:,i)$ representing to the $F_i$ matrix. Alternatively, if for the solution for the linear matrix inequality for an arbitrary $n \times n$ matrix $A$, the $F=\texttt{lyap2lmi}(n)$ function returns the three-dimensional array, the symbolic expression of $F_i$ matrices can be obtained.

**Example 9.15.** For the following matrix $A$

$$A = \begin{bmatrix} 1 & 2 & 3 \\ 4 & 5 & 6 \\ 7 & 8 & 0 \end{bmatrix},$$

the MATLAB statements can be used to solve the linear matrix inequality

```
>> A=[1,2,3; 4,5,6; 7,8,0]; F=lyap2lmi(A)
```

and the $F_i$ matrices are

$$\begin{bmatrix} 2 & 2 & 3 \\ 2 & 0 & 0 \\ 3 & 0 & 0 \end{bmatrix}, \begin{bmatrix} 8 & 6 & 6 \\ 6 & 4 & 3 \\ 6 & 3 & 0 \end{bmatrix}, \begin{bmatrix} 14 & 8 & 1 \\ 8 & 0 & 2 \\ 1 & 2 & 6 \end{bmatrix}, \begin{bmatrix} 0 & 4 & 0 \\ 4 & 10 & 6 \\ 0 & 6 & 0 \end{bmatrix}, \begin{bmatrix} 0 & 7 & 4 \\ 7 & 16 & 5 \\ 4 & 5 & 12 \end{bmatrix}, \begin{bmatrix} 0 & 0 & 7 \\ 0 & 0 & 8 \\ 7 & 8 & 0 \end{bmatrix}.$$

For an arbitrary $3 \times 3$ matrix $A$, the following commands can be issued

```
>> F=lyap2lmi(3)
```

The linear matrix inequality can be rewritten as

$$\begin{bmatrix} 2a_{11} & a_{12} & a_{13} \\ a_{12} & 0 & 0 \\ a_{13} & 0 & 0 \end{bmatrix} x_1 + \begin{bmatrix} 2a_{21} & a_{22}+a_{11} & a_{23} \\ a_{22}+a_{11} & 2a_{12} & a_{13} \\ a_{23} & a_{13} & 0 \end{bmatrix} x_2 + \begin{bmatrix} 2a_{31} & a_{32} & a_{33}+a_{11} \\ a_{32} & 0 & a_{12} \\ a_{33}+a_{11} & a_{12} & 2a_{13} \end{bmatrix} x_3$$

$$+ \begin{bmatrix} 0 & a_{21} & 0 \\ a_{21} & 2a_{22} & a_{23} \\ 0 & a_{23} & 0 \end{bmatrix} x_4 + \begin{bmatrix} 0 & a_{31} & a_{21} \\ a_{31} & 2a_{32} & a_{33}+a_{22} \\ a_{21} & a_{33}+a_{22} & 2a_{23} \end{bmatrix} x_5 + \begin{bmatrix} 0 & 0 & a_{31} \\ 0 & 0 & a_{32} \\ a_{31} & a_{32} & 2a_{33} \end{bmatrix} x_6 < 0.$$

Some particular nonlinear matrix inequalities can be converted into linear matrix inequalities. For instance, for a partitioned matrix

$$F(x) = \begin{bmatrix} F_{11}(x) & F_{12}(x) \\ \hline F_{21}(x) & F_{22}(x) \end{bmatrix}, \tag{9.55}$$

if $F_{11}(x)$ is a square matrix, the following three cases are equivalent:

$$F(x) < 0 \tag{9.56}$$

$$F_{11}(x) < 0, \quad F_{22}(x) - F_{21}(x)F_{11}^{-1}(x)F_{12}(x) < 0 \tag{9.57}$$

$$F_{22}(x) < 0, \quad F_{11}(x) - F_{12}(x)F_{22}^{-1}(x)F_{21}(x) < 0. \tag{9.58}$$

The above property is known as Schur complement.

For instance, for an algebraic Riccati inequality

$$A^\mathrm{T} X + XA + \left(XB - C\right)R^{-1}\left(XB - C^\mathrm{T}\right)^\mathrm{T} < 0, \tag{9.59}$$

where $R = R^{\mathrm{T}} > 0$. Due to its quadratic term, it is not an LMI. However, with Schur complement, the original nonlinear inequality can be converted equivalently into the following LMIs

$$X > 0, \quad \left[ \begin{array}{c|c} A^{\mathrm{T}}X + XA & XB - C^{\mathrm{T}} \\ \hline B^{\mathrm{T}}X - C & -R \end{array} \right] < 0. \tag{9.60}$$

**2. Linear objective function minimization problems**

Consider the following optimization problem

$$\min_{x \ \mathrm{s.t.}\ F(x)<0} c^{\mathrm{T}}x. \tag{9.61}$$

Since the constraints are given in linear matrix inequalities, the above optimization is, in fact, an ordinary linear programming problem.

The $\mathcal{H}_\infty$ norm of a system $\left( A, B, C, D \right)$ can be calculated with the MATLAB function `norm()` provided in Control System Toolbox. Alternatively, $\mathcal{H}_\infty$ norm can also be evaluated with linear matrix inequality method. The norm is, in fact, the solution $\gamma$ for the following problem[19]

$$\min_{\gamma, \ P \ \mathrm{s.t.}} \gamma. \tag{9.62}$$
$$\begin{cases} \left[ \begin{array}{ccc} A^{\mathrm{T}}P + PA & PB & C^{\mathrm{T}} \\ B^{\mathrm{T}}P & -\gamma I & D^{\mathrm{T}} \\ C & D & -\gamma I \end{array} \right] < 0 \\ P > 0 \end{cases}$$

**3. Generalized eigenvalue optimization problem**

The generalized eigenvalue problem is most commonly seen in LMI optimizations. Recall the generalized eigenvalue problem in Chapter 3, which is expressed as $Ax = \lambda Bx$. Such a problem can be expressed by general matrix functions as $A(x) < \lambda B(x)$, and $\lambda$ can be regarded as the generalized eigenvalue. Thus, the optimization problem becomes

$$\min_{\lambda, x \ \mathrm{s.t.}} \lambda. \tag{9.63}$$
$$\begin{cases} A(x) < \lambda B(x) \\ B(x) > 0 \\ C(x) < 0 \end{cases}$$

Other constraints can be written as $C(x) < 0$. The generalized eigenvalue problem can be expressed as a special LMI problem. In fact, if these constraints are classified into a single linear matrix inequality, it is then converted into an ordinary optimization problem.

### 9.4.2    MATLAB Solutions to Linear Matrix Inequality Problems

The LMI solver in MATLAB is currently provided in the Robust Control Toolbox. However, the way of describing the LMIs is quite complicated. An example is presented to show in detail the uses of the LMI solver.

The following procedures are used to describe LMIs in MATLAB:

(1) **Create an LMI model.** An LMI framework can be established with function `setlmis([])`. So, a framework can be established in MATLAB workspace.

(2) **Define the decision variables.** The decision variables can be declared by `lmivar()` function, with $P = \text{lmivar(key,}[n_1,n_2])$, where `key` specifies the type of the decision matrix. The variable `key` is 2 for an ordinary $n_1 \times n_2$ matrix $P$, while `key` is 1 for an $n_1 \times n_1$ symmetrical matrix. If `key` is 1, $n_1$ and $n_2$ are both vectors, $P$ is a block diagonal symmetrical matrix. If `key` is 3, $P$ is a special matrix, which is not discussed in this book. The interested readers may refer to the Robust Control Toolbox manual[8].

(3) **Describe LMIs in partitioned form.** The LMIs can be described by the `lmiterm()` function and its syntax is quite complicated

$$\text{lmiterm}([k,i,j,P],A,B,\text{flag})$$

where $k$ is the sequence number of the LMIs. Since an LMI problem may be described by several LMIs, one should number each of them. If an LMI is given $G_k(x) > 0$, then $k$ should be described by $-k$. A term in a block in the partitioned matrix can be described by `lmiterm()` function, with $i, j$ representing respectively the row and column numbers of the block. $P$ is the declared decision variables, and the matrices $A, B$ indicate the matrices in the term $APB$. If `flag` is assigned as 's', the symmetrical term $APB + (APB)^T$ is specified. If the whole term is a constant matrix, then $P$ is set to 0, and matrix $B$ is omitted.

(4) **Determine LMI model description.** After the LMI model description with the function `lmiterm()`, the function `getlmis()` can be used to determine LMI problem modeling. The syntax of the function is $G = \text{getlmis}$.

(5) **Solve the LMI problem.** For the declared $G$ model, the LMI optimization problems can be solved in one of the following three forms

$$[t_{\min}, x] = \text{feasp}(G,\text{options},\text{target}) \qquad \text{\% feasibility problem}$$
$$[c_{\text{opt}}, x] = \text{mincx}(G,c,\text{options},x_0,\text{target}) \qquad \text{\% linear objective}$$
$$[\lambda, x] = \text{gevp}(G,\text{nlfc},\text{options},\lambda_0,x_0,\text{target}) \quad \text{\% generalized eigenvalue}$$

(6) **Solution extraction.** The solution $x$ obtained is a vector, and `dec2mat()` function can be used to extract the solution. There are five components in the control option `options`, where the first describes the precision, and the default value is $10^{-5}$.

**Example 9.16.** Consider Riccati inequality $A^T X + X A + X B R^{-1} B^T X + Q < 0$, with

$$A = \begin{bmatrix} -2 & -2 & -1 \\ -3 & -1 & -1 \\ 1 & 0 & -4 \end{bmatrix}, \ B = \begin{bmatrix} -1 & 0 \\ 0 & -1 \\ -1 & -1 \end{bmatrix}, \ Q = \begin{bmatrix} -2 & 1 & -2 \\ 1 & -2 & -4 \\ -2 & -4 & -2 \end{bmatrix}, \ R = I_2.$$

The original nonlinear matrix inequality is obviously not an LMI. Using the Schur complement, this Riccati inequality can be expressed by a partitioned LMI as follows.

Also, since a positive-definite solution is expected, the second LMI can be established

$$
\left\{
\begin{array}{l}
\left[
\begin{array}{c|c}
A^{\mathrm{T}}X + XA + Q & XB \\
\hline
B^{\mathrm{T}}X & -R
\end{array}
\right] < 0 \\
X > 0, \text{ i.e., } X \text{ is positive-definite matrix.}
\end{array}
\right.
$$

When function `lmiterm()` is used, the value of $k$ can be set to 1 or 2. Besides, based on the dimensions of $A$ and $B$ matrices, it can be found that $X$ is a $3 \times 3$ symmetrical matrix. Thus, the following commands can be used to establish the feasibility problem. Since the second inequality is $X > 0$, its sequence number can be assigned to $-2$.

```
>> A=[-2,-2,-1; -3,-1,-1; 1,0,-4]; B=[-1,0; 0,-1; -1,-1];
   Q=[-2,1,-2; 1,-2,-4; -2,-4,-2]; R=eye(2);
   setlmis([]);          % establish a new LMI framework
   X=lmivar(1,[3 1]);    % declare solution matrix X, a 3 × 3 symmetrical matrix
   lmiterm([1 1 1 X],A',1,'s')  % (1,1)th block, symmetrical for A^T X + XA
   lmiterm([1 1 1 0],Q)         % (1,1)th block, add a constant matrix Q
   lmiterm([1 1 2 X],1,B)       % (1,2)th block, matrix XB
   lmiterm([1 2 2 0],-1)        % (2,2)th block, matrix -R
   lmiterm([-2,1,1,X],1,1)      % the 2nd inequility, i.e., X > 0
   G=getlmis;                   % complete LTI framework setting
   [tmin b]=feasp(G);           % solve feasibility problem
   X=dec2mat(G,b,X)             % extract the solution matrix
```

It is found that $t_{\min} = -0.2427$, and the feasibility solution to the original problem is

$$
X = \begin{bmatrix}
1.0329 & 0.4647 & -0.23583 \\
0.4647 & 0.77896 & -0.050684 \\
-0.23583 & -0.050684 & 1.4336
\end{bmatrix}.
$$

It is worth mentioning that due to possible problems in the new Robust Control Toolbox, if the command `lmiterm([1 2 1 X],B',1)` is used to describe the symmetrical term in the first inequality, wrong results were found. Thus, the symmetrical terms should not be described again in solving LMI problems.

**Example 9.17.** For the linear continuous state space equation

$$
A = \begin{bmatrix}
-4 & -3 & 0 & -1 \\
-3 & -7 & 0 & -3 \\
0 & 0 & -13 & -1 \\
-1 & -3 & -1 & -10
\end{bmatrix}, \quad
B = \begin{bmatrix}
0 \\
-4 \\
2 \\
5
\end{bmatrix}, \quad
C = \begin{bmatrix} 0, & 0, & 4, & 0 \end{bmatrix}, \quad D = 0.
$$

If the system model is entered, function `norm()` can be used to calculate its $\mathcal{H}_\infty$ norm, and the result is 0.4639. Alternatively, LMI method can also be used to calculate the norm, i.e., by solving LMIs in Eqn. (9.62), where two decision variables $\gamma$ and $P$ are used. Here, with two inequalities, the first one is a $3 \times 3$ partitioned matrix. With the following statements, the solution is 0.4651. The $c$ vector is assigned with `mat2dec()` function.

```
>> A=[-4,-3,0,-1; -3,-7,0,-3; 0,0,-13,-1; -1,-3,-1,-10];
   B=[0; -4; 2; 5]; C=[0,0,4,0]; D=0; G=ss(A,B,C,D); norm(G,inf)
   setlmis([]); P=lmivar(1,[4,1]); gam=lmivar(1,[1,1]);
```

```
lmiterm([1 1 1 P],1,A,'s'), lmiterm([1 1 2 P],1,B),
lmiterm([1 1 3 0],C'); lmiterm([1 2 2 gam],-1,1),
lmiterm([1 2 3 0],D'); lmiterm([1 3 3 gam],-1,1);
lmiterm([-2 1 1 P],1,1); H=getlmis; c=mat2dec(H,0,1);
[a,b]=mincx(H,c); gam_opt=dec2mat(H,b,gam)
```

It is obvious that there are slight differences in the two results. The problem now is, which one is more accurate? It should be noted that the default precision required in mincx() function is rather low. If the precision is set to $10^{-5}$, the following statements can be used, and the more accurate solution is 0.4640.

```
>> options=[1e-5,0,0,0,0];
   [a,b]=mincx(H,c,options); gam_opt=dec2mat(H,b,gam)
```

### 9.4.3  *Optimization Problem Solutions with YALMIP Toolbox*

The YALMIP Toolbox released by Dr. Johan Löfberg is a more flexible general purpose optimization language in MATLAB, with support also for LMI problems[20]. The description of LMI problems is much simpler and more straightforward than the ones in the Robust Control Toolbox. The YALMIP Toolbox can be downloaded for free from MathWorks Inc.'s file-exchange site. or from his own web-page at http://control.ee.ethz.ch/~joloef/yalmip.php.

Decision variables can be declared in YALMIP Toolbox with sdpvar() function, which can be called in the following ways

| | |
|---|---|
| $X = \text{sdpvar}(n)$ | % symmetrical matrix declaration |
| $X = \text{sdpvar}(n,m)$ | % rectangular matrix declarations |
| $X = \text{sdpvar}(n,n,\text{'full'})$ | % ordinary square matrix declaration |

The decision variables declared previously can further be treated, for instance, hankel() function can be applied on a decision vector to form the decision matrix in Hankel form. Similarly, the functions intvar() and binvar() can be used to declare integer and binary variables respectively, thus integer programming and binary programming problems can be handled.

For sdpvar decision variables, the symbols [ and ] can be used to describe LMIs. If there are many LMIs, they can be joined together with the , sign, to form a single LMI representation.

An objective function, when necessary, can also be described, and the LMI optimization programs can be solved with the following syntaxes

| | |
|---|---|
| $s = \text{solvesdp}(F)$ | % solve feasibility problem |
| $s = \text{solvesdp}(F,f)$ | % optimization problem with objective $f$ |
| $s = \text{solvesdp}(F,f,\text{options})$ | % options are allowed, algorithm selection |

where $F$ is the collection of constraints. After the solution, the command $X = \text{double}(X)$ can be used to extract the solution matrix $X$.

**Example 9.18.** With the use of the YALMIP Toolbox, the problem in Example 9.16 can be solved using simpler commands such that

```
>> A=[-2,-2,-1; -3,-1,-1; 1,0,-4]; B=[-1,0; 0,-1; -1,-1];
   Q=[-2,1,-2; 1,-2,-4; -2,-4,-2]; R=eye(2); X=sdpvar(3);
   F=set([A'*X+X*A+Q, X*B; B'*X, -R]<0)+set(X>0);
   sol=solvesdp(F); X=double(X)
```

and it can be seen that the results are exactly the same.

**Example 9.19.** Consider the $\mathcal{H}_\infty$ norm calculation problem in Example 9.17. With YALMIP Toolbox, the problem can be solved with more simple and straightforward commands, and the result obtained is 0.4640.

```
>> A=[-4,-3,0,-1; -3,-7,0,-3; 0,0,-13,-1; -1,-3,-1,-10];
   B=[0; -4; 2; 5]; C=[0,0,4,0]; D=0; gam=sdpvar(1); P=sdpvar(4);
   F=set([A*P+P*A',P*B,C'; B'*P,-gam,D'; C,D,-gam]<0)+set(P>0);
   sol=solvesdp(F,gam); double(gam)
```

### 9.4.4  *Simultaneous Stabilization Multiple Linear Models*

Assume that the linear system model is given by $\dot{x} = A_i x + B_i u$, $i = 1, 2, \cdots, m$. If there exists a state feedback matrix $K$, such that $u(t) = -Kx(t)$, all the closed-loop systems $A_i + B_i K$ are stabilized. Such a stabilization problem is referred to as simultaneous stabilization problem.

For each Lyapunov inequality

$$X_i > 0, \quad \left(A_i + B_i K\right)^{\mathrm{T}} X_i + X_i \left(A_i + B_i K\right) < 0, \qquad (9.64)$$

a matrix $X_i$ can be found to stabilize the closed-loop system. However, how can a unique matrix $X$ be found, to stabilize all the subsystems? The Lyapunov inequality with unique $X$ can be written as

$$X > 0, \quad \left(A_i + B_i K\right)^{\mathrm{T}} X + X \left(A_i + B_i K\right) < 0. \qquad (9.65)$$

In the inequality, the decision variables are $X$ and $K$, while the rest of the matrices are given ones. It can be seen that since the multiplication of $X$ and $K$ are contained, it should be converted to linear matrix inequalities. Then solutions can be found, and the stabilizing controller can be designed.

It can be seen by expanding Eqn. (9.65) that

$$A_i^{\mathrm{T}} X + X A_i + K^{\mathrm{T}} B_i^{\mathrm{T}} X + X B_i K < 0. \qquad (9.66)$$

With the properties of matrix transformation, i.e., $PQP^{\mathrm{T}}$ does not change the positive definiteness of matrix $Q$, the above left multiplication is $X^{-1}$, right multiplication is $\left(X^{-1}\right)^{\mathrm{T}}$, and $\left(X^{-1}\right)^{\mathrm{T}} = X^{-1}$. Thus, the above matrix inequalities can be converted to

$$X^{-1} A_i^{\mathrm{T}} + A_i X^{-1} + X^{-1} K^{\mathrm{T}} B_i^{\mathrm{T}} + B_i K X^{-1} < 0. \qquad (9.67)$$

Denote $P = X^{-1}$, $Y = KX^{-1}$, then the original matrix inequalities can be converted to the following linear matrix inequality

$$A_i P + P A_i^{\mathrm{T}} + B_i Y + Y^{\mathrm{T}} B_i^{\mathrm{T}} < 0. \qquad (9.68)$$

With $X > 0$, i.e., $P^{-1} > 0$, the whole problem can be converted to $m - 1$ LMIs. The feasibility problem can then be found for the LMIs, such that $P$ and $Y$ are obtained. Finally, the simultaneous stabilizing matrix $K$ can be found.

**Example 9.20.** Assume that there are two subsystems

$$A_1 = \begin{bmatrix} -1 & 2 & -2 \\ -1 & -2 & 1 \\ -1 & -1 & 0 \end{bmatrix}, \ B_1 = \begin{bmatrix} -2 \\ 1 \\ -1 \end{bmatrix}, \ A_2 = \begin{bmatrix} 0 & 2 & 2 \\ 2 & 0 & 2 \\ 2 & 0 & 1 \end{bmatrix}, \ B_2 = \begin{bmatrix} -1 \\ -2 \\ -1 \end{bmatrix}.$$

A simultaneous stabilizing matrix $K$ is expected. There are two decision variables, $P$ and $Y$, where $P$ is a $3 \times 3$ symmetrical matrix, $Y$ is a $1 \times 3$ row vector. Thus, the three LMIs can be written as

$$\begin{cases} P^{-1} > 0, \quad \text{or equivalently } P > 0 \\ A_1 P + P A_1^{\mathrm{T}} + B_1 Y + Y^{\mathrm{T}} B_1^{\mathrm{T}} < 0 \\ A_2 P + P A_2^{\mathrm{T}} + B_2 Y + Y^{\mathrm{T}} B_2^{\mathrm{T}} < 0. \end{cases}$$

The following statements can be used in solving the three LMIs

```
>> A1=[-1,2,-2; -1,-2,1; -1,-1,0]; B1=[-2; 1; -1];
   A2=[0,2,2; 2,0,2; 2,0,1]; B2=[-1; -2; -1]; setlmis([]);
   P=lmivar(1,[3,1]); Y=lmivar(2,[1,3]); lmiterm([1,1,1,P],-1,1);
   lmiterm([2,1,1,P],A1,1,'s'), lmiterm([2,1,1,Y],B1,1,'s')
   lmiterm([3,1,1,P],A2,1,'s'), lmiterm([3,1,1,Y],B2,1,'s')
   G=getlmis; [a,b]=feasp(G); P=dec2mat(G,b,P)
   Y=dec2mat(G,b,Y), X=inv(P); K=Y*X
```

and the following solution can be found

$$X = \begin{bmatrix} 0.13987 & 0.024173 & 0.10595 \\ 0.024173 & 0.084939 & -0.050311 \\ 0.10595 & -0.050311 & 0.21682 \end{bmatrix}.$$

The state feedback vector is $K = [2.0739, 0.5616, 2.4615]^{\mathrm{T}}$.

If the YALMIP Toolbox is used, the following statements can be used, and the same results can be found.

```
>> P=sdpvar(3); Y=sdpvar(1,3);
   F=set(A1*P+P*A1'+B1*Y+Y'*B1'<0)+set(A2*P+P*A2'+B2*Y+Y'*B2'<0);
   F=F+set(P>0); sol=solvesdp(F);
   P=double(P); X=inv(P), Y=double(Y), K=Y*X
```

### 9.4.5 *Robust Optimal Controller Design with LMI Solvers*

The norm-based robust controller design problems can be converted into linear matrix inequality problems. Some typical problems are presented below. Details can be found in [19].

(1) $\mathcal{H}_2$ **controller design.** For the state space model $(A, B, C, D)$, the $\mathcal{H}_2$ optimal controller design problem can be equivalently expressed in the following linear matrix inequalities

$$\min \quad \rho. \tag{9.69}$$

$$\rho, X, W, Z \text{ s.t.} \begin{cases} AX + B_2 W + \left(AX + B_2 W\right)^{\mathrm{T}} + B_1 B_1^{\mathrm{T}} < 0 \\ \begin{bmatrix} -Z & CX + DW \\ \left(CX + DW\right)^{\mathrm{T}} & -X \end{bmatrix} < 0 \\ \mathrm{trace}(Z) < \rho \end{cases}$$

(2) $\mathcal{H}_\infty$ **controller design.** The state feedback-based optimal $\mathcal{H}_\infty$ robust controller can be equivalently converted into the following LMIs

$$\min \quad \rho, \tag{9.70}$$

$$\rho, X, W \text{ s.t.} \begin{cases} \begin{bmatrix} AX + B_2 W + \left(AX + B_2 W\right)^{\mathrm{T}} & B_1 & \left(C_1 X + D_{12} W\right)^{\mathrm{T}} \\ B_1^{\mathrm{T}} & -I & D_{11}^{\mathrm{T}} \\ C_1 X + D_{12} W & D_{11} & -\rho I \end{bmatrix} < 0 \\ X > 0 \end{cases}$$

and the state feedback matrix is then obtained, $K = WX^{-1}$.

$\mathcal{H}_\infty$ robust controller design based on output feedback can also be converted into the following LMIs[17]

$$\min \quad \gamma. \tag{9.71}$$

$$\gamma, S, R \text{ s.t.} \begin{cases} \begin{bmatrix} N_{12} & 0 \\ 0 & I \end{bmatrix}^{\mathrm{T}} \begin{bmatrix} AR + RA^{\mathrm{T}} & RC_1^{\mathrm{T}} & B_1 \\ C_1 R & -\gamma I & D_{11} \\ B_1^{\mathrm{T}} & D_{11}^{\mathrm{T}} & -\gamma I \end{bmatrix} \begin{bmatrix} N_{12} & 0 \\ 0 & I \end{bmatrix} < 0 \\ \begin{bmatrix} N_{21} & 0 \\ 0 & I \end{bmatrix}^{\mathrm{T}} \begin{bmatrix} AS + SA^{\mathrm{T}} & SB_1 & C_1^{\mathrm{T}} \\ B_1^{\mathrm{T}} S & -\gamma I & D_{11}^{\mathrm{T}} \\ C_1 & D_{11} & -\gamma I \end{bmatrix} \begin{bmatrix} N_{21} & 0 \\ 0 & I \end{bmatrix} < 0 \\ \begin{bmatrix} R & I \\ I & S \end{bmatrix} \geqslant 0 \end{cases}$$

In Robust Control Toolbox, a dedicated LMI-based robust controller design problem can be solved with `hinflmi()` function. Optimal $\mathcal{H}_\infty$ controller can be designed directly with $[\gamma_{\mathrm{opt}}, K] = \texttt{hinflmi}(P, [p, q])$ , where $p$ and $q$ are the numbers of inputs and outputs, and $P$ is the augmented plant model, described in system matrix format. The returned argument $K$ is the controller model, also in system matrix format. Recall that we wrote a MATLAB function `sys2mat()` to convert augmented plant model into system matrix format. The state space models can also be extracted with `unpck()` function. The returned $\gamma_{\mathrm{opt}}$ is the optimal value for $\gamma$.

**Example 9.21.** Consider again the augmented plant model in Example 9.6. The function `sys2smat()` can be used to convert the model into a system matrix model. The `hinflmi()` function can be used to design directly to design optimal $\mathcal{H}_\infty$ controller

```
>> A=[0,1,0,0; -5000,-100/3,500,100/3; 0,-1,0,1; 0,100/3,-4,-60];
   B=[0; 25/3; 0; -1]; C=[0,0,1,0]; G=ss(A,B,C,0); s=tf('s');
   W1=100/(s+1); W2=1e-5; W3=s/1000; G1=augtf(G,W1,W2,W3);
   [Gc1,a,g]=hinfsyn(G1); Gc1=zpk(Gc1),  % design optimal H∞ controller
   P=sys2smat(G1); [g,K]=hinflmi(P,[1,1]);
   [a,b,c,d]=unpck(K); Gc2=zpk(ss(a,b,c,d))
   step(feedback(G*Gc1,1),'-',feedback(G*Gc2,1),'--')
   figure; bode(G*Gc1,'-',G*Gc2,'--')
```

The controllers obtained are

$$G_{c1}(s) = \frac{-587116783.7885(s + 67.4)(s + 0.06391)(s^2 + 25.87s + 4643)}{(s + 1.573 \times 10^4)(s + 1303)(s + 1)(s^2 + 23.79s + 535.7)},$$

$$G_{c2}(s) = \frac{-3191219221.354(s + 67.4)(s + 0.06391)(s^2 + 25.87s + 4643)}{(s + 1.715 \times 10^5)(s + 719.2)(s + 0.9545)(s^2 + 22.34s + 522.8)}.$$

Under these two controllers, closed-loop step responses and open-loop Bode diagrams can be obtained as shown in Figs. 9-22(a) and (b). It can be seen that the behaviors of the two controllers are very close.

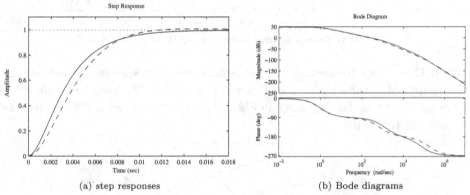

(a) step responses       (b) Bode diagrams

Fig. 9-22   Comparisons of system responses with the two controllers.

## 9.5   Quantitative Feedback Theory and Design Methods

### 9.5.1   *Introduction to Quantitative Feedback Theory*

Professor Issac Horowitz and his collaborators proposed systematically quantitative feedback theory (QFT)[21, 22]. These methods are frequency domain design methods, and can be used in designing QFT controllers with uncertainties. The plant models can be single variable as well as multivariable systems, and the methods are also applicable to nonlinear and time varying plants. Although QFT was first proposed quite a long time ago, it did not receive adequate attention. In recent years, the QFT approaches have regained much interest from the researchers in control community, and MATLAB-based QFT Toolbox has become popular[23]. In this section, single variable uncertain system design technique using QFT will be demonstrated.

### 9.5.2    QFT Design Method for Single Variable Systems

Since the design procedure for single variable minimal phase plant model is the kernel of QFT controller design, the QFT methodology will be illustrated for this kind of systems. The design procedures of QFT are:

(1) **Control system structure.**   The two-degree-of-freedom QFT control system is shown in Fig. 9-23. In the system, $\mathscr{P}(s)$ is the uncertain plant model, $C(s)$ is the controller. The characteristics of QFT controllers are that they are time invariant systems, however, they can be used to control plants with serious uncertainty or with heavy disturbances. Since the controller $C(s)$ is mainly used to ensure the stability robustness of the uncertain system, the control performance may not be satisfactory. A pre-filter $F(s)$ should be introduced to compensate the performance of the dynamics of the system.

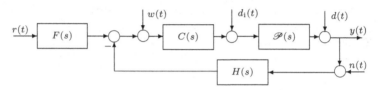

Fig. 9-23    Control system structure for QFT controller design.

(2) **Construct frequency response template.** By selecting a frequency $\omega_1$, the samples of frequency response of an uncertain system $\mathscr{P}(s)$ can be obtained and form the plant template as shown in Fig. 9-24(a). Different frequencies correspond to different templates.

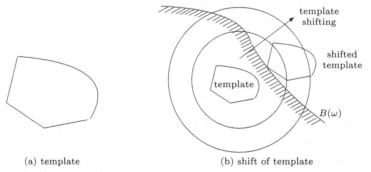

(a) template                        (b) shift of template

Fig. 9-24    Illustrations of template and template shifting.

If a frequency vector $w$ is created, the `plottmp()` function in QFT Toolbox can be used to draw the templates for each frequencies. The syntax of the function is `plottmp(w,`$k_{\text{nom}}$`,`$\mathscr{P}$`)` , where a three-dimensional array $\mathscr{P}(i,j,k)$ is the set of samples, with $i$ and $j$ representing the input and output ports, and $k$ is the serial number of the template. Each member is an uncertain transfer function (or state space) model. For single variable systems, $i = j = 1$. The variable $k_{nom}$ is the serial number of the template for the nominal system. Different serial numbers are located at different template boundaries.

With the controller $C(s)$, the template of the system may be shifted. The magnitude in horizontal shift of controller $C(s)$ is, in fact, the phase, $\angle C(j\omega_1)$, and the vertical shift is the magnitude $|C(j\omega_1)|$, as shown in Fig. 9-24(b). If the template is located outside the boundary $B(\omega)$, each member in the uncertain system $\mathscr{P}$ is stable. Similarly, each frequency correspond to a specific template.

(3) **Provide design specifications**. In the QFT design process, some inequalities are used to describe the effect of the control system, such as

(i) **Robust tracking performance**. For the uncertain plant, the frequency responses of the closed-loop system satisfy

$$T_{\mathrm{m}}(\omega) \leqslant \left| F(j\omega) \frac{\mathscr{P}(j\omega)C(j\omega)}{1 + H(j\omega)\mathscr{P}(j\omega)C(j\omega)} \right| \leqslant T_{\mathrm{M}}(\omega), \qquad (9.72)$$

(ii) **Robust stability**. The system model satisfy

$$\left| \frac{\mathscr{P}(j\omega)C(j\omega)}{1 + H(j\omega)\mathscr{P}(j\omega)C(j\omega)} \right| \leqslant M_0. \qquad (9.73)$$

Besides, other inequalities can be specified, and all the possible inequalities are listed in Table 9-1. Function `sisobnds()` in the QFT Toolbox can be used to describe different type of inequalities. The syntax of the function is `bnd = sisobnds(type, ω, W, 𝒫, C)`, where the serial number of inequality `type` is listed in Table 9-1[23]. The argument $\omega$ is the frequency vector, $W$ corresponds to the relevant $W_i$ object, $\mathscr{P}$ is the uncertain plant model.

Table 9-1　Various inequalities and descriptions.

| type | inequality constraints | interpretations of the constraints |
|------|------------------------|-------------------------------------|
| 1 | $\left\| \dfrac{\mathscr{P}CH}{1 + \mathscr{P}CH} \right\| < W_1(s)$ | magnitude and phase margin constraints |
| 2 | $\left\| \dfrac{1}{1 + \mathscr{P}CH} \right\| < W_2(s)$ | sensitivity function constraints |
| 3 | $\left\| \dfrac{\mathscr{P}}{1 + \mathscr{P}CH} \right\| < W_3(s)$ | disturbance rejection at plant input |
| 4 | $\left\| \dfrac{G}{1 + \mathscr{P}CH} \right\| < W_4(s)$ | minimization of control signal |
| 5 | $\left\| \dfrac{CH}{1 + \mathscr{P}CH} \right\| < W_5(s)$ | control effort with sensor dynamics |
| 6 | $\left\| \dfrac{\mathscr{P}C}{1 + \mathscr{P}CH} \right\| < W_6(s)$ | tracking bandwidth with sensors dynamics |
| 7 | $W_{7a}(s) < \left\| \dfrac{F\mathscr{P}C}{1 + \mathscr{P}CH} \right\| < W_{7b}(s)$ | tracking specifications of 2DOF QFT controller |
| 8 | $\left\| \dfrac{H}{1 + \mathscr{P}CH} \right\| < W_8(s)$ | disturbance rejection at output, with sensor dynamics |
| 9 | $\left\| \dfrac{\mathscr{P}H}{1 + \mathscr{P}CH} \right\| < W_9(s)$ | disturbance rejection at input, with sensor dynamics |

When the bounds $\mathrm{bnd}_1, \cdots, \mathrm{bnd}_k$ are constructed, the `grpbnds()` function can be used $\mathrm{bnd} = \mathtt{grpbnds(bnd_1,\cdots,bnd_k)}$ to construct a single boundary description `bnd`. With the combined boundary description `bnd`, function `sectbnds()` can be used to get the intersections of the bounds with $\mathrm{ubnd} = \mathtt{sectbnds(bnd)}$ . The boundary can be drawn with the MATLAB function `plotbnds(bnd)` .

(4) **Construct the lower stable boundary for different frequencies**. For the frequencies $(\omega_2, \omega_3, \cdots, \omega_m)$, the lower bounds $B(\omega_2), B(\omega_3), \cdots, B(\omega_m)$ are also processed. If an optimal controller is needed, an $L(j\omega)$ curve can be created, by selecting one point on each $B(\omega_i)$ curve, with $L(s) = \mathscr{P}(s)C(s)$. The controllers thus designed are usually very complicated, Thus, the best $L(s)$ should be selected under the constraints of $B(\omega_i)$ curves. The QFT controller $C(s)$ can then be designed. Loop shaping design is completed with the user interface opened by the `lpshape()` function. The syntax of the function is special, $\mathtt{lpshape(\omega, ubnd, P_0, C_0)}$ , where $P_0$ is the nominal plant model, $C_0$ is the initial controller. The shape of the $L(s)$ curve can be designed interactively in the interface. When the shape of $L(s)$ is created, the Apply button should be clicked to confirm the curve. When the menu File → Export is selected, a file dialog box is opened, and the QFT controller can be specified in the dialog box. For instance, when $C$ is entered, the QFT controller will be written to MATLAB workspace with the variable $C$.

(5) **Design $F(s)$ controller**. The controller $C(s)$ designed is usually not satisfactory, and the inequality in Eqn. (9.72) cannot be satisfied. A pre-filter $F(s)$ should be designed to meet the system requirements.

The pre-filter can be designed with the interface opened by `pfshape()` function, the syntax of the function $\mathtt{pfshape(type, \omega, W, \mathscr{P}, R, G, H, F_0)}$ . The menu File → Export can also be selected to return the pre-filter back to MATLAB workspace.

An example is used to illustrate the full process in QFT controller design.

**Example 9.22.** Consider the following uncertain plant model [23]

$$\mathscr{P} = \left\{ \frac{ka}{s(s+a)}, \ k \in [1, 2.5, 6, 10], a \in [1.5, 3, 6] \right\}.$$

Assume the robust stability boundary below is expected

$$\left| \frac{\mathscr{P}(j\omega)C(j\omega)}{1 + H(j\omega)\mathscr{P}(j\omega)C(j\omega)} \right| \leqslant 1.2,$$

and at low frequencies, $\omega < 10$, the robust performance inequality is

$$\frac{120}{s^3 + 17s^2 + 82s + 120} \leqslant \left| F(j\omega) \frac{\mathscr{P}(j\omega)C(j\omega)}{1 + H(j\omega)\mathscr{P}(j\omega)C(j\omega)} \right| \leqslant \frac{0.6584(s + 30)}{s^2 + 4s + 19.752}.$$

To design a QFT controller to satisfy the inequalities, the following statements can be used to describe the uncertain model. Selecting a set of frequencies, the template of the uncertain plant can be obtained as shown in Fig. 9-25(a).

```
>> c=1; a=1;
   for k=[1,2.5,6,10], P(1,1,c)=tf(k*a,[1,a,0]); c=c+1; end
   a=10; for k=[1,2.5,6,10], P(1,1,c)=tf(k*a,[1,a,0]); c=c+1; end
   k=1; for a=[1.5,3,6], P(1,1,c)=tf(k*a,[1,a,0]); c=c+1; end
   k=10; for a=[1.5,3,6], P(1,1,c)=tf(k*a,[1,a,0]); c=c+1; end
   w=[.1,.5,1,2,10,15,100]; k_nom=1; plottmpl(w,P,k_nom)
```

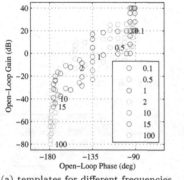 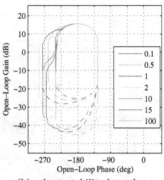

(a) templates for different frequencies  (b) robust stability boundary

Fig. 9-25  Templates and bounds for the uncertain plant.

Now the robust stable bounds can be obtained, as shown in Fig. 9-25(b). It can be seen that the robust bound for each frequency is a closed curve such that the template at that frequency should lie outside the bound, otherwise the robust stability conditions cannot be satisfied.

```
>> b1=sisobnds(1,w,1.2,P); plotbnds(b1)
```

The following statements can also be used to draw the robust performance inequality bounds as shown in Fig. 9-26(a). Note that the statement $w(w<=10)$ extracts the $\omega \leqslant 10$ frequencies from the frequency vector such that all the templates lie above the corresponding curves.

```
>> Tm=tf(120,[1 17 82 120]); TM=tf(0.6584*[1 30],[1 4 19.752]);
   b2=sisobnds(7,w(w<=10),[TM;Tm],P);
```

Considering the two robust specifications, the function **grpbnds()** can be used to create single common bound, and **sectbnds()** function can be used to extract the intersections of these bounds, as shown in Fig. 9-26(b).

```
>> bnd=grpbnds(b1,b2); ubnd=sectbnds(bnd); plotbnds(ubnd);
```

When the initial controller

$$C_0(s) = \frac{100000(s+100)(s+1)}{(s+50)(s^2+1500s+10^6)},$$

is assumed, the following statements can be used to open the controller design interface as shown in Fig. 9-27. The interactive method can be used modify $B(\omega)$ curve with mouse dragging actions. The principle of designing the $L(s)$ curve is that the curve should be dragged to the left-hand-side, but not interfering with robust boundaries. For instance, for the initial controller, the Nichols plot should be dragged upward,

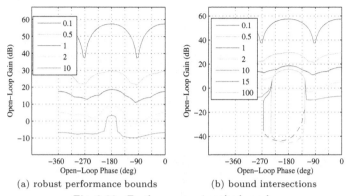

(a) robust performance bounds      (b) bound intersections

Fig. 9-26   Further processing the bounds.

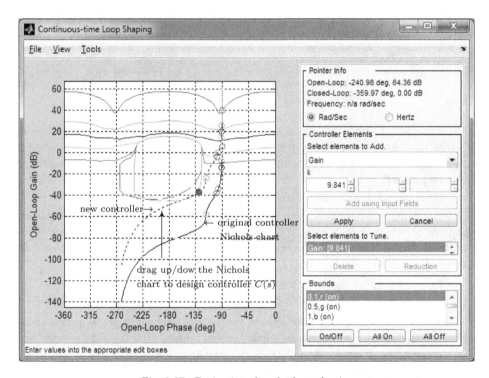

Fig. 9-27   Design interface for loop shaping.

When the modification of the curve is complete, the Apply button should be clicked to accept the modified curve. Zeros and poles can also be added to or removed from the controller to change the shape of the Nichols chart. Finally, File → Export menu can be clicked to return the controller $C(s)$ back to MATLAB workspace. For instance, the variable $C$ can be obtained

$$C(s) = \frac{4708700.2369(s + 100)(s + 1)}{(s + 50)(s^2 + 1500s + 10^6)}.$$

```
>> w=logspace(-2,4,200); s=zpk('s');
   C0=100000*(s+100)*(s+1)/(s+50)/(s^2+1500*s+1e006);
   lpshape(w(w<=10),ubnd,P(1,1,1),C0);
```

The initial model of the pre-filter $F(s)$ can be selected as a typical second-order model

$$F_0(s) = \frac{10\omega_n^2}{s^2 + 2\zeta\omega_n s + \omega_n^2},$$

and the following statements can be used to design interactively the pre-filter, in the interface shown in Fig. 9-28.

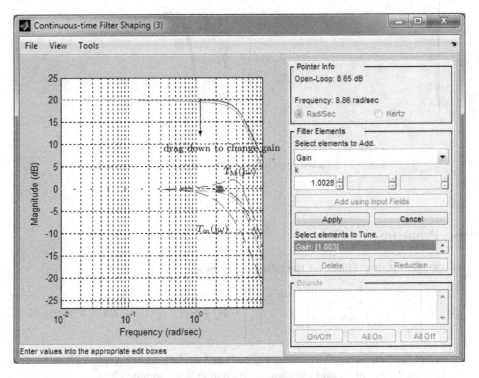

Fig. 9-28 Design interface of the pre-filter.

When the curve is well adjusted, it can be saved to `c8qft1.fsh` file. Note that if $\omega_n = 5$ is selected, no matter how the curve is adjusted, the transfer function will exceed the $[T_m(\omega), T_M(\omega)]$ boundary. Thus, $\omega_n = 4.5$ should be selected.

```
>> wn=4.5; zet=0.707; F0=10*tf(wn^2,[1,2*zet*wn,wn^2]);
   pfshape(7,w(w<=10),[TM;Tm],P,[],C,[],F0);
```

The menu File → Export can be used again to save the pre-filter back to MATLAB workspace with variable name of $F$.

$$F(s) = \frac{20.1994}{s^2 + 6.363s + 20.25}.$$

Since the model $P$ is already be declared as an uncertain model, the following statements can be used to draw the closed-loop step responses under controller $C(s)$, as shown in Fig. 9-29(a). It can be seen that although the system is stabilized, the performance is not satisfactory. The pre-filter should be used. The closed-loop responses under $C(s)$ and $F(s)$ can also be obtained, as shown in Fig. 9-29(b). It can be seen that the two degree-of-freedom QFT controller can achieve satisfactory control results for the uncertain plant.

>> FF=feedback(P*C,1); step(FF), figure, step(FF*F)

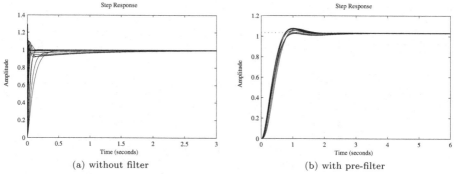

(a) without filter    (b) with pre-filter

Fig. 9-29    Closed-loop step responses under QFT controller.

## 9.6    Problems

(1) Design a Kalman filter for the following plant

$$\dot{x}(t) = \begin{bmatrix} 0 & 0 & 1 & 0 \\ 0 & 0 & 0 & 1 \\ -1.25 & 1.25 & 0 & 0 \\ 1.25 & -1.25 & 0 & 0 \end{bmatrix} x(t) + \begin{bmatrix} 0 \\ 0 \\ 1 \\ 0 \end{bmatrix} \big[ u(t) + \xi(t) \big], \quad y(t) = \big[ 2, 1, 3, 4 \big] x(t) + \theta(t),$$

where the variances of disturbance signals $\xi(t)$ and $\sigma(t)$ are $\mathrm{E}[\xi^2] = 1.25 \times 10^{-3}$ and $\mathrm{E}[\theta^2] = 2.25 \times 10^{-5}$, and the signals $\xi(t)$ and $\theta(t)$ are independent.

(2) Please select a weighting matrix $Q$, and assume $R = 1$, design a LQG controller for the plant model in the previous problem, and design an observer-based regulator. Check the magnitude and phase margins and draw time domain and frequency domain responses.

(3) Judge whether or not the return difference transfer function with the LQG controller designed in the previous problem approaches well to the one in direct state feedback. If not, please design a LQG/LTR controller, with a good value of $q$, and then compare the system responses.

(4) Write out the system matrix description to the following state space model

$$\dot{x} = \begin{bmatrix} 1 & 0 & -1 \\ 0 & -2 & 0 \\ -1 & 0 & 2 \end{bmatrix} x + \begin{bmatrix} 3 \\ 2 \\ 1 \end{bmatrix} u, \quad y = \big[ 1, 2, 3 \big] x + 4u.$$

(5) Assume that the plant model and weighting functions are

$$G(s) = \frac{1}{(0.01s+1)^2}, \quad W_1(s) = \frac{10}{s^3+2s^2+2s+1}, \quad \text{and,} \quad W_3(s) = \frac{10s+1}{20(0.01s+1)}.$$

Please solve the following problems

(i) Please write the two-port state space model of the weighted system;

(ii) Design an optimal $\mathcal{H}_\infty$ controller;

(iii) Draw the closed-loop step response and open-loop Nichols chart, and comment on the quality of the dynamic system.

(iv) Design an optimal $\mathcal{H}_2$ controller, and compare the control results.

(6) For the plant models

(i) $G(s) = \dfrac{10}{(s+1)(s+2)(s+3)(s+4)}$, (ii) $G(s) = \dfrac{10(-s+3)}{s(s+1)(s+2)}$,

design an optimal $\mathcal{H}_\infty$ controller for the minimum sensitivity problem with the concept of standard function. Analyze the system in frequency and time domain, and draw the Bode magnitude diagrams for the sensitivity and complementary sensitivity functions.

(7) In Problem 6(ii), if an optimal $\mathcal{H}_\infty$ controller is designed, and the denominator polynomial of the plant is changed to $10(s+3)$, find out the stability of the system if the same controller is used. Validate the results in frequency and time domain.

(8) Compare the sensitivity robust controller design problem in Problem 6. Analyze qualitatively the impact of the selection of natural frequency in the standard transfer function on the closed-loop system responses.

(9) For the sensitivity problem in Problem 6, please design the optimal $\mathcal{H}_\infty$ and $\mathcal{H}_2$ controllers, and perform system analysis to the systems.

(10) Consider the example in [15]

$$G(s) = \frac{-6.4750s^2 + 4.0302s + 175.7700}{s(5s^3 + 3.5682s^2 + 139.5021s + 0.0929)},$$

with sensitivity function

$$W_1(s) = \frac{0.9(s^2 + 1.2s + 1)}{1.0210(s + 0.001)(s + 1.2)(0.001s + 1)}.$$

Please design an optimal $\mathcal{H}_\infty$ controller, and draw the closed-loop step response of the system.

## Bibliography and References

[1] Sofanov M G. Stability and robustness of multivariable feedback systems. Boston: MIT Press, 1980

[2] Stein G, Athens M. The LQG/LTR procedure for multivariable feedback control design. IEEE Transaction on Automatic Control, 1987, AC-32(2):105–114

[3] Zames G. Feedback and optimal sensitivity: model reference transformations, multiplicative seminorms, and approximate inverses. Proceedings 17th Allerton

Conference, 1979, 744–752. Also, Transaction on Automatic Control, AC-26(2):585–601, 1981

[4] Doyle J C, Glover K, Khargonekar P, Francis B. State-space solutions to standard $\mathcal{H}_2$ and $\mathcal{H}_\infty$ control problems. IEEE Transaction on Automatic Control, 1989, AC-34:831–847

[5] Skogestad S, Postlethwaite I. Multivariable feedback control: analysis and design. New York: John Wiley & Sons, 1996

[6] De Cuyper J, Swevers J, Verhaegen M, Sas P. $\mathcal{H}_\infty$ feedback control for signal tracking on a 4 poster test rig in the automotive industry. Proceedings of International Conference on Noise and Vibration Engineering, 2000, 61–67

[7] Grimble M J. LQG optimal control design for uncertain systems. Proceedings IEE, Part D, 1990, 139:21–30

[8] The MathWorks Inc. Robust control toolbox user's manual, 2005

[9] The MathWorks Inc. $\mu$-analysis and synthesis toolbox user's manual, 2005

[10] The MathWorks Inc. LMI control toolbox user's manual, 2004

[11] Balas G, Chiang R, Packard A, Safonov M. Robust control toolbox user's guide, Version 3. MathWorks, 2004

[12] Anderson B D O. Controller design: moving from theory to practice. IEEE Control Systems Magazine, 1993, 13(4):16–25. Also, Bode prize lecture, CDC, 1992

[13] Anderson B D O, Liu Y. Controller reduction: concepts and approaches. IEEE Transaction on Automatic Control, 1989, AC-34(8):802–812

[14] Glover K, Doyle J C. State-space formulae for all stabilizing controllers that satisfy an $\mathcal{H}_\infty$ norm bound and relations to risk sensitivity. Systems and Control Letters, 1988, 11:167–172

[15] Doyle J C, Francis B A, Tannerbaum A R. Feedback control theory. New York: MacMillan Publishing Company, 1991

[16] Kučera K. A method to teach the parameterization of all stabilizing controllers. Proceedings of IFAC World Congress. Milan, Italy, 2011 6355–6360

[17] Boyd S, El Ghaoui L, Feron E, Balakrishnan V. Linear matrix inequalities in systems and control theory. Philadelphia: SIAM Books, 1994

[18] Willems J C. Least squares stationary optimal control and the algebraic Riccati equation. IEEE Transactions on Automatic Control, 1971, 16(6):621–634

[19] Yu L. Robust control — linear matrix inequality approaches. Beijing: Tsinghua University Press, 2002. (In Chinese)

[20] Löfberg J. YALMIP: a toolbox for modeling and optimization in MATLAB. Proceedings of IEEE International Symposium on Computer Aided Control Systems Design. Taipei, 2004 284–289

[21] Horowitz I. Quantitative feedback theory (QFT). Proceedings IEE, Part D, 1982, 129:215–226

[22] Horowitz I. Survey of quantitative feedback theory (QFT). International Journal of Control, 1991, 53(2):255–291

[23] Borghesani C, Chait Y, Yaniv O. The QFT frequency domain control design toolbox for use with MATLAB. Terasoft Inc, 2003

# Chapter 10

# Adaptive and Intelligent
# Control Systems Design

In the previous three chapters, various controller design algorithms are presented. Most of the algorithms rely heavily on the accurate plant models. If the plant model is unknown, or it is difficult to construct controllers or determine controller parameters, the advantages of new intelligent controllers such as fuzzy controllers or neural network controllers are better revealed.

The concept of intelligent control was first proposed by Professor King-Sun Fu of Purdue University in 1971[1], claiming that intelligent control is the intersection of artificial intelligence and automatic control with more focus on the combination of the concept humanized intelligence and automatic control[2]. So far, there is no unified definition on "intelligent control". A reasonable definition is given in [3]. Intelligent control is a class of automatic control which can independently drive intelligent machines to achieve the desired target without human intervention. Compared with traditional control theory, intelligent control has higher degree of adaptation for the complexity of environments and tasks.

Some of the acknowledged types of intelligent control are expert systems, fuzzy logic control, artificial neural network control, learning control, predictive control, humanized control, etc. Besides, the solutions to some of the intelligent control problems are related to optimization techniques. However, the classical optimization algorithm may sometimes obtain local minima. Better parallel global searching algorithms are needed. Some of the widely used parallel algorithms are genetic algorithms, particle swarm optimization algorithms. Equipped with these algorithms, intelligent control problems can be better solved.

The design, modeling and simulation problems are illustrated to several adaptive control systems such as model reference adaptive control, self-tuning control, which are first presented in Section 10.1. Different kinds of model predictive control system design techniques are presented in Section 10.2. In Section 10.3, the concept of fuzzy set and fuzzy inference are illustrated, and the modeling and simulation problems of several fuzzy control systems are presented. In Section 10.4, modeling and simulation of several neural network-based PID controllers are presented. Iterative learning control strategies are illustrated in Section 10.5. In Section 10.6, some of the global optimization algorithms such as genetic algorithm, particle swarm optimization algorithm are illustrated, and their applications in optimization and optimal controller design are demonstrated.

## 10.1   Design of Adaptive Control Systems

Self-tuning controllers (STC) and model reference adaptive system (MRAS)[4] are the two categories of mainly developed adaptive control systems, shown respectively in Figs. 10-1 and 10-2.

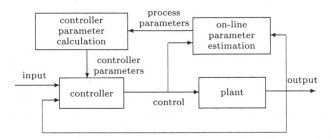

Fig. 10-1    Self-tuning adaptive control system.

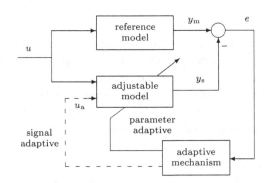

Fig. 10-2    Model reference adaptive system.

Under the self-tuning control strategy, an identification task is carried out to identify the plant model parameters on-line. This task is usually undertaken with recursive identification algorithms. With the model parameters, the control signal, or control law, the next sampling interval is calculated to control directly the plant model. This is done within one sampling interval. In the next sampling interval, the identification and control law computation are performed once again. Some of the self-tuning algorithms combine the two tasks into one task, and they are usually referred to as implicit self-tuning controllers[5].

In the model reference adaptive control systems, a reference model with good performance is introduced. The actual output of the plant is compared with that of the reference model, and the error signal is used to drive the adaptive mechanism, where the parameters or control signals can be adjusted, so that the control target can be achieved.

These two types of adaptive control structures can be used to adjust the controllers automatically so as to meet the environmental changes in the plant and external disturbances. Reference [6] shows that the two adaptive categories are actually equivalent.

In this section, the model reference adaptive control system is introduced, and simulation analysis of the adaptive control system is demonstrated. Then the presentations on forecasting and self-tuning control systems are given.

### 10.1.1   *Design and Simulation of Model Reference Adaptive Control Systems*

The concept, design algorithms and applications of model reference adaptive control systems are fully covered in [4]. In this section, only a simple kind of model reference adaptive strategy is presented, and we focus on the simulation analysis of the system.

Assume that a second-order continuous reference model is given by

$$G_{\mathrm{m}}(s) = \frac{b_0}{a_2 s^2 + a_1 s + 1}.$$

Usually the reference model can be selected as a standard transfer function, or other transfer functions with satisfied performance.

The actual plant model is given by

$$G(s) = \frac{b_0}{a_3 s^2 + a_1 s + 1}.$$

The target of the model reference adaptive control is to have the output of the plant model to follow that of the reference model. With hyper stability design approach[4], the adaptive control structure shown in Fig. 10-3 can be established[7]. In the block diagram, two multiplication blocks are used to change adaptively the gain $\hat{b}_0(t)$, such that the output of the plant follows the output of the reference model. It can be seen that the whole system model is nonlinear and can only be accurately analyzed with simulation methods.

Based on the block diagram, a Simulink model shown in Fig. 10-4 can be created. With the powerful facilities of Simulink, nonlinear manipulations can be implemented easily.

**Example 10.1.** Assume the parameters of the reference model are $b_0 = 0.5$, $a_1 = 0.447$, $a_2 = 0.1$, and the parameters of the controller are $d_0 = 1$, $d_1 = 0.5$, $k_1 = 0.03$, $k_2 = 1$, with the initial value $\hat{b}_0(0) = 0.2$. The input signal is square wave, with amplitude of 10, and frequency of 1, and the range of simulation is 0–15 s. Selecting the parameter $a_3$ to some different values, at 0.02, 0.1 $(= a_2)$, 1, 2, 5, 10, the output signals can be obtained in the following loop structure, as shown in Fig. 10-5.

```
>> b0=0.5; a1=0.447; a2=0.1; d0=1; d1=0.5; k1=0.03;
   k2=1; b01=0.2; a3v=[0.02,0.1,1,2,5,10];
```

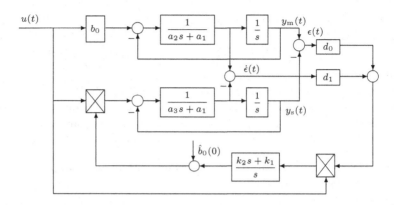

Fig. 10-3    Block diagram of model reference adaptive system.

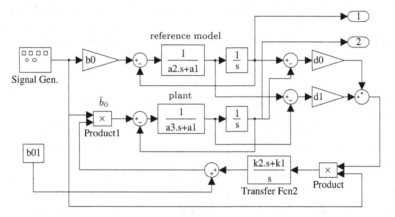

Fig. 10-4    Simulink representation    (file: c10mmras.mdl).

`for a3=a3v, [t,a,y]=sim('c10mmras',[0,15]); line(t,y(:,2)); end`

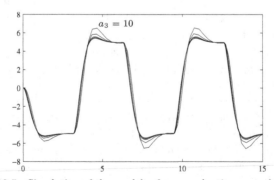

Fig. 10-5    Simulation of the model reference adaptive control system.

In the response curves, the one with smallest overshoot is obtained with $a_3 = a_2$. and with biggest overshoot is from $a_3 = 10$. With the increase of the value of $a_3$, the output of the system are all similar. It can be seen that although the plant model is different from the reference model, and the difference is significance, the adaptive control strategy is effective.

Further simulation analysis to the adaptive system can be performed. Suppose that the plant model is no longer given in the form of $b_0/(a_3 s^2 + a_1 s + 1)$. It is a high-order model with relative order of 2, the same as the reference model. For instance, the plant model can be changed to

$$G(s) = \frac{7s^2 + 24s + 24}{s^4 + 10s^3 + 35s^2 + 50s + 24}.$$

A Simulink model as shown in Fig. 10-4 can be established, where the signal $\dot{y}_s(t)$ is acquired with an approximate differentiator. Simulation result obtained is shown in Fig. 10-7. It can be seen that the adaptive control result is still satisfactory.

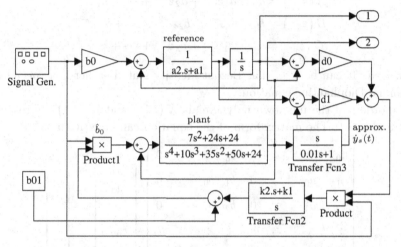

Fig. 10-6   When the plant model is replaced   (file name: 10mmras1.mdl).

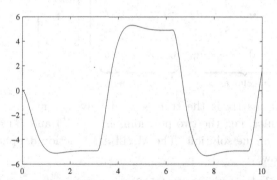

Fig. 10-7   Simulation result when the plant is changed.

## 10.1.2   *Solutions of Polynomial Diophantine Equations*

Self-tuning control is another category of adaptive control systems. The idea of self-tuning and minimum variance regulator was proposed by Karl Åström and

Björm Wittenmark in 1973[8]. The basic idea of self-tuning control is that when the plant model is uncertain or subjected to disturbances, the control law $u_0, u_1, \cdots, u_M$ for each sampling interval is designed recursively, such that the performance index reaches or approaches to minimum[9, 10].

Polynomial Diophantine equation is a very important polynomial equation in self-tuning control. The mathematical form of the equation is

$$A\left(z^{-1}\right) X\left(z^{-1}\right) + B\left(z^{-1}\right) Y\left(z^{-1}\right) = C\left(z^{-1}\right), \tag{10.1}$$

where

$$
\begin{aligned}
A\left(z^{-1}\right) &= a_0 + a_1 z^{-1} + a_2 z^{-2} + \cdots + a_n z^{-n}, \\
B\left(z^{-1}\right) &= b_0 + b_1 z^{-1} + b_2 z^{-2} + \cdots + b_m z^{-m}, \\
C\left(z^{-1}\right) &= c_0 + c_1 z^{-1} + c_2 z^{-2} + \cdots + c_k z^{-k},
\end{aligned}
\tag{10.2}
$$

and $m \leqslant n$. It can be seen that Bezout identity stated earlier is a special case of polynomial Diophantine equation.

The orders of the unknown polynomials $X\left(z^{-1}\right)$ and $Y\left(z^{-1}\right)$ are respectively $m-1$ and $n-1$. The matrix form of the equation can be written as

$$
\underbrace{\begin{bmatrix}
a_0 & 0 & \cdots & 0 \\
a_1 & a_0 & \ddots & 0 \\
a_2 & a_1 & \ddots & 0 \\
\vdots & \vdots & \ddots & a_0 \\
a_n & a_{n-1} & \ddots & a_1 \\
0 & a_n & \ddots & a_2 \\
\vdots & \vdots & \ddots & \vdots \\
0 & 0 & \cdots & a_n
\end{bmatrix}}_{m \text{ columns}}
\underbrace{\begin{matrix}
b_0 & 0 & \cdots & 0 \\
b_1 & b_0 & \ddots & 0 \\
b_2 & b_1 & \ddots & 0 \\
\vdots & \vdots & \ddots & b_0 \\
\cdot & \cdot & \ddots & b_1 \\
\cdot & \cdot & \ddots & b_2 \\
\vdots & \vdots & \ddots & \vdots \\
0 & 0 & \cdots & b_m
\end{matrix}}_{n \text{ columns}}
\begin{bmatrix}
x_0 \\ x_1 \\ \vdots \\ x_{m-1} \\ y_0 \\ y_1 \\ \vdots \\ y_{n-1}
\end{bmatrix}
=
\begin{bmatrix}
c_1 \\ c_2 \\ \vdots \\ c_k \\ 0 \\ \vdots \\ 0
\end{bmatrix}.
\tag{10.3}
$$

The coefficient matrix is the transpose of Sylvester matrix. If the Sylvester matrix is nonsingular, i.e., the two polynomials $A\left(z^{-1}\right)$ and $B\left(z^{-1}\right)$ are coprime, the equation has unique solution. The MATLAB function diophantine_eq() can be written as follows

```
function [X,Y]=diophantine_eq(A,B,C)
n=length(B)-1; m=length(A)-1; S=[];
A1=[A(:); zeros(n-1,1)]; B1=[B(:); zeros(m-1,1)];
for i=1:n, S=[S A1]; A1=[0; A1(1:end-1)]; end
for i=1:m, S=[S B1]; B1=[0; B1(1:end-1)]; end   % create Sylvester matrix S^T
C1=zeros(n+m,1); C1(1:length(C))=C(:); x=S\C1;
X=x(1:n)'; Y=x(n+1:end)';
```

**Example 10.2.** For the Diophantine equation with the polynomials

$$A\left(z^{-1}\right) = 0.212 - 1.249z^{-1} + 2.75z^{-2} - 2.7z^{-3} + z^{-4},$$

$$B\left(z^{-1}\right) = 2.04 - 1.2z^{-1} + 3z^{-2}, \quad C\left(z^{-1}\right) = -0.36 + 0.6z^{-1} + 2z^{-2},$$

the following statements can be used to solve the equation.

```
>> A=[0.212,-1.249,2.75,-2.7,1]; B=[2.04,-1.2,3];
   C=[-0.36,0.6,2]; [X,Y]=diophantine_eq(A,B,C)
```

The solutions to the Diophantine equation can be obtained, as

$$X\left(z^{-1}\right) = 2.1289 + 0.9611z^{-1}, \quad Y\left(z^{-1}\right) = -0.3977 + 1.2637z^{-1} + 0.0272z^{-2} - 0.3204z^{-3}.$$

### 10.1.3   *d-step Ahead Forecast*

Assume that at time $t$, all the input and output sequences can be measured, $y(t), u(t), y(t-1), u(t-1), \cdots$. Based on the information, if the $y(t+d)$ can be forecasted, it is referred to as $d$-step ahead forecast, denoted as $\hat{y}(t+d\,|\,t)$.

The variance of the forecast error is minimized

$$\min_{\hat{y}(t+d\,|\,t)} \; \mathrm{E}\left\{\left[y(t+d) - \hat{y}(t+d\,|\,t)\right]^2\right\}, \tag{10.4}$$

the $d$-step ahead forecast satisfies the following equation[10]

$$C\left(z^{-1}\right)\hat{y}(t+d\,|\,t) = G\left(z^{-1}\right)y(t) + F\left(z^{-1}\right)u(t), \tag{10.5}$$

where polynomial Diophantine equation can be solved

$$C\left(z^{-1}\right) = A\left(z^{-1}\right)E\left(z^{-1}\right) + z^{-d}B\left(z^{-1}\right)G\left(z^{-1}\right), \tag{10.6}$$

and then, $F\left(z^{-1}\right)$ can be calculated

$$F\left(z^{-1}\right) = E\left(z^{-1}\right)B\left(z^{-1}\right). \tag{10.7}$$

**Example 10.3.** For the discrete model of a system

$$y(t) - 0.6y(t-1) + 0.4y(t-2) = 2u(t) + 0.8\xi(t) + 0.6\xi(t-1) + 0.4\xi(t-2),$$

it can be seen that

$$A\left(z^{-1}\right) = 1 - 0.6z^{-1} + 0.4z^{-2}, \; B\left(z^{-1}\right) = 2, \; C\left(z^{-1}\right) = 0.8 + 0.6z^{-1} + 0.4z^{-2}.$$

If two-step ahead forecast is expected, i.e., $d = 2$, the following statements can be used to enter the polynomials first. Then the polynomials $E\left(z^{-1}\right)$, $F\left(z^{-1}\right)$ and $G\left(z^{-1}\right)$ can be obtained by solving the polynomial Diophantine equation

```
>> A=[1 -0.6 0.6]; B=2; B1=[0 0 B]; C=[0.8 0.6 0.4];
   [E,G]=diophantine_eq(A,B1,C), F=conv(E,B)
```

The solutions to the equation are

$$E\left(z^{-1}\right) = 0.8 + 1.08z^{-1}, \; G\left(z^{-1}\right) = 0.284 - 0.324z^{-1}, \; \text{and } F\left(z^{-1}\right) = 1.6 + 2.16z^{-1}.$$

The two-step ahead forecast model can be written as

$$\hat{y}(t+2\,|\,t) = \frac{0.284 - 0.324z^{-1}}{0.8 + 0.6z^{-1} + 0.4z^{-2}}\, y(t) + \frac{1.6 + 2.16z^{-1}}{0.8 + 0.6z^{-1} + 0.4z^{-2}}\, u(t).$$

With the forecast equation, the Simulink model shown in Fig. 10-8 can be established, and the filter blocks are shown in the model. Assume that square wave with magnitude of 4 is generated by the **Signal Generator** block with sampling interval of $T = 0.01$ s. The random noise is with zero mean, and a variance of 1. The actual signal and forecasted signal are obtained with simulation, as shown in Fig. 10-9.

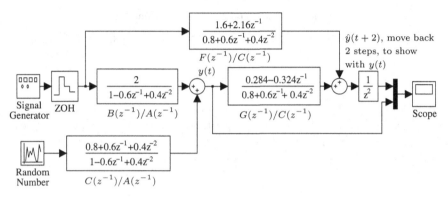

Fig. 10-8   Simulink model of two-step ahead forecast.

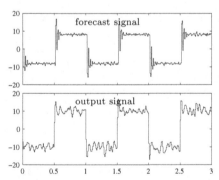

Fig. 10-9   Forecast results with two-step ahead forecast model.

### 10.1.4   *Design of Minimum Variance Controllers*

Suppose the discrete plant model can be expressed by

$$A\left(z^{-1}\right) y(t) = z^{-d} B\left(z^{-1}\right) u(t) + C\left(z^{-1}\right) \xi(t), \tag{10.8}$$

where the pure time delay is $dT$, and $\xi(t)$ is zero mean white noise signal.

The target of minimum variance self-tuning controller is to design the control sequence $u(t)$, such that the variance of actual output $y(t + d)$ and the expected output $y_{\mathrm{r}}(t + d)$ is minimized, i.e., to optimize the objective function

$$J = \min_{u} \mathrm{E}\left\{\left[y(t+d) - y_{\mathrm{r}}(t+d)\right]^2\right\}. \tag{10.9}$$

The control law for minimum variance self-tuning controller is

$$F\left(z^{-1}\right)u(t) = y_{\mathrm{r}}(t+d) + \left[C\left(z^{-1}\right) - 1\right]\hat{y}(t+d\,|\,t) - G\left(z^{-1}\right)y(t), \qquad (10.10)$$

where polynomial $F\left(z^{-1}\right)$ and $G\left(z^{-1}\right)$ can be solved from Eqns. (10.6) and (10.7).

If $y_{\mathrm{r}}(t+d) = c$, where $c$ is a constant, the minimum variance control problem is changed to minimum variance regulator one, and the control law is simplified to

$$u(t) = -\frac{G\left(z^{-1}\right)}{F\left(z^{-1}\right)}y(t) = -\frac{G\left(z^{-1}\right)}{E\left(z^{-1}\right)B\left(z^{-1}\right)}y(t). \qquad (10.11)$$

It can be seen from the control law that $B\left(z^{-1}\right)$ should be a stable polynomial. In other words, the control law is valid for minimal phase systems. If the control law is combined with the recursive identification algorithm, the following adaptive control law can be formulated

$$u(t) = \frac{1}{\hat{b}_0}\left[y_{\mathrm{r}}(t) - \boldsymbol{\psi}^{\mathrm{T}}(t)\hat{\boldsymbol{\theta}}(t)\right], \qquad (10.12)$$

where

$$\boldsymbol{\psi}^{\mathrm{T}}(t) = \left[u(t-1), \cdots, u(t-m), y(t), \cdots, y(t-n+1)\right], \qquad (10.13)$$

and

$$\hat{\boldsymbol{\theta}}(t) = \hat{\boldsymbol{\theta}}(t-1) + \boldsymbol{K}\left[y(t) - b_0 u(t-d) - \boldsymbol{\psi}^{\mathrm{T}}(t-d)\hat{\boldsymbol{\theta}}(t-1)\right]$$

$$\boldsymbol{K} = \frac{\boldsymbol{P}(t-1)\boldsymbol{\psi}(t-d)}{\lambda + \boldsymbol{\psi}^{\mathrm{T}}(t-d)\boldsymbol{P}(t-1)\boldsymbol{\psi}(t-d)} \qquad (10.14)$$

$$\boldsymbol{P}(t) = \frac{1}{\lambda}\left[\boldsymbol{I} - \boldsymbol{K}\boldsymbol{\psi}^{\mathrm{T}}(t-d)\right]\boldsymbol{P}(t-1).$$

For non-minimal phase plant model, spectral factorization should be carried out to the polynomial $B\left(z^{-1}\right)$, such that the unstable zeros can be classified in polynomial $B^-\left(z^{-1}\right)$, with $B\left(z^{-1}\right) = B^+\left(z^{-1}\right)B^-\left(z^{-1}\right)$ [9].

The simulation program of minimum variance self-tuning adaptive control system is given in [11]. Through slight modifications, the new simulation function is as follows

```
function [out,in,Rd,Sd]=adapt_sim(A,B,d,lam,sd,p0,Tend,y_ref)
out=[]; in=[]; std_y=[]; A=A(2:end); B=[zeros(1,d-1),B];
nA=length(A); nB=length(B); f=dimpulse(1,[1,A],d+nA); Rd=[]; Sd=[];
if f(1)==0, f=f(nA+1:d+nA); else f=f(1:d); end
st_opt=sqrt(ones(1,d)*(f.*f*sd*sd));
S=[1,zeros(1,nA-1)]; R=[1,zeros(1,nB-1)];
nS=length(S); nR=length(R); u=zeros(1,nR+d);
y=zeros(1,nS+d); P=p0*eye(nR+nS);
for t = 1:Tend
  y_m=-A*y(1:nA)'+B*u(1:nB)'+sd*randn(1,1);
  Phi=[u(d:d+nR-1), y(d:d+nS-1)];
  P=(1/lam)*(P-(P*Phi'*Phi*P)/(lam+Phi*P*Phi'));
  Theta=[R,S]+Phi*P*(y_m-Phi*[R,S]'); R=Theta(1:nR); Rd=[Rd,R];
```

```
S=Theta(nR+1:nR+nS); Sd=[Sd,S]; s1=R(2:nR); s2=u(1:nR-1);
if isempty(s1), s1=0; s2=0; end;
u_new=(-s1*s2'-S*[y_m,y(1:nS-1)]'+y_ref)/R(1);
u=[u_new, u(1:nR+d-1)]; y=[y_m, y(1:nS+d-1)];
out=[out, y_m]; in=[in, u_new];
end
```

where $A$, $B$ are the coefficient vectors of polynomials $A\left(z^{-1}\right)$ and $B\left(z^{-1}\right)$, $d$ is the delay term, lam is the forgetting factor $\lambda$, sd is the variance of the disturbance signal, $p_0$ is the initial values of the $\boldsymbol{P}(t)$ matrix, i.e., $\boldsymbol{P}(0) = p_0\boldsymbol{I}$. Tend is the maximum step in simulation, while y_ref is the expected output value. With this function, the output signal out, the control sequence in, and the identified numerator and polynomial coefficients are returned in variables $\boldsymbol{R}_\mathrm{d}$ and $\boldsymbol{S}_\mathrm{d}$.

**Example 10.4.** Assume that the system model is

$$A\left(z^{-1}\right) = 1 - 0.7555z^{-2} + 0.0498z^{-2}, \ B\left(z^{-1}\right) = 0.2134 + 0.081z^{-1},$$

and $d = 1$. The forgetting factor is selected as $\lambda = 1$, and the set-point is $y_\mathrm{ref} = 10$. The following statements can be used to perform simulation for the self-tuning control system as shown in Figs. 10-10(a) and (b).

```
>> A=[1 -0.7555 0.0498]; B=[0.2134,0.081]; d=1;
   lam=1; sd=1; p0=100000; Tend=200; y_ref=10;
   [y,u,num,den]=adapt_sim(A,B,d,lam,sd,p0,Tend,y_ref);
   subplot(121), stairs(num); hold on; stairs(den)
   subplot(222), stairs(y); subplot(224), stairs(u)
```

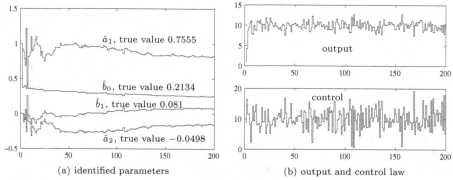

(a) identified parameters          (b) output and control law

Fig. 10-10    Minimum variance identification and control results.

## 10.1.5  *Generalized Minimum Variance Control*

In the above self-tuning control strategy, the sizes of the inputs are not considered. In real applications, the size of the control signal reflects the energy assumptions, and also if the size of the control signal is too large, it may damage the hardware system. Thus, the control signal should be taken into account in controller design. A new objective function is introduced

$$J = \min_{u} \mathrm{E}\left\{\left[P\left(z^{-1}\right)y(t+d) - R\left(z^{-1}\right)r(t)\right]^2 + \left[\Lambda\left(z^{-1}\right)u(t)\right]^2\right\}, \quad (10.15)$$

where $r(t)$ is the reference input signal, and polynomials

$$P\left(z^{-1}\right) = 1 + p_1 z^{-1} + \cdots + p_{n_p} z^{-n_p},$$
$$R\left(z^{-1}\right) = r_0 + r_1 z^{-1} + \cdots + r_{n_r} z^{-n_r}, \quad (10.16)$$
$$\Lambda\left(z^{-1}\right) = \lambda_0 + \lambda_1 z^{-1} + \cdots + \lambda_{n_\lambda} z^{-n_\lambda},$$

are the weighting functions of actual output signal, expected output signal, and control signal. In order to get optimal solutions, an auxiliary signal is introduced

$$S(t+d) = \psi(t+d) - R\left(z^{-1}\right)r(t) + \frac{\lambda_0}{b_0}\Lambda\left(z^{-1}\right)u(t), \quad (10.17)$$

where $\psi(t+d) = P\left(z^{-1}\right)y(t+d)$. The generalized minimum variance control problem is converted to the minimum variance control problem. The self-tuning law can be written as

$$u(t) = \frac{b_0\left[R\left(z^{-1}\right)r(t) - \psi(t+d\,|\,t)\right]}{\lambda_0\Lambda\left(z^{-1}\right)}. \quad (10.18)$$

Consider the adaptive prediction law in Eqn. (10.5), the variation form can be written as

$$\hat{y}(t+d\,|\,t) = \frac{G\left(z^{-1}\right)}{C\left(z^{-1}\right)}y(t) + \frac{F\left(z^{-1}\right)}{C\left(z^{-1}\right)}u(t). \quad (10.19)$$

Substituting it to Eqn. (10.18), the generalized minimum variance control law can be written as

$$u(t) = \frac{b_0\left[C\left(z^{-1}\right)R\left(z^{-1}\right)r(t) - G\left(z^{-1}\right)y(t)\right]}{\lambda_0 C\left(z^{-1}\right)\Lambda\left(z^{-1}\right) + b_0 B\left(z^{-1}\right)E\left(z^{-1}\right)}. \quad (10.20)$$

Based on the control law given above, the following MATLAB can be written

```
function [den,num1,num2]=st_contr(A,B,C,d,P,R,Lam)
B1=[zeros(1,d) 1]; [E,G]=diophantine_eq(A,B1,C);
lam0=Lam(1); b0=B(1); den=lam0*conv(Lam,C)+b0*conv(B,E);
num2=-b0*G; num1=b0*conv(C,R);
```

**Example 10.5.** Assume that the plant model is given by [10]

$$y(t) = 1.5y(t-1) - 0.7y(t-2) + u(t-1) + 0.5u(t-2) + \epsilon(t) - 0.5\epsilon(t-1),$$

and the objective function is written as

$$J = \mathrm{E}\left\{\left[y(t+1) - r(t)\right]^2 + 0.5u^2(t)\right\}.$$

It can be seen from the standard form that

$$A\left(z^{-1}\right) = 1 - 1.5z^{-1} + 0.7z^{-2}, \quad B\left(z^{-1}\right) = 1 + 0.5z^{-1},$$
$$C\left(z^{-1}\right) = 1 - 0.5z^{-1}, \quad P\left(z^{-1}\right) = R\left(z^{-1}\right) = 1, \quad \Lambda\left(z^{-1}\right) = \sqrt{0.5},$$

and $d = 1$. The polynomials $E\left(z^{-1}\right)$, $F\left(z^{-1}\right)$, and $G\left(z^{-1}\right)$ can be designed first, the generalized minimum variance control law can be obtained

```
>> A=[1 -1.5 0.7]; B=[1 0.5]; C=[1 -0.5]; d=1; P=1; R=1;
   lam=sqrt(0.5); [D,N1,N2]=st_contr(A,B,C,d,P,R,lam)
```

from which it is found that

$$D\left(z^{-1}\right) = 1.5 + 0.25z^{-1}, \ N_1\left(z^{-1}\right) = 1 - 0.5z^{-1}, \ N_2\left(z^{-1}\right) = 1 - 0.7z^{-1}.$$

From the three polynomials obtained, the control law can be written as

$$u(t) = \frac{(1 - 0.5z^{-1})r(t) - (1 - 0.7z^{-1})y(t)}{1.5 + 0.25z^{-1}},$$

and the time domain representation of the control law is

$$u(t) = \frac{1}{1.5}\Big[r(t) - 0.5r(t-1) - y(t) + 0.7y(t-1) - 0.25u(t-1)\Big].$$

## 10.2    Simulation and Design of Model Predictive Control Systems

Model predictive control is a model-based control strategy widely used in process industry[12, 13]. Dynamic matrix control (DMC) applied in Shell Oil[14] and model predictive heuristic control in ADERSA[15] are the earlier applications of model predictive controllers. The model of the system is described by past data of the plant. For linear systems, the model can also be described by state space and transfer functions. For stable linear systems, step and impulse responses of the plant systems can be used, and the error between the model output and the actual output can be used to generate a sequence of input signals $u(t), \cdots, u(t_N)$. One step control with $u(t)$ is performed, and then the next control sequence can be generated, and the control is advanced to another step. The recursive control strategy is referred to as model predictive control as illustrated in the block diagram in Fig. 10-11.

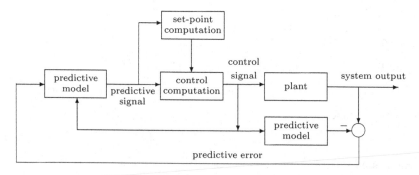

Fig. 10-11    Block diagram of model predictive control.

With the outputs and control signals in Fig. 10-12, the basic idea of model predictive control is to calculate the control sequence $u(t)$, such that the criterion of the error signals between the expected output and actual output is minimized.

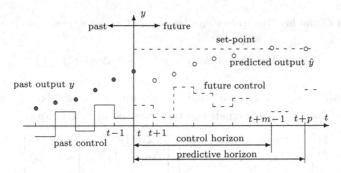

Fig. 10-12   The input and control signals.

### 10.2.1   *Dynamic Matrix Control*

Assume that a set of sample points $s_1$, $s_2$, $\cdots$, $s_p$ in step response of a linear system are obtained as shown in Fig. 10-13. The step response of the system at time $t$ can be written as

$$y(t) = \sum_{i=1}^{p} s_i \Delta u(t - i) = \sum_{i=1}^{p-1} s_i \Delta u(t - i) + s_p \Delta u(t - p), \tag{10.21}$$

where $\Delta u(t)$ is the increment in control at time $t$.

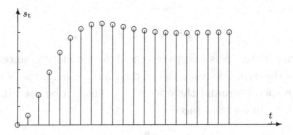

Fig. 10-13   Step response signal.

It should be noted that the point number $p$ should be selected such that the step response settles down at the steady-state region. Otherwise, the model representation may be useless in applications. For the convenience of dynamic matrix presentation, the $\Delta u(t - p)$ term is extracted. From the above formula, the $j$-step ahead prediction of the output signal can be written as

$$\hat{y}(t + j) = \sum_{i=1}^{p-1} s_i \Delta u(t + j - i) + s_p \Delta u(t + j - p), \tag{10.22}$$

where $j = 1, 2, \cdots, n$. With reference to Fig. 10-13, the inputs with subscripts $j - i < 0$ are the signals in the past, and the rest of the inputs are the current and in the future. They can be extracted from the presentation, such that

$$\hat{y}(t+j) = \sum_{i=1}^{j} s_i \Delta u(t+j-i) + \sum_{i=j+1}^{p-1} s_i \Delta u(t+j-i) + s_p \Delta u(t+j-p). \tag{10.23}$$

The sum of the last two terms can be denoted as $\tilde{y}(t+j)$

$$\tilde{y}(t+j) = \sum_{i=j+1}^{p-1} s_i \Delta u(t+j-i) + s_p \Delta u(t+j-p), \qquad (10.24)$$

the signal $\tilde{y}(t+j)$ is the prediction of the future output based on the past information. The predicted signals can be expressed in matrix form

$$
\begin{bmatrix} \hat{y}(t+1) \\ \hat{y}(t+2) \\ \vdots \\ \hat{y}(t+n) \end{bmatrix}
=
\begin{bmatrix} s_1 & & & \\ s_2 & s_1 & & \\ \vdots & \vdots & \ddots & \\ s_n & s_{n-1} & \cdots & s_1 \end{bmatrix}
\begin{bmatrix} \Delta u(t) \\ \Delta u(t+1) \\ \vdots \\ \Delta u(t-p) \end{bmatrix}
+
\begin{bmatrix} \tilde{y}(t+1) \\ \tilde{y}(t+2) \\ \vdots \\ \tilde{y}(t+n) \end{bmatrix}. \qquad (10.25)
$$

The first $m$ terms can be used, instead of all the $n$ terms to reduce computation efforts, where $m$ should be selected such that the quality of control is not sacrificed. The above equation can be approximately written as

$$
\begin{bmatrix} \hat{y}(t+1) \\ \hat{y}(t+2) \\ \vdots \\ \hat{y}(t+n) \end{bmatrix}
\approx
\begin{bmatrix} s_1 & & & \\ s_2 & s_1 & & \\ \vdots & \vdots & \ddots & \\ s_n & s_{n-1} & \cdots & s_{n+1-m} \end{bmatrix}
\begin{bmatrix} \Delta u(t) \\ \Delta u(t+1) \\ \vdots \\ \Delta u(t-m) \end{bmatrix}
+
\begin{bmatrix} \tilde{y}(t+1) \\ \tilde{y}(t+2) \\ \vdots \\ \tilde{y}(t+n) \end{bmatrix}, \qquad (10.26)
$$

and its matrix form is

$$\hat{y}(t+1) = S\Delta u(t) + \tilde{y}(t+1), \qquad (10.27)$$

where the constant matrix $S$ is referred to the dynamic matrix, since the coefficients in the matrix are the dynamic responses of the plant. Even if the plant is nonlinear, the actual step response around the operating point can be used in the matrix. A performance index can be introduced

$$J = \sum_{j=1}^{p} q(j) \left[ \hat{y}(t+j) - w(t+j) \right]^2 + \sum_{j=1}^{m} r(j) \Delta u^2(t+j-1), \qquad (10.28)$$

where $w(t+j)$ is the expected output, $\lambda(j)$ is the weight. The terms $p$ and $m$ are referred to as the prediction horizon and control horizon, respectively. Optimization techniques can be used to calculate the control sequence $u(t)$. Use the sequence to control the system in one step. The control sequence should be updated again with optimization techniques. The optimization problem is also known as the receding horizon control problem[13].

## 10.2.2    *Design of Model Predictive Controllers with MATLAB*

In the optimization problem, if $u(t)$ can be arbitrarily chosen, the original problem is unconstrained optimization problem, otherwise it is constrained optimization problem. Numerical algorithms can be used in solving the optimization problems. In the Model Predictive Control Toolbox[16], dedicated functions are provided to solve the problems with command-line format, or with graphical user interfaces. The two types of solutions are illustrated, and simulation with Simulink is demonstrated in the section.

## 1. System model and step response descriptions

If the plant model is linear, the function `poly2tfd()` can be used to describe it, with $G = \text{poly2tfd}(n, d, T, \tau)$, where $n, d$ are the coefficients of numerator and denominator of the transfer function of the plant. $T$ and $\tau$ are respectively the sampling interval and delay constant of the plant. If the plant is continuous, it can be set to $T = 0$. Here, $G$ should be a single variable transfer function. If multivariable models are involved, they can be represented by a series of single variable ones.

For the defined transfer function model $G$, the step response model `mod` can be established, with the syntax of $\text{mod} = \text{tfd2step}(t_f, T, k, G)$, where $t_f$ is the termination time, $k$ is the identifier for the output signal, with 1 for the system enters steady-state, otherwise it is 0. If multiple models $g_{11}, g_{12}, \cdots, g_{nm}$ are involved, the syntax is $\text{mod} = \text{tfd2step}(t_f, T, k, g_{11}, g_{12}, \cdots, g_{mm})$, where $k$ is an identifier vector for each output. The function `plotstep(mod)` can be used to draw the step response of the system `mod`.

**Example 10.6.** Assume a continuous plant model is given by

$$G(s) = \frac{e^{-s}}{(s+1)(2s+1)},$$

with sampling interval $T = 0.5\,\text{s}$. For a stable plant, a suitable termination time should be selected such that the step response enters the steady-state stage. With several trials, a termination time for the plant can be selected as $t_f = 12$. The step response data can be obtained as shown in Fig. 10-14. It can be seen that the last point in the response has a steady-state error of 0.82%.

```
>> t_f=12; T=0.5; G=poly2tfd(1,conv([1 1],[2 1]),0,1);
   mod=tfd2step(t_f,T,1,G); t=0:T:t_f; y=mod(1:length(t)); stem(t,y)
```

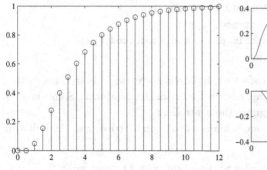

Fig. 10-14   Step response.

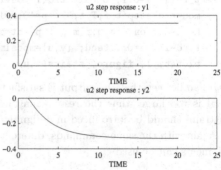

Fig. 10-15   Multivariable system.

**Example 10.7.** For the following multivariable model

$$G(s) = \begin{bmatrix} \dfrac{0.1134e^{-0.72s}}{1.78s^2 + 4.48s + 1} & \dfrac{0.924}{2.07s + 1} \\[3mm] \dfrac{0.3378e^{-0.3s}}{0.361s^2 + 1.09s + 1} & \dfrac{-0.318e^{-1.29s}}{2.93s + 1} \end{bmatrix},$$

the following statements can be used to draw the step responses as shown in Fig. 10-15.

```
>> g11=poly2tfd(0.1134,[1.78,4.48,1],0,0.72);
   g12=poly2tfd(0.924,[2.07,1],0,0);
   g21=poly2tfd(0.3378,[0.361,1.09,1],0,0.3);
   g22=poly2tfd(-0.318,[2.93,1],0,1.29);
   S=tfd2step(20,0.3,[1 1],g11,g12,g21,g22); plotstep(S)
```

## 2. Unconstrained optimal predictive controller design

The functions of Model Predictive Control Toolbox can be used in the design of the controllers. Unconstrained optimal predictive controller can be designed directly with mpccon() function $K_{\mathrm{mpc}} = \mathtt{mpccon(mod},q,r,m,p)$ , where mod is the step response data, vectors $q$ and $r$ represent the weights on the error and output increments, and $m$ and $p$ are the control and prediction horizons. The returned argument $K_{\mathrm{mpc}}$ is the controller gain matrix. With the matrix, the system response under predictive control can be obtained with mpcsim() function, with $[y,u,y_{\mathrm{m}}] = \mathtt{mpcsim(plant},\mathtt{mod},K_{\mathrm{mpc}},t_{\mathrm{f}},s_{\mathrm{p}})$ , where plant is the step response data, mod is the step response data used in controller design, the two set of data could be different. The argument $t_{\mathrm{f}}$ is the termination time, $s_{\mathrm{p}}$ is the reference input signal, and $y$ is the output of the system, $u$ is the control sequence, and $y_{\mathrm{m}}$ is the output of the reference model.

**Example 10.8.** Consider again the plant model in Example 10.6. By selecting weights $q = 1$, and $r = 0.1$, and introducing the prediction horizon as $p = 40$ and control horizon as $m = 10$, the following statements can be used to design model predictive controller. The control and output signals are shown in Figs. 10-16(a) and (b).

```
>> t_f=12; T=0.1; G=poly2tfd(1,conv([1 1],[2 1]),0,1);
   mod=tfd2step(t_f,T,1,G); p=40;m=10; q=1; r=0.1;
   Kmpc=mpccon(mod,q,r,m,p); plant=mod; sp=1;
   tend=10; t=0:T:tend; [y,u]=mpcsim(plant,mod,Kmpc,tend,sp);
   plot(t,y), figure, stairs(t,u)
```

It can be seen that the output is satisfactory, however, the expense is that the control signal is too large, thus the results may not be useful in applications. Some kind of constraint should be introduced in designing the controllers.

Again with the same commands, different horizons $m$'s can be tried, and the following statements can be used

```
>> K1=mpccon(mod,q,r,10,p); [y1,u]=mpcsim(plant,mod,K1,tend,sp);
   K2=mpccon(mod,q,r,5,p);  [y2,u]=mpcsim(plant,mod,K2,tend,sp);
```

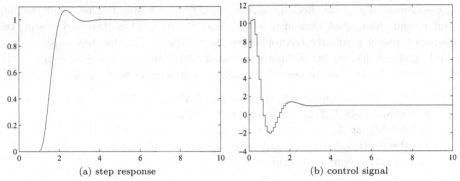

(a) step response        (b) control signal

Fig. 10-16   Simulation results of predictive control system.

```
K3=mpccon(mod,q,r,20,p); [y3,u]=mpcsim(plant,mod,K3,tend,sp);
plot(t,y1,t,y2,'-',t,y3,':')
```

and the results are obtained as shown in Fig. 10-17. For a larger $m$, for instance, $m = 20$, the output is similar to the case in $m = 10$. If $m$ is reduced, for instance, $m = 5$, there exists large difference in the results which means that the control horizon $m$ is important in controller design. If the value of $m$ is too small, the expected control target cannot be reached.

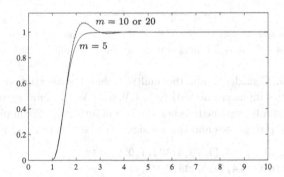

Fig. 10-17   Impact of control horizon selections.

## 3. Constrained optimal predictive controller design

If constraints are imposed on the control signals $u$, the controller design problem is changed to constrained optimization problems. The function cmpc() can be used instead in controller design

$$[y,u,y_m] = \texttt{cmpc}(\texttt{plant},\texttt{mod},q,r,m,p,t_f,s_p,u_{\text{lim}},y_{\text{lim}})$$

where the constraints are $u_{\text{lim}} = [u_m, u_M, \Delta u_m]$, and $y_{\text{lim}} = [y_m, y_M, \Delta y_m]$. Compared with the unconstrained optimization design, the cmpc() function integrates the design and simulation processes together, and simulation results can be obtained directly.

**Example 10.9.** Consider again the plant model studied in Example 10.6. Assume the expected control signal satisfies the constraints $u(t) \in (-3,3)$ with the default weights $q$ and $r$, and the control horizon $p = 40$. Selecting different control horizons $m$, the constrained model predictive controllers can be designed, and the step responses and control signals of the systems are shown in Figs. 10-18(a) and (b). It can be seen that the control is satisfactory, and the control signal is restricted in the expected interval.

```
>> t_f=12; T=0.1; G=poly2tfd(1,conv([1 1],[2 1]),0,1);
   mod=tfd2step(t_f,T,1,G); p=40; m=10; q=1; r=0.1;
   plant=mod; sp=1; tend=10; t=0:T:tend;
   [y,u]=cmpc(plant,mod,q,r,m,p,tend,sp,[-3,3,inf]);
   plot(t,y), figure, stairs(t,u)
```

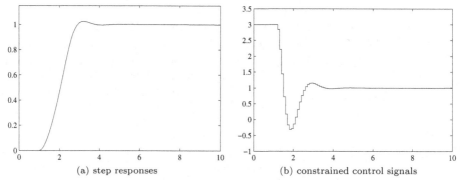

(a) step responses     (b) constrained control signals

Fig. 10-18   Simulation results with constrained optimal predictive control.

**Example 10.10.** Consider again the multivariable system studied in Example 10.7. Assume that the two input signals satisfy $|u_i(t)| \leqslant 5$. With sampling interval $T = 0.1\,\text{s}$, similar controllers can be designed. When the two input signals are applied to the system individually, the step responses and control signals are shown in Figs. 10-19(a) and (b).

```
>> g11=poly2tfd(0.1134,[1.78,4.48,1],0,0.72);
   g12=poly2tfd(0.924,[2.07,1],0,0);
   g21=poly2tfd(0.3378,[0.361,1.09,1],0,0.3);
   g22=poly2tfd(-0.318,[2.93,1],0,1.29);
   T=0.1; S=tfd2step(20,T,[1 1],g11,g12,g21,g22);
   p=20; m=15; q=[1 1]; r=[0.1 0.1]; plant=S; sp1=[1 0];
   sp2=[0,1]; tend=4; t=0:T:tend;
   [y1,u1]=cmpc(plant,S,q,r,m,p,tend,sp1,[-5,-5,5 5 inf inf]);
   subplot(211); plot(t,y1); subplot(212), stairs(t,u1)
   [y2,u2]=cmpc(plant,S,q,r,m,p,tend,sp2,[-5,-5,5 5 inf inf]);
   figure; subplot(211); plot(t,y2); subplot(212), stairs(t,u2)
```

## 4. Object-oriented design of model predictive controllers

In Model Predictive Control Toolbox, alternative object-oriented controller design function mpc() can be used to construct MPC controller object, and overload function sim() can be used to simulate systems under model predictive control.

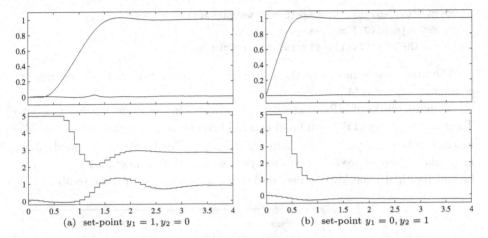

(a) set-point $y_1 = 1, y_2 = 0$        (b) set-point $y_1 = 0, y_2 = 1$

Fig. 10-19   Simulation results of multivariable predictive control systems.

Both unconstrained and constrained optimizations are supported under such a design function. The syntaxes of the functions are

> $MPCobj = \texttt{mpc}(G,T,p,m,\boldsymbol{w})$       % unconstrained optimization
> $MPCobj = \texttt{mpc}(G,T,p,m,\boldsymbol{w},Constr)$   % constrained optimization
> $[\boldsymbol{y},t,\boldsymbol{u}] = \texttt{sim}(MPCobj,N,\boldsymbol{r})$      % draw closed-loop step response

In the function call, $G$ can be an LTI object in Control System Toolbox, $T$ is the sampling interval, $m$ and $p$ are control and prediction horizons, $\boldsymbol{w}$ is weights. The option *Constr* is used to store constraints on control signals. In the simulation function, $N$ is the number of points in simulation, $\boldsymbol{r}$ is the set-points of the inputs. The returned variables in $\texttt{sim}()$ function are respectively the outputs, time and control signals of the closed-loop model predictive control system, and if they are omitted, control results will be displayed automatically.

**Example 10.11.** The following commands can be used to design model predictive controller for the multivariable plant model shown in Example 10.10, with unconstrained optimization approach.

```
>> g11=tf(0.1134,[1.78,4.48,1],'ioDelay',0.72);
   g12=tf(0.924,[2.07,1]);
   g21=tf(0.3378,[0.361,1.09,1],'ioDelay',0.3);
   g22=tf(-0.318,[2.93,1],'ioDelay',1.29); G=[g11,g12; g21 g22];
   T=0.1; p=20; m=15; MPCobj=mpc(G,T,p,m);
   tf=40; r1=[1,0]; sim(MPCobj,tf,r1)   % the first input act alone
   figure; r2=[0,1]; sim(MPCobj,tf,r2)  % second input act alone
```

If the inputs on the two channels are $|\boldsymbol{u}(t)| \leqslant 5$, the following statements can be used again to design and simulate model predictive control systems. The control results are the same as the one in Fig. 10-19. It can be seen that with these design functions, the design and simulation process is much simpler and straightforward.

```
>> MV.Min=[-5,-5]; MV.Max=[5 5]; weights=[];
   MPCobj=mpc(G,T,m,p,weights,MV);
   sim(MPCobj,tf,r1), figure; sim(MPCobj,tf,r2)
```

The state space model of the predictive controller can be retrieved with the command $G_c = \mathtt{ss}(MPCobj)$.

Simulink blocks of MPC controllers are provided in the Model Predictive Control Toolbox. Type `mpclib` command at MATLAB command window, the two MPC blocks can be displayed, as shown in Fig. 10-20(a). The blocks can be used directly in simulating model predictive control systems, with the parameter dialog box shown in Fig. 10-20(b). The MPC object designed can be entered into the toolbox.

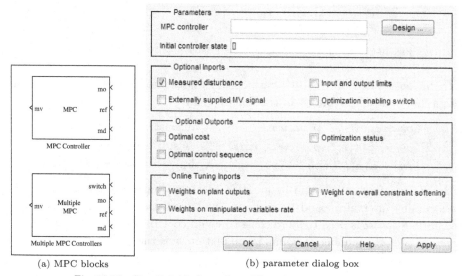

(a) MPC blocks                    (b) parameter dialog box

Fig. 10-20    Simulink blocks and model predictive control systems.

### 10.2.3 *Design and Simulation of Model Predictive Control for Complicated Plants*

Graphical user interfaces are provided in the Model Predictive Control Toolbox, and model predictive controllers for complicated plants can be designed, and a MPC block is provided in Simulink. Design and simulation can be carried out for complicated systems with Simulink.

Command `mpctool` can be given in the command window, the graphical interface for MPC controller design is invoked, as shown in Fig. 10-21.

In the interface, three items are provided on the left-hand-side — Plant models, Controllers and Scenarios, with Plant models the default one.

Click the Import Plant button, a dialog box is displayed to prompt the user to enter the plant model of the system.

In the Controllers item, a dialog box shown in Fig. 10-22 is displayed to allow

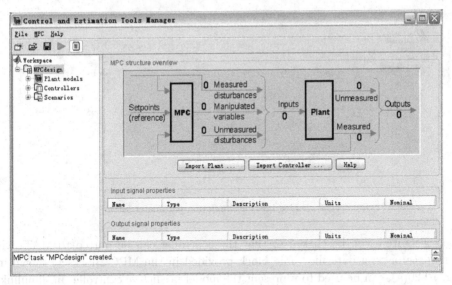

Fig. 10-21　Graphical interface of model predictive control system design.

the users to enter MPC controller parameters, such as the sampling interval and the two horizons. The panes Constraints and Weight Tuning allow the user to specify the constraints and weights in the controller.

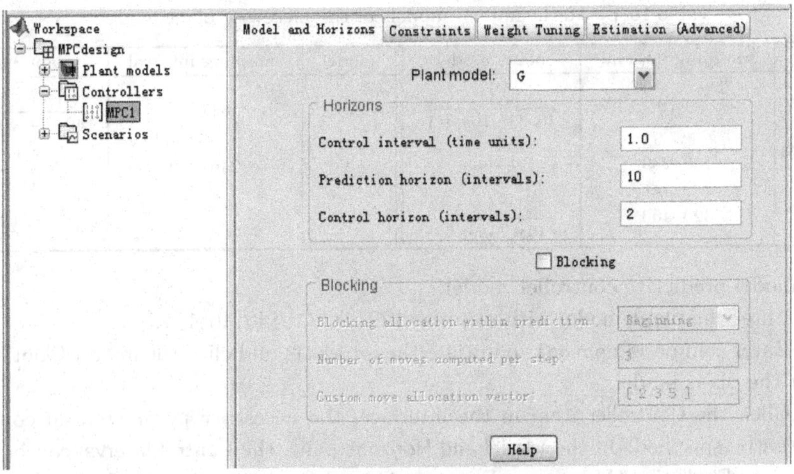

Fig. 10-22　Dialog box for controller parameters setting.

If both the plant and controller are specified, the Scenarios item can be clicked to initiate the MPC controller design. A dialog box shown in Fig. 10-23 will be displayed, and the information such as set-point, simulation terminate time can be specified.

If the control results are satisfactory, the Export Controller button under the

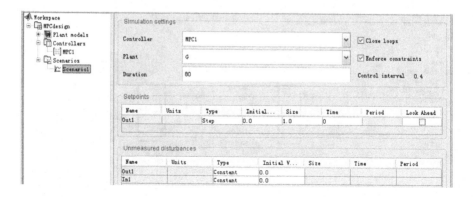

Fig. 10-23   Dialog box for simulation parameter settings.

Controllers item can be clicked so that the controller can be ported to MATLAB workspace or to a date file. The block provided in the MPC Blockset, shown in Fig. 10-20(a), can be used to represent the model predictive controller in Simulink. The design and simulation processes of model predictive control systems will be illustrated through the following example.

**Example 10.12.** Consider the piecewise plant model given in [17], given in Table 10-1. Use the first model as the nominal plant model. The following procedures can be used to

Table 10-1   Mathematical models of the piecewise plant model.

| model | sampling interval | plane model | model | sampling interval | plane model |
|---|---|---|---|---|---|
| 1 | 1–79 | $\dfrac{1}{40s^2 + 10s + 1}$ | 2 | 8–159 | $\dfrac{e^{-2.7s}}{40s^2 + 10s + 1}$ |
| 3 | 160–239 | $\dfrac{e^{-2.7s}}{10s + 1}$ | 4 | 240–319 | $\dfrac{1}{10s + 1}$ |
| 5 | 320–400 | $\dfrac{1}{10s(25s + 1)}$ | | | |

design model predictive controller model:

(1) Enter the plant model with command $G = \mathtt{tf}(1,[40,10,1])$.

(2) Enter command `mpctool` to initiate the interface, and click the Import Plant button to enter the plant model.

(3) Click the Controller item in the interface, the necessary parameters in controller design can be specified: In the Model and Horizons pane, the Control interval can be set to $T = 0.4$, and Prediction Horizon can be set to 40, and Control horizon can be set to 10. The constraints are not considered for the time being, and Constraints pane is not modified. In the Weight Tuning pane, the weight can be set to 0.1, and the rate weight can be set to 0, from the default 0.1. The output weights can be set to 1.

(4) Click the Scenarios item on the left, the information such as set-point can be specified. The set-point can be set to step signal, with step time of 0 and magnitude of 1. Start the simulation process by clicking Simulate, the input and output signals can be obtained, as shown in Figs. 10-24(a) and (b).

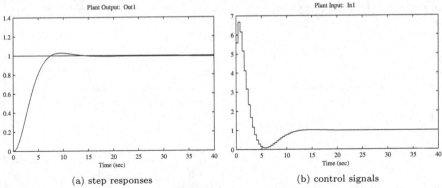

(a) step responses            (b) control signals

Fig. 10-24   Simulation results of the predictive control system.

(5) Click the Export Controller button. The controller can be saved to MATLAB workspace, as a variable c10MPC1.

With the controller, the piecewise plant model can be constructed, where model is controlled by the time in simulation. With the control system shown in Fig. 10-25, the control results can be obtained as shown in Fig. 10-26(a). It can be seen that the result is satisfactory, however, the control signal at initial time is too large. Better controller is should be used in applications.

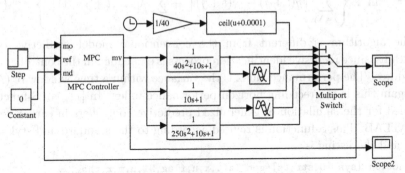

Fig. 10-25   Predictive control system for the piecewise plant (file name: c10mmpcm.mdl).

If the controller constraints are set to $|u(t)| \leqslant 2$, the predictive controller can be designed again, and the system responses can be obtained as shown in Fig. 10-26(b). It can be seen that the control results are satisfactory.

## 10.2.4   *Generalized Predictive Control Systems and Simulations*

Generalized predictive control (GPC) is a control strategy proposed by British scholar Professor David Clarke and collaborators[18, 19]. Generalized predictive control theory and applications are well documented in [20].

The plant model to be controlled is

$$A\left(z^{-1}\right) y(t) = z^{-d} B\left(z^{-1}\right) u(t) + C\left(z^{-1}\right) \xi(t) + \eta, \qquad (10.29)$$

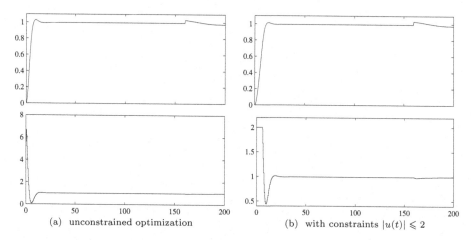

(a) unconstrained optimization          (b) with constraints $|u(t)| \leqslant 2$

Fig. 10-26   Simulation results of predictive control system.

and most part of the model are the same as the one illustrated earlier. This model can be used to handle input signal disturbed with constant bias $\eta$.

The performance index for generalized predictive control is

$$
J = \min_u \ \mathrm{E} \left\{ \sum_{j=N_1}^{p} \left[ y(t+j) - y_{\mathrm{r}}(t+j) \right]^2 + \sum_{j=1}^{m} \lambda \left[ \Delta u(t+j-1) \right]^2 \right\}. \qquad (10.30)
$$

The algorithm is different from the conventional model predictive control algorithms, since recursive identification process is embedded in the controller design procedures. The performance index is the variance within a time window of $(N_1, p)$, and again this is the receding horizon performance index. In [11], an S-function is provided for the simulation of generalized predictive controllers in earlier versions of MATLAB. This S-function is revised according to the standard and style in the book, and the listing is

```
function [sys,x0,str,ts]=gpc_1a(t,x,u,flag,N1,p,m,r,rho,...
            k_d,B_pocz,A_pocz,p_pocz,alfa,ts)
nA=length(A_pocz); nB=length(B_pocz)-1; k=nA+nB+1; kp=k*k;
kt=kp+1; ktend=kp+k; kf=ktend+1; kfend=ktend+k; ky=kfend+1;
ku=ky+1; kend=ky+k_d; P=zeros(k,k); x=x(:)';
switch flag
    case 0, % initialization of the S-function
        sizes=simsizes; sizes.NumContStates=0; sizes.NumDiscStates=kend;
        sizes.NumOutputs=1; sizes.NumInputs=2;
        sizes.DirFeedthrough=0; sizes.NumSampleTimes=1;
        sys=simsizes(sizes); str=[]; ts=[ts 0];
        x0=zeros(1,kend); x0(1:k+1:kp)=p_pocz*ones(k,1);
        x0(kt:kt+nA-1)=A_pocz; x0(kt+nA:ktend)=B_pocz;
    case 2
        Phi=[x(ky),x(kf:kf+nA-2),x(kend),x(kf+nA:kfend-1)];
```

```
P(:)=x(1:kp); P=(1/alfa)*(P-(P*Phi'*Phi*P)/(alfa+Phi*P*Phi'));
Theta=x(kt:ktend)+Phi*P*(u(2)-Phi*x(kt:ktend)');
k_m=max([nA+1,nB+k_d]);
num=[zeros(1,k_d-1),Theta(nA+1:k),zeros(1,k_m-nB-k_d)];
den=[1,Theta(1:nA),zeros(1,k_m-nA-1)]; h=dstep(num,den,p);
for i=1:m, Qt(1:p,i)=[zeros(i-1,1); h(1:p-i+1)]; end;
Q=Qt(N1:p,:); q=[1,zeros(1,m-1)]*inv(Q'*Q + r*eye(m))*Q';
[w,xw]=dlsim(rho,1-rho,1,0,u(1)*ones(p+1,1),u(2));
A=[1,Theta(1:nA)]; B=Theta(nA+1:k); Bm=[B,0]; Bm=Bm-[0,B];
Am=[A,0]; Am=Am-[0,A]; Ared=Am(2:nA+2);
Bred=[zeros(1,k_d-1),Bm]; Y=[u(2),-x(ky),-x(kf:kf+nA-2)];
U=[x(ku),x(ku:kend),x(kf+nA:kf+nA+nB-1)];
for i=1:p
    yp(i)=-Ared*Y'+Bred*U'; Y=[yp(i),Y(1:nA)]; U=[U(1),U(1:nB+k_d)];
end
nu=x(ku)+q*(w(N1+1:p+1)-yp(N1:p)');
sys=[P(:)',Theta,x(ky),x(kf:kf+nA-2), x(kend),...
    x(kf+nA:kfend-1),-u(2), nu, x(ku:kend-1)];
  case 3, sys=x(ku);
  otherwise, sys=[];
end
```

**Example 10.13.** Assume the plant model is given by

$$G(s) = \frac{1}{2s^2 + 8s + 1},$$

and the output terminal is disturbed by random signal with bias $\eta = 0.5$.

To simulate the system with a generalized predictive controller, the Simulink model shown in Fig. 10-27 can be established. Let the bias $\eta = 0$ first. Select the time window $N_1 = 1$, $m = 2$. For different values of $p$, with $p = 3, 4, 5, 6, 7$, simulation can be performed, and the output is obtained as shown in Fig. 10-28(a). It can be seen that when $p = 3$, the control results are not satisfactory. For this example, $p = 7$ is a good choice. The control signals for $p = 3$ and $p = 7$ are obtained as shown in Fig. 10-28(b).

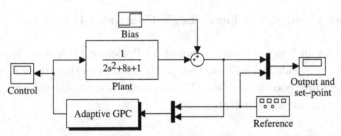

Fig. 10-27   Simulink model for generalized predictive control system (file name: c10mgpc1.mdl).

Now let the bias becomes $\eta = 0.5$, the simulation results are shown in Fig. 10-29(a), and the control results for $\eta = 0$ are also given for comparison. It can be seen that although the plant is disturbed with bias, the control results are satisfactory.

If the plant model is changed to

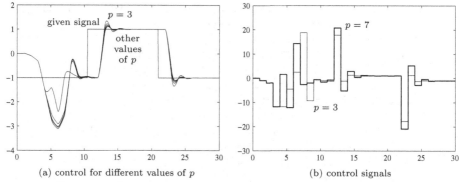

(a) control for different values of $p$          (b) control signals

Fig. 10-28     Control results and control signals for different time windows.

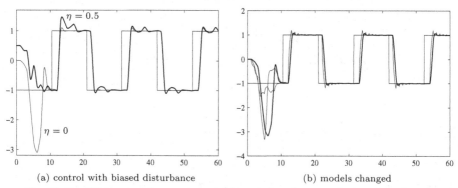

(a) control with biased disturbance          (b) models changed

Fig. 10-29     GPC control for systems with biased disturbance and plant disturbances.

$$G_1(s) = \frac{3}{3s^2 + 8s + 1}, \quad G_2(s) = \frac{2s + 1}{3s^2 + 8s + 1},$$

the control results are shown in Fig. 10-29(b). It can be seen that although the plant models are completely different, the control results are still satisfactory. In the simulation results, the original model is shown in thick lines, while thin lines are for $G_1(s)$ and $G_2(s)$.

## 10.3     Fuzzy Control and Fuzzy Logic Controller Design

The concept of fuzzy set was proposed by Professor Lotfi A Zadeh in 1965[21]. Fuzzy logic is now widely used in various fields. In this section, the concept of fuzzy logic and fuzzy inference are presented, then design and simulation analysis of fuzzy logic control systems are illustrated.

### 10.3.1     *Fuzzy Logic and Fuzzy Inference*

It is known from classical set theory that an entity either belongs to set $A$, or does not belong to it. There are no other possibilities. The fuzzy set proposed by Professor Zadeh is more and more accepted in modern sciences or engineering applications. In fuzzy set theory, an entity $a$ may belong to set $A$ to a certain extent. This is the basic idea of fuzzy set theory. The "extent" is referred to as "membership function".

Membership functions can be entered into MATLAB workspace either with MATLAB commands provided in MATLAB Fuzzy Logic Toolbox or can be entered with the editing interface.

With the `fis = newfis(`*name*`)` function provided in Fuzzy Logic Toolbox, the fuzzy inference system (FIS) can be created, where *name* is a string variable, saving the name of the fuzzy inference system. The FIS data structure variable *fis* can be created with various properties. These properties can also be defined with `newfis()` function, or they can be defined later with MATLAB function calls. When the *fis* variable is created, the `addvar()` function can be used to add input and output variables to the fuzzy inference system, with the syntaxes

`fis = addvar(fis,'input',iname,`$v_i$`)` % define an input variable `iname`

`fis = addvar(fis,'output',oname,`$v_o$`)` % define an output variable `oname`

where $v_i$ and $v_o$ are the intervals of the input/output variables, saved in row vectors. With such a function, further information can also be defined with `fis`, and each membership functions of a variable can be entered with function `addmf()`. Alternatively, the function `mfedit()` can be called to relevant information through the interface.

Suppose for a signal, three membership functions are defined. Normally, the meanings of the three membership functions are "small", "average", or "big". Signals with five membership functions are also often used, and the universe is usually expressed by $E = \{NB, NS, ZE, PS, PB\}$, meaning "negative big", "negative small", "around zero", "positive small", and "positive big". More precisely, a variable with seven membership functions can also be used, and the universe can be expressed by $E = \{NB, NM, NS, ZE, PS, PM, PB\}$. Compared with the five membership function universe, two membership functions, "negative medium" and "positive medium" are added. An accurate signal can be fuzzified into a fuzzy signal which can further be used in fuzzy inference. Exact signals can be obtained from fuzzified signals through the defuzzification process. Defuzzification of fuzzy variables can be performed with `defuzz()` function. The commonly used defuzzification options are `'mom'`, `'centriod'`.

If several input variables are fuzzified, `if-else` statement structures can be used to create the fuzzy inference system. For instance, the sentence "if input $ip_1$ signal is small, and input $ip_2$ is large, then, the output signal `op` should be set to large value", can be expressed in the fuzzy inference system as

`if `$ip_1$`== "small" and `$ip_2$`== "large" , then op = "large"`

Such a statement is referred to as a fuzzy rule which can be modeled in MATLAB as a vector. In the vector, there are $n + m + 2$ elements, where $m$ and $n$ the numbers of inputs and outputs respectively. The first $m$ contains the serial numbers of the membership functions of the input, while the next $n$ elements the serial numbers of the membership functions of the output signal. The $(n + m + 1)$th element is the weighting coefficients of the output, while the last element describes the logic relationship, with 1 for logic "and" and 2 for logic "or". A fuzzy inference system is composed of several fuzzy rules, where a matrix $R$ has several vectors.

If the fuzzy inference matrix is $R$, the command `fis = addrule(fis,R)` can be used to append rules to the system `fis`. The function `y = evalfis(X,fis)` can be used to find the inference result, where $X$ is the matrix composed of actual signals. In the function, fuzzifications are performed first to convert the signals into fuzzy signals, which are then used in fuzzy inference, and the result $y$ is the actual output, defuzzified automatically with the function.

For the fuzzy inference system created, the function `writefis()` can be used to save it to a file, with suffix "fis". Function `readfis()` can be used to load *.fis file into MATLAB workspace.

The functions discussed above can easily and straightforwardly be implemented with the graphical user interface provided in the Fuzzy Logic Toolbox. Interface-based fuzzy inference system manipulation will be illustrated through examples.

### 10.3.2 Design of Fuzzy PD Controller

Based on the error signal $e(t)$ and its derivative $de(t)/dt$ in the closed-loop feedback control system, the control signal $u(t)$ can be obtained through fuzzy inference system, and the fuzzy PD control system structure is shown in Fig. 10-30. The gains $K_p$ and $K_d$ are used to map the signals into their universe. The two signals are fuzzified into fuzzy signals, $E, E_d$, which in turn drive the fuzzy inference system to have fuzzy output $U$, and through defuzzification process, exact signal $U'$ can be generated. Through gain $K_u$, the control signal $u(t)$ can be generated to drive the plant.

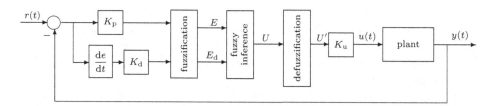

Fig. 10-30  Fuzzy PD control structure.

The universe with eight fuzzy sets shown in Fig. 10-31 can also be used and it seems to be more suitable in solving control problems. Compared with the seven fuzzy set ones, the ZE set is further divided into NZ (negative zero) and PZ (positive zero), and it describes the behaviors around zero better.

In the feedback control system, the error signal is defined as $e(t) = r(t) - y(t)$. It can be seen from the system response that if the error is PB, a positive control

Table 10-2 Rules of fuzzy PD control.

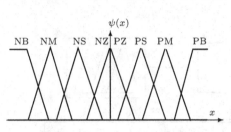

Fig. 10-31 Universe with eight memberships.

|  |  | de(t)/dt | | | | | | | |
|---|---|---|---|---|---|---|---|---|---|
|  |  | NB | NM | NS | NZ | PZ | PS | PM | PB |
|  | NB | NB | NB | NM | NM | NS | NS | NZ | NZ |
|  | NM | NB | NB | NM | NM | NS | NS | NZ | NZ |
|  | NS | NB | NB | NM | NS | NS | NZ | NZ | NZ |
| e(t) | NZ | NB | NM | NM | NZ | NS | NZ | PM | PM |
|  | PZ | NM | NM | PZ | PS | PZ | PM | PM | PB |
|  | PS | PZ | PZ | PZ | PS | PS | PM | PB | PB |
|  | PM | PZ | PZ | PS | PS | PM | PM | PB | PB |
|  | PB | PZ | PZ | PS | PS | PM | PM | PB | PB |

$u(t)$ should be given. Further, if $de(t)/dt$ is NB or NM, it means that the error is still increasing, and more control effort should be supplied. That is, set $u(t)$ to PB; However, if the $de(t)/dt$ is NS or NZ, it means that the error is decreasing, there is no need to supply large control effort. Setting $u(t)$ to PM should be a good choice; If $de(t)/dt$ is PZ or PS, smaller control effort is expected, i.e., to set the control to PS. If $de(t)/dt$ is PM or PB, there is no need to apply control signal, $u(t)$ can be set to NZ. For other $e(t)$ and $de(t)/dt$ combinations, the control rules can also be summarized. Table 10-2 contains all the possible rules for fuzzy inference[22]. Please note that the definition of the error signal is different, thus the signs of all the entities in the table are changed, i.e., P changed to N, while N changed into P.

With the membership functions and fuzzy inference rules, the fuzzy inference system can be established in the following procedures:

(1) **Start the interface**. Type `fuzzy` command at MATLAB prompt, the graphical interface shown in Fig. 10-32 will be displayed.

(2) **Set signals**. The default fuzzy inference system is assumed to be single input, single output. In the fuzzy PD control system, since the signals $e(t)$ and $de(t)/dt$ are used to drive the fuzzy inference system, and the output of the fuzzy inference is the control signal $u(t)$, a system with two input ports and output port should be constructed. An extra input should be added to the default FIS. This can be done by selecting the menu item Edit → Add Variable → Input. Now modify the labels on the interface shown in Fig. 10-32 for the three signals, the new labels should be e, ed and u, as shown in Fig. 10-33.

(3) **Setting membership functions**. Double click the input port labeled e in the interface. The default membership functions with three fuzzy sets will be displayed. Select the Edit menu, as shown in Fig. 10-34(a), then select the Remove All MFs item to remove the default fuzzy sets, and set the universe in the Range edit box to [−2, 2].

Now select the Edit → Add MFs menu, the dialog box shown in Fig. 10-34(b). In the Number of MFs edit box, fill in 8, and the default 8 triangular membership

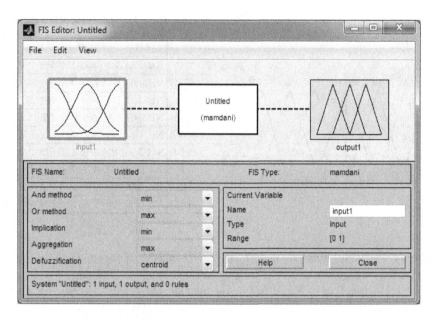

Fig. 10-32   Editing interface of the fuzzy inference systems.

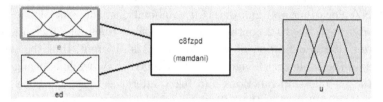

Fig. 10-33   Fuzzy PD control system structure.

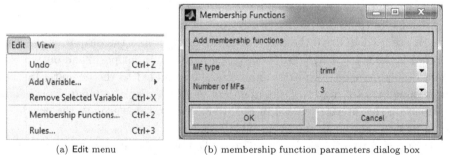

(a) Edit menu      (b) membership function parameters dialog box

Fig. 10-34   Membership functions settings.

functions will be generated as shown in Fig. 10-35(a). Change the names to NB, NM, $\cdots$. The shapes of the membership function can be adjusted manually with mouse dragging actions as shown in Fig. 10-35(b). Similarly, the membership functions for the other input and output signals can also be processed in this way.

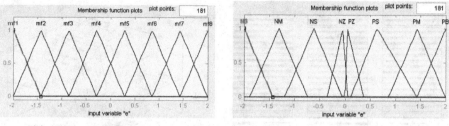

(a) default membership functions  (b) modified membership functions

Fig. 10-35   Editing of membership functions.

(4) **Edit fuzzy inference rules**. Select the Edit → Rules menu, the interface shown in Fig. 10-36 is displayed. Enter the rules one by one by clicking the Add rule

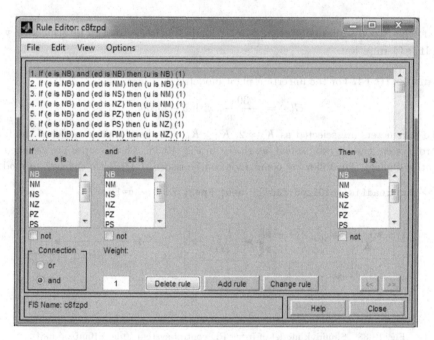

Fig. 10-36   Editing interface for fuzzy inference rules.

button, and use Change rule button to modify the rules. The 64 rules in Table 10-2 can be entered.

When the fuzzy inference system is established, the View → Rules and View → Surface menu items can be used to visualize the system as shown in Figs. 10-37(a) and (b). The fuzzy inference rules can be better understood with these figures.

(5) **Save the fuzzy inference system**. Use File → Export menu item to save the fuzzy inference system to *.fis files, or to MATLAB workspace. With the method, the established fuzzy inference system can be saved to c10fzpd.fis file.

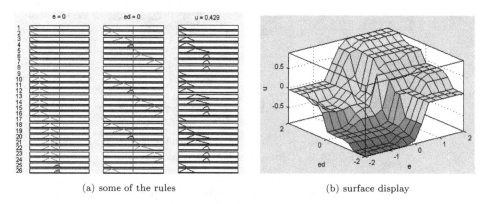

(a) some of the rules                    (b) surface display

Fig. 10-37   Graphical representation of the fuzzy inference rules.

Later, the fuzzy inference system can be loaded either with the interface, or with `readfis()` function.

**Example 10.14.** For the uncertain plant model

$$G(s) = \frac{30}{s^2 + as}, \text{ with } a \in [5, 50],$$

if the parameters are selected as $K_p = 2$, $K_d = K_u = 1$, the Simulink model of the fuzzy control system can be established, as shown in Fig. 10-38. Three scopes are assigned for the other signals. The following commands can be issued to initialize the system model.

```
>> fuz=readfis('c10fzpd.fis'); a=5; Kp=2; Kd=1; Ku=1;
```

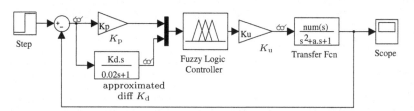

Fig. 10-38   Simulink model of fuzzy PD control system   (file: c10mfzpd.mdl).

Simulating the model, the output signal of the system can be obtained as shown in Fig. 10-39(a), and the other signals are shown in Fig. 10-39(b). It can be seen that satisfactory control results can be obtained.

Selecting other values of $a$'s, such as $a = 5, 10, 30$, the response curves are shown in Fig. 10-40(a). Again the control behavior is satisfactory, albeit for larger values of $a$, the response speed may get slower.

If the plant model is changed to $G(s) = 30/(s^2 + 5s + 1)$, and the integral action is no longer performed in the plant, the system response is obtained as shown in Fig. 10-40(b). It can be seen that the system is still well controlled, although very small oscillations may occur around the steady-state value, and the control signal $u(t)$ is also oscillating around 0. This phenomenon cannot be avoided with pure PD controller, or any kind.

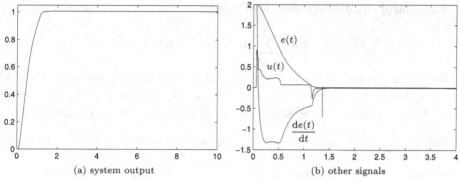

(a) system output       (b) other signals

Fig. 10-39   Simulation results of the fuzzy PD control system.

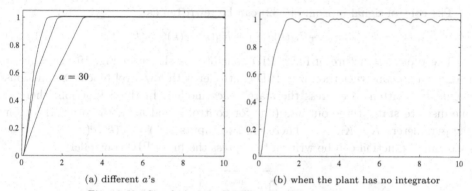

(a) different $a$'s       (b) when the plant has no integrator

Fig. 10-40   Simulation results when the plant model changes.

### 10.3.3   Design of Fuzzy PID Controllers

Fuzzy PID controller provides us a class of widely used PID type controllers. In the fuzzy PID controller, the parameters are no longer constants in the classical PID controllers. According to the changes of the error signal, the controller parameters $K_p$, $K_i$ and $K_d$ are dynamically adjusted, to get good control performance. However, it should be noted that the closed-loop control systems thus created are no longer linear systems.

The fuzzy logic PID controller can be written as

$$\begin{cases} K_p(k) = K_p(k-1) + \gamma_p(k)\Delta K_p \\ K_i(k) = K_i(k-1) + \gamma_i(k)\Delta K_i \\ K_d(k) = K_d(k-1) + \gamma_d(k)\Delta K_d, \end{cases} \qquad (10.31)$$

where $\gamma_p(k)$, $\gamma_i(k)$, $\gamma_d(k)$ are the parameters of the fuzzy PID controllers, and with the time increases, the parameters in well-designed system may decrease. Of course, all the parameters can be assumed to be constants. It can be seen from tuning formula that the controller parameters in the next step can be updated from the parameters and the increments.

The control signal can be generated with

$$u(k) = K_p(k)e(k) + K_i(k)\sum_{i=0}^{k} e(i) + K_d(k)\Big[e(k) - e(k-1)\Big]. \tag{10.32}$$

Note that the sum in the formula is not the whole integral, normally it should be multiplied by sampling interval $T$. For easy representation, this can be included in the $K_i(k)$ variable, and the same is assumed in $K_d(k)$. Due to the difficulties in calculating $\sum_{i=0}^{k} e(i)$, it can be defined as a state variable, $x(k) = \sum_{i=0}^{k} e(i)$. Thus, the state space model for the signal is

$$\overset{\bullet}{x}(k+1) = x(k) + e(k). \tag{10.33}$$

The control signal in Eqn. (10.32) can be rewritten as

$$u(k) = K_p(k)e(k) + K_i(k)x(k) + K_d(k)\Big[e(k) - e(k-1)\Big]. \tag{10.34}$$

The typical structure of fuzzy PID controller is shown in Fig. 10-41. Since it is difficult to construct the fuzzy PID controller with low-level blocks, S-functions should be written to express the state space model. In the S-function, there is one discrete state, three outputs (one for control signal $u(k)$, the other three for the parameters $K_p$, $K_i$, $K_d$. There are two inputs $\boldsymbol{u}(k) = [e(k), e(k-1)]^T$. The following S-function can be written to express the fuzzy PID controller

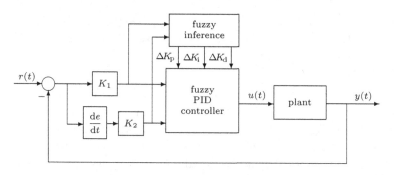

Fig. 10-41   Block diagram of fuzzy PID control system.

```
function [sys,x0,str,ts]=fuz_pid(t,x,u,flag,T,aFuz,fx0,gam)
switch flag,
    case 0, [sys,x0,str,ts] = mdlInitializeSizes(T);
    case 2, sys = mdlUpdates(x,u);
    case 3, sys = mdlOutputs(x,u,T,aFuz,fx0,gam);
    case {1, 4, 9}, sys = [];
    otherwise, error(['Unhandled flag = ',num2str(flag)]);
end;
function [sys,x0,str,ts] = mdlInitializeSizes(T) % initialization
sizes=simsizes; sizes.NumContStates=0; sizes.NumDiscStates=3;
```

```
sizes.NumOutputs=4; sizes.NumInputs=2; sizes.DirFeedthrough=0;
sizes.NumSampleTimes=1; sys=simsizes(sizes);
x0=zeros(3,1); str=[]; ts=[T 0];
function sys = mdlUpdates(x,u)        % update the discrete states
sys=[u(1);  x(2)+u(1);  u(1)-u(2)];   % PID controller
function sys = mdlOutputs(x,u,T,aFuz,fx0,gam)  % evaluate the output
Kpid=fx0+gam(:).*evalfis(x([1,3]),aFuz)';  sys=[Kpid'*x;  Kpid];
```

With the kernel S-function, the masked fuzzy PID controller block can be constructed, with the inertial structure as shown in Fig. 10-42(a). In the system model, the function fuz_pid.m is embedded with the parameters shown in Fig. 10-42(b). The whole PID controller setting is shown in Fig. 10-42(c).

The fuzzy inference rules of the controller parameters are shown in Table 10-3[23]. These rules can be entered into the fuzzy inference system, with two inputs and three outputs. The three outputs correspond to the parameters $\Delta K_p$, $\Delta K_i$, and $\Delta K_d$.

Based on the fuzzy rules, the function `fuzzy()` can be used to design the fuzzy inference system through the graphical user interface. The fuzzy inference system file c10fuzpid.fis can be constructed, and the block is with two inputs and three outputs, shown in Fig. 10-43. The input and output variable ranges, or universe, can be specified to $(-3, 3)$. The actual range can be used to adjust the values $K_1$, $K_2, \gamma_p$, $\gamma_i$, $\gamma_d$, $K_u$.

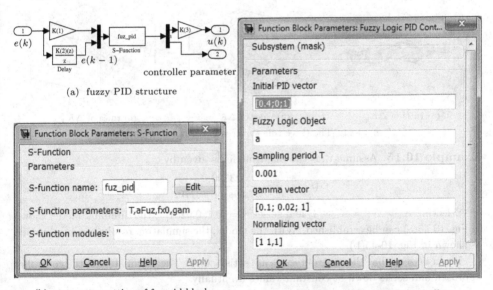

(a) fuzzy PID structure

(b) parameter setting of fuz_pid block  (c) dialog box of fuzzy PID controller

Fig. 10-42 Fuzzy PID control block design.

In the fuzzy control system, the three surfaces of rule can be obtained as shown in Fig. 10-44. More information about the fuzzy logic inference system can be obtained by opening the c10fuzpid.fis file with function `fuzzy()`.

Table 10-3  Fuzzy inference table for the PID controller.

| | | $\Delta K_\mathrm{p}$ | | | | | | | $\Delta K_\mathrm{i}$ | | | | | | | $\Delta K_\mathrm{d}$ | | | | | |
|---|---|---|---|---|---|---|---|---|---|---|---|---|---|---|---|---|---|---|---|---|---|
| | | NB | NM | NS | ZE | PS | PM | PB | NB | NM | NS | ZE | PS | PM | PB | NB | NM | NS | ZE | PS | PM | PB |
| | NB | PB | PB | PM | PM | PS | ZE | ZE | NB | NB | NM | NM | NS | ZE | ZE | PS | NS | NB | NB | NB | NM | PS |
| | NM | PB | PB | PM | PS | PS | ZE | ZE | NB | NB | NM | NS | NS | ZE | ZE | PS | NS | NB | NB | NB | NM | PS |
| | NS | PM | PM | PM | PM | ZE | NS | NS | NB | NM | NS | NS | ZE | PS | PS | ZE | NS | NM | NM | NS | NS | ZE |
| $e(t)$ | ZE | PM | PM | PS | ZE | NS | NM | NM | NM | NM | NS | ZE | PS | PM | PM | ZE | NS | NS | NS | NS | NS | ZE |
| | PS | PS | PS | ZE | NS | NS | NM | NM | NM | NS | ZE | PS | PS | PM | PB | ZE | ZE | ZE | ZE | ZE | ZE | ZE |
| | PM | PS | ZE | NS | NM | NM | NM | NB | ZE | ZE | PS | PS | PM | PB | PB | PB | NS | PS | PS | PS | PS | PB |
| | PB | ZE | ZE | NM | NM | NM | NB | NB | ZE | ZE | PS | PM | PM | PB | PB | PB | PM | PM | PM | PS | PS | PB |

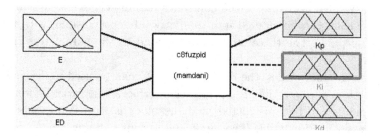

Fig. 10-43  Block diagram for fuzzy inference system.

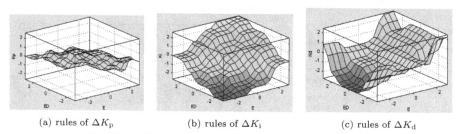

(a) rules of $\Delta K_\mathrm{p}$  (b) rules of $\Delta K_\mathrm{i}$  (c) rules of $\Delta K_\mathrm{d}$

Fig. 10-44  The three rule surfaces in fuzzy PID controller.

**Example 10.15.** Assume that the plant model is given by

$$G(s) = \frac{523500}{s^3 + 87.35s^2 + 10470s}.$$

Selecting $K_1 = K_2 = K_\mathrm{u} = 1$, and select $\boldsymbol{\gamma} = [0.1, 0.02, 1]^\mathrm{T}$, the Simulink model shown in Fig. 10-45(a) can be established. With the model, the simulation results can be obtained as shown in Fig. 10-45(b).

It can be seen that the control results are satisfactory. The parameters of the controller approach and settle down at constant values eventually.

## 10.4  Neural Networks and Neural Network Controller Design

Artificial neural networks (ANN) originated from studying and understanding the behavior of complicated neural networks of living creatures. In human brains,

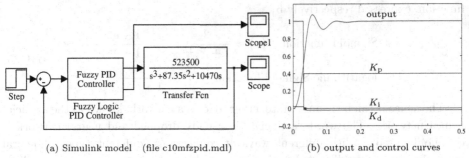

(a) Simulink model  (file c10mfzpid.mdl)        (b) output and control curves

Fig. 10-45   Fuzzy PID controller and simulation results.

there are about $10^{11}$ interlinked units known as neurons. Each neuron has about $10^4$ links with other neurons[24]. When the mathematical representations of artificial neurons are established, the interconnected neurons can be used to construct artificial neural networks. However, due to the limitations of the status of computers today, neural networks as complicated as human brains have not been built so far.

Neural network-based control is an important research area in the study of intelligent control[25]. In this section, fundamentals of neural network are illustrated first. Several neural network-based design algorithms and simulation methods are introduced. Neural network computation can also be used with Neural Network Toolbox[26], and `nntool` interface can be used to establish neural network models.

## 10.4.1   *Introduction to Neural Networks*

The basic elements of artificial neural networks, neurons, can be represented as shown in Fig. 10-46, where $x_1, x_2, \cdots, x_n$ are input signals. The weighted sum of the inputs, plus the threshold $b$, forms linear function $u_i$. The signal is further processed by the nonlinear transfer function $f(u_i)$ to generate the output signal $y$.

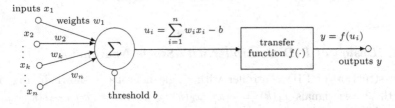

Fig. 10-46   Basic structure of a neuron.

In this artificial neuron model, the weights $w_i$ and the transfer function or activation function $f(\cdot)$ are the two important elements. The weights can be considered as the intensities of the input signals which can be determined by repeated training from the samples. Normally, the transfer function should be selected as a monotonic function such that the inverse function uniquely exists. Commonly used transfer functions are sigmoidal function and logarithmic sigmoidal function, expressed respectively by

$$\text{Sigmoid function} \quad f(x) = \frac{2}{1 + e^{-2x}} - 1 = \frac{1 - e^{-2x}}{1 + e^{-2x}},$$

$$\text{logarithmic Sigmoid function} \quad f(x) = \frac{1}{1 + e^{-x}}. \tag{10.35}$$

The neurons can be connected together to form a network, known as the artificial neural network. The word "artificial" is usually dropped and neural network is commonly used. With different ways of connections, different types of neural networks can be established. In this section, only the feedforward structure will be presented. Since in the training procedure, the error is propagated in the reversed direction, this network type is often referred to as the back-propagation (or BP) neural network. The typical structure of a BP neural network is shown in Figure 10-47. In the network, there are input layer, several intermediate layers known as hidden layers, and the output layer. In this book, the last hidden layer is, in fact, the output layer.

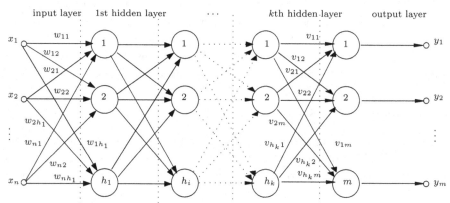

Fig. 10-47     Basic structure of neural network.

### 10.4.2     *Design of PID Controller with Single Neurons*

The structure of PID controller with single neurons is shown in Fig. 10-48, where the three signals $x_1(k) = e(k)$, $x_2(k) = \Delta e(k) = e(k) - e(k-1)$, and $x_3(k) = \Delta^2 e(k) = e(k) - 2e(k-1) + e(k-2)$ are generated with the "derivative and integral computation" unit. Improved Hebb learning algorithm is used, and the three updating laws can be written as[23]

$$\begin{cases} w_1(k) = w_1(k-1) + \eta_{\mathrm{p}} e(k) u(k) \Big[ e(k) - \Delta e(k) \Big] \\ w_2(k) = w_2(k-1) + \eta_{\mathrm{i}} e(k) u(k) \Big[ e(k) - \Delta e(k) \Big] \\ w_3(k) = w_3(k-1) + \eta_{\mathrm{d}} e(k) u(k) \Big[ e(k) - \Delta e(k) \Big]. \end{cases} \tag{10.36}$$

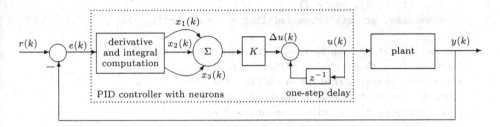

Fig. 10-48    PID controller with single neurons.

where $\eta_p, \eta_i, \eta_d$ are the learning rate of the proportional, derivative and integral of the signal. The three weights can be used as the state variables, and the control signal can be written as

$$u(k) = u(k-1) + K \sum_{i=1}^{3} w_i^0(k)x_i(k), \qquad (10.37)$$

where the normalized weights are

$$w_i^0(k) = \frac{w_i(k)}{\displaystyle\sum_{i=1}^{3} |w_3(k)|}. \qquad (10.38)$$

Based on the above algorithm, the Simulink model shown in Fig. 10-49 can be used to implement the controller, where the kernel part is represented by S-function. The signals $[e(k), e(k-1), e(k-2), u(k-1)]$ are used as the inputs, and the outputs are $[u(k), w_i^0(k)]$. To make the controller more practical, actuator saturation is used to follow the control signal $u(k)$. The Simulink model of the controller can be constructed as shown in Fig. 10-49, with the listing of the kernel S-function in the file c10mhebb.m is

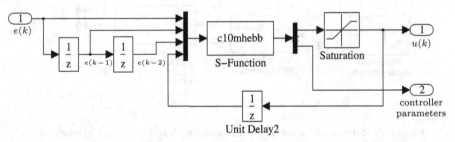

Fig. 10-49    Simulink model of PID controllers with neurons    (file name: c10shebb.mdl).

```
function [sys,x0,str,ts]=c10mhebb(t,x,u,flag,deltaK)
switch flag,
    case 0, [sys,x0,str,ts]=mdlInitializeSizes;
    case 2, sys=mdlUpdate(t,x,u,deltaK);
    case 3, sys = mdlOutputs(t,x,u);
```

```
case {1, 4, 9}, sys = [];
  otherwise, error(['Unhandled flag = ',num2str(flag)]);
end;
% model initialization function mdlInitializeSizes
function [sys,x0,str,ts] = mdlInitializeSizes
sizes = simsizes; % read the default variables of the system
sizes.NumContStates = 0; sizes.NumDiscStates = 3;
sizes.NumOutputs = 4; sizes.NumInputs = 4;
sizes.DirFeedthrough = 1; sizes.NumSampleTimes = 1;
sys = simsizes(sizes); x0 = [0.3*rand(3,1)];
str = []; ts = [-1 0]; % inherit the sampling interval of the input
% discrete state update function mdlUpdate
function sys = mdlUpdate(t,x,u,deltaK)
sys=x+deltaK*u(1)*u(4)*(2*u(1)-u(2));
% output computation function mdlOutputs
function sys = mdlOutputs(t,x,u)
xx= [u(1)-u(2) u(1) u(1)+u(3)-2*u(2)];
sys=[u(4)+0.12*xx*x/sum(abs(x)); x/sum(abs(x))];
```

**Example 10.16.** Consider the discrete plant model [23]

$$H(z) = \frac{0.1z + 0.632}{z^2 - 0.368z - 0.26}.$$

With the block of the PID controller with neurons, the control system model shown in Fig. 10-50 can be established, where the staircase input block Multi-step Signal Generator developed in Example 6.18 is used to drive the system.

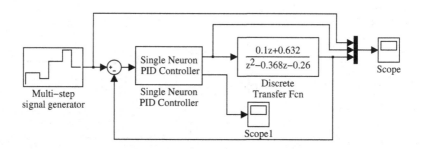

Fig. 10-50   Simulation model of PID controller with neurons   (file: c10shebb.mdl).

Simulating the system, the set-point input signal, output signal and the control signal can be obtained as shown in Fig. 10-51(a). It can be seen that the control results are satisfactory. The time responses of the three weights are also obtained as shown in Fig. 10-51(b). It can be seen that the controller parameters are no longer constants in the system, however, the control results are satisfactory.

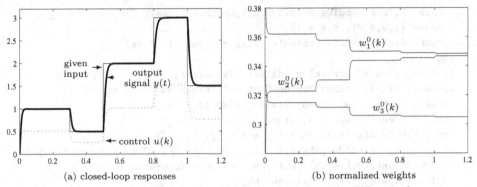

(a) closed-loop responses      (b) normalized weights

Fig. 10-51   Simulation results of the control system under PID control.

### 10.4.3   *PID Controller with Back-propagation Neural Networks*

If the incremental PID controllers are still used

$$u(k) = u(k-1) + K_{\mathrm{p}}\big[e(k) - e(k-1)\big] + K_{\mathrm{i}}e(k) + K_{\mathrm{d}}\big[e(k) + e(k-2) - 2e(k-1)\big], \quad (10.39)$$

the feedforward network with back-propagation algorithm thus used to design the PID controller parameters. With the program given in [23], a rewritten Simulink block can be constructed. Simulink model with such a controller block is shown in Fig. 10-52. The block diagram is masked, so that block for the PID control with BP network can be implemented. The block should have one input port, connected to the error signal $e(t)$ in the servo control system. Port 1 for the block generates the control signal $u(t)$, while the second port gives the PID controller properties.

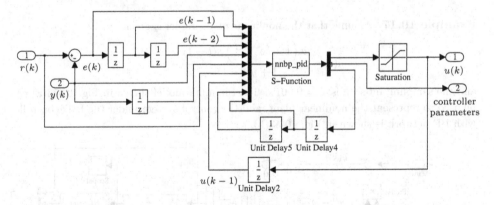

Fig. 10-52   Simulink model of a PID controller with BP network   (file: c10bp_pid.mdl).

In the Simulink model, S-function is used to describe the PID controller with BP network

```
function [sys,x0,str,ts]=nnbp_pid(t,x,u,flag,T,nh,th,alfa,kF1,kF2)
switch flag,
    case 0, [sys,x0,str,ts] = mdlInitializeSizes(T,nh);
```

```
    case 3, sys = mdlOutputs(t,x,u,T,nh,th,alfa,kF1,kF2);
    case {1,2,4,9}, sys = [];
    otherwise, error(['Unhandled flag = ',num2str(flag)]);
end
function [sys,x0,str,ts] = mdlInitializeSizes(T,nh)   % initialization
sizes=simsizes;   sizes.NumContStates=0;   sizes.NumDiscStates=0;
sizes.NumOutputs = 4+7*nh; sizes.NumInputs = 7+14*nh;
sizes.DirFeedthrough = 1; sizes.NumSampleTimes = 1;
sys = simsizes(sizes); x0 = []; str = []; ts = [T 0];
function sys = mdlOutputs(t,x,u,T,nh,th,alfa,kF1,kF2)   % compute outputs
wi_2=reshape(u(8:7+4*nh),nh,4); wo_2=reshape(u(8+4*nh:7+7*nh),3,nh);
wi_1=reshape(u(8+7*nh: 7+11*nh),nh,4);
wo_1=reshape(u(8+11*nh: 7+14*nh),3,nh);
xi=[u([6,4,1])', 1]; xx=[u(1)-u(2); u(1); u(1)+u(3)-2*u(2)];
I=xi*wi_1'; Oh=non_transfun(I,kF1); K=non_transfun(wo_1*Oh',kF2);
uu=u(7)+K'*xx; dyu=sign((u(4)-u(5))/(uu-u(7)+0.0000001));
dK=non_transfun(K,3); delta3=u(1)*dyu*xx.*dK;
wo=wo_1+th*delta3*Oh+alfa*(wo_1-wo_2)+alfa*(wo_1-wo_2);
dO=2*non_transfun(I,3);
wi=wi_1+th*(dO.*(delta3'*wo))'*xi+alfa*(wi_1-wi_2);
sys=[uu; K; wi(:); wo(:)];
function W1=non_transfun(W,key)   % approximate the activation function
switch key
    case 1, W1=(exp(W)-exp(-W))./(exp(W)+exp(-W));
    case 2, W1=exp(W)./(exp(W)+exp(-W));
    case 3, W1=2./(exp(W)+exp(-W)).^2;
end
```

**Example 10.17.** Assume that the nonlinear plant model is given by [23]

$$y(t) = \frac{a\left(1 - be^{-ct/T}\right)y(t-1)}{1 + y(t-1)^2} + u(t),$$

and the sampling interval is $T = 0.001\,$s. The Simulink model shown in Fig. 10-53(a) can be used to represent the nonlinear plant, and the control system under the PID controller with BP network is shown in Fig. 10-53(b).

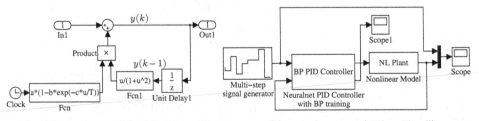

(a) nonlinear plant model   (c10plant.mdl)          (b) control system   (c10bp_pid.mdl)

Fig. 10-53   Simulation models for neural network control system.

The parameters of the PID controller with BP network can be obtained by double

clicking the masked block, as shown in the dialog shown in Fig. 10-54(a). The controller
parameters can be entered in the dialog box. When the simulation process is started, the
simulation results shown in Fig. 10-54(b) can be obtained.

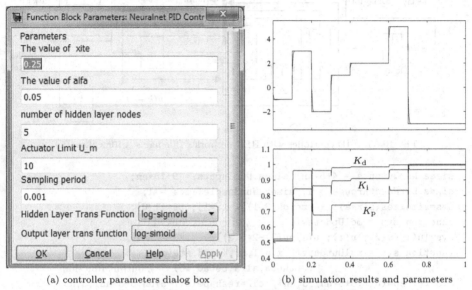

(a) controller parameters dialog box　　　　(b) simulation results and parameters

Fig. 10-54　PID control with BP neural network.

## 10.4.4　*PID Controller with Radial Basis Function-based Neural Network*

Radial basis function (RBF) neural network is a useful neural network. It is a
feedforward neural network, with one hidden layer, and the radial basis function
is used as the activation function. Based on the radial basis functions, a PID
controller can be designed[23]. The Simulink implementation model is established
of the controller is shown in Fig. 10-55, and again its kernel is the S-function
implementation shown below

```
function [sys,x0,str,ts]=nnrbf_pid(t,x,u,flag,T,nn,K_pid,...
    eta_pid,theta,alfa,beta0,w0)
switch flag,
    case 0, [sys,x0,str,ts] = mdlInitializeSizes(T,nn);
    case 2, sys = mdlUpdates(u);
    case 3, sys = mdlOutputs(t,x,u,T,nn,K_pid,eta_pid,...
                    theta,alfa,beta0,w0);
    case {1, 4, 9}, sys = [];
    otherwise, error(['Unhandled flag = ',num2str(flag)]);
end
function [sys,x0,str,ts] = mdlInitializeSizes(T,nn)    initialization
sizes = simsizes; sizes.NumContStates = 0; sizes.NumDiscStates = 3;
```

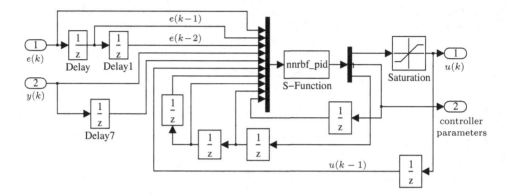

Fig. 10-55    PID controller with RBF network    (file name: c10mrbf.mdl).

```
sizes.NumOutputs = 4+5*nn; sizes.NumInputs = 9+15*nn;
sizes.DirFeedthrough = 1; sizes.NumSampleTimes = 1;
sys=simsizes(sizes); x0=zeros(3,1); str=[]; ts=[T 0];
function sys = mdlUpdates(u)      % discrete states update
sys=[u(1)-u(2); u(1); u(1)+u(3)-2*u(2)];
function sys = mdlOutputs(t,x,u,T,nn,K_pid,eta_pid,...
                         theta,alfa,beta0,w0)   % output function
ci3=reshape(u(7:6+3*nn),3,nn); ci2=reshape(u(7+5*nn:6+8*nn),3,nn);
ci1=reshape(u(7+10*nn: 6+13*nn),3,nn);
bi3=u(7+3*nn: 6+4*nn); bi2=u(7+8*nn: 6+9*nn);
bi1=u(7+13*nn: 6+14*nn); w3= u(7+4*nn: 6+5*nn);
w2= u(7+9*nn: 6+10*nn); w1= u(7+14*nn: 6+15*nn); xx=u([6;4;5]);
if t==0
    ci1=w0(1)*ones(3,nn);  bi1=w0(2)*ones(nn,1);
    w1=w0(3)*ones(nn,1);  K_pid0=K_pid;
else, K_pid0=u(end-2:end); end
for j=1: nn
    h(j,1)=exp(-norm(xx-ci1(:,j))^2/(2*bi1(j)*bi1(j)));
end
dym=u(4)-w1'*h; w=w1+theta*dym*h+alfa*(w1-w2)+beta0*(w2-w3);
for j=1:nn
    dbi(j,1)=theta*dym*w1(j)*h(j)*(bi1(j)^(-3))*norm(xx-ci1(:,j))^2;
    dci(:,j)=theta*dym*w1(j)*h(j)*(xx-ci1(:,j))*(bi1(j)^(-2));
end
bi=bi1+dbi+alfa*(bi1-bi2)+beta0*(bi2-bi3);
ci=ci1+dci+alfa*(ci1-ci2)+beta0*(ci2-ci3);
dJac=sum(w.*h.*(-xx(1)+ci(1,:)')./bi.^2); % Jacobian matrix
KK=K_pid0+u(1)*dJac*eta_pid.*x;
sys=[u(6)+KK'*x; KK; ci(:); bi(:); w(:)];
```

**Example 10.18.** Assume that the nonlinear plant model is given by [23]

$$y(k) = \frac{u(k) - 0.1y(k-1)}{1 + y^2(k-1)}.$$

The Simulink model is of the plant shown in Fig. 10-56(a), and the system model under PID controller with RBF network as shown in Fig. 10-56(b). Double click the controller block, the parameters of the controller can be specified in the dialog box shown in Fig. 10-57(a). The simulation results are shown in Fig. 10-57(b), the controller parameters plots are also given. The control behaviors is satisfactory for the given plant.

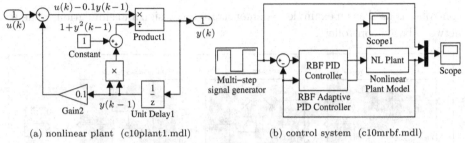

(a) nonlinear plant   (c10plant1.mdl)        (b) control system   (c10mrbf.mdl)

Fig. 10-56   Simulation models.

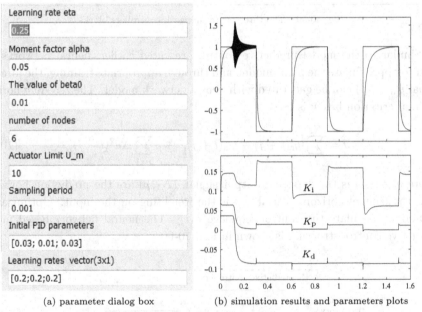

(a) parameter dialog box        (b) simulation results and parameters plots

Fig. 10-57   Simulation results.

## 10.4.5   Design and Simulation of Neural Network Controllers

In the Neural Network Toolbox provided in MATLAB, the low-level neural network elements for Simulink modeling are provided, as shown in Fig. 10-58.

In the blockset, the Control Systems icon contains three different neural network-based controllers as shown in Fig. 10-59. Here the neural network predictive

Fig. 10-58    Neural network controllers blockset.

controller is used as an example to demonstrate the design and simulations of neural network-based controllers.

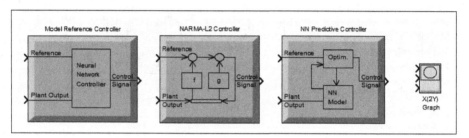

Fig. 10-59    The three neural network controllers blocks.

Similar to the model predictive control presented earlier, neural networks are used to approximate the plant model, and through appropriate training, the forecast signal $y_\mathrm{m}(t+j)$ can be generated with neural network model. The receding horizon optimal criterion below is used

$$J = \sum_{j=p}^{N_2} \left[ y_\mathrm{r}(t+j) - y_\mathrm{m}(t+j) \right]^2 + \rho \sum_{j=1}^{m} \Delta u^2(t+j), \qquad (10.40)$$

where $y_\mathrm{r}(t+j)$ is the expected output signal, $(N_1, p)$ are the prediction horizons, $m$ is the control horizon. Variable $\rho$ is the weighting on the input. Optimization is used to calculate the control sequence $u(t)$. The neural network-based model predictive control structure is shown in Fig. 10-60.

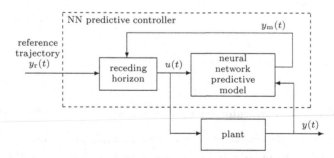

Fig. 10-60    Neural network predictive control structure.

The neural network predictive controller block shown in Fig. 10-59 can be used directly in the design and simulation of the controller with Simulink. In the following example, the application is demonstrated.

**Example 10.19.** Consider the plant model shown below

$$G(s) = \frac{(-0.2s + 1)\left(1 + \dfrac{e^{-s}}{s + 1}\right)}{(s + 1)^2},$$

and it is required that $|u(t)| \leqslant 5$. The following procedures can be used in the design and simulation of neural network-based predictive control system in Simulink.

(1) **Modeling of the plant in Simulink.** The plant model can be described with the **LTI System** block in the new versions of MATLAB as shown in Fig. 10-61(a), and the plant model can be specified with the command

```
>> s=tf('s'); g1=1/(s+1); g1.ioDelay=1; G=(-0.2*s+1)*(1+g1)/(s+1)^2;
```

where the model can be eventually converted to an SS object with internal delay. Alternatively, the plant model can be represented in Simulink with the structure shown in Fig. 10-61(b). In the two models, the input and output ports are used.

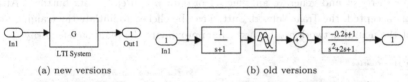

(a) new versions · · · · · · · · · · · · · · · (b) old versions

Fig. 10-61  Plant model representation in Simulink  (c10mplt1.mdl).

(2) **Closed-loop system modeling.** The closed-loop system can be modeled as shown in Fig. 10-62, where the plant model is embedded in a Simulink file. The staircase waveform constructed in Example 6.18 is used as the input of the system.

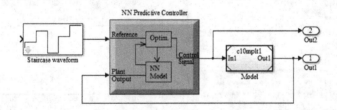

Fig. 10-62  Neural network predictive control system  (file: c10nnmpc.mdl).

(3) **Control parameter dialog box.** Double click the controller block, the parameter dialog box shown in Fig. 10-63 will be displayed. The horizons and weights in the controller can be specified in the dialog box. Of course, these parameters can be modified later according to the actual simulation process, so as to achieve satisfactory performance.

(4) **Neural network approximation of the plant model.** The neural network approximation to the original plant model can be established first automatically in simulation. Double click the **Plant Identification** button above parameter dialog box, another dialog box shown in Fig. 10-64(a) can be displayed, and in the edit box plant, the plant model name c10mplt1 should be specified. Then, click the **Generate Training**

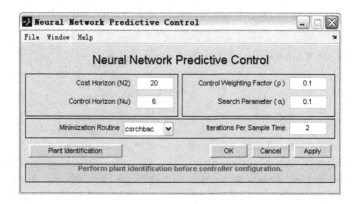

Fig. 10-63    Parameter dialog box of neural network predictive controller.

Data button, the input and output data for system identification can be generated as shown in Fig. 10-64(b). The button **Accept Data** can be clicked to accept the generated data (or to reject and generate another set of data with **Reject Data** button). After the data are accepted, the **Train Network** button can be clicked to initiate the training process, so that the neural network established can approximate the plant satisfactorily.

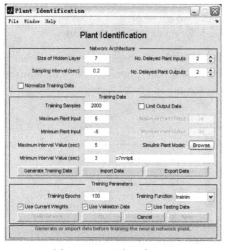

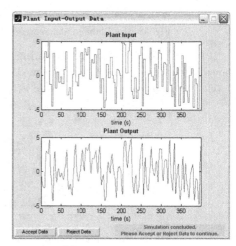

(a) parameter identification                    (b) input and output data

Fig. 10-64    Neural network approximation of the plant model.

(5) **Closed-loop simulation analysis**. With the neural network models in the controller trained, closed-loop simulation can be performed, and the output and control signals in the system are shown in Figs. 10-65(a) and (b). It can be seen that for the staircase waveform of amplitudes 1, 3, −1, 2, 4, there exist steady-state errors, however, the tracking tendencies are correct.

A neural network-based model reference adaptive controller block is also

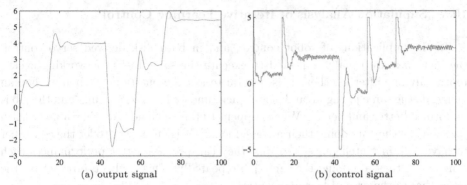

(a) output signal

(b) control signal

Fig. 10-65    Control results with neural network predictive control systems.

provided in the Neural Network Toolbox, where two neural networks are needed in the block. One of them is used to approximate the plant model, while the other is used to implement the controller. Another example is given below to demonstrate the use of the controller block.

**Example 10.20.** Consider again the plant model in Example 10.19. The neural network-based model reference adaptive controller block can be used to replace the neural network predictive controller in Example 10.19, and the Simulink model in Fig. 10-66(a) can be constructed.

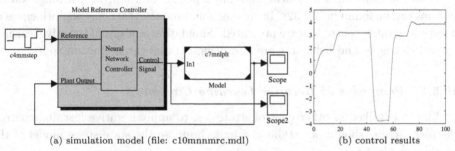

(a) simulation model (file: c10mnnmrc.mdl)                (b) control results

Fig. 10-66    Neural network MRAS and control results.

Using similar training methods with Example 10.19 to the two neural networks in the system, the Plant Identification button can be used to train the neural network model for the plant, with the interface. Similarly, the controller neural network can also be trained. After training, the control system can be simulated with the model, and the control results in Fig. 10-66(b) can be obtained.

Unfortunately, there exist large steady-state errors. Thus, for the plant model, neural network-based controllers may not be suitable.

## 10.5    Simulation Analysis of Iterative Learning Control

In the applications of robot control, and in hard disk derived servo control, the machines are usually expected to execute the same tasks, or working cycles, repeatedly one after another. It is natural to ask the question: "When we human beings do the same job again and again, each time we learn something, and the job is performed better and better. What happens to the machines, are they able to learn things while they are doing their assigned jobs?" It is our target to let the controller to have certain "intelligence", so that they can provide better performances each time, when they are doing the same job repeatedly. This is also the target for the researches in the area of learning control.

In 1978, Masaru Uchiyama proposed an idea to control high-speed mechanical arms[27]. In 1984, Suguru Arimoto extended the original ideas of Uchiyama, and proposed the concept of iterative learning control (ILC)[28]. Similar to robust control methods, iterative learning control can also be used to process the uncertainties in actual dynamical systems. Target tracking problems can be solved with this type of controllers, with simple form and less *a priori* knowledge of the systems. This kind of control strategy is suitable for the plants which have repeated movements. The first few working cycles can be regarded as the learning stage, and the control behaviors are improved gradually. The error signals and the experiences in the previous working cycles, can be used to correct the current control signal, such that the output signal can converge to the expected values. Iterative learning control is useful to the complicated systems with repeated working cycles.

Good surveys on theoretical and applications of iterative learning control systems can be found in [29–32]. In this section, fundamental concepts, principles of iterative learning controllers are presented. Simulation analysis of iterative learning control strategies and behaviors are also demonstrated through examples.

### 10.5.1    *Principles of Iterative Learning Control*

Like it is talked in other control strategies, to apply iterative learning control, the plant model should be established first. Suppose the state space model of the continuous plant is

$$
\begin{cases}
\dot{\boldsymbol{x}}(t) = \boldsymbol{f}(\boldsymbol{x}(t), \boldsymbol{u}(t), t) \\
\boldsymbol{y}(t) = \boldsymbol{g}(\boldsymbol{x}(t), \boldsymbol{u}(t), t),
\end{cases}
\tag{10.41}
$$

where $\boldsymbol{x}$ is an $n$-dimensional state vector. The system has $m$ inputs and $r$ outputs, and $\boldsymbol{f}(\cdot)$, $\boldsymbol{g}(\cdot)$ are vector functions of suitable dimensions. The iterative learning control problems can be described as follows. For the given expected output signal $\boldsymbol{y}_{\mathrm{d}}(t)$, there exist expected input signal $\boldsymbol{u}_{\mathrm{d}}(t)$, and the initial states $\boldsymbol{x}_k(0)$ in each working cycle. The processes should be executed repeatedly, so that the specific learning control law $\boldsymbol{u}_{\mathrm{d}}(t)$ will be generated for the interval $t \in [0, T]$, such that the actual output $\boldsymbol{y}_k(t)$ of the system will approach the expected output signal $\boldsymbol{y}_\mathrm{d}(t)$. Iterative learning control law can be recursively implemented as follows

$$\boldsymbol{u}_k(t) = \mathscr{L}(\boldsymbol{u}_{k-1}(t), \boldsymbol{e}_{k-1}(t)), \tag{10.42}$$

where $\mathscr{L}(\cdot)$ is linear or nonlinear operator, and $\boldsymbol{e}_{k-1}(t) = \boldsymbol{y}_\mathrm{d}(t) - \boldsymbol{y}_{k-1}(t)$ is the error of last run. It can be seen from the control law in Eqn. (10.42) that in open-loop iterative learning control, the error signal $\boldsymbol{e}_{k-1}(t)$ and input signal $\boldsymbol{u}_{k-1}(t)$ of the previous working cycle are used to construct the control sequence $\boldsymbol{u}_k(t)$ for the current working cycle.

If $k$ is large enough, and $\boldsymbol{e}_{k-1}(t)$ signal uniformly approaches to zero in $t \in [0, T]$, the above iterative learning control is convergent. Convergence problems are the most important problems in iterative learning control. Only convergent iterative learning control strategies are useful in practical control systems.

The basic open-loop iterative learning control strategy is shown in Fig. 10-67. In practical applications, the control signals at the next working cycle can be calculated. The new control sequence of the system for the next working cycle can either be obtained by the previous working cycle, or obtained with on-line computation in the previous working cycle. The new control signals are stored in the memory to refresh the old control signals. If the control signal is to be applied, they should be extracted from the memory first. If the error signal in the current working cycle is used, closed-loop control strategy can be established. It can be seen that more information has been used in iterative learning control strategy than conventional feedback structures. This include the information from the previous working cycles, as well as the information of the current working cycles.

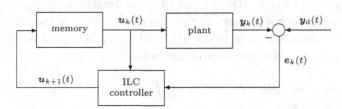

Fig. 10-67   Basic structure of open-loop iterative learning control.

In traditional studies on iterative learning control, the following assumptions are always given[33, 34]:

(1) Each working cycle of the system is in a finite interval $[0, T]$.

(2) The expected trajectories of the system in the interval $[0, T]$ is given.

(3) The initial states $\boldsymbol{x}_k(0)$ of the system at each working cycle are the same.

(4) The dynamical structure of the system is unchanged at each working cycle.

(5) The output $\boldsymbol{y}_k(t)$ of the system can be measured, and the tracking error signal $\boldsymbol{e}_k(t) = \boldsymbol{y}_\mathrm{d}(t) - \boldsymbol{y}_k(t)$ can be used to generate the control signal $\boldsymbol{u}_{k+1}(t)$ of the next time instant.

(6) The dynamic characteristics of the system are invertible, i.e., for a given expected trajectory $y_d(t)$, there is a unique control signal $u_d(t)$, such that the ideal output $y_d(t)$ of the system can be obtained.

A successful iterative learning control algorithm must not only reduce the error in each working cycle, but also have rapid convergence speed. The thus established algorithm is practical in real applications. Besides, the convergence of iterative learning control algorithms are independent of the particular tracking trajectories. If a new expected tracking trajectory is given, the iterative learning control law should be immediately used without any modifications.

### 10.5.2   *Iterative Learning Control Algorithms*

#### 1. Continuous PID-type iterative learning control algorithm

If the plant model is continuous, the following open- and closed-loop PID-type iterative learning control algorithms can be expressed as

(1) **Open-loop controller**. The earlier concept of iterative learning control was proposed in open-loop form. The most widely used algorithms are of PID-type, open-loop iterative learning control algorithms refer to control laws where the information of the current working cycle is not included. The general form of the open-loop continuous PID-type iterative learning control law can be written as

$$u_k(t) = u_{k-1}(t) + K_p e_{k-1}(t) + K_i \int_0^t e_{k-1}(\tau)\mathrm{d}\tau + K_d \dot{e}_{k-1}(t), \qquad (10.43)$$

where $K_p$, $K_i$, $K_d$ are the learning gain matrices for proportional, integral and derivative actions. If certain gain matrices are zero, the controllers can be simplified as P-type, D-type, PI-type, ID-type and PD-type iterative learning controllers.

(2) **Closed-loop controller**. In the closed-loop iterative learning control system structure, when the error in the $k$th working cycle is used as the correction term in learning, the following control law can be established

$$u_k(t) = u_{k-1}(t) + K_p e_k(t) + K_i \int_0^t e_k(\tau)\mathrm{d}\tau + K_d \dot{e}_k(t). \qquad (10.44)$$

Comparing the open- and closed-loop control strategies, it can be found that in the open-loop control law, the control and error information in the previous working cycle is used, while in the closed-loop control law, the control of the previous working cycle and the error of the current working cycle are used. Generally speaking, the performance of closed-loop iterative learning control strategies are better than the open-loop ones.

#### 2. Discrete PID-type iterative learning control algorithm

Assume that the discrete plant model is given by

$$\begin{cases} x(t+1) = f(x(t), u(t), t) \\ y(t) = g(x(t), u(t), t), \end{cases} \qquad (10.45)$$

the $k$th working cycle can be expressed as

$$\begin{cases} \boldsymbol{x}_k(t+1) = \boldsymbol{f}(\boldsymbol{x}_k(t), \boldsymbol{u}_k(t), t) \\ \boldsymbol{y}_k(t) = \boldsymbol{g}(\boldsymbol{x}_k(t), \boldsymbol{u}_k(t), t). \end{cases} \quad (10.46)$$

The output error signal can be defined as $\boldsymbol{e}_k(t) = \boldsymbol{y}_\mathrm{d}(t) - \boldsymbol{y}_k(t)$. Based on the error signal, the open- and closed-loop PID-type control laws are

$$\boldsymbol{u}_{k+1}(t) = \boldsymbol{u}_k(t) + \boldsymbol{K}_\mathrm{p}\boldsymbol{e}_k(t+1) + \boldsymbol{K}_\mathrm{i}\sum_{j=0}^{t+1}\boldsymbol{e}_k(j) + \boldsymbol{K}_\mathrm{d}\Big[\boldsymbol{e}_k(t+1) - \boldsymbol{e}_k(t)\Big], \quad (10.47)$$

$$\boldsymbol{u}_{k+1}(t) = \boldsymbol{u}_k(t) + \boldsymbol{K}_\mathrm{p}\boldsymbol{e}_{k+1}(t) + \boldsymbol{K}_\mathrm{i}\sum_{j=0}^{t}\boldsymbol{e}_{k+1}(j) + \boldsymbol{K}_\mathrm{d}\Big[\boldsymbol{e}_{k+1}(t) - \boldsymbol{e}_{k+1}(t-1)\Big]. \quad (10.48)$$

Please note, in the open-loop control law, the error signals $\boldsymbol{e}_k(t)$ of the previous working cycle are used, while in the closed-loop control law, the error signals $\boldsymbol{e}_{k+1}(t)$ of the current working cycle are used. The input signals in either cases are those used in the previous working cycle.

Of course, discrete iterative learning control algorithms can also be applied to continuous plants. If the plant is a linear single variable model, the following MAT-LAB function can be written for the above open-loop PID-type iterative learning control system. The iterative learning control algorithm can be implemented easily using the simple statements.

```
function [y,e,u,kvec,t0]=ilc_lsim(G,T,kmax,yd,Kp,Ki,Kd)
n=length(yd); y=zeros(n,kmax); e=y; t0=0:T:(n-1)*T; u=y; e(:,1)=yd(:);
kvec=[]; if G.Ts==0, G=c2d(G,T); end; G=ss(G);
for k=1:kmax, x0=zeros(size(G.a,1),1);
    for t=2:n
        x1=G.a*x0+G.b*u(t,k); y(t,k)=G.c*x1+G.d*u(t,k);
        x0=x1; e(t,k)=yd(t)-y(t,k);
        u(t,k+1)=u(t,k)+Kp*e(t,k)+Ki*sum(e(1:t,k))+... % P and I control
                Kd*(e(t,k)-e(t-1,k));                  % D control
    end,
    kvec(k)=max(abs(e(:,k)));
end
```

The syntax of the function is

$$[\boldsymbol{y}, \boldsymbol{e}, \boldsymbol{u}, \boldsymbol{k}, \boldsymbol{t}] = \texttt{ilc\_lsim}(G, T, k_\mathrm{max}, \boldsymbol{y}_\mathrm{d}, K_\mathrm{p}, K_\mathrm{i}, K_\mathrm{d})$$

where $G$ is the linear plant model. It can be continuous or discrete, and is converted to discrete state space model with sample interval $T$. The argument $k_\mathrm{max}$ is the maximum allowed number of iterations, $\boldsymbol{y}_\mathrm{d}$ is the vector containing reference input samples. The variables $K_\mathrm{p}$, $K_\mathrm{i}$ and $K_\mathrm{d}$ are PID controller parameters. The returned argument $\boldsymbol{y}$ is a matrix, whose $k$th column stores the output vector in the $k$th working cycle. The matrices $\boldsymbol{e}$ and $\boldsymbol{u}$ are the matrices of input and output signals stored in each working cycle. The argument $\boldsymbol{k}$ stores the norm of tracking error in each working cycle, and $\boldsymbol{t}$ is the time vector.

This function applies to the plants with relative order of 1. If the relative order is larger than 1, iterative learning controller with high-order derivative terms can be used[35].

**Example 10.21.** Consider the discrete plant model

$$\begin{cases} \boldsymbol{x}(k+1) = \begin{bmatrix} -0.8 & -0.22 \\ 1 & 0 \end{bmatrix} \boldsymbol{x}(k) + \begin{bmatrix} 0.5 \\ 1 \end{bmatrix} \boldsymbol{u}(k), \\ y(k) = \begin{bmatrix} 1 & 0.5 \end{bmatrix} \boldsymbol{x}(k), \end{cases}$$

with $T = 0.1\,$s and the reference input trajectory is $y_{\mathrm{d}}(t) = \sin 0.08t$. Assume that the initial states are zero, Arimoto P-type iterative learning controller can be used, by assuming $K_{\mathrm{p}} = 0.5$, and $K_{\mathrm{i}} = K_{\mathrm{d}} = 0$. The following statements can be used to simulate the iterative learning control systems, and the system responses are shown in Fig. 10-68(a).

```
>> yd=sin(0.08*[0:99])';
   G=ss([-0.8,-0.22; 1 0],[0.5;1],[1 0.5],0,'Ts',0.1);
   [y,e,u,kvec,t]=ilc_lsim(G,0.1,10,yd,0.5,0,0);
   plot(t,y), figure, plot(kvec,'-*'), figure, plot(t,u)
```

It can be seen that when $k = 1$, there is no response at the beginning, and when $k = 2$, the output signal tries to follow the given signal, however, there exist errors. The controller will learn how to control the plant with the error signals. Thus, when $k = 3$, the error will be significantly reduced, however, errors would still exist. When $k = 4$, the control behavior is further improved. This is the learning strategy of controller, such that the control behavior gets improved in each working cycle. For this example, when $k = 10$, the output signal approaches well to the given signal. It can be seen from the norm of error signal shown in Fig. 10-68(b) that there are still errors when $k = 10$, albeit the error is small. The learning control algorithm with $K_{\mathrm{p}}$ is not satisfactory, and the control signals are shown in Fig. 10-68(c).

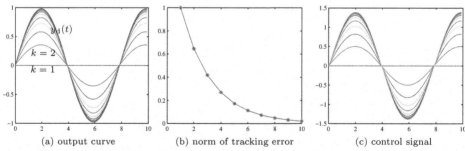

(a) output curve              (b) norm of tracking error              (c) control signal

Fig. 10-68    Control results of iterative learning control.

If different controller parameters are used, for instance, $K_{\mathrm{p}} = 0.85, 1.15, 1.5$, the control results are shown in Figs. 10-69(a)$\sim$(c). It can be seen that after a few working cycles, the output signal approaches well to the given signal $y_{\mathrm{d}}(t)$, however, the convergence speeds are different.

```
>> [y1,e,u,kv1,t]=ilc_lsim(G,0.1,10,yd,0.85,0,0);
   [y2,e,u,kv2,t]=ilc_lsim(G,0.1,10,yd,1.15,0,0);
```

```
[y3,e,u,kv3,t]=ilc_lsim(G,0.1,10,yd,1.5,0,0);
subplot(231), plot(t,y1), subplot(234), plot(kv1,'-*')
subplot(232), plot(t,y2), subplot(235), plot(kv2,'-*')
subplot(233), plot(t,y3), subplot(236), plot(kv3,'-*')
```

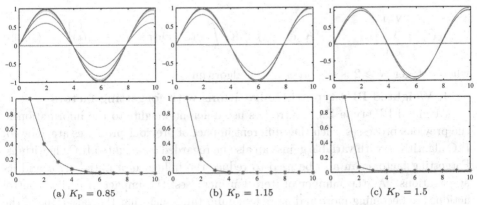

(a) $K_P = 0.85$    (b) $K_P = 1.15$    (c) $K_P = 1.5$

Fig. 10-69   ILC control with different gains.

**Example 10.22.** Suppose the plant model of a continuous system is

$$G(s) = \frac{0.2s + 1}{(0.1s + 1)^2},$$

Staircase waveform is used as the expected output of the system. The following statements can be used to describe the plant model, and generate the staircase waveform as the input of the system. Then, with the open-loop iterative learning control function ilc_lsim(), the output of the system can be obtained, as shown in Fig. 10-70.

```
>> s=tf('s'); G=(0.2*s+1)/(0.1*s+1)^2;
   yd=[2*ones(50,1); -1*ones(80,1); 1*ones(60,1); 3*ones(100,1)];
   [y,e,u,kv,t]=ilc_lsim(G,0.1,10,yd,0.5,0,0);
   subplot(131), plot(t,y), subplot(132), plot(t,u),
   subplot(133), plot(kv,'-*'),
```

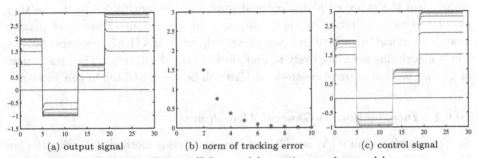

(a) output signal    (b) norm of tracking error    (c) control signal

Fig. 10-70   Discrete ILC control for continuous plant model.

## 3. High-order PID-type iterative learning control algorithms

High-order iterative learning control algorithm is proposed based upon the basic PID-type ILC algorithms. Compared with ordinary learning algorithms, the input and output information of the previous working cycle are used, besides, information of several earlier working cycles are also used. The general form of high-order ILC algorithm is

$$u_k(t) = \sum_{i=1}^{N-1} \left[ u_{k-i}(t) + K_{\mathrm{p}} e_{k-i}(t) + K_{\mathrm{i}} \int_0^t e_{k-i}(\tau)\mathrm{d}\tau + K_{\mathrm{d}} \dot{e}_{k-i}(t) \right], \quad (10.49)$$

where integer $N \geqslant 2$ is the order of the algorithm.

**4. Weighted PID-type ILC algorithms with forgetting factors**

Weighted PID-type ILC controllers use different weights to the information in the previous processes, such that different impact of previous processes are allowed. ILC algorithms with variable gains can also be regarded as weighted ILC algorithms. Forgetting factors can also be used to reduce the influence of initial error and its aggregations. As the number of iteration increases, the impact of earlier control actions are becoming more and more less important, such that the variations of the control signal become smooth.

**5. Other iterative learning control algorithms**

Apart from PID-type iterative learning algorithms, there are also other types of iterative learning algorithms, such as adaptive ILC algorithms, predictive ILC algorithms, optimal ILC algorithms, intelligent ILC algorithms, robust ILC algorithms and model-based ILC algorithms. Also, iterative learning control algorithms with interval parameters can be used[36]. The interested readers can refer to the relevant materials.

## 10.6    Design of Global Optimal Controllers

Various optimization algorithms are presented in Chapter 3. All these algorithms are started from the user selected initial points. Thus, local optimal solutions, rather than the expected global optimal solutions, are inevitable. In this section, evolution-based optimization algorithms such as genetic algorithms and particle swarm optimization algorithms are presented, with MATLAB implementations. These algorithms are more likely to find global optimal solutions. The applications of the methods in optimal controller design will be demonstrated in this section.

### 10.6.1   *Introduction to Genetic Algorithm*

Genetic algorithm (GA) is a class of evolution-based methods following the law of "survival of the fittest."[37] The method was first proposed by Professor John Holland of Michigan University in 1975. The main idea of the method is to search from a population consisting of randomly distributed individuals. The individuals are encoded, regarded as genes with chromosomes, in a certain way. The population evolves generation by generation through reproduction, crossover and mutation, until individuals with the best fitness function are found.

Global Optimization Toolbox (earlier name is Genetic Algorithm and Direct Search Toolbox) can be used to solve optimization problems with genetic algorithms, with the function `ga()`. Besides, other functions such `simulannealbnd()` and `patternsearch()` are also supported. Apart from this toolbox, there are a variety of toolboxes developed, for instance, the Genetic Algorithm Toolbox developed by Peter Fleming and Andrew Chipperfield of Sheffield University[38], and Genetic Algorithm Optimization Toolbox (GAOT)[39] developed by Christopher Houck, Jeffery Joines and Michael Kay of North Carolina State University. The major function of GAOT[39] is also `ga()`[1] For unconstrained optimization problems with simple genetic algorithm, the authors recommend the free toolbox GAOT.

The general procedure of simple genetic algorithm is

(1) Select $N$ individuals to form an initial population $P_0$. Evaluate the objective functions, known as fitness function in genetic algorithms, for all the individuals. The initial population $P_0$ can be established randomly.

(2) Set the generation to $i = 1$, i.e., the first generation.

(3) Compute the values of selective functions, i.e., select some individuals in a probabilistic way from the current population. Three selective functions are provided in GAOT, `roulette()`, `normGeomSelect()` and `tournSelect()`, with `normGeomSelect()` function the default one.

(4) Create the population of the next generation $P_{i+1}$, by reproduction, crossover and mutation.

(5) Set $i = i + 1$. If the termination conditions are not satisfied, go to step (3) to continue evolution.

Compared with traditional optimization methods, the genetic algorithms have mainly the following differences[38]:

(1) In searching the optimum points, the genetic algorithms allow searches from many initial points in a parallel way. Thus, it is more likely to find global optimum points than with the traditional methods, which initiate search from a single point.

(2) Genetic algorithms do not depend on the gradient information of the objective functions. Only the fitness functions, i.e., objective functions are necessary in optimum points search.

(3) Genetic algorithms evaluate and select the objective function in a probabilistic way rather than a deterministic way. Thus, there are slight differences among each run.

---

[1] The original name of the function is `ga()`, however, it is the same as the one provided in Global Optimization Toolbox of MathWorks, which may cause conflict. Thus, it is recommended that the function is renamed as `gaopt()` and this name is used throughout this book.
The toolbox can be downloaded from: http://www.ise.ncsu.edu/mirage/GAToolBox/gaot/

## 10.6.2    *Solving Global Optimization Problems with Genetic Algorithms*

The direct use of toolbox functions, `gaopt()` and `ga()`, are used to solve global optimization problems. Even though the reader has no knowledge about the necessary details of genetic algorithm, and they do not know what chromosomes are, how they encode, and how the crossover and mutation take place, they are still able to solve optimization problems with genetic algorithms. The syntax of the `gaopt()` functions are

> $[a,b,c] = \text{gaopt}(\text{bound}, fun)$    % the simplest syntax
> $[x,b,c,d] = \text{gaopt}(\text{bound}, fun, p, v, P_0, fun1, n)$

where $\text{bound} = [x_m, x_M]$ is the matrix composed of the lower bounds $x_m$ and $x_M$ bounds of the decision variables. The string *fun* is the MATLAB function name for the objective function. The structure of the function is different from the conventional Optimization Toolbox functions. The returned variable $a$ is the final results composed of the decision variables and the value of the objective function. It is also important to note that the standard problem of GAOT is assumed to be maximization problems. Intermediate results are returned in c. In the second syntax, vector $p$ contains the additional variables, $v$ is the precision, $P_0$ is the initial population, and *fun1* is the termination function name, with the default, `'maxGenTerm'`. The argument $n$ is the maximum allowed numbers of generations. There are other syntaxes for the function, with details given in [39].

In the Global Optimization Toolbox, function `ga()` can be used directly, and it can be used in solving constrained as well as unconstrained optimization problems[40]. The description of the objective function is the same as in the conventional Optimization Toolbox. The syntaxes of `ga()` function are

> $[x,f,\text{flag},\text{out}] = \text{ga}(fun, n, \text{opts})$
> $[x,f,\text{flag},\text{out}] = \text{ga}(fun, n, A, B, A_{eq}, B_{eq}, x_m, x_M, \text{nfun}, \text{opts})$

where the variable *fun* for objective function, again in minimization problems. The argument $n$ is the number of the decision variables, `opts` is the control options which can be set with function `gaoptimset()`. For instance, the `Generations` property represents the maximum allowed numbers of generations, `InitialPopulation` is the initial population, `PopulationSize` property is the size of the population. The property `SelectionFcn` is used to describe the selective function. After the function call, the returned $x$ is the optimal decision variable vector, and if `flag` is positive, the function call is successful.

When constrained optimization problems are considered, `gaoptimset()` function should be used to modify the mutation function properties, and the initial population size should be increased, for instance, set it to 100.

```
opts = gaoptimset('MutationFcn',@mutationadaptfeasible,...
              'PopulationSize',100);   % set mutation and population
```

**Example 10.23.** Consider the maximization problem with one decision variable $f(x) = x\sin(10\pi x) + 2$, $x \in (-1, 2)$. The following MATLAB command can be used to draw the objective function as shown in Fig. 10-71. It can be seen that there are several extreme value points with the global one marked by $x_{max}$.

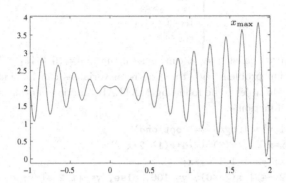

Fig. 10-71   Objective function.

```
>> ezplot('x*sin(10*pi*x)+2',[-1,2])
```

With traditional optimization functions in the Optimization Toolbox, an initial search point should be provided, and for different initial points tried, the solution obtained by `fminsearch()` function are given in Table 10-4. It can be seen that the global optimization solutions can normally be obtained with traditional search algorithms.

```
>> f=@(x)-x.*sin(10*pi*x)-2; v=[];
   for x0=[-1:0.8:1.5,1.5:0.1:2]
       x1=fmincon(f,x0,[],[],[],[],-1,2); v=[v; x0,x1,f(x1)];
   end
```

Table 10-4   Solutions and objective functions for different $x_0$ selections.

| $x_0$ | solution $x_1$ | $f(x_1)$ | $x_0$ | solution $x_1$ | $f(x_1)$ | $x_0$ | solution $x_1$ | $f(x_1)$ |
|---|---|---|---|---|---|---|---|---|
| $-1$ | $-1$ | $-2$ | 1.4 | 1.45070 | $-3.45035$ | 1.7 | 1.25081 | $-3.25040$ |
| $-0.2$ | $-0.65155$ | $-2.65078$ | 1.5 | 0.25397 | $-2.25200$ | 1.8 | 1.85055 | $-3.85027$ |
| 0.6 | 0.65155 | $-2.65078$ | 1.6 | 1.65061 | $-3.65031$ | 1.9 | 0.452233 | -2.451121 |

With function `gaopt()`, the following objective function can be written

```
function [sol,y]=c10mga1(sol,options)
x=sol(1); y=x.*sin(10*pi*x)+2;
```

Under default setting, the following statements can be used to solve the problem with function `gaopt()`. The results obtained each time are virtually the same.

```
>> [x0,a,fopt]=gaopt([-1,2],'c10mga1')
```

The solution is around $x = 1.85054746647533$, and $f_{\text{opt}}(x_0) = 3.85027376676810$. It can be seen that through 100 generations of evolution, the global optimization result can be found.

**Example 10.24.** Now consider the following linear programming problem

$$\min \quad (x_1 + 2x_2 + 3x_3).$$

$$\boldsymbol{x} \text{ s.t.} \begin{cases} -2x_1 + x_2 + x_3 \leqslant 9 \\ -x_1 + x_2 \geqslant -4 \\ 4x_1 - 2x_2 - 3x_3 = -6 \\ x_{1,2} \leqslant 0, x_3 \geqslant 0 \end{cases}$$

From the equation constraint, it can be seen that $x_3 = (6 + 4x_1 - 2x_2)/3$. Thus, the original optimization problem with three decision variables can be simplified to the one with two decision variables. The following MATLAB function can be written to describe the new objective function

```
function [sol,y]=c10mga4(sol,options)
x=sol(1:2); x=x(:); x(3)=(6+4*x(1)-2*x(2))/3;
y1=[-2 1 1]*x; y2=[-1 1 0]*x;
if (y1>9 | y2<-4 | x(3)<0), y=-100; else, y=-[1 2 3]*x; end
```

where $x_1, x_2$ are used to compute the value of $x_3$. In the objective function evaluation, the constraints are evaluated to check whether they are satisfied. If it is not satisfied, the objective function can be set to a small value, i.e., $-100$, so that the trends will be expelled from the search direction, and feasible solutions can finally be obtained.

```
>> [a,b,c]=gaopt([-1000 0; -1000 0],'c10mga4',[],[],[],...
        'maxGenTerm',1000);
    c=[c(1:15:end,:); c(end,:)]; a,c
```

Here, only $x_1, x_2$ are obtained and $x_3$ can be computed from $x_3 = (6 + 4x_1 - 2x_2)/3$, and its value is 0.00005529863957. The intermediate results in the genetic algorithm evolution are given in Table 10-5, where "gen" is for generation number.

Table 10-5    Intermediate results in GA search.

| gen. | $x_1$ | $x_2$ | $f(\boldsymbol{x})$ | gen. | $x_1$ | $x_2$ | $f(\boldsymbol{x})$ |
|------|-------|-------|------|------|-------|-------|------|
| 1 | $-269.865097$ | $-377.03111$ | $-100$ | 57 | $-1.45193811$ | $0$ | $1.2596906$ |
| 90 | $-1.59065611$ | $-0.66893063$ | $1.9532806$ | 123 | $-1.86036633$ | $-0.81042981$ | $3.30183165$ |
| 186 | $-5.897126844$ | $-9.4606018$ | $23.485634$ | 356 | $-6.38843298$ | $-10.04209934$ | $25.9421649$ |
| 613 | $-6.889962856$ | $-10.806835$ | $28.449814$ | 676 | $-6.90297178$ | $-10.80664291$ | $28.5148589$ |
| 823 | $-6.925942985$ | $-10.8757421$ | $28.629715$ | 1080 | $-6.96383795$ | $-10.92786854$ | $28.8191898$ |
| 1397 | $-6.990366303$ | $-10.9807717$ | $28.951832$ | 1768 | $-6.99734513$ | $-10.99471444$ | $28.9867257$ |
| 1849 | $-6.997368852$ | $-10.9949498$ | $28.986844$ | 1952 | $-6.99950347$ | $-10.99926216$ | $28.9975174$ |
| 1994 | $-6.999896151$ | $-10.9998524$ | $28.999481$ | 2000 | $-6.99991670$ | $-10.99991635$ | $28.9995835$ |

In fact, the problem can be solved directly with linear programming function, and precise results $x_1 = -7, x_2 = -11, x_3 = 0$ can be obtained.

```
>> f=[1 2 3]; A=[-2 1 1; 1 -1 0]; B=[9; 4]; Aeq=[4 -2 -3]; Beq=-6;
    x=linprog(f,A,B,Aeq,Beq,[-inf;-inf;0],[0;0;inf])
```

It can be seen from the optimization methods that with traditional searching algorithm, at most one solution can be found each time. For non-convex problems, local optimal points may usually be obtained. With the genetic algorithms, parallel searching is performed to start from a set of initial points. It is more likely to find better or even global optimal solutions to the same problem. Unfortunately, the speed and accuracy of the results may not be very high. In practical problems, genetic algorithm and similar algorithms can be used first to find an approximate global solution. Then the solution can be used as the initial search point, and with the traditional optimization algorithms, accurate global optimal results are likely to be obtained.

Alternatively, global optimization problem may also be solved with other functions provided in the Global Optimization Toolbox. For instance, the functions `simulannealbnd()` and `patternsearch()` can be used, with simple syntaxes.

**Example 10.25.** To use the pattern search function to solve again the optimization problem in the previous example, the following statements can be issued

```
>> f=@(x)[1 2 3]*x(:); A=[-2 1 1; 1 -1 0]; B=[9; 4];
   Aeq=[4 -2 -3]; Beq=-6; xm=[-inf;-inf;0]; xM=[0;0;inf];
   x0=[0;0;0]; x=patternsearch(f,x0,A,B,Aeq,Beq,xm,xM)
```

Unfortunately, the behavior of `ga()` function is not good in solving the problems with equation constraints. The following statements can be tried, however, each time a completely different results can be obtained.

```
>> x=ga(f,3,A,B,Aeq,Beq,xm,xM)
```

### 10.6.3 *Particle Swarm Optimization Algorithms and Applications*

Particle swarm optimization (PSO) proposed in [41] is another evolution algorithm. The algorithm is motivated by the phenomenon of a swarm of birds or fish seeking for food.

Assume that within a certain area, there is a piece of food (global optimum point), and there are a flock of randomly distributed birds (or particles). Each particle has its personal best value $p_{i,b}$, and the swarm has its best value $g_b$ up to now. The position and speed of each particle can be updated with the formula

$$v_i(k+1) = \phi(k)v_i(k) + \alpha_1\gamma_{1i}(k)\big[p_{i,b} - x_i(k)\big] + \alpha_2\gamma_{2i}(k)\big[g_b - x_i(k)\big], \quad (10.50)$$

$$x_i(k+1) = x_i(k) + v_i(k+1), \quad (10.51)$$

where $\gamma_{1i}$ and $\gamma_{2i}$ are uniform random numbers in the interval $[0,1]$, $\phi(k)$ is the momentum function, and $\alpha_1$ and $\alpha_2$ are acceleration constants.

Particle Swarm Optimization Toolbox (PSOt)[42] developed by Brian Birge can be used to solve global optimization problems. The main function of the toolbox, `pso_Trelea_vectorized()` can be used to perform the optimization process, whose syntax is [sol,tr]=pso_Trelea_vectorized(*fun*,$n$,$v_M$,[$x_m$,$x_M$],key,options)

where *fun* is used to describe the objective function, $n$ is the number of decision variables, i.e., the length of vector $x$. These two variables must be provided, while others are optional. Variable $v_M$ is the maximum allowed speed, with default value of 4; $x_m$ and $x_M$ are the vectors of minimum and maximum values of the decision variables, with default values of $\pm 100$. The variable key is used to indicate what type of optimization is to be solved, with the default 0 is for minimization, and 1 is for maximization. The variable options is the control option. The returned variable sol is an $(n+1) \times 1$ vector, the first $n$ are the optimized decision variables $x$, and the $(n+1)$th the objective function. The returned variable tr records the intermediate results. In the function, Trelea algorithm is used to implement particle swarm optimization algorithm[43], in vectorized form. Clerc algorithm is also supported in the function[44].

The "vectorized" version of the objective function is allowed, which means that the simultaneous computation for a swarm of particles is evaluated. The computational efficiency is much higher than the ordinary scalar version. Note that the argument $x$ can be a matrix, whose $i$th column corresponds to the values of the $i$th particle, thus it should be expressed by $x(:,i)$. Examples are given below to demonstrate the particle swarm optimization method.

**Example 10.26.** Particle swarm optimization algorithm can be used to solve the unconstrained optimization problem in Example 10.24. The MATLAB function written below can be used to describe the objective function

```
function y=c10mpso4(x)
x1=x(:,1); x2=x(:,2); x3=(6+4*x1-2*x2)/3; x=[x x3]';
y1=[-2 1 1]*x; y2=[-1 1 0]*x; y=[1 2 3]*x;
ii=find(y1>9|y2<-4|x3'<0); y(ii)=100; y=y(:);
```

Please note that the format of the objective function is different from those presented earlier, and the optimal solution is $x^T = [-7, -11, 0]$.

```
>> x=pso_Trelea_vectorized('c10mpso4',2);
   [x(1:2); (6+4*x(1)-2*x(2))/3]
```

### 10.6.4 *Optimal Controller Design with Global Optimization Algorithms*

It can be seen from the earlier presentations that the advantages of using genetic algorithms and particle swarm optimization algorithms are that it is more likely to find global optimization solutions. Thus, in the optimal controller design problems, the use of these global optimization approaches may be useful to further solve the behavior of the controllers. Examples will be given to demonstrate the use of optimal controller design with genetic algorithms, and point out the unapplicable problems.

**Example 10.27.** For the OCD interface presented in Chapter 7, if the plant model is unstable, conventional optimization methods may find problems with initial controller selection. If global optimization algorithms are used, the problems can be solved easily. With the global optimization methods implemented, the facilities of OCD will be significantly improved.

Consider the unstable plant model

$$G(s) = \frac{s+2}{s^4 + 8s^3 + 4s^2 - s + 0.4}.$$

The Simulink model shown in Fig. 10-72(a) can be used, where to prevent the control signal from becoming large, an actuator saturation can be introduced, with the limits $\Delta = 5$. The objective function can be written as

```
function [sol,y]=c10funun(x,options)
sol=x; assignin('base','Kp',x(1));
assignin('base','Kd',x(2)); assignin('base','Ki',x(3));
[t_time,a,y_out]=sim('c10munsta.mdl',[0,10]); y=-y_out(end,1);
```

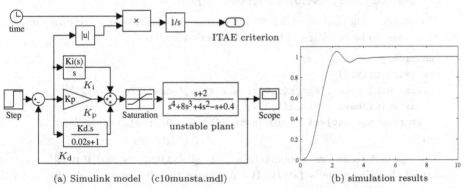

(a) Simulink model (c10munsta.mdl)        (b) simulation results

Fig. 10-72   Optimal PID controller for unstable plants.

Note that the objective function is to find the maximum values, thus a minus sign is used in the standard OCD problems. Assume that the parameters of the controllers are in the interval $(0.1, 100)$, the following MATLAB statements can be used to find the optimal PID controllers.

```
>> x1=gaopt([0.1*ones(3,1), 100*ones(3,1)],'c10funun')
   c10funun(x1(1:3))   % display the value of the objective function
```

The scope in the Simulink model should be opened to witness the optimization process. In the start of the optimization, it can be seen that very few of the entities in the population are stable. During the optimization process, it can be seen that more and more entities are stable, and the performance of the stable systems get better and better. Finally, the optimization process completes, and the optimal parameter vector is $x_1 = [71.9125, 83.2566, 0.2257]^T$, and the minimized objective function is 1.0678. The controller model can be written mathematically as

$$G_c(s) = 71.9125 + \frac{0.2257}{s} + \frac{83.2566s}{0.01s+1}.$$

The closed-loop step response can be obtained as shown in Fig. 10-72(b). It can be seen that by using the genetic algorithm, a suitable stabilizing controller can be obtained, and the behavior of the controller is satisfactory. It can also be seen that since random selective function is used in genetic algorithm, the results obtained each time are different. However, the variations in the controller parameters are very small each time, and the optimum objective function values are almost the same.

The rewritten objective function is shown below, where the objective function is written for the minimization problem

```
function y=c10funun1(x)
assignin('base','Kp',x(1)); assignin('base','Kd',x(2));
assignin('base','Ki',x(3));
[t_time,a,y_out]=sim('c10munsta.mdl',[0,10]); y=y_out(end,1);
```

With pattern search function, the optimized parameters are $x_2 = [30.6880, 35.5298, 0.2198]^T$, with minimized objective function of 1.0541. The controller parameters are not the same, while the value of objective function is similar.

```
>> x2=patternsearch(@c10funun1,rand(3,1))
```

The optimization method with PSO is a little complicated, since a vectorized objective function needs to be rewritten. The revised function is given by

```
function y=c10funun2(x)
for i=1:size(x,1)
    assignin('base','Kp',x(i,1)); assignin('base','Kd',x(i,2));
    assignin('base','Ki',x(i,3));
    [t_time,a,y_out]=sim('c10munsta.mdl',[0,10]); y(i)=y_out(end,1);
end
```

The optimal controller parameters are $x = [34.0046, 39.3404, 0.1905]^T$, and the minimized objective value is 1.0424. It can be seen that the control behavior under the three different PID controllers is very close.

```
>> x=pso_Trelea_vectorized('c10funun2',3)
```

**Example 10.28.** Now consider the fuzzy PD controller problem studied in Example 10.14. In the original example, $K_p$, $K_d$ and $K_u$ parameters are selected randomly. OCD program is now used to find the parameter setting problem. The new Simulink model for OCD program is established, where the ITAE integral is defined as the output of the model, as shown in Fig. 10-73(a). Selecting terminate time of $t_{end} = 4$, the optimal results with OCD can be obtained, $K_p = 1.9032, K_d = 0.5352, K_u = 2.2$. The objective function can be reduced from 0.228482 in that example to 0.0759. The output signal is shown in Fig. 10-73(b). It can be seen that the values of $K_p, K_d, K_u$ are reasonably chosen, and the control results are improved.

In the example, each simulation cycle may need up to 25 s of time, so genetic algorithm is not suitable for this example.

For the same plant model, if conventional PD controller is used, the Simulink model for OCD can be constructed as shown in Fig. 10-74(a). Actuator saturation can be introduced, with the limits $\Delta = 2$. With the use of OCD, the optimal PD controller can be designed, $G_c(s) = 1595.9 + 69.9s/(0.02s + 1)$. If the plant model are changed to $a = 5, 10, 30$, the

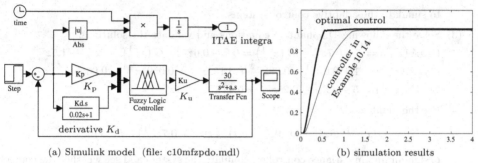

(a) Simulink model  (file: c10mfzpdo.mdl)          (b) simulation results

Fig. 10-73   Optimization results with fuzzy PD controller.

closed-loop step responses are shown in Fig. 10-74(b). It can be seen that better control results can be obtained for this example if conventional PD controller is used.

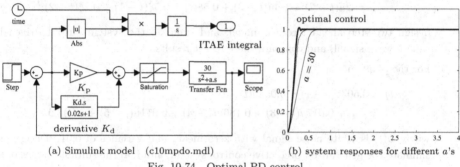

(a) Simulink model   (c10mpdo.mdl)          (b) system responses for different $a$'s

Fig. 10-74   Optimal PD control.

The genetic algorithm, particle swarm optimization algorithm, pattern search methods are all embedded in the current version of the interfaces of OCD and OptimPID. These algorithms can be selected directly from the relevant listboxes. Compared with traditional optimization algorithms, these algorithms are more likely to achieve global optimal solutions, however, the computation load is usually much higher than traditional algorithms.

## 10.7   Problems

(1) For the plant model

$$G(s) = \frac{\alpha_1 s^2 + \alpha_2 s + \alpha_3}{s^4 + 10s^3 + 35s^2 + 50s + 24},$$

try to explore the model reference adaptive control scheme, and find out the values of $\alpha_i$ which cannot be processed well with MRAS scheme.

(2) For the model reference adaptive control system shown in Fig. 10-6, remove the plant model and mask the rest of the system into a Simulink block as a model reference adaptive controller block, so that any plant model can be connected to the controller,

to simulate the adaptive control systems.

(3) Solve the following Diophantine equations and validate the solutions.
   (i)  $A\left(z^{-1}\right) = 1 - 0.7z^{-1}$, $B\left(z^{-1}\right) = 0.9 - 0.6z^{-1}$, $C\left(z^{-1}\right) = 2z^{-2} + 1.5z^{-3}$,
   (ii) $A\left(z^{-1}\right) = 1 + 0.6z^{-1} - 0.08z^{-2} + 0.152z^{-3} + 0.0591z^{-4} - 0.0365z^{-5}$,
        $B\left(z^{-1}\right) = 5 - 4z^{-1} - 0.25z^{-2} + 0.42z^{-3}$, $C\left(z^{-1}\right) = 1$.

(4) For the plant model

$$\left(1 - 1.28z^{-1} + 0.49z^{-2}\right) y(t) = \left(0.5 + 0.7z^{-1}\right) u(t - 1),$$

design minimum variance controller, simulate the system and see whether the control results are successful.

(5) For the system model

$$y(t) + 2.1y(t - 1) + 1.61y(t - 2) + 0.531y(t - 3) + 0.063y(t - 4)$$
$$= 2u(t - 2) + 1.3u(t - 3) + 0.5\xi(t) + 0.5\xi(t - 1) + 0.2\xi(t - 2),$$

design two-step ahead forecast model, and simulate the system output driven by square wave signal, and compare the forecast results.

(6) For the plant model [20]

$$y(t) = 0.503y(t - 1) - 0.053y(t - 2)$$
$$+ 0.017u(t - 3) + 0.186u(t - 4) + 0.011u(t - 5) + \omega(t)/\Delta,$$

where $\omega(t)$ is white noise signal with zero mean, and variance of 0.01. Design and simulate the generalized predictive control system, and find the suitable values of $m$, and $p$.

(7) Suppose the uncertain plant model is given by

$$G(s) = \frac{Ke^{-\theta s}}{\tau s + 1},$$

with nominal parameters $K = 5$, $\tau = 15$, and $\theta = 2$, and sampling interval of $T = 1$. Design a model predictive controller and analyze the closed-loop system. If the gain is changed to $K = 10$, simulation results.

(8) Consider the under-damped plant model [13]

$$G(s) = \frac{8611.77}{\left[(s + 0.55)^2 + 6^2\right]\left[(s + 0.25)^2 + 15.4^2\right]}.$$

Select suitable horizons and design model predictive controllers. If the plant model is changed to a non-minimum phase system, for instance, change the numerator of the plant to $28705(-s+0.3)$, redesign model predictive controller, and get the simulation results.

(9) Consider the following transfer function matrix of a multivariable plant

$$G(s) = \begin{bmatrix} \dfrac{12.8e^{-s}}{16.7s + 1} & \dfrac{-18.9e^{-3s}}{21s + 1} \\ \dfrac{6.6e^{-7s}}{10.9s + 1} & \dfrac{-19.4e^{-3s}}{14.4s + 1} \end{bmatrix}.$$

Design model predictive controller and show the simulation results.

(10) Consider the typical linear plant model

$$G(s) = \frac{e^{-10s}}{2s+1},$$

design various fuzzy and neural network controllers, and compare the results with the classical PID controllers. If the delay term is varying in a certain range, for instance, the delay constant $\tau \in (1, 30)$, compare again the control results.

(11) For the fuzzy PD controller illustrated in the text, if the values of $K_p$, and $K_d$ are very small, what kind of control behavior can be reached? Why? If better control results are expected, how to adjust the values of $K_p$, and $K_d$, or even the value $K_u$.

(12) For the sample points $(x_i, y_i)$ in Table 10-6, construct a neural network model, and fit the sample data in the interval $x \in (1, 10)$, draw the curve of the function. Try different network structures and compare the fitting results.

Table 10-6    Data in Problem (12).

| $x_i$ | 1 | 2 | 3 | 4 | 5 | 6 | 7 | 8 | 9 | 10 |
|---|---|---|---|---|---|---|---|---|---|---|
| $y_i$ | 244.0 | 221.0 | 208.0 | 208.0 | 211.5 | 216.0 | 219.0 | 221.0 | 221.5 | 220.0 |

(13) Assume that the measured data $(x, y)$ are given in Table 10-7. Use neural network to fit the surface in $(0.1, 0.1) \sim (1.1, 1.1)$ rectangle area, and show with three-dimensional plotting facilities.

Table 10-7    Data in Problem (13).

| $y_i$ | $x_1$ | $x_2$ | $x_3$ | $x_4$ | $x_5$ | $x_6$ | $x_7$ | $x_8$ | $x_9$ | $x_{10}$ | $x_{11}$ |
|---|---|---|---|---|---|---|---|---|---|---|---|
| 0 | 0.1 | 0.2 | 0.3 | 0.4 | 0.5 | 0.6 | 0.7 | 0.8 | 0.9 | 1 | 1.1 |
| 0.1 | 0.83041 | 0.82727 | 0.82406 | 0.82098 | 0.81824 | 0.8161 | 0.81481 | 0.81463 | 0.81579 | 0.81853 | 0.82304 |
| 0.2 | 0.83172 | 0.83249 | 0.83584 | 0.84201 | 0.85125 | 0.86376 | 0.87975 | 0.89935 | 0.92263 | 0.94959 | 0.9801 |
| 0.3 | 0.83587 | 0.84345 | 0.85631 | 0.87466 | 0.89867 | 0.9284 | 0.96377 | 1.0045 | 1.0502 | 1.1 | 1.1529 |
| 0.4 | 0.84286 | 0.86013 | 0.88537 | 0.91865 | 0.95985 | 1.0086 | 1.0642 | 1.1253 | 1.1904 | 1.257 | 1.3222 |
| 0.5 | 0.85268 | 0.88251 | 0.92286 | 0.97346 | 1.0336 | 1.1019 | 1.1764 | 1.254 | 1.3308 | 1.4017 | 1.4605 |
| 0.6 | 0.86532 | 0.91049 | 0.96847 | 1.0383 | 1.118 | 1.2046 | 1.2937 | 1.3793 | 1.4539 | 1.5086 | 1.5335 |
| 0.7 | 0.88078 | 0.94396 | 1.0217 | 1.1118 | 1.2102 | 1.311 | 1.4063 | 1.4859 | 1.5377 | 1.5484 | 1.5052 |
| 0.8 | 0.89904 | 0.98276 | 1.082 | 1.1922 | 1.3061 | 1.4138 | 1.5021 | 1.5555 | 1.5573 | 1.4915 | 1.346 |
| 0.9 | 0.92006 | 1.0266 | 1.1482 | 1.2768 | 1.4005 | 1.5034 | 1.5661 | 1.5678 | 1.4889 | 1.3156 | 1.0454 |
| 1 | 0.94381 | 1.0752 | 1.2191 | 1.3624 | 1.4866 | 1.5684 | 1.5821 | 1.5032 | 1.315 | 1.0155 | 0.62477 |
| 1.1 | 0.97023 | 1.1279 | 1.2929 | 1.4448 | 1.5564 | 1.5964 | 1.5341 | 1.3473 | 1.0321 | 0.61268 | 0.14763 |

(14) Select suitable initial parameters, such that the plant model in Example 10.17 can be controlled by the PID controller with radial basis neural network.

(15) Solve the nonlinear optimization problem.

$$\min_{(x,y)} \quad \sin(3xy) + xy + x + y.$$
$$\text{s.t.} \quad \begin{cases} -1 \leqslant x \leqslant 3 \\ -3 \leqslant y \leqslant 3 \end{cases}$$

(16) Consider the optimization problem of Rosenbrock's [45]

$$J = \min_{\boldsymbol{x} \text{ s.t. } -2.048 \leqslant x_{1,2} \leqslant 2.048} 100(x_1^2 - x_2) + (1 - x_1)^2.$$

Solve the problem with genetic algorithm, and compare the results with traditional optimization algorithms.

(17) De Jong's optimization problem [38] is a challenging benchmark problem of optimization problems

$$J = \min_{\boldsymbol{x}} \boldsymbol{x}^{\mathrm{T}} \boldsymbol{x} = \min_{\boldsymbol{x}} (x_1^2 + x_2^2 + \cdots + x_{20}^2).$$

If $-512 \leqslant x_i \leqslant 512, i = 1, 2, \cdots, 20$, find its solution, and compare the results with other traditional optimization algorithms.

(18) Solve the constrained optimization problem with genetic algorithm, and compare the results with traditional algorithms.

$$\min \qquad \frac{1}{2\cos x_6} \left[ x_1 x_2 (1 + x_5) + x_3 x_4 \left( 1 + \frac{31.5}{x_5} \right) \right].$$

$$\boldsymbol{x} \text{ s.t.} \begin{cases} 0.003079 x_1^3 x_2^3 x_5 - \cos^3 x_6 \geqslant 0 \\ 0.1017 x_3^3 x_4^3 - x_5^2 \cos^3 x_6 \geqslant 0 \\ 0.09939(1 + x_5) x_1^3 x_2^2 - \cos^2 x_6 \geqslant 0 \\ 0.1076(31.5 + x_5) x_3^3 x_4^2 - x_5^2 \cos^2 x_6 \geqslant 0 \\ x_3 x_4 (x_5 + 31.5) - x_5 [2(x_1 + 5) \cos x_6 + x_1 x_2 x_5] \geqslant 0 \\ 0.2 \leqslant x_1 \leqslant 0.5, 14 < x_2 \leqslant 22, 0.35 \leqslant x_3 \leqslant 0.6 \\ 16 \leqslant x_4 \leqslant 22, 5.8 \leqslant x_5 \leqslant 6.5, 0.14 \leqslant x_6 \leqslant 0.2618 \end{cases}$$

(19) Design optimal PID controllers for the following plants, with genetic algorithms

(i) non-minimum phase plant $\quad G(s) = \dfrac{-s + 5}{s^3 + 4s^2 + 5s + 6}$,

(ii) non-minimum phase unstable plant $\quad G(s) = \dfrac{-0.2s + 5}{s^4 + 3s^3 + 5s^2 - 6s + 9}$,

(iii) unstable discrete system $\quad H(z) = \dfrac{4z - 2}{z^4 + 2.9z^3 + 2.4z^2 + 1.4z + 0.4}$.

## Bibliography and References

[1] Fu K S. Learning control systems and intelligent control systems: an intersection of artificial intelligence and automatic control. IEEE Transaction on Automatic Control, 1971, AC-16(1):70–72

[2] Li R H. Theory and methods of intelligent control. Xi'an: Xi'an Electronics Science and Technology University Press, 1999. (In Chinese)

[3] Cai Z X. Intelligent control — fundamentals and applications. Beijing: National Defence Industry Press, 1998. (In Chinese)

[4] Landau I D. Adaptive control — the model reference approach. New York: Marcel Dekker, 1979

[5] Gawthrop P J. Self-tuning control. Vol X, Control Systems, Robotics, and Automation. In: Unbehauen H, ed. Encyclopedia of Life Support Sciences, UNESCO. 2004

[6] Egardt B. Stability of adaptive controllers. Berlin: Springer-Verlag, 1979

[7] Xu X H. Model reference adaptive control systems. Shenyang: Lecture notes of Northeast Institute of Technology, 1982

[8] Åström K J, Wittenmark B. On self-tuning regulators. Automatica, 1973, 9:185–199

[9] Åström K J, Wittenmark B. Adaptive control. Reading: Addison-Wesley Inc, 1989

[10] Han Z J. Adaptive control. Beijing: Tsinghua University Press, 1995. (In Chinese)

[11] Mościński J, Ogonowski Z. Advanced control with MATLAB and Simulink. London: Ellis Horwood, 1995

[12] Garcia C E, Prett D M, Morari M. Model predictive control: theory and practice a survey. Automatica, 1989, 25(3):335–348

[13] Xi Y G. Predictive control. Beijing: National Defence Industry Press, 1993. (In Chinese)

[14] Cutler C R, Ramaker B L. Dynamic matrix control — a computer control algorithm. Proceedings of Joint Automatic Control Conference, Paper WP5-B, San Francisco, 1980

[15] Richalet J, Rault A, Testud J L, et al. Model predictive heuristic control: applications to industrial processes. Automatica, 1978, 14(5):413–428

[16] Bemporad A, Morari M, Ricker N L. Model predictive control toolbox user's manual. MathWorks, 2013

[17] Richalet J. Model predictive heuristic control: applocations to industrial processes. Automatica, 1978, 14(5):413–428

[18] Clarke D W, Mohtadi C, Tuffs P S. Generalized predictive control — Part I. The basic algorithm. Automatica, 1987, 23:137–148

[19] Clarke D W, Mohtadi C, Tuffs P S. Generalized predictive control — Part II. Extensions and interpretations. Automatica, 1987, 23:149–160

[20] Wang W. Theory and applications of generalized predictive control. Beijing: Science Press, 1998. (In Chinese)

[21] Zadeh L A. Fuzzy sets. Information and Control, 1965, 8:338–353

[22] Zhu J. Principles and applications of fuzzy control. Beijing: China Machine Press, 1995. (In Chinese)

[23] J K Liu. MATLAB simulations of advanced PID controllers. Beijing: Publishing House of Electronics Industry, 2002. (In Chinese)

[24] Hagan M T, Demuth H B, Beale M H. Neural network design. PWS Publishing Company, 1995

[25] Hunt K J, Sbarbaro D, Zbikowski R, Gawthrop P J. Neural networks for control systems — a survey. Automatica, 1992, 28(6):1083–1112

[26] Nørgaard N, Ravn O, Poulsen N K, Hansen L K. Neural networks for modelling and control of dynamic systems. London: Springer-Verlag, 2000

[27] Uchiyama M. Formation of high-speed motion pattern of a mechanical arm by trial. Transactions of the Society of Instrument and Control Engineers, 1978, 14(6):706–712

[28] Arimoto S, Kawamura S, Miyazaki F. Bettering operation of robots by learning. Journal of Robotic Systems, 1984, 1:123–140

[29] Moore K L, Dahleh M, Bhattacharyya S P. Iterative learning control: a survey and new results. Journal of Robotic Systems, 1992, 9(5):563–594

[30] Moore K, Chen Y Q, Ahn H S. Iterative learning control: a tutorial and big picture view. Proceedings of IEEE Conference on Decision and Control. 2006 2352–2357

[31] Bristow D A, Tharayil M, Alleyne A G. A survey of iterative learning control: A learning-based method for high-performance tracking control. IEEE Control Systems Magazine, 2006, 26(3):96–114

[32] Ahn H S, Chen Y Q, Moore K L. Iterative learning control: brief survey and categorization. IEEE Transactions on Systems, Man, and Cybernetics, Part-C, 2007,

37(6):1099–1121

[33] Xie S L, Tian S P, Xie Z D. Theory and applications of iterative learning control. Beijing: Science Press, 2005. (In Chinese)

[34] Chen Y Q, Moore K, Yu J, *et al.* Iterative learning control and repetitive control in hard disk drive industry — a tutorial. Proceedings of IEEE Conference on Decision and Control. 2006

[35] Sugie T, Ono T. An iterative learning control law for dynamical systems. Automatica, 1991, 27(4):729–732

[36] Ahn H-S, Moore K L, Chen Y Q. Iterative learning control — parametric interval robustness and stochastic convergence. Springer-verlag, 2007

[37] Goldberg D E. Genetic algorithms in search, optimzation and machine learning. Addison-Wesley, 1989

[38] Chipperfield A, Fleming P. Genetic algorithm toolbox user's guide. Department of Automatic Control and Systems Engineering, University of Sheffield, 1994

[39] Houck C R, Joines J A, Kay M G. A genetic algorithm for function optimization: a MATLAB implementation. Electronic version, 1995

[40] The MathWorks Inc. Genetic algorithm and direct search toolbox — User's guide 2.0, 2005

[41] Kennedy J, Eberhart R. Particle swarm optimization. Proceedings of IEEE International Conference on Neural Networks. Perth, Australia, 1995: 1942–1948

[42] Birge B. PSOt, a particle swarm optimization toolbox for MATLAB. Proceedings of the 2003 IEEE Swarm Intelligence Symposium. Indianapolis, 2003: 182–186

[43] Trelea I C. The particle swarm optimization algorithm: convergence analysis and parameter selection. Information Processing Letters, 2003, 85(6):317–325

[44] Clerc M, Kennedy J. The particle swarm: explosion, stability, and convergence in a multidimensional complex space. IEEE Transactions on Evolutionary Computation, 2002, 6(1):58–73

[45] Rosenbrock H H. An automatic method for finding the greatest or least value of a function. Computer Journal, 1960, 3:175–184

# Chapter 11

# Analysis and Design of Fractional-order Systems

Fractional-order system theory is an active field of research over the last two decades. In recent years, many progresses have been made in both fractional-order calculus and fractional-order control. The research on fractional-order control has both theoretical value and practical perspectives.

The so-called "fractional-order systems" really mean that the order of the systems are no longer integers, and this is different from all discussed in the book so far. We all know that $d^n y/dt^n$ represents the $n$th order derivative of $y$ with respect to $t$. What happens if $n = 1/2$? This was the question a famous French mathematician Guillaume François Antoine L'Hôpital asked one of the inventors of calculus, Gottfried Wilhelm Leibniz[1–3], 300 years ago. From that time on, researchers began to study fractional-order calculus problems. Thus, fractional-order calculus is a 300 year-old topic, however, earlier work focused on pure mathematics. In the 19th century, various definitions on fractional-order calculus appeared, and it was not until 1960, the first publication on non-integer order integrator appeared in the field of control[4], however, few attention to the topics were received. In late 1990's, fractional-order PID controller appeared[5–7].

The operator $\mathscr{D}^\alpha$ is used in this book to describe fractional-order differentiation and integration. When $\alpha > 0$, $\alpha$th order derivative is used, while $\alpha < 0$ means $-\alpha$th order integration, and $\alpha = 0$ means the original function. This unified notation will be used throughout the book.

Strictly speaking, "fractional-order" is a misused term. The precise one should be "non-integer-order", since the order can either be fractional, or an irrational, or even complex numbers. For instance, $d^{\sqrt{2}} y/dt^{\sqrt{2}}$ means the $\sqrt{2}$th order derivative. However, the word "fractional-order" was used for a very time among the researchers. In this book, "fractional-order" is used, however, it actually means "non-integer-order".

In Section 11.1, various definitions on fractional-order calculus and their MATLAB implementations are presented. Properties of fractional-order calculus are also presented. Mittag–Leffler functions and commonly used Laplace transforms in fractional-order functions are also presented. In Section 11.2, numerical computations of fractional-order derivatives are presented. Also Mittag–Leffler functions and commonly used Laplace transforms in fractional-order functions are also presented. Section 11.3 presents the numerical and analytical solutions of linear fractional-order differential equations. The fractional-order transfer function is used as an example to demonstrate object-oriented programming in Section 11.4, where the methods of class creation, overload function design are all illustrated. With the programming technique, linear fractional-order systems analysis — stability, time and frequency domain analysis are presented. In Section 11.5, integer-order approximation to fractional-order operators and fractional-order systems are presented, and sub-optimal reduction technique are proposed. In Section 11.6, block diagram-based nonlinear fractional-order system simulation techniques are illustrated. In Section 11.7, optimal design methods and interface of fractional-order PID controllers for fractional-order plants are presented.

## 11.1    Definitions and Numerical Computations in Fractional-order Calculus

In the development of fractional-order calculus, various definitions were proposed and applied. The most widely used Cauchy integral formula, Grünwald–Letnikov definition, Riemann–Liouville definition and Caputo definition are all extended directly from integral-order calculus. In this section, the definitions and their relationships are given, then the numerical computation and properties are presented.

### 11.1.1    *Definitions of Fractional-order Calculus*

**1. Fractional Cauchy integral formula**

The formula is extended directly from its integer-order counterpart

$$\mathscr{D}_t^\gamma f(t) = \frac{\Gamma(\gamma + 1)}{2\pi \mathrm{j}} \int_C \frac{f(\tau)}{(\tau - t)^{\gamma+1}} \mathrm{d}\tau, \tag{11.1}$$

where C is the closed-path that encircles all the poles of the function $f(t)$, and $\mathscr{D}_t$ is the fractional-order differentiation operator.

**2. Grünwald–Letnikov definition**

The definition of fractional-order differentiation is

$$_{t_0}\mathscr{D}_t^\alpha f(t) = \lim_{h \to 0} \frac{1}{h^\alpha} \sum_{j=0}^{[(t-t_0)/h]} (-1)^j \binom{\alpha}{j} f(t - jh), \tag{11.2}$$

where $w_j^{(\alpha)} = (-1)^j \binom{\alpha}{j}$ is the binomial coefficients of $(1 - z)^\alpha$, and it can be obtained iteratively from

$$w_0^{(\alpha)} = 1, \ w_j^{(\alpha)} = \left(1 - \frac{\alpha + 1}{j}\right) w_{j-1}^{(\alpha)}, \ j = 1, 2, \cdots. \tag{11.3}$$

The following formula can be used in calculating fractional-order derivative

$$_{t_0}\mathscr{D}_t^\alpha f(t) \approx \frac{1}{h^\alpha} \sum_{j=0}^{[(t-t_0)/h]} w_j^{(\alpha)} f(t - jh). \tag{11.4}$$

If step size $h$ is small enough, Eqn. (11.4) can be used to directly evaluate the approximate values of fractional-order differentiation. It can be shown that[2] the accuracy of the definition is $o(h)$.

### 3. Riemann–Liouville definition

Fractional-order integral is defined as

$$_{t_0}\mathscr{D}_t^{-\alpha} f(t) = \frac{1}{\Gamma(\alpha)} \int_{t_0}^t \frac{f(\tau)}{(t - \tau)^{1-\alpha}} d\tau, \tag{11.5}$$

where $0 < \alpha < 1$, and $t_0$ is the initial instance. Normally $t_0 = 0$, and the notation is simplified to $\mathscr{D}_t^{-\alpha} f(t)$. Riemann–Liouville definition is the most widely used definition in fractional-order calculus. Especially the subscripts on both sides of $\mathscr{D}$ are the lower and upper bounds in the integral[8].

Fractional-order differentiation can also be defined. Assume that the order $\alpha$ of differentiation satisfies $n - 1 < \beta \leqslant n$, the differentiation is defined as

$$_{t_0}\mathscr{D}_t^\beta f(t) = \frac{d^n}{dt^n} \left[ _{t_0}\mathscr{D}_t^{-(n-\beta)} f(t) \right] = \frac{1}{\Gamma(n-\beta)} \frac{d^n}{dt^n} \left[ \int_{t_0}^t \frac{f(\tau)}{(t-\tau)^{\beta-n+1}} d\tau \right]. \tag{11.6}$$

### 4. Caputo definition

The definition of Caputo fractional-order differentiation is

$$_{t_0}\mathscr{D}_t^\alpha f(t) = \frac{1}{\Gamma(1-\gamma)} \int_{t_0}^t \frac{f^{(m+1)}(\tau)}{(t - \tau)^\gamma} d\tau, \tag{11.7}$$

where $\alpha = m + \gamma$, or $m = \lfloor \alpha \rfloor$ is an integer such that $0 < \gamma < 1$.

Similarly, the Caputo fractional-order integral is defined as

$$_{t_0}\mathscr{D}_t^{-\alpha} f(t) = \frac{1}{\Gamma(\alpha)} \int_{t_0}^t \frac{f(\tau)}{(t - \tau)^{1-\alpha}} d\tau, \quad \alpha > 0, \tag{11.8}$$

and it is exactly the same as Riemann–Liouville definition in Eqn. (11.5).

## 11.1.2 *The Relationship of Different Definitions*

It can be shown that for a wide class of practical functions, the Grünwald–Letnikov and Riemann–Liouville definitions are equivalent[2]. In this book, we shall not distinguish them.

The major differences of Caputo definition and Riemann–Liouville definition are that the former considers the nonzero initial condition problems. Thus, Caputo definition is more suitable to deal with fractional-order differential equations with nonzero initial conditions.

If the initial value of function $f(t)$ is nonzero, and $\alpha \in (0,1)$, compared with the definitions of Caputo's and Riemann–Liouville's, it can be seen that

$$\substack{C \\ t_0} \mathscr{D}_t^\alpha f(t) = \substack{RL \\ t_0} \mathscr{D}_t^\alpha (f(t) - f(t_0)), \tag{11.9}$$

where the fractional-order derivative of constant $f(t_0)$ is

$$\substack{RL \\ t_0} \mathscr{D}_t^\alpha f(t_0) = \frac{f(t_0)(t - t_0)^{-\alpha}}{\Gamma(1 - \alpha)}. \tag{11.10}$$

The relationship of these two definitions are

$$\substack{C \\ t_0} \mathscr{D}_t^\alpha f(t) = \substack{RL \\ t_0} \mathscr{D}_t^\alpha f(t) - \frac{f(t_0)(t - t_0)^{-\alpha}}{\Gamma(1 - \alpha)}. \tag{11.11}$$

More generally, if $\alpha > 1$, denote $m = \lceil \alpha \rceil$, then

$$\substack{C \\ t_0} \mathscr{D}_t^\alpha f(t) = \substack{RL \\ t_0} \mathscr{D}_t^\alpha f(t) - \sum_{k=0}^{m-1} \frac{f^{(k)}(t_0)}{\Gamma(k - \alpha + 1)}(t - t_0)^{k-\alpha}, \tag{11.12}$$

and the relationship shown for $0 < \alpha < 1$ is just a special case of the formula.

### 11.1.3    *Properties of Fractional-order Calculus*

Some of the important properties of fractional-order calculus are summarized below without proofs[9]

(1) The fractional-order differentiation $\substack{ \\ t_0} \mathscr{D}_t^\alpha f(t)$ of an analytic function $f(t)$ with respect to $t$ is also analytic.

(2) If $\alpha = n$, the fractional-order derivative is identical to integer-order derivative, and also $\substack{ \\ t_0} \mathscr{D}_t^0 f(t) = f(t)$.

(3) The fractional-order differentiation is linear, i.e., for any constants $c, d$

$$\substack{ \\ t_0} \mathscr{D}_t^\alpha \Big[ cf(t) + dg(t) \Big] = c \,\substack{ \\ t_0} \mathscr{D}_t^\alpha f(t) + d \,\substack{ \\ t_0} \mathscr{D}_t^\alpha g(t). \tag{11.13}$$

(4) Fractional-order differentiation operators satisfy commutative-law, i.e.,

$$\substack{ \\ t_0} \mathscr{D}_t^\alpha \Big[ \substack{ \\ t_0} \mathscr{D}_t^\beta f(t) \Big] = \substack{ \\ t_0} \mathscr{D}_t^\beta \Big[ \substack{ \\ t_0} \mathscr{D}_t^\alpha f(t) \Big] = \substack{ \\ t_0} \mathscr{D}_t^{\alpha+\beta} f(t). \tag{11.14}$$

(5) The Laplace transform of the fractional-order derivative is

$$\mathscr{L}\Big[ \substack{ \\ t_0} \mathscr{D}_t^\alpha f(t) \Big] = s^\alpha \mathscr{L}\big[ f(t) \big] - \sum_{k=1}^{n-1} s^k \Big[ \substack{ \\ t_0} \mathscr{D}_t^{\alpha-k-1} f(t) \Big]_{t=t_0}. \tag{11.15}$$

Especially, if the initial values of the function $f(t)$ and its derivatives at $t = t_0$ are all zero, $\mathscr{L}\Big[ \substack{ \\ t_0} \mathscr{D}_t^\alpha f(t) \Big] = s^\alpha \mathscr{L}\big[ f(t) \big]$. It is the same as the one in integer-order calculus, and it is the basis of fractional-order transfer functions, for the analysis and design of fractional-order systems.

## 11.2   Numerical Computations in Fractional-order Calculus

In this section, numerical computation of Grünwald–Letnikov and Caputo derivatives of given function $f(t)$ are presented. Also, the computations of the important Mittag–Leffler functions are presented.

### 11.2.1  *Numerical Solutions with Grünwald–Letnikov Definition*

With Grünwald–Letnikov definition, the following MATLAB function can be immediately written to evaluate the fractional-order differentiations[10], which implements directly Eqns. (11.3) and (11.4).

```
function dy=glfdiff(y,t,gam)
h=t(2)-t(1); w=1; y=y(:); t=t(:); a0=y(1); dy(1)=0;
if a0~=0 & gam>0, dy(1)=sign(a0)*inf; end
for j=2:length(t), w(j)=w(j-1)*(1-(gam+1)/(j-1)); end
for i=2:length(t), dy(i)=w(1:i)*[y(i:-1:1)]/h^gam; end
```

The syntax of the function is $y_1 = \texttt{glfdiff}(y,t,\gamma)$, where $y$ and $t$ are the vectors composed of sample values of the given function and time, respectively. The vector $t$ should be evenly spaced. The argument $\gamma$ is the order. The $\gamma$th order derivative of $y$ is returned in $y_1$ vector. If $y(t_0) \neq 0$, the first value in the derivative is set to infinity.

**Example 11.1.** In integer-order calculus, it is known that the derivative function of a step function is an impulse function, and first-order integral is straight line. The following statements can be used to calculate the 0.5th order derivative and integral, and the results are shown in Fig. 11-1.

```
>> t=0:0.01:5; u=ones(size(t)); y1=glfdiff(u,t,0.5);
   y2=glfdiff(u,t,-0.5); plot(t,y1,'-',t,y2,'--')
```

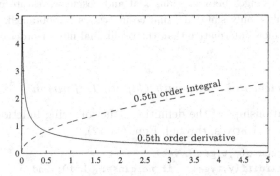

Fig. 11-1   Fractional derivative and integral of a step function.

It can be seen that the fractional integrals are no longer straight lines, and the derivatives are no longer impulse functions. Gradual changes are observed in fractional-order integrals and derivatives. The fractional-order calculus is regarded as having memories.

**Example 11.2.** Consider the sinusoidal function $f(t) = \sin(3t + 1)$. Its 0.3th order derivative is shown in Fig. 11-2(a), and the surface plots for the derivatives of different orders are shown in Fig. 11-2(b).

```
>> t=0:0.01:5; u=sin(3*t+1); ww=0:0.1:1; Y=[];
   y1=glfdiff(u,t,0.3); y2=3^0.3*sin(3*t+1+0.3*pi/2);
```

```
plot(t,y1,'-',t,y2,'--'), figure
for w=ww, Y=[Y; glfdiff(u,t,w)]; end, surf(t,ww,Y)
```

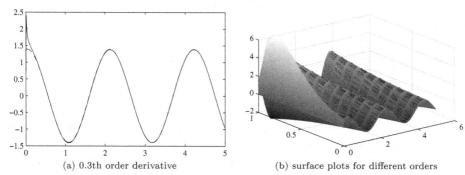

(a) 0.3th order derivative     (b) surface plots for different orders

Fig. 11-2   Fractional-order differentiation of sinusoidal function $f(t) = \sin(3t + 1)$.

The $\alpha$th order derivative under Cauchy integral formula is $3^{\alpha} \sin(3t + 1 + \alpha\pi/2)$. This derivative curve is also given in Fig. 11-2(a). It can be seen that the major difference between the two definitions is, in Grünwald–Letnikov definition, the initial values of $f(t)$ is assumed to be zero for $t \leqslant 0$. Thus, the function jumped from 0 to $\sin 1$ at time $t = 0_+$. While in the Cauchy formula, the function at $t \leqslant 0$ time is still assumed to be $\sin(3t + 1)$, thus there is no jump at $t = 0_+$.

It can be seen from the fractional-order derivatives of sinusoidal wave in Fig. 11-2(b) that gradual changes between sinusoidal and cosine waves are obtained, while in integer-order calculus, only sinusoidal and cosine waves are obtained. Thus, fractional-order calculus are more informative than the traditional integer-order calculus.

### 11.2.2   *Numerical Solutions with Caputo Definition*

From the relationships of the definitions, the following function can be used to calculate Caputo derivatives, through Eqn. (11.12).

```
function dy=caputo(y,t,gam,L,vec)
t0=t(1); dy=glfdiff(y,t,gam); if nargin<=3, L=10; end
if gam>0, m=ceil(gam); if gam<=1, vec=y(1); end
    for k=0:m-1, dy=dy-vec(k+1)*(t-t0).^(k-gam)./gamma(k+1-gam); end
    yy1=interp1(t(L+1:end),dy(L+1:end),t(2:L),'spline'); dy(2:L)=yy1;
end
```

The syntax of the function is $y_1$=caputo($y,t,\alpha,y_0,L$) , where if $\alpha \leqslant 0$, the results of Grünwald–Letnikov are returned directly; If $\alpha < 1$, the initial value of $y(t_0)$ is directly extracted from vector $y$. If $\alpha > 1$, $y_0 = [y(t_0), y'(t_0), \cdots, y^{(m-1)}(t_0)]$ should be provided, where $m = \lceil \alpha \rceil$. In numerical implementation, it is always found that the first few terms may have large errors, thus it is better to reconstruct the first $L$ terms with interpolation approaches. The default value of $L$ is 10, however, if the order of differentiation is high, $L$ should be increased.

**Example 11.3.** Consider the function $f(t) = \sin(3t + 1)$ studied in Example 11.2. It can be seen that at $t = 0$, the initial value of the function is $f(0) = \sin 1$. The difference between the two definitions is $d(t) = t^{-0.3} \sin 1/\Gamma(0.7)$. The following statements can be used to find the 0.3th order derivatives using Grünwald–Letnikov definition and Caputo definition, as shown in Fig. 11-3(a). The difference is also shown.

```
>> t=0:0.01:pi; y=sin(3*t+1); d=t.^(-0.3)*sin(1)/gamma(0.7);
   y1=glfdiff(y,t,0.3); y2=caputo(y,t,0.3); plot(t,y1,t,y2,'--',t,d,':')
```

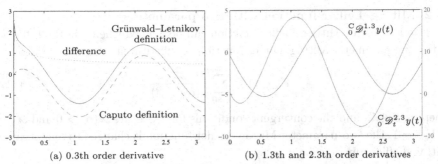

(a) 0.3th order derivative　　　　(b) 1.3th and 2.3th order derivatives

Fig. 11-3　Differentiation with Caputo definition.

Since ${}_{0}^{C}\mathscr{D}_{t}^{2.3}y(t)$ is to be calculated, the initial values $y'(0), y''(0)$ are needed. These values can be obtained with symbolic computation and convert the result back to double precision variables. The 1.3th and 2.3th order derivatives can also be obtained as shown in Fig. 11-3(b).

```
>> syms t; y=sin(3*t+1); y00=sin(1); y10=double(subs(diff(y,t),t,0));
   y20=double(subs(diff(y,t,2),t,0)); t=0:0.01:pi; y=sin(3*t+1);
   y1=caputo(y,t,1.3,[y00 y10],15); y2=caputo(y,t,2.3,[y00,y10,y20],40);
   plotyy(t,y1,t,y2)
```

### 11.2.3　*Mittag–Leffler Functions and Their Computations*

We all know that the exponential function is very important in the solutions of integer-order systems. Like exponential function in integer-order systems, the so-called Mittag–Leffler can be regarded as an extension of exponential functions to fractional-order calculus.

### 1. Mittag–Leffler function with one parameter
The definition is

$$\mathscr{E}_\alpha(z) = \sum_{k=0}^{\infty} \frac{z^k}{\Gamma(\alpha k + 1)}, \tag{11.16}$$

where $\alpha \in \mathbb{C}$. The convergent condition for the infinite series is $\mathscr{R}(\alpha) > 0$.

It is obvious that exponential function $e^z$ is a particular case of Mittag–Leffler function, with $\alpha = 1$.

$$\mathscr{E}_1(z) = \sum_{k=0}^{\infty} \frac{z^k}{\Gamma(k+1)} = \sum_{k=0}^{\infty} \frac{z^k}{k!} = e^z. \tag{11.17}$$

Other particular cases of Mittag–Leffler functions can be derived

$$\mathscr{E}_2(z) = \sum_{k=0}^{\infty} \frac{z^k}{\Gamma(2k+1)} = \sum_{k=0}^{\infty} \frac{(\sqrt{z})^{2k}}{(2k)!} = \cosh \sqrt{z}, \qquad (11.18)$$

$$\mathscr{E}_{1/2}(z) = \sum_{k=0}^{\infty} \frac{z^k}{\Gamma(k/2+1)} = e^{z^2}(1 + \operatorname{erf}(z)) = e^{z^2}\operatorname{erfc}(-z). \qquad (11.19)$$

## 2. Mittag–Leffler function with two parameters

Two-parameter Mittag–Leffler function can be defined when 1 in the $\Gamma$ function of the one-parameter Mittag–Leffler function is substituted by a free variable $\beta$

$$\mathscr{E}_{\alpha,\beta}(z) = \sum_{k=0}^{\infty} \frac{z^k}{\Gamma(\alpha k + \beta)}, \qquad (11.20)$$

where $\alpha, \beta \in \mathbb{C}$, and the convergent conditions for $z \in \mathbb{C}$ are $\mathscr{R}(\alpha) > 0$ and $\mathscr{R}(\beta) > 0$. If $\beta = 1$, the two-parameter Mittag–Leffler function is changed to one-parameter Mittag–Leffler function, i.e.,

$$\mathscr{E}_{\alpha,1}(z) = \mathscr{E}_{\alpha}(z). \qquad (11.21)$$

Besides, three- and four-parameter generalized Mittag–Leffler functions can also be defined[11]. A MATLAB function ml_func() for the computation of generalized Mittag–Leffler functions and their integer-order derivatives[5].

```
function f=ml_func(aa,z,n,eps0)
aa=[aa,1,1,1]; a=aa(1); b=aa(2); c=aa(3); q=aa(4);
f=0; k=0; fa=1; if nargin<4, eps0=eps; end
if nargin<3, n=0; end
if n==0
    while norm(fa,1)>=eps0
        fa=gamma(k*q+c)/gamma(c)/gamma(k+1)/gamma(a*k+b)*z.^k;
        f=f+fa; k=k+1;
    end
    if ~isfinite(f(1))
        if c==1 & q==1
            f=mlf(a,b,z,round(-log10(eps0))); f=reshape(f,size(z));
        else, error('Error: truncation method failed'); end, end
else
    aa(2)=aa(2)+n*aa(1); aa(3)=aa(3)+aa(4)*n;
    f=gamma(q*n+c)/gamma(c)*ml_func(aa,z,0,eps0);
end
```

The syntax of the function is $y = \texttt{ml\_func}(v,z,n,\epsilon)$, where $z$ is a vector, and the vector $v$ can be set to $v = \alpha$ or $v = [\alpha, \beta]$, to indicate one- or two-parameter Mittag–Leffler functions. Vector $v$ can also be assigned to a three or four element vector, $v = [\alpha, \beta, \gamma]$, or $v = [\alpha, \beta, \gamma, c]$, to indicate three- or four-parameter Mittag–Leffler functions. The argument $n$ is the order of derivative for the Mittag–Leffler function. The argument $\epsilon$ is the error tolerance. Since truncation algorithm is used in the function, the speed of the function is relatively fast, however, the values may sometimes become infinite. In this case, the mlf() function[12] is embedded to tackle the problem. However, the speed may become very slow. The output vector $y$ is the Mittag–Leffler function.

**Example 11.4.** The following statements can be used to draw the Mittag–Leffler function $\mathscr{E}_1(-t)$, $\mathscr{E}_{3/2,3/2}(-t)$, and $\mathscr{E}_{1,2}(-t)$, as shown in Fig. 11-4. The exponential function is also drawn. It can be seen that $\mathscr{E}_1(-t)$ is the same as $e^{-t}$, and the decay rates of the other two curves are slower than exponential function.

```
>> t=0:0.1:5; y1=ml_func(1,-t); y2=ml_func([1,2],-t);
   y3=ml_func([3/2,3/2],-t); plot(t,y1,t,y2,t,y3)
```

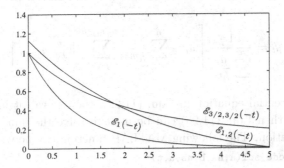

Fig. 11-4   Mittag–Leffler function curves.

## 11.3   Solutions of Linear Fractional-order Systems

Fractional-order systems are the direct extension of integer-order systems. In practical applications, there are some systems which can only be expressed accurately with fractional-order differential equations. In this section, analytical solutions for some linear fractional-order differential equations are first presented, and Mittag–Leffler functions are normally used to express the analytical solutions. For more linear fractional-order differential equation, closed-form numerical solution algorithms are presented.

### 11.3.1   *Numerical Solutions of Linear Fractional-order Differential Equations*

The typical form of linear fractional-order differential equation is given by

$$a_1 {}_{t_0}\mathscr{D}^{\eta_1} y(t) + a_2 {}_{t_0}\mathscr{D}^{\eta_2} y(t) + \cdots + a_{n-1} {}_{t_0}\mathscr{D}^{\eta_{n-1}} y(t) + a_n {}_{t_0}\mathscr{D}^{\eta_n} y(t)$$
$$= b_1 {}_{t_0}\mathscr{D}^{\gamma_1} u(t) + b_2 {}_{t_0}\mathscr{D}^{\gamma_2} u(t) + \cdots + b_m {}_{t_0}\mathscr{D}^{\gamma_m} u(t), \tag{11.22}$$

where $b_i$ and $a_i$ are real coefficients, and $\gamma_i$ and $\eta_i$ are orders.

Let us consider a simpler differential equation

$$a_1 \, {}_{t_0}\mathscr{D}_t^{\eta_1} y(t) + a_2 \, {}_{t_0}\mathscr{D}_t^{\eta_2} y(t) + \cdots + a_{n-1} \, {}_{t_0}\mathscr{D}_t^{\eta_{n-1}} y(t) + a_n \mathscr{D}_t^{\eta_n} y(t) = u(t), \quad (11.23)$$

where $u(t)$ is a given function. The Grünwald–Letnikov definition given in Eqn. (11.4) can be used directly, and the closed-form solution to the original differential equation is written as

$$_{t_0}\mathscr{D}_t^{\eta_i} y(t) \approx \frac{1}{h^{\eta_i}} \sum_{j=0}^{[(t-t_0)/h]} w_j^{(\eta_i)} y_{t-jh} = \frac{1}{h^{\eta_i}} \left[ y_t + \sum_{j=1}^{[(t-t_0)/h]} w_j^{(\eta_i)} y_{t-jh} \right], \quad (11.24)$$

where $w_0^{(\beta_i)}$ can be evaluated recursively from Eqn. (11.3). Substitute it back to the original equation, the closed-form solution of the differential equation can be written as[10]

$$y_t = \frac{1}{\displaystyle\sum_{i=1}^{n} \frac{a_i}{h^{\eta_i}}} \left[ u_t - \sum_{i=1}^{n} \frac{a_i}{h^{\eta_i}} \sum_{j=1}^{[(t-t_0)/h]} w_j^{(\eta_i)} y_{t-jh} \right]. \quad (11.25)$$

For the differential equation in Eqn. (11.22), the equivalent input $u(t)$ can be calculated first, then Eqn. (11.25) can be used to solve the numerical solution of the original equation. The following MATLAB function can be written

```
function y=fode_sol(a,na,b,nb,u,t)
h=t(2)-t(1); D=sum(a./[h.^na]); nT=length(t);
vec=[na nb]; D1=b(:)./h.^nb(:); nA=length(a);
y1=zeros(nT,1); W=ones(nT,length(vec));
for j=2:nT, W(j,:)=W(j-1,:).*(1-(vec+1)/(j-1)); end
for i=2:nT,
    A=[y1(i-1:-1:1)]'*W(2:i,1:nA);
    y1(i)=(u(i)-sum(A.*a./[h.^na]))/D;
end
for i=2:nT, y(i)=(W(1:i,nA+1:end)*D1)'*[y1(i:-1:1)]; end
```

The syntax of the function is $y = \text{fode\_sol}(a, \eta, b, \gamma, u, t)$ , where time vector $t$ and input vector $u$ should be given, and $y$ returns the numerical solution, vectors $a$ and $\eta$ are the coefficients and orders of output $y(t)$ in the equation, while $b$ and $\gamma$ are the coefficients and orders of input signal $u(t)$.

**Example 11.5.** Consider the linear fractional-order differential equation

$$\mathscr{D}^{1.6}y(t) + 10\mathscr{D}^{1.2}y(t) + 35\mathscr{D}^{0.8}y(t) + 50\mathscr{D}^{0.4}y(t) + 24y(t) = \mathscr{D}^{1.2}u(t) + 3\mathscr{D}^{0.4}u(t) + 5u(t),$$

with zero initial conditions. Assume the input $u(t)$ is unit step signal. The following statements can be used to solve the differential equation, and the solution is shown in Fig. 11-5.

```
>> a=[1,10,35,50,24]; na=[1.6 1.2 0.8 0.4 0];
   b=[1 3 5]; nb=[1.2 0.4 0]; t=0:0.01:10; u=ones(size(t));
   y=fode_sol(a,na,b,nb,u,t); plot(t,y)
```

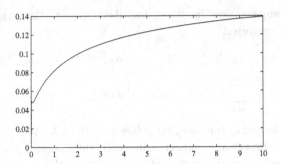

Fig. 11-5  Numerical solution of the different equation under unit step input.

### 11.3.2  *Numerical Solutions of Caputo Differential Equations*

If the initial values of the input and output signals are not zero, Caputo definition should be used, and we refer the fractional-order differential equations as Caputo differential equations.

Consider the Caputo linear differential equation

$$a_n {}_{t_0}^{C}\mathscr{D}_t^{\beta_n} y(t) + a_{n-1} {}_{t_0}^{C}\mathscr{D}_t^{\beta_{n-1}} y(t) + \cdots + a_1 {}_{t_0}^{C}\mathscr{D}_t^{\beta_1} y(t) + a_0 {}_{t_0}^{C}\mathscr{D}_t^{\beta_0} y(t) = \hat{u}(t). \quad (11.26)$$

For convenience, assume that $\beta_n > \beta_{n-1} > \cdots > \beta_1 > \beta_0 \geqslant 0$. The right-hand-side contains only $\hat{u}(t)$ function. For equations with linear combinations of $u(t)$ and its derivatives, the right-hand-side $\hat{u}(t)$ should be calculated first.

If $m = \lceil \beta_n \rceil$, $m$ initial values, $y(t_0)$, $y'(t_0)$, $\cdots$, $y^{(m-1)}(t_0)$, are expected to uniquely solve the Caputo differential equations. Thus, the auxiliary variable $z(t)$ can be introduced

$$z(t) = y(t) - y(t_0) - y'(t_0)\, t - \cdots - y^{(m-1)}(t_0)\, t^{m-1}. \quad (11.27)$$

The initial values of the first $(m-1)$th order derivatives of $z(t)$ are zero. Slightly change the form of the expression yield

$$y(t) = z(t) + y(t_0) + y'(t_0)\, t + \cdots + y^{(m-1)}(t_0)\, t^{m-1}. \quad (11.28)$$

Since the initial values of $z(t)$ are zeros, ${}_{t_0}^{C}\mathscr{D}_t^{\beta_i} z(t) = {}_{t_0}^{RL}\mathscr{D}_t^{\beta_i} z(t)$. The $\beta_i$th order Caputo derivative of the polynomial $y(t_0) + y'(t_0)\, t + \cdots + y^{(m-1)}(t_0)\, t^{m-1}$ can be obtained with the following function

```
function s=poly2caputo(a,r), syms u tau;
s=int(diff(poly2sym(a,'tau'),ceil(r))/((u-tau)^(r-ceil(r)+1))...
     /gamma(ceil(r)-r),tau,0,u);
```

The syntax of the function is $s = \texttt{poly2caputo}(a, \beta)$, where $a$ is the initial condition vector $a = [y^{(m-1)}(t_0), \cdots, y'(t_0), y(t_0)]$, $\beta$ is the order of differentiation. The returned variable $s$ is symbolic expression of the polynomial, with independent variable $u$.

With the compensation function described earlier, the original differential equation can be converted to

$$a_n {}^{RL}_{t_0}\mathscr{D}_t^{\beta_n} z(t) + a_{n-1} {}^{RL}_{t_0}\mathscr{D}_t^{\beta_{n-1}} z(t) + \cdots + a_1 {}^{RL}_{t_0}\mathscr{D}_t^{\beta_1} z(t) + a_0 {}^{RL}_{t_0}\mathscr{D}_t^{\beta_0} z(t)$$

$$= \hat{u}(t) - \sum_{i=0}^{n} a_i {}^{C}_{t_0}\mathscr{D}^{\beta_i}\Big[y(t_0) + y'(t_0)t + \cdots + y^{(m-1)}(t_0)t^{m-1}\Big]. \quad (11.29)$$

Similar to `fode_sol()` function, the following MATLAB function can be written to solve Caputo differential equation. Currently, this function can only be used in solving differential equations with right-hand-side of the equation contains only $u(t)$. The syntax of the function is $y = \mathtt{fode\_caputo}(a, n_a, y_0, u, t)$, where $u$ is the sample of the input signal, and $t$ is the evenly spaced time vector.

```
function [y,z]=fode_caputo(a,na,y0,u,t)
h=t(2)-t(1); D=sum(a./[h.^na]); nT=length(t); nb=0; b=1;
vec=[na nb]; D1=b(:)./h.^nb(:); nA=length(a);
y1=zeros(nT,1); W=ones(nT,length(vec));
for i=1:length(a), u=u-a(i)*subs(poly2caputo(y0,na(i)),'u',t); end
for j=2:nT, W(j,:)=W(j-1,:).*(1-(vec+1)/(j-1)); end
for i=2:nT,
    A=[y1(i-1:-1:1)]'*W(2:i,1:nA); y1(i)=(u(i)-sum(A.*a./[h.^na]))/D;
end
z=y1'; y=z+polyval(y0,t);
```

**Example 11.6.** Consider the Caputo linear differential equation

$$\mathscr{D}_t^{3.5} y(t) + 8\mathscr{D}_t^{3.1} y(t) + 26\mathscr{D}_t^{2.3} y(t) + 73\mathscr{D}_t^{1.2} y(t) + 90\mathscr{D}_t^{0.5} y(t) = 90\sin t^2,$$

with initial conditions, $y(0) = 1$, $y'(0) = -1$, $y''(0) = 2$, and $y'''(0) = 3$.

The initial condition vector can be entered, and with the following statements, the Caputo differential equation can be solved, as shown in Fig. 11-6.

```
>> a=[1,8,26,73,90]; n=[3.5,3.1,2.3,1.2,0.5]; t=0:0.001:10;
   u=90*sin(t.^2); y0=[3 2 -1 1]; y=fode_caputo(a,n,y0,u,t); plot(t,y)
```

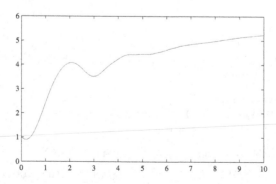

Fig. 11-6   Numerical solutions of Caputo differential equations.

### 11.3.3 *Some Important Laplace Transforms*

In the analytical solution approach presented later, some of the important Laplace transforms are needed. Here, we list some of the useful formula. All the Laplace transforms presented later are the variations of the following formula[11, 13]

$$\mathscr{L}^{-1}\left[\frac{s^{\alpha\gamma-\beta}}{(s^\alpha+a)^\gamma}\right] = t^{\beta-1}\mathscr{E}^\gamma_{\alpha,\beta}\left(-at^\alpha\right). \tag{11.30}$$

For different values of the parameters, the following formula can be derived

(1) If $\gamma = 1$, and $\alpha\gamma = \beta$, or $\beta = \alpha$, the above formula can be written as

$$\mathscr{L}^{-1}\left[\frac{1}{s^\alpha+a}\right] = t^{\alpha-1}\mathscr{E}_{\alpha,\alpha}\left(-at^\alpha\right). \tag{11.31}$$

This formula can be regarded as the analytical solution of the impulse response of the fractional-order transfer function $1/(s^\alpha+a)$. It can be seen that the essential representation in fractional-order system is Mittag–Leffler function, just as the exponential function in integer-order systems.

(2) If $\gamma = 1$, and $\alpha\gamma - \beta = -1$, or $\beta = \alpha + 1$, Eqn. (11.30) can be written as

$$\mathscr{L}^{-1}\left[\frac{1}{s(s^\alpha+a)}\right] = t^\alpha\mathscr{E}_{\alpha,\alpha+1}\left(-at^\alpha\right). \tag{11.32}$$

The formula can be regarded as the analytical solution of the step response of the transfer function $1/(s^\alpha+a)$. The above equation can also be written as

$$\mathscr{L}^{-1}\left[\frac{1}{s(s^\alpha+a)}\right] = \frac{1}{a}\left[1 - \mathscr{E}_\alpha\left(-at^\alpha\right)\right]. \tag{11.33}$$

(3) If $\gamma = k$ is an integer, and $\alpha\gamma = \beta$, i.e., $\beta = \alpha k$, Eqn. (11.30) is written as

$$\mathscr{L}^{-1}\left[\frac{1}{(s^\alpha+a)^k}\right] = t^{\alpha k-1}\mathscr{E}^k_{\alpha,\alpha k}\left(-at^\alpha\right). \tag{11.34}$$

and the formula can be regarded as the impulse response of $1/(s^\alpha+a)^k$.

(4) If $\gamma = k$ is an integer, and $\alpha\gamma - \beta = -1$, i.e., $\beta = \alpha k + 1$, Eqn. (11.30) can be written as

$$\mathscr{L}^{-1}\left[\frac{1}{s(s^\alpha+a)^k}\right] = t^{\alpha k}\mathscr{E}^k_{\alpha,\alpha k+1}\left(-at^\alpha\right). \tag{11.35}$$

which can be regarded as the unit step response of $1/(s^\alpha+a)^k$.

### 11.3.4 *Analytical Solutions of Commensurate-order Linear Differential Equations*

Consider the orders in Eqn. (11.22). If a greatest common divisor $\alpha$ can be found among the orders, such that the original equation can be written as

$$\begin{aligned} &a_1\mathscr{D}^{n\alpha}_t y(t) + a_2\mathscr{D}^{(n-1)\alpha}_t y(t) + \cdots + a_n\mathscr{D}^\alpha_t y(t) + a_{n+1}y(t) \\ &= b_1\mathscr{D}^{m\alpha}_t v(t) + b_2\mathscr{D}^{(m-1)\alpha}_t v(t) + \cdots + b_m\mathscr{D}^\alpha_t v(t) + b_{m+1}v(t), \end{aligned} \tag{11.36}$$

the original differential equation is referred to as commensurate-order differential equations of the base order $\alpha$. Denote $\lambda = s^{\alpha}$, the original differential equation can be expressed by the integer-order transfer function of $\lambda$. If there is no repeated poles in the system, the original transfer function can be written as the following form with the partial fraction expansion technique

$$G(\lambda) = \sum_{i=1}^{n} \frac{r_i}{\lambda + p_i} = \sum_{i=1}^{n} \frac{r_i}{s^{\alpha} + p_i}. \tag{11.37}$$

From the formula of Laplace transform given in Eqns. (11.31) and (11.32), the analytical solution of the impulse and step responses of the system can be obtained as

$$\mathscr{L}^{-1} \left[ \sum_{i=1}^{n} \frac{r_i}{s^{\alpha} + p_i} \right] = \sum_{i=1}^{n} r_i t^{\alpha-1} \mathscr{E}_{\alpha,\alpha} \left( -p_i t^{\alpha} \right), \tag{11.38}$$

$$\mathscr{L}^{-1} \left[ \sum_{i=1}^{n} \frac{r_i}{s(s^{\alpha} + p_i)} \right] = \sum_{i=1}^{n} r_i t^{\alpha} \mathscr{E}_{\alpha,\alpha+1} \left( -p_i t^{\alpha} \right). \tag{11.39}$$

The latter can alternatively written as

$$\mathscr{L}^{-1} \left[ \sum_{i=1}^{n} \frac{r_i}{s(s^{\alpha} + p_i)} \right] = \sum_{i=1}^{n} \frac{r_i}{p_i} \left[ 1 - \mathscr{E}_{\alpha} \left( -p_i t^{\alpha} \right) \right]. \tag{11.40}$$

If the system has repeated poles, Eqns. (11.34) and (11.35) should be used to write the analytical solutions to impulse and step responses.

**Example 11.7.** Consider the fractional-order differential equation

$$\mathscr{D}^{1.2} y(t) + 5 \mathscr{D}^{0.9} y(t) + 9 \mathscr{D}^{0.6} y(t) + 7 \mathscr{D}^{0.3} y(t) + 2 y(t) = u(t),$$

with zero initial conditions, where $u(t)$ is the unit step signal. If base order is selected as $\lambda = s^{0.3}$, the transfer function can be written as

$$G(\lambda) = \frac{1}{\lambda^4 + 5\lambda^3 + 9\lambda^2 + 7\lambda + 2}.$$

The following MATLAB statements can be used to find its partial fraction expansion regarding to $\lambda$,

```
>> num=1; den=[1 5 9 7 2]; [r,p]=residue(num,den)
```

and the results can be obtained as

$$G(\lambda) = -\frac{1}{\lambda + 2} + \frac{1}{\lambda + 1} - \frac{1}{(\lambda + 1)^2} + \frac{1}{(\lambda + 1)^3},$$

and the Laplace transform of the output signal can be written as

$$Y(s) = \frac{1}{s} G(\lambda) = -\frac{1}{s(s^{0.3} + 2)} + \frac{1}{s(s^{0.3} + 1)} - \frac{1}{s(s^{0.3} + 1)^2} + \frac{1}{s(s^{0.3} + 1)^3}.$$

Thus, the analytical solution to the step input can be obtained as

$$y(t) = -t^{0.3} \mathscr{E}_{0.3,1.3} \left( -2t^{0.3} \right) + t^{0.3} \mathscr{E}_{0.3,1.3} \left( -t^{0.3} \right) - t^{0.6} \mathscr{E}_{0.3,1.6}^2 \left( -t^{0.3} \right) + t^{0.9} \mathscr{E}_{0.3,1.9}^3 \left( -t^{0.3} \right)$$

$$= \frac{1}{2} + \frac{1}{2} \mathscr{E}_{0.3}(-2t^{0.3}) + \mathscr{E}_{0.3} \left( -t^{0.3} \right) - \left[ 1 - \mathscr{E}_{0.3} \left( -t^{0.3} \right) \right]^2 + \left[ 1 - \mathscr{E}_{0.3} \left( -t^{0.3} \right) \right]^3.$$

### 11.3.5  Analytical Solutions of Linear Fractional-order Differential Equations

Consider the following $(n+1)$-term fractional-order differential equation

$$a_n \mathscr{D}_t^{\beta_n} y(t) + a_{n-1} \mathscr{D}_t^{\beta_{n-1}} y(t) + \cdots + a_0 \mathscr{D}_t^{\beta_0} y(t) = u(t), \qquad (11.41)$$

with step input. The analytical solution can be written as

$$y(t) = \frac{1}{a_n} \sum_{m=0}^{\infty} \frac{(-1)^m}{m!} \sum_{\substack{k_0+k_1+\cdots+k_{n-2}=m \\ k_0 \geqslant 0, \cdots, k_{n-2} \geqslant 0}} (m; k_0, k_1, \cdots, k_{n-2})$$

$$\prod_{i=0}^{n-2} \left( \frac{a_i}{a_n} \right)^{k_i} t^{(\beta_n - \beta_{n-1})m + \beta_n + \sum_{j=0}^{n-2}(\beta_{n-1}-\beta_j)k_j - 1} \qquad (11.42)$$

$$\mathscr{E}^{(m)}_{\beta_n-\beta_{n-1},\ \beta_n+\sum_{j=0}^{n-2}(\beta_{n-1}-\beta_j)k_j} \left( -\frac{a_{n-1}}{a_n} t^{\beta_n - \beta_{n-1}} \right),$$

where $(m; k_0, k_1, \cdots, k_{n-2})$ is defined as

$$(m; k_0, k_1, \cdots, k_{n-2}) = \frac{m!}{k_0! k_1! \cdots k_{n-2}!}. \qquad (11.43)$$

It is difficult to write out analytical solutions to a certain system, since the solution form is too complicated. This method is quite useful in practical problems.

## 11.4  Modeling and Analysis of Fractional-order Transfer Functions

Consider the linear fractional-order system shown in Eqn. (11.22). If the initial values of the input signal $u(t)$ and output $y(t)$ and their derivatives are all zero, with Laplace transform, the fractional-order transfer function when appended a time delay $T$ can be written as

$$G(s) = \frac{b_1 s^{\gamma_1} + b_2 s^{\gamma_2} + \cdots + b_m s^{\gamma_m}}{a_1 s^{\eta_1} + a_2 s^{\eta_2} + \cdots + a_{n-1} s^{\eta_{n-1}} + a_n s^{\eta_n}} e^{-Ts}. \qquad (11.44)$$

Compared with the integer-order transfer functions, apart from the numerator and denominator coefficients, the orders can also be declared. Thus, normally four vectors and a delay constant can be used to describe uniquely the fractional-order transfer function model in Eqn. (11.44).

Since this model is useful in the analysis and design of linear fractional-order systems, we can construct a MATLAB class FOTF to describe the model as it is done in TF class, in Control System Toolbox. When the class is created, overload functions can be written to implement the modeling, analysis and design tasks, in a simple and straightforward way.

In this section, creation of class, and object-oriented programming technique are demonstrated first, then based on the class, the modeling and analysis of fractional-order transfer functions are presented.

### 11.4.1   *FOTF — Creation of a MATLAB Object*

If one wants to create a MATLAB class, a name of the class should be selected. For instance, for fractional-order transfer function, we selected FOTF as its name. A folder @fotf should be created for it, and all the files related io the class should be placed in the folder. Normally for a new class, at least two functions should be written, fotf.m is used to define the class, and display.m is used to display the class. The programming of the two functions and other supporting functions are illustrated below:

(1) **Defining FOTF class**. A function fotf.m should be written and placed in the @fotf folder. The listing of the function is

```
function G=fotf(a,na,b,nb,T)
if nargin==0,
   G.a=[]; G.na=[]; G.b=[]; G.nb=[]; G.ioDelay=0; G=class(G,'fotf');
elseif isa(a,'fotf'), G=a;
elseif nargin==1 & isa(a,'double'), G=fotf(1,0,a,0,0);
elseif nargin==1 & a=='s', G=fotf(1,0,1,1,0);
else, ii=find(abs(a)<eps); a(ii)=[]; na(ii)=[];
   ii=find(abs(b)<eps); b(ii)=[]; nb(ii)=[];
   if nargin==5, G.ioDelay=T; else, G.ioDelay=0; end
   G.a=a; G.na=na; G.b=b; G.nb=nb; G=class(G,'fotf');
end
```

The command $G=\texttt{fotf}(\boldsymbol{a},\boldsymbol{n}_{\mathrm{a}},\boldsymbol{b},\boldsymbol{n}_{\mathrm{b}},T)$ can be used to enter a FOTF object, where $\boldsymbol{a}=[a_1,a_2,\cdots,a_n], \boldsymbol{b}=[b_1,b_2,\cdots,b_m]$, $\boldsymbol{n}_{\mathrm{a}}=[\eta_1,\eta_2,\cdots,\eta_n]$ and $\boldsymbol{n}_{\mathrm{b}}=[\gamma_1,\gamma_2,\cdots,\gamma_m]$ can be used to represent the coefficients and orders of the numerator and denominator of the system, and $T$ is the delay constant. If there is no delay in the model, the variable can be omitted.

Similar to tf() function, function $s=\texttt{fotf('s')}$ command can be used to declare an $s$ operator for the fractional-order model. The command $G=\texttt{fotf}(k)$ can be used to convert a constant to FOTF object. If $G$ is an LTI object in Control System Toolbox, the command $G=\texttt{fotf}(G)$ can be used to convert the TF object into an FOTF object.

(2) **Writing display function**. Another function, display.m, should be written in that folder, which is used to display the FOTF object, once it is created. The listing of the function is

```
function display(G)
strN=fpoly2str(G.b,G.nb); strD=fpoly2str(G.a,G.na);
nn=length(strN); nd=length(strD); nm=max([nn,nd]);
disp([char(' '*ones(1,floor((nm-nn)/2))) strN]), ss=[];
T=G.ioDelay; if T>0, ss=[' exp(-' num2str(T) 's)']; end
disp([char('-'*ones(1,nm)), ss]);
disp([char(' '*ones(1,floor((nm-nd)/2))) strD])
function strP=fpoly2str(p,np)
if isempty(np), p=0; np=0; end
```

```
P='';  [np,ii]=sort(np,'descend');  p=p(ii);
for i=1:length(p),  P=[P,num2str(p(i)),'s^',num2str(np(i)),'+'];  end
P=strrep(strrep(strrep(P,'s^0+','+'),'s^1+','s+'),'s^1-','s-');
P=strrep(strrep(strrep(P,'+-','-'),'+1s','+s'),'-1s','-s');
strP=P(1:end-1);  nP=length(strP);
if nP>=2 &  strP(1:2)=='1s',  strP=strP(2:end);  end
```

**Example 11.8.** For the fractional-order transfer function model

$$G(s) = \frac{0.8s^{1.2} + 2}{1.1s^{1.8} + 1.9s^{0.5} + 0.4} e^{-0.5s},$$

the following MATLAB commands can be used to directly enter the model. The display result is displayed as

```
>> G=fotf([1.1,1.9,0.4],[1.8,0.5,0],[0.8,2],[1.2,0],0.5)
```

It should be noted that these files must be placed in @fotf folder, and should not be placed elsewhere. Otherwise, the files cannot be called, and they may affect the existing MATLAB files with the same names.

(3) **Other facilities.** Further, apart from the two essential functions fotf.m and display.m, if we want to access the members in the FOTF object directly with MATLAB, the following two files are written. With these functions, commands like $G$.nb and $G$.na $= [0.1, 0.2]$ are supported

```
function A=subsasgn(G,index,InputVal)
switch index.subs
    case {'a','na','b','nb','ioDelay'},
        eval(['G.' index.subs,'=InputVal;']);
        if length(G.a)~=length(G.na) | length(G.b)~=length(G.nb)
            error('Error: field pairs (na,a) or (nb,b) mismatched.')
        else, A=fotf(G.a,G.na,G.b,G.nb,G.ioDelay); end
    otherwise, error('Error: Available fields are a, na, b, na, ioDelay.');
end
```

```
function A=subsref(G,index)
switch index.subs
    case {'a','na','b','nb','ioDelay'}, A=eval(['G.' index.subs]);
    otherwise,
        error('Error: Available fields are a, na, b, na, ioDelay.');
end
```

(4) **Conversion function from TF to FOTF object.** The following function should be placed in the @tf folder.

```
function G1=fotf(G)
[n,d]=tfdata(tf(G),'v'); nn=length(n)-1:-1:0;
nd=length(d)-1:-1:0; G1=fotf(d,nd,n,nn,G.ioDelay);
```

### 11.4.2  *Interconnections of FOTF Blocks*

It has been shown in Chapter 4 that integer-order models can be calculated with +, * and feedback() functions to process the parallel, series and feedback connection. Similar to the idea, the following overload functions can be written. These files should be placed in the @fotf folder. Most of the functions are from the book [5], however, some of them are modified and extended.

(1) **Multiplications of FOTF blocks.** To define the expression $G = G_1*G_2$, the overload function mtimes() should be written. This function is used to evaluate the series connection of two FOTF blocks, $G_1(s)$ and $G_2(s)$, the algorithm is

$$G(s) = G_1(s)G_2(s) = \frac{N_1(s)N_2(s)}{D_1(s)D_2(s)}. \tag{11.45}$$

The overload function can be written as

```
function G=mtimes(G1,G2)
G1=fotf(G1); G2=fotf(G2); na=[]; nb=[];
a=kron(G1.a,G2.a); b=kron(G1.b,G2.b);
for i=1:length(G1.na), na=[na,G1.na(i)+G2.na]; end
for i=1:length(G1.nb), nb=[nb,G1.nb(i)+G2.nb]; end
G=simple(fotf(a,na,b,nb,G1.ioDelay+G2.ioDelay));
```

(2) **Adding FOTF blocks.** The expression $G = G_1 + G_2$ should be described by the overload function plus() to evaluate the parallel connection of two FOTF blocks, with the algorithm

$$G(s) = G_1(s) + G_2(s) = \frac{N_1(s)D_2(s) + N_2(s)D_1(s)}{D_1(s)D_2(s)}. \tag{11.46}$$

The following overload function is implemented

```
function G=plus(G1,G2)
G1=fotf(G1); G2=fotf(G2); na=[]; nb=[];
if G1.ioDelay==G2.ioDelay
  a=kron(G1.a,G2.a); b=[kron(G1.a,G2.b),kron(G1.b,G2.a)];
  for i=1:length(G1.a),
     na=[na G1.na(i)+G2.na]; nb=[nb, G1.na(i)+G2.nb];
  end
  for i=1:length(G1.b), nb=[nb G1.nb(i)+G2.na]; end
  G=simple(fotf(a,na,b,nb,G1.ioDelay));
else, error('cannot handle different delays'); end
```

(3) **Feedback function.** The function $G = \text{feedback}(G_1, G_2)$ evaluates the negative connection of the two FOTF blocks. If the positive structure is used, the forward path can be converted to $-G_2$, such that negative feedback structure can still be used.

$$G(s) = \frac{G_1(s)}{1 + G_1(s)G_2(s)} = \frac{N_1(s)D_2(s)}{D_1(s)D_2(s) + N_1(s)N_2(s)}. \tag{11.47}$$

The listing of the overload function is

```
function G=feedback(F,H)
F=fotf(F); H=fotf(H); na=[]; nb=[];
if F.ioDelay==H.ioDelay
   b=kron(F.b,H.a); a=[kron(F.b,H.b), kron(F.a,H.a)];
   for i=1:length(F.b),
      nb=[nb F.nb(i)+H.nb]; na=[na,F.nb(i)+H.nb];
   end
   for i=1:length(F.a), na=[na F.na(i)+H.na]; end
   G=simple(fotf(a,na,b,nb,F.ioDelay));
else, error('cannot handle blocks with different delays'); end
```

(4) **Simple supporting functions.** Function $\texttt{uminus()}$ is used to evaluate $G_1(s) = -G(s)$, with the syntax $\boxed{G_1 = -G}$; Function $\boxed{G = \texttt{inv}(G_1)}$ is used to evaluate $G(s) = 1/G_1(s)$; Function $\texttt{minus()}$ is used to evaluate $G(s) = G_1(s) - G_2(s)$, with $\boxed{G = G_1 - G_2}$. Function $\texttt{eq()}$ judges whether two FOTF blocks $G_1$ and $G_2$ equal or not, with $\boxed{\texttt{key} = G_1 == G_2}$, if equal, the returned $\texttt{key}$ is 1.

```
function G=uminus(G1), G=G1; G.b=-G.b;
function G=inv(G1), G=fotf(G1.b,G1.nb,G1.a,G1.na,-G1.ioDelay);
function G=minus(G1,G2), G=G1+(-G2);
function key=eq(G1,G2), key=0; G=G1-G2;
if length(G.nb)==0 | norm(G.b)<1e-10, key=1; end
```

(5) **Right division.** With $\boxed{G = G_1/G_2}$ to evaluates $G(s) = G_1(s)/G_2(s)$

```
function G=mrdivide(G1,G2)
G1=fotf(G1); G2=fotf(G2); G=G1*inv(G2);
G.ioDelay=G1.ioDelay-G2.ioDelay;
if G.ioDelay<0, warning('block with positive delay'); end
```

(6) **Power function.** With $\boxed{G = G_1{}^{\wedge}n}$, the power of $G_1$ can be evaluated, if $n$ is integer. Otherwise, only the case $G_1$ is a Laplace operator can be handled.

```
function G1=mpower(G,n)
if n==fix(n),
   if n>=0, G1=1; for i=1:n, G1=G1*G; end
   else, G1=inv(G^(-n)); end, G1.ioDelay=n*G.ioDelay;
elseif G==fotf(1,0,1,1), G1=fotf(1,0,1,n);
else, error('mpower: power must be an integer.'); end
```

(7) **Simplification function.** With $\boxed{G = \texttt{simple}(G)}$, the coefficients of numerator and denominator are collected to simplify the description. Sub-function $\texttt{polyuniq()}$ can be used to collect coefficients of polynomials. The sub function cannot be called directly.

```
function G=simple(G1)
[a,n]=polyuniq(G1.a,G1.na); G1.a=a; G1.na=n; na=G1.na;
[a,n]=polyuniq(G1.b,G1.nb); G1.b=a; G1.nb=n; nb=G1.nb;
if length(nb)==0, nb=0; G1.nb=0; G1.b=0; end
nn=min(na(end),nb(end)); nb=nb-nn; na=na-nn;
G=fotf(G1.a,na,G1.b,nb,G1.ioDelay);
```

```
function [a,an]=polyuniq(a,an)
[an,ii]=sort(an,'descend'); a=a(ii); ax=diff(an); key=1;
for i=1:length(ax)
    if ax(i)==0, a(key)=a(key)+a(key+1); a(key+1)=[]; an(key+1)=[];
    else, key=key+1; end
end
```

**Example 11.9.** The following commands can be used to express the fractional-order PID controller $G_c(s) = 5 + 2s^{-0.2} + 3s^{0.6}$ into MATLAB workspace

```
>> s=fotf('s'); Gc=5+2*s^(-0.2)+3*s^0.6
```

**Example 11.10.** The fractional-order transfer function model

$$G(s) = \frac{(s^{0.3}+3)^2}{(s^{0.2}+2)(s^{0.4}+4)(s^{0.4}+3)},$$

can be entered into MATLAB workspace, with the following MATLAB statements, the expanded model can be obtained

$$G(s) = \frac{s^{0.6}+6s^{0.3}+9}{s+2s^{0.8}+7s^{0.6}+14s^{0.4}+12s^{0.2}+24}.$$

```
>> s=fotf('s'); G=(s^0.3+3)^2/(s^0.2+2)/(s^0.4+4)/(s^0.4+3)
```

**Example 11.11.** Assume that typical unity negative feedback control system is

$$G(s) = \frac{0.8s^{1.2}+2}{1.1s^{1.8}+0.8s^{1.3}+1.9s^{0.5}+0.4}, \quad G_c(s) = \frac{1.2s^{0.72}+1.5s^{0.33}}{3s^{0.8}},$$

the following statements can be used to enter the model into MATLAB workspace

```
>> G=fotf([1.1,0.8 1.9 0.4],[1.8 1.3 0.5 0],[0.8 2],[1.2 0]);
   Gc=fotf([3],[0.8],[1.2 1.5],[0.72 0.33]); GG=feedback(G*Gc,1)
```

and the closed-loop model obtained is

$$G(s) = \frac{0.96s^{1.59}+1.2s^{1.2}+2.4s^{0.39}+3}{3.3s^{2.27}+2.4s^{1.77}+0.96s^{1.59}+1.2s^{1.2}+5.7s^{0.97}+1.2s^{0.47}+2.4s^{0.39}+3}.$$

### 11.4.3    *Analysis of FOTF Objects*

#### 1. Stability analysis

The stability assessment of commensurate-order systems can be carried out directly. If the base order of the commensurate-order system is $\lambda = s^\alpha$, the stable regions for the commensurate-order system are shown in Fig. 11-7. If the poles of the system of $\lambda$ are located in the stable regions, then the system is stable, otherwise the system is unstable[14]. For the base order $\alpha$, the boundaries of stable regions are the straight lines with slopes of $\pm \alpha \pi/2$. When the base order is $\alpha = 1$, the system is of integer-order, and the stable boundary is changed to the imaginary axis, which agrees well with the cases in integer-order systems.

Based on the idea, the following MATLAB function can be written. The function can be used to convert FOTF object to commensurate-order system first, and then

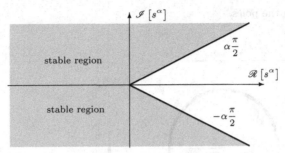

Fig. 11-7   Stable regions for commensurate-order systems.

the poles of the system can be evaluated. Although sometimes the order of the commensurate-order system is extremely high, it can also be processed by MATLAB easily. The syntax $[\texttt{key},\alpha,\epsilon,a_1]=\texttt{isstable}(G,a_0)$ can be used to assess the stability of the FOTF object, where key is one for stable. The argument $\alpha$ returns the base order, $\epsilon$ is the error tolerance in root finding, $a_1$ is the slopes of $\pm\alpha\pi/2$, and $a_0$ is the user selected base order, with default of 0.01.

```
function [K,alpha,err,apol]=isstable(G,a0)
if nargin==1, a0=0.01; end
a=G.na; a1=fix(a/a0); n=gcd(a1(1),a1(2));
for i=3:length(a1), n=gcd(n,a1(i)); end
alpha=n*a0; a=fix(a1/n); b=G.a; c(a+1)=b; c=c(end:-1:1);
p=roots(c); p=p(abs(p)>eps); err=norm(polyval(c,p));
plot(real(p),imag(p),'x',0,0,'o')
apol=min(abs(angle(p))); K=apol>alpha*pi/2;
xm=xlim; xm(1)=0; line(xm,tan(alpha*pi/2)*xm)
title('Pole-Zero Map'), xlabel('Real Axis'), ylabel('Imaginary Axis')
```

**Example 11.12.** Consider the fractional-order transfer function

$$G(s) = \frac{-2s^{0.63} - 4}{2s^{3.501} + 3.8s^{2.42} + 2.6s^{1.798} + 2.5s^{1.31} + 1.5}.$$

The following statements can be used to enter the model into MATLAB workspace first, then assess the stability of the system.

```
>> b=[-2,-4]; nb=[0.63,0];
   a=[2,3.8,2.6,2.5,1.5]; na=[3.501,2.42,1.798,1.31,0];
   G=fotf(a,na,b,nb); [key,alpha,err,apol]=isstable(G,0.001)
```

It is obvious that the base order is $\alpha = 0.001$, the commensurate-order model of the system can be rewritten as an integer-order transfer function of $\lambda$

$$G(\lambda) = \frac{-2\lambda^{630} - 4}{2\lambda^{3501} + 3.8\lambda^{2420} + 2.6\lambda^{1798} + 2.5\lambda^{1310} + 1.5}.$$

The roots of the polynomials of $\lambda$ can be obtained automatically in the function, as shown in Fig. 11-8(a). The zoomed plots around the $x$-axis can be obtained in Fig. 11-8(b). It can be seen that all the poles of the system are located in the stable regions. Thus, the system is stable. Since $\alpha = 0.001$, the polynomial is of 3501th order. It may take some time to find all the poles.

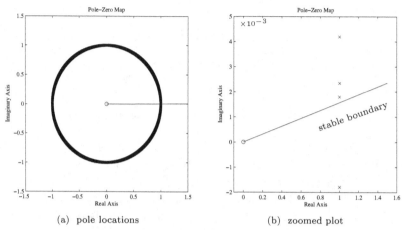

(a)  pole locations                    (b)  zoomed plot

Fig. 11-8    Pole positions and stability assessment.

## 2. Norms of fractional-order systems

The norms of the systems are important quantities in robust control design. The evaluation algorithms of the norms of fractional-order systems are illustrated here. The $\mathcal{H}_2$ and $\mathcal{H}_\infty$ norms of $G(s)$ are defined respectively as

$$||G(s)||_2 = \sqrt{\frac{1}{2\pi j} \int_{-j\infty}^{j\infty} G(s)G(-s)\mathrm{d}s}, \tag{11.48}$$

$$||G(s)||_\infty = \sup_\omega |G(j\omega)|. \tag{11.49}$$

It can be seen that the $||G(s)||_2$ norm can be evaluated through numerical integration methods, while $||G(s)||_\infty$ norm can be obtained with numerical optimization approaches. The overload function `norm()` can be written and placed in the `@fotf` folder, with the syntaxes `norm(G)` and `norm(G,inf)`. In old versions of MATLAB, the `integral()` function can be replaced with `quadgk()`.

```
function n=norm(G,eps0)
j=sqrt(-1); dx=1; f0=0; if nargin==1, eps0=1e-6; end
if nargin==2 & ~isfinite(eps0) % H∞ norm, find the maximum value
    f=@(w)[-abs(freqresp(j*w,G))];
    w=fminsearch(f,0); n=abs(freqresp(j*w,G));
else % H2 norm, numerical integration
    f=@(s)freqresp(s,G).*freqresp(-s,G)/(2*pi*j);
    while (1)
        n=integral(f,-dx*j,dx*j);
        if abs(n-f0)<eps0, n=sqrt(n); break; else, f0=n; dx=2*dx;
end, end, end
```

where the low-level frequency response function `freqresp()` is given by

```
function H1=freqresp(w,G)
a=G.a; na=G.na; b=G.b; nb=G.nb; j=sqrt(-1); T=G.ioDelay;
for i=1:length(w)
    P=b*(w(i).^nb.')); Q=a*(w(i).^na.')); H1(i)=P*exp(-T*w(i))/Q;
end
```

**Example 11.13.** Consider the fractional-order model given in Example 11.12. The norms of the system can be evaluated, and the results are $n_1 = 2.7168$, and $n_2 = 8.6115$.

```
>> a=[2,3.8,2.6,2.5,1.5]; na=[3.501,2.42,1.798,1.31,0];
   b=[-2,-4]; nb=[0.63,0]; G=fotf(a,na,b,nb);
   n1=norm(G), n2=norm(G,inf)
```

### 11.4.4  *Frequency Domain Analysis of FOTF Objects*

Consider a fractional-order transfer function $G(s)$. If $j\omega$ is used to substitute $s$, through simple complex number computation, the exact frequency response data can be obtained directly. The data can be written in the form of the `frd()` function in the Control System Toolbox, so that the frequency domain analysis functions such as `bode()` can be used to draw frequency domain plots. Overload functions for these can also be written, and placed in `@fotf` folder. The listing of the overload function `bode()` is as follows, with the supporting function `freqresp()` as its kernel.

```
function H=bode(G,w)
if nargin==1, w=logspace(-4,4); end
j=sqrt(-1); H1=freqresp(j*w,G); H1=frd(H1,w);
if nargout==0, bode(H1); else, H=H1; end
```

Similarly, overload functions for Nyquist plots and Nichols chart are

```
function nyquist(G,w)
if nargin==1, w=logspace(-4,4); end, H=bode(G,w); nyquist(H);
function nichols(G,w)
if nargin==1, w=logspace(-4,4); end, H=bode(G,w); nichols(H);
```

**Example 11.14.** Consider again the fractional-order model in Example 11.12. The following statements can be used to draw the Body diagram and Nyquist plot as shown in Figs. 11-9(a) and (b).

```
>> b=[-2,-4]; nb=[0.63,0]; w=logspace(-2,2);
   a=[2,3.8,2.6,2.5,1.5]; na=[3.501,2.42,1.798,1.31,0];
   G=fotf(a,na,b,nb); bode(G,w);
   figure, w=logspace(-2,4,400); nyquist(G,w); grid
```

### 11.4.5  *Time Domain Analysis of FOTF Objects*

Based on the closed-form solutions of linear fractional-order differential equations, and its MATLAB implementation in function `fode_sol()`, the overload step

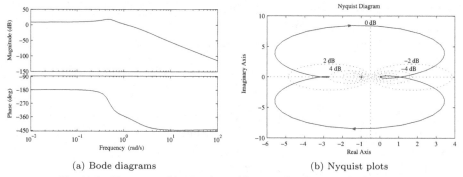

(a) Bode diagrams                    (b) Nyquist plots

Fig. 11-9    Frequency domain plots of fractional-order transfer function.

response function `step()` and arbitrary input time response function `lsim()` of the fractional-order transfer functions can easily be written

```
function y=step(G,t)
y1=fode_sol(G.a,G.na,G.b,G.nb,ones(size(t)),t);
ii=find(t>G.ioDelay); lz=zeros(1,ii(1)-1);
y1=[lz, y1(1:end-length(lz))];
if nargout==0,
    plot(t,y1,t,c_term(G.b,G.nb)/c_term(G.a,G.na),'--'),
    title('Step Response'), xlabel('Time (Sec)'), ylabel('Magnitude')
else, y=y1; end
function c=c_term(a,na) % this function is to find constant term in polynomials
i=find(na==0); c=0; if length(i)>0, c=a(i(1)); end
```

```
function y=lsim(G,u,t)
y1=fode_sol(G.a,G.na,G.b,G.nb,u,t);
ii=find(t>G.ioDelay); lz=zeros(1,ii(1)-1);
y1=[lz, y1(1:end-length(lz))];
if nargout==0, plot(t,y1,t,u,'--'),
    title('Step Response'), xlabel('Time (Sec)'), ylabel('Magnitude')
else, y=y1; end
```

The syntaxes of the two functions are

$$y = \text{step}(G,t), \quad \text{and} \quad y = \text{lsim}(G,u,t)$$

where $G$ is the FOTF model, $t$ is an evenly spaced time vector, $u$ is a vector of the input samples. We tried to make the syntaxes of these overload functions similar to those in the Control System Toolbox. It should be noted that vector $t$ cannot be omitted here.

**Example 11.15.** Consider the following fractional-order differential equation

$$\mathscr{D}_t^{3.5}y(t) + 8\mathscr{D}_t^{3.1}y(t) + 26\mathscr{D}_t^{2.3}y(t) + 73\mathscr{D}_t^{1.2}y(t) + 90\mathscr{D}_t^{0.5}y(t) = 90\sin t^2,$$

and it can be seen that the fractional-order transfer function is

$$G(s) = \frac{90}{s^{3.5} + 8s^{3.1} + 26s^{2.3} + 73s^{1.2} + 90s^{0.5}},$$

and the input is $u(t) = \sin t^2$. The following statements can be used to draw the time response of the output $y(t)$ as shown in Fig. 11-10, where the solid curve is the output while the dash plot is the input.

```
>> a=[1,8,26,73,90]; n=[3.5,3.1,2.3,1.2,0.5];
   G=fotf(a,n,90,0); t=0:0.002:10; u=sin(t.^2); lsim(G,u,t);
```

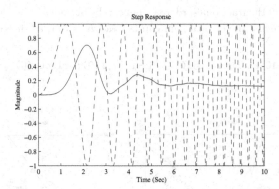

Fig. 11-10 Input and output signals of the system.

Similar to other computation problems in MATLAB, the results obtained should be validated. Smaller step sizes can be tried to seen whether the same results can be obtained. If the results with smaller step sizes are the same, the results can be accepted, otherwise the step size should be reduced again. For this example, the results are validated.

### 11.4.6 *Root Locus for Commensurate-order Systems*

For commensurate-order systems, if the base order is $\alpha$, we can let $\lambda = s^\alpha$, and the original system can be written as the integer-order model of $\lambda$, denoted by $G_1(\lambda)$. Function rlocus() in Control System Toolbox can be used to draw the root locus of integer-order model $G_1(\lambda)$, and superimpose the stability boundaries $\pm\alpha\pi/2$ on the root locus. Based on the idea, the overload function rlocus() can be designed. The syntax of the function is $\boxed{\text{rlocus}(G)}$, where $G$ is a FOTF object.

```
function rlocus(G)
nx=unique(round(1000*[G.na,G.nb])); nx=nx(nx~=0); nd=max(nx);
for i=1:length(nx), nd=gcd(nd,nx(i)); end
alpha=nd*0.001; na=round(G.na/alpha); nb=round(G.nb/alpha);
b=G.a; den(a+1)=b; den=den(end:-1:1);
b=G.b; num(x+1)=b; num=num(end:-1:1); G1=tf(num,den);
rlocus(G1), xm=xlim; if xm(2)<=0, xm(2)=-xm(1); end
xm(1)=0; line(xm,tan(alpha*pi/2)*xm)
```

Interactive method in the original rlocus() function is inherited to get the critical gain of the system with mouse clicks.

**Example 11.16.** Assume that the fractional-order transfer function is given by

$$G(s) = \frac{1}{s^{3.5} + 10s^{2.8} + 35s^{2.1} + 50s^{1.4} + 24s^{0.7}}.$$

It can be seen that the base order is $\alpha = 0.7$. Let $\lambda = s^{0.7}$, the integer-order transfer function can be written as

$$G(\lambda) = \frac{1}{\lambda^5 + 10\lambda^4 + 35\lambda^3 + 50\lambda^2 + 24\lambda}.$$

The root locus of the fractional-order system can be obtained as shown in Fig. 11-11(a). Zooming the root locus, the critical gain can be read $K = 371$, as shown in Fig. 11-11(b).

```
>> G=fotf([1 10 35 50 24 0],0.7*[5:-1:0],1,0); rlocus(G)
```

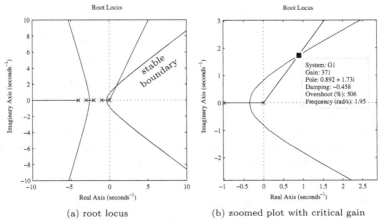

(a) root locus          (b) zoomed plot with critical gain

Fig. 11-11    Root locus analysis of fractional-order system.

### 11.4.7    *State Space Models of Commensurate-order Systems*

If the fractional-order system can be expressed as the commensurate-order transfer function $G(\lambda)$ with base order $\alpha$, the matrices $(A, B, C, D)$ for integer-order model $G(\lambda)$ can be obtained, and the state space representation of the fractional-order system can be written as

$$\begin{cases} \mathscr{D}^\alpha x(t) = Ax(t) + Bu(t) \\ y(t) = Cx(t) + Du(t). \end{cases} \tag{11.50}$$

The state space models of fractional-order system are not covered in the book. The interested readers are advised to create their own FOSS class and overload functions. These tasks are left as a problem.

## 11.5 Approximation and Reduction of Fractional-order Systems

### 11.5.1 *Oustaloup Filter for Fractional-order Differentiators*

The Grünwald–Letnikov definition presented earlier can be used to evaluate accurately the fractional-order derivatives for given functions. However, there are certain limitations in control systems. Control systems are always described by block diagrams, for instance, the input signal to the plant model is often generated by its previous block, i.e., the controller. Thus, the control signal is not known precisely before numerical derivatives can be calculated. Thus, block diagram approximations, usually with filters, to the fractional-order derivative actions are expected.

Normally, filters are classified as continuous and discrete ones, here, continuous filters to fit the Laplace operator $s^\gamma$ are mainly discussed. It can be seen that fractional-order derivatives can be approximated by filters.

### 1. Oustaloup filter approximation

Several filter approximation approaches are summarized in [9], including continued fraction approximation, Charef approximation[15] and Oustaloup approximation[16]. Here, only Oustaloup algorithm is presented.

Since pure fractional-order derivative can be represented by straight lines in Bode diagrams, it is not possible to fit them at the whole frequency range with integer-order filters. A specific interested frequency interval $(\omega_b, \omega_h)$ should be assigned, with the continuous transfer function

$$G_f(s) = K \prod_{k=1}^{N} \frac{s + \omega_k'}{s + \omega_k}, \tag{11.51}$$

where the poles, zeros and gain can be obtained from

$$\omega_k' = \omega_b \omega_u^{(2k-1-\gamma)/N}, \quad \omega_k = \omega_b \omega_u^{(2k-1+\gamma)/N}, \quad K = \omega_h^\gamma, \tag{11.52}$$

with $\omega_u = \sqrt{\omega_h/\omega_b}$. Based on the algorithm, the following MATLAB function can be written to implement Oustaloup filter. If $y(t)$ is the input signal to the filter, the output of the filter can be approximately regarded as $\mathscr{D}_t^\gamma y(t)$.

```
function G=ousta_fod(gam,N,wb,wh)
k=1:N; wu=sqrt(wh/wb); wkp=wb*wu.^((2*k-1-gam)/N);
wk=wb*wu.^((2*k-1+gam)/N); G=zpk(-wkp,-wk,wh^gam); G=tf(G);
```

with the syntax $G = \text{ousta\_fod}(\gamma, N, \omega_b, \omega_h)$, where $\gamma$ is the order of derivative, $N$ is the order of the filter. The variables $\omega_b$ and $\omega_h$ are the lower- and upper-bounds of the frequency of users' choice. Normally within the frequency range, the Bode diagram fractional-order operator are satisfactory, while the fitting outside the range is not. The algorithm presented here avoided the restriction on $\omega_b\omega_h = 1$, the two frequencies can be selected independently.

In the function, $\gamma$ can either be positive or negative, for differentiation and integrals. Also, the absolute values of $\gamma$ can be larger than 1, for instance, $\gamma = 3.7$.

However, in this case, it is suggested to keep $-1 < \gamma < 1$, and leave the remaining integers as TF object. For instance, better to use $s^{3.7} = s^3 s^{0.7}$, or $s^{3.7} = s^4 s^{-0.3}$.

### 2. Improved Oustaloup filter

In practical applications, the orders of the numerator and denominator are the same, and if at the boundaries of the frequency the fitting is not good, improved Oustaloup filters[17] and optimal filter design method[18] can be used. The latter can also be extended to fit complex orders, however, its implementation is rather complicated.

The following improved Oustaloup filter is presented[17]. The limitations of the filter is that the order should be between 0 and 1. The improved filter is

$$s^\gamma \approx \left( \frac{d\omega_h}{b} \right)^\gamma \left( \frac{ds^2 + b\omega_h s}{d(1-\gamma)s^2 + b\omega_h s + d\gamma} \right) \prod_{k=1}^{N} \frac{s + \omega'_k}{s + \omega_k}, \qquad (11.53)$$

and the definitions of $\omega_k$, $\omega'_k$ are the same as in Oustaloup filter. Two adjustable parameters $b$, $d$ are introduced, and normally they can be set to $b = 10$, $d = 9$. The MATLAB implementation is given by

```
function G=new_fod(r,N,wb,wh,b,d)
if nargin==4, b=10; d=9; end, k=1:N; wu=sqrt(wh/wb);
wkp=wb*wu.^((2*k-1-r)/N); wk=wb*wu.^((2*k-1+r)/N);
G=zpk(-wkp,-wk,(d*wh/b)^r)*tf([d,b*wh,0],[d*(1-r),b*wh,d*r]);
```

### 3. Filter approximation of high-order fractional-order systems

Based on Oustaloup filter and its improved form, high-order integer-order approximation to fractional-order transfer function, i.e., each fractional-order term can be approximated with the filters. Based on the idea, the following MATLAB function is designed, and placed in the @fotf folder.

```
function Ga=high_order(G,filter,wb,wh,N)
if nargin==1, filter='ousta_fod'; wb=1e-3; wh=1e3; N=5; end
Ga=pseudo_poly(G.b,G.nb,filter,wb,wh,N)...
          /pseudo_poly(G.a,G.na,filter,wb,wh,N);
Ga=minreal(Ga);
function G1=pseudo_poly(a,na,filter,wb,wh,N), G1=0; s=tf('s');
for i=1:length(a), na0=na(i); n1=floor(na0);
   if na0>n1, g1=eval([filter '(na0-n1,N,wb,wh)']);
   else, g1=1; end
   G1=G1+a(i)*s^n1*g1;
end
```

The syntax of the function is $G_1 = \text{high\_order}(G, \text{filter}, \omega_b, \omega_h, N)$, where $G$ is the FOTF object, filter can be selected as 'ousta_fod' or 'new_fod'. The arguments $\omega_b$, $\omega_h$ and $N$ are the parameters of the Oustaloup filters. The default values are $\omega_b = 10^{-3}$, $\omega_h = 10^3$, $N = 5$, and the default filter is Oustaloup filter.

It is interesting to note that if the FOTF object $G$ is, in fact, an integer-order model, $G_1 = \text{high\_order}(G)$ will convert it into a TF object $G_1$.

**Example 11.17.** Consider high-order fractional-order transfer function

$$G(s) = \frac{-2s^{0.63} - 4}{2s^{3.501} + 3.8s^{2.42} + 2.6s^{1.798} + 2.5s^{1.31} + 1.5}.$$

Selecting frequency interval $(\omega_1, \omega_2)$, and suitable order $N$, the high-order integer-order approximation can be obtained, with examples $s^{3.501} = s^3 s^{0.501}$. The low-level command is rather complicated and tedious

```
>> N=9; w1=1e-3; w2=1e3; g1=ousta_fod(0.501,N,w1,w2); s=tf('s');
   g2=ousta_fod(0.42,N,w1,w2); g3=ousta_fod(0.798,N,w1,w2);
   g4=ousta_fod(0.31,N,w1,w2); g5=ousta_fod(0.63,N,w1,w2);
   G1=(-2*g5-4)/(2*s^3*g1+3.8*s^2*g2+2.6*s*g3+2.5*s*g4+1.5)
```

Alternatively, **high_order()** function can be used directly

```
>> b=[-2 -4]; nb=[0.63 0]; a=[2 3.8 2.6 2.5 1.5];
   na=[3.501 2.42 1.798 1.31 0]; G=fotf(a,na,b,nb);
   G2=high_order(G,'ousta_fod',w1,w2,N); order(G2)
   bode(G1,G2); hold on; bode(G); t=0:0.004:30;
   figure; y=step(G,t); step(G1,G2,30); line(t,y)
```

It can be seen that a 45th order integer-order model can be obtained. The exact Bode diagram and its integer-order approximation can be obtained as shown in Fig. 11-12(a). It can be seen that the magnitude curves are almost the same in the specified frequency interval, and the phase difference is $360°$, thus they are effectively the same as well. For larger frequency intervals, the frequency response fitting are also satisfactory. Step responses of the fractional-order model and the integer-order approximation can also be obtained as shown in Fig. 11-12(b). It can be seen that the approximation of step response is also satisfactory.

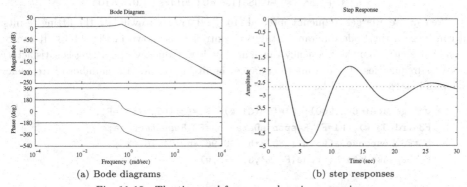

(a) Bode diagrams        (b) step responses

Fig. 11-12   The time and frequency domain comparisons.

## 11.5.2   *Approximations of Fractional-order Controllers*

In control system design, the controller obtained may be rather complicated, and may not be easy to implement. For instance, if $[(as+b)/(cs+d)]^\alpha$ term is contained in the controller, the following procedures can be used in controller approximation:

(1) Generate exact frequency response samples to the fractional-order controller;

(2) Select suitable orders in numerator and denominator for the controller;

(3) Use function `invfreqs()` to get the frequency response fitting model;

(4) Validate the fitting results. If it is not satisfactory, the orders should be increased in step (2), or go to step (1) to select again the interested frequency range until a satisfactory model can be obtained.

**Example 11.18.** Consider the following fractional-order QFT controller model [5]

$$G_c(s) = 1.8393 \left( \frac{s + 0.011}{s} \right)^{0.96} \left( \frac{8.8 \times 10^{-5} s + 1}{8.096 \times 10^{-5} s + 1} \right)^{1.76} \frac{1}{(1 + s/0.29)^2}.$$

The controller is rather complicated, so that approximate integer-order controllers are expected, with frequency response fitting approach. Since the `frd()` function in MATLAB can only be used to deal with integer-order systems, its member variable `ResponseData` can be used to complete the computation with non-integer powers. Thus, the frequency response data of $G(s)$ can be obtained. Function `invfreqs()` can then be used to get the fitting model, within the frequency range of $\omega \in (10^{-4}, 10^0)$ rad/s, with the following statements

```
>> w=logspace(-4,0); G1=tf([1 0.011],[1 0]); F1=frd(G1,w);
   G2=tf([8.8e-5 1],[8.096e-5 1]); F2=frd(G2,w);
   s=tf('s'); G3=1/(1+s/0.29)^2; F3=frd(G3,w); F=F1;
   h1=F1.ResponseData; h2=F2.ResponseData; h3=F3.ResponseData;
   h=1.8393*h1.^0.96.*h2.^1.76.*h3; F.ResponseData=h;
   [n,d]=invfreqs(h(:),w,4,4); G=tf(n,d)
```

The approximate controller obtained is

$$G(s) = \frac{2.213 \times 10^{-7} s^4 + 1.732 \times 10^{-6} s^3 + 0.1547 s^2 + 0.001903 s + 2.548 \times 10^{-6}}{s^4 + 0.5817 s^3 + 0.08511 s^2 + 0.000147 s + 1.075 \times 10^{-9}}.$$

We can use a larger frequency interval $(10^{-6}, 10^2)$ rad/s to validate the fitting results. It can be seen the Bode diagram of the two controllers is shown in Fig. 11-13. It can be seen that apart from the frequency range at very low frequency, the fitting is satisfactory in other frequencies. If we want to enhance the fitting results, the number of frequency samples in step (1) should be increased.

```
>> w=logspace(-6,2,200); F1=frd(G1,w); F2=frd(G2,w); F=F1;
   F3=frd(G3,w); h1=F1.ResponseData; h2=F2.ResponseData;
   h3=F3.ResponseData; h=1.8393*h1.^0.96.*h2.^1.76.*h3;
   F.ResponseData=h; bode(F,'-',G,'--',w)
```

### 11.5.3    *Optimal Reduction Algorithm for Fractional-order Models*

To get better reduction model, the error between the original model and reduced model to the same input signal should be defined, and the target is to minimize the error criterion. The optimal reduced model can be converted to the minimization of the following objective function

$$J = \min_{\theta} \left\| \widehat{G}(s) - G_{r/m,\tau}(s) \right\|_2, \tag{11.54}$$

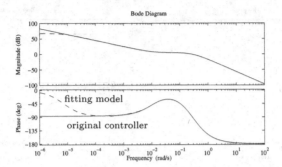

Fig. 11-13 Comparisons of fractional-order QFT controller and integer-order approximation.

where $\boldsymbol{\theta}$ is the vector of undetermined model parameters, i.e.,

$$\boldsymbol{\theta} = \left[ \beta_1, \beta_2, \cdots, \beta_r, \alpha_1, \alpha_2, \cdots, \alpha_m, \tau \right]^{\mathrm{T}}. \tag{11.55}$$

Since there is delay terms in Eqn. (11.54), Padé approximation is used for them, and the objective function can be changed to the following norm evaluation form

$$J = \min_{\boldsymbol{\theta}} \left\| \widehat{G}(s) - \widehat{G}_{r/m}(s) \right\|_2. \tag{11.56}$$

There is no analytical solution to the problem, thus numerical optimization technique can be used. Based on the optimal model reduction algorithm in Chapter 4, we can solve directly the optimal model reduction problem.

**Example 11.19.** Consider again the fractional-order transfer function in Example 11.17, the following commands can be used to get 45th order approximate model

```
>> b=[-2 -4]; nb=[0.63 0]; a=[2 3.8 2.6 2.5 1.5];
   na=[3.501 2.42 1.798 1.31 0]; G=fotf(a,na,b,nb);
   G1=high_order(G,'ousta_fod',1e-3,1e3,9); order(G1)
```

Since the order of the original approximation is too high, model reduction techniques can be used with MATLAB function `opt_app()` presented in Chapter 4. The third-order reduced model is obtained as

$$G_r(s) = \frac{0.6122s^2 + 0.6244s + 0.02588}{s^3 + 0.2014s^2 + 0.1972s + 0.01494}.$$

Comparisons on step responses and Bode diagrams are shown in Figs. 11-14(a) and (b). It can be seen that the approximate third-order model is very close to that of the original system. For high frequency magnitude fitting, it appears that the fitting is not good. However, since logarithmic scale is used, there should not be too much difference.

```
>> Gr=opt_app(G1,2,3,0); step(G1,Gr,'--',30);
   hold on, step(G,0:0.01:30);
   figure; bode(G1,Gr,'--'); hold on; bode(G);
```

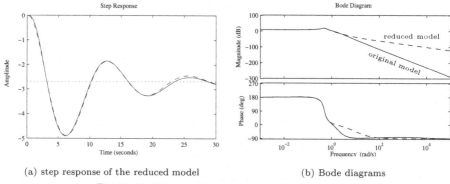

(a) step response of the reduced model          (b) Bode diagrams

Fig. 11-14   Time and frequency domain comparisons.

## 11.6   Simulation Methods for Complicated Fractional-order Systems

### 11.6.1   *Simulation with Numerical Laplace Transform*

It has been shown that inverse Laplace transforms can be used to solve simulation problems. However, Laplace and inverse Laplace transforms are not always solvable for complicated systems. For instance, the system with the controller in Example 11.18 cannot be easily solved. Thus, numerical techniques have to be used instead. The INVLAP() function is a powerful tool for performing numerical inverse Laplace transforms[19, 20], with the syntax  $[t, y] = \text{INVLAP}(\text{fun}, t_0, t_f, n)$ .

The essential input arguments are: fun, which is a string describing the Laplace transform form $F(s)$, and $(t_0, t_f)$, which is the time interval, with $n$ points.

There was a bug in the original code when $t_0 = 0$, and this is fixed in the package of the book. The remaining input arguments are internal parameters and the use of default values is suggested. More input arguments can be used in the function call, details can be found in doc INVLAP.

**Example 11.20.** Considering a fractional-order transfer function

$$G(s) = \frac{(s^{0.4} + 0.4s^{0.2} + 0.5)}{\sqrt{s}(s^{0.2} + 0.02s^{0.1} + 0.6)^{0.4}(s^{0.3} + 0.5)^{0.6}},$$

where the input is $u(t) = e^{-0.2t} \sin t$, the Laplace transform of it can be obtained and converted to a string. The output signal can be obtained as shown in Fig. 11-15. The execution speed of INVLAP() is extremely fast, the whole process needing only 0.3 s.

```
>> G='(s^0.4+ 0.4*s^0.2+0.5)/(s^0.2+0.02*s^0.1+0.6)^0.4/(s^0.3+0.5)^0.6';
   syms t; u=exp(-0.2*t)*sin(t); Y=['(' G ')*' char(laplace(u))];
   [t,y]=INVLAP(Y,0.01,25,1000); plot(t,y)
```

To further illustrate the topic, suppose that the input signal is given by a set of sample points. Of course, using the symbolic Laplace transform is not possible for functions given by sample points. Interpolation, and then numerical integration,

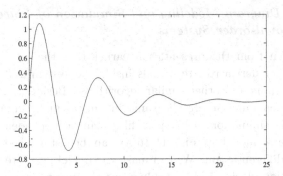

Fig. 11-15   Response to complicated fractional-order system.

should be performed to find the numerical Laplace transform. Based on the source code of INVLAP(), numerical Laplace transform functions can be embedded to solve complicated problems. A new MATLAB function is written, with the syntax

$$[t,y] = \text{num\_laplace}(\text{fun}, t_0, t_f, n, x_0, u_0)$$

where fun is a string describing the transfer function of the system. The extra arguments $x_0$ and $u_0$, specify the sample points of the input signal. Note that the function is extremely slow. The listing of the M-function is

```
function [t,y]=num_laplace(G,t0,tf,nnt,x0,u0)
FF=strrep(strrep(strrep(G,'*','.*'),'/','./'),'^','.^');
a=6; ns=20; nd=19; t=linspace(t0,tf,nnt);
if t0==0, t=t(2:end); nnt=nnt-1; end  % the original bug is fixed here
n=1:ns+1+nd; alfa=a+(n-1)*pi*1j; beta=-exp(a)*(-1).^n; n=1:nd;
bdif=fliplr(cumsum(gamma(nd+1)./gamma(nd+2-n)./gamma(n)))./2^nd;
beta(ns+2:ns+1+nd)=beta(ns+2:ns+1+nd).*bdif; beta(1)=beta(1)/2;
for kt=1:nnt
    tt=t(kt); s=alfa/tt; bt=beta/tt;
    U=integral(@(x)interp1(x0,u0,x,'spline').*exp(-s.*x),...
                t0,tf,'ArrayValued',true);
    btF=bt.*eval(FF).*U; y(kt)=sum(real(btF));
end
```

**Example 11.21.** If the analytical form of the input function is not known, but instead only a set of sample points is given, the following statements can be given to calculate the output signal. After around 30 s, the numerical solution can be found and it is exactly the same as the one shown in Fig. 11-15. It can be seen from the example that extremely complicated problems can be solved in this way.

```
>> x0=0:0.5:25; y0=exp(-0.2*x0).*sin(x0);
   [t,y]=num_laplace(G,0,25,200,x0,y0); plot(t,y)
```

### 11.6.2    *Block Diagram Modeling and Simulation of Linear Fractional-order Systems*

It can be seen from the presentation earlier that the best way to evaluate the fractional-order derivatives to signals inside the system is to use filters with Oustaloup algorithms and other similar algorithms. Besides, since the orders of numerator and denominator are the same in Oustaloup filter and may lead to algebraic loops in simulation, a low-pass filter can be appended with bandwidth $\omega_h$. The Simulink model in Fig. 11-16(a) can be established to approximate fractional-order differentiation. We can mask the model into a reusable fractional-order differentiation block. With suitably selected frequency ranges and order, the block can be used in the block diagram-based modeling of complicated nonlinear fractional-order systems.

The masked block is given in Fig. 11-16(b). Double click the block, the dialog box is shown in Fig. 11-16(c). The necessary parameters can be assigned in the dialog box. In the initialization column in the masking process, the following statements can be specified, and the labels in the icon can correctly be displayed.

```
wb=ww(1); wh=ww(2);
if key==1, G=ousta_fod(gam,n,wb,wh); else, G=new_fod(gam,n,wb,wh); end
num=G.num{1}; den=G.den{1}; T=1/wh; str='Fractional\n';
if isnumeric(gam)
    if gam>0, str=[str, 'Der  s^' num2str(gam) ];
    else, str=[str, 'Int  s^{' num2str(gam) '}']; end
else, str=[str, 'Der  s^gam']; end
```

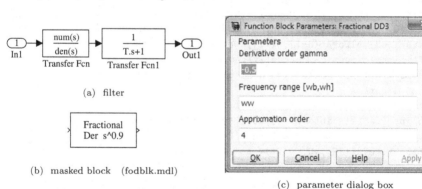

(a)  filter

(b)  masked block   (fodblk.mdl)

(c)  parameter dialog box

Fig. 11-16    Design of fractional-order differentiator block.

In real simulation processes, the algorithms **ode15s** or **ode23tb** are recommended, since the model is likely to be stiff equations. The following examples are used to demonstrate of fractional-order differential equations.

**Example 11.22.** Consider the linear fractional-order differential equation studied in Example 11.15, expressed as

$$\mathscr{D}_t^{3.5}y(t) + 8\mathscr{D}_t^{3.1}y(t) + 26\mathscr{D}_t^{2.3}y(t) + 73\mathscr{D}_t^{1.2}y(t) + 90\mathscr{D}_t^{0.5}y(t) = 90\sin t^2.$$

Let $z(t) = \mathscr{D}_t^{0.5} y(t)$, the original model can be rewritten as

$$z(t) = \sin t^2 - \frac{1}{90} \left[ \mathscr{D}_t^3 z(t) + 8\mathscr{D}_t^{2.6} z(t) + 26\mathscr{D}_t^{1.8} z(t) + 73\mathscr{D}_t^{0.7} z(t) \right].$$

Simulink model for the differential equation can be established, as shown in Fig. 11-17. After simulation, the output signal can be obtained and it is exactly the same as the one obtained in Example 11.15.

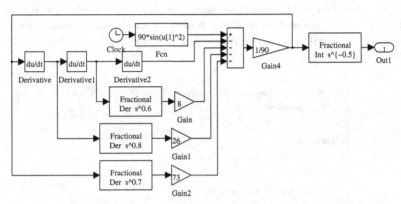

Fig. 11-17   Simulink representation for the linear fractional-order model (c11fode1.mdl).

Two more masked blocks are established for the package of the book, one for fractional-order transfer function, and the other for fractional-order PID controller. These blocks can be used directly in Simulink as shown in Fig. 11-18(a).

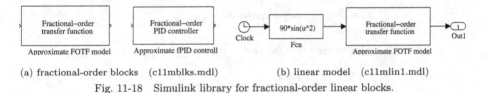

(a) fractional-order blocks   (c11mblks.mdl)          (b) linear model   (c11mlin1.mdl)

Fig. 11-18   Simulink library for fractional-order linear blocks.

The code for the Initialization pane of the Approximate FOTF model block can be expressed as

```
if strcmp(class(na),'fotf'), G=na;
else
    if length(na)~=length(a),
        errordlg('Error','Mismatch on the denominator')
    end
    if length(b)~=length(nb),
        errordlg('Error','Mismatch on the denominator')
    end
    G=fotf(a,na,b,nb);
end
if kFilter==1, str='ousta_fod'; else, str='new_fod'; end
```

```
wb=ww(1); wh=ww(2);
GO=high_order(G,str,wb,wh,N); [numG,denG]=tfdata(GO,'v');
```

**Example 11.23.** With the Approximate fractional-order transfer function block, the Simulink model for the differential equation in Example 11.15 can be established as shown in Fig. 11-18(b). Double click the Approximate fractional-order transfer function block, the parameters of the system can be entered as shown in Fig. 11-19. Alternatively, if the FOTF object $G$ is established in MATLAB workspace, we can simply enter $G$ in the Orders of denominator edit box. It can be seen that the model is much simpler than the one in the previous example. Simulation result with the new model is exactly the same as the one in the previous example.

Fig. 11-19    Parameter dialog box for the FOTF block.

### 11.6.3    *Block Diagram Modeling and Simulation of Nonlinear Fractional-order Systems*

For complicated nonlinear fractional-order systems, the overload functions `step()`, `lsim()` and the numerical inverse Laplace transforms cannot be used. Block diagram-based modeling and simulation strategies are more important. Here, the modeling and simulation methods are illustrated through an example.

**Example 11.24.** Consider the following nonlinear fractional-order differential equation

$$\frac{3\mathscr{D}^{0.9}y(t)}{3 + 0.2\mathscr{D}^{0.8}y(t) + 0.9\mathscr{D}^{0.2}y(t)} + \left|2\mathscr{D}^{0.7}y(t)\right|^{1.5} + \frac{4}{3}y(t) = 5\sin 10t.$$

Based on the equation, the explicit form of the $y(t)$ signal is written as

$$y(t) = \frac{3}{4}\left[5\sin 10t - \frac{3\mathscr{D}^{0.9}y(t)}{3 + 0.2\mathscr{D}^{0.8}y(t) + 0.9\mathscr{D}^{0.2}y(t)} - \left|2\mathscr{D}^{0.7}y(t)\right|^{1.5}\right].$$

A Simulink model can be constructed as shown in Fig. 11-20(a). It can be seen from the simulation model that the accuracy of the simulation results are to some extent, related to the specifications of the filters. Different frequency intervals and filter orders may affect the simulation results. Simulation results for different frequency intervals and filter orders are obtained in Fig. 11-20(b). It can be seen that all the curves agree well.

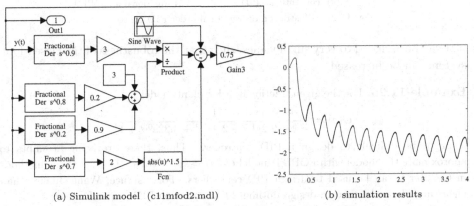

(a) Simulink model (c11mfod2.mdl)  (b) simulation results

Fig. 11-20  Simulink model and simulation results.

## 11.7 Design of Optimal Fractional-order PID Controllers

### 11.7.1 *Optimal Design of $PI^\lambda D^\mu$ Controllers*

The structures of the fractional-order PID controllers are different from the PID controllers studied in Chapter 8. The fractional $PI^\lambda D^\mu$ model can be expressed as

$$G_c(s) = K_p + \frac{K_i}{s^\lambda} + K_d s^\mu. \tag{11.57}$$

In the illustration shown in Fig. 11-21, the orders of integral and differentiation are used as the two axes. It can be seen that the conventional PID-type controllers are just a few specific points on the order planes. However, the orders of the controllers in fractional-order PID controllers can be relatively arbitrarily chosen. Normally with stability considerations, $0 < \lambda, \mu < 2$. Because there are two more parameters to tune than the conventional PID controller, the fractional-order PID controllers are usually more flexible, and may expect better performances[21].

From loop shaping point of view, the slopes in Bode magnitude plots are multiples of $20\,\mathrm{dB/dec}$ in integer-order systems, while in fractional-order systems there is no such restrictions. Thus, the shape can be arbitrarily shaped. For instance, at the places around the crossover frequency, the slope of the magnitude

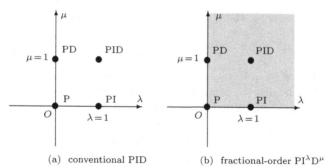

(a)  conventional PID          (b)  fractional-order $PI^{\lambda}D^{\mu}$

Fig. 11-21    Illustration of fractional-order PID controllers.

plot can be assigned to very small values, such that the robustness of the closed-loop system can be increased.

**Example 11.25.** For the given fractional-order plant model

$$G(s) = \frac{1}{s^{2.6} + 2.2s^{1.5} + 2.9s^{1.3} + 3.32s^{0.9} + 1},$$

it might be difficult to design a PID controller. Thus, there are some attempts to approximate the model with FOPDT model $G_{\text{p}}(s) = ke^{-Ls}/(Ts+1)$, so that the methods in Chapter 8 can be used to design PID controllers. For instance, Wang–Juang–Chan algorithm [22] can be used to design optimal ITAE criterion PID controller

$$K_{\text{p}} = \frac{(0.7303 + 0.5307T/L)(T + 0.5L)}{K(T+L)}, \quad T_{\text{i}} = T + 0.5L, \quad T_{\text{d}} = \frac{0.5LT}{T + 0.5L}. \quad (11.58)$$

It can be seen that the FOPDT model can be obtained with

```
>> N=5; w1=1e-3; w2=1e3; s=fotf('s');
   G=1/(s^2.6+3.3*s^1.5+2.9*s^1.3+3.32*s^0.9+1);
   G0=high_order(G,'ousta_fod',w1,w2,N); Gr=opt_app(G0,0,1,1)
```

The reduced model can be obtained as $G_{\text{r}}(s) = 0.1836e^{-0.827s}/(s + 0.1836)$. Then a PID controller can be designed with the following statements

```
>> L=Gr.ioDelay; [n,d]=tfdata(Gr,'v'); K=n(2)/d(2); T=d(1)/d(2);
   Ti=T+0.5*L; Kp=(0.7303+0.5307*T/L)*Ti/(K*(T+L));
   Td=(0.5*L*T)/(T+0.5*L); s=tf('s'); Gc=Kp*(1+1/Ti/s+Td*s),
   w=logspace(-4,4,200); C=fotf(Gc);
   H=bode(G*C,w); bode(G0*Gc,'-',H,'--');  figure;
   t=0:0.01:20; step(feedback(G0*Gc,1),20),
   y=step(feedback(G*C,1),t); hold on; plot(t,y,'--')
```

The PID controller can be designed as $G_{\text{c}}(s) = 3.9474\,(1 + 1/(5.8232s) + 0.3843s)$. Under such a controller, the open-loop Bode diagram and closed-loop step response can be obtained as shown in Figs. 11-22(a) and (b). It can be seen that the two systems are quite close.

**Example 11.26.** Consider the plant model in the previous example. Now the searching algorithm can be used to design optimal $PI^{\lambda}D^{\mu}$ controller. The following MATLAB

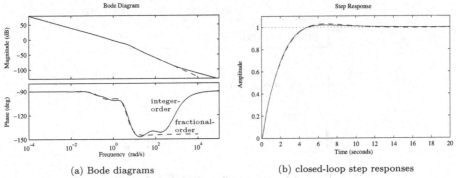

(a) Bode diagrams         (b) closed-loop step responses

Fig. 11-22   Fractional-order PID control results.

function can be written to describe the objective function

```
function fy=fpidfun(x,G,t,key)
s=fotf('s'); C=x(1)+x(2)*s^(-x(4))+x(3)*s^(x(5));
dt=t(2)-t(1); y=step(feedback(G*C,1),t); e=1-y;
if key==1, fy=dt*sum(t.*abs(e)); else, fy=dt*sum(e.^2); end
disp([x(:); fy].')
```

where in the last statement, the intermediate results can be obtained. The function has three additional arguments, $G$ is the FOTF plant model, $t$ is the evenly spaced time vector, and key is the criterion, with 1 for ITAE criterion, otherwise for ISE criterion.

Assume the terminate time is 10 s, and assume the parameters of the $PI^\lambda D^\mu$ controller are all smaller than 10, and the orders are in the interval $(0,2)$. The function fminsearchbnd() is recommended to find optimal $PI^\lambda D^\mu$ controller

```
>> xm=zeros(5,1); xM=[10; 10; 10; 2; 2];
   x0=[Kp,Kp/Ti,Kp*Td,1,1].'; t=0:0.01:20;
   x=fminsearchbnd(@fpidfun,x0,xm,xM,[],G,t,1)
   s=fotf('s'); Gc1=x(1)+x(2)*s^(-x(4))+x(3)*s^(x(5));
   step(feedback(G*Gc1,1),t);
   y=step(feedback(G*C,1),t); hold on; plot(t,y,'--')
```

The optimal controller is $G_c(s) = 10 + 2.3088s^{-0.9877} + 8.9811s^{0.4286}$. The step responses of the systems under this controller and the one obtained in the previous example, are obtained as shown in Fig. 11-23. It can be seen that the fractional-order PID controller is better than the integer-order controller.

Based on the above idea, an optimal fractional-order PID controller design function can be designed for linear fractional-order plants

```
function [Gc,x,y]=fpidtune(G,type,t,key,x0,xm,xM,ff)
if nargin==7, ff=optimset; ff.MaxIter=50; end
x=fminsearchbnd(@fpidfuns,x0,xm,xM,ff,G,t,key,type);
[y,Gc]=fpidfuns(x,G,t,key,type);
```

The syntax of the function is

$$[G_c, x, y] = \text{fpidtune}(G, \text{type}, t, \text{key}, x_0, x_m, x_M, \text{ff})$$

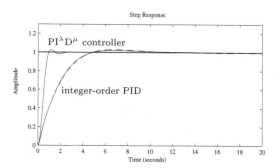

Fig. 11-23   Comparisons of different PID controllers.

where $G$ is the FOTF plant model, type is the expected controller type, with options 'fpid', 'fpi', 'fpd', 'fpidx', and 'pid', with 'fpidx' for PID$^\mu$ controller with integer integral. The argument $t$ is the evenly spaced time vector, key is the type of criterion, with options 'itae', 'ise', 'iae' and 'itse', with 'itae' recommended. The definitions of variables $x_0$, $x_\mathrm{m}$, $x_\mathrm{M}$ are the same as defined earlier. Variable ff is the optimization control template, and it can be omitted.

For different types of fractional-order controllers and criteria, the supporting MATLAB function describing the objective function can be written as

```
function [fy,C]=fpidfuns(x,G,t,key,type), s=fotf('s');
switch type
   case 'fpid', C=x(1)+x(2)*s^(-x(4))+x(3)*s^(x(5));
   case 'fpi', C=x(1)+x(2)*s^(-x(3));
   case 'fpd', C=x(1)+x(2)*s^x(3);
   case 'fpidx', C=x(1)+x(2)/s+x(3)*s^x(4);
   case {'pid','PID'}, C=x(1)+x(2)/s+x(3)*s;
end
dt=t(2)-t(1); y=step(feedback(G*C,1),t); e=1-y;
switch key
   case {'itae','ITAE'}, fy=dt*sum(t.*abs(e));
   case {'ise','ISE'}, fy=dt*sum(e.^2);
   case {'iae','IAE'}, fy=dt*sum(abs(e));
   case {'itse','ITSE'}, fy=dt*sum(t.*e.^2);
   otherwise, error('Error: available criteria are itae, ise, iae, itse.')
end
disp([x fy])
```

Since this is an open structure with switch commands, other controller structures and criteria selections can be added to the source code directly by the readers, if necessary.

**Example 11.27.** Consider again the problem in Example 11.26. The optimal fractional-order PID controller can be obtained directly with the following MATLAB function, and the results are exactly the same as the ones in the previous example.

```
>> s=fotf('s'); G=1/(s^2.6+3.3*s^1.5+2.9*s^1.3+3.32*s^0.9+1);
```

```
xm=zeros(5,1); xM=[10; 10; 10; 2; 2]; x0=[1;1;1;1;1].';
t=0:0.01:20; [Gc,x]=fpidtune(G,'fpid',t,'itae',x0,xm,xM)
```

The following statements can also be used to design the optimal PID controller

```
>> xm=zeros(3,1); xM=[10; 10; 10]; x0=[1;1;1].';
   t=0:0.01:20; [Gc1,x]=fpidtune(G,'pid',t,'itae',x0,xm,xM)
   step(feedback(G*Gc,1),t); hold on; step(feedback(G*Gc1,1),t);
```

with an optimal conventional PID controller $G_{c1} = 9.9945+1.5107/s+9.1101s$. The closed-loop step responses under the two controllers are shown in Fig. 11-24. It can be seen that the closed-loop response under $PI^\lambda D^\mu$ controller is much better than the conventional PID controller for the fractional-order plant model.

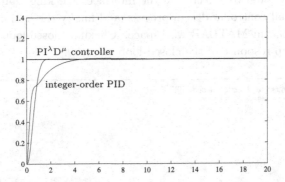

Fig. 11-24 Comparisons of different PID controllers.

If the plant model and controller model are both approximated with Oustaloup filters, the following statements should be specified, and integer-order closed-loop model, usually of extremely high order (for this example, a 43th order closed-loop model is obtained, with 7th order Oustaloup filter), can be obtained. The closed-loop step response of the high order integer-order system is almost the same as the one obtained in Fig. 11-24.

```
>> Gc0=high_order(Gc,'ousta_fod',1e-3,1e3,7);
   G0=high_order(G,'ousta_fod',1e-3,1e3,7); G1=feedback(G0*Gc0,1);
   order(G1), step(G1,t); hold on; step(feedback(G*Gc,1),t)
   Gc10=high_order(Gc1); step(feedback(G0*Gc10,1),t)
```

**Example 11.28.** The fractional-order PID control system is modeled with Simulink as shown in Fig. 11-25. When the parameters in the plant and fractional-order PID controller are specified, simulation results can be obtained. It can be seen that the control results are exactly the same as the one obtained in the previous example.

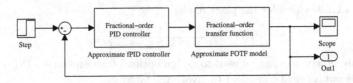

Fig. 11-25 Fractional-order PID controller system (file name: fPID_simu.mdl).

### 11.7.2　*OptimFOPID — An Optimal Fractional-order PID Controller Design Interface*

Based on the algorithms presented earlier, a graphical user interface, Optim-FOPID, is designed. This function can be used to design optimal fractional-order PID controllers with user interface[23].

The plant model $G$ in FOTF format should be entered into MATLAB workspace first. Then type `optimfopid` command at MATLAB prompt. The user interface shown in Fig. 11-26 will be displayed. Click Plant model, the model $G$ can be loaded into the interface. Then the controller type, object function type and terminate simulation time should be selected in the interface. Clicking Optimize button will invoke the optimal controller design process, and finally the optimal controller can be obtained in $G_c$, in MATLAB workspace. Clicking Closed-loop response button will show the step response of the closed-loop system.

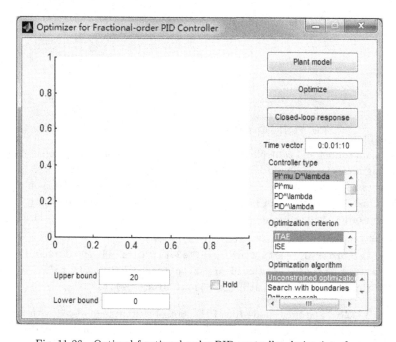

Fig. 11-26　Optimal fractional-order PID controller design interface.

**Example 11.29.** Consider the plant model

$$G(s) = \frac{1}{0.8s^{2.2} + 0.5s^{0.9} + 1},$$

The following procedures can be used to design optimal fractional-order PID controller.

(1) Type `optimfopid` command to invoke the interface.

(2) Enter the FOTF model $G$ into MATLAB workspace, and click Plant model to load the model into the interface.

```
>> G=fotf([0.8 0.5 1],[2.2 0.9 0],1,0)
```

(3) Set the upper bounds of the controller parameters to 15, and terminate time at 8. It should be noted that the upper bounds of controller parameters may affect the final search results.

(4) Click the Optimize button to initiate the optimization process, and the optimal fractional-order controller can be obtained, and for this example, the optimal vector is

$$x = [6.5954 \quad 15.7495 \quad 11.4703 \quad 0.9860 \quad 1.1932].$$

The controller model can be written as

$$G_c(s) = 6.5954 + \frac{15.7495}{s^{0.986}} + 11.4703s^{1.1932}.$$

(5) Click Closed-loop response to draw the closed-loop step response of the system, as shown in Fig. 11-27(a). Since the order of integrator is very close to 1, PID^mu item from the controller type listbox can be selected, and optimal PID$^\mu$ controller can be designed. The result is very close to the one obtained by PI$^\lambda$D$^\mu$ controller.

```
>> t=0:0.01:8; y=step(feedback(G*Gc,1),t); plot(t,y)
```

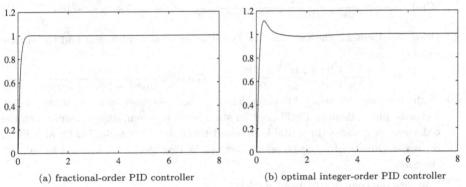

(a) fractional-order PID controller          (b) optimal integer-order PID controller

Fig. 11-27   Comparisons of optimal fractional-order and integer-order PID controllers.

If the PID item from the Controller Type listbox is selected, and then if Optimize button is clicked, the optimal integer-order PID controller can be designed, and the closed-loop step response can be obtained as shown in Fig. 11-27(b). It can be seen that for this example, the results of fractional-order PID controller is better than the integer-order one.

For linear fractional-order plant models, the OptimFOPID interface can be used to directly design fractional-order PID controllers in a user friendly manner. There are also limitations in the interface. For instance, in the current version, the plant should not contain time delays. Also, controllers with actuator saturation cannot be processed.

## 11.8   Problems

(1) Assume that the fractional-order differential equation is [2]

$$0.8 \mathscr{D}_t^{2.2} y(t) + 0.5 \mathscr{D}_t^{0.9} y(t) + y(t) = 1, \ y(0) = y'(0) = y''(0) = 0,$$

find the numerical solutions. If orders 2.2 and 0.9 are approximated by integers 2 and 1, the original differential equation can be approximated by integer-order differential equation. Please compare the approximation results.

(2) With the code for Mittag–Leffler functions, verify the following

(i) $\mathscr{E}_{\alpha,\beta}(x) + \mathscr{E}_{\alpha,\beta}(-x) = 2\mathscr{E}_{\alpha,\beta}(x^2)$,  (ii) $\mathscr{E}_{\alpha,\beta}(x) - \mathscr{E}_{\alpha,\beta}(-x) = 2x\mathscr{E}_{\alpha,\alpha+\beta}(x^2)$,

(iii) $\mathscr{E}_{\alpha,\beta}(x) = \dfrac{1}{\Gamma(\beta)} + \mathscr{E}_{\alpha,\alpha+\beta}(x)$,  (iv) $\mathscr{E}_{\alpha,\beta}(x) = \beta\mathscr{E}_{\alpha,\beta+1}(x) + \alpha x \dfrac{d}{dx}\mathscr{E}_{\alpha,\beta+1}(x)$.

(3) Two filter approximation approaches are proposed in the chapter on fractional-order derivatives. Please compare the two filters for the following fractional-order system, in frequency and step response fitting.

$$G(s) = \frac{s+1}{10s^{3.2} + 185s^{2.5} + 288s^{0.7} + 1}.$$

(4) Analyze the stability of the closed-loop system, and draw Bode diagram and closed-loop step response for the following system.

$$G(s) = \frac{s^{1.2} + 4s^{0.8} + 7}{8s^{3.2} + 9s^{2.8} + 9s^2 + 6s^{1.6} + 5s^{0.4} + 9}, \quad G_c(s) = 10 + \frac{9}{c^{0.97}} + 10s^{0.98}.$$

(5) Draw root locus for the following fractional-order plant models and find the critical gains of them.

(i) $G_1(s) = \dfrac{s^{1.5} + 9s + 24s^{0.5} + 20}{3s^2 + 16s^{1.5} + 9s + 20s^{0.5}}$,  (ii) $G_2(s) = \dfrac{s+1}{10s^{3.2} + 185s^{2.5} + 288s^{0.7} + 1}$.

(6) With reference to the FOTF class definition and overload function programming methods, please define a FOSS class for state space representation of commensurate-order systems, and write suitable overload functions. Write out FOTF and FOSS conversion functions. The transfer functions in Problem 5 can be used to validate the class.

(7) Consider the complicated plant models

$$G(s) = \frac{(s^{0.2} + 3s^{0.1} + 3)^{0.6}}{s^{0.7}(s^{0.1} + 2)^{0.5}(s^{0.4} + 2)^{0.3}}.$$

It is obvious that FOTF class cannot be used to handle the plant model. Thus, the overload bode() function cannot be used directly. Please draw the Bode diagram of the system through low-level commands.

(8) Please consider the following fractional-order control system with

$$G(s) = \frac{1}{s^{0.5}(s^{0.2} + 2)^{0.7}} e^{-1.3s}, \ \text{with} \ G_c(s) = 0.8 + \frac{2}{s^{0.45}} + 0.6s^{0.3}.$$

Again the FOTF class cannot be used to handle the closed-loop system representation. Please try to draw the unit step response of the closed-loop system through numerical inverse Laplace transform approach.

(9) Solve the following nonlinear fractional-order differential equation with zero initial conditions, where $f(t) = 2t + 2t^{1.545}/\Gamma(2.545)$.

$$\mathscr{D}^2 x(t) + \mathscr{D}^{1.455} x(t) + \left[\mathscr{D}^{0.555} x(t)\right]^2 + x^3(t) = f(t).$$

(10) For the fractional-order model

$$G_1(s) = \frac{5}{s^{2.3} + 1.3s^{0.9} + 1.25}, \quad G_2(s) = \frac{5s^{0.6} + 2}{s^{3.3} + 3.1s^{2.6} + 2.89s^{1.9} + 2.5s^{1.4} + 1.2},$$

please find integer-order approximations, and find out the suitable order of the filters. Find also a suitable reduced order model, and compare frequency domain and step response of the reduced order systems.

(11) Find suitable low-order approximations to the following fractional-order models, and compare frequency domain fitting results.

(i) $G(s) = \dfrac{25}{(s^2 + 8.5s + 25)^{0.2}}$, (ii) $G(s) = \dfrac{562920(s + 1.0118)^{0.6774}}{(s^2 + 54.7160s + 590570)^{0.8387}}$.

(12) Design optimal integer-order PID controller and $\mathrm{PI}^\lambda\mathrm{D}^\mu$ controller, and observe the control results.

$$G(s) = \frac{5s^{0.6} + 2}{s^{3.3} + 3.1s^{2.6} + 2.89s^{1.9} + 2.5s^{1.4} + 1.2}.$$

(13) Consider the `fpidfuns()` function. If the following controller and criterion are used, please extend the function

$$G_c(s) = K_p \left(1 + \frac{K_i}{s}\right)\left(1 + \frac{K_d s}{Ts + 1}\right), \quad I = \int_0^\infty t^2 e^2(t)\mathrm{d}t.$$

(14) Extend the OptimFOPID interface, such that more optimization algorithms can be used, to design optimal $\mathrm{PI}^\lambda\mathrm{D}^\mu$ controllers with global optimization algorithms.

(15) Consider the following uncertain fractional-order plant model $G = b/(as^{0.7} + 1)$, with nominal values $a = b = 1$, approximate the plant model with integer-order transfer function, and design robust optimal $\mathcal{H}_\infty$ controller, and observe control results with simulation methods for $a \in (0.2, 5)$, and $b \in (0.2, 1.5)$.

## Bibliography and References

[1] Miller K S, Ross B. An introuction to fractinal calculus and fractional differential equations. New York: John Wiley & Sons, 1993

[2] Podlubny I. Fractional differential equations. San Diago: Academic Press, 1999

[3] Vinagre B M, Chen Y Q. Fractional calculus applications in automatic control and robotics. Las Vegas: 41st IEEE CDC, Tutorial workshop 2, 2002

[4] Manabe S. The non-integer integral and its application to control systems. Japanese Institute of Electrical Engineers Journal, 1960, 80(860):589–597

[5] Monje C A, Chen Y Q, Vinagre B M, Xue D Y, Feliu V. Fractional-order systems and controls — fundamentals and applications. London: Springer, 2010

[6] Lakshmikantham V, Leela S. Theory of fractional dynamic systems. Cornwall, UK: Cambridge Scientific Publishers, 2010

[7] Caponetto R, Dongola G, Fortuna L, Petráš I. Fractional order systems — modeling and control applications. Singapore: World Scientific Publishing, 2009

[8] Hilfer R. Applications of fractional calculus in physics. Singapore: World Scientific Publishing, 2000

[9] Petráš I, Podlubny I, O'Leary P, Dorčák L, Vinagre B M. Analogue realization of fractional order controllers. Fakulta BERG, Technical University of Košice, 2002

[10] Xue D Y, Chen Y Q. Solving applied mathematical problems with MATLAB. Boca Raton: CRC Press, 2008

[11] Shukla A K, Prajapati J C. On a generalization of Mittag–Leffler function and its properties. Journal of Mathematical Analysis and Applications, 2007, 336(1):797–811

[12] Podlubny I. Mittag–Leffler function, 2005. http://www.mathworks.cn/MATLAB central/fileexchange/8738-mittag-leffler-function

[13] Kilbas A A, Saigob M, Saxena R K. Generalized Mittag–Leffler function and generalized fractional calculus operators. Integral Transforms and Special Functions, 2004, 15(1):31–49

[14] Matignon D. Stability properties for generalized fractional differential systems. Matignon D, Montseny D, eds., Proceedings of the Colloquium Fractional Differential Systems: Models, Methods and Applications, 5. Paris, 1998 145–158

[15] Charef A, Sun H H, Tsao Y Y, Onaral B. Fractal system as represented by singularity function. IEEE Transactions on Automatic Control, 1992, 37(9):1465–1470

[16] Oustaloup A, Levron F, Mathieu B, Nanot F M. Frequency-band complex noninteger differentiator: characterization and synthesis. IEEE Transaction on Circuit and Systems-I: Fundamental Theory and Applications, 2000, TCS-47(1):25–39

[17] Xue D Y, Zhao C N, Chen Y Q. A modified approximation method of fractional order system. Proceedings of IEEE Conference on Mechatronics and Automation. Luoyang, China, 2006: 1043–1048

[18] Meng L, Xue D Y. An approximation algorithm of fractional order pole models based on an optimization process. Proceedings of Mechatronics and Embedded Systems and Applications. Qingdao, China, 2010: 486–491

[19] Valsa J, Brančik L. Approximate formulae for numerical inversion of Laplace transforms. International Journal of Numerical Modelling: Electronic Networks, Devices and Fields, 1998, 11(3):153–166

[20] Valsa J. Numerical inversion of Laplace transforms in MATLAB. MATLAB Central File ID: #32824, 2011

[21] I. Podlubny. Fractional-order systems and $PI^{\lambda}D^{\mu}$controllers. IEEE Transactions on Automatic Control, 1999, 44(1):208–214

[22] Wang F S, Juang W S, Chan C T. Optimal tuning of PID controllers for single and cascade control loops. Chemical Engineering Communications, 1995, 132:15–34

[23] Xue D Y, Chen Y Q. OptimFOPID: a MATLAB interface for optimum fractional-order PID controller design for linear fractional-order plants. Proceedings of Fractional Derivatives and Its Applications. Nanjing, China, 2012 #307

# Chapter 12

# Hardware-in-the-loop Simulation and Real-time Control

In the previous chapters, Simulink was used to modeling and simulation of complicated control systems. It can be seen that single variable and multivariable systems, continuous, discrete and hybrid systems, linear and nonlinear systems, time invariant and time varying systems can all be modeled and simulated easily with Simulink. For even more complicated systems, S-functions, Stateflow and SimScape can all be used in the system simulation tasks.

However, the discussions up to now are carried out on the pure numerical simulation problems. The links to the real-time outside world is not at all considered. In many actual applications, the plant models cannot be obtained accurately, thus exact Simulink models cannot be constructed. Even if the models are available, it may not be accurate for certain systems, since some of the less important factors are neglected. Thus, in control engineering, the actual plant can be embedded inside the simulation loop. This kind of simulation is referred to as hardware-in-the-loop (HIL) simulation, and sometimes it is also called real-time simulation.

Real-Time Workshop provided by MathWorks can translate the Simulink models into C code, and the standalone executable files can also be generated using this tool, so that real-time control can be performed. Also, third-party software and hardware provide interfaces to Simulink. Good examples of these products are dSPACE, with its Control Desk and Quanser plus WinCon (which can be used to implement hardware-in-the-loop simulation and real-time control experiments).

In Sections 12.1 and 12.2, the related products of dSPACE and Quanser are introduced briefly, and in 12.3, a real-time control problem is used to demonstrate it under Quanser and dSPACE. In Section 12.4, low-cost implementation of hardware-in-the-loop simulation and real-time experimentation with Arduino is presented.

## 12.1 Introduction to dSPACE and Commonly Used Blocks

dSPACE (digital signal processing and control engineering) real-time simulation system was developed by dSPACE in Germany[1]. The dSPACE real-time system has high-speed computation capabilities in hardware systems, with processers and

I/O ports, and it can easily be used in real-time code generation.

dSPACE real-time control systems have certain advantages. The blocks provided are adequate for constructing real-time control systems, and the real-time facilities are ideal, since the on-board PowerPC processor can be used directly. Seamless connection with MATLAB and Simulink can be used to directly convert the numerical simulation structure to real-time control. dSPACE systems are now widely used in automotive, aerospace, robots, industrial automation and other fields. By using dSPACE systems, product development cycles can be significantly reduced, and the control quality significantly increased.

Software and hardware environments of the dSPACE real-time simulation system are presented below. The widely used hardware in education and scientific research is the ACE1103 and ACE1104 R&D controller boards. Real-time control software Control Desk, real-time interface RTI and real-time data acquisition interface MTRACE/MLIB are provided on the dSPACE package, and it is very flexible and convenient to use. The DS1104 R&D controller board, which is equipped with a PCI interface and a PowerPC processor, is a cost-effective entry-level control system design product. Here, the DS1104 R&D controller board is used to illustrate the applications in hardware-in-the-loop simulation.

When the hardware and software of dSPACE are installed, there will be a dSPACE group in the Simulink model library; double click its icon, and the group will be opened as shown in Fig. 12-1.

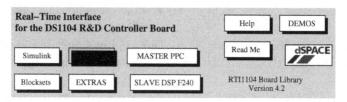

Fig. 12-1    dSPACE 1104 block library.

Double click the **MASTER PPC** block, and the model library shown in Fig. 12-2 will be opened. It can be seen that a lot of components on the board, such

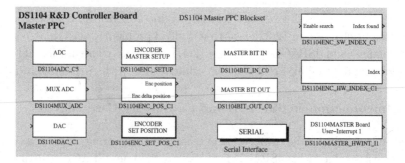

Fig. 12-2    Master PPC group.

as A/D converter, are represented by blocks in the group. Also, double clicking the Slave DSP F240 icon will open the slave DSP F240 blocks shown in Fig. 12-3. Many practical servo control blocks, such as PWM signal generator and frequency sensor are provided in the group, and they can be dragged to Simulink models. The signals generated by the computer can also be used to drive the actual plant, so that hardware-in-the-loop simulation can be completed.

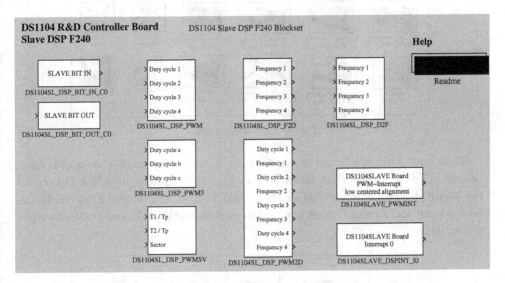

Fig. 12-3   Slave DSP F240 group.

## 12.2   Introduction to Quanser System and Its Blocks

### 12.2.1   *Introduction to Commonly Used Blocks in Quanser*

Quanser products are developed by Quanser Inc., who provide various plants for control education. Quanser has interfaces to MATLAB/Simulink and to LabView of National Instruments. It also provides real-time control software WinCon, which is similar to Control Desk from dSPACE. Quanser products are suitable for control education and laboratory research and experimentation, where different control algorithms are being tested.

Quanser experimental plants include linear motion control series, rotary series and other special experimental devices. WinCon software enables Simulink modes to directly control the actual plants.

MultiQ and other kinds of interface boards are provided in Quanser series products. The boards all provide D/A and A/D converters, and motor encoder input and output ports, such that the actual plants can be connected to the computers to construct closed-loop control structures.

WinCon is a Microsoft Windows-based application program implementing real-time control. The program can be used to execute code generated by Simulink models and exchange data with the MultiQ card to achieve real-time control. When WinCon is installed, a WinCon Control Box group will appear in the Simulink model library as shown in Fig. 12-4, where the subgroups for different MultiQ boards are provided.

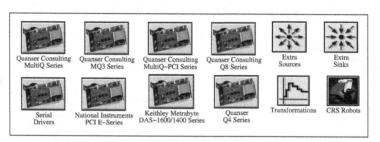

Fig. 12-4   WinCon library.

Here, the MultiQ4 board is used as an example for further demonstration. Double click the Quanser Q4 Series icon in Fig. 12-4 and the Simulink library for the MultiQ4 board is opened as shown in Fig. 12-5. It can be seen that the blocks Analog Input and Analog Output are used to implement the A/D and D/A converters respectively.

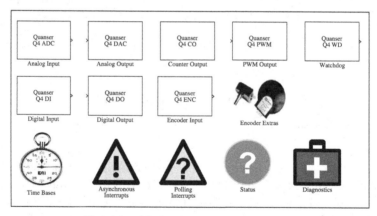

Fig. 12-5   All the blocks in MultiQ4 group.

Double click the Analog Input and Analog Output blocks, the parameter dialog boxes can be opened as shown in Figs. 12-6(a) and (b). The key parameter Channel should be set according to the actual hardware connection, otherwise, the system cannot work properly.

### 12.2.2   *Brief Introduction to Plants in Quanser Rotary Series*

Quanser experimental plants are mainly the linear motion series and the rotary motion series.  The components in the linear series can be used to compose

**Block Parameters: Analog Output** ☒

**Q4 Analog Output (mask) (link)**

Writes to the selected analog output channels of the Q4 Series I/O Boards

**Parameters**

Board number:

`0`

Channel(s) to use:

`0`

Mode(s): (0 = bipolar, 1 = unipolar)

`0`

Range(s): (5 or 10)

`10`

Initial output(s):

`0`

Final output(s):

`0`

Sample time (sec):

`-1`

☑ Input Volts

☐ Simulation output

[ OK ]  [ Cancel ]  [ Help ]  [ Apply ]

**Block Parameters: Analog Input** ☒

**Q4 Analog Input (mask) (link)**

Reads the selected analog input channels of the Q4 Series I/O Boards

**Parameters**

Board number:

`0`

Channel(s) to use:

`0`

Sample time (sec):

`simget(bdroot,'FixedStep')`

☑ Read after conversions complete

☑ Output Volts

☐ Simulation input

[ OK ]  [ Cancel ]  [ Help ]  [ Apply ]

(a) Analog Input          (b) Analog Output

Fig. 12-6   Parameter dialog boxes of two blocks.

different experiments such as linear speed and position servo control, linear inverted pendulum, double inverted pendulum. In the rotary series, experiments such as rotary inverted pendulum, planar inverted pendulum, ball-beam system and flexible link can be composed. Other plants such as helicopter attitude control and magnetic levitation systems can also be composed. Some of the plants in the Quanser series system are shown in Fig. 12-7.

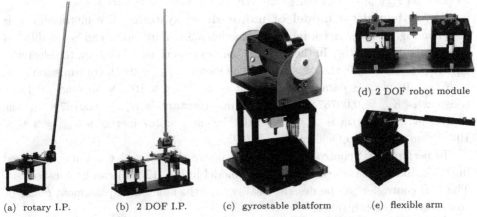

(d) 2 DOF robot module

(a) rotary I.P.      (b) 2 DOF I.P.      (c) gyrostable platform      (e) flexible arm

Fig. 12-7   Some plant models  (I.P. for inverted pendulum, DOF for degree-of-freedom).

## 12.3   An Example of Hardware-in-the-loop Simulation and Real-time Control

### 12.3.1  *Mathematical Description of the Plant Model*

The ball-beam experimental system illustrated here is provided in the Quanser rotary series. The photograph of the experiment system is shown in Fig. 12-8(a), and the principles of the system are illustrated in Fig. 12-8(b). The control principle of the system is to adjust the angle $\alpha$ of the beam by adjusting the angle $\theta$ driven by the motor, so that the ball can be rapidly stabilized at certain specified position. The arm AB is the fixed supporting arm.

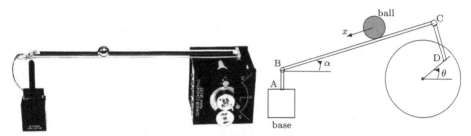

(a) photograph of the ball-beam system       (b) sketch of ball-beam system

Fig. 12-8   Ball-beam system.

In the ball-beam system, the position $x(t)$ of the ball is the output signal, the voltage $V_m(t)$ of the motor is the control signal. A controller is needed to generate the control signal $u(t)$ from the error signal $e(t) = c(t) - x(t)$, where $c(t)$ is the expected position. The ball behaves like a variable resistor on the steel beam, and its position $x(t)$ can be measured directly as the value of the resistance.

(1) **Mathematical model of motor drive system.** The motor model is shown in Fig. 12-9(a). According to the model, a Simulink model can be established as shown in Fig. 12-9(b). In the current Quanser experimental system, the electrical efficiency is $\eta_m = 0.69$, the resistance of the motor is $R_m = 2.6\Omega$, transmission ratio is $K_g = 70$, viscous damping coefficient is $B_{eq} = 4 \times 10^{-3}\text{N} \cdot \text{m}/(\text{rad/s})$, EMF constant is $K_m = 0.00767\text{V}/(\text{rad/s})$, torque constant is $K_t = 0.00767\text{N} \cdot \text{m}$, the equivalent load inertia is $J_{eq} = 2 \times 10^{-3}\text{kg} \cdot \text{m}^2$, motor inertia is $J_m = 3.87 \times 10^{-7}\text{kg} \cdot \text{m}^2$, gearbox efficiency is $\eta_g = 0.9$.

To perform PID control to the motor, where the derivative action is assigned in the feedback path, the control system model in Fig. 12-9(b) can be constructed. The PID controller can be designed easily, and the angular displacement $\theta$ can be controlled by the controller.

In the Quanser experimental system, the Simulink model of the motor system can be constructed as shown in Fig. 12-10. The transfer function between the motor

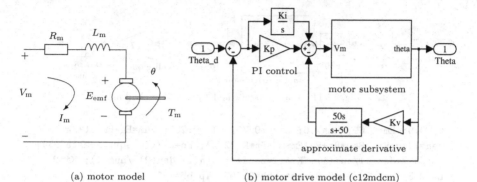

(a) motor model        (b) motor drive model (c12mdcm)

Fig. 12-9   Motor and control model.

voltage signal $V_m(t)$ and the angle $\theta$ can be derived[2]

$$G_1(s) = \frac{\theta(s)}{V_m(s)} = \frac{\eta_g \eta_m K_t K_g}{J_{eq} R_m s^2 + (B_{eq} R_m + \eta_g \eta_m K_m K_t K_g^2)s} = \frac{61.54}{s^2 + 35.1s}. \quad (12.1)$$

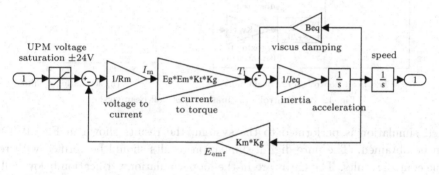

Fig. 12-10   Motor model and its Simulink model.

**(2) Mathematical of the ball-beam system.** Assume the length of the beam is $l = 42.5$cm, and the radius of the ball is $R$. The gravity component of the ball along the direction of $x$ is $F_x = mg \sin \alpha$, with $m = 0.064$g, and the inertia of the ball is $J = 2mR^2/5$. The dynamic model of the ball can be derived as $\ddot{x} = 5g \sin \alpha/7$.

Since the angle $\alpha$ is usually very small, a simplified version is $\sin \alpha \approx \alpha$. Thus, the nonlinearity can be approximated by linear model. Besides, if the bias of the discus is $r = 2.54$cm, it can be found that $l\alpha = r\theta$, i.e., $\theta = l\alpha/r$. Thus, the Simulink model in Fig. 12-11 can be constructed[3].

The control and simulation model for the whole ball-beam system can be constructed as shown in Fig. 12-12(a), where PD controllers are used, and the parameters in the models and controllers can be assigned with the following statements

```
clear all;  % file name: c12dat_set.m
Beq=4e-3; Km=0.00767; Kt=0.00767; Jm=3.87e-7; Jeq=2e-3; Kg=70;
```

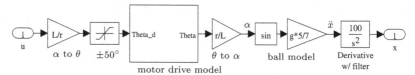

Fig. 12-11    Plant model (model name: c12mball.mdl).

```
Eg=0.9; Em=0.69; Rm=2.6; zeta=0.707; Tp=0.200; num=Eg*Em*Kt*Kg;
den=[Jeq*Rm, Beq*Rm+Eg*Em*Km*Kt*Kg^2 0]; Wn=pi/(Tp*sqrt(1-zeta^2));
Kp=Wn^2*den(1)/num(1); Kv=(2*zeta*Wn*den(1)-den(2))/num(1); Ki=2;
L=42.5; r=2.54; g=9.8; zeta_bb=0.707; Tp_bb=1.5;
Wn_bb=pi/(Tp_bb*sqrt(1-zeta_bb^2)); Kp_bb=Wn_bb^2/7;
Kv_bb=2*zeta_bb*Wn_bb/7; Kp_bb=Kp_bb/100; Kv_bb=Kv_bb/100;
```

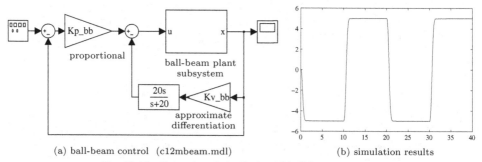

(a) ball-beam control (c12mbeam.mdl)        (b) simulation results

Fig. 12-12    Control and simulation of ball-beam system.

If simulation is performed to the system, the results shown in Fig. 12-12(b) can be obtained. The pure digital simulation results should be verified with real-time control results. The hardware-in-the-loop simulation verification below will be presented next.

### 12.3.2    *Real-time Experiments with Quanser*

It can be seen that the inner PID controller in the system generate the control signal $V_m$ to the motor. The position $x$ and the angle $\theta$ of the motor are measured in real-time. The control signal can be implemented with the Analog Output block, and the positions of the ball can be measured with the Analog Input block. The angular displacement $\theta$ can be measured with the Encoder Input block. In real applications, filter blocks should be used in measurement, and the real-time Simulink model in Fig. 12-13 can be constructed. It should be noted since real-time simulation is involved, fixed-step simulation algorithms must be used. This can be set with Simulation → Parameters menu in the Simulink model window, and when the dialog box appears, the relevant items in the Solver pane should be assigned, and the step size can be set to 0.001 s, with the simulation algorithm set to ode4.

Select Tools → Real-Time Workshop → Build Model menu, the simulation model

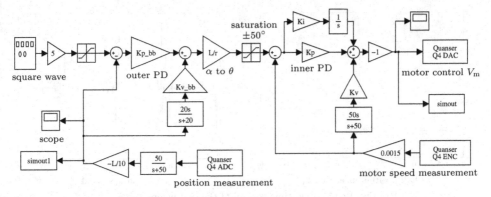

square wave    outer PD    $\alpha$ to $\theta$    inner PD    motor control $V_m$

scope    position measurement    motor speed measurement

Fig. 12-13    Simulink model for real-time control    (file name: c12mbbr.mdl).

can be compiled, and a dynamic link library file can be generated. The WinCon control interface shown in Fig. 12-14 can be opened automatically. The plant model can be controlled directly with the interface. Click the START button in the interface, the real-time simulation facilities can be started. The Analog Output block applies the control signal directly to the motor, and the angle and ball position are measured in real-time and fed back to the computer, so that closed-loop control structure can be established.

The scope button in the interface can be clicked to display the waveforms of the ball positions and control signals, as shown in Fig. 12-15. It should be noted that there are differences in the actual control results and the numerical simulation results. The differences may be caused by modeling error or other minor discrepancies. With the WinCon real-time control interface, the Simulink model runs in the External mode. In this mode, if you modify the variables in the MATLAB workspace, real-time control results will also change.

Fig. 12-14    WinCon control interface.

In real-time control systems, the scope data can be saved to the MATLAB workspace with the File → Save → Workspace menu item. The amount of data is determined by the size of the buffer. The buffer size can be selected with the Buffer menu; it is set to 50 s in this example.

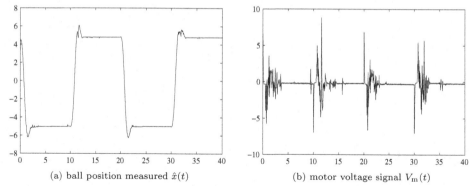

(a) ball position measured $\hat{x}(t)$          (b) motor voltage signal $V_{\mathrm{m}}(t)$

Fig. 12-15    Real-time control of the ball-beam system.

### 12.3.3    Real-time Experiments with dSPACE

From the Simulink model constructed by the interfaces to the Quanser MultiQ4 components shown in Fig. 12-13, a new Simulink model can be constructed, with the corresponding components replaced by dSPACE blocks, as shown in Fig. 12-16. In the dSPACE blockset, the settings of the A/D and D/A converters are different from those in Quanser. We need to multiply the Quanser A/D converter figures by 10, and the D/A figures by 0.1, so that the units are unified. Also, since the motor encode input block of dSPACE is different from that of Quanser, this should be multiplied by 0.006.

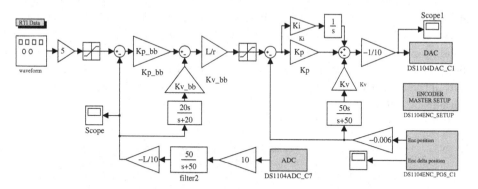

Fig. 12-16    Simulink model for dSPACE    (file name: c12mdsp.mdl).

With the model established, the Tools → Real-Time Workshop → Build Model menu in Simulink model window can be used to compile it, and the description file c12mdsp.ppc for PowerPC platform can be generated. Open Control Desk[4] software window, and with File → Layout menu, a virtual instrumentation editing interface is opened. With the controls provided in the Virtual Instruments toolbox, the control interface can be established. For instance, sliders can be used to tune the parameters of the PD controllers, and scopes can be used to display the speed and position of the ball. The control interface in Fig. 12-17 can be constructed.

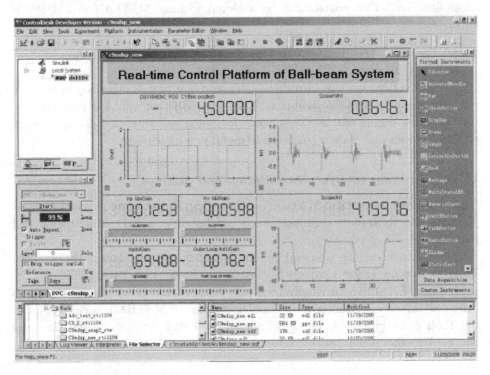

Fig. 12-17   Control interface constructed with Control Desk.

Select the Platform pane, connections can be established to the c12mdsp.ppc file, with standard file name dialog box. The association of the variables in Simulink should also be established with the controls in the interface so that they can be tuned in the interface directly. This can be done by dragging the relevant Simulink variable names to the corresponding controls in the interface. For instance, the Simulink variables displayed in the Control Desk interface can be dragged to the controls, such as the scroll bars, so that they are associated with the controls.

With the control interface constructed, real-time control of the actual plant can be performed. The responses of the ball and beam system are as shown in Fig. 12-17. Note that the control signal obtained here is the actual signal written to the DAC block from dSPACE, and this should be multiplied by 10 to get the physical signal in the system, which varies in the interval $(-10, 10)$, and it is similar to that obtained with Quanser.

It can be seen that the controller established in Simulink can be used to directly control the practical plant in real time. Also, on-line controller parameter tuning is allowed. For instance, in the example, the scroll bars can be used to change the parameters of the PD controller, and the control results can be immediately obtained.

The controller and parameters thus created can be downloaded to the actual controllers, such that control can be achieved without MATLAB and dSPACE environments.

## 12.4    Low-cost Realizations of Hardware-in-the-loop Simulation

In this section, we will introduce a low-cost hardware-in-the-loop simulation solution based on Arduino products. This solution is not only low cost but also very portable and it can be taken home for doing real-time closed-loop systems control experiments. This is particularly useful in a mobile age.

### 12.4.1    *Arduino Interface Installation and Settings*

In the latest versions of MATLAB such as R2012b, Simulink provides support packages for third-party products such as Arduino, LEGO Mindstorms and PandaBoard.

This feature can be accessed in any Simulink model window through the Tools → Run on Target Hardware → Install/Update Support Package menu item, as shown in Fig. 12-18, or simply by typing `targetinstaller` in the MATLAB command window. Alternatively, in older versions of MATLAB, users can go to the Tools menu in a Simulink model window and click Add-Ons → Get Hardware Support Packages menu item.

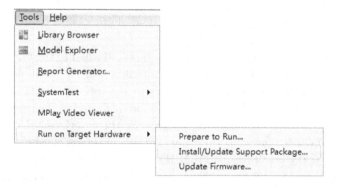

Fig. 12-18    Additional package support menu.

After the above action, users will be directed to the Target Installer in which the target support packages are listed. For a complete list of the supported products, see [5]. On completing the installation procedure described previously, the "Simulink Arduinolib" is automatically embedded into the Simulink Library Browser and is ready to use. It includes the blocks shown in Fig. 12-19.

The Simulink model created in this way is set up to run on the target, which is the Arduino board in this case. Hence, pre-settings need to be performed prior to execution. Again, referring to Fig. 12-18, clicking the Prepare to Run menu item

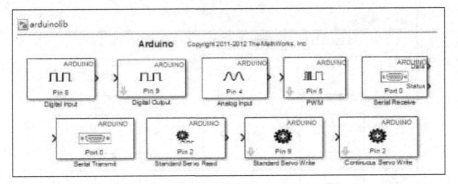

Fig. 12-19  Simulink Arduinolib blockset.

will pop up the standard Simulink configuration dialog box. From the dialog box, if the Run on Target Hardware is selected, the Arduino Uno item can be specified from the Target hardware list box.

Follow the steps of specifying the serial communication port and Baud rate, then the popup menu appears as in Fig. 12-18. Now, the Simulink model can run on the Arduino target as a stand-alone application.

### 12.4.2  *Applications of Arduino Control*

There are two main ways of interfacing with the open-source hardware Arduino:
(1) interfacing with it as a normal target through code generation
(2) "virtual machine style" host-target communication.

The block library given earlier can be regarded as the first approach, while the Simulink model can be executed directly with the connected hardware.

Here, the second approach is presented as a case study on Arduino Uno. This interfacing approach does not support code generation, meaning that it does not generate code to download to the Arduino target. Instead, an I/O description file needs to be fed into the Arduino in advance as if it were firmware. Afterwards, all the I/Os on the Arduino board can be accessed either through Simulink or through MATLAB commands using serial communication. This is similar to the mechanism of a "Java virtual machine", which manages the bottom layer hardware while providing users with generic APIs.

To use this approach, a third-party Arduino support package is needed which is freely available from MATLAB Central[6], and it can be initiated with `arduino_io_lib`. The blocks in the package are shown in Fig. 12-20.

**Example 12.1.** This example shows a simple closed-loop control system developed on the Simulink Arduino support package. The hardware set-up is shown in Fig. 12-21(a). The control objective is to make the ball track the height set-point and, after settling down, maintain its height against disturbances.

A MATLAB GUI, shown in Fig. 12-21 (b), is designed to visualize the control and response. Users can adjust the height set-point by sliding the bar in the GUI. The Simulink

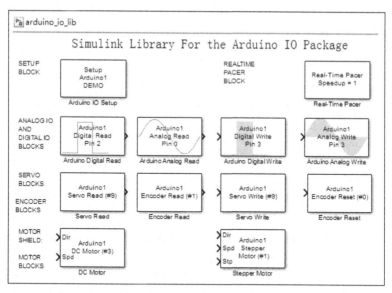

Fig. 12-20　The blocks in the Arduino support package.

model is displayed in Fig. 12-22, in which the Arduino analog read Pin 0 is connected to an infrared (IR) sensor on top of the tube, and Arduino analog write Pin 3 is connected to a motor-driven fan to blow the ball. The IR sensor is used to detect the height of the ball within the tube.

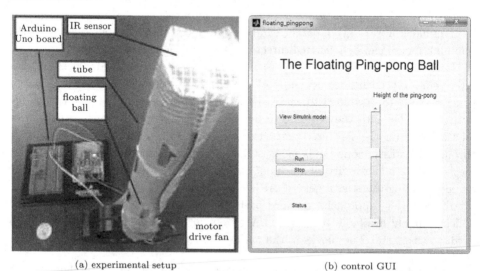

(a) experimental setup　　　　　　　　　　　　(b) control GUI

Fig. 12-21　The ping-pong ball floating experiment.

It is worth mentioning that during the running of such an application, the serial communication between the host PC and the Arduino target cannot be interrupted because the signal processing is, in fact, being carried out on the PC and only the sensing and

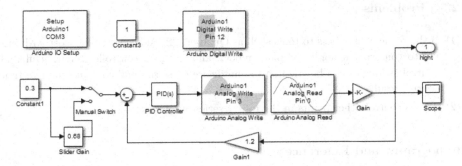

Fig. 12-22   The Simulink model   (model name: pingpong_sim.mdl).

actuation is performed on the Arduino.

### 12.4.3   *The MESA Box*

An educational experimental toolbox, named MESA box, based on the Arduino Uno core and peripheral hardware components was developed in the MESA Laboratory in University of California Merced for the purpose of making the traditionally cumbersome mechatronics laboratories into a small-sized portable handset[7]. The cost of the key components in MESA box is approximately $180. The assembled box is shown in Fig. 12-23.

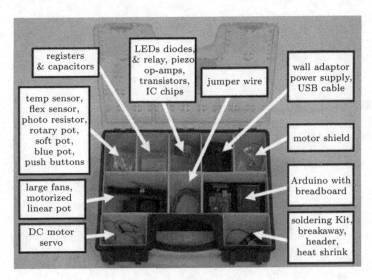

Fig. 12-23   MESA box.

In MATLAB R2012b, varieties of "Apps" such as the "Floating ball" and "Fan-plate" have been developed for the MESA box to support its educational usage. They are seamlessly integrated into MATLAB as a Toolbox/App.

## 12.5   Problems

(1) If the reader has access to tools such as Quanser, dSPACE, or the low-cost Arduino, try to construct a nonlinear plant model, and design a controller for it. Different control strategies can be tried on the hardware platform, and compare the real-time control results.

(2) Try to control other plants in the rotary series of Quanser.

## Bibliography and References

[1] dSPACE Inc. DS1104 R&D controller board installation and configuration guide, 2001

[2] Quanser Inc. SRV02Series rotary experiment # 1: Position control, 2002

[3] Quanser Inc. SRV02Series rotary experiment # 3: Ball & beam, 2002

[4] dSPACE Inc. Control Desk — experiment guide, Release 3.4, 2002

[5] MathWorks.   Hardware for  project-based  learning.  http://www.mathworks.com/academia/hardware-resources/index.html, 2012

[6] MathWorks Classroom Resources Team. MATLAB support package for Arduino (aka ArduinoIO package). MATLAB Central # 32374, 2011

[7] Stark B, Li Z, Smith B, and Chen Y Q.  Take-home mechatronics control labs: a low-cost personal solution and educational assessment. Proceedings of the ASME 2013 International Design Engineering Technical Conferences & Computers and Information in Engineering Conference, Portland, Oregon, USA, 2013

# Appendix A

# Some Practical Plant Models

In the early stage of the development of computer simulation and design software, various benchmark problems were proposed, such as the well-known F-14 aircraft model[1, 2], and complicated continuous/discrete test model[3] and ACC models[4, 5]. The target of the benchmark problems is to assess the flexibility and accuracy of computer software. With specific and dedicated computer languages and tools, the representation of the systems is no longer a difficult problem. These benchmark problems can be used to assess the controller design algorithms. Various control algorithms can be tested on the models to compare the benefits of the control design algorithms.

In the appendix, some of the well known benchmark plant models are presented, the readers are advised to evaluate their own control algorithms on these models.

## A.1 Well-known Benchmark Problems

### A.1.1 *Control of the F-14 Aircraft Model*

Before the emergence of tools like Simulink, some of the benchmark problems were proposed to assess the modeling capabilities of computer modeling tools. F-14 aircraft model[1] is one of them. The block diagram of the system model is shown in Fig. A-1. There are two input signals, with vector form $\boldsymbol{u} = [n(t), \alpha_c(t)]^{\mathrm{T}}$, where $n(t)$ is the white noise signal with unity variance, and $\alpha_c(t) = K\beta(\mathrm{e}^{-\gamma t} - \mathrm{e}^{-\beta t})/(\beta - \gamma)$ generates the angle of attack, with $K = \alpha_{c_{\max}} \mathrm{e}^{\gamma t_{\mathrm{m}}}$, and $\alpha_{c_{\max}} = 0.0349$, $t_{\mathrm{m}} = 0.025$, $\beta = 426.4352$, $\gamma = 0.01$. There are three output signals, $\boldsymbol{y}(t) = [N_{z_{\mathrm{p}}}(t), \alpha(t), q(t)]^{\mathrm{T}}$, and $N_{z_{\mathrm{p}}}(t)$ signal is defined as

$$N_{z_{\mathrm{p}}}(t) = \frac{1}{32.2}[-\dot{w}(t) + U_0 q(t) + 22.8\dot{q}(t)].$$

The parameters of the system are given by
$\tau_{\mathrm{a}} = 0.05$, $\sigma_{\mathrm{wG}} = 3.0$, $a = 2.5348$, $b = 64.13$, $\sigma_\alpha = 5.236 \times 10^{-3}$,
$V_{T_0} = 690.4$, $Z_{\mathrm{b}} = -63.9979$, $M_{\mathrm{b}} = -6.8847$, $U_0 = 689.4$, $Z_{\mathrm{w}} = -0.6385$,
$M_{\mathrm{q}} = -0.6571$, $M_{\mathrm{w}} = -5.92 \times 10^{-3}$, $\omega_1 = 2.971$, $\omega_2 = 4.144$, $\tau_{\mathrm{s}} = 0.10$,
$\tau_\alpha = 0.3959$, $K_{\mathrm{Q}} = 0.8156$, $K_\alpha = 0.6770$, $K_{\mathrm{f}} = -3.864$, $K_{\mathrm{F}} = -1.745$.

The original problem is to compute all the closed-loop poles of the system with the computer tools to be assessed. Another problem is, when the loop is broken at $\Delta$ point, what are the open-loop poles.

The original problems can be solved easily with today's leading-edge software systems. The new problem now is how to design the controllers for the system, such that the attack angle $\alpha(t)$ can follow the given command signal $\alpha_c(t)$ as fast as possible, with minimum error. Besides, how to design the relevant controller to reduce the impact of the noise signal $n(t)$?

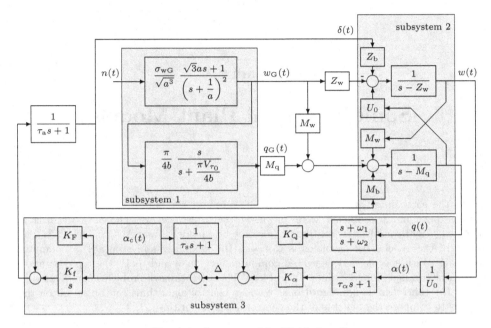

Fig. A-1   System model of F-14 aircraft.

## A.1.2   ACC Benchmark Problem

ACC benchmark problems are proposed in [4,5]. Since they are proposed at American Control Conference (ACC), they are widely known as ACC benchmark problems. Three benchmark problems were proposed in the first paper, and a new problem was added in the second paper.

The first benchmark problem is described in Fig. A-2. In the model, $m_1$ and $m_2$ are the masses of two carts. The variables $x_1$ and $x_2$ are the displacement of the two carts. Variable $u$ is the acceleration of the first cart, and it is regarded as the input of the system. Signal $w$ is the disturbance signal on the acceleration of the second cart. The variable $k$ is the elastic coefficient of the string linking the two carts.

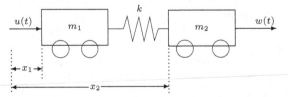

Fig. A-2   ACC benchmark problem.

According to the description in Fig. A-2, the state variables are assigned as $x_1$ and $x_2$, and the third state variable $x_3 = \dot{x}_1$ and $x_4 = \dot{x}_2$ are introduced, as the speed of the two carts. The state space equation of the system can be established as

$$\dot{x}(t) = \begin{bmatrix} 0 & 0 & 1 & 0 \\ 0 & 0 & 0 & 1 \\ -k/m_1 & k/m_1 & 0 & 0 \\ k/m_2 & -k/m_2 & 0 & 0 \end{bmatrix} x(t) + \begin{bmatrix} 0 \\ 0 \\ 1/m_1 \\ 0 \end{bmatrix} u(t) + \begin{bmatrix} 0 \\ 0 \\ 0 \\ 1/m_2 \end{bmatrix} w(t), \qquad (A.1)$$

and $y(t) = x_2(t)$.

The control target is to let the position $x_2(t)$ of the second cart to reach the assigned position rapidly under the control of $u(t)$ and the inevitable noise signal $w(t)$.

## A.2 Other Engineering Models

### A.2.1 *Servo Control System Model*

A well-established servo control model is presented in the manual of Model Predictive Control Toolbox[6]. This model can be used in testing controller design and control algorithms.

Assume that the system structure is shown in Fig. A-3. The motor speed can be controlled through adjusting the voltage $V$. The target is to have the angular velocity $\theta_L$ reaches and maintain at constant value as fast as it can. The parameters of the system are shown in Table A.1.

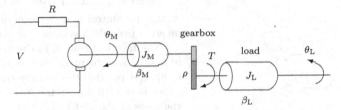

Fig. A-3   System structure of motor servo control.

Table A.1   Parameters of the servo system.

| variable | definition | values | variable | definition | values |
|---|---|---|---|---|---|
| $k_\theta$ | torsional rigidity | 1280.2 | $k_T$ | motor constant | 10 |
| $J_M$ | motor inertia | 0.5 | $J_L$ | load inertia | $50 J_M$ |
| $\rho$ | gear ratio | 20 | $\beta_M$ | motor viscous friction coefficients | 0.1 |
| $R$ | armature resistance | 20 | $\beta_L$ | load viscous friction coefficients | 25 |

The following differential equations can be derived

$$\begin{cases} \dot{\omega}_L = -\left(\theta_L - \dfrac{\theta_M}{\rho}\right) - \dfrac{\beta_L}{J_L}\omega_L , \\[4mm] \dot{\omega}_M = \dfrac{k_T}{J_M}\left(\dfrac{V - k_T\omega_M}{R}\right) - \dfrac{J_M}{\beta_M}\omega_M + \dfrac{k_\theta}{\rho J_M}\left(\theta_L - \dfrac{\theta_M}{\rho}\right). \end{cases} \qquad (A.2)$$

Besides, we have $\omega_M = \dot{\theta}_M$, $\omega_L = \dot{\theta}_L$. Selecting the state variables $\boldsymbol{x} = [\theta_L, \omega_L, \theta_M, \omega_M]^T$, the following state space model can be obtained.

$$\dot{\boldsymbol{x}} = \begin{bmatrix} 0 & 1 & 0 & 0 \\ -\dfrac{k_\theta}{J_L} & -\dfrac{\beta_L}{J_L} & \dfrac{k_\theta}{\rho J_L} & 0 \\ 0 & 0 & 0 & 1 \\ \dfrac{k_\theta}{\rho J_M} & 0 & -\dfrac{k_\theta}{\rho^2 J_M} & -\dfrac{\beta_M + k_T^2/R}{J_M} \end{bmatrix} \boldsymbol{x} + \begin{bmatrix} 0 \\ 0 \\ 0 \\ \dfrac{k_T}{R J_M} \end{bmatrix} V. \tag{A.3}$$

If the output signals are $\boldsymbol{y} = \begin{bmatrix} \theta_L, & T \end{bmatrix}^T$, where $T$ is the torque output, the output equation can also be written

$$\boldsymbol{y} = \begin{bmatrix} 1 & 0 & 0 & 0 \\ k_\theta & 0 & k_\theta/\rho & 0 \end{bmatrix} \boldsymbol{x}. \tag{A.4}$$

The control target is to design a servo controller such that the load's angular position $\theta_L$ reaches desired value quickly under the following conditions,
   (1) the controller voltages $V$ does not exceed the range of $\pm 220$, i.e., $|V| \leqslant 220$;
   (2) the control torque $T$ does not exceed 78.5 N·m, i.e., $|T| \leqslant 78.5$.

## A.2.2    *Mathematical Model of Inverted Pendulum*

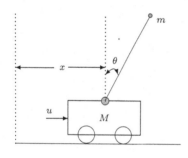

Inverted pendulum system is the often used system in control systems experiment[7]. The inverted pendulum system is shown in Fig. A-4.

The target of control in the inverted pendulum system is to maintain the pendulum stay at upright position through the control signal $u$, which is used to control the speed of the cart. If the mass of the cart is $M$, and the mass of the pendulum is $m$. The length of pendulum is $l$. The following system model can be derived[7]

Fig. A-4   Inverted pendulum system.

$$\ddot{x} = \frac{u + ml\sin\theta\dot{\theta}^2 - mg\cos\theta\sin\theta}{M + m - m\cos^2\theta}, \tag{A.5}$$

$$\ddot{\theta} = \frac{u\cos\theta - (M + m)g\sin\theta + ml\sin\theta\cos\theta\dot{\theta}}{ml\cos^2\theta - (M + m)l}. \tag{A.6}$$

If the state variables are selected as $x_1 = \theta$, $x_2 = \dot{\theta}$, $x_3 = x$, $x_4 = \dot{x}$, the state space model of the inverted pendulum system can be written as

$$\frac{\mathrm{d}}{\mathrm{d}t} \begin{bmatrix} x_1 \\ x_2 \\ x_3 \\ x_4 \end{bmatrix} = \begin{bmatrix} x_2 \\ \dfrac{u\cos x_1 - (M + m)g\sin x_1 + ml\sin x_1\cos x_1 x_2}{ml\cos^2 x_1 - (M + m)l} \\ x_4 \\ \dfrac{u + ml\sin x_1 x_2^2 - mg\cos x_1\sin x_1}{M + m - m\cos^2 x_1} \end{bmatrix}, \tag{A.7}$$

and $y = \begin{bmatrix} x_1, x_3 \end{bmatrix}^{\mathrm{T}}$.

Selecting operating point at $x_0 = 0$, $u_0 = 0$, linearization process can be performed, and the linearized model is

$$\Delta\dot{x} = A\Delta x + Bu, \; y = C\Delta x, \tag{A.8}$$

where

$$A = \begin{bmatrix} 0 & 1 & 0 & 0 \\ \dfrac{(M+m)g}{Ml} & 0 & 0 & 0 \\ 0 & 0 & 0 & 1 \\ -\dfrac{mg}{M} & 0 & 0 & 0 \end{bmatrix}, \; B = \begin{bmatrix} 0 \\ -\dfrac{1}{Ml} \\ 0 \\ \dfrac{1}{M} \end{bmatrix}, \; C = \begin{bmatrix} 1 & 0 & 0 & 0 \\ 0 & 0 & 1 & 0 \end{bmatrix}. \tag{A.9}$$

The Simulink model can be constructed. The error between the original nonlinear model and the linearized model can be compared. Based on the linearized model, controllers can be designed. The effectiveness of the controllers can be compared and assessed.

### A.2.3 AIRC Model

In [8, 9], a linearized model of vertical-plane dynamics of an aircraft is given, called AIRC model. The state space equation of the model is

$$A = \begin{bmatrix} 0 & 0 & 1.1320 & 0 & -1 \\ 0 & -0.0538 & -0.1712 & 0 & 0.0705 \\ 0 & 0 & 0 & 1 & 0 \\ 0 & 0.0485 & 0 & -0.8556 & -1.013 \\ 0 & -0.2909 & 0 & 1.0532 & -0.6859 \end{bmatrix}, \; B = \begin{bmatrix} 0 & 0 & 0 \\ -0.120 & 1 & 0 \\ 0 & 0 & 0 \\ 4.419 & 0 & -1.665 \\ 1.575 & 0 & -0.0732 \end{bmatrix},$$

and $C = I_{5\times5}$, $D = 0_{5\times3}$. In the model, there are three inputs, $u_1$ is the spoiler angle, $u_2$ is the forward acceleration, and $u_3$ is the elevator angle. There are five state variables, $x_1$ is the altitude relative to some datum, $x_2$ is the forward speed, $x_3$ is the pitch angle, $x_4$ is the pitch rate, and $x_5$ is the vertical speed. The five outputs of the model are, in fact, the states of the system.

If there exist coupling among different inputs and outputs, the design of the system might be rather difficult. If a fully decoupled system can be reached, individual control loops can be designed easily, such that the controller design task is simplified.

### A.3 Problems

(1) Construct the open- and closed-loop model for F-14 aircraft, with MATLAB/Simulink. Find the poles and zeros of the model. The original model is controlled with PI controller. See whether the system response can be improved if PID controller is used.

(2) Use MATLAB to express the ACC benchmark problem, and design controller for the model, with certain robustness. If the disturbance is not considered, what kind of controller can be used, and how can the parameters of the controllers can be tuned.

(3) Read the relevant materials in the Model Predictive Control Toolbox manual[6] for the servo system. Follow the instructions in the manual to design a MPC controller. If

the original problem is converted to a constrained optimization problem, is it possible to design PID controllers, and what are the best parameters in the controller? Please compare the designed PID controller with the model predictive controller designed in the manual.

(4) Please compare the linearized model and the original nonlinear model of the inverted pendulum. Is it possible to design some kind of controller to achieve the target?

(5) Please mask the inverted pendulum plant into a Simulink block, with options to describe it in original nonlinear system and the linearized model. If the parameters of the system are given by $m = 0.3$kg, $M = 0.5$kg, $l = 0.3$m, design an optimal PID controller for the linearized model, and observe the results. If the original nonlinear plant is used, use OptimPID interface to design optimal PID controller and compare the results.

(6) A sub-model of AIRC problem was studied in Example 7.17, using parameterization design algorithm, and satisfactory results were obtained. Try other control methods, or try to use OCD interface to design practical controllers, and compare results.

## Bibliography and References

[1] Frederick D K, Rimer M. Benchmark problem for CACSD packages. Abstracts of the Second IEEE Symposium on Computer-aided Dontrol System Design, 1985. Santa Barbara, USA

[2] Rimvall C M. Computer-aided control system design. IEEE Control Systems Magazine, 1993, 13:14–16

[3] Hawley P A, Steven T R. Two sets of benchmark problems for CACSD packages. Proceedings of the Third IEEE Symposium on Computer Aided Control System Design, 1986. Arlington

[4] Wie B, Bernstein D S. A benchmark problem for robust controller design. Proceedings of American Control Conference, 1990. San Diego, USA

[5] Wie B, Bernstein D S. Benchmark problems for robust control design. Proceedings of American Control Conference, 1992. Chicago, USA

[6] Bemporad A, Morari M, Ricker N L. Model predictive control toolbox user's manual. MathWorks, 2013

[7] Ogata K. Modern control engineering. Englewood Cliffs: Prentice Hall, 4th edition, 2001

[8] Hung Y S, MacFarlane A G J. Multivariable feedback: a quasi-classical approach. In: Lecture Notes in Control and Information Sciences, Volume 40. New York: Springer-Verlag, 1982

[9] Maciejowski J M. Multivariable feedback design. Wokingham: Addison-Wesley, 1989

# Index of Functions

# Index

551

Printed in the United States
By Bookmasters